Internet Business Models and Strategies

Text and Cases

Second Edition

Allan Afuah
University of Michigan

Christopher L. Tucci
New York University
Stern School of Business

McGraw Hill

Boston   Burr Ridge, IL   Dubuque, IA   Madison, WI   New York   San Francisco   St. Louis
Bangkok   Bogotá   Caracas   Kuala Lumpur   Lisbon   London   Madrid   Mexico City
Milan   Montreal   New Delhi   Santiago   Seoul   Singapore   Sydney   Taipei   Toronto

McGraw-Hill Higher Education

A Division of The **McGraw-Hill** *Companies*

INTERNET BUSINESS MODELS AND STRATEGIES: TEXT AND CASES
Published by McGraw-Hill/Irwin, a business unit of The McGraw-Hill Companies, Inc., 1221 Avenue of the Americas, New York, NY, 10020. Copyright © 2003, 2001 by The McGraw-Hill Companies, Inc. All rights reserved. No part of this publication may be reproduced or distributed in any form or by any means, or stored in a database or retrieval system, without the prior written consent of The McGraw-Hill Companies, Inc., including, but not limited to, in any network or other electronic storage or transmission, or broadcast for distance learning.

Some ancillaries, including electronic and print components, may not be available to customers outside the United States.

This book is printed on acid-free paper.

domestic   1 2 3 4 5 6 7 8 9 0 FGR/FGR 0 9 8 7 6 5 4 3 2
international 1 2 3 4 5 6 7 8 9 0 FGR/FGR 0 9 8 7 6 5 4 3 2

ISBN 0-07-251166-4

Publisher: *John E. Biernat*
Sponsoring editor: *Ryan Blankenship*
Editorial assistant: *Tammy Higham*
Marketing manager: *Lisa Nicks*
Media producer: *Craig Atkins*
Project manager: *Catherine R. Schultz*
Senior production supervisor: *Michael R. McCormick*
Designer: *Adam Rooke*
Senior digital content specialist: *Brian Nacik*
Cover design: *Adam Rooke*
Interior design: *Adam Rooke*
Typeface: *10.5/12 Times New Roman*
Compositor: *Lachina Publishing Services*
Printer: *Quebecor World Fairfield Inc.*

Library of Congress Cataloging-in-Publication Data

Afuah, Allan.
  Internet business models and strategies : text and cases / Allan Afuah, Christopher L. Tucci.— 2nd ed.
    p. cm.
  Includes bibliographical references and index.
  ISBN 0-07-251166-4 (alk. paper) — ISBN 0-07-115123-0 (international : alk. paper)
  1. Business enterprises—Computer networks. 2. Electronic commerce. 3. Internet. I. Tucci, Christopher L. II. Title.
  HD30.37 .A33 2003
  658.8'4—dc21

                                                                    2002069233

INTERNATIONAL EDITION ISBN 0-07-115123-0
Copyright © 2003. Exclusive rights by The McGraw-Hill Companies, Inc. for manufacture and export. This book cannot be re-exported from the country to which it is sold by McGraw-Hill. The International Edition is not available in North America.

www.mhhe.com

To my grandmother, Veronica Masang-Namang Nkweta, and the Peace Corps

—A.A.

To my parents, Michael A. Tucci and Isabella A. Di Giulio Tucci

—C.L.T.

Contents

About the Authors

Allan Afuah

Allan Afuah holds a Ph.D. from the Massachusetts Institute of Technology. He is co-chair and associate professor of corporate strategy and international business, and Michael & Mary Kay Hallman fellow of electronic business at the University of Michigan Business School, where he teaches the core course in strategy to first-year M.B.A. students and an elective in strategies for technology and innovation management. He has also worked as an engineer in the Silicon Valley and Route 128.

Christopher L. Tucci

Christopher L. Tucci is assistant professor of entrepreneurship and innovation at the New York University Stern School of Business, where he teaches the M.B.A. course in technological innovation and new product development. He received the degrees of Ph.D. in management of technological innovation and the S.M. in technology & policy from MIT. He also received an M.S. in computer science, a B.S. in mathematical sciences, and an A.B. in music from Stamford University. His prior work experience was as an industrial computer scientist in Palo Alto, California.

Preface

The phrase "business model" has found its way into the vocabulary of just about everyone who must manage or work in businesses with an Internet content, from venture capitalists to CEOs. Despite the enormous importance of the Internet and business models to firms, and the explosive interest in both subjects, there are no business school texts that address the impact of the Internet on firm performance.

In *Internet Business Models and Strategies: Text and Cases,* we draw on research in strategic management and the management of technology to develop an integrative framework that allows readers to put their minds around what determines firm performance and the central role that business models play in the face of the Internet. We offer concepts and tools that students of management need to analyze and synthesize business models, especially Internet business models. The framework developed in the book allows its users to make more informed concept- and theory-grounded arguments about Internet start-ups, bricks-and-mortar firms that must face challengers, the relative merits of formulating and implementing Internet business models and strategies, and how much ventures might be worth.

In the first part of the book, we explore the concepts on which Internet business models rest and the tools that can be used to analyze and appraise them. In addition to building a conceptual framework, the chapters include discussion questions and key terms to engage readers further with the subject matter. The second part of the book offers cases of both pure-play Internet firms as well as bricks-and-mortar firms that must formulate and execute successful business models and strategies in order to gain, defend, or reinforce a competitive advantage in the face of the Internet.

To the best of our knowledge, no other book addresses the central issues of the impact of the Internet on business performance. This is not to say that there are no books on e-commerce or the impact of the Internet from a functional perspective, simply that they do not centrally address business issues, particularly the impact of the Internet on business models and firm performance.

INTENDED AUDIENCE

The book should be of particular interest to those who are interested in managing a business with an Internet component. It is designed for those who want to pursue new ventures related to digital markets, manage such ventures, compete with such ventures, or interact with them. This includes individuals who plan to work for venture capital firms that must understand the viability of the business models they are financing, start-up ventures, bricks-and-mortar firms that must adopt or exploit the Internet to fend off challengers or reinforce an existing competitive advantage, consulting firms that must undertake Internet-related assignments for clients, investment bankers who must value Internet businesses, and even those in government who must formulate policies that influence firm performance in the face of the Internet. Thus, students and managers alike will find this book useful. These potential users can refer to this book at different stages of their careers.

Graduate Business School Programs

There are four different contexts in which the book can be used in business schools: It can be used (1) in a stand-alone e-business strategy course in a strategy group, marketing department, entrepreneurship area, or any of the functional departments that contribute to an e-commerce track; (2) as a module in a core strategy course where as much attention must be given to Internet business models as traditionally has been given to business strategy; (3) as a module in management information systems (information technology, computer information systems) courses that provides a link between the Internet as an information technology and firm performance—that is, a module that emphasizes profiting from an information technology; and (4) as an Internet business models elective in one of the many e-commerce/digital economy tracks, concentrations, departments, and degree programs in business schools.

Undergraduate Programs

Undergraduates are increasingly sophisticated about the Web. Moreover, many of them graduate to take jobs that have an Internet or business model content. Some of them will start their own businesses while in college or right after they graduate. A large number of the Internet courses taught to undergraduates usually dwell on the technology, transactions, and connectivity, and pay little or no attention to the link between these technologies and firm performance. This book helps readers focus on profiting from the Internet. Thus, the material can be useful in undergraduate courses offered in the fields of strategy, e-commerce, computer/management information systems, information technology, entrepreneurship, or marketing.

Practicing Managers

Any manager or functional specialist who must contribute to formulating and executing Internet business models and strategies should find the book useful. It may also be appropriate for those, such as consultants and venture capitalists, who must analyze, appraise, and sometimes synthesize business models and strategies for start-ups or bricks-and-mortar firms.

Our interest in the Internet, management of technology, and the strategic issues on which profiting from technological change rests has built up over the last 20 years. That interest kicked off when we worked at different times in Silicon Valley before meeting at MIT as PhD students in the Management of Technological Innovation Area. Subsequently, Allan went to the University of Michigan Business School to teach Technology & Innovation Management as well as Strategic Management, while Chris went to the NYU Stern School of Business to teach Technological Innovation & New Product Development, Strategic Management, and Operations Management. We hope that you, the reader, will share our passion for this timely subject! We welcome your thoughts and suggestions as well at our website, www.mhhe.com/afuahtucci2e.

Allan and Chris

Ann Arbor and New York City

From the Publisher

INSTRUCTOR SUPPORT MATERIAL

Instructor's Manual Online

The instructor's manual, prepared by the authors, contains teaching suggestions, case notes, sample syllabuses, and additional helpful materials. It can be accessed through the book's companion website at www.mhhe.com/afuah tucci2e.

Website: www.mhhe.com/afuahtucci2e

Instructor resource materials are contained at this website and include an opportunity for instructors to contact the authors; to post and share syllabi, resources, and other materials; and to gain access to relevant e-commerce education links. Please contact your McGraw-Hill/Irwin sales representative for the password to this protected material.

Customized Publication and Updated Cases Available through Primis

The content of this text is also available through Primis Online, a large and growing database that provides you the flexibility of choosing only the material that matches your course. You can easily build a custom version of this text at mhhe.com/primis/online. In addition, you will find updated cases that accompany this text.

PageOut: Your Own Course Website for Free

With PageOut you will receive a unique website address that is home for all of the courses you teach. It requires no prior knowledge of HTML, no long hours of coding, and no design skills on your part. Easy-to-follow templates help you create your site quickly with a professional design. The PageOut interactive syllabus offers a place where you can add your own content, create Web links, and post assignments. PageOut also has an online gradebook and discussion area.

PageOut is hosted by McGraw-Hill and, best of all, is free with the adoption of a McGraw-Hill title. To learn more, please contact your McGraw-Hill/Irwin sales representative.

STUDENT SUPPORT MATERIAL

Website: www.mhhe.com/afuahtucci2e

There is a companion website for this text that provides students with access to study tools, an opportunity to contact the authors and to review relevant e-commerce and e-strategy links, and more.

Acknowledgments

This book has been a collective task, and we would like to express our gratitude to several people who contributed to it. First, we are basing many of the frameworks and concepts of this book on several streams of literature, including those of strategic management, management of technology, economics, and organizational theory. We would like to thank those academics, consultants, practicing managers, and other researchers whose work we have cited throughout the book. We also owe a debt of gratitude to our mentors in the Strategy and Management of Technological Innovation groups at MIT, especially Michael Cusumano, Rebecca Henderson, Ed Roberts, and James Utterback.

We heartily thank our students at the University of Michigan Business School and the New York University Stern School of Business. Many of the ideas in the book were pretested on them, and all the cases in the last part of the book were written by them under our supervision. Our stimulating interactions in the classroom gave us energy for the project and also led us to believe that there was deep interest in a textbook that focused on the strategic implications of the Internet. Two of our students deserve special mention. Denise Banks was an expert reader, making many nuanced suggestions for the manuscript. Alison Matochak was an incredible research assistant who made many helpful comments on the manuscript and drafted chapter summaries, key words, and discussion questions. We also benefited from the research assistance of Angel Cordero, Jennie Ma, Monica Malhotra, and Bryan Sloane.

The book was refereed in a peer-review process and we are grateful to the referees for their helpful suggestions, insightful comments, and constructive criticism of the drafts. We would like to thank Robert Brooker (Gannon University), Anthony F. Chelte (Western New England College), George S. Cole (Shippensburg University), Stéphane Gagnon (McGill University), John H. Gerdes, Jr. (University of California, Riverside), Benjamin Gomes-Casseres (Brandeis University), Haym Hirsh (Rutgers University), James A. Howard (University of Maryland), Ronald Lamprecht (Columbia University), Brian Lindquist (University of Phoenix), Timothy Mills (University of Phoenix), James G. Morris (University of Wisconsin, Madison), B. P. S. Murthi (University of Texas at Dallas), d.t. ogilvie (Rutgers University), Ralph Oliva (Pennsylvania State University), Mihir Parikh (Polytechnic University and Institute for Technology & Enterprise), Srinivasan Ragothaman (University of South Dakota), Kenneth Sardoni (University of Phoenix), Bindiganavale S. Vijayaraman (University of Akron), and four anonymous reviewers.

Jennifer Roche was the executive editor in charge of the first edition of this book and she took up this task with aplomb, shepherding the project through the various stages in a professional, fair, and enthusiastic way. It was clear from our early interactions with Jennifer and with Mike Junior, the editor-in-chief, that McGraw-Hill/Irwin "got it" in terms of their thinking about the Internet and its impact on the educational curricula of business schools. In addition to our main contacts, there was an entire production team behind the publication of the first edition of the book, including Barb Block, Ellen Cleary, Elizabeth Degenhard, Laura Griffin, Tracy L. Jensen, Michael R. McCormick, and Jennifer McQueen. Ellen Cleary deserves great praise for her masterful marketing of the first edition. For the second edition, we have enjoyed working closely with Tammy Higham and Cathy Schultz, and also appreciate the behind-the-scenes efforts of John Biernat, Marianne Rutter, Lisa Nicks, Adam Rooke, Craig Atkins, Michael McCormick, and Ryan Blankenship. We have been quite impressed by everyone's professionalism and ability to make things happen.

Finally, we would like to express our warmest thanks to Chris's wife, Carolyn, who went well beyond the call of duty, not only for obliging our (and her) hectic work schedules, but also for lending her own editorial prowess to the manuscript.

Part **One**

The Internet

Chapter **One**

Introduction and Overview

Most firms are in business to win, to outperform their competitors. They are in business to make money. They adopt new technologies to fend off new competitors, reinforce an existing competitive advantage, leapfrog competitors, or just to make money in new markets. Performance is critical. If performance is so significant to firms and their managers, an important question is: What determines performance to begin with? Only by understanding the determinants of business performance can firms better formulate their business models—how they plan to make money over the long term. By understanding the determinants of **firm performance**, firms are in a better position to comprehend how a technology such as the Internet impacts that performance and how firms can exploit the new technology. In this chapter, we briefly describe the determinants of firm performance and the role played by business models, especially Internet business models. We sketch the framework on which the book is built.

DETERMINANTS OF PERFORMANCE

There are three major **determinants of business performance**: business models, the environment in which businesses operate, and change (see Figure 1.1).[1] Before delving into these determinants, we need to define what performance means in this book. What exactly constitutes firm performance can be the subject of passionate debate and even controversy. One can make a strong argument for defining performance as profits, cash flow, economic value added (EVA), market valuation, earnings per share, sales, return on sales, return on assets, return on equity, return on capital, economic rents, and so on. Throughout this book, except where noted, performance means accounting profits. Now, let's return to the determinants of performance.

FIGURE 1.1
Determinants of
Business
Performance

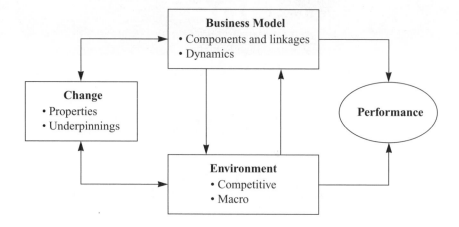

Business Models

The first determinant of a firm's performance is its **business model**. This is the method by which a firm builds and uses its resources to offer its customers better value than its competitors and to make money doing so. It details how a firm makes money now and how it plans to do so in the long term. The model is what enables a firm to have a sustainable **competitive advantage**, to perform better than its rivals in the long term. A business model can be conceptualized as a system that is made up of components, linkages between the components, and dynamics.

Components and Linkages

A business model is about the value that a firm offers its customers, the segment of customers it targets to offer the value to, the scope of products/services[2] it offers to which segment of customers, the profit site it chooses, its sources of revenue, the prices it puts on the value offered its customers, the activities it must perform in offering that value, the capabilities these activities rest on, what a firm must do to sustain any advantages it has, and how well it can implement these elements of the business model. It is a system, and how well a system works is not only a function of the type of components, but also a function of the relationships among the components. Thus, if the value that a firm offers its customers is low cost, then the activities that it performs should reflect that. Take the bricks-and-mortar example of Southwest Airlines. In the 1980s and 1990s, it offered its customers low-cost frequent flights.[3] Two of the activities that the firm performed—no meals on its flights and flying only out of uncongested airports—were consistent with this low-cost strategy. In addition to the relationships among the components of a firm's business model, there is the relationship between the business model and its environment. A good business model always tries to take advantage of any opportunities in its environment while trying to dampen the effects of threats from it.

Dynamics

The right business model components and linkages do not last forever. Managers often have to change some components or relationships before competitors do it for them. In some industries, firms have to keep reinventing their business models. They have to cannibalize themselves before someone else does. It is these actions associated with change, whether initiated by a firm to preempt competitors or to fend them off, or in response to any other opportunities and threats, that we refer to in this text as **dynamics**. In the 1990s Dell Computer was often cited as a firm that was good at reinventing its business model.

Environment

Competitive Environment

Firms do not formulate and execute their business models in a vacuum. They do so in a **competitive environment**. They face competitors who have their own business models, who are just as interested in making money, and who may be equally capable of offering the same level of value to customers. They also face suppliers and customers who may be just as interested in maximizing their own profits as the firms are.

A firm's competitors can, and often do, force down the prices that a firm can charge for its products or force it to offer higher value to customers at a smaller price premium.[4] The lower the prices or the higher the costs, the lower the profits that a firm can make. Rivals do not compete only in the value that they offer customers. They also compete for talent and other resources. Although suppliers can be partners or allies, they are in a sense competitors because their actions can increase a firm's costs and lower the prices that the firm can charge its own customers. Powerful suppliers can extract high prices from a firm, thus raising its costs. They may even force a firm to take lower-quality products, making it difficult for it to offer the kind of value that it would like to offer customers. Similarly, although customers can be loyal allies, their actions often have the same results as those of competitors. If customers are very powerful, they may be able to extract lower prices from a firm or force it to ship products of higher quality than the price warrants. If the market in which a firm is operating is easy to enter, then the firm faces the constant threat of other firms entering its competitive space. This puts a lot of pressure on the prices that a firm can charge because higher prices tend to attract more entrants. Of course, the higher the number of substitute products, the more difficult it is for the firm to make money since higher prices or lower quality will drive customers to substitute products. Finally, the type of technology on which industry products and activities rest also has an impact on firm performance.

Macro Environment

Beyond the competitive environment is the overarching **macro environment** of government policies, natural environment, national boundaries, deregulation/regulation, and technological change. In other words, industries themselves do not operate in a vacuum.[5] The government plays one of the most important roles of the macro environment in terms of firm profitability. Without the government, for example, there would be no Internet. Moreover, government policies worldwide will go a long way in determining the extent to which the Internet thrives and to which firms within their domains profit from the new technology.

Change

The last determinant of firm performance is change. Its role is more indirect than direct. Change impacts business models or their environments, which can translate into higher or lower profitability. Change can come from competitors, suppliers, customers, demographics, the macro environment, or the firm itself. It can be present in firm strategies, demographics, demand and supply, government regulation/deregulation, or the technologies that underpin an industry's products. For example, the microprocessor and personal computer (PC) transformed a computer industry once dominated by makers of mainframes like IBM and makers of minicomputers such as Digital Equipment Corporation into one in which PCs and workstations/servers dominated. Better still, witness the change brought about by the Internet that we explore in this book.

The impact of change on a firm's business model or industry is a function of the type of change. Radical, architectural, or disruptive change can render existing business models obsolete and drastically alter the competitive landscape in existing industries or create entirely new industries while killing old ones. It can result in what the economist J. A. Schumpeter (1883–1950) termed "creative destruction" when it gives rise to new entrepreneurial firms creating wealth and old, established incumbents dying off.[6] The Internet may be doing just that to some industries.

The Internet

The Internet is a technology with many properties that have the potential to transform the competitive landscape in many industries while at the same time creating whole new industries. The **Internet** is a low cost standard with fast interactivity that exhibits network externalities, moderates time, has a universal reach, acts as a distribution channel, and reduces information asymmetries between transacting parties. These properties have a profound impact on the 5-Cs of coordination, commerce, community, content, and communications. Since nearly every firm's activities rest on some subset of the 5-Cs, one can expect the Internet to have a profound effect on all firms. It plays a critical and profound role in the way firm activities (internal or external) are coordinated, how commerce is conducted, how people and machines communicate, how communities are defined and how they interact, and how and when goods are made and delivered. The Internet has the potential to influence established ways of conducting business while creating new ones and new businesses.

INTERNET BUSINESS MODELS

Given such landscape-transforming properties of the Internet, the question is, How can a firm take advantage of them and make money? An **Internet business model** spells out how. It is the method by which a firm plans to make money long term using the Internet. The Internet business model is the system—components, linkages, and associated dynamics—that takes advantage of the properties of the Internet to make money. It takes advantage of the properties of the Internet in the way it builds each of the components—choice of profit site, value, scope, revenue sources, pricing, connected activities, implementation, capabilities, sustainability, and cost structure—and crafts the linkages among these components. For example, the Internet's universality and time-moderation properties allow employees of a firm located in different parts of the world to collaborate on product development, thus decreasing the time needed to bring a product to market. They also allow retailers to stay open 24 hours a day to shoppers, in the privacy of their homes, from different parts of the world.

For expository purposes, Internet business models can be categorized as pure play or clicks-and-mortar. A firm is said to have a pure play Internet business model if, at the model's conception, the firm did not have an existing bricks-and-mortar business model. With a clean slate, a firm can conceive and execute a business model that is free of some of the baggage that old ways of doing things can carry. A clicks-and-mortar model is an Internet business model conceived when a bricks-and-mortar model is already in place. A firm with such a model must concern itself with the impediments—and advantages—of its past models. Which components and linkages of a firm's bricks-and-mortar business model are influenced by the Internet is a function not only of those components and linkages but also of the type of competitive and macro environments in which the firm operates.

Internet business models, whether pure play or clicks-and-mortar, come in all forms. They include brokerage, advertising, infomediary, merchant, manufacturer, affiliate, community, subscription, and utility.[7] All, however, have one goal: to make money. Each model's ability to achieve this goal rests on its components and the linkages between them and its resilience, flexibility, and ability to take advantage of change.

INTERNET BUSINESS MODELS AND STRATEGIES

This book is about Internet business models and strategies and what it takes for them to allow firms to make money. There are five parts to the book (see Figure 1.2). Part I explores the Internet—the technology and its properties. Part II examines the components, linkages, dynamics, taxonomy, appraisal, and valuation of a business model. Part III turns to the role of the competitive and macro environment in firm profitability. Part IV considers applications of the concepts, models, and tools discussed in the text. Part V presents the cases.

FIGURE 1.2 **Conceptual Framework: Where Chapters Fit in the Context of Business Performance**

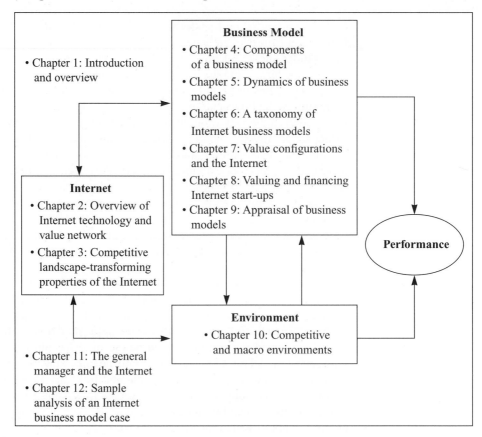

Part I: The Internet

An important part of profiting from an innovation is understanding where one is located or should be located in the innovation value-added configuration. In Chapter 2 we explore the Internet value-added network. We examine infrastructure providers, Internet service providers (ISPs), applications service providers (ASPs), suppliers (of hardware, software, and content) to the Internet infrastructure, complementors, and end users. We pay attention to the relationships between the different members of the configuration and the evolving terminology.

In Chapter 3 we explore those properties of the Internet that promise to transform the competitive landscape in many industries. In particular, we examine 10 properties: mediating technology, universality, network externalities, distribution channel, time moderator, information asymmetry shrinker, infinite virtual capacity, low cost standard, creative destroyer, and reducer of transaction costs. We pay particular attention to how these properties impact the 5-Cs of coordination, commerce, community, content, and communications. We also discuss the limits to the Internet because any good business model must recognize the limitations of the driving force on which it rests.

Part II: Components, Linkages, Dynamics, and Evaluation of Business Models

Having examined the Internet and its properties, we move on to explore Internet business models. In Chapter 4 we examine the components of a business model and the linkages among them. In particular, we discuss the profit site, value, scope, revenue sources, price, connected activities, implementation, capabilities, cost structure, and sustainability, and relationships among them, all of which determine the impact of a business model on firm performance. In Chapter 5 we recognize that the elements of a business model are not static but dynamic as firms initiate or respond to both exogenous and endogenous changes. We explore some of a firm's actions and reactions to attain and maintain a profitable business model in the face of change. In exploiting a technological change, different firms usually pursue different business models. In Chapter 6 we explore the categories or taxonomy of business models that different scholars have developed in an attempt to better understand Internet business models. Thus, while Chapter 4 explores those components of a business model that are critical to gaining and maintaining a competitive advantage, irrespective of the type of business model, Chapter 6 answers the question, What types of business models are out there in the Internet world?

An important part of offering superior customer value is performing the activities that underpin the value. In Chapter 7 we examine the three different value configurations on which value rests: the value chain, the value shop, and the value network. Each has its own characteristics; treating an industry that has a value network as if it had a value chain can be misleading. Understanding these configurations also provides a strong basis for comprehending the extent to which the Internet impacts bricks-and-mortar models and the viability of clicks-and-mortar models.

In Chapter 8 we confront two interesting questions: how to value a start-up company and how to finance it. We explore different methods of valuing a firm or Internet business model: price-earnings (P/E) ratio, price-earnings growth (PEG) ratio, cash flows, and business model attributes. We also explore the role of intellectual capital in valuations, and examine different methods of financing entrepreneurial activity.

If firms have different business models, it becomes important to ask, How can one tell whether one business model is better than another? In Chapter 9 we offer a method for appraising a business model, that is, a method for determining the attractiveness of a business model.

Part III: The Role of Competitive and Macro Environments

In Chapter 10 we recognize that business models do not operate in a vacuum and examine the role of a firm's competitive and macro environments as determinants of profitability and as influencers of business models. We also explore how these environments impact and are impacted by the Internet.

Part IV: Applying the Concepts, Models, and Tools

Chapter 11 takes the point of view of a general manager who must conceive and execute a business model. It walks through some of the things to which the manager must pay attention in formulating and executing business models and strategies. This is a summary of the book from a practitioner's point of view with the addition of a few corporate-level examples. The chapter also explores some of the differences between bricks-and-mortar firms and pure play Internet firms. In Chapter 12 we present an example of how to analyze cases with the focus on an Internet business model case.

Part V: Cases

Relationship between the Text and Cases

The text part of this book explores those concepts, theories, tools, and models that allow students and managers to understand how to gain and maintain a competitive advantage using the Internet. The cases present some of the complex contexts in which managers often must make decisions. Thus, such decisions often require more than one concept, tool, or model. As such, a good analysis of each of the cases in Part V usually requires an understanding of the material from more than one topic.

Summary

Firms are in business to make money. A business model plays a critical role in achieving that goal. The type of environment in which a firm operates and the type of changes that it faces also play important roles. The Internet stands to establish new game strategies for business as it renders existing bricks-and-mortar strategies obsolete while creating opportunities for wealth creation. To take advantage of the Internet entails conceiving and executing a good Internet business model. Such a model must have not only the right components but also the right linkages between them and its environment. It also must have the resilience and flexibility to take advantage of change. This book explores all these factors.

Key Terms

business model, *4*

competitive advantage, *4*

competitive environment, *5*

determinants of business performance, *3*

dynamics, *5*

firm performance, *3*

Internet, *6*

Internet business model, *7*

macro environment, *5*

Discussion Questions

1. By including customers and suppliers in the competitive environment, we imply that they are competitors. Why might we think of suppliers and customers as competitors?

2. It has been argued that the extent to which each determinant of performance impacts a firm's performance is a function of the measure of performance. Do you agree or not? Support your answer with examples.

3. The arrows in Figure 1.1 suggest that a firm can, through its business model, influence both its competitive and macro environments. Do you agree or not? Does the type of industry make a difference? the type of environment?

4. What is the difference between business models and Internet business models?

Notes

1. A firm's performance is determined by its firm-specific resources and capabilities, the type of activities in which it is engaged, the type of industry, and the type of regional or national environment in which it lies. See R. Rumelt, "How Much Does Industry Matter?" *Strategic Management Journal* 12 (1991), pp. 167–85; R. R. Nelson, "Why Do Firms Differ, and How Does It Matter?" *Strategic Management Journal*, Winter Special Issue 12 (1991), pp. 61–74; B. Wernerfelt, "A Resource-Based View of the Firm," *Strategic Management Journal* 5 (1984), pp. 171–80; M. E. Porter, *Competitive Strategy: Techniques for Analyzing Industries and Competitors* (New York: Free Press, 1980); M. E. Porter, *The Competitive Advantage of Nations* (New York: Free Press, 1990).

2. Unless specified otherwise, the word "product" means "product or service" throughout this book.

3. M. E. Porter, "What Is Strategy?" *Harvard Business Review*, November–December 1996, pp. 61–78.

4. Porter, *Competitive Strategy*.

5. Porter, *The Competitive Advantage of Nations*.

6. J. A. Schumpeter, *The Theory of Economic Development* (Boston: Harvard University Press, 1934), a translation from the German, *Theorie der Wirtschaftlichen Entwicklung* (Leipzig: Duncker & Humboldt, 1912).

7. Michael Rappa, "2000. Managing the Digital Enterprise: Business Models," ecommerce.ncsu.edu/topics/models/models.html.

Chapter **Two**

Overview of Internet Technology and Value Network

DEFINITION AND HISTORY

What Are the Internet and the World Wide Web?

This book is about Internet business models and how to analyze them. So far, we have only briefly discussed the Internet and said nothing about the World Wide Web. In this chapter, we fully explore both. The Internet is a vast collection of networks of computers that are interconnected both physically and through their ability to encode and decode certain specialized communications protocols called the Internet Protocol (IP) and the Transmission Control Protocol (TCP).[1] A *protocol* in this sense is simply a specification of how computers exchange information. IP describes how information to be transmitted should be broken down into small *packets*, while TCP describes how a "stream" of packets should be reconstructed at the other end and what to do, for example, if a packet is missing.[2]

The Internet infrastructure consists of five major components: the backbone, routers (digital switches), points of presence (POPs), computer servers, and users' connected computers (see Figure 2.1).[3] This system allows authorized users connected to the network anyplace in the world to have access to data stored on computers anywhere else in the world.

The **backbone** is a collection of high-speed telecommunications lines (what used to be called "trunk lines" or simply "telephone lines" but now have a much higher capacity) that are connected by high-speed computers. It is made up of fast fiber-optic lines that allow computers to transfer data at very high speeds. The **bandwidth** of the telecommunications line refers to the capacity or speed of data transfer: the amount of information—the digital 1s or 0s that

FIGURE 2.1 **Internet Components**

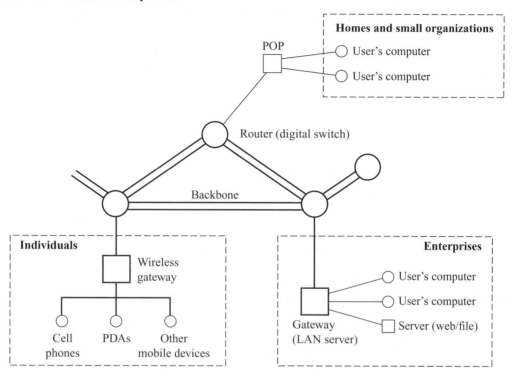

are called **bits**—the line is capable of carrying per unit time, usually expressed in the number of bits per second (bps) or millions of bits per second (Mbps) or, for very high-capacity lines, billions of bits per second (gigabits per second, or Gbps). Thus the backbone of the Internet is made up of high-bandwidth lines that crisscross North America and extend throughout the world. For example, in 2002 MCI Worldcom's backbone lines from New York to the San Francisco Bay Area had a capacity of 10 Gbps (10,000 Mbps or 10 billion bits per second) and they had several of those lines.[4] In 1999, forty backbone carriers transported almost all of the long-distance traffic.[5]

Connecting each backbone line to another is a high-speed **digital switch** such as an asynchronous transmission mode (ATM) switch. These switches are actually very fast dedicated computers that move "traffic" (information) along the backbone lines. The switches take the information and pass it along to the next backbone line. Switches that perform a "routing" function, deciding on which direction to pass traffic, are called **routers**. For example, suppose you request information from a computer in a different part of the country. This generates "**traffic**" in the form of a request to a remote computer and a response from that computer, if the information is available.[6] We will shortly discuss what happens at each end of this transaction. Between the two ends, the information "flows" along the backbone lines as it is forwarded from one digital switch to the next. Many of these intermediate switches are connected to more than two backbone lines. Based on the destination and the congestion along the lines, they decide which line information should be "routed" (forwarded).

To gain access to this network requires other specialized computers. The three most common types of end users are (1) individuals, (2) small- to medium-sized organizations, and (3) large organizations or "enterprises." Individuals and small organizations are often grouped together because their access is usually identical. They gain access to the Internet by means of an Internet service provider's (ISP) **point of presence (POP)**. A POP is simply a point of access to the network and consists of a switch (computer) that knows how to route traffic to the end users connected directly to it.[7] Individuals may also gain access to the Internet via personal communications and electronic devices, such as mobile telephones and personal digital assistants, via wireless gateways. The means of access are a little more complicated as the individual may be moving from one location to the next, but conceptually speaking it is similar to the case of the home user. The wireless gateway serves as an interface between the Internet and the wireless operator's own network. Information within the operator's network, that is, from the mobile device to and from the operator's equipment, is treated as any voice call would be.

Large enterprises connect to the Internet by means of a similar kind of switch called a *gateway* or **local area network (LAN)** server, which may or may not be behind a "**firewall**"—a combination of specialized hardware and software that provides protection from users and requests outside the LAN. LANs consist of various types of hardware devices and other resources that organizations can share. Large LANs such as those that serve enterprises are usually connected directly to a high-speed switch through the LAN server, which also knows how to route local traffic to end users on the LAN (see Figure 2.1). End users can be physically connected to the LAN (the so-called **fixed-line** or **wire-line Internet**) or can be connected wirelessly through the combination of a network access point that is physically attached to the network and a wireless card (antenna) that sends and receives data from the access point. This setup is often called **fixed wireless**. All computers that can interconnect with the Internet are considered part of the Internet.

The **World Wide Web** (WWW or the Web, for short) is the collection of computers on the Internet that support a certain hypertext function. **Hypertext** is different from "normal" text in that it does not follow a linear path from top to bottom; instead, one can follow items of interest in a nonlinear fashion by selecting words or pictures of interest and immediately gaining more information on the items selected. Not all potential items (words or pictures) can be selected, so how does the user-reader know which items are available? The *author* of the page decides which items are worthy of more information and creates a special link from the current page to the page (or pages) that has additional information. The pages are also called the **content**; thus, the author is often referred to as the *content creator*. In the language of the World Wide Web, a user *clicks on* (selects) the link to gain the desired information.

For example, imagine that you wish to post your resume online to improve your chances of getting a job. When you contact recruiters, you tell them to go to your Web page to see the latest version of your resume. There are many tools available to translate your document into HTML (HyperText Markup Language), which will be discussed shortly. Simply posting the text of the resume is entirely possible. Recruiters will see only the text of the resume and will not be able to follow links to other sites. However, you decide that it is appropriate to provide more information in two areas. First, your university, Best University, has its own website, so on your resume you create a link between the words "Best University" and the website, http://www.best.edu. Therefore, users viewing your resume see the link underlining Best University; when they click on it, they are connected to the Best University website. As the author, you determine which links are "clickable."

The above link was to an external source of the additional information. However, you may want to develop some further content. For example, in the section under Additional Information, you may want to have a picture of you at age 12 shaking hands with Bill Gates. Let's say that you do not want that picture, which you have scanned into a file, to be on your resume, but you do want anyone who wants to look at the picture to be able to gain access to it from your resume. So, in the Additional Information section on your resume, you link the words "shook hands with Bill Gates" to the new file. Thus, you now have two links in your resume, one to content created and maintained by someone else (the university website), the other to content created, or at least maintained, by you (the picture). This is part of the process that content authors go through whenever they design content for the Web.

The World Wide Web works because the Internet infrastructure is in place to support it. Thus, the WWW performs a function (hypertext) that is a subset of all the functions available on the Internet (e.g., file transfers, remote login, electronic mail—see the appendix to this book for more details). Because the WWW is the most famous function of the Internet, many people use the terms interchangeably; as we have seen from the above discussion, this is slightly inaccurate.

A Brief History of the Internet and the World Wide Web[8]

During the Cold War the United States military and its think tanks such as the RAND Corporation were faced with a problem. The threat of nuclear attack loomed in the minds of military strategists: specifically, any centralized "control center" would be a prime target in a nuclear attack. This problem gave birth to the idea of a decentralized "network" with redundant connections. The research was sponsored for many years by the Advanced Research Projects Agency (ARPA), a government agency affiliated with the Department of Defense. When a few computers (e.g., one at UCLA and another at the

Stanford Research Institute—SRI) were connected in the late 1960s and early 1970s, the precursor of the Internet, the **ARPAnet**, was born.

By design, the system was intended to be redundant; that is, it would have many paths of delivering data so that if one part of the network was disabled, other paths could be found automatically. In this decentralized environment, the network grew from a handful of U.S. universities to practically all universities in the United States and many overseas, in addition to many research institutes and some companies, usually defense-oriented companies with some affiliation with DARPA (Defense Advanced Research Projects Agency, as ARPA became known). At one point, the National Science Foundation took over responsibility for providing the backbone (high-speed trunk line) services. As the number of commercial users grew from year to year and it became clear that users were willing to pay for such services, private telecommunications companies stepped into the void and began providing their own high-speed lines, the use of which they rented or sold to companies wanting access.

Most of the traffic in the early days of the Internet, as the network eventually became known, was generated by just four applications. The most widely used service was *electronic mail*, or **e-mail**. E-mail service allowed a user at one end-user computer (also known as a *host*) to send a text message and have this message stored for delivery at the recipient's host for retrieval by the recipient when convenient. In addition to e-mail, **discussion lists/newsgroups** became popular. Users posting messages to a newsgroup or a discussion list had their messages copied to all other subscribers of the list. Another popular application, especially among the scientific community, was **file transfer protocol (ftp)**. With a file transfer, one could either send a file to or retrieve one from a remote host. The advantage of this was that a user could move large blocks of data very quickly, much more quickly than backing up a file on tape and carrying or mailing it to the remote site. Finally, a highly useful application was **telnet** or *remote login* capability. This allowed the user to log in to a remote host and perform functions on the remote computer as if the user were connected to the host on-site. For example, a user in California could log in to a computer in Korea and be indistinguishable from a user sitting at a terminal in Korea.

These four applications were popular enough to drive the growth of the Internet for many years. The Internet infrastructure—the backbone, digital switches, computer servers, POPs, users' computers, software, and protocols—was created to help users gain access to information on computers anywhere in the world. The problem in the early days was that to find information on the Internet, a user had to specify the address of the computer on which the information resided. This made finding information on different computers tedious and limited to those with computer science skills.

Tim Berners-Lee, a researcher at CERN,[9] the particle physics laboratory near Geneva, Switzerland, would change all of that. The scientists who worked at CERN came from all over the world and had immense problems exchanging incompatible documents and e-mail messages from their own proprietary systems. Berners-Lee revived an earlier idea of his from 1980 that was a precursor to a hypertext storage and retrieval system. He proposed that CERN's scientists could combine their knowledge by linking their documents contextually. He developed a language called **HyperText Markup Language (HTML)** that he could use not only to create links to different computers but also to display graphics associated with some files. To the user, such links, or hypertext, are highlighted; all the user needs to do to gain access to the information associated with the link is to click on it. These hypertext links and the associated information stored on the Internet nodes became known as the World Wide Web. CERN made the source code for the first WWW browser and server freely available, which spurred growth in their development as programmers from all over the world began contributing to the infrastructure of the WWW.[10]

In recent years, a slew of **wireless protocols** have been developed to help bridge the gap between the information available on the Internet (e-mail, instant messaging, Web pages, and so on) and portable devices ranging from laptops to cell phones. We mention just a few of the most important ones here with the proviso that the wireless sector is in a great deal of flux. IEEE 802.11b (and its eventual successor, the quicker 802.11a or 802.11g), also known as "Wi-Fi" (short for wireless fidelity), is a standard that defines how information is passed between a wireless access point (also known as a base station) and a wireless client (such as a laptop with a wireless card) or between two wireless clients. Bluetooth is another, albeit slower but more energy-efficient. For communications with cell phones, several broad classes of technology have been developed, starting with so-called 2G (second generation) digital PCS (personal communications service, see the Sprint case in this book), which is used for voice but enables limited data exchange. After 2G, a transitional technology known as 2.5G was developed. This is an extension of 2G that allows for packet-switched data services (see the Appendix for more information on packet switching). Late in 2001, 3G (third generation) technology was introduced and is meant for higher bandwidth on data transfer to and from cellular phones and other mobile clients. The bandwidth is much lower than Wi-Fi, but the advantage is that the power requirements are also much lower and thus more suited to personal mobile devices. To gain access specifically to Internet content, these 3G-compatible devices utilize such protocols as Wireless Access Protocol (WAP), which is an open protocol designed to request, receive, and transform Internet content. Proprietary services such as NTT DoCoMo's i-Mode can also take advantage of 3G. In addition, in principle, 3G devices can run IP applications directly on the devices.

THE INTERNET VALUE NETWORK

Associated with each of the components of the Internet is an industry or group of firms that market similar or related products. In this section, we describe the various sectors of the Internet economy and give the names of the largest companies in each sector. We call this the "**Internet value network**" because in the broadest sense, all the components described below and their interrelations create value for the end users, the customers, and organizations that actually use the network.[11]

Generally speaking, we propose that the Internet value network can be divided into three major groups: users, communications service providers, and suppliers. This division into three groups is an abstraction; many firms are both users and suppliers, or users and communications service providers, or communications service providers and suppliers. For example, Cisco Systems is a supplier of communications equipment *and* a large user (a Web merchant) in its own right; that is, Cisco not only makes routers that Internet service providers (ISPs) buy but also sells directly to those ISPs over the Internet.

In addition, some segments might just as easily be classified as both suppliers and users. To give a specific case, media and content companies, such as AOL Time Warner, supply editorial content to firms as well as run "**portals**," which are entry and focal sites for consumers and businesses. For this reason, we have included a category under both users and suppliers. Thus, the categorizations of any one firm or even subsegment are slightly arbitrary; however, the broad trends will be evident as we discuss the logic of each group and segment.

The three large groups—users, communications services, and suppliers—can be further subdivided into segments or what we are calling **profit sites**. We will examine each group in turn and provide examples of the largest companies in each segment (see Table 2.1).

I. Users

Users are companies that use the Internet intensively in the core of their business. We exclude from consideration here large companies that use the Internet intensively but only at the periphery of their business (see Chapters 5, 6, and 9). Users may be subdivided further into five categories (see Figure 2.2): (1) *e-commerce*, those companies that sell goods over the Internet; (2) *content aggregators*, those that gather content from multiple sources and display that content on their sites; (3) *market makers,* which act as intermediaries and run electronic markets; (4) brokers/agents, which act as intermediaries by facilitating transactions for a particular party (e.g., a buyer or a seller); and (5) *service providers* that furnish all other Internet-based services.[12] Technically, individuals and non-Internet organizations (e.g., automobile manufacturers) are also "users," but they will not be discussed here because our main concern in this chapter is to describe the interrelations that comprise the Internet infrastructure.

1. E-commerce Companies

E-commerce (electronic commerce) companies exchange "real products for real money through online channels."[13] While some people refer to e-commerce as any business having anything to do with the Internet, we will be more precise in our classification and limit ourselves only to those companies that sell over online channels. Some companies manufacture or assemble the goods

TABLE 2.1 **The Largest Companies in Each Profit Site**

Source: *Internet World, Network World, Red Herring, Business 2.0, Boardwatch Magazine,* Telecommunications Reports International, Yahoo Finance, *Business Week,* SEC Filings, and company websites.

Profit Site	Company	Revenues (in millions), Market Share, and Users
1. E-commerce		
	1. Dell Computer	$31,200 (online)
	2. Cisco Systems	22,300
	3. AOL Time Warner	8,700
	4. IBM	3,500
	5. Amazon	3,300
2. Content aggregators		
	1. AOL Time Warner	$ 8,700 (online)
	2. MSN	2,500
	3. Yahoo!	720
	4. Terra Lycos	670
	5. CNET	290
3. Brokers/agents		
	1. Charles Schwab	$ 4,400 (online)
	2. E*Trade	2,100
	3. Citigroup	800
	4. Ameritrade	500
	5. Harrisdirect	340
4. Market-makers		
	1. Priceline	$ 1,200 (online)
	2. eBay	750
	3. VerticalNet	130
	4. Sotheby's	60
	5. ImageX	50
5. Service providers		
	1. IBM	$34,900 (services)
	2. EDS	19,200
	3. Computer Sciences	10,500
	4. Automatic Data Processing	9,500
	5. EMC	7,400
6. Backbone operators		
	1. MCI Worldcom/UUNet	27.9% (market share)
	2. AT&T	10.0%
	3. Intermedia	7.7%
	4. Sprint	6.5%
	5. Genuity	6.3%
7. ISPs/OSPs		
	1. AOL Time Warner	28.5 M (subscribers)
	2. MSN	7.7 M
	3. United Online	5.2 M
	4. Earthlink	4.9 M
	5. CompuServe	3.0 M

(continued)

TABLE 2.1 *(continued)*

Profit Site	Company	Revenues (in millions), Market Share, and Users
8. Last Mile		
	1. NTT	$103,100
	2. Verizon	67,200
	3. AT&T	52,600
	4. SBC Communications	45,900
	5. British Telecom	43,800
9. Content creators		
	1. AOL Time Warner	$ 38,200 (content)
	2. Viacom	23,200
	3. Bertelsmann	16,400
	4. Walt Disney	15,700
	5. New York Times	3,000
10. Software suppliers		
	1. Microsoft	$ 25,300 (software)
	2. Oracle	10,900
	3. SAP	7,400
	4. NCR	5,900
	5. Computer Associates	3,000
11. Hardware suppliers		
	1. Hewlett-Packard*	$ 37,200 (hardware)
	2. IBM	33,400
	3. Dell	31,200
	4. Motorola	29,900
	5. Compaq*	26,700

*Merger/acquisition activity in 2002.

themselves; others simply resell goods made by other companies. The largest companies in this space sell over the Internet products that they manufacture themselves (see Table 2.1). As mentioned above, Cisco Systems manufactures communications equipment (mainly routers) and sells them directly over the Internet to ISPs. Some e-commerce companies sell only over the Internet; others sell both over the Internet and in standard bricks-and-mortar distribution channels. When the downstream buyers' (not those of the end-user customers) needs conflict with the Internet channel, it is called *channel conflict*. Many companies are involved in multiple segments, especially the e-commerce segment, where companies can compete in any other segment and take orders over the Internet. For example, Intel is one of the largest hardware components manufacturers, but it also sells several billion dollars worth of those components online. America Online (AOL) is the largest online service provider (OSP), and it books all of its revenues online. Thus, the e-commerce segment is a catch-all for any segment selling online and can be treated in tandem with the other segments.[14] In late 2001, **m-commerce** (mobile commerce), or

FIGURE 2.2 **Value Network Profit Sites with Representative Companies**

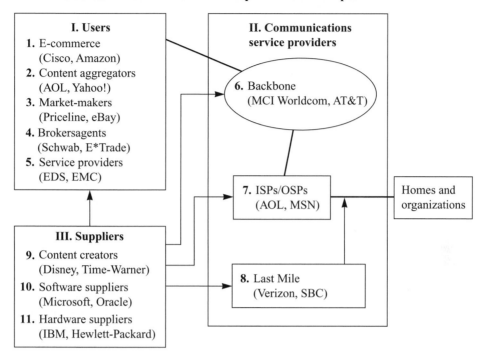

e-commerce over wireless channels, has been a particular focus of attention, probably due to its massive potential rather than its realization.

2. Content Aggregators

The next category of users encompasses *media companies* and *content providers*. Note that media companies and content providers are listed under both users and suppliers because most of them are intensive users of the Internet as well as suppliers (of information) to other users. In this section, we discuss the companies whose business revolves around intensive use of the Internet, such as America Online, Netscape (which was acquired by AOL in 1999), and Yahoo! These companies, while they are content providers, are mainly information aggregators and portals.

3. Market-Makers and 4. Brokers/Agents

In contrast to expectations, many famous names in Internet business are *intermediaries*. We say "in contrast to expectations" because much of what you read in the business press is how the Internet *reduces* intermediation. As we will see in Chapter 7, this is not quite true; indeed, the Internet may actually *increase* intermediation. The Internet allowed and continues to allow a new class of intermediaries that bring buyers and sellers together and make money by charging one or the other party a small transaction fee. A *market-maker* acts as a neutral intermediary that provides a place to trade and also sets the rules of the market. Thus this profit site includes companies that run or set up electronic markets, such as electricity markets, and electronic auctioneers, such as eBay or Sotheby's. Priceline makes a market in airline tickets, among other areas. They all have the same logic of bringing buyers and sellers together. Note the relatively small size of intermediaries in general and market-makers in particular.

We also see a large number of brokerages (buyers and sellers of securities), banks (borrowers and lenders), and travel agents (buyers and sellers of travel services) migrating or extending their businesses to the Internet. These are all examples of *brokers* or *agents*, who facilitate transactions for one party to a transaction. We call attention to brokers like Charles Schwab, which has grown from a bricks-and-mortar discount stock brokerage—where clients visited branch offices or telephoned in their orders—into the largest Internet broker because of the migration of orders to the Internet. Schwab takes orders from a buyer (or seller) and then attempts to complete the transaction by finding someone for the other side of the deal.

5. Internet Services

Internet services include support services such as consulting, outsourcing, website design, electronic data interchange, firewalls, and data storage backups. Any service beyond communications services belongs in this category.[15] Thousands of companies perform these services, but the companies in this segment tend to be very small. Five of the largest service companies are listed in Table 2.1. These companies make money by selling their services or their expertise on a fee-for-service basis. Electronic Data Systems (EDS), for example, has made a name for itself in the outsourcing of information technology services. When a company in a noncomputer industry grows tired of managing its own data processing (e.g., databases, payroll, hardware upgrades, software upgrades), the original firm may decide to hire another firm to completely run its own data processing, freeing up management to run its original business. This is referred to as **outsourcing**. Some of these services offered by EDS and other companies have now begun migrating to the Internet; for example, EDS can completely manage the software upgrade process for an entire company over the Internet.

II. Communications Services

Communications service providers may also be divided into several segments: backbone service providers, ISPs/OSPs, and Last Mile providers. **Backbone service providers** are those companies that maintain their own backbone lines, as described at the beginning of this chapter. An **Internet service provider (ISP)** delivers access to consumers and small- to medium-sized organizations, while **online service providers (OSPs)** do the same but also provide content to subscribers. **Last Mile providers** develop, maintain, and provide the physical connection (e.g., the telephone, cable, or wireless connections) to consumers and small- to medium-sized organizations. The companies in this group all provide telecommunications services to each other, to the users' segment, and to consumers. They develop communications networks that enable the connectivity of their customers. Their key expertise is in designing and developing new products (e.g., *69, ISDN, DSL, cable modems), developing sophisticated billing systems, and maintaining equipment and lines. They also all face a similar problem: recovering fixed costs.

Anyone who has used a telephone in recent years has probably noticed that long-distance rates have fallen dramatically from 28 cents per minute to 15 cents (remember 10-cent Sundays?) to 10 cents per minute, 24 hours a day, seven days a week. In 2002 the rate is pushing down further to 2.9 cents a minute and lower! How do we explain this relentless price movement? The problem for the companies, not for the consumer, is that the fixed cost of buying and installing a switch and developing a billing system is very high, but the marginal cost of connecting an additional telephone call is essentially nil. This was not much of an issue when one telephone company, AT&T, dominated the telephone industry. It simply charged enough to recover its fixed costs and make a profit. But after the long-distance market was opened to competition, any company that had made the high fixed investment was—and continues to be—in a battle for revenues; hence the price competition and the "race to the bottom." This is an extreme example of a more general problem in so-called knowledge-based industries which we will discuss further in Chapter 4.

In any case, the telecommunications service providers in the Internet sphere have not had to face this problem yet, perhaps because of the tremendous growth of the market, perhaps because many of them still hold monopolies in local telephone service. Most of the companies in the communications services segment rely on a subscription-based model for making money.

6. Backbone Operators

The first segment of the Internet infrastructure is the companies that run the backbone. The companies in this segment control large-bandwidth lines and are able to handle a large volume of digital traffic. Table 2.1 shows the market share of the five leading companies in the industry. MCI Worldcom dominates with one-third of the market, followed by AT&T at 10 percent. MCI Worldcom (which was itself formed by the merger of MCI and Worldcom) attempted to acquire Sprint in 2000. These companies make money by selling Internet connectivity services to Internet service providers and large companies on a subscription basis. For information purposes, the median charge in 2001 for tapping into the network through the backbone operators was about $1,800 per T1 line (1.544 Mbps) per month.[16]

7. ISPs/OSPs

How do individuals or small organizations without LANs access the Web? A group of firms called Internet service providers (ISPs) provide the hardware and software that enable individuals to gain access to the Web. ISPs have their own servers, switches, and software to connect individuals to the Internet.

ISPs include firms such as AT&T, MCI Worldcom, Sprint, UUNet, Netcom, Online, PSI, and others. In addition to ISPs that offer their customers access to the free content of the Internet, proprietary online service providers (OSPs) not only offer their subscribers access to the Internet but also, for a fee, offer access to a private, closed network whose content is only for fee-paying members. OSPs include America Online (AOL), CompuServe, Prodigy, and Microsoft Network. Table 2.1 lists the companies by the number of subscribers each ISP/OSP serves. These companies make money by providing Internet access through their points of presence (POP) to small organizations and to individuals, usually for a flat monthly fee.

8. *Last Mile*

The connection to consumers is sometimes known as the Last Mile because it represents the physical connection between the POP—which is usually considered to be local, such as the local telephone switch—and the end user. These connections can take many forms, such as telephone wire ("twisted pair"), fiber optics, cable, and wireless. More generally, the Last Mile is the category of the industry supporting these types of communications services. As shown in Table 2.1, this segment is dominated by telecommunications companies, mainly local phone companies. We would have to move all the way down to #12 before we even get to a cable company. Also note the sheer size of the companies in the Last Mile category, which is much bigger on average than any of the other segments. Most of these companies grew to their vast size as a result of the monopoly they had as local telephone companies. Now they make money by investing in local lines and selling access to these lines on a subscription basis.

Many researchers believe that controlling the Last Mile is a battle in its infancy. The former AT&T local telephone monopolies (the Regional Bell Operating Companies) have done a creditable job of maintaining their control over the Last Mile, perhaps through their development of new products or their influence on the regulatory process.[17] Two developments over the last decade that count as new products are Integrated Services Digital Network (ISDN) and the Digital Subscriber Lines (DSL). Both technologies allow for higher-bandwidth transfers, using the normal twisted-pair telephone wiring, and enable the end user to talk on the telephone while sending and receiving digital data at rates higher than those available from a modem.

AT&T itself, though, has chosen a two-pronged approach to wrest control of the Last Mile from the regional Bell operating companies. The first is a "wireless" strategy (e.g., giving away cellular telephones, promoting flat-rate long-distance service from cellular telephones, eliminating roaming charges, providing complimentary services such as traffic reports) that attempts to supplant the wireline telephone from its primacy in the hearts of consumers. In fact, in much of the rest of the world, wireless access to the Internet via cell phones is predicted to surpass wire-line access.[18] AT&T's second approach relates to the use of cable television lines as an alternative Last Mile conduit.

Cable lines can provide high-speed Internet access. Therefore, in 1999 AT&T acquired MediaOne—one of the largest cable television companies—with the intention of providing an alternative to the regional Bells. In addition, other media firms that own cable companies, such as AOL Time Warner, have been developing products based on high-speed Internet access over the cable. Even electric utilities have contemplated entering this market, using the electricity lines they have already installed and maintained!

Why do these companies care so much about the Last Mile? There are several reasons for this intense interest. The first is control over strategic resources. Just about every page served, every commerce transaction, and every download will pass through that Last Mile, so it is natural that certain firms do not want to leave to chance or historical accident who controls that Last Mile. In the past the regional Bell operating companies controlled that last mile, which turned out to be immensely profitable. Thus, the Last Mile has attracted entry precisely because of its profitability. This entry represents the first time the regional Bells have faced any serious competition; it was only a matter of time before other companies with a different technology jumped in to shave off a piece of that gigantic market. As mentioned above, all consumers go through a Last Mile provider before attaining access to the Internet, and it seems that consumers are quite willing to pay for high quality/bandwidth in the Last Mile.[19]

III. Suppliers

Finally, suppliers can be divided into three segments: (1) content creators, (2) software suppliers, and (3) hardware suppliers. These segments belong with "suppliers" because they typically supply upstream products or services to users and communications service providers, and in some cases to each other. Content creators are in the business of developing news- and entertainment-oriented content in many forms, including text, music, and video. Computer software suppliers develop the software, usually in packaged form, and sell the software that runs on consumer and enterprise computers, including personal computers and engineering workstations. Computer hardware companies manufacture the desktop computers, workstations, mobile devices, servers, telecommunications, and switching hardware that end users and communications service providers need. Hardware suppliers also manufacture components such as the internal devices that control or interact with computer hardware systems.

9. Content Creators

Media/content suppliers are the developers and owners of intellectual capital. They produce such works as music, games, graphics, video/motion pictures, and text (articles, news, and other sorts of information). The two largest companies, Disney and AOL Time Warner, are fully integrated in the content business, producing and developing all of the above, such as motion pictures, videos, music, games, and news in their business units. In contrast to the bricks-and-mortar economy, this category of the Internet economy has been the most in flux with no dominant model of making money. The subscription model applies to few content creators, mainly those dispensing financial information. For example, Dow Jones supports its Wall Street Journal Interactive Edition with subscriptions from *The Wall Street Journal* subscribers and even nonsubscribers, who are charged more for the content.[20] Fee-for-service is another model pursued by some of these companies, although users are apparently unwilling to pay for most intellectual content (with the exception of pornography).

Part of the problem is that it is extremely inexpensive to reproduce digital media, thus making it very difficult to enforce intellectual property ownership of media content. We will discuss this further in Chapter 3, but for now most media/content suppliers have been satisfied to give away their content for free, raise the number of "**eyeballs**" (the number of unique viewers), and pin their hopes on an advertising model. Some sell complementary goods and make money from that rather than the content. For example, Sony sells gaming hardware that is Internet-enabled so that consumers can play games with other Internet users. While there is nothing (or little) to prevent the copying of the gaming software, the hardware itself is more difficult to imitate.[21]

10. Software Suppliers

Software suppliers provide software products, such as word processing or spreadsheet applications, operating systems, printer drivers, databases, electronic commerce software, and so on. These companies operate on the principle of selling software products to end users or to companies interested in starting or maintaining an Internet presence. They are like manufacturers, investing in software development and marketing and selling products, presumably for a profit. While fixed-cost recovery and easy replication are also theoretically issues—and may be so in the future—the insatiable appetite of the public for increased features (coupled with Microsoft's dominant position) keeps the industry growing.[22] Microsoft is the largest of these companies; it is the software company of choice for desktop personal computers and, in the late 1990s, some servers. Oracle has made the transition from database company to Internet-database company and has maintained its position as the second-largest software company.

To provide a taste of some kinds of Internet-based software suppliers, consider electronic commerce (e-commerce) software. Electronic commerce software companies produce software that enables e-commerce, which can be one of several different types. Prior to the advent of the Internet, the most important and popular kind of e-commerce was electronic data interchange (EDI). EDI allowed companies to exchange ordering and inventory information up and down the supply chain; for example, when a distributor ran low on inventory for a certain product, an EDI system passed that information to the manufacturer. In the past EDI was implemented on private data networks; in the late 1990s this technology has migrated to the Internet.[23]

There are a variety of other e-commerce applications having to do with retailing products on a website, such as "shopping cart" technology, order/payment processing, and "micro-payments."[24] Shopping cart technology keeps track of purchases that consumers make. While this might sound like a trivial task, most people do not realize the complexity of tracking such information from page to page on a website. It operates on the principle that the Web server for the retailer does not know who you are when you make repeated shopping selections without some form of identification. The companies that make the browsers allow an identification number of sorts to be stored on your computer, which can be passed to the retailer every time you interact with it.[25] In this way you can keep adding items to your shopping cart and the retailer always knows that it is you placing the order.

Order/payment processing software is designed to track orders, track inventories, and, most importantly, process credit card transactions. As you can imagine, the security considerations of processing payments are immense. Most of the effort in this area has been to design systems that prevent credit card numbers from falling into the wrong hands through the use of encryption.[26] Micropayment or microcash software is designed to handle very, very small transactions. For example, imagine that you wanted to listen to a piece of music only once over the Internet. The recording studio would like to charge you a royalty fee of 1/20¢ (i.e., if you listened to it 20 times, you would owe 1 cent). How can companies keep track of such small payments? Micropayment systems are designed to do just that.

In 1999 a new type of software business sprang up: the **application service provider (ASP)**. The ASP service, also referred to as an "app-on-tap," provides a centralized repository for software applications which individuals can "borrow" or "rent" to run on their own desktop personal computers. This end-user system is called a **thin client** because the applications no longer reside on the end-user system. The applications are delivered over the Internet to the thin client on demand. Applications envisioned for this type of service span the full range from database software packages to word processing applications to corporate business process analysis programs. Large enterprises also appreciate the ASP system because it enables the centralized information technology (IT) function to regain control over employees' desktop software. In recent years, as corporate computer systems have become more decentralized, it has become more difficult for companies to control the versions of software that employees store on their own personal computers.

11. Hardware Suppliers

The hardware category comprises three interrelated areas: communications equipment manufacturers, computer equipment manufacturers, and hardware component manufacturers. The *communications equipment* manufacturers are the producers of the various kinds of routers and other digital switches. Cisco Systems and Lucent Technologies (formerly part of AT&T) dominate this industry, although 3Com is also well known for its communications equipment. Motorola also gains much of its revenue from communications equipment, cellular telephones, and semiconductors. These companies make money by selling their manufactured products, which are hardware/software systems that enable the Internet to move data traffic. The customers of these companies include backbone operators, ISPs, and large organizations that have their own internal networks.

Computer hardware contains both client and server hardware—that is, end-user computers (personal computers and workstations) and server devices (Web servers, file servers, e-mail servers, LAN servers).[27] The largest computer hardware company is undoubtedly IBM, which brought in almost $86 billion dollars in 2001, much of which came from hardware sales. Other large computer manufacturers include Hewlett-Packard and Compaq, which attempted to merge in 2002. These companies also produce servers, as does Sun Microsystems, which is one of the largest server manufacturers. These companies sell their hardware to end users and to other businesses. They are the main customers of the *hardware components* companies, which sell computer chips and peripherals such as disk drives to the computer hardware companies and the communications equipment companies. The hardware components segment also operates under the producer model where the largest companies are Motorola and Intel (processors and other semiconductor chips) and Seagate (disk drives).

Summary

This chapter has provided a brief introduction to the history and terminology of the Internet along with the key segments of the Internet industry. The Internet and the World Wide Web, often used interchangeably, are not the same. The Internet is a vast system of computers that are connected by high-speed communications lines and can understand the IP/TCP protocols. The WWW is linked content that is accessible through the Internet, written in HTML and viewed through a browser. In addition to the WWW protocol (http), the main four applications on the Internet are e-mail (electronic mail), discussion lists/newsgroups, FTP (file transfer protocol), and remote login (telnet). Companies in the Internet infrastructure are found in 1 of 11 market categories, or profit sites, grouped into three segments: users, communications service providers, and suppliers. Users are divided into e-commerce companies, content aggregators, market-makers, brokers/agents, and service providers. Communications service providers are divided into backbone operators, ISPs/OSPs, and Last Mile providers. Finally, suppliers can be divided into content creators, software suppliers, and hardware suppliers.

Key Terms

application service
 provider (ASP), *27*
ARPAnet, *16*
backbone, *12*
backbone service
 providers, *22*
bandwidth, *12*
bits, *13*

content, *14*
digital switch, *13*
discussion lists, *16*
e-commerce, *18*
e-mail, *16*
eyeballs, *26*
file transfer protocol
 (ftp), *16*

firewall, *14*
fixed line Internet, *14*
fixed wireless, *14*
hypertext, *14*
HyperText Markup
 Language
 (HTML), *17*

Discussion Questions

1. Step by step, draw a map of what happens when you buy a new widget online. Start with pressing the "Add to Shopping Cart" button on the vendor's website. End with the vendor packing your order. Who makes money in this transaction? Where is value added?

2. Discuss the benefits and pitfalls of being in the content creation business. Name a content creation company and describe the weaknesses in its business plan.

3. Is an Internet service provider different from a backbone operator? How?

4. Looking at a company such as Amazon.com (see Chapter 12), would you classify it as an e-commerce company, a content aggregator, a market-maker, or a service provider? Why? How about a company such as eBay (see the eBay case in Part V)?

5. Think of another industry besides telecommunications where fixed-cost recovery is an important challenge.

6. Pick one of the profit sites and discuss the differences between being a wire-line and wireless participant in that profit site.

Notes

1. These protocols are almost always used in tandem, hence the terms IP/TCP and TCP/IP. Technically, a computer does not have to be able to understand IP/TCP itself; it simply has to be connected with a gateway computer that does.

2. See the appendix to this book for more detail on these protocols.

3. See Haim Mendelson, "A Note on Internet Technology," Stanford University Graduate School of Business #S-OIT-15, January 1999; see also www.whatis.com/tourenv.htm; finally, refer to Charles W. Hill, "America Online and the Internet," in C. W. Hill and G. R. Jones, *Strategic Management,* 4th edition (Boston: Houghton Mifflin, 1999), pp. C92–C106.

4. www1.worldcom.com/global/about/network/maps/northam

5. The backbone carriers do not carry all of the traffic for several reasons: local area networks (LANs) carry local traffic; some large companies have their own networks, usually based on IP/TCP (called *intranets* if operating solely within one company and *extranets* when outside organizations have direct access); and the existence of alternate media controlled by other companies, such as microwave and satellite service.

6. The technical details of how this works are given in the appendix.
7. POP should not be confused with POP3, which stands for Post Office Protocol and is used for electronic mail delivery. See the appendix for further details.
8. See Stephen Segaller, *Nerds$^{2.0.1}$: A Brief History of the Internet* (New York: TV Books, 1999); Mendelson,"A Note on Internet Technology"; and info.isoc.org/guest/zakon/Internet/History/HIT.html.
9. Conseil Européen pour la Recherche Nucléaire, also known as the European Laboratory for Particle Physics.
10. For more details, see Segaller, *Nerds$^{2.0.1}$*, pp. 284–89, or Tim Berners-Lee and Mark Fischetti, *Weaving the Web: The Original Design and Ultimate Destiny of the World Wide Web by its Inventor* (San Francisco: Harper-Collins, 1999).
11. The "Internet value network" is a broad term for all the components and their interrelations. In Chapter 6, we will explore the term *value network* that is one of three generic value configurations. Thus, within the sphere of the broader Internet value network, there can be many, smaller value networks.
12. This is not to be confused with Internet service providers (ISPs), which provide homes and small organizations with Internet connectivity. ISPs are described under communications services.
13. Jeffrey F. Rayport, "The Truth about Internet Business Models," *Strategy and Business* 16 (3rd quarter 1999), pp. 5–7.
14. Some companies will be categorized only as e-commerce: those that purely sell (retailers or resellers) and those that compete in non-Internet businesses that also sell online.
15. Communications services are not considered part of this category; as the Internet is a communications medium, the communications service provider segment is large enough to rate its own segment as described in the next section.
16. *Boardwatch Magazine's Directory of Internet Service Providers.*
17. In Chapter 11 we will briefly discuss the role of government and regulation and how it relates to the external environment.
18. Tom Standage, "The Internet, Untethered," in Survey of the Mobile Internet, *The Economist*, October 11, 2001.
19. Subscriptions for telephone DSL and high-speed cable access lines were being billed out at approximately $50 per month in 2000.
20. Dow Jones & Company, Inc., Quarterly Report, SEC Form 10-Q, November 12, 1999.
21. At least one company has manufactured a Sony-compatible gaming device by reverse-engineering it.
22. Some have argued that illegal copying of software is not harmful to software producers because copying builds up the installed base of users, thus exploiting network externalities evident in the industry. See Chapter 3 for more information.

23. See Ravi Kalakota, Marcia Robinson, and Don Tapscott, *E-Business: Roadmap for Success* (Reading, MA: Addison-Wesley, 1999).

24. This is just a smattering of e-commerce software applications; see Ravi Kalakota and Andrew B. Whinston, *Electronic Commerce: A Manager's Guide* (Reading, MA: Addison-Wesley, 1997); see also Marilyn Greenstein and Todd Feinman, *Electronic Commerce: Security, Risk Management, and Control* (New York: Irwin/McGraw-Hill, 2000) for more information on commerce applications.

25. This information is stored in a so-called *cookie* on your computer. The cookie contains three main pieces of information: the information the retailer wants to store (IDs, etc.), the domain name of the retailer (i.e., who has authorized access to that piece), and the expiration of the information. See home.netscape.com/newsref/std/cookie_spec.html for the exact specification.

26. See Greenstein and Feinman, *Electronic Commerce*, for more information on Internet security and how it relates to e-commerce.

27. See the appendix for more details on the client-server model.

Chapter Three

Competitive Landscape-Changing Properties of the Internet

In Chapter 2 we examined the Internet value network and the roles of different players in adding customer value. While that examination tells us who is located where in the configuration and what each group of players does and the relationship between them, it still leaves two very important questions unanswered: What makes the Internet a better technology than its predecessor technologies? Does it really have the potential to transform competitive landscapes? Answering these questions is critical to conceiving and executing business models that exploit the Internet. We will focus on those properties that have the potential to influence business models and industry profitability and examine their impact on the 5-Cs of electronic transactions—be they commerce, business, or otherwise. Many business models rest on elements of the 5-Cs, so by understanding the impact of the Internet on them, we can better understand how Internet business models can be conceived and executed, and how they influence existing bricks-and-mortar models.

PROPERTIES OF THE INTERNET

The Internet has many properties, but 10 of them stand out: mediating technology, universality, network externalities, distribution channel, time moderator, information asymmetry shrinker, infinite virtual capacity, low cost standard, creative destroyer, and transaction-cost reducer.

1. Mediating Technology

The Internet is a **mediating technology** that interconnects parties that are interdependent or want to be.[1] The interconnection can be business-to-business (B2B), business-to-consumer (B2C), consumer-to-consumer (C2C), or consumer-to-business (C2B). It can also be within a firm or any other organization, in which case it is called an intranet. In either case, the Internet facilitates exchange relationships among parties distributed in time and space. In some ways, it is like the technology that underpins bricks-and-mortar bank services. A bank acts as a medium for lenders and borrowers, taking money from some customers and lending it to others. In other ways, the Internet is like print, radio, and TV media which mediate between their audience and paying advertisers. The Internet's interactivity gives it some unique advantages over these media as parties can interact, asking and answering questions rather than one party sending and another only receiving messages. Most important, anyone connected to the Internet has the power to broadcast information to anyone on it. In the older media, broadcasting is limited to a select few.

2. Universality

Universality of the Internet refers to the Internet's ability to both enlarge and shrink the world. It enlarges the world because anyone anywhere in the world can potentially make his or her products available to anyone anywhere else in the world. For example, a musician in Ann Arbor, Michigan, can make his music available to the rest of the world by posting it on the World Wide Web. A software developer in Egypt can sell her software to customers all over the world simply by posting it on a website in Alexandria. A steelmaker in Korea can post the prices, availability, and quality of its steel on a website in Seoul. People anywhere in the world can access these varied postings on the Web. Ford Motor Company can put bids for the new components that it needs for its cars on its website, allowing anyone in the world with the capabilities to supply the component to bid for their supply.

The Internet shrinks the world in that a skilled worker in South Africa does not have to move to California to work in the Silicon Valley. Software developers in the Silicon Valley can have access to programming skills in a country as far away as Madagascar. As we will see throughout this book, this property has many implications for many industries. For example, it suggests that we can expect more software firms to enter the software industry and salaries for certain skills to be more competitive, no matter where the owners of such skills are located.

3. Network Externalities

A technology or product exhibits **network externalities** when it becomes more valuable to users as more people take advantage of it.[2] To understand what this means, the reader might think of owning a telephone in a system that is connected only to the authors of this book. Such a phone would be much less useful to the reader than if it were connected to members of the reader's family and the rest of the world. Clearly, the more people who are connected to a telephone system, the more valuable it is to its users. The Internet clearly exhibits this property: The more people connected to it, the more valuable it is. The more people that are connected to a network within the Internet, the more valuable that network is. Suppose a collector wants to auction off a rare work of art. The auction firm that she selects is more valuable to her only if the firm has a large number of clients since she will then have a large set of bidders for her work of art. If she instead wants to buy a work of art, she is still better off going to the firm with the large network; the larger the auction firm is, the better the selection and her chances of finding what she wants. For individuals looking for a chat group, the larger the network, the better the chances of finding others with similar tastes with whom they can share ideas and further their sense of community. Since a network is more attractive the more members that it has, one can expect larger networks to gain new members at a faster rate than smaller ones; that is, the larger a network, the larger it is going to become. This is the positive feedback in which a firm—once it finds itself ahead in network size—is likely to see its lead increase rather than decrease.[3] The question is, When does this snowballing stop? It usually ends when a change, especially a technological change, comes along that renders the basis for the advantages of the network obsolete.

At least two estimates of the value of network size have been offered. Bob Metcalfe, founder of 3Com and inventor of the Ethernet, advanced what is now called **Metcalfe's law:** The value of a network increases as the square of the number of people in the network.[4] That is, value is a function of N^2, where N is the number of people in the network. It has also been argued that the increase in value from size is exponential.[5] That is, the value of a network increases as a function of N^N.

The phenomenon of network externalities is not limited to connected networks like telephone systems and the Internet. It also applies to products whose value to customers increases with complementary products. Computers, even stand-alone ones, are a good example. Software is critical for their use, so the more people who own computers of a particular standard, the more likely that software will be developed for them. And the more software that is available for them, the more valuable they are to users since users have more software to choose from. And the more computers, the more people who are willing to develop software for it. These events lead to the positive feedback effect. We will suggest in later chapters that one goal of a firm may be to build a large network early because the size of the network can act as *switching costs* for members of the network while attracting others at a faster rate than smaller networks.

It is important to remember that large network size on the Internet does not always mean large network effect benefits. That is, it is not always the case that the larger the network size, the more valuable it is to users of the network. Two networks of equal size do not necessarily endow their members with equal benefits. Take an online auction house and an online book retailer. The larger the network size for an auction house like eBay, the better for a customer who wants, say, to buy a work of art. This is because a large network size increases a member's chances of finding another member of the network who has the work of art. Belonging to an online book retailer's large network, on the other hand, does not do as much for a customer who wants to buy a book online; it does not increase the customer's chances of finding the right book as much.

4. Distribution Channel

The Internet acts as a **distribution channel** for products that are largely information—bits (zeros and ones). Software, music, video, information, tickets for airlines or shows, brokerage services, insurance companies, and research data can all be distributed over the Internet. When the product itself cannot be distributed by means of the Internet, information on its features, pricing, delivery times, or other useful information about the product can. The Internet has two kinds of effects on existing distribution channels: replacement or extension. There is a **replacement effect** if the Internet is used to serve the same customers served by the old distribution channel without bringing in new customers. The replacement of travel agencies in distributing airline tickets is a good example.[6] Few customers will start flying simply because they can buy airline tickets over the Internet. On the other hand, investors who ordinarily cannot afford to buy stocks from stockbrokers can use the Internet to participate in the stock market where they can afford the lower online brokerage fees. This is the **extension effect**. Very often, the extension effect is also accompanied by some replacement effects. Some investors who previously went to stockbrokers to buy their securities have likely switched to doing it themselves over the Internet.

5. Time Moderator

The fifth property of the Internet is **time moderation,** or its ability to shrink and enlarge time. For example, it shrinks time for a potential customer who wants information on a new car or the way houses look in a particular neighborhood in the Netherlands; the customer can get it instantaneously using the Web. It enlarges time for a customer who might not be able to attend an auction held from 12:00 noon to 3:00 P.M. on a Saturday, but who will find the material is auctioned on the Internet 24 hours a day, seven days a week, to anyone anywhere in the world. Work can continue on a microchip design 24 hours a day: Engineers in Japan work on the chip and at the end of their workday, turn it over to engineers in Israel who, at the end of their own workday, turn it over to engineers in the United States and back again to Japan.

6. Information Asymmetry Shrinker

An **information asymmetry** exists when one party to a transaction has information that another party does not—information that is important to the transaction. Such asymmetries, for example, were a source of advantage for car dealers. They often knew the costs of the cars they were selling while the average buyer did not. The Web reduces some of these information asymmetries. Since an automobile manufacturer's suggested prices are easily obtainable from the Web, customers can go to a car dealer armed with the same information that the dealer has about the car.

7. Infinite Virtual Capacity

More than 30 years ago, Gordon Moore of Intel predicted that every 18 months, computer processing power would double while the cost would stay about the same. This is known as Moore's law. As of 2002, his prediction has proved true. While these outstanding technological advances have boosted processing speed, similar advances have been made to storage and network technologies. Using these technologies, the Internet often gives customers the feeling that it has **infinite virtual capacity** to serve them. If you want to buy a stock or book, you do not have to wait on hold or in a long line. Suppliers and vendors now have more memory and computing power. Therefore, they can collect more data on customers, enabling them to offer personalized service to better help customers discover their needs. Virtual communities like chat houses have infinite capacity for members who can talk anytime of the day for as long as they want.

8. Low Cost Standard

Firms could not exploit the properties of the Internet if they did not adopt it. For two reasons, adoption has been easy. First and most important, the Internet and the Web are standards open to everyone everywhere and are very easy to use. Whether users are in a jungle in the Congo or in New York City, they use the same point-and-click and create a Web page that can be accessed anywhere in the world. Information is transmitted and received using the same protocol. Second, the cost of the Internet is a lot lower than that of earlier means of electronic communications such as proprietary electronic data interchange (EDI).[7] The U.S. government underwrote much of the development costs for the Internet. Many of the remaining costs are shared among the millions of users since it is a standard. If instead of one standard Internet, many proprietary networks that do not talk to each other existed, then users would be paying for the many networks instead of the one network. That's more costly. Firms still have to invest in adopting the Internet, but the costs are considerably lower than they would have been had the Internet not been an open standard and had most of the costs not already been underwritten by the U.S. government.

9. Creative Destroyer

These properties of the Internet have enabled it to usher in a wave of what J. A. Schumpeter called **"creative destruction"** in many industries.[8] Newspapers, for example, offer their readers editorials, news, stock prices, weather forecasts, classified and want ads, advertising, and promotions.[9] Offering this value to customers requires an investment in a printing press, distribution network, content, and brand name. This investment constitutes a barrier to potential new entrants. The Internet is a low cost standard printing press of sorts and a distribution network with unlimited capacity that reaches more people than any newspaper could ever hope to reach. This tears down a large part of the barriers to entry that exist in the newspaper business. Furthermore, this network allows instantaneous, low cost interactive communication. With such low entry cost, flexibility, and virtually unlimited possibilities, one does not have to bundle editorials, news, stock prices, weather forecasts, classified and want ads, advertising, and promotions together to make money. Entrepreneurs can focus on each. For example, a firm can focus on auctioning what used to be in the want ads. This is creative destruction for the newspaper industry— the old giving way to the superior new. In general, creative destruction is taking place in three forms. First, brand-new industries have been created. Suppliers of Web software (e.g., browsers) or services [e.g., those provided by Internet service providers (ISPs)] have the Internet to thank for their business. Second, the Internet is transforming the structure, conduct, and performance of other industries, in many cases rendering the basis for competitive advantage obsolete. Travel, newspapers, and insurance are the tip of an iceberg of industries that are likely to experience creative destruction. As we will see later, these are industries whose basis for offering value to customers is overturned by one or more of the properties of the Internet. Third, the basis for competitive advantage in other industries has been enhanced. A firm like Intel, which has always pushed the frontier of semiconductor technology, finds the demands a match for its technological prowess and strategies in an industry that is critical to the Internet.

10. Transaction-Cost Reducer

The Internet also reduces transaction costs for many industries—thanks in part to the universality, distribution channel, low cost standard, and information asymmetry reduction properties. **Transaction costs** are the costs of searching for sellers and buyers; collecting information on products; negotiating, writing, monitoring, and enforcing contracts; and the costs of transportation associated with buying and selling.[10] Firms often must conduct searches to find the right suppliers to provide the components they want. Buyers must learn about suppliers' reputations, product features, and prices. Sellers must learn about buyers' financial standing and other characteristics of a good customer.[11] Buyers and sellers must negotiate contracts, sign them, monitor their execution, and enforce them. All these activities cost money. The Internet reduces these transaction costs. It reduces search costs because information on buyers, sellers, and products can be obtained more easily through the Web. The ability of the Internet to shrink information asymmetry also means a reduction in the cost of contract negotiation, monitoring, and enforcement. For products like software, music, and video that are in digital form, transportation costs are also greatly reduced since they can be "shipped" over the Internet. We will see later in this book that the reduction in transaction costs has some implications for the boundaries of the firm.

IMPACT OF THE INTERNET ON THE 5-CS

Conceiving and delivering value to customers entail the performance of many activities that rest on information exchange. Five of these activities are coordination, commerce, community, content, and communication. We will call them the **5-Cs**. The properties of the Internet just described potentially have a huge impact on these 5-Cs in intrafirm, business-to-business (B2B), business-to-consumer (B2C), consumer-to-consumer (C2C), and consumer-to-business (C2B) transactions (see Figure 3.1).

Coordination

For just about every firm, performing a task T often requires the performance of interdependent subtasks A, B, and C which may require common resources R. The **coordination** of these tasks entails ensuring that each of the subtasks is performed, that information from A needed to accomplish B or C does indeed get to each of them and does so on time and efficiently, and that resources R are available for A, B, and C when needed and with little waste. Coordination—whether of the schedules of three people who want to attend a meeting, the design and development of a Pentium III, or the design and building of a Boeing 777—can be critical. The cost, completion time, features, and quality of the final task rest on the coordination of subtasks and resources. In adding value along its value configuration, a firm often has to coordinate many activities between groups within the firm and groups from outside. Most of what is exchanged in the coordination is information, and the Internet, as an informa-

FIGURE 3.1   **Properties of the Internet and the 5-Cs**

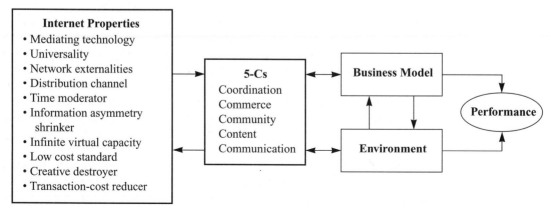

tion technology, can help tremendously. The construction industry narrated in Illustration Capsule 3.1 points to the importance of coordination and the enormous role that the Internet can play in coordinating activities. With the help of the Internet, much of the $200 billion lost annually in the industry to inefficiencies, mistakes, and delays could be recovered by better coordination of the activities of the dozens of businesses involved. The mediating and interactivity property of the Internet means that the thousands of transactions recorded on paper in the bricks-and-mortar world can be recorded electronically and any changes made during construction are immediately available to architects, engineers, and contractors. Blueprints and thousands of other documents do not have to be shipped over long distances overnight, saving some of the $500 million spent each year to transport them. Mistakes are reduced, cutting down on costs, delays, and possible litigation.

The Internet can be equally valuable during product development. Automobile product development, for example, entails the coordination of thousands of people within the automaking firm and dozens of suppliers outside the company. The Internet can greatly simplify the process. Potentially, automakers can implement the type of build-to-order processes that PC makers such as Dell Computer employ in building computers. By choosing what they want in their cars, customers do not have to, for example, take heated seats and power mirrors just because these features come with the antilock brakes that customers want. Fewer components can mean lower cost and better reliability. Moreover, Daimler-Chrysler engineers located in Europe and the United States developing a new car do not have to travel to Detroit or Stuttgart. They can use the Internet or intranet to coordinate their activities. The properties of time moderation and universality suggest that these engineers do not have to work on the car at the same time either. Engineers working on a car today can share in the knowledge accumulated in previous projects and stored in the firm's databases that can be made available over an intranet. Moreover, as development is going on, the purchasing group and suppliers can monitor development progress, taking note of any changes that they may have to make in the design of components.

Commerce

There are many advantages to purchasing and selling goods and services over the Internet—or performing e-commerce. The low cost standard and universality properties, for example, suggest that firms and individuals who engage in **commerce** over the Internet have potential access to customers all over the world since customers everywhere potentially have access to the Internet. E-commerce can be business-to-business (B2B), business-to-consumer (B2C), consumer-to-consumer (C2C), or consumer-to-business (C2B).

Business-to-Business

In **business-to-business (B2B),** businesses buy and sell goods and services to and from each other. In 1999 B2B commerce was estimated to be about $1.3 trillion by 2002.[12] The universality property suggests that buyers can put out

Building Construction and the Internet

The Economist had this to say about the impact of the Internet on the building and construction industry:

> Anyone who has ever hired a builder knows that even the simplest job tends to be plagued by cost overruns and delays. And the bigger the project, the bigger the problems: according to one estimate, inefficiencies, mistakes and delays account for $200 billion of the $650 billion spent on construction in America every year. It is easy to see why. A building project, whether it is a hotel or a cement plant, involves dozens of businesses—architects, engineers, material suppliers—working together for months or years. Each project entails thousands of transactions, all of them currently recorded on paper. A typical $100m building project generates 150,000 separate documents: technical drawings, legal contracts, purchase orders, requests for information and schedules. Project managers build warehouses just to store them. Federal Express reputedly garnered $500m last year just shipping blueprints across America. Worse, construction is a slow affair, regularly held up by building regulations, stroppy [belligerent] unions and bad weather. Owners, architects and engineers must physically visit sites. With everything still done by fax or telephone, requests for the size of a roof tile can take weeks and seemingly minor changes can lead to long delays as bits of paper wind through approval processes. Even then, mistakes are common. Wrong supplies arrive and bills go unpaid. Given onerous shipping costs and the high value of commercial contracts, mistakes matter. Building is one of the world's most litigious industries.
>
> Help is at hand. A group of new business-to-business companies plan to turn all construction into an efficient virtual process. Daryl Magana, chief executive of Bid.com, says his company creates a separate website for every building project for clients including the city of San Francisco, The Gap and General Electric. Everyone involved from the architect to the carpenters can then have access to this site to check blueprints and orders, change specifications and agree on delivery dates. Moreover, everything from due dates to material specifications is permanently recorded.
>
> Clients love this approach. Harlan Kelly, city engineer at the city of San Francisco, says Bid.com has cut project time by six months: "We can do things quicker, faster and better and there are fewer arguments about whether information has reached people." Charlie Kuffner, Northern California business manager for Swinerton & Walberg Builders, a large contractor, says that using Bid.com has reduced by two-thirds the time needed to deal with requests for information. . . . The scale economies are potentially enormous. . . .

requests for new bids for supplies on their websites and sellers from all over the world have a chance to bid. More buyers means sellers have more customers for their goods. More sellers means more choices for buyers. The more sellers, the better things can be for all sellers. This is the case especially when sellers can learn from each other or produce complementary goods.

A problem arises when sellers and buyers are highly fragmented; that is, there are a great many small sellers and buyers. Because buyers are fragmented, a seller may not even know who all the buyers are. The buyer may not know who all the sellers are either. Each supplier has to search through the

Web pages of all buyers to find out what they want, give them the product descriptions that they need, find out about their creditworthiness, complete the buyer's requests for quotation (RFQs), and so on. Thus, the more sellers and buyers and the more fragmented both are, the higher the transaction costs. To see why, consider Figure 3.2. Figure 3.2(*a*) shows only two sellers S_1 and S_2, and two buyers B_1 and B_2. It takes each of the two sellers just two searches for a total of four contacts with buyers. When the number of sellers and buyers goes up to four each, the number of contacts that sellers have to make goes up to 16 as each of the four sellers must look for the four buyers as shown in Figure 3.2(*b*). Thus, the costs of sellers and buyers undertaking transactions with each other increase rapidly as the number of buyers and sellers increases. This is where **B2B hubs**—also known as B2B intermediaries or **B2B exchanges**—come in. They provide a central point in the value system where sellers and buyers can go to find each other. Figure 3.2(*c*) shows Figure 3.2(*b*) with a B2B hub added. Now, instead of 16 contacts (N^2), only 8 ($2N$) are needed. The four sellers make four postings on the hub's website and four buyers view the postings for the total of eight. Thus, sellers enjoy the benefits of a network of size N^2 but only have to make $2N$ contacts. More importantly, the hubs can offer software to further reduce the number of contacts.

Two types of hubs have been identified: vertical and functional.[13] **Vertical hubs** usually focus on an industry or market and provide content that is specific

FIGURE 3.2
B2B Networks

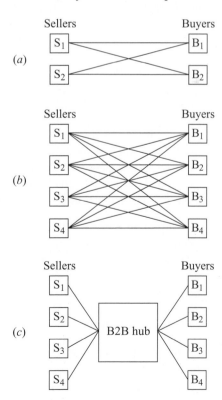

to the industry's value system of sellers, buyers, and complementors. This allows them to develop industry-specific capabilities. Examples include any firm that acts as an intermediary between steelmakers and users, or acts as a hub for suppliers to the life sciences industry. VerticalNet focuses on more than one industry. It provides hubs for many industries including electronics, process, telecommunications, and utilities. **Functional hubs** provide the same function for different industries, allowing them to build function-specific capabilities. Examples include any firm that acts as an intermediary between sellers and buyers of used capital equipment in different industries. Whether vertical or functional, B2B hubs require detailed industry-specific or function-specific knowledge and capabilities.

Business-to-Consumer

In **business-to-consumer (B2C)** commerce, businesses sell to consumers. Two of the most famous examples are Dell Online and Amazon.com. The time moderator effect means that customers have access to e-shops 24 hours a day, everyday. The infinite virtual capacity property means that consumers face no lines anytime they go shopping. It also means that there is almost no limit to the number of goods that an online retailer can display on its virtual storefront or mall. Furthermore, it means that firms can collect rich data sets on customers and use them to personalize service for these customers. The distribution channel effect means that some goods (e.g., music and software) bought over the Internet can be received instantaneously. The low cost standard and universality effects mean that consumers can shop in the privacy of their own homes.

The exchange between business and consumer may or may not involve an intermediary. Where the cost of finding a seller is high, a consumer may prefer to go to an intermediary. For example, rather than worry about which of the thousands of book publishers produces a particular book, a consumer may prefer to go to Amazon.com to look for the book. On the other hand, a consumer who wants to buy a computer may purchase one directly from Dell or one of the other major PC makers. Laws can also dictate that intermediaries must be where they would not necessarily have to be. As of early 2002, for example, U.S. law did not permit consumers to buy automobiles directly from manufacturers. Consumers had to go through car dealers.

Consumer-to-Consumer

In **consumer-to-consumer (C2C),** consumers sell to other consumers. Because there are millions of sellers with different items to sell and millions of buyers who want different items, the cost to sellers and buyers of finding each other can be exorbitant. The solution is to have an intermediary as shown in Figure 3.2*(c)*. Auction houses such as eBay are such an intermediary. They mediate between consumers who want to buy or sell.

Consumer-to-Business

In early 2000, **consumer-to-business (C2B)** was not as developed as B2B, B2C, or C2C. In C2B, consumers state their price, and firms either take it or leave it. Under Priceline's model, for example, potential customers name their prices for a flight and leave them for the airline to accept or reject. This contrasts with B2C where a firm usually states its price for a product or service and customers take it or leave it. Again, an intermediary plays an important role. In our example, Priceline is the intermediary.

Intermediary Models

Where **intermediaries** play a role in commerce, different models are usually used in pricing the goods that are exchanged in transactions. These models include auction, reverse auction, fixed or menu pricing, bargaining, and barter. Again, one of the most popular models used by intermediaries in C2C is the auction model as practiced by eBay. We will explore these models in Chapter 6.

Community

Groups with like interests, or **community,** can congregate online through chat rooms or message boards. Electronic communities have many advantages over physical communities. The universality and low cost standard properties mean that anyone from anywhere can join the group if he or she meets the group's criteria. Distance is no longer a drawback to belonging to a community. The time moderator effect also suggests that groups do not have to meet at the same time.

Some of the most important communities for firms are user groups. Lead users, for example, are customers whose needs are similar to those of other users except that they have these needs long before most of the marketplace and stand to benefit significantly by satisfying those needs earlier.[14] A community of lead users that can discuss their needs as they use early versions of a design can be extremely valuable in helping each other discover their needs. More important, the developer of the product has access to this critical information. Customer user groups, in general, can be important resources for firms. For example, users of Cisco products learned so much from each other that they did not have to ask many questions of Cisco about how to use the products in their own system. This not only freed Cisco applications engineers to develop more products (instead of hand-holding customers), but also meant happier customers who wanted more Cisco products.

The network externality property suggests that the larger the community, the more valuable it is. This in turn suggests that once one belongs to a large network, the less easy it is to switch to a smaller network. One strategic implication is that firms might want to build such communities early.

Content

Content is the information, entertainment, and other products that are delivered over the Internet. Entertainment includes Disney online, MTV online, interactive video games, and sportscasting. A person can play games with friends and relatives located thousands of miles away. Information content includes current news, stock quotations, weather forecasts, and investment information. Both contents rest on the distribution channel, low cost standard, and mediating technology properties—all of which suggest that more content is available to more people.

Communication

At the heart of the four Cs that we have just explored is the fifth: **communication.** Its uses go beyond coordination, commerce, community, and content. People use electronic mail (e-mail), Web phones, or real-time video to exchange messages for numerous bricks-and-mortar activities. Mediating and interactivity properties mean that people can exchange electronic messages in real-time. The time moderator, low cost standard, and universality properties mean that one can send many messages at any time to many people. The infinite virtual capacity effect means that one can send many messages, each of which can have a high content. Every user also has the capability to broadcast messages. Broadcasting is no longer limited to the owners of radio and television stations.

Implications for Industries

Because the Internet has so great an impact on the 5-Cs (see Table 3.1), any firm whose activities involve coordination, commerce, community, content, and communication must take a good look at it as either a potential threat or opportunity. Consider again the automobile industry. In early 2002, it took 60 to 100 days from the forming of sheet metal to build a car to delivery of the finished vehicle to a customer.[15] Since it takes so long to build the cars, customers are unwilling to commit to buying one before it is built. Consequently, automakers have to build the cars and send them to dealers in hopes that they will sell. If the cars don't sell, they resort to rebates, advertising, and redistribution of cars that can account for as much as 30 percent of the price. Using the Internet to find out what customers want and then building to order could trim these costs. But building to order also means trimming the lead time from the previous 60 to 100 days. This means that the Internet must be used to coordinate information from customers and suppliers as well as for internal information. It also means using the Internet to collaborate with suppliers to meet these customer needs. All of this means that even the automobile industry is at risk with the Internet. We will say more about which firms and industries are at risk in Chapters 5 and 10.

LIMITATIONS TO TRANSACTIONS OVER THE INTERNET

The Internet is an information technology. The information sent over it must at some point be encoded into bits (ones and zeros) to be transmitted and received. Sooner or later, the information sent over the Internet must be handled by people. Therefore, the choice of transactions that can be performed over the Internet is a function of the nature of the knowledge on which the transactions rest and of the type of people who undertake the transactions. Thus, the nature of knowledge and people limits the extent to which the Internet can be used to conduct business.

TABLE 3.1   The 5-Cs and Key Internet Properties

Internet property	5-Cs				
	Coordination	Commerce	Community	Content	Communication
Mediating technology	X	X	X	X	X
Universality	X	X	X	X	X
Network externality		X	X		X
Distribution channel		X		X	
Time moderator	X	X	X	X	X
Information asymmetry shrinker	X	X			
Infinite virtual capacity		X	X	X	
Low cost standard	X	X	X	X	X
Creative destroyer		X		X	
Transaction-cost reducer	X	X			

Tacit Knowledge

Whatever is transmitted over the Internet usually has been knowledge at some point—knowledge that has resided in individuals or in organizational routines. E-mail messages sent by individuals derive from their stock of knowledge. The design of a car sent over the Internet is knowledge that has resided in individuals who work for the automaker or in its organizational routines and archival knowledge banks. For knowledge to be effectively transmitted over the Internet, it must be encoded in a form that can be transmitted; that is, knowledge transmitted over the Internet is **explicit knowledge,** not tacit. Knowledge is explicit if it is codified, spelled out in writing, and verbalized or coded in drawings, computer programs, or other products. It is also sometimes referred to as articulated or codified knowledge.[16] Knowledge is tacit if uncoded and nonverbalized. It may not even be possible to verbalize or articulate **tacit knowledge.** It can be acquired largely through personal experience by learning or by doing. Tacit knowledge is often embedded in the routines of organizations and the actions of an individual, and therefore is very difficult to copy. Thus, carrying out transactions over the Internet becomes a problem when the tacit knowledge on which the transactions rest cannot be encoded into a form that can be put onto the Internet and transmitted. How can you transmit the smell and feel of a car over the Internet?

People

The other problem with transacting over the Internet is that human beings and their organizations, smart as they can be, are still limited cognitively. They have **bounded rationality.** According to Oliver Williamson:

> Bounded rationality involves neurophysiological limits on the one hand and language limits on the other. The physical limits take the form of rate and storage limits on the powers of individuals to receive, store, retrieve, and

process information without error. . . . Language limits refer to the inability of individuals to articulate their knowledge or feelings by use of words, numbers, or graphics in ways which permit them to be understood by others. Despite their best efforts, parties may find that language fails them (possibly because they do not possess the requisite vocabulary or the necessary vocabulary has not been devised) and they resort to other means of communications instead. Demonstrations, learning-by-doing, and the like may be the only means of achieving understanding when such language difficulties develop.[17]

Because individuals and organizations are cognitively limited, they may not be able to encode their knowledge into a form that can be transmitted over the Internet. Even if they could articulate this knowledge well, cognitively limited individuals at the receiving end might not understand. How does one describe the smell of a new car to other people and give them the sensation that they would get by themselves? Even if one could, would this other person get it?

Tacit knowledge and cognitive limitations of people make it difficult to perform some transactions over the Internet. Technological advances such as virtual reality may help to remove some of these limitations. In any case, as a firm develops its business models and strategies, it is important to understand some of the limitations of the Internet.

Summary

The Internet has numerous properties that have the potential to transform the competitive landscape in many industries. Ten properties—mediating technology, universality, network externalities, distribution channel, time moderator, information asymmetry shrinker, infinite virtual capacity, low cost standard, creative destroyer, and transaction-cost reducer—have an impact on the way activities in a firm are carried out. In particular, they have a major impact on coordination, commerce, community, content, and communication—the 5-Cs. In coordination, the Internet reduces the cost of transactions, cuts lead times, and improves product-service features and quality. It takes commerce—business-to-business, business-to-consumer, consumer-to-consumer, or consumer-to-business—to a different level. The Internet redefines communities, making them virtual, larger, and much more valuable. More content is available to more people. Communication now has the potential to offer everyone not only large virtual capacity but also the ability to broadcast information. The Internet also has the potential to change the way the 5-Cs are carried out—thus having a large impact on the way business models are conceived and executed—and to have a huge impact on nearly every industry.

Key Terms

B2B exchanges, *41*
B2B hubs, *41*
bounded rationality, *45*
business-to-business
    (B2B), *39*

business-to-consumer
    (B2C), *42*
commerce, *39*
communication, *44*
community, *43*

consumer-to-business
    (C2B), *42*
consumer-to-consumer
    (C2C), *42*
content, *43*

Discussion Questions

1. Where do you expect network externalities to have the most impact: intrafirm, business-to-business (B2B), business-to-consumer (B2C), consumer-to-consumer (C2C), or consumer-to-business (C2B) transactions? Start by estimating the network size in each case.

2. Of the 10 major properties of the Internet, which one do you consider the most powerful in terms of the impact on firm activities? (*Hint*: What is the impact of each property on each of the 5-Cs?) Does the type of industry in which these activities are performed matter?

3. Which of the 5-Cs stands to be most affected by the Internet and why? Does the type of industry matter?

4. Which industries stand to benefit the most from the Internet?

5. Which activities are least likely to be impacted by the Internet?

Notes

1. J. D. Thompson, *Organizations in Action* (New York: McGraw-Hill, 1967); C. B. Stabell and O. D. Fjeldstad, "Configuring Value for Competitive Advantage: On Chains, Shops, and Networks," *Strategic Management Journal* 19 (1998), pp. 413–37.

2. M. L. Katz and C. Shapiro, "Technology Adoption in the Presence of Network Externalities," *Journal of Political Economy* 94, no. (4) (1986), pp. 822–41.

3. B. Arthur, "Positive Feedbacks in the Economy," *Scientific American*, February 1990, pp. 80–85.

4. See, for example, L. Downes and C. Mui, *Unleashing the Killer App: Digital Srategies for Market Dominance* (Boston: Harvard Business School Press, 1998).

5. Kevin Kelly, *New Rules for the New Economy: 10 Radical Strategies for a Connected World* (New York: Penguin, 1999).

6. These examples are from N. Kumar, "Internet Distribution Strategies: Dilemmas for the Incumbent," *Financial Times*, March 15, 1999.

7. "The Net Imperative: Survey of Business and the Internet," *The Economist*, June 26, 1999.

8. J. A. Schumpeter, *Capitalism, Socialism and Democracy*, 3rd ed. (New York: Harper, 1950).

9. This example is from "Newspapers and the Internet: Caught in the Web," *The Economist*, July 17, 1999, pp. 17–19.

10. R. H. Coase, "The Nature of the Firm," *Econometrica* 4 (1937), pp. 386–405; O. Williamson, *Markets and Hierarchies* (New York: Free Press, 1975).

11. Downes and Mui, *Unleashing the Killer App*, pp. 35–39.

12. A. Marlatt, "Creating Vertical Marketplaces," *Internet World*, February 1999, pp. 85–92.

13. M. Sawhney and S. Kaplan, "Let's Get Vertical," *Business 2.0*, September 1999.

14. E. Von Hippel, "Lead Users: A Source of Novel Product Concepts," *Management Science* 32 (1986), pp. 791–805.

15. "Cars: Wheels and Wires," *The Economist*, January 8, 2000, pp. 58–60.

16. See, for example, M. Polanyi, *Personal Knowledge: Towards a Post Critical Philosophy* (London: Routledge, 1962); G. Hedlund, "A Model of Knowledge Management and the N-form Corporation," *Strategic Management Journal* 15 (1994), pp. 73–90.

17. Williamson, *Markets and Hierarchies*, p. 21; K. Conner and C. K. Prahalad, "A Resource-based Theory of the Firm: Knowledge versus Opportunism," *Organization Science* 7, no. 5 (1995), pp. 477–501.

Part Two

Components, Linkages, Dynamics, and Evaluation of Business Models

Chapter **Four**

Components of a Business Model

In Chapter 3 we explored those properties of the Internet that could transform the competitive landscape in many industries. The question now is, How can a firm take advantage of these properties to gain and maintain a competitive advantage? That is, how can a firm use the Internet to be more profitable than its competitors over the long term? How a firm plans to make money long term using the Internet is detailed in its Internet business model. In this chapter, we explore the components of an Internet business model and the linkages between these components. We will begin with a definition of business models. We will then examine the components of a business model and the linkages between them, paying particular attention to the role of the properties of the Internet that we explored in Chapter 3. The dynamics of business models and their appraisal will be discussed in Chapter 5.

INTERNET BUSINESS MODEL

Each firm that exploits the Internet should have an Internet **business model**—how it plans to make money long term using the Internet. This is a set of Internet- and non-Internet–related activities—planned or evolving—that allows a firm to make money using the Internet and to keep the money coming. If well formulated, a firm's business model gives it a competitive advantage in its industry, enabling the firm to earn greater profits than its competitors. Whether implicit or explicit in a firm's actions, a business model should include answers to a number of questions: The profit site to enter, what value to offer customers, which customers to provide the value to, how to price the value, who to charge for it, what strategies to undertake in providing the value, how to provide that value (see Figure 4.1), and how to sustain any advantage from providing the value. Answering these questions entails an understanding of the firm's industry and the key drivers of value in that industry, customers and what they value, the activities that undergird delivering value to these customers, the impact of

FIGURE 4.1
Determinants of
Firm Performance

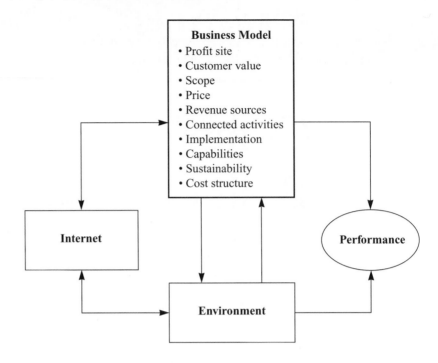

the Internet on the industry and these activities, and the firm's distinctiveness and how best to exploit it. The firm can be a supplier to the Internet, a service provider within the Internet infrastructure, or a user.

COMPONENTS AND LINKAGES

Rationale for Components

While all these models are different and serve their owners well, they have one thing in common: They are designed to make money for their owners long term. Rather than try to enumerate the numerous and changing business models in different industries, we will explore those elements that are common to all business models and on which making money rests. For a firm to keep making money, it must keep offering customers something that they value and that competitors cannot offer.[1] **Customer value** can take the form of differentiated or lower-cost products. Such a firm must also target the right market segments with products or services that have the appropriate value mix since not all customer value is meant for all customers. That is, market and product *scope* are also important. Offering the right customers the right value is only part of the equation. The firm must *price* them properly. To offer value to customers, firms must perform the *activities* that underpin the value.[2]

These activities must be carried out or *implemented* by people who have to be managed well. How well these individuals and firms perform the value-adding activities is a function of the superiority of their **capabilities.**[3] How much of a competitive advantage they have is a function of the distinctiveness of the capabilities. Often a firm has more than one *revenue source* and should take all sources into consideration as it decides what value to offer customers, how to price it, what activities to perform, and so on. A well-conceived business model with all these components can be profitable. Once a firm starts making money, however, competitors usually want a piece of the action. A firm with such an advantage must also worry about **sustainability** of profits. It must find ways to keep making money. It must find ways to retain its competitive advantage. Its profit site and cost structures also play critical roles.

Table 4.1 summarizes some questions that a firm should ask itself at all times about its business model in general, and Internet business models in particular.

PROFIT SITE

A firm's **profit site,** as we saw in Chapter 2, is its location in a value configuration vis-a-vis its suppliers, customers, rivals, potential new entrants, complementors, and substitutes. In the case of the Internet, for example, firms positioned themselves as Internet Service Providers (ISPs), backbone suppliers, content suppliers, network providers, network infrastructure providers, network utility providers, applications service providers (ASPs), online content providers, or users of the Internet such as online brokers, online retailers, online market-makers, business-to-business (B2B) exchanges, business-to-consumer (B2C), consumer-to-consumer (C2C), and so on. A firm's profit site determines the competitive pressures from rivals, suppliers, customers, potential new entrants, complementors, and substitutes. A profit site is said to be attractive if the pressure exerted by competitive forces is low and unattractive otherwise. It is a function of the type of industry in which the profit site happens to be located and of the type of strategy pursued by the firm. Some industries are, by their nature, more attractive than others. In 2001, for example, being a supplier to infrastructure firms was more attractive than being an online retailer. A firm's profit site impacts or is impacted by the type of value that the firm offers, the customer segment that it can pursue, the prices that it charges, its sources of revenues, the activities that it chooses to perform, its capabilities, how it implements its business model, how sustainable its business model is, and its cost structure. Locating in an unattractive site—a site where competitive forces are strong—makes it more difficult to cultivate and execute a winning business model. Firms that are located in such a site would have a more difficult time being profitable. Customers with bargaining power can extract higher prices or better quality products from profit-site firms thereby influencing both the pricing strategies that firms can pursue and the type of customer value they can offer. Suppliers with bargaining power can

TABLE 4.1   Elements of a Business Model

Component of Business Model	Questions for All Business Models	Questions Specific to Internet Business Models
Profit site	What is the relative (dis)advantage of a firm vis-a-vis its suppliers, customers, rivals, complementors, potential new entrants, and substitutes?	What is the impact of the Internet on the firm's relative (dis)advantage over suppliers, customers, rivals, complementors, potential new entrants, and substitutes?
Customer value	Is the firm offering its customers something distinctive or at a lower cost than its competitors?	What is it about the Internet that allows your firm to offer its customers something distinctive? Can the Internet allow you to solve a new set of problems for customers?
Scope	To which customers (demographic and geographic) is the firm offering this value? What is the range of products/services offered that embody this value?	What is the scope of customers that the Internet enables your firm to reach? Does the Internet alter the product or service mix that embodies the firm's products?
Pricing	How does the firm price the value?	How does the Internet make pricing different?
Revenue source	Where do the dollars come from? Who pays for what value and when? What are the margins in each market and what drives them? What drives value in each source?	Are revenue sources different with the Internet? What is new?
Connected activities	What set of activities does the firm have to perform to offer this value and when? How connected (in cross section and time) are these activities?	How many new activities must be performed as a result of the Internet? How much better can the Internet help you to perform existing activities?
Implementation	What organizational structure, systems, people, and environment does the firm need to carry out these activities? What is the fit between them?	What does the Internet do to the strategy, structure, systems, people, and environment of your firm?
Capabilities	What are the firm's capabilities and capabilities gaps that need to be filled? How does a firm fill these capabilities gaps? Is there something distinctive about these capabilities that allows the firm to offer the value better than other firms and that makes them difficult to imitate? What are the sources of these capabilities?	What new capabilities do you need? What is the impact of the Internet on existing capabilities?
Sustainability	What is it about the firm that makes it difficult for other firms to imitate it? How does the firm keep making money? How does the firm sustain its competitive advantage?	Does the Internet make sustainability easier or more difficult? How can your firm take advantage of it?
Cost structure	What drives costs in each component of the business model?	What is the impact of the Internet on those cost drivers that underpin the components of a business model?

force firms to take lower-quality inputs or pay higher prices for the inputs that they buy from these suppliers. Accepting lower-quality inputs can reduce the level of customer value that firms can offer, increase their cost, or erode their brand-name reputation. Paying more for inputs increases costs. High rivalry may increase costs since firms may have to, for example, advertise to differentiate themselves. Increased rivalry may force firms out of certain market segments to niche markets. It may also influence which activities a firm performs. For example, firms may decide to locate manufacturing in countries with lower manufacturing costs. Effectively, where a firm locates in an innovation value configuration influences or is influenced by the customer value that it offers, the customer segment that it pursues, the prices that it charges, its sources of revenues, the activities that it chooses to perform, its capabilities, how it implements its business model, how sustainable its business model is, and its cost structure. As we explore in Chapter 10, the Internet stands to alter the relative bargaining position in many industries.

CUSTOMER VALUE

Customers would buy a product from a firm only if the product offers them something that competitors' products do not.[4] This something, or customer value, can take the form of differentiated or low cost products/services.

Differentiation

A product is differentiated if customers perceive it to have something of value that other products do not have. A firm can differentiate its products in eight different ways: product features, timing, location, service, product mix, linkage between functions, linkage with other firms, and reputation.[5]

Product Features

A firm can differentiate its products/services by offering features that competitors' products do not have. For example, a manufacturer of memory microchips might differentiate its products by emphasizing the speed of its chips. Distinctive features are probably the most familiar form of product differentiation, and better coordination of activities within and outside a firm using the Internet can result in better product features for customers. For example, the Internet offers the possibility of made-to-order cars, customized to individual taste. The Internet also offers 24-hour service, no lines, and access to a community of customers. It also can offer personalized service for everyone.

Timing

A firm can differentiate a product by being the first to introduce it. Since such a product is the only one on the market, it is, by default, differentiated because no other product has its features. Thus, two personal computers with identical physical attributes—speed, main memory capacity, disk capacity, operating system, and the number of applications running on it—are seen as highly differentiated if one was produced in 1999 and the other in 2000. For a time, Compaq differentiated its IBM-compatible personal computers by being the first to introduce computers that used the latest version of Intel microprocessors. The Internet allows product developers to reduce the lead times of their products. Improved coordination using the Internet allows a manufacturer to complete the design of a product faster and to bring the product to market earlier than it might otherwise have done. Again using our chip design example, if Intel can have engineers in Japan work on a design, turn it over to engineers in Israel who continue the work on it before handing it over to engineers in the United States, Intel can finish the product faster than it could if engineers in only one country worked on the design. The building construction case in Chapter 3 is another example of the importance of timing.

Location

Two products with identical features can still be differentiated by virtue of their location. One differentiating factor may be the ease of access to the products. For example, if an Internet service provider (ISP) in Ann Arbor, Michigan, offers identical service to that offered by another ISP in New York, the two services are differentiated because a customer in Ann Arbor does not have access to the services in New York. The universality property, however, suggests that the Internet may take away some of the advantages of location for many products and services. The most popular example is the bricks-and-mortar bookstore whose differentiating factor was its location. Now customers worldwide have the potential to buy books from anywhere in the world. With products that are bits of zeros and ones, such as music, videos, and books or services like insurance, banks, and brokerage firms, location is less of a differentiator.

Service

A firm's products may also be differentiated by how quickly they can be repaired if they break down. For example, an automaker in a developing country can differentiate itself by the amount of service that it offers. With the Internet, the role of user groups is larger than ever before. Users of most systems and complex products such as the automobile can exchange information on how to service their cars. The larger such groups are, the better the service will be since size increases the chances that someone in the group can solve a problem and then share the knowledge with other members of the group.

Product Mix

The mix of products that a firm sells can also be a source of product differentiation. Customers who prefer one-stop shopping or variety would find such product mixes valuable. Virtual stores offer a tremendous amount of choice. Bookseller Amazon.com, for example, offered 16 million items for sale on its storefront in May 1999,[6] differentiating it from other retailers. Furthermore, the firm can use data gathered on its customers to suggest personalized choices for them.

Linkages

Association with another firm can also be a source of differentiation. An Internet upstart or bricks-and-mortar firm associated with AOL gains some credibility in the eyes of the many customers who perceive AOL as reputable. The network externalities property suggests that the larger a Web community is, the more valuable its membership, which distinguishes the community from others.

Brand-Name Reputation

Finally, a firm's brand-name reputation can go a long way in making customers perceive that its products are different. The Internet offers one more channel to establish brand-name reputations. This time, however, the channel can be more worldwide than anytime before since the Internet reaches many more people.

Low Cost

Low cost means just that—a firm's products or services cost customers less than those of its competitors. The idea is that it costs the firm less to offer customers the product/service, so the firm passes some of the cost savings on to customers. Reduction in information asymmetry means savings in transaction costs. The distribution channel effect means large savings and better ways of disposing of a firm's output. For example, a software developer or musician who sells her products by posting them on the Internet saves on distribution, packaging, and transportation costs. Better coordination of activities also means lower costs for producers. The savings can then be passed on to customers.

SCOPE

While customer value is about offering low cost and/or differentiated products, **scope** is about the market segments or geographic areas to which the value should be offered as well as how many types of products that embody versions of this value should be sold.[7] A firm can market either to businesses or households. Within the business markets are different industries and, within each of these industries, firms of different sizes and technical sophistication. Households also consist of many segments that are a function of demographics, lifestyles, and incomes. iVillage, for example, is targeted largely toward women. Then there is geography. Often a firm must decide where in the world it wants to market its products—North America, Europe, or Africa—and within each continent, which country to serve. The universality property of the Internet makes geographic expansion a great deal more feasible than in the bricks-and-mortar world. For example, a person in South Africa with an Internet connection can shop in Amazon.com's Seattle storefront.

A firm's task of making decisions on scope is not limited to the choice of market segment. A firm must also decide how much of the needs of the segment it can profitably serve.[8] For example, an Internet firm that targets teenagers must decide how many of their needs it wants to meet. It could provide them only with basic hookup services and chat rooms or provide content such as movies and math tutoring. It might also decide to provide the same type of service to all demographic groups.

PRICE

An important part of profiting from the value that firms offer customers is to price it properly. A bad **pricing strategy** can not only leave money on the table, but also kill a product or stifle its prosperity. Most products and services in the so-called knowledge economy are, well, knowledge-based.[9] **Knowledge-based products** are heavy on know-how and have very high up-front costs relative to the variable cost of producing and offering each unit to customers. For example, a software developer can spend millions of dollars to develop a software application while the cost of selling a copy to customers is almost zero because all the developer has to do is post the software on the Web for customers to download. It cost AOL hundreds of millions of dollars to build its software, hardware, brand, and subscriber base, but once the initial amount is spent, the monthly relative cost of maintaining each member is negligible. To illustrate some of the underpinnings of the pricing strategies for knowledge-based products and services, let's start with a simple but revealing example.

Example Consider two firms, A and B, each of which has developed a proprietary software package. Each spends $500 million (M) a year on research and development (R&D), marketing, and promotion, with the bulk of that sum on R&D.[10] Since the software can be downloaded by customers, let's assume that it costs both A and B $5 to sell each copy (for credit card verification and management of the marketing website) at a unit price of $200. Suppose firm A, through the right strategic decisions and endowments, has a market share of 80 percent of the 10 million units in 1999 while B has the remaining 20 percent.
    Using the extremely simple but enlightening relation:

$$\text{Profits} = \Pi = (P - V_c)Q - F_c$$

where P is the price per unit of the product,
         V_c is the per unit variable cost,
         Q is the total number of units sold, and
         F_c is the up-front or fixed costs,

we find that in 1999:

Firm A's profits = $(200 - 5) \times 8M - 500M = 1,560M - 500M = \$1,060M$
Firm B's profits = $(200 - 5) \times 2M - 500M = 390M - 500M = -\$110M$

Thus, while firm A earned more than $1 billion in profits in 1999, firm B actually *lost* $110 million. What a difference market share makes for high fixed cost, low variable cost products! This very simple example brings out several underpinnings of pricing strategies for products with high fixed costs and low variable costs—both characteristics of knowledge-based products. To illustrate the role of market share, margins, revenues, and growth, we have extended our simple calculation to include the years 1998 and 2000. The results are shown in Table 4.2.

Market Share and Margins Are Critical!

As we have noted, market share is critical to knowledge-based products. In our example, the firm with an 80 percent market share in 1999 earned more than $1 billion in profits while the one with 20 percent lost money. A firm's strategy early in the life of such products, then, is to strive for high market share. Strategies for attaining such a high market share include (1) giving away a product and charging for later versions, (2) giving away product X and charging for related product Y, and (3) pricing low to penetrate the market. Note that if firm A gives away its product in 1998 and 1999 to help it attain the 80 percent market share in 2000, it loses $1.044 billion in those two years but more than makes up for it with a $15.1 billion profit in 2000. Also note that firm A can cut its sales price by half and still make over $7 billion. One way of looking at this is that A's profit margins are higher because its fixed costs are spread over more units.

It's Growth! It's Revenues!

Notice in Table 4.2 that although firm A's market share in 1998 was 80 percent, it actually lost $344 million even though its losses were less than those of firm B. However, firm A earned $1.06 billion in profits in 1999 and a whopping $15.1 billion in 2000 even though in both years its market share was still 80 percent. The difference is that it sold only 800,000 units in 1998, but 8 million units in 1999 and 80 million in 2000. Indeed, even firm B earned $3.4 billion in 2000. The most important strategy, then, is to develop the market. Sell more units! It is in the interest of both firms to increase the size of the market. It is not so much the fractional share as the revenue share that matters.

Lock-in

An important question is, Why can't firm B reduce its price low enough to grab some of the market share from firm A? One answer is that such pricing strategies work best for products that not only have a very high ratio of fixed

TABLE 4.2   **Market Share and Profitability for Knowledge-Based Products**

	1998			1999			2000		
	Market Share (%)	Market Share (1,000 units)	Profits ($ millions)	Market Share (%)	Market Share (1,000 units)	Profits ($ millions)	Market Share (%)	Market Share (1,000 units)	Profits ($ millions)
Firm A	80	800	344	80	8,000	1,060	80	80,000	15,100
Firm B	20	200	−461	20	2,000	−110	20	20,000	3,400

to variable costs but also exhibit **lock-in,** which means that the products have certain characteristics that lock in customers. First, switching to a new product means users must learn how to use the new one if both old and new products are not compatible. Unless the benefits of the new product outweigh those of the old one, customers may not be willing to switch. For example, a person who has learned how to use Microsoft's Windows operating system and decides to switch to UNIX must now learn how to use this new operating system. Many customers regard **switching costs** as important. The required new learning may not be worth the cost savings, if any. Second, the product may have complementary products that are not compatible with those of competing products. In this case switching could mean buying a new set of compatible products. In the Windows example, switching to UNIX could mean having to abandon all the applications programs that the user has accumulated over the years. Third, these products sometimes exhibit **network externalities**— the more users who own them, the more valuable they are to users. If many people already own an IBM-compatible PC, it makes sense to stay with that type of computer when you need a new one or go with what most people have when you buy your first computer. That way, you can share user tips and software with other users. These lock-in properties allow firms that are already ahead of the competition to increase the distance between themselves and competitors.

Types of Pricing and the Influence of the Internet (Dynamic Pricing)

There are actually five main types of pricing: menu, one-to-one bargaining, auction,[11] reverse auction, and barter.

Menu

In **menu pricing,** or fixed pricing, the seller sets a price and buyers can either take it or leave it. This is the most common form of pricing, used by nearly every retail store in the United States. Menu pricing has two shortcomings. First, given the value they are getting from the product, customers may be willing to pay more than the menu prices set by the seller. In such a case, the seller is leaving money on the table. There is also the possibility that the menu price is too high, cutting off many buyers who would have bought the product at a lower price. At the same time, the seller is forgoing extra revenue. These prices are also sticky because, once set, they are difficult to change. The stickiness is a result of two factors. First, it is not easy to detect changes in consumer preferences quickly enough to effect price changes since menu prices reveal little about customer preferences. Second, it is difficult to implement price changes. It takes time and costs money to change the labels on products. Just think of how much it would cost to keep changing all the prices in your grocery store as a function of the day of the week or time of day. This could also be extremely confusing to customers. With the Internet, however, customer preferences can be detected more easily. Moreover, it costs a lot less to change prices since they are all virtual.

One-to-One

In **one-to-one bargaining,** a seller negotiates with a buyer to determine at what point the buyer considers the price appropriate for the value that he or she is getting. This overcomes the disadvantage of menu pricing which lets some customers get away with a price that is less than they would be willing to pay, and misses out on customers who would prefer to pay less. This type of pricing is very common on the streets of most developing countries. The first disadvantage of one-to-one bargaining is that it is impractical in most large bricks-and-mortar stores; imagine customers trying to negotiate prices on all the items in a supermarket. The second disadvantage is that the seller cannot be sure that the prospective buyer is willing to pay what he or she believes the product is worth, nor can the buyer be sure that the seller necessarily wants to sell for the least price. With the Internet, changing prices is as easy as clicking a mouse. Moreover, customer personalization helps better determine each customer's willingness to pay and prices can be adjusted accordingly.

Auction

In **auction pricing** the seller solicits bids from many buyers and sells to the buyer with the best bid. This removes the second disadvantage of one-to-one bargaining. One problem with auctions is that buyers can collude to hold down the price of an item or sellers can limit the number of items up for bid at any time. The other problem with auctions in the bricks-and-mortar world is the difficulty in bringing together many buyers and sellers. This difficulty still exposes auction participants to some of the risk of not getting the best buyers and sellers that one-to-one bargaining faces. The large communities of the Internet, however, bring together many sellers and buyers, greatly reducing this problem. Moreover, on the Web auctioneers like eBay have developed programs that allow buyers to rate each other, helping to establish a rating reputation for performance. This goes a long way in reducing the fear of collusion and opportunism.

Reverse Auction

In a **reverse auction,** sellers decide whether to fulfill the orders of potential buyers. A buyer proposes a price for a good or service. Sellers then decide whether to accept or reject the bid. Priceline.com was one of the pioneers of the reverse auction model. A user of Priceline proposes a price he or she is willing to pay for, say, air transportation, between points A and B on a certain day. Priceline then presents this information to the airlines to see whether any are interested. If an airline is willing to sell tickets at that price, the deal is consummated and Priceline gets a commission from the seller.[12] This system also allows price discrimination by sellers because buyers do not know how much other buyers are willing to pay. The reverse auction is not as good for sellers as an auction since an astute buyer can capture all of the seller's surplus.

Barter

Probably one of the oldest pricing models first employed by our ancestors, **barter** refers to the swapping of goods for goods, or goods for services, and the use of those goods or services by the parties involved. Although it works for young companies strapped for cash, in general, barter is a relatively weak pricing model that has little long-term potential.

REVENUE SOURCES

A critical part of a business model analysis is the determination of the sources of a firm's revenues *and* profits. In the bricks-and-mortar world, many firms receive their **revenue sources** directly from the products they sell. Others receive their revenues from selling products *and* servicing them, with a larger share of their profits coming from the service. For example, a jet engine maker or earth-moving equipment manufacturer may receive large amounts of revenue from selling its products but make much greater profits from spare parts and servicing of the equipment. An understanding of the sources of profits allows a firm to make better strategic decisions. For example, the jet engine maker may decide to sell the engines at giveaway prices and depend on after-sales service to make money.

With the Internet, the need to determine the sources of revenues and profits is even more critical largely because of its properties of mediating and network externalities. Consider an online stockbrokerage firm, for example. It has three sources of revenues: (1) the commissions that it collects on the stock trades it executes for clients; (2) the interest that it charges clients who must borrow from the cash reserves of other clients (deposited with the broker) to pay for any securities they buy on margin; and (3) the spread between the bid and ask prices of stocks. Thus, an online stockbrokerage may decide to charge extremely low commissions to increase the number of its clients with large assets. More such clients mean more revenues and profits from interest charges and spreads.

The mediating property also suggests that the revenue model of radio, print, and television media in the United States and Canada provides useful information in determining the sources of revenues and profits for the Internet. In the media model, firms offer value to their audience but charge advertisers, not the audience, for it. A firm may therefore sell its products at a discount but make money from selling advertising to merchandisers who value the firm's audience. An online auto dealer may collect a fee for referring customers to automakers but make its money by selling insurance to visitors to its site. Some firms might lose money in selling to customers but collect information on these customers that they can sell to other vendors. In early 2000, there were two problems with this model. First, almost anyone with a website had an audience and therefore the potential to sell advertising or capture customer data. Second, exactly what advertisers should be paying for has not been very clear. Table 4.3 traces some of the evolution of online advertising metrics.

TABLE 4.3   **Evolution of Advertising Metrics for Portals**

Metric	Definition	Comment
Number of hits	Count of each time data is requested from a server while a Web surfer is at a website. There may be more than one hit each time a user clicks a mouse.	Number of hits does not say much about the types of customers and what they were doing.
Page views	The number of individual HTML pages that a surfer pulls out while at a website.	Number of surfers who respond to an ad still not given.
Click-through	Percent of prospective customers who respond to an online advertisement.	No information on the customers themselves.
Unique visitors	Count of individuals using their internet protocol (IP) address.	
Reach	Percent of sampled users who visit a page on a specific website in a given month.	
Length of stay	How long the user has been on the website.	
Registered users	Measure of website users likely to come back.	
Repeat visitors	The number of visitors at a website for two or more times.	

Source: S. V. Haar, "Web Metrics: Go Figure." *Business 2.0* (June 1999), pp. 46–47.

CONNECTED ACTIVITIES: WHAT ACTIVITIES AND WHEN

To deliver value to different customers, a firm must perform the activities that underpin the value. If Intel is going to offer very fast microprocessors to its customers and charge a premium price for them, it must be able to perform some of the **connected activities** that underpin the making of microprocessors: R&D, product design, wafer fabrication, testing, marketing and sales, and field support. A set of these connected activities is normally called a value chain because value is added to materials or knowledge as it moves up the chain.[13] We will say more about value chains in Chapter 6. To offer better value to the right customers, a firm must carefully choose *which* activities it performs and *when* it performs them.

Which Activities to Perform

Five criteria guide a firm's choice of which activities to perform (see Table 4.4). First, the activities should be consistent with the value that the firm is offering. If a firm positions itself as a low cost or product differentiator, the activities

TABLE 4.4 **Which Activities to Perform and When**

In choosing which activities to perform, management should ask itself if the activities:
- Are consistent with customer value and the scope of customers served.
- Reinforce each other.
- Take advantage of industry success drivers.
- Are consistent with any distinctive capabilities that the firm has or wants to build.
- Make the industry more attractive for the firm.

In choosing when to perform the activities, management should ask:
- What are the characteristics of the industry at this stage of the life cycle and what will they be down the line?
- What are existing competitors doing and what are potential ones likely to do?
- Are the activities consistent timewise?

that it performs should be consistent with that position. Dell Computer, for example, by going direct not only cut the cost of offering PCs to its customers (consistent with a low cost strategy) but also considerably cut down the time between the production of a computer and the time a customer receives it. If an e-tailer is going to offer 24-hour-a-day shopping, it must not only have the right software and customer service (easy-to-use website and Web reps) to match but also should have the logistics to deliver the products on time.

Second, the activities should reinforce each other.[14] A well-constructed virtual storefront should be accompanied with appropriate promotions to help establish brand-name reputation. The performance of the storefront helps reinforce the effectiveness of the campaign while the campaign further boosts the perceived performance of the storefront. AOL may have all the portal services and content, but if the Last Mile to the house is very slow and its customers have to wait a long time for responses to their inquiries, the value perceived by these customers will not be as high as if the Last Mile were faster.

Third, the activities should take advantage of industry success drivers—the factors that are likely to have the most impact on cost or differentiation. For example, Dell's excellent performance in the 1990s is often credited to the firm's decision to sell directly to business customers instead of going through distributors. The apparent success of the decision may rest on two key characteristics of the PC industry. The first is that the rate of technological change is very rapid, so PCs that sit on distributors' shelves can become obsolete if not sold quickly. By selling directly to customers, Dell was able to get the products to customers early enough for them to enjoy the latest that processors can offer, before new products rendered them obsolete. The second is that the prices of PCs drop very fast so the more the PCs wait at distributors, the less the manufacturer will get for the PCs when they are eventually sold. Moreover, by going direct Dell also avoids the large number of returns that PC makers often have to take from dealers.

The fourth criteria for choosing which activity to perform is that the activities should take advantage of any distinctive capabilities that a firm may have or that it can build. Wal-Mart claims that one of its core capabilities is logistics.[15] Thus, it would make sense for logistics to be one of the activities that it performs in e-tailing.

Finally, and probably most important, the activities should be geared toward making the industry more attractive to the firm. As we will see in Chapter 8, one benefit of performing an analysis of industry attractiveness is finding out why the industry is attractive or unattractive so that a firm can make the industry more attractive for itself; that is, through strategic action, a firm can increase its bargaining power over suppliers and customers, reduce rivalry, raise barriers to entry, and reduce the power of substitutes. Offering customers better value than competitors is a necessary condition for making profits, but it is not a sufficient condition. A good example illustrates this. Suppose an entrepreneurial firm uses its proprietary technology to develop a custom electronic fuel injector that uses microprocessors from Intel and is 30 percent more fuel efficient, but it works only with Ford cars. Clearly this is a highly differentiated product with enormous customer value, but it probably will not be very profitable for the entrepreneur. For one thing, Ford has bargaining power over the entrepreneur since it is the only automaker that can use the product. For another, Intel is the only firm that manufactures the microprocessor and, because sales to the entrepreneur are so small compared to the millions of microprocessors sold to PC makers, Intel also has bargaining power over the entrepreneur. Thus, the choice of activities should go beyond providing better value than competitors. The activities chosen should allow a firm to be in a better position to exploit the value that it offers customers—to make the industry more attractive for itself.

When to Perform Activities

When a firm decides to perform an activity is also critical. Industry characteristics evolve and so should the kinds of activities a firm performs to take advantage of industry profitability. The activities that firms perform in an industry are a function of where the technology is in that industry's life cycle. In the emerging phase, firms must decide how they are going to adopt the technology and what role they see that technology playing in their revenue streams. In the growth phase, firms must decide what the basis for their competitive technological advantage should be and invest accordingly.[16] For example, if an online stockbrokerage firm decides that its profits will come more from the interest that it earns from members who borrow on margin than from commissions, the firm may want to invest in acquiring clients with large accounts who are less likely to switch. A portal firm may want to invest in building its brand name to differentiate its website from those of numerous potential competitors. It is also important to take cues from the point at which customers are in their own technological evolution. For example, timing was one reason why going direct worked for Dell. The company implemented that strategy when its industry had evolved to a point where many businesses had management information systems (MIS) groups that could better determine their PC needs without the help of distributors.[17] Before then, most customers needed the hand-holding that dealers provided. The PC had also evolved to a point where some kind of a standard had emerged making it easier for firms to specify their needs in a PC.

Additionally, when a firm chooses to perform some activities is also a function of what competitors are doing. If a firm's major competitors are acquiring cable companies to allow them to offer broadband service over the Last Mile to homes, the firm may want to do something about that. Finally, the sequence in which activities are performed is also important. If a firm advertises its financial services to lure customers, but then lacks the computer services to match, its reputation may be damaged.

IMPLEMENTATION

A firm's decision concerning what value to offer customers, which customers to offer this value to, how to price it, and what activities to perform is one thing. Actually carrying out the decision—its **implementation**—is another. We next discuss the role of implementation, highlighting the relationships between strategy, structure, systems, people, and environment.[18]

Structure

The structure of a firm tells us who is supposed to report to whom and who is responsible for what so that the activities a firm has chosen to perform are carried out. In searching for the right structure, three questions must be explored. First is the question of *coordination*. While performing their own activities, how do inbound logistics and operations, for example, manage to exchange information at the right times in order to offer customer value? How does the firm ensure that the right resources are available at the right cost when needed? Second is the problem of *differentiation* and *integration*. A firm's logistics and marketing groups are maintained as separate functions because each necessarily has to specialize in what it does in order to keep building the stock of knowledge that underpins its activities—each one has its own unique tasks and roles to play. This is differentiation. At the same time, offering customers value often entails cross-functional interaction; that is, the differentiated activities of the different functions must be integrated for optimal value.[19]

Organizational structures are some variation of two major types: *functional* and *project*. In the **functional organizational structure**, people are grouped and perform their tasks according to traditional functions such as inbound logistics, R&D, operations, marketing, and so on. Grouping people together with similar competencies and knowledge enables them to learn from each other and to increase the firm's stock of knowledge in the particular area. Communication is largely vertical, up and down the hierarchy of each function.

In the **project organizational structure**, employees are organized not by functional area but by the project they are working on. For example, if the project is to develop a minivan, employees from marketing, design, manufacturing, engines, and other relevant functions are assigned to the project and work for the project manager, not their functional managers. Communication is largely lateral, an advantage for innovation.

Organizational structures also can be characterized as *organic* or *mechanistic*.[20] First, in the **organic organizational structure**, communications are lateral, not vertical as with **mechanistic organizational structures**; that is, product designers talk directly to marketing employees rather than through their boss. This allows for a better exchange of ideas. Second, in the organic structure, employees with the most influence are those with technological skills or marketing knowledge and not those ranking high in the organizational hierarchy. This allows them to make the best-informed decisions. Third, job responsibilities are more loosely defined in the organic structure, giving employees more opportunities to be receptive to new ideas and more objective about how best to use these ideas. Finally, the organic structure emphasizes the exchange of information rather than a one-way flow of information from some central authority as in the mechanistic structure.

Systems

An organizational structure tells us who does what but very little about how to keep people motivated as they carry out their assigned tasks and responsibilities.[21] Management must be able to monitor performance and reward and punish individuals, functions, divisions, and organizations in some agreed upon and understood way. For employees of many start-ups, the payoff at the initial public offering (IPO) is a strong incentive. In these firms, systems must be in place whereby information will flow in the shortest possible time to the right targets for decision making. In addition to performance and reward systems, information flow systems are critical. These can be grouped into information and communication technologies and the physical layout of the building. The Internet makes it possible for the CEO of Microsoft, for example, to see new product ideas from an engineer deep down the organizational hierarchy via electronic mail or an intranet. If such information had to pass up the organizational ladder, it would take much longer and face a good chance of distortion. An area manager for a U.S. multinational corporation who is resident in France does not have to go through loops to obtain information on a new product being developed in the United States. All she needs to do is go to the company's website in the company's intranet to get undistorted, up-to-date information on the product. A German driver should be able to test-drive a car in a virtual reality site in Stuttgart knowing that the results will be fed instantly to designers in Detroit, Los Angeles, and Tokyo.

People

Establishing control and reward systems to motivate employees, and building information systems that provide them with the best information for decision making, is one thing. Whether these people are motivated or not, or make the right decisions with the available information, is another. This is a function of many questions: To what extent do employees share common goals? Is the manager of the brake division of an automobile manufacturer interested in building a personal empire or doing the best he can to make sure that the company builds the best car possible in the shortest possible time with the best brake system that can be manufactured in the most efficient manner? Does the manufacturing group see R&D as a "bunch of ivory tower, money-spending snobs" or colleagues with whom they can work to build the best cars in the shortest possible time at the lowest cost? To what extent do employees have the knowledge that underpins the various activities of the firm's value chain? How much is such knowledge valued? What really is the core competence of the firm and where does it reside—in people or organizational routines and endowments of the firm? What does it take to motivate employees? Paychecks, job security, stock options, implementation of their ideas, earning respect, or being "seen" as a person? Does management see unions as the adversary or part of a team with shared goals that is there as part of the checks and balances necessary to keep on course toward the firm's goals? Are managers leaders or systematic planners?

Recognizing the Potential of Innovation

The literature in technology management suggests that five kinds of individuals have been identified to play key roles in recognizing the potential of an innovation: idea generators, gatekeepers, boundary spanners, champions, and sponsors.[22] The more effective each of these individuals is, the better the chance a firm has in recognizing the potential of an innovation. For example, **champions** are individuals who take an idea (theirs or that of an idea generator) for a new product/service and do all they can within their power to ensure its success. By actively promoting the idea and communicating and inspiring others with their vision of the innovation, champions can help their organization realize its potential. Thus, champions with charisma and an ability to articulate their vision of a product/service to others are more effective than those who do not.[23]

Having **gatekeepers** and **boundary spanners** is critical to collecting information. A gatekeeper is an individual within a firm who understands the idiosyncrasies of the firm and those of the outside. He or she acts as a transducer between the firm and the outside world during the exchange of information that often takes place during technological innovation. Without ties to any particular functional organization, project, or product in the firm, gatekeepers are more likely to be objective when collecting new ideas from the outside. The danger is that a gatekeeper may also develop the same information filters that successful functions have. Some human resource practices ensure that two promotional ladders are present in their firms: a technical ladder and the more traditional administrative one. The idea is to free inventors or gatekeepers from administrative tasks so they can spend their time doing what they do best and still get rewarded as much as the administrative stars who get promoted to management positions. Boundary spanners play the role of gatekeepers between a team and an organization.

Organizational Culture

How well people perform their roles in the firm is a function of a firm's culture. **Organizational culture** is a system of shared values (what is important) and beliefs (how things work) that interact with the organization's people, organizational structures, and systems to produce behavioral norms (the way we do things around here).[24] Whether a culture is good at recognizing the potential of an innovation is a function of the type of culture. An entrepreneurial culture that keeps employees on the lookout for new ideas and holds the employees in high esteem when they turn those ideas into new products can be an asset in recognizing the potential of an innovation. However, some cultures can lead to evils such as the Not Invented Here (NIH) syndrome.

Different firms use different strategies to avoid such evils. For example, Sony looks for people who are *neyaka*, that is, open-minded, optimistic, and wide-ranging in their interests. It also prefers generalists compared to specialists. Sony's founder, Masuru Ibuka, says "Specialists are inclined to argue why you can't do something, while our emphasis has always been to make something out of nothing."[25]

CAPABILITIES

Resources

To perform the activities that underpin customer value, firms need resources. These **resources** can be grouped into tangible, intangible, and human.[26] *Tangible resources* are both physical and financial, the types usually identified and accounted for under assets in financial statements. These include plants, equipment, and cash reserves. For some Internet start-ups, these are their computers, pipes over the Last Mile to homes, and the money raised through IPOs. *Intangible resources* are the nonphysical and nonfinancial assets that are usually not accounted for in financial statements.[27] These include patents, copyrights, reputation, brands, trade secrets, relationships with customers, relationships between employees, and knowledge embedded in different forms such as databases containing the vital statistics of customers and market research findings. For many portals, ISPs, and e-tailers, these are their software, databases of visitor or customer profiles, copyrights, brands, and client communities. *Human resources* are the skills and knowledge that employees carry with them. For Internet firms, these are the knowledge and skills embedded in employees on everything from how to code software to how to design and implement business plans.

Competencies

Resources in and of themselves do not make customer value and profits. Customers would not scramble to a firm's doors because the firm has great plants, geniuses, or a war chest from an initial public offering. Resources must be converted into something that customers want. The ability or capacity of a firm to turn its resources into customer value and profits is usually called a capability or **competence**.[28] This usually entails the use or integration of more than one resource. G. M. Hamel and C. K. Prahalad argued that a firm's capabilities or competencies are core when they meet three criteria: customer value, competitor differentiation, and extendibility.[29] The *customer value* criteria requires that a core competence must make an unusually high contribution to the value that customers perceive. For example, in the late 1980s and early 1990s Apple Computer's expertise in developing graphical user interface (GUI) software made its computers among the most user-friendly. A competence is *competitor differentiating* if it is uniquely held or, if widely held, the firm's level of competence is higher than that of its competitors. Many companies have the ability to develop user-friendly interfaces, but Apple Computer's Macintosh GUI remains, arguably, the most user-friendly. A competence is *extendable* if it is used in more than one product area. For example, Honda's ability to design excellent engines has allowed it to offer engines not only for cars but also for portable electric generators, lawn mowers, and marine vehicles.

Competitive Advantage

A firm's core competencies allow it to have a **competitive advantage** because, by definition, they allow the firm to offer its customers better value than competitors. The extent to which this advantage is sustainable is a function of how inimitable and difficult to substitute the capabilities are. Three reasons have been offered for why it may be very difficult to replicate or acquire distinctive capabilities.[30] First, it may be difficult to replicate the historical context in which the capabilities were developed. Caterpillar's worldwide service network of people trained in servicing its earth-moving equipment has its foundation in World War II, when its machines were the machines of choice by Allied forces in Europe. After the war many servicepeople who returned to the civilian workforce had the skills and knowledge to service Caterpillar equipment. A firm would find it very costly to build an identical network. Second, it may take time to develop these capabilities, giving first movers an advantage that is difficult to overcome. Merck's ability to get its drugs through clinical testing and approval by the U.S. Food and Drug Administration is outstanding. It rests on the relationships that the firm has created over the years with different physicians, research centers, and hospitals. These relationships cannot be created overnight. Third, it may be very difficult at first to identify the core competence and even more difficult to find out how to copy it. What really constitutes Honda's ability to offer outstanding engines? How does one copy that? Answering these questions is difficult, suggesting that replicating the capability is also very difficult.

SUSTAINABILITY

If a firm's business model enables it to gain a competitive advantage, the chances are that its competitors would like to catch up or maybe even leapfrog it. What can a firm do to maintain its competitive advantage? To sustain a competitive advantage, a firm can—depending on its capabilities, environment, and technology in question—pursue some subset of three generic strategies: *block, run,* and *team-up.*[31]

Block Strategy

In the **block strategy**, a firm erects barriers around its product market space. A firm can block in two ways. First, if its capabilities in any of the components of the business model are inimitable and distinctive enough to offer customers unique value, the firm can limit access to them and thereby keep out competitors. That would be the case, for example, when a firm has **intellectual property** (e.g., patents, copyrights, software applications, domain assets, service marks, trademarks, and trade secrets) that can be protected and sends signals to potential imitators that it means business in protecting the property. Amazon.com's 1999 lawsuit against barnesandnoble.com, charging the latter with copying its "1-Click" technology, is one such signal. Second, if all firms are equally capable of performing these activities, incumbents may still prevent entry by signaling that post-entry prices will be low. There are several ways a firm can achieve this.[32] For example, it can establish a reputation for retaliating against anyone who tries to imitate any component of its business model. It can also do so by making heavy, nonreversible investments in relevant assets. For example, if a firm spends billions of dollars installing fiber optics capability for all the households in a town, the chances are that it will lower prices if another firm wants to offer high-speed access to the same customers. In general, such signals can prevent profit-motivated potential competitors from entering.

Blocking works only as long as a company's capabilities are unique and inimitable or as long as barriers to entry last. But competitors can, for example, circumvent patents and copyrights or challenge them in court until they are overturned. Moreover, the usefulness of such capabilities lasts only until discontinuities such as deregulation/regulation, changing customer preferences and expectations, or radical technological change render them obsolete. The information asymmetry reduction property of the Internet also suggests that blocking is not going to be very effective. With the Internet, learning about competitors' products, the technologies that underpin them, and how to reverse-engineer these products is considerably easier. A software developer that once depended on the scarcity of distribution channels to keep out competitors, for example, can no longer do so since new entrants can now sell their products over the Internet. With the databases on patents available on the Internet, an imitator can quickly search through its own patents and those of its target competitors and be in a better position to challenge the patents or to determine what it needs to leapfrog the competitor. Special relations with customers that gave a firm an advantage may no longer do so because customers can solicit bids from many more suppliers over the Internet.

Run Strategy

The **run strategy** admits that blockades to entry, no matter how formidable they may appear, are often penetrable or eventually fall. Sitting behind these blockades only gives competitors time to catch up or leapfrog the innovator. An innovator often has to run. *Running* means changing some subset of components or linkages of business models or reinventing the whole business model to offer customers better value. In the 1990s Dell Computer often introduced new ways of selling its personal computers (PCs) before competitors copied its existing sales strategy. Running can give a firm many first-mover advantages, including the ability to control parts of its own environment. In an age of rapid technological change, the run strategy becomes extremely important because blocking is more difficult. Running sometimes means the **cannibalization**—introduction of new products that render existing ones less competitive, thereby eating into existing sales—of one's own products before competitors do. Intel Corporation offers a very good example. In the late 1980s and 1990s it usually introduced a new generation of microprocessors before unit sales of an existing one had peaked. If Intel had not done so, despite its microcode copyrights, other firms would have found a way to catch up.[33]

Team-up Strategy

Sometimes, a firm simply cannot do it all alone. It must pursue a **team-up strategy** with others through some kind of strategic alliance, joint venture, acquisition, or equity position. Teaming up allows a firm to share in resources that it does not possess and may not want to acquire or cannot acquire even if it wanted to. Shared resources also facilitate knowledge transfer. Teaming up has its disadvantages too. It is not easy for a firm to protect its technology or other aspects of its business model that it would like to keep proprietary. In teaming up, a firm also risks becoming too dependent on another firm's resources. Often, running also requires teaming up. For example, developing some chips on time may require more resources than one firm can afford, necessitating teaming up—witness the Toshiba, IBM, and Siemens alliance to develop the 256M memory chip.

Attaining and maintaining a competitive advantage often requires some combination of the three strategies. An important question is, When is each strategy or combination of strategies appropriate? Two factors influence the choice of strategy. First, the choice depends on what it takes for a firm to build a profitable business model. It depends on what determines profitability in the face of the technology in question. After all, a business model is about how to make money over the long term. Second, timing is of the essence. The strategy pursued is a function of the stage of evolution of the technology—the Internet in our case. It is also a function of when existing and potential competitors have pursued related strategies or plan to.

COST STRUCTURE

Offering customer value to different market segments, performing value-adding activities, pursuing different sources of revenues or pricing strategies, building firm capabilities, executing business models, and sustaining firm competitive advantages all cost money. Every dollar of revenues is associated with some cost. A firm's **cost structure** expresses the relationship between its revenues and the underlying costs of generating those revenues. Irrespective of whether it pursues a low cost or differentiation strategy, a firm would like to keep its cost per revenue dollar per unit customer value very low. To keep these costs low, a firm must understand the determinants of its costs. A firm's cost structure is determined by how it exploits its industry's cost drivers as it adds and delivers value to its customers while positioning itself well vis-a-vis its co-opetitors. A firm's **co-opetitors** are the suppliers, customers, and complementors with whom it must compete and co-operate. Key cost drivers include economies of scale, input-to-output transformation technology on which value-adding activities rest, capacity unitilization, and transaction costs.[34] Where such cost drivers are themselves driven by information rather than by materials, the Internet stands to have a more profound impact on cost structure. Take the software industry for example. Since the product is made up of ones and zeros, software developers can reside anywhere in the world and use the Internet to co-develop new software. Moreover, software can be distributed to customers over the Internet, which is less costly than the bricks-and-mortar distribution model of packaging the software in disks and transporting it by land, sea, or air.

In general, having a low cost structure entails paying careful attention to the cost of the other nine components of a business model and making sure that they are planned and executed efficiently. Thus, in delivering value to customers, it is always important to keep asking how much it costs to deliver the value, how much it costs to acquire customers in each market segment, which activities a firm is better off outsourcing and which should remain internal, and so on.

Summary

A firm's business model is critical to its ability to gain and maintain a competitive advantage—it is critical to the firm's profitability. The success of a firm's business model in the face of the Internet challenge is a function of the type of value that it offers customers, the type of customers to which it offers that value, the range of products or services that contain the value, how it prices that value, the types of revenue sources it pursues, the way the activities that undergird customer value creation work as a system, the implementation of the activities and value creation, the capabilities on which value-creating activities rest, and the strategies used to sustain the firm's competitive advantage. How much of a competitive advantage is also a function of the extent to which the firm, in designing and executing its business model, takes advantage of those factors that make its industry attractive or unattractive as a result of the impact of the Internet.

Again, using the deceptively simple relationship, Profits = $\Pi = (P - V_c)Q - F_c$, we can see how each of the components of a business model affects profitability. If a firm can offer its customers something distinctive (i.e., competitors cannot imitate it), it can afford to charge premium prices, P, for it. This leads to higher profits. If its per unit costs, V_c, are low, Π is higher. The more people in a particular market segment that can buy the product, the higher the quantity Q will be. The more each of the customers in the segment is willing to pay for the product, the higher P becomes. Pricing ensures that a firm gets paid for the value that it offers customers and does not leave money on the table. It can also be used to gain a large market share early and build switching costs at customers ensuring a higher Q. Different revenue sources mean a higher Q and the appropriate $P - V_c$. Well-connected activities and good implementation reinforce higher P, lower V_c, and higher Q. So does a good sustainability strategy.

Key Terms

auction pricing, *61*
barter, *61*
block strategy, *71*
boundary spanners, *68*
business model, *51*
cannibalization, *72*
capabilities, *53*
champions, *68*
competence, *70*
competitive
    advantage, *70*
connected activities, *63*
co-opetitor, *73*
cost structure, *73*
customer value, *52*
functional
    organizational
    structure, *66*

gatekeepers, *68*
implementation, *66*
intellectual property,
    71
knowledge-based
    products, *58*
lock-in, *60*
mechanistic
    organizational
    structures, *67*
menu pricing, *60*
network
    externalities, *60*
neyaka, *69*
one-to-one
    bargaining, *61*
organic organizational
    structure, *67*

organizational
    culture, *69*
pricing strategy, *58*
profit site, *53*
project organizational
    structure, *66*
resources, *69*
revenue sources, *62*
reverse auction, *61*
run strategy, *71*
scope, *57*
sustainability, *53*
switching costs, *60*
team-up strategy, *72*

Discussion Questions

1. What is the relationship between profitability, fixed costs, variable costs, margins, and market share for knowledge-based products? What is the significance of this relationship for strategy formulation?

2. Name three firms that are key players in e-business. What is the competitive advantage of each? Are these competitive advantages sustainable? If so, brainstorm possible events or circumstances which could reduce their sustainability.

3. Is the magnitude of the role played by each component of a business model a function of industry? If so, which components have the most impact in which industries?

4. Name an e-business company that has an innovative pricing model. How has the company benefited from this strategy? Is such a model sustainable?

5. Look for news on an e-business firm introducing a new product and/or service. Does this new activity fit the criteria listed in Table 4.4?

6. What is the relationship between core competencies and competitive advantage?

7. Search the news for the latest merger in the Internet business. Does this alliance make sense? Why or why not?

Notes

1. M. E. Porter, "Towards a Dynamic Theory of Strategy," *Strategic Management Journal* 12 (1991), pp. 95–117.

2. M. E. Porter, *Competitive Advantage: Creating and Sustaining Superior Performance* (New York: Free Press, 1985).

3. R. Amit and P. Schoemaker, "Strategic Assets and Organizational Rent," *Strategic Management Journal* 14 (1993), pp. 33–46; J. Mahoney and J. R. Pandian, "The Resource-Based View within the Conversation of Strategic Management," *Strategic Management Journal* 13 (1992), pp. 363–80; C. Helfat, "Know-how and Asset Complementarity and Dynamic Capability Accumulation: The Case of R&D," *Strategic Management Journal* 18 (1997), pp. 339–60; B. Wernerfelt, "A Resource-based View of the Firm," *Strategic Management Journal* 5 (1984), pp. 171–80.

4. M. E. Porter, *Competitive Strategy: Techniques for Analyzing Industries and Competitors* (New York: Free Press, 1980).

5. M. E. Porter, *Competitive Strategy*; J. B. Barney, *Gaining and Sustaining Competitive Advantage* (Reading, MA: Addison-Wesley, 1997).

6. R. D. Hof and L. Himelstein, "eBay vs Amazon.com." *Business Week*, May 31, 1999.

7. For a more detailed treatment of this very important marketing subject, see P. Kotler, *Marketing Management* (Englewood Cliffs, NJ: Prentice Hall, 1994).

8. M. E. Porter, "What Is Strategy?" *Harvard Business Review*, November–December 1996, pp. 61–78.

9. W. B. Arthur, "Increasing Returns and the New World of Business," *Harvard Business Review*, July–August 1996, pp, 100–9.

10. For a related example, see A. James, "Give It Away and Get Rich," *Fortune*, June 10, 1996, pp. 90–98.

11. "The Heyday of the Auction," *The Economist*, July 24, 1999.

12. See Amy Cortese, "E-Commerce: Good-Bye to Fixed Pricing?" *Business Week*, May 4, 1998.

13. Porter, *Competitive Advantage*.

14. The first two criteria are from Porter, "What Is Strategy?" pp. 61–78.

15. According to Wal-Mart's CEO in 1999, the firm's core competencies are logistics and information technology.

16. R. M. Grant, *Contemporary Strategy Analysis: Concepts, Techniques, Applications* (Oxford: Blackwell, 1998).

17. D. B. Yoffie, J. Cohn, and D. Levy, "Apple Computer 1992," Harvard Business School case #9-792-081.

18. This section draws heavily on *Innovation Management: Strategies, Implementation and Profits,* Oxford University Press, 1998, pp. 99–106.

19. P. R. Lawrence and J. W. Lorsch, *Organization and Environments: Managing Differentiation and Integration* (Burr Ridge, IL: Richard D. Irwin, 1967).

20. See, for example, T. Burns and G. M. Stalker, *The Management of Innovation* (London: Tavistock, 1961) and S. P. Robbins, *Organizational Theory: Structure, Design and Applications* (Englewood Cliffs, NJ: Prentice Hall, 1987).

21. C. W. L. Hill and G. R. Jones, *Strategic Management: An Integrated Approach* (Boston: Houghton Mifflin, 1995), p. 352.

22. See, for example, *Innovation Management.*

23. J. M. Howell and C. A. Higgins, "Champions of Technological Innovation," *Administrative Sciences Quarterly* 35 (1990), pp. 317–41.

24. B. Uttal and J. Fierman, "The Corporate Culture Vultures," *Fortune,* October 17, 1983, pp. 66–73. For a detailed discussion on culture, see, for example, E. Schein, *Organizational Culture and Leadership* (San Francisco: Jossey-Bass, 1990).

25. B. Schlender and S. Solo, "How Sony Keeps the Magic Going," *Fortune,* February 24, 1992, pp. 76–83.

26. R. M. Grant, *Contemporary Strategy Analysis* (Malden, MA: Blackwell, 1995), p. 120.

27. Given the critical role that intangible resources play in market value, many firms are taking another look at their financial statement reporting. See, for example, T. A. Stewart, *Intellectual Capital: The New Wealth of Organizations* (New York: Currency/Doubleday, 1997).

28. There is a lot of outstanding research done in the so-called resource-based view of the firm. For the tip of the iceberg, see, for example, R. Amit and P. J. H. Schoemaker, "Strategic Assets and Organizational Rent," *Strategic Management Journal* 14, no. 1, (1993), pp. 33–46; J. B. Barney, "Firm Resources and Sustained Competitive Advantage," *Journal of Management* 17, no. 1 (1991), pp. 99–120; C. Helfat, "Know-how and Asset Complementarity and Dynamic Capability Accumulation: The Case of R&D," *Strategic Management Journal* 18 (1997), pp. 339–60. The terms *resources, endowments, assets, competencies,* and *capabilities* have been used to mean different things by different authors. The terminology we use here is the most common. See, for example, G. M. Hamel and C. K. Prahalad, "Letter," *Harvard Business Review,* May–June 1992, pp.164–65.

29. G. M. Hamel and C. K. Prahalad, *Competing for the Future* (Boston: Harvard Business School Press, 1994).

30. J. B. Barney, "How a Firm's Capabilities Affect Boundary Decisions," *Sloan Management Review* 40, no. 3 (Spring 1999), pp. 137–45.

31. See *Innovation Management,* chap. 12.

32. There is an immense literature on this topic with its roots in economics. See, for example, P. Ghemawat, *Commitment: The Dynamics of Strategy* (New York: Free Press, 1991); and S. Oster, *Modern Competitive Analysis,* 3rd ed. (Oxford: Oxford University Press, 1999).

33. In 2000, Advanced Micro Devices made considerable progress but was far from catching up with Intel in revenues and profits.

34. For a more detailed treatment of the determinants of costs, please see R. M. Grant, *Contemporary Strategy Analysis: Concepts, Techniques, Applications* (Oxford: Blackwell, 1998), chap. 7.

Chapter **Five**

Dynamics of Internet Business Models

In Chapter 4, we explored the components of a business model and the linkages between them. This exploration was largely static because we described a business model at a point in time and said nothing about the impact of change on the model. We said very little about the changes in the components and linkages of dot.coms as the Internet evolves. Nor did we say much about the impact of the Internet on bricks-and-mortar business models that existed prior to the emergence of the Internet. But as Figure 5.1 reminds us, change has a direct impact on business models and for these models to continue to give a firm a competitive advantage, they too must change—they must be dynamic. In this chapter, we examine the dynamics of business models. We explore several models of technological change that are helpful in formulating and executing business models as firms create or respond to technological change. We begin by exploring a simple but important question: Who profits from technological change? We then examine several technological change models—incremental/radical, architectural innovation, disruptive change, innovation value-added chain, and technology life cycle models—that explore how best to develop a new technology. Finally, we discuss the implications of these technological change models for Internet business models.

WHO PROFITS FROM TECHNOLOGICAL CHANGE?

By definition, business models are about making money. Therefore, to formulate and execute the right business models in the face of a technological change, it is important to first understand what it takes to make money from technological change. One of the first models to explore the question of who profits from a technological change is the complementary assets model.

Complementary Assets Model

What does it take to make money from a technology or invention? David Teece argued that two things determine the extent to which a firm can profit from its

FIGURE 5.1
Change and
Business Models

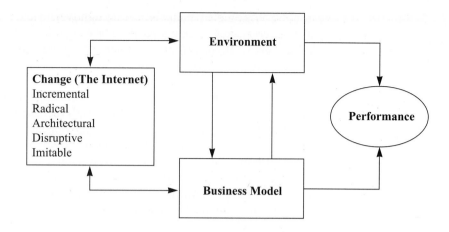

FIGURE 5.2
Who Profits from
Innovation

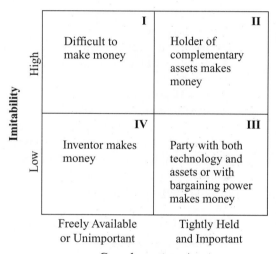

invention or technology: imitability and complementary assets (see Figure 5.2).[1] **Imitability** is the extent to which the technology can be copied, substituted, or leapfrogged by competitors. Low imitability may derive from the intellectual property protection of the technology, from the failure of potential imitators to have what it takes, or from the inventor's strategies to sustain its lead. **Complementary assets** are all other capabilities—apart from those that underpin the technology or invention—that the firm needs to exploit the technology. These include brand name, manufacturing, marketing, distribution channels, service, reputation, installed base of products, relationships with clients or suppliers, and complementary technologies.

Figure 5.2 suggests when a firm is likely to profit from an innovation in this model. When imitability is high, it is difficult for an innovator to make money if complementary assets are easily available or unimportant (cell I in Figure 5.2).

If, however, complementary assets are tightly held and important, the owner of such assets makes money (cell II). For example, CAT scanners were easy to imitate and EMI, the inventor, did not have complementary assets such as distribution channels and the relations with U.S. hospitals that are critical to selling such expensive medical equipment. General Electric had these assets and quickly captured the leadership position by imitating the innovation. Coca-Cola and Pepsi were able to profit from RC Cola's diet and caffeine-free cola inventions because they had the brand-name reputation and distribution channels that RC did not, and the innovations were easy to imitate.

When imitability is low, the innovator stands to profit from it if complementary assets are freely available or unimportant (cell IV). For example, the inventor of the Stradivarius violin profited enormously because no one could imitate it, and complementary assets for it were neither difficult to acquire nor important. When imitability is low and complementary assets are important and difficult to acquire as in cell III, whoever has both or the more important of the two wins. The better negotiator can also make money. Pixar's interaction with Disney is a good example. Imitability of some of its digital studio technology is somewhat low given the software copyrights it holds and the combination of technology and creativity it takes to deliver a compelling animation movie. But offering customers movies made with that technology requires distribution channels, brand-name recognition, and financing which are tightly held by the likes of Disney and Sony Pictures. Before *Toy Story*, Disney had the bargaining power because it had all the complementary assets and the technology had not been proven. After the success of *Toy Story*, when Pixar proved that it could combine technology and creativity—something that is more difficult to imitate than plain computer animation—there was a shift in bargaining power to Pixar, which was then able to renegotiate a better deal.[2]

Implications for the Internet

This model has some important implications for the Internet, which we will see throughout this chapter and the other chapters that follow. Since the use of the Internet is relatively easy to imitate, we can say that imitability of the technology is high. This leaves us in cell I or II of Figure 5.2. Firms that are in industries where complementary assets are easy to get or unimportant (cell I) have a difficult time making money from the Internet. If firms are in industries where complementary assets are important and difficult to get (cell II), those firms that own complementary assets are more likely to make money.

Strategic Implications of Complementary Assets Model

Does this mean that a firm that finds itself in cell I should give up on making money? Of course not! It means that such a firm should take this important piece of information—that it is easy to imitate its technology and that complementary assets are either unimportant or easy to come by—into consideration as it develops and executes its business model. A firm in cell I can pursue a run strategy (see Figure 5.3); that is, since its technology can be easily imitated, the firm keeps innovating. By the time competitors catch up with yesterday's technology, the firm has moved on to tomorrow's technology. The more frequently encountered case is that of cell II: although complementary assets are tightly held and important, the technology is easy to imitate. The firm must develop the complementary assets internally or get them by teaming up with someone else. Either way, the key thing is timing. If the firm decides to build internally, it must do so before competitors with complementary assets have had a chance to copy the technology. If the firm is going to team up, it must do so while it still has something to bring to the table—while potential partners have not yet imitated the technology. As defined earlier, teaming up means forming some kind of partnership (e.g., joint venture, strategic alliance, or an acquisition) with a firm that has the important complementary assets (Figure 5.3). It can also mean offering the firm for acquisition by another firm that has the complementary assets.

In the early part of their life cycles, many Internet start-ups are positioned in either cell I or cell II, but they are chiefly in cell II since their exploitation of the technology is easy to imitate or substitute and complementary assets are important. By carefully determining what complementary assets are critical to them, these start-ups can build them before incumbent competitors have had time to imitate their technologies or build similar complementary assets. For this strategy of developing complementary assets to be successful, it is important that the firm builds in switching costs for its clients and customers. Given the network externalities feature of the Internet, switching costs can be network size where network externalities are important. For example, the larger a community or number of clients, the more valuable it is to members and the more difficult it is for a member to switch to a lesser community. eBay pursued these strategies early in its life cycles.

FIGURE 5.3
Strategies for Building Business Models

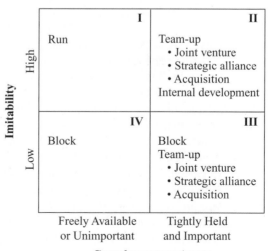

In cell III, a firm can pursue one of two strategies: block or team-up. If it has both the technology and complementary assets, it can protect both. The danger is that sooner or later most technologies are imitated or become obsolete. Imitation or obsolescence moves the firm from cell III to cell II (in Figure 5.3) where it can use its complementary assets to team up with someone who has the new technology. In a world where technology is difficult to imitate but complementary assets are easy to come by (cell IV), a firm depends on protecting that technology if it is going to make money. Very few firms, especially those exploiting the Internet, can be found in cell IV.

Determining One's Complementary Assets

We defined a firm's complementary assets above as all other capabilities—apart from those that underpin the technology or invention—that the firm needs to exploit a technology. This definition suggests that a good way for a profit-seeking firm to determine its complementary assets involves the following two steps: First, the firm should understand what **product-market position** it occupies or wants to occupy. By product-market position here, we mean the customer value, scope, and positioning (relative bargaining position vis-a-vis co-opetitors) that a firm attains or wants to attain. For most start-ups, this is not an easy tasks since such a position is not always clear early in the life of a technology. Second, the firm should understand its value configuration (value chain, value network, or value shop) and determine what capabilities, other than the technology, are critical not only to offering the right customer value to the right market segments but also to increasing the firm's relative positioning vis-a-vis suppliers, customers, and complementors. To avoid ending up with a laundry list, it is important to understand what drives value in the industry and limit the list to those capabilities that are critical to these value drivers.

One way to determine which capabilities are critical is to ask two simple questions for each stage of the value chain of activities that need to be performed for the firm to offer value to its customers: (1) Do the complementary assets make an unusually high contribution to the value that customers perceive? and (2) How quickly and to what extent can other firms duplicate or substitute the complementary assets? The first question is about customer value. In the end, customers must find some value in a technological innovation if it is going to be successful. This customer value is in the form of low cost or differentiated attributes as perceived by customers. Complementary assets that make an unusually high contribution to the value that customers perceive are more likely to help a firm profit from a technological change. An example of complementary assets that made an unusually high contribution to customer value was Caterpillar's worldwide service and supplier networks which, in the early 1980s, enabled the firm to deliver any part, for any of its equipment, to any part of the world, in two days or less. For many customers in remote construction sites who must meet tight completion schedules, this was a very valuable complementary asset.[3] If complementary assets make an unusually high contribution to customer value, the next question is, How long can such complementary assets last before they can be duplicated or substituted? For example, Komatsu substituted the service network by designing and building machines that were so reliable that the company did not need as efficient a service and supplier network as Caterpillar did.

Thus, in determining one's complementary assets, it is important to sort out those that make a relatively high contribution to customer value and also to understand the extent to which they can be imitated or substituted. This avoids generating a laundry list of assets that can be more confusing than helpful.

DEVELOPING THE TECHNOLOGY

Whether a technology is imitable or not, developing it is often not easy. In fact, the inability of firms to develop products or services using a new technology is often the reason why such firms fail to exploit the new technology despite having the right complementary assets. Five models of technological change provide some guidance for successfully developing a new technology: (1) Radical versus incremental change, (2) architectural innovation, (3) disruptive change, (4) innovation value-added chain, and (5) technology life cycle. Before we explore these models, it is important to recall that a business model can be conceptualized as a mapping of capabilities into the three business model components of customer value, scope, and positioning, which make up the firm's product-market position (Figure 5.4). Low cost capabilities, for example, allow a firm to offer its customers lower-cost products/services than its competitors, support customer segments that are cost conscious, and help the firm's position vis-a-vis rivals and potential new entrants. Thus the changes that must take place in a firm's business model for the firm to stay profitable in the face of a technological change depend on the type of capabilities that are needed to support the potential new product-market positions.

Since the Internet is an information technology and information needs vary from industry to industry, we can expect the impact of each of the properties of the Internet that we saw in Chapter 3—mediating technology, universality, network externalities, distribution channels, time moderator, information asymmetry shrinker, infinite virtual capacity, low cost standard, creative destroyer,

FIGURE 5.4
Mapping of Capabilities into Product-Market Positions

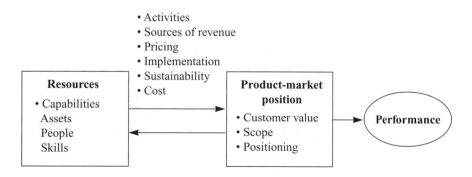

and transaction-cost reducer—on capabilities and product-market positions to vary from industry to industry. The models of technological change that we explore provide frameworks for understanding the impact of change on capabilities and product-market positions, and by doing so, we understand the impact on Internet business models since capabilities and product-market positions are the core components of business models.

Models of Technological Change

Existing models of technological change focus on the impact that technological change has on the existing or new product-market positions and the capabilities on which such positions rest.

Radical/Incremental Change Model

The radical/incremental innovation framework argues that the type of firm that is likely to exploit a technological change is a function of the type of change. It is a function of the extent to which the change impacts the firm's product-market position and capabilities.

Product-Market Position View

A technological change usually results in products or services that render existing products and services noncompetitive, enhances them, or allows the old and new to coexist. If the change results in products that render existing products noncompetitive, it is said to be **radical in the economic sense.** In that case, incumbents with dominant market positions in the industry may be reluctant to invest in the new technology for fear of cannibalizing their existing products or services.[4] Thus, one can expect new entrants to be more likely than incumbents to invest in radical technological change and therefore improve their chances of being successful in developing the new technology. The electronic point-of-sale (EPOS) cash register is an example of a radical technological change in the economic sense because it rendered existing mechanical cash registers noncompetitive. Often, however, the realization that if they do not cannibalize their own products, someone else will, gives incumbents the incentive to invest in the new technology.

If a technological change results in enhancing existing products or allows them to remain competitive, it is said to be an **incremental innovation in the economic sense.** Since such an innovation does not threaten incumbents' existing product-market positions, but rather stands to reinforce such positions, incumbents have an incentive to invest in the new technology. As a result, incumbents are more likely to develop incremental technological changes than new entrants. Both diet and caffeine-free cola were incremental innovations in the economic sense because they allowed classic cola drinks to stay competitive in the market. Electric razors are also an incremental innovation over traditional mechanical razors since they allow the former to remain competitive.

Technological Capabilities View

It is not unusual that some firms that invest in a technological change still fail to successfully develop products or services using the new technology.[5] This suggests that it takes more than incentive to invest in a new technology to profit from it. Success is also a function of the extent to which the capabilities (knowledge, skills, assets, resources) that underpin the new technology build on existing ones or are radically different from them. If the capabilities to develop the new technology are very different form existing ones, the change is said to be radical in the organizational sense, or competence destroying.[6] For example, the capabilities that were required to develop electronic calculators were very different from those required to develop mechanical calculators. Making mechanical calculators required knowledge of gears, ratchets, belts, levers, and methods to combine them to generate calculations whereas electronic calculators required knowledge of microchips with very different core concepts. Thus, electronic calculators were a radical (competence destroying) technological change to makers of mechanical calculators.

For several reasons, incumbents that face radical or **competence-destroying** technological changes are likely to have difficulties hanging onto any competitive advantage that they held prior to the change. First, in attaining the competitive advantage using an old technology, incumbents would have developed technological assets, resources, and capabilities that helped give the firm the advantage. It would also have developed a **culture**—a system of shared values (what is important) and beliefs (how things work) that interact with the organization's people, organizational structures, and systems to produce behavioral norms (the way we do things around here)[7]—that is embedded in the technology. Each incumbent is also likely to have had a business model: delivered some value to its customers, targeted particular segments of customers, focused on certain revenue sources, had pricing strategies, developed well-connected sets of activities, implemented the bricks-and-mortar strategy well, and may have sustained an advantage over some period. In the face of a radical technological change, these capabilities and cultures that were an advantage with the old technology may not only be useless, but they may also actually constitute a handicap. Learning new ways of doing things that are radically different from old ways usually means discarding the old ways first.[8] But cultures are difficult to change, especially in radical ways. Moreover, processes established to support an old technology that become embedded in organizational values and culture are difficult to uproot fast enough to catch up with new entrants who do not have such processes in place. Second, if those in power at the incumbent derive their power from the old technology, they will not let the old technology die since their power will die with it. One reason why IBM had problems with the PC was because most of its executives derived their power from the mainframe computers threatened by the PC.

New entrants do not have old capabilities and culture to handicap them in their efforts to exploit a new technology. They do not have old knowledge to unlearn either and are therefore less likely to have as much difficulty in developing products/services using a new technology as do incumbents.

In general, most radical technological changes are likely to be radical to one or a few of the stages of a firm's value chain but may leave other stages intact. Thus, in the face of many competence-destroying technological changes, many of a firm's complementary assets such as distribution channels, relations with customers, and brand-name reputations are likely to be useful assets for the incumbent.[9] New entrants usually do not have these complementary assets.

On the other hand, a technological change is said to be **incremental** (in the organizational sense) or **competence-enhancing** if the capabilities required to exploit the new technology build on existing firm capabilities. In that case, the capabilities and culture that incumbents have developed give them an advantage over new entrants. Most technological changes are incremental and incumbents usually use such changes to reinforce their competitive advantages.

Implications for the Internet The Internet is likely to be radical—both in the economic and organizational sense—to firms in industries whose competitive advantage rested largely on information asymmetries. Firm capabilities and product-market positions (customer value, scope, and positioning) are likely to be impacted. Recall from Chapter 3 that one of the properties of the Internet is its ability to reduce information asymmetries. The industries that are likely to experience this reduction in information asymmetry include real estate, tour ticketing, airline and concert ticketing, car dealerships, investment banking, commercial banking, and stock brokerages. Prior to the Internet, real estate agents had easy access to multiple housing listings, local chamber of commerce information, and knowledge of neighborhoods. Travel agents had access to airline schedules and pricing that travelers did not have. Car dealers had information on car features and prices that customers lacked. Stockbrokers had access to investment research and to timely stock quotes that most investors did not have. The Internet makes most of that information available directly to customers without intermediaries. Firm positioning vis-a-vis co-opetitors is also likely to change where the basis of bargaining power was information asymmetries. For example, car dealers do not have the type of information advantages that they had over customers and therefore no longer have as much power. Incumbents who face any of these changes have to be careful how they go about the change since old capabilities can handicap the decision to change. As Compaq found out, for example, a firm's links with channels that were critical in the bricks-and-mortar world can stifle its attempts to take full advantage of the Internet. The PC dealers that had served Compaq so well successfully resisted the company's efforts to sell directly to customers like its archrival Dell Computers.

Separate Entity or a Unit Within? In industries where the Internet is a radical technological change, incumbents often face the question of whether to develop the technology within the existing bricks-and-mortar organization or create a separate legal entity. There are many arguments for creating a separate legal entity. Doing so avoids the dominant managerial logic and culture of the old bricks-and-mortar organization, which can only hurt the new endeavor. It avoids the political haggling that can crush a fledgling group within the incumbent. At the peak of the dot.com boom, a separate legal entity attracted more talent that would prefer to work in the entrepreneurial environment of a start-up and participate in the potential payoff of an initial public offering (IPO). The fear of the cannibalization of existing products/services takes attention away from the longer-term issues of the Internet. Finally, if the valuations of dot.com companies are high relative to their bricks-and-mortar competitors, a separate legal entity could raise a lot more and cheaper capital through an IPO. There are also good arguments for developing new technology within. Most incumbents have complementary assets that can be used. By developing the group within, the bricks-and-mortar personnel can learn from it. Moreover, the firm would not have to worry about the painful process of integrating the entity into the larger organization later. In any case, the option that is best for a firm depends on the firm, its business model, and its industry. A firm may decide, for example, to keep the unit within itself but physically locate it far away to reduce some of the cultural and political power problems.

Architectural Innovation Model

Professors Kim Clark and Rebecca Henderson were puzzled by why some incumbents have so much difficulty exploiting what appear to be incremental technological changes—seemingly minute changes in existing technologies: Xerox stumbled for many years before finally developing a good small plain-paper copier despite being the inventor of the core technology of xerography.[10] RCA was never able to lead in the market for portable transistor radios despite its experience in the components (transistors, audio amplifiers, and speakers) that went into the portable radio. From their research, Clark and Henderson suggested that since products are normally made up of components connected together, building them must require two kinds of knowledge: knowledge of the components and knowledge of the linkages between them, which they called *architectural knowledge*. An architectural change is therefore one which requires different knowledge of linkages between components. Thus, although the core concepts that underpin the primary components of large and small copiers may be the same, knowledge of how these components interact in large copiers may be very different from knowledge of how they interact in small copiers. In moving from large copiers to small copiers, a Xerox that does not take the time to understand the changes in interactions between components (architectural knowledge) and change its processes and culture to match is likely to face more difficulties than a new entrant without a culture entrenched in large copiers.

An architectural change does not imply that there is no change in components at all. Quite the contrary. Architectural change is often triggered by a change in one component. For example, building a computer requires not only knowledge of components such as the microprocessor, main memory, secondary memory, software, and input/output (component knowledge) but also knowledge of how these components interact (architectural knowledge). A new design that wants to take advantage of the speed of a much faster processor is an architectural innovation and must consider the changes in the linkages between this new processor and other components of the computer.

With an understanding of the concept of architectural innovation, it became clear why firms had problems with what appeared to be incremental innovations. They may have mistaken architectural innovation for incremental innovation. While the component knowledge required to exploit the innovations had not changed (and therefore the semblance of incremental innovation), architectural knowledge had changed. Architectural knowledge is often tacit and embedded in the routines and procedures of an organization, making changes in it difficult to discern and respond to.

Implications for the Internet The architectural innovation model can help us explore the potential impact of the Internet on some industries. Take the automobile industry, for example, where distribution can account for one-third of the sticker price of an automobile in the industry's bricks-and-mortar value system.[11] The primary reason for the high distribution cost is the industry's supply-push system—especially in the United States—in which automakers have been known to build large numbers of cars without paying enough attention to customer needs and then put pressure on dealers to sell the cars. Where supply outweighs demand, automakers offer huge discounts and marketing promotions. With the Internet, firms can better collect and analyze data on their customers and offer them the cars they want. This reduces unnecessary discounting, marketing promotion, and inventory holding costs. But offering customers the cars that they want may require so-called build-to-order, where carmakers build cars to customers' specifications when customers want them. Thus, although the core concepts that underpin the different functions of an automaker's value chain have not changed, the linkages between the functions have changed. That is, although the core concepts that underpin R&D, manufacturing, marketing, and other primary functions of an automobile value chain may not have changed, knowledge of how these functions can more effectively interact using the Internet has changed. Architectural knowledge in this industry has changed. Automobile makers that see the Internet as just one more channel to sell cars may be missing out on critical information that could help them in their business models. Effectively, bricks-and-mortar firms, even in manufacturing industries such as automobiles, may have to adjust their business models appropriately so as to take advantage of the Internet. They may have to adjust their capabilities, especially architectural competencies.

Cisco is another less obvious example of how the Internet impacts knowledge of linkages between value-chain functions. It was estimated that Cisco, which earned $1.4 billion in profits in 1999, saved about $500 million that year by using the Internet.[12] Customers placed their orders on the company's website. Prior to the creation of the site, as many as 33 percent of customer orders were inaccurate. The website eliminated nearly all the errors. After-sales support groups also use the Web for help in configuring and integrating the network equipment bought from Cisco into their own systems, freeing Cisco engineers to tackle other tasks. Furthermore, Cisco's customers not only share information with each other on how to use Cisco's products in different systems but also share information with Cisco so that the firm can develop better next-generation products. Closing the company's quarterly accounts, which used to take 10 days, was performed in only 2 days when Cisco started using the Web. Travel and expenses were also put on the Web and reimbursement time fell to two days. Procurement, employee benefits, and recruitment are also placed on the Web. Suppliers know which components to ship to what Cisco manufacturing site by accessing the company's custom software on its website. Most firms, like Cisco, not only save on costs but also gain in accuracy of performing activities and in offering better customer value.

Disruptive Change Model

The disruptive change model was advanced and championed by Professor Clayton Christensen.[13] According to this model, **disruptive technologies** have the following four characteristics:

1. They create new markets by introducing a new kind of product or service.

2. The new product or service from the new technology costs less than existing products or services from the old technology.

3. Initially, the products perform worse than existing products when judged by the performance metrics that existing mainstream customers value. Eventually, however, the performance catches up and addresses the needs of mainstream customers.

4. The technology should be difficult to protect using patents.

Incumbents fail to exploit disruptive technologies not so much because they do not "get it," as suggested by the architectural innovation model, but because they spend too much time listening to and meeting the needs of their existing mainstream customers, who initially have no use for products from the disruptive technology.

To understand the disruptive change model, consider a firm that presently exploits a technology to offer products to its customers. Its capabilities—what it can or cannot do—are a function of three factors: resources, processes, and values. Its **resources** are assets such as product designs, brands, relationships with suppliers, customers, distribution, people, plants and equipment, technologies, and cash reserves. **Processes** are "patterns of interaction, coordination, communication, and decision making employees use to transform resources into products and services of greater worth."[14] Such processes are designed to make task performance more efficient and are not meant to change. If they must change, however, there are other processes that must be used to effect the change. An organization's **values** are "the standards by which employees set priorities that enable them to judge whether an order is attractive or unattractive, whether a customer is more important or less important, whether an idea for a new product is attractive or marginal, and so on."[15] A firm's capabilities allow it to offer products to its customers. Suppose one of those products is A, which in year 1 more than meets the key performance attributes that the firm's customers want (B) in the product (Figure 5.5). Also suppose that in year 2 a new product C, which costs less than A, is introduced. Initially, C's performance is inferior to that of A and clearly does not meet the performance requirements demanded by B. Producers of A—given their processes, values, and culture that rest partly on being good in offering A—focus their attention on satisfying the requirements of their key existing customers and therefore do not pay attention to developing the necessary capabilities, processes, and culture to build product C, which meets the performance attributes D that are needed by a different market. New entrants produce C and keep improving its performance. Eventually, say in year 5, C's performance has improved to a point where it also meets the needs of the market with demand B. By this time, it's too late for producers of A to shed the processes, values, and culture that served them so well with the old technology to develop C and gain a product advantage. New entrants who did not have the old baggage—the processes, values, culture, and cost structures associated with producing A—have taken the leadership position in producing C.

Professor Christensen used examples from the disk drive industry to develop this model. At some point, makers of 8-inch disk drives (A in Figure 5.5) produced disk drives that had storage capacity, measured in Megabytes, that met the needs of minicomputers with memory storage capacity demand B. When

FIGURE 5.5
**Disruptive
Technological
Change**

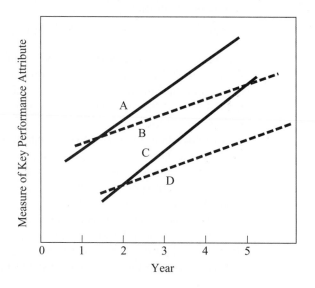

5.25-inch disk drives (C in Figure 5.5) were introduced, their storage capacity was below what minicomputers needed but was more than adequate for desktop PCs. In addition, 5.25-inch drives cost less than their 8-inch counterparts. Makers of 8-inch disk drives did not pay much attention to 5.25-inch disk drive technology; instead, they concentrated on satisfying the needs of their customers who wanted 8-inch drives for their minicomputers. Makers of 5.25-inch drives, however, kept improving the capacity of the drives. Eventually, 5.25-drives could meet the needs of minicomputer makers. By this time, it was too late for makers of 8-inch drives to beat their attackers, the makers of 5.25-inch drives.[16]

According to Professor Christensen, management that faces a disruptive technology must create a new organizational space that is conducive to developing the new capabilities that they need. Three options proposed by Professor Christensen are to (1) create a group within the firm in which new processes can be developed; (2) spin out an independent entity from the existing firm and develop new processes, values, and culture within this new entity; and (3) acquire another entity whose processes and values are a close match for what is needed. The option that a firm chooses is a function of the extent to which the firm's existing values and processes differ from the values and processes that are needed to exploit the disruptive technology. The larger the differences, the more a firm should think of acquisition rather than creating a group within the firm to develop the new processes and values needed.

Implications for the Internet In the late 1990s, the Internet exhibited many of the characteristics of disruptive technology in some industries. Take the stock brokerage industry. People could use the Internet to buy and sell stocks. Buying stocks on the Internet cost less than buying through a traditional bricks-and-mortar broker. Initially, buying stocks on the Internet did not have as much information as would be available through a broker with analysts' reports but that quickly changed as more information about firms became available online. Most implementations of the Internet were not protected by patents. This exhibition of the characteristics of disruptive technologies by online brokerages suggests that incumbents in the stock brokerage industry risked being replaced by new entrants if they did not pursue one of the organizational options stated above. As of 2002, many incumbent brokerage firms, such as Merrill Lynch, which had not pursued the suggested organizational arrangement, had not been replaced. One reason may be that these incumbents had complementary assets such as large client base, cash, relationships with clients, brand-name reputation, and so on that they could use to exploit the imitable technology.

Innovation Value-Added Chain

The **innovation value-added chain** model argues that the value that a firm offers its customers is often a function not only of the firm's capabilities but also of the capabilities of its suppliers, customers, and complementors.[17] For example, the value that a customer gets from using a Dell personal computer is a function not only of Dell's capabilities but also of the capabilities of Intel (the maker of the microprocessor), of Microsoft (the maker of the Windows operating system), and of the customer's skill in using the computer. Therefore, in the face of a technological change, it is important also to consider the impact of the change on suppliers, customers, and complementors as well, not just the impact on the focal firm.[18] This differs from previous models in that while these other models focus on the impact of a technological change on firm capabilities and competitiveness, the value-added chain model focuses on the effects to the competitiveness and capabilities of co-opetitors—of the suppliers, customers, and complementors with whom the firm must often cooperate and compete at the same time. That is, previous models addressed the question, What does the electric car do to the capabilities and competitiveness of automobile makers such as Ford? Is it disruptive, radical, or architectural to Ford? This model emphasizes the fact that the electric car will not only have a direct impact on Ford, but will also have an impact on suppliers of mechanical components for the internal combustion engine automobile, on complementors such as gas station owners and oil companies, and on users of cars. The model explores the impact of a technological change on co-opetitors and the resulting impact on focal firms.[19] An innovation that is incremental to a manufacturer can be radical to its customers and complementors but incremental to its suppliers. For example, the DSK (Dvorak Simplified Keyboard) arrangement that by many estimates performed 20 to 40 percent better than the QWERTY arrangement that most of today's keyboards have, was competence-enhancing to its innovator, Dvorak, and other typewriter manufacturers.[20] All they had to do was rearrange the position of the keys if they wanted to manufacture the DSK. But it was competence-destroying to customers who had already learned how to type with the QWERTY keyboard, since to use the new keyboard, they would have to relearn how to touch-type again. The various faces of this innovation at the different stages of the innovation value-added chain are shown in Figure 5.6.

Another example (also illustrated in Figure 5.6) is Cray Computer's decision in 1988 to develop and market a supercomputer that would use gallium arsenide (GaAs)[21] chips—a technology that yields very fast chips and consumes very little power but that was still relatively unproven then—instead of proven silicon chip technology that its suppliers had built their competencies in. While the supercomputer design was competence-enhancing to Cray, its decision to use gallium arsenide was competence-destroying to its traditional silicon chip supplier base.

These examples suggest that an innovation which is incremental to the manufacturer may not be to suppliers, customers, or complementors. Thus, incumbents for whom an innovation is competence-destroying may still do well if the innovation is competence-enhancing to their co-opetitors, and relations with co-opetitors are important and difficult to establish. The implications are that a firm's success in exploiting an innovation may depend as much on what the innovation does to the capabilities of the firm as on what it does to the capabilities of its co-opetitors.

FIGURE 5.6   **Impact of a Technological Change on Co-opetitors**

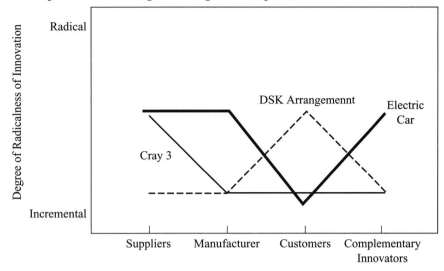

Implications for the Internet   The innovation value-added chain model suggests that a book publisher that wants to exploit the Internet should be concerned not only about the extent to which the technology is disruptive to it, but also about the extent to which it is disruptive to its suppliers (e.g., authors, copy editors, and printers), customers (book wholesalers and resalers), and complementors. A book publisher that does not include in its strategy what Amazon.com has done to book wholesalers and retailers may be missing important strategic information.

Technology Life Cycle Model

The technological change models that we have explored so far have been about one-shot change: there is a change, and depending on the type of change—whether it is incremental, radical, architectural, value-added chain-based, or disruptive—one can make certain decisions to better exploit the change. The models do not take into consideration the fact that following a technological change, the new technology usually evolves. **Technology life cycle** models have been used as a framework for understanding the evolving competitive landscape following a technological change and the consequences for firm strategy (see Figure 5.7). According to these models, a technology usually goes through three phases: Fluid, transitional, and stable.[22] In the **fluid phase,** at the onset of an innovation, there is a great deal of product and market uncertainty. Firms are not quite sure what should go into the product. Customers too may not know what they want in the product. There is competition between the new and old technologies as well as between different designs using the new technology. Firms interact with their local environment of suppliers, customers, complementors, and competitors to resolve both technological and market

FIGURE 5.7   **Internet Technology Life Cycle**

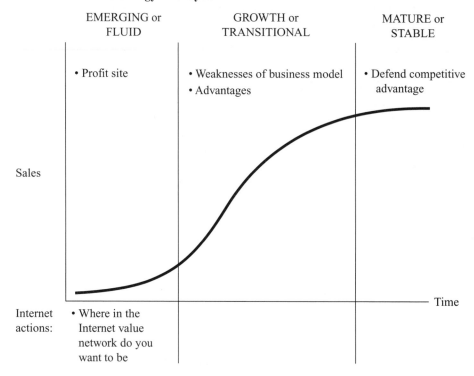

uncertainties. Product quality is low, and cost and prices are high, as economies of scale and learning have yet to set in. Market penetration is low and customers are largely **lead users**—customers whose needs are similar to those of other users except that they have these needs months or years before most of the marketplace[23]—or high-income users. At this time, firms must place their strategic bets by choosing where in the value chain or network of the technology they want to exploit the technological change.

As a vision of the type of customer value that can be offered and the potential profits that can be made are articulated, profit-motivated entrepreneurs flock to different profit sites. Since product/service and market requirements are still ambiguous, there are very few failures. Early in the life of the U.S. automobile industry, for example, over a thousand firms entered. As more and more firms enter, there is competition to develop products or services. There is also competition for resources—for capital, for talented employees—and for customers and suppliers. There may, for example, be tens or hundreds or even thousands of firms in an industry, each of which wants, say, a 20 percent market share. By the year 2001, this stage had passed for many industries using the Internet. This was the stage when firms made their initial decisions about their location in the Internet value network: as, for example, an ISP, backbone supplier, content supplier, network provider, network infrastructure provider, network utility provider, applications service provider (ASP), online content provider, or user of the Internet such as online brokers, online retailers, online market makers, B2B exchanges, B2C, and C2C.

The technology enters the **transitional phase** when some standardization of components, market needs, and product design features takes place, and a standard or common framework for offering products or services emerges signaling a substantial reduction in uncertainty, experimentation, and major changes. The customer base increases from lead and high-income users to mass market during the growth phase. Many firms find out that they do not have what it takes to compete for customers, suppliers, and resources and then are forced to file for bankruptcy, be bought, or merge. Thus the number of entries decreases drastically while the number of exits increases tremendously. Firms that win the standard or happen to have the capabilities that underpin the common framework are likely to fare better. In the automobile industry example, hundreds of firms were forced to exit the market when a dominant design emerged. In the transitional phase, a firm should determine where it excels or wants to excel and try to reinforce or build upon that.

As of the year 2002, the Internet was in the transitional phase for many industries. The Web had emerged as a standard. The dot.com burst had taken place with many firms being forced to file for bankruptcy, merge with others, or totally restructure their business models. Firms continued building their networks (for externalities), establishing brands, winning customers, and modifying their initial bets as uncertainty unfolded. Thus, even as many firms died, others like eBay gained yet more registered users and boosted their brands, and America Online (AOL) merged with Time Warner to form AOL Time Warner.

In the **stable phase** (or mature phase), products built around the common framework or standard proliferate. Products are highly defined with differences fewer than similarities between competing products. Demand growth slows considerably with most output earmarked to satisfy replacement needs. The total number of firms in each industry decreases considerably from the peak of the growth phase. In the automobile industry, for example, there were only three U.S. firms that remained from the thousands that had entered the market at one time or another. In this phase, a firm's strategies focus on defending its position and watching out for the next technological change that could start the life cycle over again. As of 2002, this next phase had yet to arrive for most of the new markets created by the Internet.

Implications for Internet business models Before exploring the implications of the life cycle model for Internet firm strategies, it is important to note that different industries usually experience a technological change at different times.[24] For example, computers, cash registers, calculators, and watches were mechanical or electromechanical devices before their transformation to electronic devices. The technological change from mechanical to electronic took place at different times for each industry. Thus, we can expect the technology life cycle of the Internet to vary from industry to industry with, for example, backbone suppliers, content suppliers, and network providers all having different life cycles.

In the fluid phase, potential new entrants make their bets concerning where they want to locate in the value network that we discussed in Chapter 2. Choosing where to locate is not an exact science, but an entrepreneur can make a more informed decision with data on three factors. First, an entrepreneur can brainstorm with customers, especially lead users, on the problems that can be solved at each of the potential product-market positions, what kind of value the firm can offer customers in solving the problem, and what it takes to get the other components of a business model in place. Second, an entrepreneur should perform an industry analysis to learn more about the attractiveness of the industry in question. (We will say more about industry analysis in Chapter 10.) Third, it should evaluate its capabilities and capabilities gaps in what it takes to craft and execute a winning business model for each product-market position. Data from all three factors are critical in making a choice of what product-market position to locate in. Since a standard or dominant design/solution has not yet emerged in the fluid phase, it is important for the firm to learn as much as possible about the different design/solution options while establishing relationships with those who can tip the scales in the standards/dominant design race. In particular, teaming up with lead users can be critical because a firm can learn much from such customers about the emerging applications of the technology. It is also important to pay attention to lead products/services or so-called killer applications. Adult entertainment appears to be one of the early killer applications in the B2C and C2C businesses and can provide some valuable lessons. The choice of revenue can also be critical. Many dot.coms chose to go after advertising revenues. This turned out not to be a very good decision.

During the growth phase, when a dominant solution or design has emerged, a firm should appraise its business model and determine its strengths and weaknesses. From this appraisal, the firm can determine which elements to reinforce and which ones to build. In the case of the Internet, this may mean teaming up with firms that have complementary assets. It may also mean teaming up to build a larger network of clients, customers, or community. Advertising (to build brand equity) and nonreversible investments all prepare for blocking later in the life cycle. Given how easy it is to imitate Internet business models, firms may have to keep introducing changes in the models or their components. Amazon.com's continuous extension of its capabilities illustrates how a firm keeps making incremental innovations in its business model.

EXAMPLE: THE DOT.COM BOOM AND BURST

In 1998, 1999, and early 2000, just about any dot.com that went to the public to raise money through initial public offerings (IPOs) was very well received. For example, on November 13, 1998, theGlobe.com went public with its shares priced at $9 each. The stock price shot up to $90 before eventually closing at

$63.50. Slightly more than a year later on December 9, 1999, VA Linux Systems, a company that built computer servers, also went public with an IPO offer price of $30. Again, investors wanted to pay about 10 times as much and the price shot up to $299 before settling down to $239.25 at the end of the day. There was nothing distinctive about VA Linux's business model either. It planned to build systems using commodity components and a free operating system in Linux. It seemed no dot.com company could go wrong even though most of them did not make any money and had no potential to do so. Sometimes, all it took to get investors to invest was the suffix ".com" in a company name. Many dot.coms were touted as attackers who would destroy the bricks-and-mortar firms that they targeted.

By April of 2000, however, things had changed. The Internet bubble, as the inflated stock prices had come to be known, burst. On March 20, for example, theGlobe.com's share price had dropped to $3.56, a decline of 94 percent from its first day closing price, while that of VA Linux Systems had dropped to $38.02, a drop of 84 percent from its first day closing price. By 2001, the valuations of many dot.coms had dropped considerably and many had filed for bankruptcy. In fact, VA Linux Systems' value had dropped to less than $5.00. Many more firms had died without reaching the IPO stage and with them the dreams of many entrepreneurs. Many individuals who invested in these dot.coms lost a lot of money.

These events raise some interesting questions: Should we have expected the boom and burst of the dot.coms? Can we better predict when dot.coms are likely to successfully attack bricks-and-mortar firms and when they are not likely to? The technological change models that we have explored in this chapter can help us answer these questions.

Should the Dot.com Bubble and Burst Have Been Expected?

According to the technology life cycle model that we explored, we should have expected the dot.com bubble and burst. The Internet allowed firms to offer new customer value in existing markets and new ones. Entrepreneurs who recognized this value, or its potential, located at different profit sites. In the fluid phase of the technology, there is a lot of entry. In 2000, for example, there were over nine thousand ISPs, and ISPs are just one of many profit sites. As the number of entries increased, competition for resources such as capital, talented employees, and standards increased. So did competition for market share, customers, and suppliers. Each firm wanted to win. Each one wanted a 20 percent market share. As competition heated up, some firms were forced to exit or to be bought by rivals with better potential.

Who Wins in a Dot.com versus Bricks-and-Mortar Battle?

Who is expected to win in a new entrant versus incumbent battle? One answer to this important question can be arrived at by using the complementary asset model. First, we determine how easy it is to imitate the technology. In the case of the Internet, the technology is easy to imitate for most industries. Second, we take a look at complementary assets. If complementary assets are important and difficult to come by, then the owner of the complementary assets will make money. Thus, in a dot.com versus bricks-and-mortar battle in any industry, who wins depends on who has the complementary assets. In most industries, bricks-and-mortars have such complementary assets as brands, relationships with customers and suppliers, etc. They can leverage these assets in formulating and executing their business models. Dot.coms that do not have such assets are not likely to do as well.

Summary

Most business models are not static. The technology on which they rest and the environments in which they operate continually change. The firms and competitors who design them initiate or react to change. In responding to or initiating change to sustain or attain a competitive advantage, it is important to understand the nature of change so as to better take advantage of it in crafting and executing a business model. Where that change is from a new technology such as the Internet, one of the first things to remember is that profiting from the new technology will take more than mastering the new technology. Profiting from a new technology depends both on how easy it is to imitate the new technology and the extent to which complementary assets are important and readily available. In short, it takes more than technology to make money from technology. It also takes complementary assets. Imitable or not, being able to develop the new technology is important since many firms that fail to profit from a new technology, despite having complementary assets, do so because they do not know how to develop the new technology. Various models have explored who is most likely to more effectively develop a new technology. The incremental/radical, architectural innovation, disruptive change, innovation value-added chain, and technology life cycle models all argue that the type of firm that can best exploit a technological change depends on the type of change. Table 5.1 summarizes the elements of these models.

TABLE 5.1   Summary of Models

Model	Key Points about Model	Implications for the Internet
Complementary assets	• It takes more than technology to profit from a technology. The imitability of the technology and complementary assets are also important. • Explains why inventors are not always the ones that profit from an innovation.	• Since the Internet is an imitable technology, we can expect bricks-and-mortar firms that have complementary assets to win bricks-and-mortar versus dot.com battles in those industries where such assets are important and difficult to acquire.

(continued)

TABLE 5.1 *(continued)*

Model	Key Points about Model	Implications for the Internet
Incremental/Radical dichotomy	• Focuses on technological component of innovation. • Bundles component and architectural knowledge. • The type of technological change determines the type of firm that is able to exploit it. • Capabilities and cultures that are embedded in the old technology are likely to handicap firms in the face of radical technological change. Incumbents are more likely to exploit incremental technological changes while new entrants are more likely to exploit incremental changes.	• Whether the Internet is radical or incremental depends on the industry. • Where the Internet is radical, firms with capabilities and cultures that are embedded in the old technology run the risk of these capabilities handicapping Internet efforts. Different organizational arrangements can alleviate the problem. • Complementary assets are likely to help bricks-and-mortar firms in battles with dot.coms
Architectural innovation	• Unbundles technological knowledge into component and architectural innovations. • Explains why incumbents fail at what appear to be incremental innovations—they are actually architectural innovations.	• Can expect impact of the Internet to have a larger long-term effect on value chains of manufacturing companies than would appear at first glance. • Knowledge of interactions between value-chain functions likely to change enough to influence functional activities and firm performance.
Disruptive change	With disruptive technologies, • New markets are created by introducing new products or services. • The new products or services cost less than existing products or services. • New products initially perform worse than existing products when judged by the performance metrics that existing mainstream customers value. Eventually, performance catches up. • The technology should be difficult to protect using patents.	• This model suggests that the Internet is a disruptive technology in many industries. In such industries, firms need organizational arrangements that allow for development of Internet resources, processes, and values without being handicapped by bricks-and-mortar resources, processes, and values. • Some firms may need to have separate Internet entities.
Innovation value-added chain	• The impact of a technological change on co-opetitors may be just as important as that on focal firms. (Recall that co-opetitors are the suppliers, customers, and complementors with whom the firm must cooperate and compete.) • Explains why incumbents may fail at incremental innovations and why they may succeed at radical innovations.	To really understand the impact of the Internet on a firm's business model, it is important to understand the impact on the firm's co-opetitors as well.

(continued)

TABLE 5.1 *(continued)*

Model	Key Points about Model	Implications for the Internet
Technology life cycle	There are three phases in an innovation's life cycle: • In the *fluid* phase, firms place their bets: e.g., new entrants choose the profit sites in which they want to locate. • In the *transitional* phase, where a standard or dominant design defines a critical point in the life of an innovation, competition forces many firms to exit. • In the *specific* phase, firms may want to determine their competitive advantage and focus on it.	• We should have expected the dot. com boom and burst to take place although the timing was not predictable. • Firms that want to improve their chances of survival during a burst need a good business model.

Key Terms

architectural
  innovation
  model, *87*
competence-
  destroying, *85*
competence-
  enhancing, *86*
complementary
  assets, *79*
culture, *85*
disruptive
  technologies, *89*

fluid phase, *93*
imitability, *79*
incremental in the
  economic sense, *84*
incremental
  innovation, *86*
innovation value-added
  chain, *91*
lead users, *94*
new entrants, *85*
processes, *89*

product-market
  position, *82*
radical in the economic
  sense, *84*
radical/incremental
  change model, *84*
resources, *89*
stable phase, *95*
technology life
  cycle, *93*
transitional phase, *95*
values, *90*

Discussion Questions

1. What is the significance of this statement from the text: "It takes more than technology to profit from a technology"?
2. Consider a bricks-and-mortar retailer that wants to enter the online retailing business. Is it better off (1) creating a separate legal firm, (2) establishing a separate unit within the firm, or (3) scattering employees with Internet skills in its bricks-and-mortar units? Would it be different for a bank or an automaker? Does industry matter for each of the three possibilities?
3. When would you advise a start-up Internet firm to offer itself for acquisition by another firm? Does the type of purchaser matter?
4. Why might an incumbent want to buy a start-up Internet firm?
5. What are the differences between an architectural technological change and a disruptive technological change?

6. Why have so many bricks-and-mortar firms survived the Internet dispite the disruptive technology model's predictions otherwise?

7. Can you think of bricks-and-mortar innovations that are radical in the organizational sense but incremental in the economic sense?

Notes

1. D. J. Teece, "Profiting from Technological Innovation: Implications for Integration, Collaboration, Licensing and Public Policy," *Research Policy* 15 (1986), pp. 285–306. See also A. Afuah, *Innovation Management: Strategies, Implementation, and Profits* (Oxford: Oxford University Press, 1998).

2. C. Crane, W. Johnson, K. Neumark, and C. Perrigo, "PIXAR, 1996," University of Michigan Business School case, 1998.

3. U. S. Rangan and C. A. Bartlett, "Caterpillar Tractor Co." Harvard Business School Case #9-385-276, 1985.

4. R. Henderson, "Underinvestment and Incompetence as Responses to Radical Innovation: Evidence from the Photolithographic Alignment Industry," *Rand Journal of Economics* 24, no. 2 (Summer 1993). See also A. Afuah, *Innovation Management,* chapter 12.

5. R. Henderson and K. B. Clark, "Architectural Innovation: The Reconfiguration of Existing Product Technologies and the Failure of Established Firms," *Administrative Sciences Quarterly* 35 (1990), pp. 9–30.

6. M. L. Tushman and P. Anderson, "Technological Discontinuities and Organizational Environments." *Administrative Science Quarterly* 31, pp. 439–65.

7. B. Uttal and J. Fierman, "The Corporate Culture Vultures." *Fortune*, October 17, 1983. For a detailed discussion on culture, see, for example, E. Schein, *Organizational Culture and Leadership* (San Francisco, CA: Jossey-Bass, 1990).

8. C. M. Christensen, *The Innovator's Dilemma* (Boston: Harvard Business School Press, 1997); and R. A. Bettis and C. K. Prahalad, "The Dominant Logic: Retrospective and Extension," *Strategic Management Journal* 16 (1995), pp. 5–14.

9. W. Mitchell, "Whether and When? Probability and Timing of Incumbents' Entry into Emerging Industrial Subfields," *Administrative Sciences Quarterly* 34 (1989), pp. 208–30; and M. Tripsas, "Unraveling the Process of Creative Destruction: Complementary Assets and Incumbent Survival in the Typesetter Industry," *Strategic Management Journal* 18 (1997), pp. 119–42.

10. R. Henderson and K. B. Clark, "Architectural Innovation."

11. This example is from "Breakdown," *The Economist*, May 22, 1999, pp. 69–70.

12. The Cisco case comes from "Cisco Business and the Internet," *The Economist*, July 26, 1999, p. 12.

13. C. M. Christensen, *The Innovator's Dilemma.* See also C. M. Christensen and M. Overdorf, "Meeting the Challenge of Disruptive Change," *Harvard Business Review* (March–April 2000), pp. 67–76.

14. C. M. Christensen and M. Overdorf, "Meeting the Challenge."

15. C. M. Christensen and M. Overdorf, "Meeting the Challenge."

16. C. M. Christensen, *The Innovator's Dilemma.*

17. Complementors are firms that provide complementary products or technologies for the manufacturer's product or technology, usually directly to customers. For example, Microsoft is a complementary innovator for makers of personal computers.

18. A. N. Afuah, "Do Your Co-opetitors' Capabilities Matter in the Face of a Technological Change?" *Strategic Management Journal* 21, no. 3 (2000), pp. 387–404.

19. A. N. Afuah and N. Bahram,"The Hypercube of Innovation," *Research Policy* 24 (1995), pp. 51–76.

20. For a good account of the QWERTY story, see P. A. David, *American Economic Review* 75, no. 2 (1985), pp. 332–6.

21. Gallium arsenide is a chip technology that can result in chips that are three-and-a-half times as fast and consume half as much power as their silicon counterparts. The technology still has many problems.

22. J. M. Utterback, *Mastering the Dynamics of Innovation* (Cambridge: Harvard Business School Press, 1994); and A. N. Afuah with J. M. Utterback, "Responding to Structural Industry Changes: A Technological Innovation Perspective," *Industrial and Corporate Change* 6, no. 1 (1997).

23. E. von Hippel, *The Sources of Innovation* (New York: Oxford University Press, 1998).

24. See Afuah, *Innovation Management*, chap. 6.

Chapter Six

A Taxonomy of Business Models

In this chapter, we continue our exploration of business models by enumerating a taxonomy of business models. This taxonomy is based on a synthesis of the literature on business models. We first describe in detail seven major business models with dozens of variants. We then summarize these business models by how they are described by four variables or dimensions based on material from Chapters 2 through 4: the profit site, the revenue model, the commerce strategy, and the pricing model. We emphasize that no matter how a business model is named or described, for it to be viable, it must exhibit some strength in several of the components we discussed in Chapter 4. We still need to analyze the components to know which of the many competitors that use these business models will succeed. But as it turns out, almost all the models discussed in the literature can be described by these four elements.

A TAXONOMY OF BUSINESS MODELS

As mentioned above, our goal in this chapter is simply to fill in the major areas of business concentration dealing with the Internet as begun in Chapter 2 and analyzed in Chapter 4. Again, this is not intended to be an appraisal of specific strategies, but rather a taxonomy of generic business models that make up how the Internet can be used in business.[1] Some readers may want to know how well-known work in the area of business models—specifically, the seminal article by Paul Timmers,[2] the pioneering online work of Michael Rappa,[3] and more recent work by Thomas Eisenmann[4] and by Laudon and Traver in a traditional e-commerce textbook[5]—relate to our framework and to each other. Timmers's article was the first attempt to classify the different ways of doing business in the Internet era and gave some preliminary categories, such as "e-shop," "e-auction," and "e-mall." Rappa's later work, built on Timmers's and others', has further refined the categories and attempted to enumerate them.

Below we offer our synthesis, based on the dominant revenue model for each category. We try to stay consistent with Rappa's naming conventions where possible, although this is not always possible since Rappa does not strictly organize by revenue model. It should be emphasized that the groupings below are based on the traditional (or dominant) revenue model for each category, but as we will see at the end of this chapter, non-traditional combinations of profit sites, revenue models, commerce models, and pricing models may be beneficial and even preferred. Our taxonomy has as its basis seven revenue models: commission, advertising, markup, production, referral, subscription, and fee-for-service. These are summarized in Table 6.1 and discussed in more detail below.

TABLE 6.1 **Summary of Business Model Taxonomy**

Dominant Revenue Model	Basic Idea	Variants
Commission	Fees levied on transactions based on the size of the transaction	Buy/Sell Fulfillment, Market Exchange, Business Trading Community, Buyer Aggregator, Distribution Broker, Virtual Mall, Metamediary, Auction Broker, Reverse Auction, Classifieds, Search Agent, Bounty Broker, Matchmaker, Peer-to-peer Content Provider
Advertising	End users subsidized by advertising	Generalized Portal, Personalized Portal, Specialized Portal, Attention/Incentive Marketing, Free Model, Infomediary Registration Model, Recommender System, Bargain Discounter, Community Provider
Markup	Value added in sales	Virtual Merchant, Catalogue Merchant, Click and Mortar, Bit Vendor
Production	Value added in production	Manufacturer Direct, Content Producer, E-Procurement, Networked Utility Provider, Brand Integrated Content
Referral	Fees for referring customers to a business	Lead Generator
Subscription	Fees for unlimited use	ISPs/OSPs, Last Mile Operators, Content Creators
Fee-for-service	Fees for metered service	Service Provider, B2B Service Provider, Value Chain Service Provider, Value Chain Integrator, Audience Broker, Collaboration Platform Provider, Application Service Provider

Commission-Based

A **commission** is a fee that is levied on a transaction by a third party (usually an intermediary). A commission-based model is one that relies on commissions as a mainstay of the business. For example, when a broker helps a customer sell a stock (by pairing the seller with a buyer), the broker takes a commission on the transaction. In this regard, the most common example is the commission that E*Trade charges its brokerage customers for trading stocks.[6] However, the commission model goes well beyond financial brokerages. Perhaps the two most famous examples are eBay and Travelocity. eBay is the online auction house that makes a market for buyers and sellers of mainly household goods. The company also provides a referral or rating system for sellers and an escrow service to facilitate transactions. When a sale is made over eBay, the company receives a commission based on the amount of the sale.

In a similar vein, Travelocity brings together airlines and customers who want to travel by air. When the customer buys a ticket online through Travelocity, the airline pays a small commission. The commission model has only two ways of being sustainable. The first is volume. All of the examples above rely on a large volume of completed transactions to make the commission model worthwhile. This is the way most Internet intermediaries think about commissions. The second, less common one is to offset low volume with very expensive transactions.

As hinted above, commission-based models are usually associated with intermediaries, which explains why some researchers call the commission-based model an **intermediary model** or **brokerage model.** In Rappa's brokerage model, for example, firms act as market-makers that bring buyers and sellers together and charge a fee for the transactions that they enable. They can be business-to-business, business-to-consumer, or consumer-to-consumer brokers. Examples include travel agents, online brokerage firms, and online auction houses. As we did in Chapter 2, some scholars distinguish between "brokers," who primarily assist one party to the transaction in finding the other party, and "market-makers" or "market-creators," who set the rules of the market itself, allowing buyers and sellers to find each other.

Commission-based models can also be further specified by the following variations:

1. *Buy/sell fulfillment* (what Laudon and Traver call a transaction broker and Eisenmann calls an online broker), which enables consumers to consummate transactions (e.g., E*Trade, Travelocity, CarsDirect).

2. *Market exchange* (what Laudon and Traver call a marketplace/exchange/ B2B hub, Timmers calls a third-party marketplace, and Eisenmann classifies as an online market maker with transaction type of exchange), which facilitates transactions between businesses by setting up a market (e.g., New View).

3. *Business trading community,* which enables market participants to exchange information and contribute to dialogue in a vertical market (e.g., Vertical-Net—see Case 4 in this volume).

4. *Buyer aggregator,* which facilitates purchasing consortia so that individuals or businesses can have greater purchasing power (e.g., Market Mile).

5. *Distribution broker* (called a distributor model by Rappa or E-distributor by Laudon and Traver[7]), which connects manufacturers with large-volume producers (e.g., Grainger).

6. *Virtual mall* (or what Timmers calls an E-mall), in which a firm provides links to (or "hosts") many merchants usually through a shopping interface (e.g., MySimon, Yahoo![8] Shopping).

7. *Metamediary,* which is a virtual mall that also provides transaction and clearing services (e.g., Amazon zShops—see Chapter 12).

8. *Auction broker* (or what Laudon and Traver call a market creator, Timmers calls an E-auction, and Eisenmann classifies as an online market maker with transaction type of auction), which facilitates auctions (for sellers) and charges a commission to the sellers (e.g., eBay—see above and Case 10 in this book).

9. *Reverse auction,* which facilitates auctions for buyers; that is, the buyer makes a bid and sellers then bid to provide the good or service to the buyer, with the market-maker often keeping the difference between the buyer's and seller's bid (e.g., Priceline).

10. *Classifieds,* in which individuals advertise to sell goods or services (e.g., Apartments, Monster).

11. *Search agent,* in which the firm provides personalized shopping or information services via the mechanism of intelligent "agents" or "shopbots" that search out the desired information by scanning many sites for the buyer (e.g., MySimon shopbots).

12. *Bounty broker,* in which the company acts as a broker for hard-to-find information or goods for a "reward" that buyers pay (e.g., BountyQuest).

13. *Matchmaker* (what Timmers calls an information brokerage), which according to Laudon and Traver helps businesses (as opposed to consumers) find what they need (e.g., iShip).

14. *Peer-to-peer content provider,*[9] which enables users to share files or services (e.g., Napster, my.MP3.com).

15. *Transaction broker,* in which a third party enables a buyer and seller to consummate a transaction (e.g., PayPal).

Advertising-Based

In the **advertising-based model**, the owner of a website provides to end users subsidized or free content, services, or even products that attract end-user visitors. Some of the most famous, or infamous, users of the advertising model are Yahoo, Excite@Home, and Altavista. The advertising model does not refer to the public relations strategy of the company; rather, *it refers to advertising as a source of revenue in and of itself.* The website owner attempts to make money by charging advertisers fees for banners, permanent buttons, pop-up windows, and other ways of getting a client's messages to visitors.[10] The advertising on the Internet often takes the form of banners that appear at the top of a Web page. This is similar to how broadcast television and radio sustain their businesses.

There are two ways in which an advertising-based model might be successful. The first is based on reaching the broadest possible audience, analogous to advertising on television during the Super Bowl. The higher the number of viewers/readers/visitors/so-called eyeballs, the broader the appeal to most advertisers. The number of viewers is also called the volume of viewers; hence this model has become known as the **volume-based approach**. The classic example of the advertising-based model is Yahoo, which has made the transition from Internet search engine to generalized portal to personalized portal to a host of value-added services, such as e-mail, calendar, and stock quotes. In this transition, the company has built up an impressive number of customers who visit the site for one reason or another. The volume of customers allows Yahoo to charge a premium relative to most Internet sites for banner advertising.[11]

The second way in which advertising might be successful is to have a highly targeted and specialized audience. For example, from the point of view of an audio speaker company (the paying customer of a firm with an advertising-based model), it might be preferable (i.e., more efficient and better use of its money) to be able to reach users of home theater systems via a site targeted to audio- and videophiles rather than a general-purpose site where only one in a million consumers own a home theater. Again, to make the television analogy, it depends on the product (or service) and the marketing strategy of the advertiser whether the advertiser chooses to buy ad time during the Super Bowl (broad-based audience) or during late-night reruns of *Star Trek* (a narrower, more specialized audience).

The advertising-based approach, while certainly a popular one among Internet companies, is also the most controversial as a means of sustaining profitability. Proponents claim that "if it works for television and newspapers, it can work for the Internet," while detractors point out that only two cities in the entire country can support more than one newspaper (!) and that broadcast television networks are not exactly the most profitable enterprises. Almost anyone with a website that attracts visitors has the potential to compete in this model. *i*Village is an example of a well-run company that witnessed the trend of declining advertising rates that their community-based business was dependent upon, causing them to look for new sources of revenue.[12]

Advertising models can be further classified into

1. *Generalized portal* (also called a horizontal/general portal by Laudon and Traver, a horizontal online portal by Eisenmann, and—in one sense—an information brokerage by Timmers), in which the content coverage is broad

and the target audience is both large and diffuse, making advertising revenues a possibility (e.g., Yahoo, MSN).

2. *Personalized portal,* which is a generalized portal that is customized to the user's preference, building loyalty and switching costs due to the time invested in the personalization process (e.g., my.yahoo.com).

3. *Specialized portal* (also called a vertical/specialized portal by Laudon and Traver, a vertical online portal by Eisenmann, and known as a "Vortal"), which is a vertically oriented portal focusing on a narrow audience with much deeper coverage (e.g., iBoats).

4. *Attention/incentive marketing,* in which the company pays users (usually indirectly through incentive "points" or entry into sweepstakes) for their viewing of content or entry of information (e.g., My Points).

5. *Free model,* in which some service or product is given for free in exchange for viewing ads (e.g., Wunderground).

6. *Bargain discounter,* in which the company sells goods at a steep discount to attract the traffic which then enables advertising revenues (e.g., Buy.com).

7. *Infomediary[13] registration model,* in which the service is free but the user must register, enabling the company to track usage and viewing patterns (e.g., NYTimes).

8. *Recommender system,* in which users exchange information about goods and services that they have experience with (e.g., Epinions).

9. *Community provider* (what Timmers calls the virtual community model), which rests on community loyalty rather than traffic. Users have invested in developing relationships with members of their community and are likely to visit the website frequently (i.e., attractiveness for advertisers is how long each person spends on the site rather than just the number of people who visit the site). Members of such a community can be a very good market target. A good example is *i*Village. Variants include voluntary contributor, in which the business is supported by voluntary donations from community members, and knowledge networks, in which experts (usually employed by the site but not necessarily so) provide information in response to queries from community members.

Markup-Based

Markup refers to value added in sales rather than in production, and thus the **markup-based model** is one in which firms' primary source of revenues is via markup. This model has been traditionally used by wholesalers and retailers, which is why some scholars such as Rappa call it the merchant model. Goods can be sold by list prices or through auctions. For example, a company may buy finished goods from a manufacturer and then sell them to the public (in other words, the company is a retailer) or to other firms (i.e., the company is a wholesaler or distributor). The most famous example is undoubtedly Amazon.com, which revolutionized both the book business and online selling. The key here is clearly the size of the markup. If the company has distribution efficiencies or marketing muscle, the chances of the markup being positive are good. Amazon, while being at the center of the revolution, has not yet definitively proven that the model is viable. While Amazon does show decent operating margins in the book business and in 2002 announced a quarterly profit, as of 2002 it has yet to show a yearly profit. We suspect that the main problem is competition. Just about anybody who was previously restricted to a geographic area can hang a shingle and start reselling merchandise over the Internet. In addition, comparison shopping for price is becoming extremely easy, putting pressure on the size of the markup that firms are able to pass on.

Other variants of the merchant model include:

1. *Virtual merchant* (what Eisenmann calls an online retailer and Timmers calls an E-shop),[14] which is a pure-play Internet e-tailer (e.g., Amazon).

2. *Catalogue merchant,* which is a traditional catalogue company that now also sells and fulfills orders over the Internet (e.g., L. L. Bean, Lands End).

3. *Click-and-mortar,* which is a traditional store that also sells over the Internet (e.g., BN [Barnes & Noble], WalMart).

4. *Bit vendor,* which not only sells over the Internet but whose products are also purely digital such that the product can be delivered over the Internet (e.g., Eyewire).

Production-Based

In the **production model**, or what Rappa calls the **manufacturing model**, manufacturers try to reach customers or end users directly through the Internet. By doing so, they can save on costs and better serve customers by finding out directly what they want. This model is based on revenues from production: the classic manufacturer/producer/assembler/value-added-in-production model. That is, the company transforms raw materials into a higher-value product. Most of the hardware and software suppliers fall into this model. For example, Compaq brings in components such as memory chips and disk drives and assembles them into a finished product, a personal computer. Software, as mentioned above, is an analogous example, although the product is not tangible. Software companies such as Microsoft "develop" software by hiring programmers who develop pieces of larger applications by coordinating their efforts with other programmers on the team to produce new programs or to add functions to old ones. At a certain point, the software application is sold to customers. The distinguishing feature of the production model is therefore that the price sold in the market be higher than the cost of production.

Volume plays a role in this through economies of scale and learning curve effects.[15] By economies of scale, we mean the cost savings that a company realizes by having higher volume. The key behind economies of scale is fixed versus variable costs. In a business with high fixed costs and low variable costs, economies of scale will be more evident as the fixed costs are spread among more units. Learning curve effects are improvements in productivity that are gained by cumulative production. The Internet version of the production model can also be based on other efficiencies such as disintermediation. These topics will be discussed further in Chapter 7.

Channel conflicts present a challenge for such manufacturers. In the late 1990s, Compaq decided to drop the computer dealers who had been its distributors and go directly to customers. The distributors fought the changes and Compaq had to reconsider its decision.

Variants of the model also include:

1. *Manufacturer-direct,* in which, according to Laudon and Traver, manufacturers sell directly to end-user customers (e.g., Dell).

2. *Content producer*, in which firms produce entertainment, information, art, or other content and sell the content (e.g., Sony Entertainment).

3. *E-procurement,* in which, according to Timmers, companies tender and procure goods and services over the Web, increasing the choice of suppliers and keeping costs down (e.g., Ford Motor Company's increasing use of electronic procurement in purchasing parts from suppliers).

4. *Networked utility provider,* which, according to Eisenmann, is a producer of a software program that connects an end user either to a destination website or to other users to augment the capabilities of browsers or e-mail, relying on establishing a standard in its marketplace to beat the competition (e.g., Adobe).

5. *Brand integrated content,* in which a company attempts to more fully integrate advertising, branding, and the product via the Internet (e.g., BMWFilm's "advertainment" for BMW cars).

Referral-Based

In the **referral-based model,** firms rely on fees for steering visitors to another company. This referral fee is often a percentage of the revenues of the eventual sale but can also be a flat fee. The flat fee can be collected if an order is made (or more generally speaking if a deal is consummated, called "pay-per-sale"), it can be collected regardless of whether an order is made (called "pay-per-click"), or it can be collected every time a lead is generated (call "pay-per-lead"). This referral-based structure is often used with corporate affiliate programs, which is why some researchers such as Rappa refer to an **affiliate model,** wherein a merchant has affiliates whose websites have **click-through** (selecting a link that connects to another organization's site) to the merchant. Each time a visitor to an affiliate's site clicks through to the merchant's site and buys something, the affiliate is paid a referral fee. Examples include frozenpenguin.com and americanracefan.com. A variant includes:

1. *Lead generator,* proposed by Laudon and Traver to mean a company that collects data about customers and then uses the data to steer businesses toward the customers (e.g., AutoByTel).

Subscription-Based

In the **subscription-based model** a company charges a flat rate on a periodic basis (such as a month) that qualifies the user for a certain amount of service. The user pays this subscription fee whether or not the service is actually used. This is analogous to the monthly charge you pay on your telephone bill whether or not you make any telephone calls. As mentioned in Chapter Two, most businesses that operate at zero marginal cost usually migrate to a subscription model. The classic examples from our value network profit sites, as mentioned above, are ISPs/OSPs, Last Mile companies, and content creators. For example, most ISPs, such as AT&T Worldnet, charge a flat monthly rate for unlimited usage. Likewise, most Last Mile arrangements, such as local telephone service or cable television, charge a monthly fee for unlimited local service. Content creators such as Dow Jones also charge a subscription to obtain access to their content. It takes very valuable content, though, to sustain a subscription model for content purposes on the Internet. Subscriptions do not appear to be feasible for most content businesses due to competitive pressures. So far they have been feasible in segments with little competition. Subscriptions also have a *moral hazard* component to them: once customers have paid the subscription fee, they occasionally use the service much more than they normally would have. AOL discovered this when they introduced flat-rate pricing. Customers stayed on all day without using the system, tying up the telephone lines to the local access numbers.

Thus, variants include:

1. *ISPs/OSPs* (what Eisenmann calls internet access providers), which provide Internet access and sometimes additional content (e.g., AT&T Worldnet).

2. *Last Mile operators,* which provide local loop and end-user access points and telecommunications services (e.g., Verizon).

3. *Content creators* (or what Laudon and Traver call content providers and Eisenmann calls online content providers), in which information and entertainment are offered to end-user consumers (e.g., WSJ, Sportsline, CNN).

Fee-for-Service–Based

In the **fee-for-service model**, or what Rappa calls the **utility model**, firms pay as they go. Activities are metered and users pay for the services that they consume. In this model, customers pay for only the service that they actually use. In fact, the example of brokerages making additional revenue from margin interest is an example of the fee-for-service model: you pay a fee (margin interest) for the service of borrowing money from the brokerage. The fee continues until you pay back the loan. Other examples include some ISP plans in which the user pays for metered Internet service (only pay for as long as you are connected), customers paying ASPs for renting an application, or even paying airlines directly for transportation from one place to another, that is, buying tickets directly from an airline. The hallmark of these is always that the customer pays only for the usage. The method of making this model into a sustainable business is, of course, to convince customers to intensively use the service or to have a large volume of customers, or both. There is no subscription base to cushion the company if usage drops off.

Variants include (according to Laudon and Traver, unless noted otherwise):

1. *Service provider,* in which firms make money by selling services rather than products to end users (e.g., xDrive, myCFO).

2. *B2B service provider,* which supports businesses by selling services to other businesses (e.g., Employeematters).

3. *Value chain service provider,* which, according to Timmers, specializes in one specific piece of the value chain such as logistics (e.g., FedEx).

4. *Value chain integrator,* which, according to Timmers, focuses on integrating multiple steps of the value chain with the possibility of exploiting the information flow between the multiple steps (e.g., Exel, EDS).

5. *Collaboration platform providers,* which, also according to Timmers, are companies that manage collaborative platforms and sell collaboration tools that enable businesses to improve internal design and engineering (e.g., Vastera).

6. *Application service provider,* which, as discussed in Chapter 2, "rents" software applications to businesses (e.g., Corio).

7. *Audience broker,* which is a company that collects information on consumers and uses the information to help advertisers target their audience most effectively (e.g., DoubleClick).

PUTTING IT ALL TOGETHER: THE FOUR ELEMENTS AND THE TAXONOMY

When examining the taxonomy presented in this chapter, certain patterns emerge. We organized the taxonomy by dominant revenue model, but the revenue model is only one of at least four dimensions that determine the classification of business models. Further, as we mentioned at the beginning of this chapter, it is not necessary or possibly even desirable to stick with a traditional revenue model. We note here that most if not all the models developed in this chapter can be characterized in terms of the revenue model, profit site, commerce strategy, and pricing model. Table 6.2 shows how several of the business models compare to each other along these four dimensions.

TABLE 6.2 Business Model Taxonomy vs. Typology: Examples from the Literature

Term	Short Definition	Profit Site	Revenue Model	Commerce Strategy	Pricing Model
Timmers					
e-Shop	"Web marketing of a company or shop"	E-commerce	Markup	B2C	Fixed
e-Auction	"Electronic implementation of the bidding mechanism"	Market-maker	Commission	N/S	Auction
Virtual community	"Members add their information onto a basic environment"	Service provider	N/S	P2P	N/S
Rappa					
Buy/sell fulfillment	"An online . . . brokerage"	Broker/agent	Commission	B2C	Fixed
Generalized portal	"Generic or diversified content or services"	Content aggregator	Advertising	B2C	Fixed (ads), infomediary
Subscription model	"Users pay for access to the site"	N/S	Subscription	N/S	N/S
Reverse auction	"'Name your price' business model"	Market-maker	Commission	C2B	Reverse auction
Registration model	Free content but requires users to register	Content aggregator	Infomediary	B2C	N/S
Eisenmann					
Online portal (horizontal)	Direct users to a broad range of content and commerce	Content aggregator	Advertising	B2C	Fixed (ads)
Online content provider	Delivery of professionally produced, copywritten content	Content creator	Advertising	B2C	Fixed (ads)
Online retailers	Companies that "use a website to merchandise newly manufactured physical goods"	E-commerce	Markup	B2C	Fixed

(continued)

TABLE 6.2 *(continued)*

Term	Short Definition	Profit Site	Revenue Model	Commerce Strategy	Pricing Model
Online brokers	An entity "hired to act as an agent or intermediary in making contracts"	Broker/agent	Primarily commission; also subscrip-, tion, advertis-, ing, and fee-for-service	B2C	Fixed
Internet access provider	Provides "residential and business custom-ers with connections to the Internet . . . "	Communica-tions service provider	Primarily subscription; also fee-for-service and advertising	B2C, B2B	Primarily fixed
Online market-makers	Intermediaries that provide "a place to trade, rules to govern trading, and an infra-structure to support trading"	Market-maker	Primarily commission; also markup, subscription, infomediary, fee-for-service, or advertising	Mainly B2B; also B2C and C2B	Fixed, auction, or one-to-one
Networked utility providers	Producers of software that allows users to "complete specialized tasks that are beyond . . . Web browsers" (e.g., "plug-ins")	Software supplier	Production	B2B (servers), B2C (client)	Fixed (server and premium client software)
Application service providers	A company that allows other compa-nies "to access appli-cation software on remote servers"	Service provider	Fee-for-service	B2B	One-to-one and fixed

N/S=not specified.

Profit Sites

The column called "profit site" refers to the value network profit sites as dis-cussed in Chapter 2. We consider there to be 11 major profit sites within the Internet infrastructure: (1) E-commerce, (2) content aggregators, (3) brokers/ agents, (4) market makers, (5) service providers, (6) backbone operators, (7) ISPs/OSPs, (8) Last Mile, (9) content creators, (10) software suppliers, and (11) hardware suppliers.

Revenue Models

Revenue models refer to the primary sources of revenue for the firm. The seven we have featured were: (1) advertising, (2) subscription, (3) commission, (4) fee-for-service, (5) production, (6) markup, and (7) referral. While these business models have been organized by revenue model according to work done by scholars in this area, we propose that revenue models and profit sites are intertwined but actually somewhat independent. For example, we claim that a commission is a fee levied on a transaction by an intermediary. However, an intermediary (either a broker/agent or market-maker) might just as well work on a subscription basis (for example, pay a flat rate and trade all you want) or a fee-for-service basis (pay for the time spent by the agent regardless of whether the deal is consummated). Likewise, firms operating in other profit sites could use a commission-based model. For example, a software company might produce a catalogue-processing product. Rather than collecting a flat licensing fee (production-based model), the firm could collect a percentage on goods sold using its catalogue-processing system (a commission-based model). Thus, even though intermediaries usually use commissions and others do not, that does not mean that commissions must be associated with intermediaries. That is why we claim that these two dimensions are more or less independent. Examples of new and different combinations of profit sites and revenue models are appearing every day. In fact, there may be some advantage to non-traditional pairings, as we saw in Chapter 4.

Commerce Strategy

The column in Table 6.2 called **commerce strategy** refers to the strategy that identifies the customer base of or population served by the business as discussed in Chapter 3. The most obvious case is that of an e-commerce company that chooses to sell to consumers (a retailer, or *e-tailer* as they are often called) rather than businesses (a wholesaler or distributor model). The retailer is involved in the B2C market, while the wholesaler is involved in the B2B market. For example, based on the discussion in Chapters 2 and 3, Amazon.com is mainly involved in the B2C market, while Cisco is mainly involved in B2B.

The commerce strategies go beyond simply identifying who your customers are. For example, how do you classify a company such as eBay, which arranges for individuals to sell to each other? Each individual pays eBay once an item is sold, so does that make eBay a B2C company? Technically, it does, but this characterization misses some information, which is that *eBay as an intermediary enables consumers to sell to each other*. And so, it might be more accurate to characterize intermediaries and perhaps other segments as well by the kinds of interactions among customers. And so we also have the term person-to-person (P2P), also known as consumer-to-consumer (C2C).[16] Other potential areas have been identified, such as business-to-employees (B2E). Note that this could refer to a business selling services to its own employees, but more likely it refers to the concept of providing services to other businesses that facilitate the relationship between that business and its employees.

Content aggregators might also usefully employ this terminology to describe "community" sites. For example, *i*Village brings consumers—primarily women—together to communicate with each other. In addition to relaying content from major sources, one of the primary purposes of *i*Village's site is the content that is created by the community itself. Thus, one might characterize *i*Village's business as a content aggregator, mainly based on advertising, with a P2P population that reflects the reality that the content is created by the community itself, in contrast with other sites, such as the *New York Times* on the Web, where the content is created by the company and directed toward the customers in more of a B2C model.

Pricing Models

The last column refers to the pricing model. As discussed in Chapter 4, the main pricing models are (1) fixed (menu) pricing, (2) one-to-one bargaining, (3) auction, (4) reverse auction, (5) barter, and (6) free. These again can be combined in almost any combination with the prior elements. Thus, a backbone provider could auction off bandwidth rather than charge a fixed price, or a content company could barter with another company rather than sell content. A further complication is that market-makers can facilitate and charge a commission for any of these pricing models, too.

A note on the free pricing model. We do not really classify "free" as a viable pricing model. Although giving away products or services usually builds a customer base, there should be some long-term plan for charging somebody something, which is called **monetization**. For example, it may be desirable to give products away for free to build volume, but then charge advertisers to advertise on the site. Or a company could give away computers if customers watch advertising on their free computers. We would classify these as advertising-based revenue models where products were given away to boost volume. Thus, "free" can only be a piece of a legitimate business and not the centerpiece of any business.

Each of the models proposed by the scholars referenced above and others can be broken down into the four elements and thus described more succinctly. The framework presented here is more theoretically complete: there are $11 \times 7 \times 4 \times 6 = 1848$ possible combinations, excluding the fact that each of the 11 profit sites can use more than one revenue model, commerce type, and even pricing model! Thus, the number of combinations is in the millions. Again, we emphasize that the firm should strive to understand the strength of the components of the business model relative to competitors to determine whether the business model is viable.

Summary

We enumerated a taxonomy of Internet business models involving dozens of variants of seven basic revenue models and related them to the work of other researchers in the field. We also proposed a framework that succinctly summarized the essential elements of these models based on four dimensions:

profit site, revenue model, commerce strategy, and pricing model. These are summarized below. Businesses can use any combination of these four elements when making strategic decisions about the basic structure of their activities and how they would like to exploit the Internet.

Companies with online businesses earn revenue through the employment of one or several of the following seven revenue models:

- Advertising.
- Subscription.
- Commission.
- Fee-for-service.
- Production.
- Markup.
- Referral.

The different types of commerce strategies are:

- B2B—business-to-business.
- B2C—business-to-consumer.
- P2P—person-to-person, also called C2C—consumer-to-consumer.
- C2B—consumer-to-business.
- Possibly even B2E—business-to-employee.

Finally, the different pricing models are made up of:

- Fixed (menu) pricing.
- One-to-one bargaining.
- Auctions.
- Reverse auctions.
- Barter.

Key Terms

advertising model, *106*
affiliate model, *110*
brokerage model, *105*
click-through, *110*
commerce strategy, *115*
commission, *105*
fee-for-service model, *111*

intermediary model, *105*
manufacturing model, *109*
markup, *108*
markup-based model, *108*
monetization, *116*
production model, *109*

referral-based model, *110*
subscription-based model, *111*
utility model, *111*
volume-based approach, *107*

Discussion Questions

1. Why do ISPs use a subscription-based, as opposed to a fee-for-service, model? Will this change over time? Why or why not?
2. Which types of online companies have the hardest time making money? Why?
3. A company is considering selling its excess inventories to other businesses. What are some reasons to use fixed pricing over auctions or reverse auctions? What about a company reselling compact discs?
4. Think of a company that gives away a service or product for free. What revenue model does it employ? How does it plan to monetize its service or product?

Notes

1. See K. C. Laudon and G. C. Traver, *E-commerce* (Boston: Addison Wesley, 2002). The authors point out that any of the above business models can be extended to wireless technology.
2. P. Timmers, "Business Models for Electronic Markets," *Electronic Markets* 8, no. 2 (1998), pp. 3–8.
3. M. Rappa, "Business Models on the Web," http://ecommerce.ncsu.edu/business_models.html.
4. T. R. Eisenmann, *Internet Business Models* (New York: McGraw-Hill/Irwin, 2002).
5. Laudon and Traver, *E-commerce.*
6. Again, note that commissions are not E*Trade's (or any online broker's) sole source of revenue. The company also makes money from interest spreads between depositors and borrowers.
7. Note that elsewhere in this book we emphasize that a distributor is usually thought to carry inventory risk.
8. Henceforth we will omit the exclamation point.
9. "Peer-to-peer" refers to a protocol that allows direct sharing of files between end users without going through servers. Thus, an individual's files could be made available to other individuals as popularized by Napster's song-swapping service (although Napster did employ a server to organize the song selections and therefore was not considered peer-to-peer by purists, it would be considered a peer-to-peer content provider).
10. "Advertising That Clicks," *The Economist,* October 9, 1999. Note that in several of these models in general, and advertising-based models in particular, there is a distinction between paying customers (the advertiser) and the consumer (the end user).
11. Advertising is not Yahoo's only source of revenue. For example, it also charges companies such as travel agencies a fee when someone uses the travel.yahoo.com site to book tickets. See M. Halper, "Portal Pretense," *Business 2.0,* September 1999, pp. 43–49.
12. See C. Foley et al., "*i*Village: Innovation among Women's Websites," in Case 9 of this book.

13. Actually, the concept of selling information on a firm's own customers has been around much longer than the Internet, but the ease of collecting the information and the concept of tracking how customers use the product or service have been greatly enabled by the Internet.

14. Timmers originally conceived of the E-shop as "Web marketing" but correctly foresaw ordering, paying, and fulfilling orders through the E-shop.

15. Note that the use of the word "volume" here is not necessarily exactly the same as discussed in the advertising model: here we are referring to the number of units produced or assembled rather than the number of customers.

16. P2P also refers to "peer-to-peer," as discussed in note 9 above.

Chapter **Seven**

Value Configurations and the Internet

In Chapter 4 we introduced the idea of customer value as a prime component of analyzing a business model. We also discussed the importance of connected activities and how the execution of connected activities was a source of competitive advantage for firms. In this chapter we elaborate on the concept of customer value and how it relates to three proposed value creation logics based on Professor James Thompson's typology of long-linked, intensive, and mediating technologies.[1] These three value creation logics are related to three generic "value configurations": the value chain, value shop, and value network.[2] We discuss each value configuration in turn and demonstrate the primary "activities" associated with each. Finally, we show how the misapplication of a proposition oriented more toward manufacturing and products—the value chain framework—to Internet services and brokering can lead to the building of the wrong kinds of capabilities. The result of this misapplication could be an uncompetitive position in the market. Likewise, we show how firms building capabilities consistent with the correct value configuration can develop and maintain a competitive advantage. Thus, in this chapter we go beyond value chain analysis to the kind of value configuration analysis that may be aligned more with the kinds of services that are proliferating in the Digital Economy.

This chapter serves as a basis for analyzing the connected activities of two types of firms. For incumbents, it aids in understanding the impact of the Internet on the current value configuration (in any industry) and in choosing the most appropriate response in terms of connected activities. For new entrants, it aids in understanding the three value configurations so entrants can choose the most appropriate value configuration and the most appropriate set of connected activities.

VALUE CREATION AND ORGANIZATIONAL TECHNOLOGIES

Recall from Chapter 4 that companies are mainly concerned with creating value in terms of differentiated products or services, or in offering undifferentiated products at a lower price to customers. In which areas should companies focus if they want to build competencies that create the most value? At the heart of every business is a **value configuration:** The company is adding value in some way that makes customers willing to pay. One might imagine that there is a huge number of value configurations in the world. However, management researchers in Norway found that these value configurations can be grouped into only three fundamental "value creation configurations" in the economy.[3] These models are based on the notion of a value chain, value shop, and value network and are themselves derived from Thompson's three generic "organizational technologies."

In his landmark book, *Organizations in Action,* Thompson proposed a **typology of organizational technologies.**[4] He categorized technologies as long-linked, intensive, and mediating. In a **long-linked technology,** interdependencies are sequential and tasks are accomplished serially. Thompson cited the continuous process (e.g., continuous chemical processing) and assembly lines (e.g., automobile manufacturing) as the ultimate embodiment of long-linked technology. Other hallmarks of long-linked technologies are continuous output of standardized products, repetitive tasks, the conversion of raw materials into finished goods, clear-cut criteria for the selection of capital and labor, and continuous improvement in production.

An **intensive technology** is oriented toward solving highly specific problems. Thompson called this type of technology "intensive" to signify that the choice of techniques needed to solve a problem was based in an iterative fashion on the progress made toward solving the problem. There would likely be an intensive interaction between the problem solvers and the object of their attention. Professors Charles Stabell and Øystein Fjeldstad named the value configuration analogous to the value chain, but one based on intensive technologies, the **value shop.** The value shop is based on most types of service provision (with the exception of intermediaries, as discussed below). Thus, a hospital's primary business—healing—may be thought of as creating value as a value shop based on an intensive technology:

> At any moment an emergency admission may require some combination of dietary, X-ray, laboratory, and housekeeping or hotel services, together with the various medical specialties, pharmaceutical services, occupational therapies, social work services, and spiritual or religious services. Which of these, and when, can be determined only from evidence about the state of the patient.[5]

A **mediating technology** provides the service of a connection between two or more customers who wish to be interdependent, such as borrowers and lenders (depositors) or buyers and sellers. Thus, mediating technologies facilitate the role of the aptly named intermediary service, with the associated value configuration named the **value network.** Thompson stressed the importance of standardized criteria and decision making, as well as scale of operations. As an example of standardized criteria for taking on a customer (providing the intermediary service), decisions on creditworthiness of a potential borrower must be done in a standardized fashion to avoid bank solvency problems later on.

As mentioned in Chapter 4, a company can make money in only two ways: (1) to add value that customers are willing to pay for and (2) to have the lowest possible costs.[6] The model built on the value chain and reproduced in Figure 7.1 involves the production and sale of manufactured goods.[7] This does not necessarily involve selling to the general public (retailing), although it could.[8] Many businesses have a tangible product that is sold, so "adding value" involves the transformation of "raw materials" into that tangible product. For example, a manufacturer of chairs may take in materials such as wood stain and blocks of wood, and transform them into finished chairs. The value chain concept was popularized by Professor Michael Porter as a way to catalog the kinds of activities that add value. Using this model, we see that there are several areas in which a manufacturer such as the chair manufacturer can add value. One is inbound logistics: moving the raw materials into the plant in a more efficient way. The next is operations or transforming the raw materials into a more finished product. Next we have outbound logistics, marketing, sales, and service. These activities are called the **primary activities** of the value chain because they are most closely associated with transforming inputs into outputs and with the customer interface—the most important additions to value in the short term. The primary activities are backed up by the longer-term **secondary (support) activities** of firm infrastructure, human resource management, technology development, and procurement.

Stabell and Fjeldstad, however, proposed that the value chain does not apply to all industries and is not always a useful metaphor for managers searching for competitive advantage. For example, how does a hospital fit into the value chain analysis? Are the sick patients the "raw materials" and healthy patients the "product"?* They concluded that for most services, *value shop* was a more apt analogy.

Finally, Stabell and Fjeldstad proposed a third type of value configuration, the *value network,* which involves brokering and intermediating. Companies competing under the value network model facilitate transactions between diverse communities, for example, by bringing buyers and sellers together.

In the next three sections we explore these three value configurations and relate them to the profit sites of the Internet economy developed in Chapter 2 and the properties of the Internet described in Chapter 3. While most students will be familiar with the concept of the value chain, we briefly summarize the basic framework in the next section. We then devote one section each to the value shop and value network.

FIGURE 7.1
A Typical Value Chain

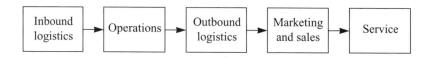

*MBA students may also recognize the mismatched concept of being called the "customers" of an educational system, a fact that the faculty often heatedly dispute! Are they instead the "raw materials" of the educational system?

THE VALUE CHAIN

To deliver low-cost or differentiated products, a firm must perform a series of activities. The different functions that perform each of these activities are called the firm's **value chain.** Most students should have had some exposure to the value chain from a course on introductory business strategy. In this section we briefly examine a value chain for manufacturing products.

A Manufacturer's Value Chain

The typical assembler/manufacturer's value chain should at this point be fairly well understood. For review purposes, we use the example of a manufacturer of computer hardware, such as a personal computer. The *inbound logistics* stage involves raw materials handling, such as computer CPU chips, memory modules, disk drives, fans, and so forth. A manager would also have to worry about an inspection of the materials, selection of parts, and delivery issues. The *operations* involve the production of in-house components, assembly of the computer, testing and tuning, maintenance of equipment, and operation of the plant. The *outbound logistics* stage involves order processing and shipping. The *marketing and sales* stage is concerned with advertising, pricing, promotion, and management of the sales force. Finally, the *service* stage involves managing technical support and service representatives and replacement and repair of computers.

In performing the activities of its value chain, a firm must interact with suppliers, customers, and firms in related industries. The other firms also have value chains of their own. What we really have, then, is a system of value chains called the value chain system (see Figure 7.2).

If you think about it, the value chain is more about efficiency than about new product development. It is about process more than product. And it is about low cost more than differentiation. The value chain describes the necessary activities once a product and its features have been conceived, and it is not necessarily concerned with developing a continual stream of innovations. However, marketing does have two roles in the value chain. The first was implied above: to stimulate demand for the product. The second role, however, is to provide input into the product specifications themselves, along with estimates of expected volume. This allows for limited differentiation.

FIGURE 7.2 **The Value Chain System**

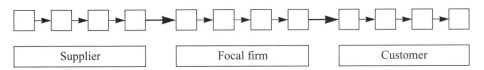

How Does the Internet Affect the Primary Activities of the Value Chain?

The seminal article on Internet business models by Paul Timmers is an important touchstone in understanding how the Internet affects the connected activities of the value chain.[9] Timmers made the first attempt to classify the different ways of doing business in the Internet era and provided some preliminary categories, such as "e-shop," "e-procurement," and "e-mall." In some sense, Timmers was concerned with a virtual value chain and how the Internet was affecting that chain.[10] Abstracting from Timmers's categories, we will demonstrate that several properties of the Internet developed in Chapter 3 influence the connected activities of the value chain.

Mediating Technology Property

The connections enabled by the Internet might allow a firm to learn more about end users; that is, a denser social web may allow the marketing and sales functions to be in more direct contact with downstream (direct customers) and end users (final users). This will allow a two-way flow of information corresponding with the dual role of marketing: By becoming more familiar with end-user customers, marketing may be better able to assess market needs or facilitate user-developed or -induced innovations.[11] Likewise, by having more direct contact with end users, it may be easier to stimulate demand from the downstream end of the channel. This process has been used with some success in the software industry, where companies prerelease free beta versions and employ user input to improve and debug their product releases.[12]

Universality, Time Moderation, and Distribution Channels

The geographic scope argument is perhaps the best known and understood story in electronic commerce. The Internet, by enabling a wider geographic scope, represents another medium in which to market and sell to customers. Local companies without a large national or international presence can now serve a larger audience outside their geographic area. The best-known story is Amazon.com's book business and its geographic reach which would have been viewed as impossible before the advent of the Internet. The marketing function thus sees the Internet as, at a minimum, an additional catalog venue. For example, L.L.Bean and most other retailers were early in putting catalogs on the Web. In addition, advertising on Internet portals and other Web pages has grown from nothing in 1995 to a projected $4.7 billion in 2002.[13] This, however, represents only 2.6 percent of total advertising spending. Other geographic effects of the Internet include the ability of existing sales and service representatives to expand their geographic reach by being in contact with a larger number of people without necessarily having to be in close physical proximity.

The ability to cover a larger geographic area and to shift in time also affects the earlier stages of the value chain; specifically, it may allow a wider choice of inputs, distributed manufacturing, and remote testing. These benefits are especially relevant to software production but may apply to other industries as well. Companies are experimenting with round-the-clock software production that can take place in the United States, Europe, and India with each team picking up where the last one left off.

Information, software, and content can also be delivered instantaneously, affecting the outbound logistics part of the chain. For example, firms such as Intuit now offer customers the ability to download their products rather than wait for a diskette or a CD to be shipped.[14] This saves the company in several ways: It eliminates the costs of the disks, the storage of information on the disks, and shipping costs. Some of those savings are passed on to the customer, who finds value in the timely delivery, in the lower price, and in the product itself. Most of the major record labels, including Capitol Records and Sony, have begun experimenting with the delivery of music over the Internet,[15] perhaps in response to audio formats such as MP3 that promise reasonable audio quality over the Internet. The reasoning is that if the labels do not control the Internet distribution by means of antipiracy digital watermarks or the equivalent, the intellectual property of the labels loses any ability to generate rents. Thus, we see both the positives and negatives of instantaneous delivery.

Information Asymmetries and Transaction Costs

The main and most celebrated effect of the Internet on the value chain is a company's ability to carry lower amounts of inventory by ordering directly from a manufacturer and shipping directly to a customer. This argument can be extended to all sorts of value chain bypassing.[16] The news and business press in the late 1990s often used the term **disintermediation** and foretold its inevitability in the Digital Economy. The concept behind disintermediation springs directly from the value chain system discussed above.

Here we draw a distinction between the downstream (direct) customer—henceforth called the *broker* or *distributor*—and the end-user (or final) consumer. Note that in many cases the direct downstream customer is not the same as the end-user consumer. Why would the upstream firm ever enter into business with the downstream customer (*not* the end-user customer) in the first place? It could be that the firm has a specific capability in manufacturing and does not know much about marketing the products. Further, the distributor might aggregate orders from other manufacturers and have large warehouses and distribution capabilities. Or the distributor might know a certain geographic area very well, but the firm is too far away to devote much time, attention, and money to that remote area.

The concept of disintermediation is that a firm upstream may **leapfrog** a downstream firm and sell directly to the distributor's customer. This is also referred to as "cutting out the middleman." Why would a firm want to do this? For one thing, the distributor might be in a more profitable line of business. For another, the distributor usually marks up the price of the firm's products through a commission or margin, thereby charging a higher price to the end user and thus dampening demand for the product.

Prior to the widespread use of the World Wide Web, the only story behind disintermediation was vertical integration: The firm could buy out the broker or try to match internally the distributor's capabilities—for example, in marketing or distribution. However, since the diffusion of the World Wide Web, it occurred to many manufacturers that they might be able to sell directly to end users. This is the travel agency story that we referred to earlier. Before the Web, airlines could sell to the public over the telephone, but it was much easier to simply let travel agents sell to the public and pay the travel agents a commission to sell tickets. The travel agents had the specialized knowledge of schedules and fares, and people were willing to go to a travel agent close to home to find out the available fares and schedules. Following the advent of the Web, the airlines began selling tickets in large volume to the general public by making their schedules and fares available to anyone with an Internet connection. When direct sales rose to a sufficiently high level, the airlines cut commissions to travel agents from 20 percent to 10 percent, then to 8 percent with a $50 cap for domestic and $100 for international flights, then, in 2002, to zero.[17] Travel agents responded by charging end users a $10 fee to book a ticket. This further reduced demand for travel agents.

The most famous example of disintermediation is no doubt Amazon.com.[18] Legend has it that Amazon cut out several middlemen in offering books for sale to the public directly from its website. Specifically, as a retailer the company could bypass both wholesalers and distributors and buy directly from the publishers. It could generate more volume from its website than a store that was wedded to a geographic area.

Dell Computer, with its famous "direct method" and the Internet version of that, Dell Online, followed a similar logic by cutting out distributors and retailers. The public can buy directly from Dell, which cuts out the reseller's markup and also keeps channel inventories low. This means that the computers in the channels are more up-to-date on average than those of Dell's competitors, thereby avoiding the problem of "fire sales" when new chips or other highly depreciating components hit the market.[19] In 1999 Apple began selling direct to the public, using the same method in its "Apple Store."

Scalability and Infinite Virtual Capacity

For many information-intensive businesses, advances in computer technology, combined with the larger customer base provided through the Internet, enable a much larger scale of operations than was previously possible. For example, the ability of online retailers such as barnesandnoble.com to serve millions of customers simultaneously sets them apart from bricks-and-mortar retailers, such as Barnes and Noble's retail outlets.

In sum, the Internet has had a profound impact on many if not all the primary activities of firms in information-based industries and of many retailers. For most other businesses, the Internet primarily interacts with the value chain's primary activities in the marketing and sales stage, which may in turn trigger substantial changes in the other stages of the value chain.

THE VALUE SHOP

Since Porter's work on the topic of value chains, much business analysis has focused squarely on improving the position of the firm relative to its competitors by **benchmarking** (comparing in a carefully controlled and objective way) its performance against the primary activities of the value chain. However, Stabell and Fjeldstad pointed out that benchmarking against the primary activities of the value chain was forcing the company into a business model centered around manufactured goods. Should an e-mail service, consulting company, travel agent, or other service provider really care about inbound logistics? Stabell and Fjeldstad argued that they should not, that **service provisioning** has a different **value creation logic.** Service providers tend to customize their service to the needs of their clients rather than mass-produce— or even mass-customize—as in the value chain model. This distinction is key: Service providers tend to work in real time to come up with new solutions, rather than fixing on one solution and reproducing it time and again.

Value Creation Logic and Service Provision

The basic example of this sort of value creation logic is the travel agent. When a client visits a high-end, service-oriented travel agent,[20] the agent must first determine what the customer wants. Compared to a manufacturer, who knows mainly what the customer wants, a travel agent has a much wider latitude of possible solutions. For example, there are various means of transportation (e.g., car, airplane, cruise ship, train), locations, dates, and potential services (e.g., hotel, car, plane). Some clients simply want to "go someplace warm" for a low price, while others want to travel by train to a specific location on a specific day. Therefore, the travel agent must ascertain exactly what the customer needs and then propose a method of filling that need. Then the agent must see if the proposed plan meets with customer approval and charge the customer the appropriate amount.

One can see that this is similar to the value chain logic described above, yet different from it. The logic of the value shop is not the logic of producing anything in particular, but honing in on what the customer actually wants and finding a way to fulfill it. One might argue that an automaker is in the same position, trying to figure out what kinds of cars the clients want and fulfilling those orders. However, that is not where the automaker adds the most value; it adds value by manufacturing and assembling cars, albeit with some design input from marketing. In any case, marketing's job is mainly to promote cars that have already been designed, not to design new ones, especially not in real time.

To give another example, consider the case of Yahoo![21] as a service provider. Yahoo started as a search engine, cataloging and categorizing sites on the World Wide Web. As that business became more commoditized, competitive, and more efficiently operated, Yahoo began searching for other services that would enable it to continue attracting visitors. First, they developed my.yahoo.com, one of the first personalized content pages. Then came the free e-mail followed by pager services. This is a type of value shop logic, although it is not targeted at a specific customer. There is a constant, real-time search for a service that will provide value to the customer, then a quick response developing that service. Time horizons are important in distinguishing value shops from value chains. With value chains, the time lag between searching for a solution and commercializing one may take years while it is only a matter of hours with the value shop.

Finally, the entire business does not have to be a service provider for a value shop logic to prevail. Service-oriented divisions or parts of larger companies can operate under the value shop logic. For example, many retailers such as L.L.Bean have customer service organizations. Even though the business itself operates under the logic of the value chain, the customer service area is more of a value shop. Likewise, internal service departments (e.g., software engineering organizations or even new product development teams) can also be thought of as value shops.

Primary Activities of the Value Shop

The hallmark of these examples is the primary concentration on **iterative problem solving** in real time; that is, a firm concentrates on discovering what the client wants, figuring out a way to deliver value, determining whether the customer's needs were fulfilled, and, if necessary, repeating the process all over again. Stabell and Fjeldstad proposed the following *primary activities* of the value shop as shown in Figure 7.3: (1) problem finding and acquisition, (2) problem solving, (3) choice, (4) execution, and (5) control and evaluation. We briefly discuss each of these.

Problem Finding and Acquisition

Problem finding and acquisition involves working with the customer to determine the exact nature of the problem or need. It also involves deciding on the overall plan of approaching the problem. As mentioned above, this is highly related to the marketing function in the traditional value chain framework.

Problem Solving

Problem solving is the actual generation of ideas and action (or treatment) plans.

Choice

Choice represents the decision of choosing between alternatives. While the least important primary activity of the value shop in terms of time and effort, it is also the most important in terms of customer value. Indeed, one of the hallmarks of the value shop compared to other value configurations is the *information asymmetry* between the service provider and the customer. The service provider has information or expertise that the customer lacks. Thus, the choice activity represents real value to the customer.

FIGURE 7.3 **Primary Activities of the Value Shop**

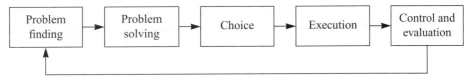

Execution

Execution represents "communicating, organizing, and implementing" the decision, or performing the treatment.

Control and Evaluation

Control and evaluation activities involve monitoring and measurement of how well the solution solved the original problem or met the original need. This feeds back into our first activity, problem finding and acquisition, for two reasons. First, if the proposed solution is inadequate or did not work, it feeds back into learning why it was inadequate and begins the problem-solving phase anew. Second, if the problem solution was successful, the firm might enlarge the scope of the problem-solving process to solve a bigger problem related to or dependent upon the first problem being solved.

How Does the Internet Affect the Primary Activities of the Value Shop?

The activities of the value shop have been influenced in several important ways by the development of the Internet. The Internet affects these activities in four main ways:

1. It enables a larger scale of operations.

2. It widens the geographic scope of the area the firm represents.

3. It allows more information to be collected and processed by the service provider.

4. It enables a new delivery medium or mechanism.

Note that these influences are not unequivocally good for the service providers. Each has advantages and disadvantages, which we describe below.

Universality, Time Moderation, and Distribution Channel

The ability to deliver service in distant regions is another aspect of the value shop that has changed considerably. Certainly such services as haircuts remain distinctly local, but clearly others are now turning to a wider geographic base than ever before. These include bill payment, consulting (especially information technology consulting), travel agencies, real estate agencies, and possibly law services, architecture, engineering, and even medical services. This geographic expansion is both an opportunity and a threat to value shop–oriented companies. A wider geographic base allows companies to serve a larger population, but, as above, the threat of competition from distant locales is very real.

For the sheer number of resources to throw at solving a problem, the Internet opens up some interesting possibilities involving collaboration. Problem solving can be enhanced in two ways. The first is collaboration on group decisions. Several systems centered on collaborative groupware are currently in use, such as Lotus Notes. These systems allow input by means of the Internet from geographically dispersed participants, allowing the participation of many more people than could physically meet together and providing a higher level of brainstorming or input selection while exploring options.

The second way problem solving can be enhanced is for single-decision makers. A single-decision maker now has the option of researching information to aid in the decision-making process, not from other people, as above, but from information archives now available on Web servers worldwide. For example, an art appraiser could easily search the latest auction prices for a certain artist over the Web, an endeavor that formerly was very time and resource consuming.

The disadvantage of the sheer number of resources is **information overload.** Decision-making quality might actually drop if the decision makers are not careful. Further, the decision maker must have some confidence in the authenticity of the research sources available over the Web. A medical doctor, for example, may not necessarily believe everything he or she reads about a certain condition on every website. Likewise, in our example of the art appraiser, unless the appraiser goes to the websites of major auction houses, there is always the possibility that the prices quoted on a website are incorrect, or worse, that the work auctioned was not an authentic piece by the artist in question.

For some services, the Internet may be used as a delivery medium. Fax service from overseas is one example of using the Internet for service delivery. From a computer in France, one sends an e-mail message to a certain address in the United States. The computer at that address forwards the message to an address near the intended recipient, where the computer converts it into a fax that is sent to the recipient. The sender is charged only a nominal fee for the service, which enables customers overseas to send documents to people who do not have e-mail access and without having to pay for an international telephone call. Thus, the existence of high-speed connections may become a viable method for service providers to deliver services themselves— clearly in telecommunications as in the above example, but also potentially in any virtual, information-based service such as stock quotations and architectural design.

Information Asymmetries and Transaction Costs

Value shops are both made and unmade by information asymmetries. The entire value proposition of the value shop is its ability to solve problems that the client cannot. Thus, the Internet represents a fundamental hazard to the very core of the value shop: As an increasing amount of information is available online, the more competition the general knowledge base provides against the value shop firm. This does not mean that there will be no more consulting companies, architects, or professional service firms. Reputation, information from a trusted source, and personalization will always have value to many customers. However, the information-based value shop businesses will be expected to encounter competition from the general knowledge base available over the Internet. This will be especially true for information asymmetries based on explicit rather than tacit knowledge.

Scalability and Infinite Virtual Capacity

The advantage of the Internet is its ability to serve more customers at once, especially in information-intensive services. Previously a firm was limited by the number of people it could hire to perform customer service. Now the number of inputs can be greatly increased by allowing many more simultaneous connections. For example, many companies, such as L.L.Bean, are allowing live "chat" with customer service agents over the Web. This allows the same number of agents to serve more customers; in addition, it increases the total number of customers that L.L.Bean can serve at the same time.

Getting basic information back to customers *without* the intervention of customer service agents in a timely and cost-efficient fashion is also an advantage of the Internet. It is clear that value shops are the primary beneficiaries of the ability to store information on servers and pass it along to customers on demand. For example, airlines have moved to a system whereby not only the fares and schedules are available over the Web, but also flight status, airplane layouts, seat locations, and more. In 1999 Delta Airlines tried to charge more for customers who purchased a ticket over the telephone because of the higher cost structure. However, after a firestorm of criticism, Delta decided to drop this charge. We believe that the Web-based approach must be providing cost savings for Delta in addition to providing more information for customers.[22] Likewise, diverse organizations such as the Vanguard Group (mutual funds and financial services) and the Internal Revenue Service have put all of their customer service forms online. This allows many more customers to be served simultaneously, gets the information to the customer more quickly (see below), saves printing and postage costs, and reduces the need for staffing customer service telephone centers.

The disadvantage of these approaches, again, is that as the size and scale of service providers increase, surviving competitors will tend to grow bigger while the smaller, less aggressive firms will find themselves under more intense competitive pressure. This is a potential hazard to the smaller companies that have been playing comfortably in a niche market for many years.

In sum, the Internet touches most, if not all, of the primary activities of the value shop. Information-based value shops cannot expect that all of the changes will be positive.

THE VALUE NETWORK

Despite the story related above about travel agents, we believe that the inevitability of disintermediation has been greatly exaggerated. In fact, the third value configuration we will explore—the value network—is a direct outgrowth of *brokering.* The value network is the value configuration that exists when a firm is an intermediary, such as a broker (or agent or market-maker in the terminology of Chapter 2). The broker brings buyers and sellers together and makes money by doing so. While the above concerns about disintermediation are very real in the bricks-and-mortar world, one needs only to look at the list of top retailers to see that most of them are intermediaries. Indeed, most of the top consumer websites are either travel agents or brokerage houses. Let us briefly examine each of these.

Examples of Value Network Businesses

Online travel agents, such as Travelocity and Expedia, provide convenient summaries of fares and schedules. They also allow the user to search for the lowest fare across several airlines and to search by schedule, type of ticket (restricted or unrestricted), number of connecting flights, and so forth. These agencies get the same commissions as bricks-and-mortar travel agencies, but they are able to sustain huge volumes owing to the scalability of their Internet services; that is, Internet travel agencies can handle thousands (even millions) of users simultaneously while a typical corner travel agency can handle only three or four. Thus, the fixed costs are spread over a great many more users and the marginal costs of servicing each additional user are much lower than they are in a bricks-and-mortar organization. The Internet travel agencies make money by taking a low commission on a large volume of purchasers while the bricks-and-mortar agencies make money by taking a higher commission on a low volume. Now that the services are virtually indistinguishable, however, the Internet agencies are putting competitive pressure on the bricks-and-mortar agencies because customers are unwilling to pay the higher commissions.[23]

Another growing area of electronic commerce is Internet brokerage houses such as E*Trade or Ameritrade. Once again, we have a similar brokering value configuration. The online brokerages bring buyers and sellers together and shave off a small commission, in some cases as low as $7, for each trade. The very high volumes of trading allowed by high-speed servers and the ability to service many people at the same time compensate for the lower per-trade commission.

To summarize, we can see that there is money to be made by an intermediary if both buyers and sellers perceive value from that intermediary. Customers must perceive that there is value in being part of the "network" that the intermediary controls or supports. In the case of the travel agencies, airlines want to sell more tickets. Customers, however, cannot trust the airlines to offer them the lowest possible fares. Therefore, customers are willing to use the online travel agency which acts as an information broker to find the lowest fares across all the airlines. The same logic applies to online brokerages. Any individual company could (subject to securities regulations) theoretically sell stock directly to the public; however, most would-be buyers could not be sure that they were getting a suitable price and therefore go through an online broker to get the best price. The more companies an online brokerage interacts with, the more valuable the service to the end-user customers.

Likewise, a bank (online or otherwise) performs a service, which is to bring together people with capital (savers) with those who need capital (borrowers). The value to each of these sets of customers depends on the bank's capabilities in building a network of savers and borrowers.

Primary Activities of the Value Network

Generally speaking, a broker, distributor, or other intermediary must pursue several activities if it wants to remain or become competitive. Rather than focusing on logistics such as the importation and delivery of raw materials and how they are transformed into finished goods, the intermediary must focus on the following items:

1. Network promotion and contract management.

2. Service provisioning.

3. Infrastructure operations.

We discuss each of these in turn.

Network Promotion and Contract Management

This activity involves promoting and building the network, acquiring customers, and managing contracts for service provision. The management of contracts involves the initiation, maintenance, and termination of contracts to provide whatever service the intermediary proposes to furnish. This activity is distinguished from sales and marketing in the value chain by its active selection of customers to join the network. As the level of commitment rises, the complexity of the contracting process and of the contracts themselves rises.

Service Provisioning

Service provisioning involves linking people in the network and then collecting payment from them for making the connection. Specifically, it involves setting up contacts—directly, as in real-time chat telephone service, or indirectly, as in banking or electronic mail—seeing that the contacts are maintained for the appropriate amount of time, and ending the contact at the appropriate moment. Collecting payment is about tracking the usage (both *volume* and *time*) and billing for direct contact or, in the case of indirect contacts, collecting a commission for putting the two parties together. Upon receiving a service request, the intermediary needs to check the feasibility of making the connection as well as the eligibility of the requestor.

Infrastructure Operations

These activities allow the infrastructure to operate efficiently and remain in a state of readiness to provide service to the next customer. It can include both a physical and information infrastructure. Stabell and Fjeldstad provided examples of different types of infrastructure activities that vary with the type of network: For telecommunications providers, the main infrastructure is embedded in switches and distribution centers; for financial services companies, it is embedded in the branch offices, financial assets, or connections to trading floors.[24] Figure 7.4 provides an example of the value network activities of a financial services provider.

How Does the Internet Affect the Primary Activities of the Value Network?

Analogous to the case of the value shop, the Internet also influences the activities of the value network in three main ways:

1. It compounds network externalities.

2. It widens the geographic scope of the network.

3. It enables a larger scale of the network.

Note that these influences are not unequivocally good for service providers. Each of them has advantages and disadvantages, which we describe below.

Mediating Technology and Network Externalities

The network externality effect is the most important property influencing the value network. Arguably, the network externality property enables the large number of Internet intermediaries. The size of the network is the most important criterion of merit for users evaluating a value network–oriented business. A bank that has no lenders, only borrowers, will not be solvent for long. A used-car service with access to one dealer is of little use to potential buyers. Likewise, a music service that recommends CDs based on one you recently bought will not make very good recommendations if it has only three customers. As described in Chapter 3, this is a virtuous cycle (or vicious cycle, depending on where the firm starts and what competitors do) with a larger network attracting more users and complementors. For example, not only will car purchasers shun the "network" of one dealer, but other dealers will also be reluctant to sign up with so few customers. In contrast, a large network of dealers and customers encourages more customers to want to use the service (more dealers) and more dealers to participate (more customers).

This can lead to a kind of "crowd mentality" behavior in value network–oriented businesses. Initially, there may be several firms providing similar intermediary services. Eventually—because of the company's strategy, chance, or something else—one or a small number of the firms may enjoy a small lead in the size of their network. Once this happens, the crowd will rush to the doors of the larger networks, leaving the smaller rivals with no customers. Thus, as

FIGURE 7.4
Activities of the Value Network

Adapted from Charles B. Stabell and Øystein D. Fjeldstad, "Configuring Value for Competitive Advantage: On Chains, Shops, and Networks," *Strategic Management Journal* 19 (1998), p. 430.

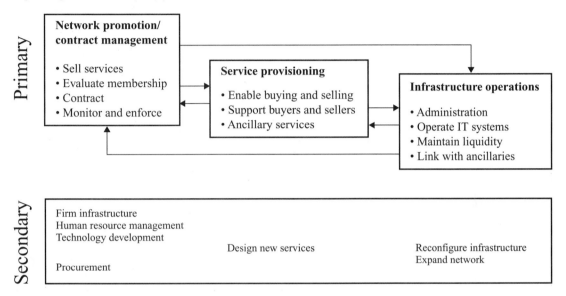

we discussed with lock-in in Chapter 4, it is extremely important for inter-mediaries to think about how they will develop the size of the network.[25] *We emphasize that there must be both lock-in (switching costs) and network effects for this to be successful, however.*

Universality, Time Moderation, and Distribution Channel

The Internet, as in all previous examples, widens the geographic scope of the network. This is especially important for value networks, as the size of the network affects its usefulness to users. A larger geographic base of users allows the network to grow more quickly. Thus, businesses that were once constrained to a small geographic area (and slow growth for their networks) are now free to expand more quickly. The downside, as always, is that once comfortable, slow-growth networks can now be won and lost in a matter of months or even weeks.

In terms of a distribution channel, Qwest Communications, among others, is experimenting with providing long-distance telephone service over the Internet. Long-distance service works in one of two ways: with or without special equipment. With special equipment, your phone is connected directly to the Internet, and the receiver must also have the same specialized phone.

The voice traffic is broken into packets and reassembled at the other end. For people with standard phones, the voice data are connected through a circuit to the switch of the long-distance carrier, at which point it is broken into packets and transmitted to a remote switch where it is reassembled and sent through a circuit to the destination. In both cases, the current capacity of Internet bandwidth means that the packet connection is of low quality (e.g., missing packets are "dropped" due to the real-time requirement of voice communication). With expected advances, however, packet-switched voice communications may become a viable option in the next few years. Other examples include the development of electronic markets that use the Internet for trading, not simply for entering orders.

Scalability and Infinite Virtual Capacity

Again, infrastructure operation enables the network to have a larger scale, which is the primary way that a firm oriented to the value network adds value. Thus, in addition to a larger geographic reach, the increase in computing power has made it possible to serve many more customers. Businesses that were originally constrained by their capacity (and were also found in comfortable, slow-growth niches) now find themselves able to expand their networks rapidly, which in turn raises the value of their networks.

MAKING A FIRM'S VALUE CONFIGURATION CONSISTENT WITH ITS ACTIVITIES

One main conclusion that we might draw is that it is better to figure out the value configuration and then pursue the activities that are more appropriate for that particular value configuration. An interesting example is the progression of the state of real estate brokerages and the evolution in the way they make money. Real estate agencies at one point offered "exclusive" listings; that is, a seller who wanted to sell a house would go to one real estate office, which would "list" the house. If anyone else wanted to buy the house, that buyer would have to contact the listing agent directly. Therefore, the value of an agency was in the number of direct connections it had to sellers: a classic value network. Upon sale of the house, the seller paid the real estate agency a commission for listing and selling the house—a practice that has continued to the present.

At one point the Multiple Listing Service (MLS) came into being and agents could choose to adopt it. The concept behind the MLS should be familiar to anyone with an interest in e-commerce. If an agency chose to join the MLS, the agency would report all of its listings to the MLS, which would pass them along to all the other members. While the MLS is clearly a value network as we understand it, it should be noted that with the advent of the MLS, the uniqueness of a real estate agency began to diminish from the point of view of the value network. In an abstract way, the value of the agency was still the value of its connections, but because of its membership in the MLS, the agency's connections became in some sense a commodity. Real estate agencies began at this point to look more like value shops than value networks. We also began at this point to see the use of "buyers' brokers" whose role was to work for the buyer. Agencies made money on volume (more people could see their own listings) and competition drove down or held in check the commissions that agencies could charge.

The Internet has now enabled a new form of real estate firm: an online agency that again looks like a value network, possibly supplanting the MLS, and further driving the agency into the role of a pure service provider (a value shop) rather than a value network. In the latest phase, home owners can list their own homes on the websites of certain online brokerages for a low flat fee, or even for free. The MLS is also available on some websites such as Cyberhomes.com, bringing the listing information directly into the hands of potential buyers. Yahoo, for example, has grown the network quickly by integrating information from several diverse networks and allowing free listings and easy search facilities. In response, some bricks-and-mortar agencies began introducing fee-for-service plans, where an agent would work with a client on an hourly basis rather than on commission. It has begun to look as if the bricks-and-mortar agencies are in danger of being bypassed by online brokerages or becoming fee-for-service providers.

An oft-quoted example of disintermediation is Amazon.com which, when analyzed from a value chain standpoint, seems to be eliminating book distributors from the value chain. If Amazon thought of itself as primarily a bookseller/retailer, then it should concentrate entirely on value chain activities such as logistics (e.g., shipping, warehousing, distribution) and operations (e.g., order processing). From this point of view, Amazon's celebrated hiring of Wal-Mart's information technology/logistics experts seems like a brilliant move.

There is, however, another point of view on Amazon.com. It could also be thought of as a firm in the value network configuration. Its success would therefore spring not from efficiency of ordering and delivery of books, but from brokering information about book-buying behavior. By selling the largest number of books, Amazon collects information on what other customers with similar tastes do. For example, if a customer buys book A, Amazon can inform that person that customers who bought book A also bought book B. Further, descriptions of books are accompanied by reviews written by the publishers, authors, critics, and anyone who wants to contribute a review. Thus, the value of the information that Amazon has increases with the size of the network, which is represented by the number of book purchasers. If the firm considered itself a value network, it would focus its efforts on personalization, collaborative filtering, and information brokering.

Summary

Eliminating geographic distance is the most important property of the Internet for all three value configurations, but the reduction in distance interacts with other properties uniquely for each configuration. Table 7.1 summarizes these important interactions. For the value chain, it is keeping costs low through more efficient procurement and logistics. For the value shop, it is the increasing amount of available exploitable information while simultaneously recognizing that value shops based on explicit rather than tacit knowledge will be rendered uncompetitive. For the value network, it is the ability to build the network quickly to take advantage of network externalities.

Value configurations, such as the value chain, are based on Thompson's three generic organizational technologies:

- Long-linked—sequential interdependencies, serial tasks, continuous output of standardized products, clear criteria for capital and labor selection.

- Intensive—for solving highly specific problems in an iterative fashion.

- Mediating—facilitate intermediary services; focus on standardized criteria and decision making and scale of operations.

The value chain is a value configuration (or value creation logic) that is applied most appropriately to manufacturing and product-oriented businesses. In light of the growing service and digital economies, other models are needed to explain value creation for competitive advantage.

The focus of the value chain (that is, firms oriented toward a value chain logic) is on efficiency, process, and lowering cost. Disintermediation is a possibility for both logistics and procurement. The focus of the value shop is on customizing service(s) to the need(s) of clients, new product development, and differentiation. The value shop is based on constant, iterative problem solving in real time (solving problems the client cannot solve). For value shop–oriented firms, the Internet allows for a larger scale of operations, a wider geographic scope, more information to be collected and processed, and a new delivery medium or mechanism. The focus of the value network is on brokering, building the network of users (buyers) and suppliers, contract management, service provisioning and infrastructure operations. For value network–oriented firms, the Internet allows for a larger scale of the network, a wider geographic scope of the network, and a speedier compounding of network externalities.

TABLE 7.1 The Most Important Properties of Each Value Configuration

Value Configuration	Most Important Properties
Value chain	Universality
Value shop	Reduces information asymmetries
Value network	Compounds network externalities
Support activities	Reduces transaction costs

Key Terms

benchmarking, *127*
disintermediation, *125*
information
    overload, *130*
intensive
    technology, *121*
iterative problem
    solving, *128*
leapfrog, *125*

long-linked
    technology, *121*
mediating
    technology, *121*
primary activities, *122*
secondary (support)
    activities, *122*
service
    provisioning, *127*

typology of
    organizational
    technologies, *121*
value chain, *123*
value configuration, *121*
value creation logic,
    127
value network, *121*
value shop, *121*

Discussion Questions

1. Why should a firm bother to choose the most appropriate value configuration?

2. List one firm for each value configuration. Why is the value configuration you assigned the most appropriate?

3. How do the three firms you listed in your answer to No. 2 make money? What are the core competencies of each firm? Which competence is the most extensible? Why?

4. In the value shop example, what is the problem that the firm is solving for clients/customers?

5. Give an example of:
   • a long-linked technology
   • an intensive technology
   • a mediating technology
   Show how each fits into the value configurations mentioned above.

6. To what value configuration does America Online (AOL) most closely conform? Is this true of the many companies it has acquired (e.g., Netscape, Time Warner)?

Notes

1. James D. Thompson, *Organizations in Action* (New York: McGraw-Hill, 1967).

2. See Charles B. Stabell and Øystein D. Fjeldstad, "Configuring Value for Competitive Advantage: On Chains, Shops, and Networks," *Strategic Management Journal* 19 (1998), pp. 413–37. The value chain configuration has been the dominant value creation logic in the economy for the last century. However, over the last 10 to 20 years, the "service economy" has equaled, and recently surpassed, the manufacturing economy. The Internet has played a role in speeding up this transition. Thus, management researchers prior to the rise of the Internet and the service economy had little need to describe a different type of value creation logic.

3. Stabell and Fjeldstad, "Configuring Value for Competitive Advantage," pp. 414–15.

4. Thompson, *Organizations in Action,* pp. 15–18.

5. Thompson, *Organizations in Action,* p. 17.

6. These are not mutually exclusive: A company could have both differentiated products and a low cost structure.

7. Michael Porter, *Competitive Strategy* (New York: Free Press, 1985).

8. Some question the concept of the value chain as it relates to retailing. Retailers can also be thought of as intermediaries, bringing buyers and sellers together (although they do not facilitate a spot transaction, most hold inventory). This will be discussed further in the next section.

9. Paul Timmers, "Business Models for Electronic Markets," *Electronic Markets* 8, no. 2 (1998), pp. 3–8.

10. Timmers also introduced the categories of "e-auction" and "virtual communities" which were primarily value network configurations as described below.

11. Eric von Hippel, *The Sources of Innovation* (New York: Oxford University Press, 1988).

12. Raghu Garud, Sanjay Jain, and Corey Phelps, "From Vaporware to Betaware," *STERNBusiness* 4, no. 2 (1997), pp. 20–23.

13. Myers Reports, www.jackmyers.com/research/reports/advertisingspending .html.

14. www.quickenstore.com.

15. Mihir Parikh, "The Music Industry in the Digital World: Waves of Change," Working paper, Institute for Technology and Enterprise, 1999; see also G. Raik-Allen, "Players Line Up for Battle over Online Music Industry," *Red Herring,* February 1999, www.redherring.com/insider/1999/0202/news-music.com; "Music over the Web," *Business Week,* March 2, 1998, p. 89; and "Diamond Multimedia and the Rio Player," NYU Stern School of Business, Case #991-071, 1999.

16. It should be noted that the disintermediation argument can be equally applied to the secondary or support activity of procurement. Procurement is a secondary activity that supports all three value configurations. See Timmers, "Business Models for Electronic Markets," p. 5 ("e-procurement").

17. Joel J. Smith, "Northwest Bypasses Agents," *Detroit News,* February 18, 1999, p. B1.

18. See below why this might not really be the only story, or even the story at all.

19. "Selling PCs like Bananas," *The Economist,* October 5, 1996, p. 63.

20. Travel agents, especially those who only sell tickets to people who already know what they want, might be thought of as intermediaries. This will be discussed in the next section.

21. Henceforth we will eliminate the exclamation point from the name to minimize distraction.

22. It could also be that Delta's marginal costs are higher with the telephone while the fixed costs are higher with the Internet. Therefore, even though one might argue that the total cost is lower with the telephone, Delta is attempting to discourage its use to exploit lower marginal costs.

23. Expedia, owned by Microsoft, had not made a profit as of early 2000; Microsoft uses its deep pockets to fund the fixed costs of Expedia's capacity. However, the trend mentioned above—the replacement of bricks-and-mortar agencies by Internet agencies—is expected to continue.

24. Stabell and Fjeldstad, "Configuring Value for Competitive Advantage," p. 429.

25. For more information about the dynamics of the Internet's effect on value networks, see Larry Downes and Chunka Mui, *Unleashing the Killer App* (Boston: Harvard Business School Press, 1998); see also Carl Shapiro and Hal R. Varian, *Information Rules* (Boston: Harvard Business School Press, 1999).

Chapter **Eight**

Valuing and Financing an Internet Start-Up

As we noted in Chapter 1, most people go into business to make money. If the business has what it takes to be profitable, its founders often have to decide when to take out their share of the profits. They usually face at least two options: They can (1) collect the profits over the life of the business or (2) sell part or all of the business to investors who, for a price, get the right to collect some or all of the future cash flows from the business. To carry out the second option, it is important to determine how much the company is worth—it is important to value the business. In the first part of this chapter, we explore the cash flow, price-earnings (P/E) ratio, price-earnings growth (PEG), and business model based methods for valuing technology start-ups. We also take a look at the role of intellectual capital in valuing companies. We begin with a brief discussion of the initial public offering (IPO) process.

In the second part of the chapter, we recognize that somewhere in the process of conceiving and executing a business model, a firm usually needs money; that is, before a firm can start making money, it needs money. Finding, obtaining, and allocating this money to the right components of the business model is called financing. We explore the different sources of financing for a start-up and suggest that although low-cost money is important, the complementary assets and intellectual capital that often come with some financing sources can be even more important for start-ups.

WHEN TO CASH OUT

Over a Firm's Life Cycle

Over each accounting period, a firm receives money from its revenue sources but must also spend money to cover the costs that it incurs in offering value to its customers. The cash that the company generates is normally called *cash inflows* while the cash that it consumes is called *cash outflows.* The excess of cash inflows over cash outflows is the amount of money available to the owners of the business to take out or plow back into the business.

Collecting Early

Rather than wait to collect profits over the life of a firm, an entrepreneur may decide to collect today by selling his or her right to collect future profits to someone else. Very early in the life of a start-up, this someone is usually a venture capital firm. The funds collected at this stage, however, usually go to meet the large cash outflows required to keep the fledgling start-up going, not for the owners to take out. In return for the funding, the venture capital firm usually gets a share of the company and the right to a piece of future cash flows. Founders can also sell part of their company to institutional investors such as retirement funds or to rich individuals often known as angel investors. A popular way, however, is to sell shares of the company to the public by means of an **initial public offering (IPO).** In an IPO, anyone can buy shares of the company and, in return, is entitled to an appropriate share of the company's future free cash flows. Indeed, the primary motivation for venture capital firms and other early investors is the anticipation of cashing out at the time of the IPO or shortly thereafter. They usually do not invest in a start-up with the intention of waiting to share in future earnings from the firm.

THE IPO PROCESS

In the late 1990s, wealth in the billions of dollars was created for many Americans through the IPO process. The process of issuing an IPO starts with building a viable business.[1] The firm then finds an underwriter, usually an **investment bank** such as Goldman Sachs, Solomon Smith Barney, or Morgan Stanley Dean Witter (see Figure 8.1). The investment bank determines how much the firm is worth, how many shares to issue to the public, when to issue the shares, and what to price the shares. According to the full disclosure requirement of the Securities Act of 1933, the investment bank must file a registration statement with the Securities and Exchange Commission (SEC) in which it provides a description of the business, financial statements, the purposes of the money raised from the stock issue, any legal proceedings involving the firm, biographical information on the officers of the firm, and the number of shares owned by officers of the company and any shareholder who owns more than 10 percent of the stock. Following the filing date is a **cooling off period** during which the SEC verifies that full disclosure has been made. When the SEC is satisfied, it gives its approval for the issue to be offered to the public. The date on which this approval comes is called the effective date since from that day on the firm can hold its IPO. While waiting for approval from the SEC, the investment bank usually tries to generate interest in the issue. The

FIGURE 8.1   **The IPO Process**

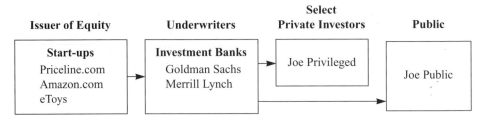

amount of interest from investors is an important factor in determining the price of the issue. Each of these investors, usually a select group (called Joe Privileged in Figure 8.1), makes a commitment to buy a certain number of shares at the **public offering price.**

If public interest in the issue is high on the IPO date, the price of the stock may rise quickly from the offering price, making Joe Privileged very rich. In 1999 most Internet-related issues closed higher than their public offering prices. Of course, if interest from the public is very low, then Joe Privileged may not be so lucky after all and the start-up firm that issued the stock gets a lower price than the public offering price.[2] The difference, also called the *spread,* is used to pay the underwriter. The underwriter usually enters one of two types of agreements with the firm. In a firm commitment, the underwriter guarantees to sell a certain number of shares. If the public does not buy all the shares, the underwriter will buy the rest. In a "best efforts" agreement, the underwriter only commits to do the best that it can to sell the shares, leaving the issuing firm responsible for any unsold shares.

Impact of the Internet on the IPO Process

Technically, start-up firms could go straight to the public to sell their stocks. One main reason why such firms have traditionally hired investment banks is that these banks have information on how to value issues and drum up interest in an IPO through their established relations with clients—information that start-ups usually do not have. The backing of a stock issue by an investment bank lends credibility to the valuation and viability of the firm issuing the shares. Thus, investment banks act as intermediaries between issuing firms and investors. The Internet may make these benefits become less important. Now, an issue's prospectus can be posted on the Internet and instead of a select number of clients buying the shares at a guaranteed price before the rest of the public, the issues can be auctioned to the public through an Internet auction house such as eBay without passing through an investment bank. In any case, to determine the number of shares to be sold and at what price, the investment bank or the firm must value the business.

VALUATION OF A BUSINESS

We next explore several methods that have been used to value firms and businesses: Cash flow, price-earnings (P/E) ratio, price-earnings growth (PEG) ratio, and one based on the business model.

Cash Flows

In the *Theory of Investment Value,* written over 50 years ago, John Burr Williams set forth the equation for value, which we condense here: The value of any stock, bond or business is determined by the cash inflows and outflows—discounted at the appropriate interest rate—that can be expected to occur during the remaining life of the asset.

Warren Buffett

The value of a business or firm, then, is the **present value** of its future free cash flows discounted at its cost of capital. Thus, the value of a firm V is given by:[3]

$$V = C_0 + \frac{C_1}{(1 + r_{k)}} + \frac{C_2}{(1 + r_k)^2} + \ldots + \frac{C_n}{(1 + r_k)^n}$$

$$= \sum_{t=0}^{t=n} \frac{C_t}{(1 + r_k)^t} \tag{1}$$

where

C_t is the free cash flow at time t, and
r_k is the firm's cost of capital.

This discounting reflects the higher value of money today than its value tomorrow.

If the value of a stock is determined by the present value of the cash inflows and outflows that can be expected to occur during the remaining life of the business, valuing a business boils down to determining what those cash inflows and outflows will be over the life of the business and the appropriate discount rate.

Free Cash Flow

Free cash flow is the cash from a business's operations that is available for distribution to its claim holders—equity investors and debtors—who provide capital. It is the difference between cash earnings and cash investments. A firm's free cash flow, C_t, in period t is given by:[4]

C_t = Cash earnings (from income statement) – Cash investments (from balance sheet)

= Operating income − Taxes on operating income + Depreciation + Noncash charges

  − Increase in **working capital** (current assets – current liabilities) in period t

  − Cash expenditures on investments in period t **(2)**

Operating income, taxes on operating income, depreciation, and noncash charges are from the firm's income statement while increase in working capital and cash expenditures on investments are from the balance sheet.

Discount Rate

The **discount rate,** r_k, is the firm's opportunity cost of capital. It is the expected rate of return that could be earned from an investment of similar risk. It reflects the systematic risk that is specific to the firm and therefore undiversifiable. The discount rate can be estimated using a model such as the **capital asset pricing model (CAPM):**

$$r_k = r_f + \beta_i(r_m - r_f)$$ **(3)**

That is, the discount rate is equal to r_f, the risk-free rate such as the interest rate on Treasury bills, plus a risk premium. This **risk premium** is equal to the **systematic risk** or beta coefficient, β_i, for the business or firms, and the excess return over the market return r_m.

Bricks-and-Mortar vs. Internet Cash Flows

One advantage that Internet companies have over their bricks-and-mortar competitors is that they can take advantage of the Internet's properties in crafting their business models to improve their cash flows. Consider again Amazon.com. Before it built its own warehouses, it carried no inventory. Whenever a customer placed an order for a book, the customer paid with his or her credit card and Amazon collected the cash almost immediately. Amazon then ordered the book from a wholesaler or publisher who delivered it directly to the customer right away but did not collect the cash for the book from Amazon until 30 to 45 days later. Effectively, Amazon kept the customer's money for 30 to 45 days before paying the book wholesaler or publisher. This meant that Amazon had negative working capital for that particular transaction and from expression (2) above, this means positive cash flow for Amazon. Even after building its own warehouses, Amazon kept inventory for an average of only two weeks. Additionally, whenever Amazon doubled its sales it did not have to double the number of physical stores—as would a bricks-and-mortar competitor like Borders—because it had none. That also saved on cash expenditures for investment, effectively increasing free cash flow.

Free cash flow gains do not come only from pure play Internet firms like Amazon.com. Bricks-and-mortar firms could also boost their free cash flows by adopting the Internet. Consider automakers. In 1998 alone, automakers had an estimated $100 billion in inventory, much of it because of their inability to forecast what customers wanted. By using the Internet to "go direct" to customers using a Dell-type model,[5] much of the inventory could be eliminated. Less inventory means less working capital and therefore more free cash flow.

The main problem with using equation (1) for determining the value of a firm is that it is very difficult to predict what the cash flows and cost of capital will be in the future. The situation is particularly challenging for start-up firms, most of which do not have positive cash flows. One way to circumvent this problem is to find a firm whose systematic risk or beta coefficient is similar to that of the start-ups and use that firm's cash flows with the necessary adjustments to estimate the cash flows of the start-up. This procedure is analogous to the more widely used price-earnings methods that we discuss next.

Price-Earnings (P/E) Ratio

In the **price-earnings (P/E) ratio** method of valuing firms, a P/E ratio for the firm is first determined. By multiplying this P/E ratio by the firm's earnings, the price per share can be obtained. Also called the capitalization factor, the P/E ratio reflects investors' expectations of future earnings. The question is, How does one determine the P/E ratio for the firm to begin with? One thing to do is to find firms with similar beta coefficients and use their P/E ratio as a base; that is, look for firms whose systematic risk is similar to that of the firm in question. The P/E ratio from the reference group is then adjusted for any differences between the firm and the reference firms. The ratio is further adjusted for general conditions. For example, the ratio is adjusted upward in a bull market and downward in a bear market.[6] After all the adjustments have been made to the ratio, it is multiplied by the firm's earnings to obtain its share price.

Simple Example: It is now 2003 and back in 2001 you had founded an online auction firm that earned $3 million in 2002. You are about to go public. With the help of the venture capital firm that financed many of your start-up activities, you have found an investment bank which suggests that you issue 5 million shares in an initial public offering. What should be the share price of your firm? The P/E ratio of other online auction firms is 80. The earnings per share of your company is $3M/5M = $0.60. Since the P/E ratio is 80,

$$\frac{P}{E} = \frac{p}{\$0.6} = 80 \Rightarrow p = \$48$$

Thus, the share price that you should expect is $48.

This method, although very popular, has several shortcomings. First, although earnings are highly correlated with cash flows, they are not free cash flows. A firm can be profitable but have negative free cash flows and vice versa. Second, there is more than one type of earnings, so deciding on which one to use is not easy. Third, there is always the question of whether historical earnings are a good predictor of future earnings.

Price-Earnings Growth (PEG) Ratio

The **price-earnings growth (PEG) ratio** method more explicitly incorporates the role of growth. Calculations are similar to those that use the P/E with adjustments made for growth. Consider our online auction example. Suppose the firm is growing at 90 percent annually. Since its P/E ratio is 80, we obtain the PEG ratio by dividing the P/E ratio by its annual growth rate:

$$\frac{80}{90} = .89$$

What is considered a good PEG ratio is a matter of debate. Traditionally, stocks with PEG ratios of less than 1.00 were considered good buys. Anything above that was thought to be overpriced. Such generalizations are no substitute for careful research that digests a firm's business model to understand why one can expect profits from the company down the line.

The PEG ratio suffers from the same types of problems as the P/E ratio. In addition, ratios lose some useful information when data are simplified for better absorption. Consider firms A and B, each with a PEG ratio of 1. However, firm A has a P/E ratio of 50 and a growth rate of 50 percent while B has a P/E ratio of 4 and a growth rate of 4 percent. These seem to be two very different firms in different industries; therefore, each stock is likely to attract a different type of investor. Firm B may be early in its life in a fast-growing industry where it has invested a large amount of up-front capital that should pay off soon, while A is in a mature industry with high variable costs and not much hope of growth. In any case, using both methods to value start-ups is particularly problematic because most start-ups have negative earnings, even those that are going to be profitable later.

VALUATION OF BUSINESSES THAT ARE NOT YET PROFITABLE

Most start-up companies lose money and have negative cash flows in their formative years. In the late 1990s many Internet firms that went public had not yet become profitable. How do you estimate the value of a firm that has negative earnings? Nothing in our discussion of price-earnings and price-earning growth said anything about negative earnings. We explore two methods of accomplishing this task.

Firm and Industry Proxies

In the firm and industry proxy method, a firm's share price is estimated using the P/E ratios of analogs—firms and industries that the analyst deems representative of the subject firm. This method is best illustrated by Henry Blodget's 1998 estimates of Amazon.com's share price (see Illustration Capsule 8.1).

Estimating Share Prices of Firms with Negative Earnings

He starts by looking at the size of Amazon's target market. Worldwide, the market for books, music, and videos is around $100 billion. So how big a slice of that can the company get? Blodget draws an analogy between Amazon, the leader in its category, and Wal-Mart, the leader in discount retailing, which has a 10 percent market share. Since Amazon is adding to its product mix, he thinks it's fair to estimate that it could hit a 10 percent share in the next five years, which would amount to $10 billion in revenues. Then, he asks, what could the company's profit margin be? Traditional retailers typically achieve net margins of 1 percent to 4 percent. But Blodget believes Amazon will be able to run leaner than land-based types by paying less rent, keeping less inventory, and

hiring fewer employees. Its net margin, he assumes, could be more like Dell's—a fatter 7 percent. So, 7 percent of $10 billion is $700 million in net income. The last question is, what price/earnings multiple will the market assign Amazon at that point? P/Es normally range from 10 or so for a slow-growth company to about 75 for one that's growing quickly. That means that a slow-growing Amazon could have a $7 billion market cap, or $44 per share (post-split), while a fast-growing Amazon could be worth $53 billion, or $332 per share. Using these assumptions, Amazon's current $25 billion market cap and $160 share price start to seem plausible.

Source: *Fortune*, February 1, 1999, p. 148.

Business Models Approach: Earnings and Cash Flow Chain

Instead of finding proxy firms and industries, we could turn to a firm's business model for some indication of future earnings potential. When we explored the pricing component of a business model in Chapter 4, we showed how a firm—with high up-front costs and relatively low variable costs—could lose a great deal of money early in the life of a product or technology but become very profitable later. We argued that the primary indicators of whether such a firm would be profitable in the future were its profit margins, market share, and revenue share growth. If a start-up is not profitable, some of the measures upstream of its profit/cash flow chain (see Figure 8.2) could be used in estimating share prices.

Profitability Predictor Measures

Since profit margins, market share, and revenue share growth are good **profitability predictor measures** of future profits, we can use price-margins, price-share, and price-share growth, rather than P/E or PEG ratios to determine a firm's share price. Their use is analogous to that of P/E and PEG. For example, if a new Internet service provider (ISP) is going public and we know of other ISPs that recently went public, we can estimate its value by comparing its margins, market share, or revenue share growth rate to that of the proxy firms.

Business Model Component Attribute Measures

Where margins, market share, and revenue share growth rates are not available, we could use measures of those business model component attribute measures that drive them (Figure 8.2). In valuing an ISP, for example, these

FIGURE 8.2
Profits/Cash Flow
Chain of an ISP

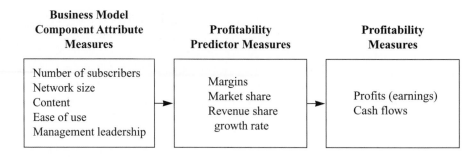

Business Model Component Attribute Measures	Profitability Predictor Measures	Profitability Measures
Number of subscribers Network size Content Ease of use Management leadership	Margins Market share Revenue share growth rate	Profits (earnings) Cash flows

measures are the number of subscribers, network size, amount and quality of content available, ease of use of system, and management talent. For a biotechnology start-up, for example, the number of patents that the firm owns or the number of staff scientists with Ph.D.s would be a good metric.

Implications of Market Value for Financing and Investment Strategies

The primary indication of the bursting of the dot.com boom was the crash in market valuations that became very visible in the Spring of 2000. One question that was on the minds of many investors who lost money in the burst and of many financial analysts as well was, How can one tell when a firm is overvalued? One answer is to compare the P/E ratios of the firms in question to the historical P/E ratios of firms in the same industry. PEG ratios can also be compared. In this section, we describe another method of estimating whether a stock is overvalued.

Recall from (1) that a firm's market valuation, V, is given by

$$V = \sum_{t=0}^{t=n} \frac{C_t}{(1 + r_k)^t}$$

If we assume that after n years the firm in question will start receiving constant cash flows C_f, then (1) reduces to

$$V = \frac{C_f}{r_k(1 + r_k)^n} \qquad \textbf{(4)}$$

If we assume that the constant cash flows start in the present year so that $n = 0$, (4) reduces to

$$V = \frac{C_f}{r_k} \qquad \textbf{(5)}$$

Using expressions (4) and (5), one can obtain useful information on how overvalued or undervalued a firm's stocks are. Such information can help individuals in their decisions to invest in a firm. It can also provide more information for firms to use in their decisions to use their market valuations to purchase other companies.

Example   At one point in early 2000, Cisco's market capitalization (market value) was about $500 billion. Some analysts expected the company to earn about $4 billion on sales of $17 billion and about 3.7 billion shares outstanding. Given this information, would you have invested in Cisco in early 2000? Assume that in 2000 you expected to earn 20 percent in stocks that you invested in.

From (5)

$$\$500 \text{ billion} = \frac{C_f}{r_k} = \frac{C_f}{0.20}, \text{ assuming that the cost of capital is 20 percent}$$

$$C_f = \$100 \text{ billion}$$

This suggests that in the future, you should expect Cisco to have steady positive cash flows of $100 billion (at least that much in profits). The $100 billion number is astronomical given that Cisco's 2000 profits were expected to be only $4 billion. Not that many companies have revenues of $100 billion, let alone that much in profits or positive cash flows. This suggests that Cisco may have been overvalued. A firm that knows that it is overvalued can use its stock valuation as currency to make acquisitions. Investors might want to be a little more cautious when purchasing the stocks of such companies.

INTELLECTUAL CAPITAL: VALUING THE PARTS

If a firm with three major product lines were to be broken up, one could value each product line because it is possible to estimate earnings and free cash flows from each. Now suppose a key individual threatened to leave a start-up company. What is his or her worth to the company? How much are a firm's client network, repeat customers, patents, and copyrights worth? Valuation of such "assets" can be problematic even for firms that have gone public and have stable cash flows and earnings. Valuing such intangibles is becoming increasingly important, especially in a knowledge economy, and has led to the term *intellectual capital,* which we will define soon. For the moment, however, consider the simple but useful balance sheet equation:

$$\text{Assets} = \text{Liabilities} + \text{Shareholder equity}$$

Whence:

$$\text{Assets} - \text{Liabilities} = \text{Book value} = \text{Shareholder equity} \quad \textbf{(6)}$$

One way to interpret this equation is if a firm were to close its doors to business, then what is left over to pay shareholders is the assets less liabilities—the **book value.** Prior to the decision to close its doors, however, what shareholders would get from the company if they were to sell their shares would be the **market value** of the firm (shares outstanding multiplied by share price). This suggests that market value ought to be close to book value. Table 8.1, however, indicates otherwise. Look at Microsoft. In 1994 its book value was $4.45

TABLE 8.1   **Sample Book and Market Values**

| Firm | March 15, 1994 | | March 15, 1997 | | March 15, 1999 | |
| | Book Value | Market Value | Book Value | Market Value | Book Value | Market Value |
	($ million)	($ million)	($ million)	($ million)	($ million)	($ million)
Intel	$ 9,267	$35,172	$19,295	$125,741	$23,371	$196,616
Microsoft	4,450	41,339	10,777	199,046	16,627	418,579
General Motors	12,823	33,188	17,506	54,243	14,984	63,839
General Electric	26,387	92,321	34,438	260,147	38,880	360,251
Cisco			4,289	64,568	7,106	166,616
Dell			1,293	41,294	2,321	111,322

billion while its market value was $41.34 billion, or almost 10 times as much. In 1997 Microsoft's book value was $10.77 billion and its market value $199 billion, almost 20 times as much. Compare this to General Motors 1997 book value of $18 billion and market value of $54 billion. In 1999 Microsoft's market value was about 25 times its book value. While the differences in other firms' book and market values are not as astounding as Microsoft's, they are still very large.

The differences between book value and market value suggest that there is something else about each of these firms, other than the assets on their books, that makes investors believe that they will keep generating free cash flows or earnings. Why is it important to understand this difference? Because managers would like to know how to manage it, given its enormous significance. This difference has been called **intellectual capital** and has been attributed to several factors: (1) underpriced physical assets or intangible assets such as patents, trade secrets, and trademarks; (2) human capital—the people who must turn assets, underpriced or otherwise, into products or services that customers want;[7] (3) the product market positions that firms chose in industries that are, by their nature, more profitable than others; (4) unique resources or capabilities that are difficult to imitate or substitute, the source of the enduring advantage that allows firms to keep earning profits; and (5) knowledge, whether embedded in employees, encoded in some physical form, or resident in organizational routines that firms use to offer better value to their customers than competitors.[8] Such knowledge gives a firm a sustainable competitive advantage so long as it is difficult to copy, replicate, or substitute.[9]

Components of Intellectual Capital

We can distinguish between three components of intellectual capital: intellectual property, human capital, and organizational capital.[10] All three are a function of where knowledge resides and of how it can be converted into customer value. Understanding these components and their contribution to the market value of a firm may enable us to determine the worth of, say, human capital and therefore the worth of key individuals within a firm.

Intellectual Property

The **intellectual property** component refers to codified knowledge in a form that enables a company to claim ownership, including patents, copyrights, trademarks, brand names, databases, microcodes, engineering drawings, contracts, trade secrets, documents, and semiconductor masks, as well as intangibles such as reputation, network size, installed base, client relationships, and special licenses.[11] These are the "havings" since they are things that a firm *has* opposed to the things that it *does*.[12] The extent to which intellectual properties are protectable, difficult to replicate, or substitute determines the extent to which firms can profit from any products or services that rest on them.

Human Capital

Intellectual property, in and of itself, will not give a firm a competitive advantage. It also takes employees with the skills, know-how, experience, and competencies to build intellectual property or use it to deliver value to customers.[13] It also takes **human capital** which is the specialist knowledge that is resident in employees. A top-notch scientist's knowledge of combinatorial chemistry is an example. Human capital is what Richard Hall calls the "doing" since it refers to the ability to perform value-adding activities—the ability to get things done.[14]

Organizational Capital

Intellectual property and human capital, in and of themselves, may not be sufficient to give their owners a competitive advantage. For example, a cache of patents and Nobel laureates alone is not likely to give a firm a competitive advantage. Factors internal and external to a firm allow firms to turn their intellectual property and human capital into customer value and to cultivate more intellectual property. For lack of a better name, we will call these factors **organizational capital**.[15] Internal to a firm, the factors of organizational capital are the firm's structure, systems, strategy, people, and culture that it uses to create, share, coordinate, and integrate the knowledge and skills embodied in individual employees to make intellectual property and to convert the intellectual property into products that customers want.[16] A project structure, for example, is more conducive to tasks of short duration in environments that are not fast moving while, in some industries, projects with "heavyweight" project managers perform better than those without. Still, in other industries, the culture that firms have cultivated—the "system of shared values (what is important) and beliefs (how things work) that interact with the organization's people, organizational structures, and systems to produce behavioral norms (the way we do things around here)"—can be a source of competitive advantage.[17] Sometimes, factors external to the firm are also critical to the ability of firms to innovate. For example, firms in a region with a system that provides financial support and rewards for innovation, a culture that tolerates failure, the right suppliers, customers, complementors, competitors, universities and other research institutions, and supportive government policies are conducive to the creation of intellectual property and their conversion into new products.[18]

FINANCING A START-UP

A firm has several instruments for financing entrepreneurial activity: Internal assets in which the firm reallocates the resources it already has to the entrepreneurial activity; equity financing in which the firm issues equity to venture capital firms, private individuals, or the public in return for financing; debt in which the firm issues some form of debt; and complementary asset financing in which a firm reaches out for complementary assets through a strategic alliance or an acquisition.[19] The balance sheet relation in Figure 8.3 shows the relationships between the financing instruments.

Internal Sources: Assets and Activity

A firm has several internal sources to which it can turn for financing an entrepreneurial activity. First, a firm can use its retained earnings. As shown in Figure 8.3, retained earnings come from the profits that a firm makes, net of any dividends that the firm pays out to shareholders. Thus, a very profitable firm does not have to seek outside financing.[20] Second, a firm can use existing assets, originally earmarked for another project, for the innovation. Chrysler's need for outside financing of its blockbuster minivan was reduced because it already had a front-wheel-drive engine and transmission—critical components in the minivan—that it used in its Dodge Omni and Plymouth Horizon cars.[21] Entrepreneurs often use personal assets. Hewlett Packard and Apple began in garages in the Silicon Valley.

Equity

To finance its activities, a firm can issue equity; that is, through **equity financing,** a firm can sell shares of the company to investors in return for money that the firm needs. Figure 8.4 provides some elements of the equity market. Equity can be issued to the public through a stock exchange such as the NASDAQ (National Association of Securities Dealers Automated Quotations) or the London Stock Exchange. The issue can take the form of an initial public offering (IPO) in which, for the first time, a firm offers its shares to the public for purchase. For many Internet start-ups in the late 1990s, this was one of the most popular sources of financing.

For many start-ups whose products have not yet been proven, the most likely buyers of their equity are private equity firms. Private equity can be venture or nonventure. **Venture equity** is issued by start-ups in the early or later stages of their start-up cycle. In return for part ownership in the start-up, a venture capital firm or other financier will finance the start-up. Their primary motivation is to cash in during the IPO which will eventually come

FIGURE 8.3   **Sources of Financing: The Balance Sheet Context**

Source: Reprinted from *Innovation Management: Strategies, Implementation, and Profits* (New York: Oxford University Press, 1998), p. 200.

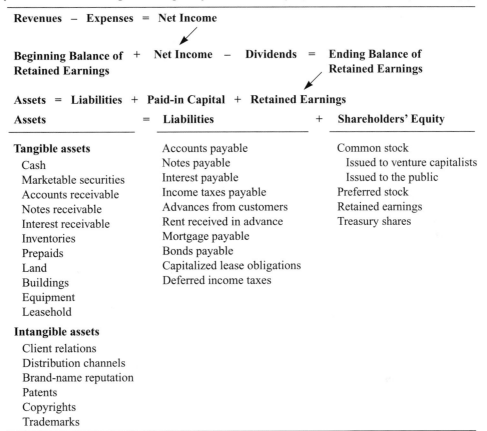

Revenues – Expenses = Net Income

Beginning Balance of + Net Income – Dividends = Ending Balance of
Retained Earnings   Retained Earnings

Assets = Liabilities + Paid-in Capital + Retained Earnings

Assets	=	Liabilities	+	Shareholders' Equity
Tangible assets		Accounts payable		Common stock
Cash		Notes payable		Issued to venture capitalists
Marketable securities		Interest payable		Issued to the public
Accounts receivable		Income taxes payable		Preferred stock
Notes receivable		Advances from customers		Retained earnings
Interest receivable		Rent received in advance		Treasury shares
Inventories		Mortgage payable		
Prepaids		Bonds payable		
Land		Capitalized lease obligations		
Buildings		Deferred income taxes		
Equipment				
Leasehold				
Intangible assets				
Client relations				
Distribution channels				
Brand-name reputation				
Patents				
Copyrights				
Trademarks				

after the start-up has proven itself dynamic enough to go public. In addition to providing the much-needed money, venture capital firms can also offer management expertise which can be critical for a start-up. Some venture capital firms have networks of firms in which they have stakes, and such firms can become the start-up's first customer or supplier. Such intangibles are often critical in the life of a start-up. One major drawback to obtaining venture capital is that the start-up firm often loses control of a large part of the company to the venture capital firm. The money that venture capital firms use to finance ventures can be their own or that of limited partners. In the United States, venture capital can also come from small business investment companies (SBICs). These are private corporations that have been licensed by the Small Business Administration to provide financing to risky companies. To encourage them to undertake these risky loans, the federal government gives SBICs tax breaks and Small Business Administration (SBA) loans.

FIGURE 8.4   **Different Elements of Equity**

Source: Reprinted from *Innovation Management: Strategies, Implementation, and Profits* (New York: Oxford University Press, 1998), p. 202.

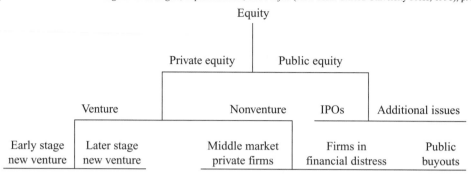

Major players
- Venture capital firms such as
  Kleiner, Perkins, Caufield, and
  Byers; and Asset Management
- SBICs

Source of funds for major players
- Own money
- "Angels"
- Partnerships

Major players
- Buyout groups such as Kohlberg,
  Kravis, Roberts

Source of funds for major players
- Partnerships

Debt

A firm can also borrow money from a money-lending institution such as a bank, or sell bonds or notes; that is, it can acquire debt. The problem with **debt financing** is that the financier usually wants some physical assets as collateral—something that most start-ups usually do not have. Their assets are often intangible, largely intellectual capital, which may not be enough collateral for some banks. The drawback in borrowing is that interest payments may drain off profits that could have been plugged back into the business or paid out as dividends to investors. If a start-up does issue debt, sometimes the debt is convertible to equity.

A smart form of debt financing for start-ups is the one undertaken by Amazon.com, which we described earlier in our discussion of cash flows. Recall that the firm collected from its customers right away but did not pay its vendors until 30 to 45 days later. During that time, it used the money that it owed its vendors to finance its activities. This is sometimes called **working capital financing.**

Complementary Assets

As we saw in Chapter 5, complementary assets are critical to profiting from an innovation. Unfortunately, most start-up firms lack these assets. We also said that some complementary assets are difficult to replicate or substitute. For example, it is very difficult for a fledgling Web advertising firm to replicate the kinds of relationships that bricks-and-mortar advertising firms have had for decades with Fortune 500 clients. Money from a venture capital firm or bank may not be able to buy such relations right away. An alternative is to enter some form of strategic alliance with an owner of the complementary assets, buy that owner, or sell your firm to the owner.

Summary

Firms are in business to make money. But to make money, they often need money up front to get going. Thus, a firm has two finance-related problems: How to find and use the money that it needs, and how to cash out. An entrepreneur can collect the money from the free cash flows of his or her business over the life of the business or sell the right to collect some of the future free cash flows to venture capitalists, angels, or to the public through an initial public offering (IPO). In either case, the business must be valued so that the financier can know the value of his or her investment. Many methods have been used to value firms: free cash flow, price-earnings (P/E) ratios, price-earnings growth (PEG) ratios, and the business model. Valuing Internet start-ups is particularly troublesome because most of them have neither positive free cash flows nor positive earnings. In such a case, proxies together with predictors of earnings and cash flows such as profit margins, market share, and revenue share growth rate can be used to value a firm. Beyond that, measurable business model component attributes can be used.

There are several sources of financing for a start-up: a firm's own assets, venture capital, debt, IPO, and some form of teaming up with a firm that has complementary assets. The most important thing about financing a start-up is that money purchased with the lowest interest rate is not always the best money because start-ups usually need important complementary assets that are difficult to acquire or substitute. And teaming up with another firm that has such assets or selling an equity share to a venture capital firm may be the best way to get access to such assets.

Key Terms

book value, *151*
capital asset pricing
    model (CAPM), *146*
cooling off period, *143*
debt financing, *156*
discount rate, *146*
equity financing, *154*
free cash flow, *145*
human capital, *153*
initial public offering
    (IPO), *143*
intellectual capital, *152*

intellectual
    property, *153*
investment bank, *143*
market value, *151*
organizational
    capital, *153*
present value, *145*
price-earnings growth
    (PEG) ratio, *148*
price-earnings (P/E)
    ratio, *147*

profitability predictor
    measures, *149*
public offering
    price, *144*
risk premium, *146*
systematic risk, *146*
venture equity, *154*
working capital, *146*
working capital
    financing, *156*

Discussion Questions

1. What is the difference between earnings and cash flows? Can an unprofitable firm have positive free cash flows?
2. What are the drawbacks of using P/E and PEG ratios to value firms?
3. Why is negative working capital a good thing?
4. Why might a firm that is still unprofitable have a very high market value? How would you value such a firm?
5. When might a start-up give up an interest-free loan from a bank and take venture capital money even though the owners of the start-up may lose the control of and equity in their firm?

Notes

1. See, for example, S. C. Blowers, P. H. Griffith, and T. L. Milan, *The Ernst & Young Guide to the IPO Value Journey* (New York: John Wiley, 1999).
2. www.internetnews.com/stocks/ipodex/.
3. See, for example, R. A. Brealey and S. C. Myers, *Principles of Corporate Finance* (New York: McGraw-Hill, 1995).
4. See, for example, C. P. Stickney and R. L. Weil, *Financial Accounting,* 7th ed. (New York: Dryden, 1994); W. Petty, "Harvesting," in *The Portable MBA in Entrepreneurship,* ed. by W. D. Bygrave (New York: John Wiley, 1997), pp. 414–41.
5. In the United States, however, franchise laws do not permit direct sales of cars to customers.
6. M. J. Dollinger, *Entrepreneurship: Strategies and Resources* (Burr Ridge, IL: Richard D. Irwin, 1995).
7. D. Ulrich, "Intellectual Capital = Competence × Commitment," *Sloan Management Review* 39, no. 2 (1998), pp. 15–27.
8. L. Edvinsson and P. Sullivan, "Developing a Model for Managing Intellectual Capital," *European Management Journal* 14, no. 4 (August 1996), p. 356; I. Nonaka, "A Dynamic Theory of Organizational Knowledge Creation," *Organization Science* 5, no. 1 pp. 477–501; T. A. Stewart, *Intellectual Capital: The New Wealth of Organizations* (New York: Currency/Doubleday, 1997).
9. M. A. Peteraf, "The Cornerstones of Competitive Advantage: A Resource-based View," *Strategic Management Journal* 14 (1993), pp. 179–91.
10. Edvinsson and Sullivan, "Developing a Model for Managing Intellectual Capital," p. 356; H. Saint-Onge, "Tacit Knowledge: The Key to the Strategic Alignment of Intellectual Capital," *Strategy and Leadership* 2 (March–April 1996), p. 1014.
11. Edvinsson and Sullivan, "Developing a Model for Managing Intellectual Capital," p. 356.
12. R. Hall, "A Framework Linking Intangible Resources and Capabilities to Sustainable Competitive Advantage," *Strategic Management Journal* 14 (1993), pp. 607–18.
13. C. K. Prahalad and G. Hamel, "The Core Competencies of the Corporation," *Harvard Business Review,* May–June 1990, pp. 79–91.

14. Hall, "A Framework," pp. 607–18.
15. In Edvinsson and Sullivan's (1996) and Saint-Onge's (1996) taxonomy, structural capital includes both organizational capital and human capital.
16. Saint-Onge, "Tacit Knowledge," p. 1014.
17. B. Uttal and J. Fierman, "The Corporate Culture Vultures," *Fortune,* October 17, 1983; J. Barney, "Organizational Culture: Can It Be a Source of Sustained Competitive Advantage?" *Academy of Management Review* 11 (1986), pp. 656–65.
18. This draws on A. N. Afuah, *Innovation Management, Strategies, Implementation, and Profits* (New York: Oxford University Press, 1998), chap. 12.
19. Ibid., chap. 10.
20. The type of financing that is best for a firm and how the firm should go about obtaining that financing are very important topics in corporate finance. See, for example, Brealey and Myers, *Principles of Corporate Finance.*
21. A. Taylor III, and J. E. Davis, "Iacocca's Minivan: How Chrysler Succeeded in Creating the Most Profitable Products of the Decade," *Fortune,* May 30, 1994, pp. 56–63.

Chapter **Nine**

Appraisal of Business Models

Given the central role that business models play in firm performance, it is important to be able to understand how one business model compares with another. Such an appraisal is important for several reasons. First, when making choices about components and linkages of a business model, a firm needs to be able to determine which business model alternatives are best. Second, a good analysis of competitors ought to include a comparison of business models; such a comparison needs some way of appraising business models. In this chapter, we explore the appraisal of business models. We explore how one can tell if one business model is better than another. Our discussion is divided into three sections. First, we present the elements of such an appraisal. Second, we present the case of Juniper Networks. Finally, we appraise Juniper Networks' business model.

ELEMENTS OF APPRAISING BUSINESS MODELS

When we explored the pricing component of a business model in Chapter 4, we encountered the following simple but useful equation:

$$\text{Profits} = \Pi = (P - V_c)Q - F_c$$

where
P is the price per unit of the product,
V_c is the per unit variable cost,
Q is the total number of units sold, and
F_c is the up-front or fixed costs.

From this relation, we said that profit margins, market share, and revenue growth were good predictors of profits. These in turn were driven by the components and linkages of a business model. This suggests that we can measure how good a business model is at three levels: measures of profitability, profitability prediction, and business model component attributes (see Table 9.1).

TABLE 9.1 **Business Model Appraisal Levels**

	Profitability measures
Level 1	• Earnings • Cash flow
	Profitability predictor measures
Level 2	• Margins • Market share • Revenue share growth rate
	Component attribute measures
Level 3	• Positioning • Value • Scope • Price • Revenue • Activities • Implementation • Capabilities • Sustainability • Cost structure

Profitability Measures

The raison d'être of a business model is to make money, so what better way to measure how good a business model is than to compare its profitability to that of its competitors. Any one of many **profitability measures** can be used. Here we use *earnings* and *cash flows* because analysts use them most frequently in valuing businesses. If a firm's earnings or cash flows are better than those of competitors, we say that it has a competitive advantage. This suggests that the firm has a good business model. The problem with using profitability as a measure of the soundness of a business model is that many businesses with solid business models, especially start-ups, are not profitable even though down the line they might become very profitable. Moreover, a business that is profitable today may have a poor business model whose effects are still trickling down the profit chain. These two reasons suggest that we need to find a more reliable measure.

Profitability Predictor Measures

As we saw in Chapter 4, profit margins, revenue market share, and revenue growth rate are good **profitability predictor measures** for knowledge-based products, and we can use them to appraise Internet business models. The procedure is to compare a firm's profit margins, revenue market share, and revenue growth rate with those of industry competitors. Again, a firm has a competitive advantage if it scores higher in these measures than do industry competitors.

Since these profitability predictor measures rest on the components of a business model and the linkages between them, there may be things about the model that have not trickled down the chain to profit margins, market share, and revenue growth rate. We next turn to the components of a business model.

Business Model Component Measures

While not as objective or as easily available as the measures of the first two levels of Table 9.1, **business model component measures** get to the source itself: the business model. Table 9.2 provides some benchmark questions that can be used to appraise each component.

Positioning

When we explored the components of a business model, we argued that the profit site in which a firm locates plays an important role in the profitability of the firm. Firms that locate in an unattractive site, for example, are less likely to be as profitable as those that locate in a more attractive site. We also argued that a profit site's attractiveness influences the customer value that it offers, the customer segment that it pursues, the prices that it charges, its sources of revenues, the activities that it chooses to perform, its capabilities, how it implements its business model, how sustainable its business model is, and its cost structure. For example, suppliers with bargaining power can force firms to accept lower-quality inputs. Accepting lower-quality inputs can reduce the level of customer value that firms can offer, increase their cost, or erode their brand-name reputation. Suppliers with bargaining power can also force industry firms to pay higher prices for the inputs that they buy from these suppliers. Paying more for inputs increases costs and may influence the activities that firms perform in their efforts to lower cost.

Appraising a firm's positioning in a profit site, then, consists of determining the forces that are exerted on profit site firms. Effectively, it consists of determining Porter's competitive forces for the profit site. Where the forces—bargaining power of suppliers, bargaining power of customers, power of substitutes, potential new entry, power of complementors, and rivalry—are high, positioning in Table 9.2 gets an L. Note that we have used an L when the forces are high because low forces mean an attractive site and an attractive site means higher profitability. Where they are low, positioning gets an H.

Customer Value

When customers buy a product, they do so because they value something in it. As we saw in Chapter 4, this value could be in product features such as location and the timing of the product's delivery. For a portal, value could be in the number of subscribers, repeat clients, unique visitors, or page views. For a manufacturer of cholesterol drugs, value could be in how much its drugs reduce high cholesterol levels. The first question (see Table 9.2) that a firm should be asking itself is, Is the firm's customer value distinct from that of competitors? If not, Is the firm's level of value higher than that of competitors? If the answer is yes, an H for "high" can be placed in the "rank" column. If the

TABLE 9.2   **Appraising a Business Model: Component Measures**

Component of Business Model	Benchmark Questions	Rank
Positioning	What are the competitive forces from: • Rivalry • Customers • Complementors • Suppliers • Potential new entry • Substitutes	H/L
Customer value	• Is customer value distinct from that of competitors? If not, is the firm's level of the value higher than that of competitors? • Is the firm's rate of increase in customer value high relative to that of competitors?	H/L
Scope	• Is the growth rate of market segments high? • Is the firm's market share in each segment high relative to that of competitors'? • Is potential erosion of products high? If so, in what segments?	H/L
Price	• Is the quality-adjusted price low?	H/L
Revenue source	• Are margins and market share in each revenue source high? • Are margins and market share in each revenue source increasing? • Is the firm's value in each source of revenue distinctive? If not, is the level of value higher than that of competitors?	H/L
Connected activities	What is the extent to which activities: • Are consistent with customer value and scope? • Reinforce each other? • Take advantage of industry success drivers? • Are consistent with the firm's distinctive capabilities? • Make the industry more attractive for the firm?	H/L
Implementation	• Is the quality of the team high?	H/L
Capabilities	To what extent are the firm's capabilities: • Distinctive? • Nonimitable? • Extendible to other product markets?	H/L
Sustainability	• Has the firm been able to maintain or extend its lead in its industry?	H/L
Cost structure	What is its cost structure relative to strategic competitors': • Cost per revenue dollar? • Cost per unit of customer value?	H/L

answer is no, an L for "low" can be placed in the "rank" column. The next question—Is the firm's rate of increase high in customer value relative to that of competitors?—addresses the issue that while a firm's value may be higher or more distinct than that of the competition, the firm should be worried if competitors are closing the gap. Such a threat might come from a competitor's new strategies or a technological change that allows competitors to catch up or leapfrog a firm. A ranking of H means the firm is increasing its lead or competitors are not catching up.

Scope

Recall from Chapter 4 that *scope* refers to the market segments to which a firm offers customer value and the range of products that contain the value. Here we appraise a firm's strength in each market segment and in each product that embodies the value. The first question—Is the growth rate of market segments high?—tells us how the segment itself is doing. But we also want to know how well the firm itself is doing in each segment relative to its competitors. Hence the question: Is the firm's market share in each segment high relative to that of competitors? Finally, the firm may want to know how well each product is doing in each segment, particularly if the products are threatened by new products in competitors' pipelines. The answers to these questions tell us how much pressure is being exerted on the firm in each of its market segments. An overall ranking of H indicates that the products embodying value and the market segments served are doing well, suggesting that the firm's choices in the scope element of its business model are good.

Price

If a firm offers its customers something distinctive or a higher level of value, the question is, How much is the firm charging for it? What is the value for the customer's dollar? What is the bang for the buck? How much does a patient pay for a 1 percent drop in bad cholesterol? The less a firm charges per unit of value, the more difficult it is for other firms to take away its market share. A high value per dollar may also be an indication of customer bargaining power or pressure from potential new entrants or rivals.

Revenue Sources

The questions to be asked in this component are (1) Are the market share and margins in each revenue source high? (2) More importantly, are the market shares and margins increasing at each revenue source? If the competitive forces in a market are high, the margins may be decreasing. This was the case in 1999, for example, with online brokerage firms where the margins for brokerage fees were dropping. (3) Is the firm's value in each revenue source distinctive? If not, is the level of it higher than that of competitors? The third question addresses the matter that high and even growing margins may be determined by a firm's bargaining power and may hide the actual decline in value of the firm's products/services. Again, if all the answers in the revenue sources category are yes, place an H in column 3. This is an indication of the strength of the firm in each revenue source.

Answers to the remaining business model elements are more qualitative than quantitative but nonetheless are very important.

Connected Activities

Recall from Chapter 4 the following questions for connected activities. Are the activities consistent with customer value and scope? Do they reinforce each other? Do they take advantage of industry success drivers? Are they consistent with a firm's distinctive capabilities? Do they make the industry more attractive for the firm? If the answers to these questions are yes, column 3 gets an H, indicating a sound strategy.

Implementation

Implementation is critical to the success of a business model. Unfortunately, much less research has been done on what constitutes good or bad implementation than on the other components of a business model. In any case, the idea is to get a feel for the extent to which a firm's strategy, structure, systems, people, and environment fit. One measure of the likelihood of good execution is the type of people on the team. The rationale is that people are central to everything, especially at a start-up firm. The right people can structure the organization well and set up the right systems to implement the business model. In deciding whether to invest in a venture, venture capital firms usually put a lot of emphasis on the quality of the team members who are going to carry out the business model. The quality of the team is measured not only by the quality of individuals within the team, but also by how much the skills of individuals complement each other. The quality of each individual is measured by his or her relevant knowledge and a number of intangibles such as enthusiasm.

Capabilities

If a firm's value to customers rests on its capabilities, then the extent to which competitors can replicate this value is determined by how easy it is to duplicate or substitute capabilities. The ease of doing this can be determined by answers to the questions: Are the capabilities distinctive? Inimitable? As Prahalad and Hamel pointed out that another desirable characteristic of capabilities is **extendibility**—the degree to which those capabilities can be used to offer other products.[1] Thus, another question is, Are capabilities extendible to other product markets? If the answer to these questions is yes, place an H in column 3.

Sustainability

Appraising sustainability entails a determination of the extent to which a firm's block, run, or team-up strategies work. If the firm opts for a block strategy, then the appraisal process focuses on determining what is inherent in the firm and its competitors that will make *blocking* work. For example, does the firm have many patents, copyrights, and trade secrets that are difficult to imitate or substitute? If the run strategy is used, the firm must then ask whether it has what it takes to run. For example, does it have the personnel and financing to keep innovating? Can it afford to reinvent itself? If the firm relies on teaming up, then it must determine what it can bring to the table in teaming up and how much complementarity its partners have. Also, what kinds of partners does it attract? If the ingredients exist for making the firm's strategy work, sustainability gets an H rank.

Cost Structure

Recall that a firm's cost structure is the relationship between its revenues and the underlying costs of generating the revenues. The lower the costs per dollar of sales, the better off a firm is. High revenues can also be a result of market power—a result of the fact that a firm has bargaining power over customers and can charge higher prices than it would if it were a price taker. Moreover, a firm with very low costs may decide to pass on its cost savings to customers by charging very low prices for its products or services. Such a firm may have a very low revenue-to-cost ratio. This should not be mistaken for a high cost structure. Therefore, in comparing cost structures, it may also be valuable to measure the cost per unit of customer value offered. Appraising a cost structure therefore consists of measuring the cost per revenue dollar relative to rivals' and the cost per unit of customer value offered relative to competitors'. If both are lower than competitors', column 3 gets an H. If both are higher than comeptitors', column 3 gets an L.

If column 3 of Table 9.2 has many highs, the business model is strong. If it has many lows, the model is weak. This is important information for the development of strategy and the business model.

Important!

Often the most important thing to take away from the appraisal of an Internet business model is not so much that the business model is strong or weak, but to identify *why* it is strong or weak. In this way, the strong components and links in the model can be reinforced and the weak ones strengthened. In competitor analysis, the important thing is not so much to find out whether competitors have a stronger or weaker business model, as to find out *where* and *why* they are stronger or weaker.

THE CASE OF JUNIPER NETWORKS*

Following the Spring 2000 dot.com crash, Juniper Networks' management and many of its shareholders faced an interesting question: How could Juniper sustain its profitability and phenomenal growth in the face of intensifying competition and changing market conditions?

*This case was prepared by Todd Bottger, Brad Carmody, Peter Lyons, Drew O'Malley, Ben Resnick, and Brandon Schmidt under the supervision of Professor Allan Afuah. © 2000 Allan Afuah.

The Networking Industry

The networking industry, broadly defined as networking equipment, supplies, and support products and services, experienced spectacular growth from 1990 to 2000. Fueled by the growing acceptance of the Internet, players in the industry enjoyed a rapidly expanding market. The market saw growth in almost all segments.[2]

Routers and Router Markets

At the heart of the expanding networking industry is the router. Routers are the Internet's "traffic cops," directing traffic from one network to another as packets of information travel through the interconnected router-serviced networks (Figure 9.1). Routers have two main purposes: to determine the most efficient route to direct data (in the form of data packets) over a network and to forward the data packets along this route to the next router. To perform these functions, the routers use data tables to look up information on all of its "peer" routers (the other routers that this particular router can communicate with) using standardized routing protocols. These routing protocols, determined by an international standards body called the Internet Engineering Taskforce (IETF), allows for interoperability and the sharing of information among the routers so that the routers can adjust to changing conditions. Without these protocols, routing decisions would be made at the beginning of the path and could not be

FIGURE 9.1   Relationship between Enterprise and Carrier-Class Routers

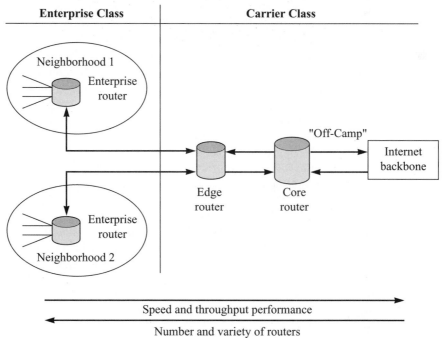

changed during the journey to the end destination. Once the router has determined the appropriate path, it forwards the data packets to the next router.

The market for these important devices can be divided into two primary customer segments, enterprise and carrier.

The enterprise routers are dedicated to a particular organization's network. The enterprise router can direct traffic within an organization's local area network (LAN), within an organization's wide area network (WAN), and/or provide access to the Internet by coordinating traffic between a LAN or WAN and the organization's network service providers that connect them to the Internet. Given the diverse nature and size of customers and applications in this market, the enterprise class of routers includes a very broad array of different functionalities and performance levels. In 2000, Cisco Systems controlled 66 percent of the estimated $10 billion enterprise router market.[3]

Carrier-class routers direct traffic over the interconnected networks that make up the Internet. These can be divided into core and edge subsegments. Edge devices are the aggregators and local access boxes that serve ISPs, Web hosting companies, data centers, and local exchanges. Additionally, edge devices are used by carrier facilities to direct traffic into and out of the backbone. Core boxes take electrical traffic aggregated by edge routing devices and run that traffic through to the primarily optical Internet backbone. By comparison, edge routers are more numerous and variable in their specific functionality than core routers, which are specialized and built with primarily throughput and speed in mind.

As illustrated in Figure 9.2, one can look at the entire Internet as a hypothetical road system made up of neighborhoods, major thoroughfares, and interstates. Enterprise routers are the traffic lights directing traffic within local neighborhoods for consumers, corporations, and other organizations. Edge devices are traffic lights on the major thoroughfares running to the interstate highway systems from those neighborhoods. The core routers are traffic lights leading traffic onto the on-ramps and off-ramps of the interstate highway. The interstate highway in this case is made up of the primarily optical fiber "backbone" networks that connect major access points, normally over long distances or between major metropolitan areas. These backbone networks (interstate highways) are controlled by a relatively few number of carriers. Between 2000 and 2003, the total market for carrier-class routers was expected to increase 208 percent to $23.7 billion for edge routers and increase 53 percent to $15.8 billion for core routers.[4]

Key Router Attributes

As outlined above, extremely high-end, core router functionality is needed by only a few very large-scale backbone ISPs or carriers. This need is driven by rapidly expanding demand. For example, UUNet's annual traffic growth is 800 percent. Furthermore, industry analysts anticipate traffic growing from 0.47 terabits (trillions of bits) per second per month to 2,200 terabits per second per month between 2000 and 2004.[5] Considering the rapid expansion of

FIGURE 9.2   **Basic Deployment of Enterprise, Edge, and Core Routers**

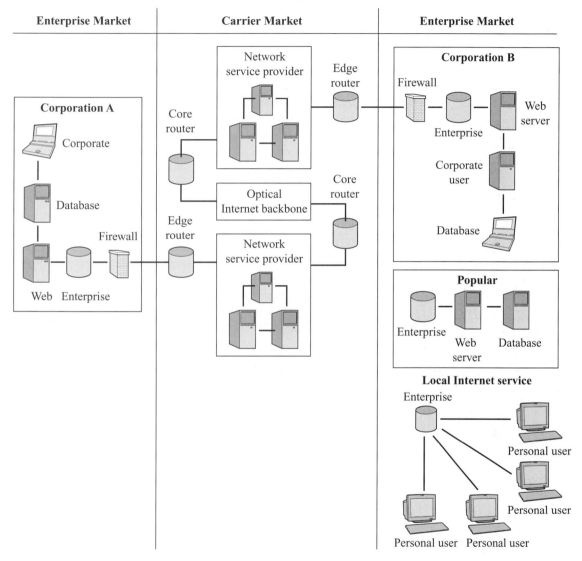

traffic over the Internet and the increasing deployment of optical fiber on the backbone, core router performance has not kept up with traffic demand and, hence, has become a source of congestion on the Internet road system.[6] With traffic growing exponentially while router performance grows by a factor of four every 18 to 24 months, demand for core routers should continue to explode.[7] In turn, as core traffic grows, edge traffic grows, so older core routers rotate into an edge role as new, faster core routers are introduced.

Because of these rapid changes in traffic characteristics and progression of core devices to the edge, the life cycle of a core device has decreased to 16 to 24 months.

In addition to speed, the performance uptime (time not down due to technical difficulties) is a critical core router attribute. The uptime necessary to satisfy carrier-class customers is based on "telco-grade" performance requirements for switching systems. One primary feature of uptime in these high-performance systems is the ability to service the hardware and/or upgrade the software without shutting down the unit (this is called "hot-swapping"). These stringent requirements force 12- to 18-month testing periods by carrier customers before actual deployment into their networks. Once the initial testing is complete for core routers, edge devices see the benefit of significantly reduced trial periods for similar technologies, whereby testing is reduced to approximately 2 months.[8] Thus, suppliers of core devices find it easier to introduce edge devices to the same customers once their core devices have been approved.

For enterprise customers, the primary needs are considerably different. Enterprise IT capital expenditures are driven by cost and customer service considerations. Access to service and support for installation, configuration, and long-term management are important features. In practice, networking equipment companies with specific product lines often have cooperative marketing agreements to broaden product and service offerings to compete with Cisco's one-stop shop advantage.

Juniper Networks' Company History

The seeds of Juniper Networks were planted in 1995 when the burnt-out principal scientist of Xerox's Palo Alto Research Center, Pradeep Sindhu, quit Xerox, headed for the south of France, and returned with an idea to capitalize on the exploding market for the networking technology underlying the Internet.[9]

Upon securing some initial seed money from Kleiner Perkins Caufield & Byers,[10] Sindhu moved rapidly to bring in the top minds in the industry to cofound Juniper—Bjorn Liencres, a leading server architect from Sun Microsystems, and Dennis Ferguson, a networking designer from MCI Communications.[11] After officially establishing the company in February 1996 with $2 million in first-round financing, Sindhu recognized the need to bring in an experienced hand to help the company develop its strategy and business model. Forty-year-old Scott Kriens, former vice president of data-switch maker StrataCom, was hired in April 1996 as CEO of Juniper Networks; this allowed Sindhu to assume the mantle of chief technology officer.

Juniper's Corporate Strategy

Juniper's mission was simple—build high-end equipment to route traffic across the largest Internet backbones.[12] By focusing on the large phone companies and carrier-class ISPs that handle the bulk of Internet traffic (a strategy Kriens would later call "survival of the focused"[13]), Juniper could to some degree avoid directly competing with routing giant Cisco Systems, which focused primarily on the enterprise market.

Still, Juniper faced the daunting challenge of developing a product from scratch, without the help of legacy technologies to follow for guidance.[14] Additionally, the networking industry was fast-paced and unforgiving; Sindhu and Kriens believed they would have only one chance to convince ISPs that their product was better than the competition's.[15]

In spite of the many challenges, Kriens believed the environment was ripe for a challenger to Cisco. If it could develop a viable router product, major industry players looking to avoid overreliance on a single supplier could welcome Juniper. Following an innovative strategy he successfully employed at StrataCom, Kriens sought equity investments in Juniper's developing technology from companies that represented Juniper's potential clients. On September 2, 1997, a collection of some of the most prominent names in networking and telecom—including 3Com, Lucent Technologies, Ericsson, and Worldcom/UUNet—announced a $40 million investment in Juniper, providing for future growth.

The strategic distribution deals with its equity partners and others allowed Juniper to maintain focus on product development. Key to these deals were the instant access to customers who were also investors (i.e., UUNet), as well as distribution deals providing access to the sales forces of Alcatel and Nortel. In addition, manufacturing was outsourced. For example, Juniper's ASIC production was contracted to IBM, and Kriens signed an early deal with California-based Solectron to manufacture its routers.[16] This focused allocation of resources would soon allow Juniper to claim one of the highest revenues per employee in the business, exceeding even Cisco's.[17]

Initial Success for Juniper

In September 1998, one year after receiving the $40 million investment, Juniper shipped its first product: a 35-inch-high by 19-inch-wide box called the M40 Internet Backbone Router.[18] The M40 represented a major advance in core routing technology, able to send packets of data at 10 times the speed of the routers available at the time from market-leader Cisco.

To build the M40, Juniper made significant strides in both hardware and software technology. It collaborated with IBM to develop and manufacture a unique set of high-performance ASICs, which dramatically increased processing speed and reliability by shifting more functionality from the software to the chip than in previous versions. At the same time, Juniper internally developed an innovative software routing package.

This new routing software, called JUNOS, operates on Intel-based architecture and uses an approach whereby the two distinct router functions of route determination and data forwarding are separated, allowing these two activities to be carried out simultaneously and to run independently. Therefore, as one is updated, the other continues to operate simultaneously. This splitting of functionality results in significantly faster performance than the competitors' software, which performs the two activities sequentially. In addition to greater processing speed, JUNOS also enhances stability, a key attribute of a core router given its responsibility for tremendous loads of traffic and that traffic's revenue generation for carrier. As a final improvement, JUNOS was the first software system that allowed for "hot-swapping" of components and software upgrades, thereby overcoming a historic problem of previous core routers which had to be shut down to perform maintenance.

By comparison, the Cisco Internet Operating System (IOS) software was originally developed for enterprise applications as opposed to the core market. Therefore, IOS had not incorporated these high-speed, telco-grade features, was not scalable to high volumes, and offered less stability.

The M40 became enormously successful, catching on quickly in the networking industry. In addition to its sheer speed, the M40 benefited from latent customer dissatisfaction with Cisco. Customers frustrated with a lack of responsiveness from Cisco suddenly found they had an alternative. In the words of one executive, the first time he purchased Juniper equipment he did it because he "finally figured out that the only way to get Cisco's attention was to show them a purchase order with eight zeros and another company's name on it."[19] By the end of 1998, Juniper had already carved out a 7 percent market share in the core router market.[20]

The success of the M40 router rapidly increased Juniper's revenues and market share. The company averaged 90 percent quarter-to-quarter growth in 1999, achieving total year-end sales of $102.6 million.[21] Market share leapt to 17 percent by the end of 1999, largely at the expense of Cisco, whose pre-Juniper market share of 91 percent had dropped to 80 percent by the end of 1999.[22] Despite these incursions into Cisco's share of the market, Kriens continued to insist publicly that Juniper was not directly competing with Cisco, focusing instead on the power of both companies to grow overall market size, which would in turn leave plenty of room for both of them.

In June 1999, Kriens took the company public, foregoing the potentially lucrative option of selling out to a larger company. Explained Kriens, "We'll stay independent. Not for the ego of it, but because we can build more value than anyone would be willing to pay for us now."[23] The market showed its willingness to pay, pushing the company's IPO price of $34 per share to nearly $100 by the end of its first day of trading, and to $304 within five months.[24] The stock price was bolstered by earnings expectations. Due in large part to its strict focus on product development, with manufacturing and distribution outsourced, Juniper was able to post positive net income of $4.8 million in the fourth quarter of 1999, a remarkably quick path to profitability for a high-tech start-up company.

Juniper's technology has been the key to this rapid success. The company has been widely recognized as being at the forefront of networking applications, winning several industry awards, including the Best Internet Product for the 1999 Technical Innovations Awards from *PC Magazine* for its M40 router.[25] To date, Juniper continues to enjoy a six-month lead on advances in throughput speed over Cisco and other competitors.[26]

Juniper Gains Market Share

With the turn of the millennium, Juniper raised the stakes in its quest for market share, launching the M20 router, a smaller-version Internet router designed for the edge of the network and for smaller core backbones.[27] This launch into edge routers began an alternating product cycle which would typify Juniper's strategic business model: The M40 strengthened the core of the Internet backbone, but in turn, burdened the edge (end-users); the M20 rescued the edge, putting more demand on the core and necessitating more powerful core routers.[28] Juniper's product launches in 2000 followed this alternating product approach, with its M160 core router, launched in March, able to manage Internet flows of 10 billion digital bits per second (see Table 9.3).

As Juniper continued to introduce more powerful routers, it made greater inroads into the major existing players' market share in the networking industry. Though Juniper continued to expand its customer base (increasing from 113 to 136 customers in the third quarter of 2000 alone), over half of its revenues came from four key customers—Cable & Wireless, MCI Worldcom, Qwest, and Metromedia Fiber Network (MFN).[29] The credibility gained from such prominent customers allowed Juniper to make further inroads into the core router market, capturing a 24 percent market share by the third quarter of 2000 with no signs of slowing. Indeed, with industry experts forecasting a doubling of demand for network capacity *every three months,*[30] Juniper continued to enjoy tremendous growth prospects. Year 2000 revenues were expected to be $643 million,[31] with most analysts expecting that number to more than double in 2001.[32]

As 2000 drew to a close, Kriens found himself in an enviable position. His company had captured a quarter of the fiercely competitive core router market in less than two years, and industry analysts estimated Juniper's technological lead at about six months over both potential and actual rivals in this market. The company's cash holdings reached $500 million and it had been profitable for over a year, with estimates for 2000 net income at $162 million (Table 9.4).[33] Still, with emerging players such as Avici and

TABLE 9.3   **Juniper Product Releases**

Router Product	Target Market	Release Date	Approximate Sales Price* (in $ thousands)	Speed
M40	Core	9/16/98	$400	40+ Gbps
M20	Edge	12/7/99	100	20+ Gbps
M160	Core	4/28/00	800	160+ Gbps
M5	Edge	9/9/00	20	5+ Gbps
M10	Edge	9/9/00	20	10+ Gbps

*From an interview with Muayyad Al-Chalabi, November 14, 2000.

Pluris in the midst of successful trials of competing products, and rival Cisco with much deeper financial and technological resources, Kriens could hardly afford to rest easy.

Juniper's Competitors

Juniper's tremendous success came at the expense of Cisco and other industry players. The market for core routers in 2000 was dominated by a Cisco–Juniper duopoly (see Table 9.5). In edge devices, Juniper joined strong competitors that offered routers and other hardware necessary for enterprisewide solutions. Market entry and exit were common, new partnerships surfaced almost daily,

TABLE 9.4   **Summary of Juniper's Income Statement (in thousands, except per share amounts)**

	Consolidated Statements of Operations Year Ended December 31			
	2000	**1999**	**1998**	**1997**
Net revenues(1)	$673,501	$102,606	$ 3,807	—
Cost of revenues	237,554	45,272	4,416	—
Gross profit (loss)	435,947	57,334	(609)	—
Operating expenses:				
Research and development	87,833	41,502	23,987	9,406
Sales and marketing	89,029	20,931	4,216	1,149
General and administrative	21,176	5,235	2,223	1,043
Amortization of goodwill and purchased intangibles and deferred stock compensation	43,820	4,286	1,235	—
Total operating expenses	241,858	71,954	31,661	11,598
Operating loss	194,089	(14,620)	(32,270)	(11,598)
Interest income, net	88,960	8,011	1,301	1,235
Income (loss) before income taxes	230,372	(6,609)	(30,969)	(10,363)
Provision for income taxes	82,456	2,425	2	—
Net income (loss)	$147,916	$ (9,034)	$(30,971)	$(10,363)
Basic net income (loss) per share	$ 0.49	$ (0.05)	$ (0.40)	
Diluted net income (loss) per share	$ 0.43	$ (0.05)	$ (0.40)	
Shares used in computing net income (loss)				
Basic	304,381	189,322	77,742	
Diluted	347,858	189,322	77,742	

TABLE 9.5   **Core Router Market Share***

	98 Q3	98 Q4	99 Q1	99 Q2	99 Q3	99 Q4	00 Q1	00 Q2
Cisco	91%	87%	85%	82%	83%	80%	81%	75%
Juniper	0	7	12	14	16	17	18	24
Lucent	9	6	3	2	1	1	0	0
Nortel	0	0	0	2	1	2	1	0

*Lehman Brothers, MSDW, Dain Rauscher Weiss Analyst Reports.

and innovation frequently redefined product categories. In general, router producers were telecom and electronics giants, recent spin-offs, or venture-funded start-ups.

Cisco Systems and Other Competitors

In November 2000, Cisco Systems, Inc., with an approximate market capitalization of $350 billion, was the third most valuable company in the world (behind General Electric and Microsoft). Cisco finished the fiscal year 2000 with $18.9 billion in revenues and net income of $2.7 billion. Founded in 1984 by a pair of then-married Stanford University computer science professors, Sandy Lerner and Len Bosack, the company first sold shares to the public in February 1990 at $18 a share.[34] Since then Cisco's stock had undergone nine splits, seven 2-for-1 splits, and two 3-for-2 splits. Cisco began as a one-product company selling routers, but in 2000 it had more than 150 different networking products. Unlike Juniper, which focused on organic growth through product development, Cisco focused more on technology growth via acquisitions, breadth of product line, the customer experience, and retaining top talent. Using its rising stock as currency, Cisco makes one acquisition every two to three weeks, and since 1993 has purchased more than 60 companies.[35] Other competitors included Nortel Networks, Lucent, Alcatel, Avici Systems, Procket Pluris, IronBridge, Charlotte's Web, Caspian, Redback Networks, Riverstone, and Unisphere.

Juniper at Crossroads

With rapid advances in technology and an onslaught of potential new competitors, Juniper could not be sure if and for how long its technology advantage would last. Could the dot.com gold rush be over? Was Juniper there to stay? Did it have the right business model? Should it enter the router market? How would Cisco react?

APPRAISING JUNIPER NETWORKS' BUSINESS MODEL

We will explore two primary questions: (1) How viable is Juniper Network's business model? and (2) should it enter the enterprise router market?

How Viable Is Juniper Networks' Business Model?

We determine the viability of Juniper Networks' business model by appraising it. We use all three appraisal measures: profitability measures, profitability predictor measures, and business model component measures.

Profitability Measures

Juniper became profitable in only its fourth year since being founded, with an estimated 2000 year-end net income of $162 million. This was phenomenal performance when compared to the thousands of dot.coms that accumulated huge losses over the same period. The firm also had cash reserves of $500 million.

Profitability Predictor Measures

In November 2000, only two years since shipping its first M40 core-carrier router in September 1998, Juniper had gained a 24 percent market share in core routers. Its profit margins were 64 percent in the nine months that ended in September 2000.

Business Model Components Measures

The appraisal of the components of Juniper's business model is summarized in Table 9.6. We examine each component measure.

Positioning [HIGH] A Porter's five-forces analysis shows that Juniper's position in carrier routers was attractive in 2000 and expected to be attractive in the future. Details of the analysis are given in Table 9.7. Therefore positioning is ranked as a HIGH. Juniper's most important decision may have been its choice of profit site in the Internet value network—choosing to be a supplier of carrier-class routers rather than becoming another B2B, C2C, or B2C as many dot.coms at the time chose to do. High demand from high industry growth not only reduced rivalry but also reduced the power of buyers. Complementary assets were important and tight thereby increasing barriers to entry. Switching costs were high with no clear substitutes. Many ASIC chip suppliers competed to supply Juniper and other router makers. Long qualification times for testing also reduced potential new entry. The fact that there were only two players, Cisco and Juniper, that sold a differentiated product also gave them bargaining power over buyers and may have reduced rivalry. Customers wanted an alternative to Cisco and found one in Juniper.

Customer Value [HIGH] Router speed and uptime were critical in the industry. Juniper beat Cisco in both. The M40 was 10 times faster than rival Cisco's model. Moreover, Juniper had another important differentiator: hot-swapping, which Cisco did not have. Juniper's routers were the most technologically advanced in the industry in 2000.

Scope [HIGH] In 2000, the growth rate of core routers was 53 percent while that of edge routers was 208 percent. Juniper had 24 percent of the core router

TABLE 9.6   **Appraising Juniper Networks' Business Model: Component Measures**

Component		Rank
Positioning	Juniper's position in carrier routers was attractive in 2000 and expected to be attractive in the future.	High
Customer value	Juniper was better than Cisco in speed and uptime, which were critical in industry. M40 was 10 times faster than rival Cisco model. Cisco did not have hot-swapping. Juniper's routers were the most technologically advanced in the industry.	High
Scope	Growth rate of core (53%) and edge (208%) routers in 2000 was high. Had 24% of core router market in 2000 compared to Cisco's 75% but had gained the 24% market share in only 2 years. Potential erosion of carrier routers from Cisco and new entrants was high.	High
Pricing	If Cisco's prices were comparable to Juniper's, then Juniper must have had better quality-adjusted prices since its products were much faster than Cisco's and it had hot-swapping, an important feature that Cisco did not have.	High
Revenue source	Major sources of revenues were core and edge routers. Its margins and market share were high in both. Margins and market share increased from 1999 to 2000. Juniper offered higher value in each source of revenues than did Cisco since its products had superior product attributes compared to Cisco's.	High
Connected activities	Concentrated on product development and innovation, which reinforced the superior product differentiation that it offered. Outsourced manufacturing to IBM and Solectron, and some sales activities to Alcatel and Nortel. Developed alternating product cycle for core and edge routers to push technology to new limits.	High
Implementation	Management team added genetic mix. Funding from a renowned VC firm may have lent credibility to the firm. Such credibility can attract top talent in a tight resource-limited market and may also attract more financing. Juniper's timing was good: Customers were eager to have a second supplier.	High
Capabilities	Superior product technology allowed it to offer best performance and hot-swapping. Proprietary routing software, JUNOS. In 2000, Juniper had not been imitated but probably would be. Capabilities potentially extendible to other product-market positions.	High
Sustainability	Had not held a high market share for long. Higher market share was vulnerable. However, Juniper was employing a combination of run, block, and team-up to maintain advantage.	Medium

(continued)

TABLE 9.6 *(continued)*

Component		Rank
	• Kept innovating. • Collaboration with leading high-tech companies, such as IBM, Solectron, etc. • Teamed up with future customers, making them equity partners and giving them partial ownership and distribution rights. • Kept routing software, JUNOS, proprietary. • Risk from the majority of revenues coming from four customers in a market with short product life span.	
Cost structure	Juniper's cost structure in 2000 was comparable to Cisco's, despite the fact that the former did not yet have the scale economies of Cisco.	Low

market in 2000 compared to Cisco's 75 percent but had gained the 24 percent market share in only two years. To maintain its growth rates and profits, Cisco was likely to fight back and recapture some market share from Juniper or at least decrease the rate of increase of Juniper's market share. Router traffic was growing exponentially while router performance grew by a factor of four every 18 to 24 months.

Pricing [HIGH] If Cisco's prices were comparable to Juniper's, then Juniper must have had better quality-adjusted prices since its products were much faster than Cisco's and it had hot-swapping, an important feature that Cisco did not have.

Revenue Source [HIGH] Juniper's two primary sources of revenues were core and edge router product sales. Its margins and market share were high in both core and edge routers. Margins and market share increased from 1999 to 2000. Juniper's routers were faster than Cisco's and had hot-swapping, which Cisco's did not.

Connected Activities [HIGH] Juniper concentrated on product development and innovation, which reinforced the superior product differentiation that it offered. Its activities were geared toward ensuring an alternating product cycle in which its core routers like the M40 were able to route signals through the Internet backbone quickly, thereby burdening edge routers. A new faster edge router like the M20 would then be brought in to rescue the routing at the edge level. This, in turn, created the need for faster core routers. And faster core routers again meant faster edge routers, continuing the virtuous cycle. Juniper outsourced manufacturing to IBM and Solectron, and some sales activities to Alcatel and Nortel, rather than try to do it all alone. Moreover, its strength was in product development. It developed and kept its JUNOS routing software proprietary. These activities gave the firm an attractive position in an already attractive industry in 2000.

TABLE 9.7   **A Porter's Five-Forces Attractiveness Analysis of Juniper's Positioning in Carrier (Core and Edge Routers)**

Force	In 2000	Exertion on Juniper	In the Long Term	Exertion on Juniper
Supplier power	Many ASIC chip manufacturers. Mobile, limited talent but Juniper could attract the right people.	Low	Many ASIC chip manufacturers. Mobile, limited talent but Juniper could attract the right people.	Low
Buyer power	High demand from high industry growth. Long production evaluation cycles to get a vendor qualified and high cost of delayed deployment. Few (Cisco and Juniper) carrier router makers. High switching costs since differences in human interface and configuration procedures existed despite standard protocols for interoperability. Reputation and brand were important.	Low	High demand may not last for long. Long production evaluation cycles to get a vendor qualified and high cost of delayed deployment. High switching costs since differences in human interface and configuration procedures existed despite standard protocols for interoperability. Reputation and brand still important.	Med
Rivalry	Two large players, Cisco and Juniper, dominated a growing market. Rivalry could be good or bad depending on how they "played the game." Large growing market that reduced the bad effects of rivalry.	Low	More entry likely to increase rivalry. Slow-down in industry might increase rivalry—Cisco might decide to fight back.	Low–Med
Threat of entrants	Capital-intensive industry. Complementary assets important and tight. Shortage of skilled routing engineers. Plenty of venture capital money being invested in the area might increase entry. Large potential for new entrants such as Seimens and Fujitsu.	Low	Large, profitable, growing market likely to attract new entrants in the near term. Lots of available financing (VC) to fund start-ups with potential.	Med–High
Substitutes	Not clear what substitutes were.	Low	Substitutes might emerge from emerging alternate technologies.	Low
Overall	**Attractive market**		**No longer as attractive**	

Implementation [Limited data] Despite being the first founder, Sindhu decided to concentrate on technology and appoint Kriens as CEO. Management team had a genetic mix: Sindhu as CTO, industry-experienced CEO (Kriens), leading server architect from Sun Microsystems, and networking designer from MCI. Funding from Kleiner Perkins Caufield & Byers, a renowned venture-capital firm, may have lent credibility to Juniper. Such credibility usually can attract top talent in a tight resource-limited market and may also attract more financing. Juniper's timing was good. It entered the industry at a time when customers were eager to have another choice.

Capabilities [HIGH] Its superior product capabilities allowed it to offer best performance and hot-swapping. Such performance helped start the building of a brand-name reputation among customers. In 2000, Juniper had not been imitated but probably would be—especially by Cisco. Its capabilities were potentially extendible to other product-market positions such as enterprise routers.

Sustainability [MODERATE] In 2000, Juniper had not held a high market share for long. For two reasons, Juniper's high market share appeared to be vulnerable. With venture capital readily available for this profit site and temptation from the potential profits of the profit site, new entrants were likely to enter the market for carrier routers. Moreover, Cisco was likely to fight back to regain some of the market share that it had lost to Juniper. Juniper's technology was imitable and since Cisco had complementary assets such as brand, large customer base, cash, and the ability to acquire new start-ups with new technologies, Cisco posed a very real threat. Juniper would need a good combination of run, block, and team-up to maintain its advantage. It would have to keep running by innovating and offering newer and faster products. (As we saw in the ranking of "activities," Juniper was better able to run by concentrating its efforts where it believed its advantage laid while outsourcing less important activities to others.) It kept its JUNOS routing software proprietary even as it gunned for a standard. It had teamed up with future customers, making them equity partners and giving them partial ownership and distribution rights. It had also collaborated with leading high-tech companies, such as IBM, Solectron, etc. Throughout, it had resisted trying to replicate Cisco's activities. For example, it had resisted using its high market valuation to make acquisitions, a strategy that rival Cisco had utilized in the mid-to-late 1990s.

Cost Structure [HIGH] The only cost data provided are the financial statements from the 2000 income statement of each firm. Compared to Cisco's, we can assume that cost of product development and innovation was likely high.

Conclusion In 2000, Juniper had an excellent business model. However, Cisco and other competitors still posed a potential threat to Juniper's advantage. Radical technological changes also posed a threat. For example, optical technology could usher in a new era in which Juniper would become an incumbent facing more nimble new entrants. In 2000, core routers were connected by fiber-optics cables that carried optical signals. These optical signals had to be converted into electrical signals for the routers to decide their next destinations, and then converted back to optical signals in order to be sent over fiber-optics cables for delivery to the next router. Predictions in 2000 were that eventually routers would have to be optical. The electrical to optical router change would be a radical technological change.

Should Juniper Enter the Enterprise Router Market?

At first glance it might be tempting to suggest that Juniper should enter the enterprise router market for the following reasons. First, it was a growing market. Second, core router technology usually moved to the edge routers and then to enterprise routers. Thus, Juniper could use its edge router technology to enter the enterprise router market without much more technology development. Finally, entering the enterprise router market where Cisco dominates would keep Cisco busy and delay its efforts to fight Juniper in the carrier router market. However, a more detailed analysis would suggest otherwise.

A Porter's five-forces analysis of the enterprise router market suggests that it was neither attractive in 2000 nor promised to be attractive in the future (see Table 9.8). Growth is just one factor in determining a market's attractiveness.

TABLE 9.8 **A Porter's Five-Forces Attractiveness Analysis of the Enterprise Router Market**

Force	In 2000	Exertion on firms	In the Long Term	Exertion on firms
Supplier power	Many ASIC chip manufacturers.	Low	Many ASIC chip manufacturers.	Low
Buyer power	Many product choices from many diverse players.	High	Many product choices from many diverse players.	High
Rivalry	Many diverse players, many product choices. Firms competed on price and service. Cisco already dominated the market.	High	Smaller number of players when market matured.	Moderate
Threat of entrants	Low barriers to entry.	High	Low barriers to entry in the short term but increasing with time.	Moderate
Substitutes	Obsolete carrier routers could be substitutes.	High	Obsolete carrier routers could be substitutes. New technologies could give rise to more substitutes.	Low
Overall	**Unattractive market**		**Remains unattractive market**	

Moreover, it usually takes more than technology to do well in a market; it usually also takes complementary assets. Thus, the question here should be whether Juniper had what it would take to have a competitive advantage in this unattractive market that was already dominated by Cisco and other large vendors. In this more mature enterprise router market, it was not technological prowess that would give firms an advantage. Rather, it was complementary assets such as a sales force, a large installed base, and a service network that could give a firm an advantage. Juniper had none of these tight complementary assets. Its core capability was technological. Engaging Cisco in a fight where Cisco dominated and had the core complementary assets would probably not be advisable. Rather, it might be more advisable for Juniper to concentrate its efforts where its core capabilities laid—the more attractive core and edge router markets.

Summary

Appraising a business model helps a firm to make choices. It tells a firm how good its business model is compared to that of competitors or how good alternative business models under different scenarios can be. More importantly, it enables a firm to understand which components and linkages of its business model are weak or strong compared to those of competitors. With this information, a firm can keep building a better business model. Like most models, this appraisal model is static in that it appraises a business model at a point in time. It does not say much about what today's good business model may look like tomorrow.

We used the Juniper Networks case to illustrate how a business model might be appraised. Appraisal suggested that, in 2000, Juniper had a viable business model. Since the firm is in a fast-changing industry, its competitive environment might change, necessitating changes in the business model.

Key Terms

business model
    component
    measures, *162*
extendibility of
    capabilities, *165*

profitability
    measures, *161*
profitability predictor
    measures, *161*

Discussion Question

1. What do you consider the most important thing gained from appraising a business model?

Notes

1. C. K. Prahalad and G. Hamel, "The Core Competences of the Corporation," *Harvard Business Review,* May–June 1990, pp. 79–91.
2. "Cisco's European Consultant," *Business Week,* March 20, 2000.
3. Interview with Muayyad Al-Chalabi, November 14, 2000.
4. Morgan Stanley Dean Witter, "Two Years of Stunning Growth," October 13, 2000.
5. Cowen Securities, Inc., "Key Takeaways form RHK's STARTRAX2000 Conference," November 16, 2000.
6. Morgan Stanley Dean Witter, "Two Years of Stunning Growth."
7. Interview with Muayyad Al-Chalabi, December 13, 2000.
8. Interview with Muayyad Al-Chalabi, November 14, 2000.
9. "Juniper: Fresh Competitor? Fresh Meat?" *Fortune,* May 15, 2000.
10. Silicon India, April 2000 "Pradeep Sindhu"
11. "Start-up Snags $40M in a Bid to Redefine Routers," *Electronic Engineering Times,* September 1, 1997.
12. "Juniper: The Upstart That's Eating Cisco's Lunch," *Business Week Online,* September 11, 2000.
13. Ibid.
14. "Technology Guru Scott Kriens of Juniper Networks Named 2000 E&Y EOY," Business Wire, November 13, 2000.
15. Ibid.
16. Morgan Stanley Dean Witter Analyst Report, October 13, 2000.
17. "Juniper: The Upstart That's Eating Cisco's Lunch," *Business Week Online,* September 11, 2000.
18. "Mountain-View, Calif.-Based Juniper Kicks Off Internet Roto Routers," *San Jose Mercury News,* September 21, 1998.
19. "Juniper: The Upstart That's Eating Cisco's Lunch," *Business Week Online,* September 11, 2000.
20. "Mountain-View, Calif.-Based Juniper Kicks Off Internet Roto Routers," *San Jose Mercury News,* September 21, 1998.
21. Lehman Brothers Analyst Report, October 16, 2000.
22. Morgan Stanley Dean Witter Analyst Report.
23. "Technology Guru Scott Kriens of Juniper Networks Named 2000 E&Y EOY," Business Wire, November 13, 2000.
24. Lehman Brothers Analyst Report.
25. www.zdnet.co.uk/pcmag/tinas/1999/41.html.
26. Interview with Muayyad Al-Chalabi, November 14, 2000.
27. "Technology Guru Scott Kriens of Juniper Networks Named 2000 E&Y EOY," Business Wire, November 13, 2000.
28. Lehman Brothers Analyst Report.
29. "Juniper: The Upstart That's Eating Cisco's Lunch," *Business Week Online,* September 11, 2000.
30. Lehman Brothers Analyst Report.
31. Lehman Brothers, MSDW, Dain Rauscher Weiss Analyst Reports.

32. "Companies & Finance: Shooting Star Juniper in Race Against Time," *Financial Times London,* March 28, 2000.

33. Morgan Stanley Dean Witter, "Two Years of Stunning Growth," Juniper Equity Research Report, October 13, 2000.

34. John A. Byrne, "The Corporation of the Future," *Business Week,* August 24–31, 1998.

35. Andy Serwer, "There's Something about Cisco," *Fortune,* May 15, 2000.

Part Three

The Role of Competitive and Macro Environments

Chapter **Ten**

Competitive and Macro Environments

So far in this book, we have focused on business models and the Internet, only sparingly referring to the environment in which firms and their business models must operate. But as we pointed out in Chapter 1, a firm's profitability rests as much on its business model as on its environment. In this chapter we explore the role of a firm's environment in determining its business model and profitability (see Figure 10.1). In particular, we explore the impact of the Internet on the competitive and macro environments of a firm and the resulting consequences for business models.

THE ENVIRONMENT AS DETERMINANT OF FIRM PERFORMANCE

As Figure 10.1 shows, a firm's environment is not only a determinant of its performance. It also influences the type of business model that the firm adopts as well as how the Internet evolves. The business model itself is influenced by the Internet and firms. Two types of environments can impact firm performance.[1] First is the **industry** or **competitive environment:** the suppliers, customers, complementors, rivals, substitutes, and potential new entrants with which a firm must interact or take into consideration in making its strategic decisions. Then there is the **macro environment,** the overarching environment of regional and national governments and institutions in which firms in an industry must operate.

The Competitive Environment

For an industry to be profitable, the firms in it must be able to provide products or services whose value to customers considerably exceeds the cost of providing them. But as Michael Porter pointed out, there are five forces—bargaining power of suppliers, bargaining power of buyers, threat of new entrants, rivalry among existing firms, and threat of substitute products—that can prevent firms in the industry from being profitable.[2] The impact of **Porter's five forces** on

FIGURE 10.1 **The Role of the Environment**

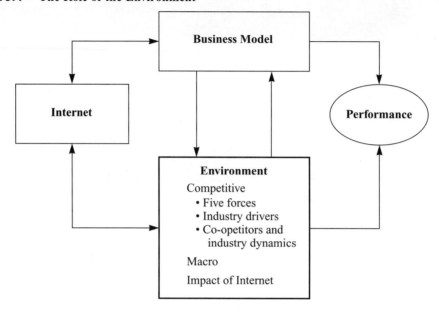

firm profitability can be understood by considering the simple relationship of equation (1), which states that the profits that firms make are equal to the revenues that they receive from customers in exchange for the products or services that they offer, less the costs of offering them.

$$\text{Profits} = \text{Revenues} - \text{Costs} = P(Q) \times Q(P) - C(Q) \quad \textbf{(1)}$$

If suppliers have high enough bargaining power to extract higher prices from industry firms, the costs to the firms are higher and their profits reduced. If these powerful suppliers instead get away with offering firms lower-quality inputs, these firms will end up with inferior products for their customers. This in turn will reduce their ability to charge premium prices for the products or they may have to spend more to improve product quality. Either way, industry profits are reduced.

Powerful customers have an analogous effect on firm profitability. They can extract lower prices and higher-quality products from firms. Lower prices and higher quality mean less profitability. A high threat of new entrants forces firms to charge less for their products. They may also be forced to take costly measures to create barriers to entry or differentiate their products. Either way, firm profitability is reduced. Increased rivalry among existing firms can lead to price wars or costly attempts to differentiate products, both of which reduce profitability. Substitute products provide a powerful alternative to firms' products, thereby putting pressure not only on the prices that firms can charge, but also on the quantities that they can sell. An industry in which suppliers and buyers have bargaining power, and in which rivalry, the threat of new entry, and the power of substitutes are high, is said to be **unattractive** because, on the average, the industry's profits are low.

Industry Characteristics and Critical Success Drivers

Every industry has its idiosyncrasies. These may be in the customers, customer value, distribution channels, activities performed to deliver the value, or technology that underpins the value and activities. These can lead to certain **industry success drivers** or factors that are critical to success. Firms must exploit these factors if they are going to gain and maintain a competitive advantage in the industry. Critical factors are those that have the most impact on a firm's cost or the distinctive value that it can offer customers. In consulting, for example, capacity utilization is critical. Few firms can afford to have MBAs, who cost over a quarter of a million dollars a year each, idling. Relations with clients are also critical if the consultants are going to win contracts and complete them successfully. So is the ability to create and share knowledge since, when all is said and done, consulting is a knowledge management business. In pharmaceuticals, two industry success drivers are R&D and the ability to perform clinical trials quickly and efficiently. Both determine the efficacy and safety of drugs.

In formulating Internet business models, it is important to identify these industry success drivers and go after them. In the automobile industry, for example, distribution accounts for 30 percent of the price of a car while an inability to forecast what customers want accounts for most of the cost. Well-conceived and well-executed Internet business models for automakers could trim many distribution costs by using the Internet to better forecast. In auctions, the size of the network is critical. Thus, a firm may want to build a loyal clientele early and quickly.

These idiosyncrasies on which industry success drivers rest often distinguish one business model from another.

THE INTERNET AND ENVIRONMENTAL DETERMINANTS OF PERFORMANCE

The question is, though, How do the properties of the Internet that we explored in Chapter 3 impact industry profitability and, in turn, a firm's ability to profit in this new frontier? To explore this question, we focus first on the industry environment and then on the macro environment.

Impact of the Internet on Industry Environment

One way to explore the impact of the Internet on industry profitability is to use Porter's five forces model.[3]

Suppliers

As we saw earlier, suppliers in an industry may be powerful enough to extract the industry's profits through high input prices or low-quality inputs. One source of this power is the information that suppliers may have on their products, prices, and costs that no one else has. The better informed that firms are about their suppliers and the products they are buying, the better their bargaining position. The World Wide Web equalizes this firm-supplier bargaining power somewhat because it reduces the information asymmetry that often exists between firms and their suppliers. Information on products, prices, and firms is more available to more people. For example, by accessing one of many websites, a potential car buyer can obtain detailed information on cars, their prices, and financing—information that was once the main source of power for car dealers. The result is that firms have more power over their suppliers, all else being equal. The distribution channel property means that more suppliers can reach industry firms than could do so before the Internet. For example, a software developer whose products were shunned by computer dealers (stores) can now post its products on the Web. This effectively increases the number of suppliers, giving more power to industry firms (their customers). The universality property has a dual effect. On the one hand, it means that firms in one region do not have to depend as much on local firms for supplies as they did before the Internet. Firms can solicit bids from suppliers worldwide. On the other hand, it also means that suppliers can sell their products to more firms worldwide.

Customers

For the same reasons why the Internet gives more power to firms over their suppliers, it also gives more bargaining power to customers over firms. Customers have more information on firms' products, prices, and costs; more firms compete for customers' attention; and distribution costs are lower, allowing more firms to reach customers. However, the mediating technology nature of the Internet suggests that the relationship between customers and firms is much more than analogous to that between suppliers and firms. Mediating technologies usually have more than one type of customer who is interdependent through the mediating firm. Consider a newspaper, for example. It has customers who buy the paper for the news, and customers who buy the advertising space to sell their products or services to those who read the newspaper. Effectively, the newspaper is a medium of exchange for the two groups of customers.[4] The larger a newspaper audience, the more power the newspaper has over advertisers. The network externality property also suggests that for certain applications, firms with large networks have some bargaining power since the larger the network, the less likely customers are to switch.

Rivalry

Recall that rivalry between existing firms may result in price wars that lower their prices, or advertising and promotion wars that increase their costs. Both result in lower profits for firms in the industry. For many products, the advent of the Internet means more rivalry. Why? Well, look at book retailing. A local bookseller used to face competition only from its bricks-and-mortar neighbors whose stores were located in the same or neighboring towns. With the Internet, the number of competitors increases rapidly because local customers can now buy from Web sellers, which greatly increases rivalry. The universality property also has two opposing effects. On the one hand, competitors can come from anywhere in the world. This increases rivalry. On the other hand, the market is also the whole world, which decreases rivalry since there is a larger pie to be shared.

Threat of New Entrants

Recall that the threat of new entrants forces incumbents to charge less for their products or take costly steps to keep them out. The result is that incumbent profits are lower. Such a threat is reduced if potential new entrants have little information available about incumbents, their products, costs, and prices. Potential new entrants would enter the new industry if they believe that they stand to make money in it. Making such a determination entails knowledge of incumbent costs and prices. Again, where the Web makes such information available to potential new entrants, the threat of entry increases and potentially reduces profits for incumbents. The threat of new entry also increases where the Internet serves as a distribution channel for some products. Consider, for example, a software developer who, prior to the Internet, had no chance of getting shelf space at computer and software retailers. With the Internet, all the developer has to do is develop the software and post it on the Web for customers. This increases the number of firms that can enter the industry. The universality property also suggests that the threat of new entrants increases since a firm from Bali is as likely to sell software to customers in Tokyo as one from Tokyo itself or one from Boston.

Finally, since the Internet is a low cost standard, the threat of new entry looms large for nearly all industries whose barriers to entry rest on some form of mediating technology. These range from telephone long-distance service to newspapers to television, radio, and financial services.

Substitutes

Substitute products or services reduce demand by providing buyers with alternative products. The Internet increases this possibility because it offers more information on the prices and attributes of substitutes and the extent to which they can substitute for industry products, making it easier for customers to find and use these substitutes. For substitutes that can be distributed over the Internet, the threat to industry firms is even higher. The universality property also suggests that there are more of such substitutes because makers of substitutes from all over the world can participate.

Complementors

Complementors are firms that produce complementary goods and services for industry products. For example, gasoline makers are complementors to the automobile industry because gasoline is a complementary product essential to the operation of automobiles. Complementary products increase demand for firm products. Thus, the more software that is developed for a particular computer standard, the more valuable the computer. The Internet provides more information on complementary products, thus increasing rivalry (in offering complementary products) and the number of complementary products that are sold. This in turn increases the number of industry products that are sold, augmenting industry profits.

The Internet's Multiple Forces

One underlying assumption in Porter's five forces is that customers are the ones who pay firms for the customer value offered by these firms. When an automaker sells a car, the buyer pays for it. The more power the customer has, the less a firm can expect for the customer value it offers. The mediating and network externalities properties of the Internet, however, suggest that frequently the customer who gets value from a firm is not the one who pays for it. This has significant implications for the competitive forces that impact an industry. Take the newspaper industry, which we said has two interdependent types of customers: its audience and advertisers. A newspaper actually has two types of rivals: those in the news business and those who sell and buy the kinds of things advertised in newspapers. Thus, with the Internet, a newspaper's rivals are not only other newspapers (or online news services), but also the auctioneers like eBay who advertise *and* sell many of the same items that are—or used to be—advertised in newspapers. The threat of new entry also takes a different dimension since anyone with a website and the capability to offer any of the content that newspapers do (e.g., news, weather, advertising, sports scores, and stock prices) is a potential competitor for newspapers.

In the bricks-and-mortar world, a retail store in Bentonville, Arkansas, does not compete intensively with one that is 200 miles away. In the virtual world, it competes with one that is thousands of miles away. Also, any store can potentially compete with any other store. This takes rivalry to a different dimension.

For many industries, then, the Internet shifts the bargaining power from suppliers to firms and in turn from firms to customers. To determine how attractive an industry is, however, we still need to perform a five forces analysis for that particular industry. The Internet service provider (ISP) industry serves as our example.

A Five Forces Analysis of ISPs

Internet service providers (ISPs) in 1998 provided their customers with basic Internet access to information, e-commerce, entertainment, community, and communications.[5]

Threat of Entry

The threat of entry was high. There was plenty of communications capacity available from competing telephone, cable, and wireless providers. The computer hardware, such as servers and routers, and the basic software required to enter the industry were inexpensive and readily available. There was no clear product differentiation; strong brand loyalties were yet to be established. There was no fear of retaliation since this was a new industry with no incumbents.

Suppliers

Suppliers were the owners of communications infrastructure, makers of hardware and software, and the providers of content (e.g., entertainment, e-commerce, information, and communications) such as Disney, Playboy, and news networks (see Chapter 2). Some of these suppliers had their own ISPs, demonstrating a credible threat of forward vertical integration into ISPs. They were also relatively less fragmented than the thousands of ISPs in business in 1998. Effectively, suppliers of content had bargaining power over ISPs while suppliers of equipment such as hardware and software did not.

Buyers

Buyers in 1998 were the businesses and individuals that used the Internet. Since the service ISPs provided was undifferentiated with little switching costs, customers had the bargaining power.

Rivalry

In 1998 the Internet service provider industry was highly fragmented, with over a thousand ISPs and no sign of a slowdown of entry (see Chapter 2). The service offerings were still largely undifferentiated with low switching costs. On the other hand, the industry was experiencing high growth. Competition also tended to be regional; for example, ISPs that served Ann Arbor might not serve Los Angeles. Overall, despite the high industry growth and regional competition, rivalry was high.

Substitutes

In 1998 customers used ISPs to communicate and access information, e-commerce, entertainment, and community. Many customers still had plenty of alternative ways to satisfy these needs at low cost. The telephone and traditional hard-copy mail still allowed customers to communicate inexpensively. Television and theaters still provided entertainment while bricks-and-mortar stores still supplied low-cost shopping alternatives.

An Important Point about Industry Analysis

Our analysis suggests that the ISP industry in 1998 was very unattractive. Does this mean that in 1998 no firms could make money in the industry and that firms such as America Online (AOL) should have pulled out of ISP activities? Of course not! Does it mean that an industry analysis is useless? Of course not! It provides us with critical information. It tells us that the industry is, on average, not very profitable at the time the cross-sectional analysis was performed (1998). More important, an industry attractiveness analysis tells us why the industry is unattractive or attractive and a firm can, through appropriate strategic actions, make the industry more attractive for itself by influencing the competitive forces in it. For example, this analysis suggests that the service offered by ISPs in 1998 was, on average, undifferentiated. Thus, firms could differentiate themselves, for example, by building strong brands. AOL has taken several strategic steps to differentiate its service, including building a brand name. Since a critical success driver in the ISP industry is network size, AOL has also taken strategic steps to build loyal subscribers in a larger network. Brand and membership loyalty can help AOL stand out in the ISP market. Thus, a five forces analysis allows a firm to ask itself the following questions:

What can we do to moderate rivalry in this industry?

What can we do to reduce the viability of substitutes?

How can we create and maintain barriers to entry?

What can we do to increase our power over buyers and suppliers?

In general, firms should be asking, If the Internet has caused power to shift from suppliers to firms and from firms to customers, what strategic steps must we undertake to prosper from these shifts? The answers to these questions should be incorporated in the firm's business model.

In any case, our five forces analysis of the industry so far has two major shortcomings. First, it sees suppliers and customers as competitors over whom firms fight to gain bargaining power. But we know that suppliers and customers are more than just competitors. Second, the analysis is static because it considers industry attractiveness at a particular point in the life cycle of the industry.

CO-OPETITORS AND INDUSTRY DYNAMICS

Co-opetitors

The sole focus on the competitive relationship between a firm and its **co-opetitors**—the rivals, suppliers, customers, complementors, and potential new entrants with which a firm must compete *and* cooperate[6]—does not do justice to the critical role that these co-opetitors can play in helping firms exploit the Internet. First, the value that customers perceive is very difficult to break down into the contributions from firms, suppliers, customers, and complementors. Look at a tantalizing game played over the Internet. Is it fascinating because of the ISP's portal site, the speed with which signals are delivered over the Last Mile to the house, the backbone provider, or the way the game is designed? The point is that it takes all of these players to deliver the right value to customers. Thus, an industry analysis should also include an analysis of the industries of major suppliers, customers, and complementors. It should consider that customers are there not only to exercise any bargaining power they may have, but also that they may be interested in cooperating with firms. Much of the advantage that Japanese automobile companies had over their U.S. and European competitors in the 1980s came from cooperative relations with suppliers.[7]

Industry Dynamics and Evolution

In the five forces industry analysis, in which we predicted the likely outcome of the impact of the Internet on competition and profitability in industries, we assumed that these industries were static. However, following a major technological change such as the Internet, competition is a dynamic process in which firms fight for competitive advantage and survival. Industry structure and conduct change as the industry evolves.

Evolution of Technology

The rate at which firms enter or exit an industry parallels the evolution of the technology.[8] Early in the life of a technology, venture capitalists and other investors want to invest in it, entrepreneurs want to take advantage of the opportunities it offers, the product/service and its components are still ambiguous, and there are a large number of entries and few failures. In the late 1990s, for example, plenty of venture capitalists and many entrepreneurs took advantage of the Internet. The ISP industry alone attracted hundreds of new entrants. In the growth stage, firms fight for standards, establish relationships with customers, build brand-name loyalty, and struggle for market share. For most Internet start-ups, this has meant acquiring subscribers and clients, building large communities and infrastructures, winning "mindshare," and establishing brands. At the same time, customers are trying to "discover" their needs. Eventually, some product/service designs emerge as dominant designs. Some firms are forced to exit, others merge, and the number of surviving firms is greatly reduced as the evolution enters the stable state. As of 2002, the Internet had not yet reached the mature phase in any industry.

Example   The automobile industry illustrates what may be in the future of the Internet and the many industries exploiting it. In the early and growth phases of the automobile industry from the 1890s to the 1930s, more than 2,000 companies entered the industry in the United States. Just as the catchword in the late 1990s was "dot.com," the catchword in the automobile industry was "motor." In 2000, there were only two major U.S. automobile companies (Chrysler is now considered a German company since it merged with Daimler Benz to form DaimlerChrysler). In the mature phase of the Internet, there is likely to be a lot fewer dot.com firms than existed in 2000.

THE MACRO ENVIRONMENT

Firms, suppliers, customers, and complementors do not operate in a vacuum either; they are surrounded by the macro environment of government policies and laws, social structure, technological environment, demographic structure, and the natural environment which directly impact the industry environment.

Regulation and deregulation can increase or decrease barriers to entry and therefore the profits that firms can make. By issuing a limited number of taxicab licenses, for example, a city is creating industry barriers to the taxicab market and how much cab owners can make. The increasing number of people who have grown up with the computer and see it as an integral part of their work and social lives means different customer expectations and preferences and different opportunities for creating new industries that depend on computers. National and international economic factors such as interest rates, exchange rates, employment, income, and productivity also impact an industry. Government plays a critical though indirect role in creating new industries. The Internet itself and the World Wide Web derived from government research and development.

Impact on Performance

A firm's macro environment indirectly impacts its performance by influencing the competitive environment and business models. As we indicated earlier, it does so by impacting the industry environment; that is, the properties of the Internet may suggest, for example, that the retail book industry is a good candidate for transformation and that anyone anywhere can start an online retail bookstore to sell to customers anywhere in the world. But it still takes a certain kind of environment to launch an Amazon.com. In other words, some environments are more conducive to innovation than others.[9] We consider four attributes of such environments: (1) a system that provides financial support and rewards for innovation; (2) a culture that tolerates failure; (3) the presence of related industries, universities, and other research institutions; and (4) government policies.[10]

Financial Support and Rewards: IPOs and Venture Capital

Money still talks, even on the Internet. It takes money to finance Internet activities. Many entrepreneurs or employees are attracted to the Internet by expected future earnings. Thus, an environment that provides both would be more conducive to Internet businesses than others. Let's start with the reward system, which differs from country to country. In the United States, for example, the rewards for innovation can be astronomical. These rewards come in several forms. First, as we described in Chapter 8, there is the initial public offering (IPO) in which firms sell their stock to the public for the first time. In one day, following one to five years' work, an entrepreneur can become a billionaire while many others see their personal wealth go up by millions of dollars. A firm can also push up its net worth by spinning off an entrepreneurial unit and offering its stock for purchase. Expectation of such rewards can be an excellent incentive to start new Internet businesses and work hard at them. Money raised in IPOs and subsequent stock valuations can be a valuable resource for pursuing a strategy. As James H. Clark, cofounder and former chairman of Netscape, explained, "Without IPOs, you would not have any start-ups. IPOs supply the fuel that makes these dreams go. Without it, you die."[11] Internet firms, such as Amazon.com and many others, did not even have to be making a profit at the IPO date. Unfortunately, not all environments offer such rewards and sources of financing. In Japan, for example, firms must show several years of decent profits in order to be listed on that country's over-the-counter (OTC) market.[12] That can take as many as 10 years compared to 5 or less in the United States, and even less in 1998 and 1999 for Internet-based IPOs.

The availability of venture capital, partly a result of the expectations of financial rewards, also plays a critical role in Internet business formation. By making money available for projects that banks and other financing sources would normally consider too risky, venture capitalists allow firms to be more daring in their pursuit of new ideas. Some entrepreneurs use personal or family savings or loans from friends to finance their innovations, again in anticipation of the rewards. Anticipation of such rewards, coupled with readily available venture capital, allows more people to search for more innovative ideas. Many of those who succeed usually reinvest in other innovation-searching activities.

Culture That Tolerates Failure

Many start-up firms never get to the payoff at an IPO, or they fail right after it. For several reasons, such failures stop neither the entrepreneurs nor the venture capitalists who finance the innovations from founding other start-ups. First, those who fail learn in the process and that can improve their chances of doing well the next time around. They acquire competencies that can be used to tackle another innovation. Even if all they learn is what not to do next time, that can be useful too. Second, venture capital firms have seen many failures before and have found ways to reduce their risk, for example, by offering management expertise to ventures. Moreover, some of the venture capital comes from entrepreneurs who had succeeded only after having failed earlier. During their stints in Silicon Valley, the authors do not remember seeing anyone point a finger at a person and say, "That's an entrepreneur who failed." Whereas in Europe bankruptcy laws are harsh and entrepreneurs who fail are stigmatized, in the Silicon Valley, "bankruptcy is seen almost as a sign of prowess—a dueling scar."[13] In general, firms in the United States, be it in New York City's Silicon Alley or California's Silicon Valley, have these conditions in their favor.

Presence of Related Industries, Universities, and Other Research Institutions

The environment constitutes a very important source of innovations. Since tacit technological and market knowledge is transferred best by personal interaction, local environments that are good sources of innovation can make it easier for local firms to recognize the potential of an innovation. The presence of related industries is an example; being close to suppliers or complementary innovators increases a firm's chances of picking up useful ideas from them. Amazon.com's founder Jeff Bezos went west where he could find a large number of computer software developers and be located close to book distributors.

The proximity of universities or other research institutions helps innovation in two ways. First, these institutions train personnel who can go on to work for firms or found their own firms. From Yahoo! founded by graduate students at Stanford to Netscape started by students from the University of Illinois, examples abound. The knowledge that they acquire gives them the **absorptive capacity** to assimilate new ideas from competitors and related industries. Second, scientific publications from the basic research often act as a catalyst for investment by firms in applied research.

Government Policies

Finally, governments play a critical role—direct or indirect—in creating environments conducive to innovation.[14] The direct role may be in sponsoring research at the National Institutes of Health or the Defense Department. The Internet itself traces its roots to the Defense Department's DARPA project. More important, the U.S. government sponsored research in computer science and communication networks while training hundreds of thousands of people in electrical engineering and computer science who now fill Internet business jobs.

The government's indirect role is in regulation and taxation. Lower capital gains taxes or other regulations that allow firms to keep more of what they earn allow them to spend more on innovation. Taxing e-commerce can have a huge impact on the Internet. Other regulations also can be critical. In July 1999, for example, Internet signatures were not available; that is, people could not sign documents over the Internet. This meant that people still had to personally deliver documents or send them by "snail" mail to be signed. Making signatures delivered over the Web legal could increase the use of the Web. Government laws on intellectual property protection also influence the effectiveness of block strategies.

Summary

A firm's performance is determined by three factors: its business model, its environment, and change such as the Internet. In this chapter we explored the environmental factors and the impact of the Internet on these factors and vice versa. Two environmental factors determine firm profitability: industry and macro environment. Some industries are, on average, more profitable than others. The profitability of these industries is determined by the extent to which suppliers, customers, rivals, potential new entrants, and substitutes exert competitive pressures on industry firms. These competitive pressures are themselves a function of the macro environment—the overarching political/legal, national/international, social, technological, and demographic forces.

Industry analysis provides information that firms can employ in formulating their business models and strategies. For example, a Porter's five forces analysis of an industry in the face of the Internet tells a firm how attractive that industry is, but more importantly, it tells the firm what this industry has that makes it attractive or unattractive. With this information, a firm can take the necessary strategic steps, in building its business model, to make the industry more attractive for itself. By developing more content, building a large network of subscribers, and establishing a brand name, AOL made an otherwise unattractive ISP industry more attractive for itself. An analysis of industry success drivers provides firms with key information that they can use in making decisions about business model components and linkages. In understanding how the macro environment can shape the extent to which an industry can profit from the Internet, firms in that industry can do something about the macro environment. For example, automakers are not allowed to sell cars directly to customers in the United States; they have to sell their products through dealers. But they might choose to lobby to scrap these laws so that they can better exploit the Internet. An industry analysis also has implications for policy makers: They can know better what kinds of macro environments they must create to make firms in their jurisdictions more innovative. For example, countries with low financial reward systems for Internet entrepreneurs and little or no venture capital may find it difficult to compete with the United States, which has a generous reward system and plenty of venture capital. Therefore, policy makers in other countries may want to find ways to change their environments.

Key Terms

absorptive capacity, *198*
competitive environment, *187*
complementors, *191*
industry environment, *187*

industry success drivers, *189*
macro environment, *187*
Porter's five forces, *187*
unattractive industry, *189*

Discussion Questions

1. Name an industry in which new entrants have an advantage over incumbents. What factors allow them to have this advantage?
2. How might the Internet be different if it had been developed commercially instead of by the government?
3. Which properties of the Internet increase industry rivalry?
4. Name an industry that was created as a result of the Internet. What "traditional" industries could be threatened by this emerging industry? Why? Be specific.
5. Give examples of co-opetitors. Why do they cooperate? How do they compete?
6. Why do e-business "hotbeds" such as Silicon Valley emerge? What contributes to their formation?
7. Give an example of an instance when offering customer value is a necessary but insufficient condition for a firm's profitability.

Notes

1. C. W. L. Hill and G. R. Jones, *Strategic Management: An Integrated Approach* (Boston: Houghton Mifflin, 1995).
2. M. E. Porter, *Competitive Strategy: Techniques for Analyzing Industries and Competitors* (New York: Free Press, 1980); A. M. McGahan and M. E. Porter, "How Much Does Industry Matter? Really?" *Strategic Management Journal* 18 (Summer special issue, 1997), pp. 15–30.
3. Porter, *Competitive Strategy*.
4. Newspapers are often referred to as a print medium because they are a medium through which news and information are delivered to readers, not because they are a medium through which advertisers and producers are brought together.
5. C. W. L. Hill, "America Online and the Internet," in C. W. L. Hill and G. R. Jones, *Strategic Management: An Integrated Approach* (Boston: Houghton Mifflin, 1998), pp. C92–C106.
6. A. M. Brandenburger and B. J. Nalebuff, *Co-opetition* (New York: Doubleday, 1997).
7. K. B. Clark and T. Fujimoto, *Product Development Performance: Strategy, Organization, and Management in the World Automobile Industry* (Boston: Harvard Business School Press, 1991).
8. J. M. Utterback, *Mastering the Dynamics of Innovation* (Boston: Harvard Business School Press, 1994).
9. M. E. Porter, *The Competitive Advantage of Nations* (New York: Free Press, 1990).
10. This section draws heavily on A. N. Afuah, *Innovation Management: Strategies, Implementation and Profits* (New York: Oxford University Press, 1998).
11. C. Farrell et al., "The Boon in IPOs," *Business Week,* December 18, 1995, p. 64.
12. "Japanese Venture Capital: In Need of Funds," *The Economist,* October 16, 1993, pp. 91–92.
13. "Please Dare to Fail," *The Economist,* September 28, 1996, pp. 21–22.
14. See Chapter 15 of Afuah, *Innovation Management*.

Part Four

Applying the Concepts, Models, and Tools

Chapter **Eleven**

The General Manager and the Internet

A general manager can be a chief executive officer (CEO), president, chief operating officer (COO), vice president, director, administrator, product line manager, profit center manager, or any other person who is responsible for the performance of an organization that has more than one functional area. This executive's primary responsibility is to guide his or her organization to meet its performance goals and mission or, better still, to attain and maintain a competitive advantage. In the face of the Internet, the general manager's responsibility includes using the new technology to reinforce an existing competitive advantage or to gain and maintain a new one. The extent to which he or she can meet this challenge is a function of three factors: (1) whether the firm is an incumbent or a pure-play Internet new entrant, (2) the formulation and execution of a good strategy, and (3) the characteristics of the general manager. We explore these three factors.

We begin by defining competitive advantage and explaining why it is an important performance goal of many firms. Then we explore the characteristics of incumbents or so-called legacy or bricks-and-mortar firms that must adopt the Internet, and those of new entrant or so-called pure-play Internet firms. In the face of the Internet, each exhibits some characteristics that make managing it a challenge. Next, we examine the process of formulating and implementing an Internet strategy that entails answering four important questions:[1] Where is the firm now as far as the Internet is concerned? Where does the firm go next? How does it get there? How does it implement the decisions to get there? Finally, we examine some traits that would serve a general manager well in the face of the Internet.

COMPETITIVE ADVANTAGE AND THE GENERAL MANAGER

An organization's **competitive advantage** lies in those characteristics that allow it to outperform its rivals in the same industry or market.[2] As we noted in Chapter 1, performance has many definitions but we will focus on profitability.

Thus, we say that a firm has a competitive advantage over its rivals if it earns a higher rate of profits than those rivals or has the potential to do so.[3] Why is having a competitive advantage so important? First, investors are more likely to invest in firm A than in firm B if A is more profitable than B, even if both A and B are profitable. There are three types of investors here: the equity investors who prefer the better price-earnings (P/E) ratios, cash flows, profit margins, or business model attribute; suppliers who extend lines of credit, or debtors; and potential employees who would rather work for a winner. Second, during bad times for an industry, firms with a competitive advantage are more likely to survive than those with a disadvantage. During such times, the industry is less profitable, making it more likely that marginal firms that made money in good times will lose money. With fewer investors likely to invest in them, their chances of being forced out of business are higher. A general manager's primary responsibility, then, is to develop and sustain a competitive advantage for his or her organization. How successful the manager is in doing so is a function of the type of firm.

INCUMBENTS VERSUS NEW ENTRANTS

Managing Bricks-and-Mortar Incumbents

Incumbents are firms that were in existence prior to the adoption of the Internet by their industries. These are the so-called bricks-and-mortar or **legacy firms.** In early 2000 the vast majority of firms belonged to this category. Many of them were grappling with the question of what to do about the Internet. As incumbents in their industries, they had disadvantages and advantages that promised to have a large impact on their abilities to successfully adopt the Internet and the ability of their managers to guide them through the change.

Incumbent Advantages

Complementary Assets   Incumbents have some advantages over dot.coms. Recall from Chapter 5 that it takes more than technology to profit from technology. It also takes **complementary assets** such as brand name, distribution channels, client relations, important clients, marketing, manufacturing, shelf space, supplier relations, and so on. Many incumbents have these complementary assets and while the Internet may render some of them obsolete or turn them into handicaps, it leaves many intact for use with the new technology. Those complementary assets that can be used to profit from the Internet are a primary asset for the general manager of an incumbent firm. Where such assets are difficult to acquire and new entrants have difficulty obtaining them, the general manager can use them to improve the firm's chances of catching up or overtaking new entrants who moved first. Merrill Lynch was late entering the online brokerage business, but its reputation, strong relationships with clients, large clients, and monetary assets gave it a chance to catch up and overtake Internet firms like Ameritrade. Earlier, IBM was late in entering the PC market, but the IBM name helped it gain a huge market share as soon as it entered the PC market. In making acquisitions or entering strategic alliances, useful complementary assets are an important part of what the general manager of an incumbent firm brings to the table in any negotiating process.

Technology Is Easy to Imitate   Another thing that incumbents have going for them is that parts or the whole of an Internet business model are usually easy to imitate or outdo. Although Merrill Lynch was late to adopt the Internet, it still was able to develop and execute a good business model. The complementary assets model presented in Chapter 5 suggests that if technology is easy to imitate and complementary assets are important and difficult to get, owners of complementary assets are usually the firms that make money from the technology. Thus, incumbents have an advantage in industries where incumbents have the important complementary assets and the Internet technology is easy to imitate.

Potential Disadvantages for Incumbents[4]

Certain characteristics of incumbents make them particularly vulnerable in some areas to new entrants in the face of the Internet. Many of the characteristics served these firms well prior to the Internet—in some cases they were the cornerstones of their competitive advantage—but are now useless or may have become handicaps. If an incumbent has a chance to defend or maintain its competitive advantage in the face of the Internet, it must pay particular attention to these advantages-turned-handicaps and find ways to overcome them.

Dominant Managerial Logic   Each manager brings to each decision a set of biases, beliefs, and assumptions about the market served by the firm, whom to hire, who the firm's competitors are, what technology to use to remain competitive, and how to develop and execute a business model.[5] This set of biases, assumptions, and beliefs is a manager's **managerial logic.** It defines the frame within which a manager is likely to scan for information and approach problem solving. It is the mental model that a manager brings to each decision. Depending on a firm's strategies, systems, technology, organizational structure, culture, and record of success, there usually emerges a **dominant managerial logic,** a common way of viewing how best to do business as a manager in the firm. The longer a management team has been at the company and in the industry, and the more successful the firm has been, the more dominant and pervasive the managerial logic.

In relatively stable environments or in the face of competence-enhancing changes, dominant managerial logic can be a competitive weapon because it is business as usual, and management has the capabilities in place which, combined with its dominant logic, reinforce or extend the firm's competitive advantage. However, in the face of radical or disruptive change, dominant managerial logic can have disastrous consequences. It prevents managers from understanding the rationale behind the new technology—from "getting it." And when they eventually do get it, they still have difficulty in carrying out their new functions efficiently because managers imbued with the dominant logic tend to think and act as if it were business as usual, and they fight to maintain the status quo.[6]

Competency Trap Even if management overcomes its dominant logic handicap and sees a disruptive change for what it is and decides to exploit it, the same capabilities that may have given a competitive advantage to a firm can become a handicap.[7] For example, an important part of Wal-Mart's bricks-and-mortar capabilities is in logistics—its ability to move goods into and out of its large distribution centers to the shelves in its retail stores. Online retailing requires a completely different logistics system—one that can efficiently sort out single item orders, package them, and deliver single packages to individual households on time with few errors. A **competency trap**—an inability to shed old successful ways of doing things and to embrace new ones—can occur because of several reasons. The firm's managers may not want to spend so much money building a new logistics system when they believe that the firm already has one. Their dominant bricks-and-mortar logic may prevent them from seeing the differences in the requirements of the two types of retailing. Also, they cannot ditch the old logistics system because they still need it for bricks-and-mortar activities. Moreover, it takes more than the decision alone to build a new logistics system that will be successful. It also requires building and developing the capabilities to integrate it into the firm's retail system and running it. But doing this requires skills, knowledge, and routines which the firm must learn. Learning in the face of a disruptive change, however, usually requires *un*learning the old ways of doing things first.[8] Anyone who has had to break longtime personal habits or routines knows how difficult it is to unlearn old ways of doing things. Thus, in the face of the Internet, old capabilities not only are sometimes rendered obsolete, but also become a handicap to performing some value configuration activities.

Fear of Cannibalization and Loss of Revenue Sometimes the Internet renders a firm's existing products/services noncompetitive. The new product/service often offers better customer value than the old one. Offering these new products means the **cannibalization** of existing ones since fewer customers would buy the older product. The fear of cannibalizing existing products often makes firms reluctant to adopt technologies such as the Internet that render existing products/services noncompetitive. An increasing number of managers are, however, beginning to realize that if their firms do not perform cannibalization themselves, someone else will do it for them and they will miss out on both the old and new revenues.

Channel Conflict The Internet renders some existing distribution channels and some sales skills obsolete. In that case, **channel conflict** often occurs because existing sales forces and the distributors fight hard against the new channel rather than see their revenues go to the new channel. Consider the popular example of Compaq's attempts to emphasize selling its PCs directly to customers over the Internet, rather than depending largely on dealers. The PC dealers fought hard against Compaq's decision to go direct as Dell Computer had done. Prior to the World Wide Web and the use of the Internet as a distribution channel, Compaq's relationship with dealers had been a key factor in its rise to the top of the personal computer manufacturing industry. The Internet not only radically reduced the importance of these relationships, but also turned them into a handicap. When Merrill Lynch decided to offer online brokerage, its own sales force fought hard to keep it out.

Political Power   Throughout most of this book, we have treated a firm as if it were a homogeneous entity with congruent goals and employees whose primary interest is to pursue these goals. Often, however, top management does not share a common purpose and the interest of the firm may not be the primary consideration in every manager's decision. As such, firms can be thought of as composed of political coalitions formed to protect and enhance their vested interests.[9] The extent to which each of these coalitions can influence the decisions a firm makes is a measure of how much power it has. **Political power** is defined here as the ability to have one's preferences or inclinations reflected in any actions taken in the firm or organization.[10] A coalition whose interests are often reflected in a firm's decisions is said to be a **dominant coalition.** Each of these coalitions acts in its own interests. One can expect incumbents to be more likely to adopt the Internet if it enhances the power of its dominant coalition. If it appears that the Internet will destroy the power of the firm's elite, the elite may work hard to impede its adoption.[11]

Co-opetitor Power   The customers, suppliers, and complementors with whom a firm has to compete and cooperate also play a role in how successful a firm can be in adopting the Internet. If a firm's customers do not want the new technology, it risks not adopting it early. If such customers possess **co-opetitor power**—that is, they are powerful and are the primary source of revenues for a firm—the firm will tend to listen to the customers in an effort to satisfy their needs. However, listening too much to powerful customers can be detrimental to a firm's adoption of the new technology.[12] One can imagine a case where a firm that leans too much on a supplier who dominates the supplier-firm relationship and also has no incentive to invest in the Internet will also be detrimental to the firm's ability to adopt a new technology. Complementors who have power may not want to change either, further slowing down a firm's efforts.

Emotional Attachment   Many general managers were promoted to their top position or brought in because of the valuable contributions they had made to the invention and commercialization of an existing technology or to existing business models. In some cases a firm's competitive advantage also rests on such a technology. In either case, these managers may—in the face of a disruptive technology that potentially might replace the technology that made them what they are—have such strong **emotional attachments** to the existing technology that they will delay adoption of the Internet. For example, some of Intel's managers were reluctant to get out of the DRAM (Dynamic Random Access Memory) business and concentrate on microprocessors.[13] They were emotionally attached to DRAMs, which Intel had invented and from which it had, for a while, earned a lot of money.

Overcoming the Disadvantages

For the general manager, the most important question is a simple one: How can he or she overcome these disadvantages while exploiting the advantages?

Genetic Mix C. K. Prahalad and Gary Hamel wrote that firms need some kind of **genetic mix** in their management if they are to overcome the dominant logic problem and exploit new opportunities.[14] A firm whose management is made up entirely of electrical engineers is more likely to miss out on disruptive marketing changes than one that has a mix of engineers and marketers, all else being equal. The goal is to find people with complementary skills who share the overall objectives and mission of the firm.

S³PE A genetic mix of people in a company is only one of the elements of the strategy, structure, systems, people, and environment **(S³PE) system.** Many of the disadvantages that incumbents face can be mitigated by the right S^3PE system. At 3M, for example, at least 25 percent of a division's sales in any given year must be from products introduced within the last five years.[15] Resources are then allocated to back the expectations: Employees are expected to spend 15 percent of their workweek on anything they want, so long as it is product related. Employees who come up with a viable product are given grants to pursue the idea. An environment as vibrant as the Silicon Valley is likely to keep a firm on its toes and reduce its chance of lapsing into complacency. Employees are constantly reminded of why paying attention to change is good.

Separate Entity One way to avoid the problems of dominant managerial logic, emotional attachment, political power, co-opetitor power, and the competency trap is to form a separate unit that is organizationally and physically separated from the incumbent but is still a unit within the firm. Another is to go even further and create a separate start-up company. A separate company attracts more talent who prefer to work in the entrepreneurial environment of a start-up and earn the rights to the potential payoff at the IPO. Moreover, given the valuations of dot.com companies relative to their bricks-and-mortar competitors in the late 1990s and 2000, a separate legal entity could raise much more and cheaper capital through an IPO. A key decision for the general manager is whether to keep the Internet unit within the firm or spin it off as a separate unit. Charles Schwab created a separate unit and later reabsorbed it. General Electric decided to have its own units cannibalize themselves. The company did not see why there should be different Internet units within GE with different compensation systems from those of its bricks-and-mortar units. Some firms form **joint ventures** with venture capital firms that provide not only financing, but also some of the nurturing that start-ups need. Procter and Gamble formed a joint venture with a venture capital firm to launch Reflect.com to offer beauty products directly to customers.

Managing New Entrants

There are two kinds of **new entrants** or so-called pure-play firms: Those that enter markets that rest on the Internet and were nonexistent prior to the Internet, and those that use the Internet to enter existing markets.

New Entrant Advantages

Less Inertia   New entrants do not have many of the handicaps of incumbents: no dominant managerial logic, no competency traps, no channel conflicts, no fear of cannibalization, no emotional attachment to an older technology, no co-opetitor power, and less internal politics. New entrants do not have any legacy systems to handicap them. Thus, they are more nimble and can adopt the new technology more easily.

Equity Capital   In the late 1990s and early 2000, the market valuations of many pure-play Internet companies were high relative to those of the bricks-and-mortar firms that they were attacking. Whether they were worth those high valuations was the topic of debate. But their high valuations constituted a source of **equity capital** for new entrants that their bricks-and-mortar competitors did not have. Managers can take advantage of such high valuations to team up.

Attraction for Talent   Partly attracted by stock options and the potential pay-off at the IPO, young, educated talent would rather work for a pure-play start-up than for an established bricks-and-mortar firm. In the late 1990s and early 2000, young talent found Amazon.com more attractive to work for than Borders. The belief that they could learn more from an Akamai Technologies, Vertical Net, or Commerce One than from a Ford or General Motors also attracted college graduates to the start-ups.

New Entrant Disadvantages

New entrants frequently lack the requisite complementary assets and must develop them from scratch. Some complementary assets such as brand names can be expensive and elusive. In 1999, for example, many dot.coms spent as much as 70 percent of the money raised from venture capital on marketing. Another disadvantage is that the technology could be easy to imitate; therefore, any lead that new entrants have over incumbents may be difficult to protect. This suggests that new entrants may want to develop complementary assets that are more difficult to imitate, rather than depend on their early lead in technology.

Overcoming the Disadvantages

Taking Advantage of the Internet's Properties Although adoption of the Internet is easy to imitate by competitors, some of its properties give new entrants a better chance at first mover advantages. The network externalities effect, for example, suggests that if a firm is able to enter a market first, it can build a large network before competitors come in. Since the larger the network, the more valuable it is, followers that enter later have less of a chance because first movers have the opportunity to capture a large network. Moreover, first movers can advertise and build brand loyalty before incumbents can recover from dominant logic and other incumbent problems.

Run and Extendability Since most business models or parts of them are easy to imitate, a firm may want to emphasize a run strategy. It may want to innovate parts of it or reinvent the whole model before competitors catch up or leapfrog it. Since distinctive capabilities are at the heart of business models, a firm may want to build capabilities that can be extended so that different or better value is offered to the same or different customers in order to generate greater revenues and profits. Amazon.com is a good example of a firm extending its capabilities, although it had not made a profit by early 2001. With capabilities in selling books, music, and videos, Amazon's marginal cost of adding toys was lower than the cost to a new entrant of entering the toy retail market with the same scale as Amazon.

Incumbent/New Entrant Race

Where new entrants are attacking markets, they are in a race of sorts with incumbents: New entrants have the technology and are racing to develop the complementary assets while incumbents have many of the complementary assets and must develop the technology. A new entrant's general manager's responsibility is to decide when and how to go after the complementary assets. If a new entrant wants to develop its own complementary assets rather than team up with another firm that has them, it may want to start early, especially with complementary assets such as network size and brand-name reputation where first mover advantages are important. If a new entrant wants to team up with an incumbent that has the assets, the timing has to be right. If it moves too early, the incumbent's dominant logic may still be too much of a problem for it to understand the value of the new technology. If it waits too long, incumbents might have developed their own technologies and no longer need those of the new entrant.

FORMULATING AND IMPLEMENTING A STRATEGY

Change and the Strategic Management Process

Change is one thing that we can be sure about in a technology that is in its early growth phase. The technology is changing, firms are changing their business models, and the environment is changing. To take advantage of change or avoid competitors taking advantage of them, firms may frequently want to undergo a **strategic management process,** that is, to answer the four strategy formulation and implementation questions: Where is the firm now concerning the Internet? Where does the firm go next? How does it get there? How does it implement the decisions to get there?

Where Is the Firm Now?

This is an analysis of how well the firm is performing, what determines that performance, and how the forces of change may or may not impact that performance (see Figure 11.1). Understanding where a firm is now entails an analysis of the firm's performance, its business model, its competitive (industry) environment, its macro environment, and the change that it is likely to experience. The analysis explores the firm's strengths and weaknesses as well as the threats and opportunities that it faces.

FIGURE 11.1   Where Is the Firm Now?

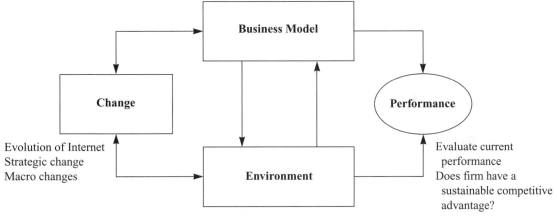

Appraisal of firm's business model
What are the firm's strengths and weaknesses?
What are the sources of competitive advantage?
Are the sources sustainable?

Evolution of Internet
Strategic change
Macro changes

Evaluate current
 performance
Does firm have a
 sustainable competitive
 advantage?

Competitive analysis
 Appraisal of competitors' business models
 Porter's five forces
 Likely actions and reactions of competitors

Industry value drivers
 What are the major drivers of cost
  and differentiation?
 How has the Internet impacted them?

Macro environment
 Economic, social, demographic,
  and political forces

Opportunities and threats

Performance Evaluation

Profitability Measures The analysis of where a firm is now starts with an evaluation of the firm's performance. It explores such basic questions as, How profitable is the firm? What are its cash flows? What are the firm's profit margins, market share, and revenue share growth rate? (Recall that profit margins, market share, and revenue share growth can be predictors of future profitability for knowledge-based products.) For bricks-and-mortar firms facing attack from new entrants, the question might be: How much market share is being captured by the attackers? The bottom line is whether the firm has a competitive advantage and, if so, whether it is sustainable.

Intellectual Capital Rather than assess a firm's performance using profitability measures, a general manager may also want to pay attention to its market valuations. Table 11.1 shows the differences between the book values and market values of a sample of leading firms. Two things stand out. First, the differences between book value and market value are very large. Second, the differences vary considerably from firm to firm. In any case, what each difference says is that there is something about each firm—about its competitive and macro environments and, above all, *something* about its business model—that makes investors believe that its future free cash flows and profits will be higher than its book value. The differences say that there is something about each firm, other than the assets on its books, that makes investors believe that it will be profitable enough or generate enough free cash flows to be worth that much. This something, as we suggested in Chapter 8, has been called *intellectual capital,* intangible assets, human capital, or knowledge. Thus, Cisco's intellectual capital in March 1999 was $159 billion while that of General Motors, a company with about 20 times Cisco's revenues, was only $49 billion. Amazon.com's intellectual capital is more than 20 times that of its bricks-and-mortar foe Barnes & Noble. Rather than dismiss other firms' val-

TABLE 11.1 Market Valuations and Intellectual Capital

Source: Company Financial Statements, *Fortune,* April 26, 1999.

	1998 Revenues ($ millions)	1998 Profits ($ millions)	March 15, 1999		
			Market Value (MV) ($ millions)	Book Value (BV) ($ millions)	Intellectual Capital MV − BV ($ millions)
General Motors	$161,315	$2,956	$63,839	$14,984	$48,855
Ford	144,416	22,071	70,881	23,409	47,472
Cisco	8,458	1,350	166,615	7,106	159,209
Amazon.com	610	−125	22,383	139	22,244
Barnes & Noble	3,006	92	2,045	679	1,366

uations as ridiculously high or a market bubble, the responsibility of general managers is to understand why the intellectual capital in their industry is lower than that in other industries, why their firms' intellectual capital is higher or lower than that of rivals, and, above all, what the relationship between intellectual capital and the Internet is.

Business Model Appraisal

A primary determinant of a firm's performance is its business model. Thus, determining where a firm is now entails an appraisal of the firm's *Internet* business model. This is the appraisal that we explored in Chapter 9, in particular, the questions in Table 9.2. The result is a determination of the firm's strengths and weaknesses in the components and linkages of the business model. For a bricks-and-mortar firm under attack, the appraisal should include a comparison and "what if" analysis for both its bricks-and-mortar business model and potential Internet business models.

Environmental Analysis

The other key determinant of a firm's performance is its environment—both the competitive (industry) and macro environments.

Competitive Environment The first thing in a competitor analysis is to appraise the Internet business models of key competitors. This appraisal reveals to the general manager the strengths and weaknesses of competitors. With this information, the manager can better know where his or her firm may be attacked, which competitors would make for good team-up partners, and what the actions and reactions of competitors are likely to be. The second important analysis is one of industry attractiveness. This consists of the now-familiar Porter's five forces to identify what makes an industry attractive or unattractive. The focus is on the potential impact of the Internet on industry attractiveness. Recall that because of the Internet's information asymmetry property, there is a shift in bargaining power from suppliers and firms to customers. The exact nature of this shift should be analyzed.

Industry Value Drivers The analysis here focuses on those things that drive cost or differentiation in a firm's industry—more importantly, the extent to which the Internet has or can impact them. The analysis entails a value chain, value shop, or value network detailed analysis that determines the firm's cost and differentiation structures. This is then followed by an analysis of how the Internet is likely to impact the structure. Recall the automobile example in Chapter 8 in which the cost structure is heavily skewed toward the back end of the value chain where 30 percent of the price of a car covers the cost of distribution attributed largely to the inability to forecast, which in turn leads to unnecessary advertising, promotion, discounting, and transportation costs. Information movement inefficiencies are also partly to blame for the length of time (60–100 days) it takes from the bending of metal to the customer receiving the car. These are examples of opportunities in the value chain of an industry that a manager can target so that the firm can take advantage of the Internet.

Macro Environment Recall that an environment with a good financial support and reward system for entrepreneurs, a culture that tolerates failure, the right co-opetitors, and innovation-friendly government policies is more conducive to innovation than an environment that is void of these elements. An analysis of the macro environment should include an examination of the strength of the environment in each of these factors. Government policies and rulings on patents and other intellectual property issues related to the Internet should be carefully analyzed. This has an impact on whether a firm pursues a block strategy or not. Demographic, sociological, political, and legal trends should also be surveyed. Particular attention should be given to legislation that affects the Internet. Increasingly, the natural environment also plays a critical role and its potential impact on the Internet should be examined too.

Change

There are three external sources of change: the Internet, competitors, and the macro environment.

The Evolving Internet Recall that technology usually evolves from an early phase through a growth phase to a stable phase, and each phase requires different capabilities and strategies. In many industries the Internet is in the early or the growth phase. Also recall that over the life cycle of the automobile industry, more than 2,000 companies were started in the United States. The catchword that had to be in each company's name was "motor" just as in the growth phase of the Internet the catchword was "dot.com."[16] In 2000 there were just two major automobile companies left in the United States. Along the way, all the horse-driven cart companies that the automobile firms replaced also disappeared. The point is that eventually most of the existing dot.com companies will exit their industries or merge with others. General managers must take this into consideration as they explore the threats and opportunities that face their firms.

In focusing on the Internet, it is easy to forget about other technologies that might complement a firm's Internet strategy. Technologies such as wireless communications can offer alternative or complementary infrastructures for data communications.

Competitive Environmental Change Rivals are constantly changing their strategies and such changes, especially new game strategies, have to be watched very carefully. A firm is said to pursue a **new game strategy** if by performing value chain, value shop, or value configuration activities that differ from what the dominant logic of the industry dictates, or by performing the same activities differently than the logic dictates, the firm is able to offer superior customer value. Wal-Mart's early strategies were new game strategies. It decided to move into small towns, saturate adjoining towns with stores, build distribution centers, and improve logistics, with an empowering culture and information technology to match. This allowed Wal-Mart to achieve high economies of scale and bargaining power over its suppliers. This in turn allowed the firm to offer its customers lower prices than its competitors. Kmart's management did not pay attention to this new game strategy, which resulted in the firm being overtaken by Wal-Mart. Kmart has never recovered.

Changes from Macro Environment   Many changes from the macro environment have the potential to cripple even the best of strategies and must therefore be watched. Managers should note any changes in the environmental factors cited above as conducive to innovation. Potential changes in exchange rates, especially unanticipated large ones, central bank policies that raise interest rates, and taxation laws, along with demographic and sociopolitical changes, all have the potential to impact firm strategies. Managers should examine them carefully for potential threats and opportunities. In particular, they should examine the potential impact of changes in tax policies concerning the Internet.

This analysis of a firm's current performance, appraisal of its business model, appraisal of its competitors' business models, analysis of industry attractiveness, assessment of its macro environment, projection of the evolution of the Internet, and a forecast of its environmental changes is sometimes called a strengths and weaknesses, opportunities, and threats **(SWOT)** analysis.[17]

Where Does the Firm Go Next?

From the exploration of where a firm is now, a manager has many strategic alternatives from which to choose. After such an analysis, for example, AOL might discover that to maintain its subscription pricing model successfully, it needs more content. It may then decide to add more content. A manager may find out that its fledgling Internet start-up does not have the complementary assets that it needs to offer competitive customer value and must get them if the start-up is to gain a sustainable advantage. An Amazon.com may find out that, in selling books, it has developed capabilities that can be extended to sell music, videos, electronics, home improvement, toys, and even to create online malls. So it decides to move into these areas.

After an analysis of where the firm is now, a manager may also decide not to pursue profits as previously planned but to hone the firm's capabilities to fit another firm's portfolio of capabilities so that it can be acquired by the other firm. On the other hand, a firm whose exit strategy had been to be acquired, with no intention of ever making profits, may decide that it now wants to become profitable after all.

In all these cases, a firm has decided to move into new areas. It is now intent on doing certain things that it had not done before. If moving into these new areas requires entirely new capabilities, the objective to do so is sometimes referred to as a firm's **strategic intent.**[18]

How Does the Firm Get There?

Take the example of the fledgling start-up that needs complementary assets to offer the right customer value. The question now becomes, How does the start-up get the complementary assets? It has the option of developing the assets internally or teaming up with a firm that already has them. In teaming up, the firm may decide to be acquired rather than form a strategic alliance. An AOL, for example, could develop the content alone or team up with a Disney to do so. It might also buy a Time Warner company that has the content. By and large, getting there usually requires new capabilities. When a firm wants to get somewhere but lacks the capabilities to do so, it is said to have a **capabilities gap.** To fill this gap, a firm usually must decide whether to develop the capabilities internally or obtain them from outside. E. B. Roberts and C. A. Berry developed a model that can be used to guide managers in their choice of how to get the capabilities that they need.

Roberts and Berry Model

Offering new value to customers or assuming a new product-market position usually requires both technological and marketing capabilities. The more unfamiliar firms are with the technology or market, the higher their risk of failure since they will have a difficult time building the capabilities from scratch. Since these capabilities take time to build, a firm may be better off teaming up with another firm that has them. The **Roberts and Berry model**[19] of Figure 11.2 depicts this. In other words, the mechanism that a firm uses to build the capabilities that it needs is a function of the extent to which it is familiar with the technology and market. Roberts and Berry explored seven such mechanisms for acquiring new capabilities: internal development, acquisitions, licensing, internal ventures, joint ventures, venture capital, and educational acquisitions.[20]

If the technology and market are familiar, the firm may be better off developing the innovation internally because it has the capabilities to do so. If the market is new but familiar while the technology exists in the firm, the firm can also pursue internal development since the required marketing capabilities build on existing ones and the firm already has the technological capabilities. Amazon.com's move from books, music, and videos to toys, auctions, and electronics is a good example. A similar strategy applies when the technology is new but familiar, and the market is an existing one; that is, a firm can also develop the technology internally since the required capabilities build on existing ones. In both cases, the firm can also buy the technology or license it from someone because it has the absorptive capacity to assimilate it.

When the technology is familiar but the market is new and unfamiliar, a joint venture becomes a very attractive mechanism. Why? Because, in a joint venture, two or more firms set up a separate and legal entity that they own, and pool their capabilities to achieve a common goal. Thus, a firm that is familiar with the technology but not with the market can form a joint venture with others that are familiar with the market. With their complementary capabilities, they can offer customer value to the market earlier while learning from each other and building capabilities in the areas they lack.

When both the market and technology are new but familiar, a firm can use other mechanisms such as internal ventures, acquisitions, and licensing. In an

FIGURE 11.2   Roberts and Berry Model on Acquiring Capabilities

Source: Adapted from: E. B. Roberts and C. A. Berry, "Entering New Businesses: Selecting Strrategies for Success," *Sloan Management Review* 26, no. 3 (1985), pp. 3–17.

	Existing	New but familiar	New and unfamiliar
New and unfamiliar	Joint venture	Venture capital Educational acquisition	Venture capital Educational acquisition
New but familiar	Internet market capabilities development Acquisition	Internal ventures Acquisitions Licensing	Venture capital Educational acquisition
Existing	Internal development (or acquisition)	Internal technological capabilities development Acquisitions Licensing	Strategic alliance

*(Vertical axis label: **Market**; Horizontal axis label: **Technology**)*

internal venture, a firm sets up a separate entity within itself to develop a new product, usually employing those entrepreneurial individuals who would otherwise move out on their own to found a competing firm. A firm can also buy another firm that has the capabilities that it needs. This gives it immediate access to the necessary capabilities and it can start learning right away. Rather than buy, a firm can also license the product from another firm.

When both the technology and market are new and unfamiliar to a firm, the required capabilities are different from its existing capabilities. Roberts and Berry suggested using venture capital and educational acquisitions. In venture capital, a firm makes a minority investment in a young firm that has the capabilities (usually technological). In either case, by taking interest in the start-up, the investing firm obtains a window on technology and markets, and can learn. **Educational acquisition** is the purchase of a firm by another one for the sole purpose of learning from it, not to keep it as a subsidiary. It is the reverse engineering of an organization—buy, open up, and learn from.

Implementation

Deciding where a firm should go and how to get there is one thing. Implementing the decision is another. If an AOL has decided to add more content and wants to develop it internally, the questions now include: How should the organization that will develop the content be structured? Who will report to whom? How will performance be measured and rewarded? Who should be hired? The strategy, structure, systems, people, and environment (S^3PE) framework that we described when exploring the implementation component of a business model applies here. If an AOL decides to team up with someone, who should that be, who will stay where, and what type of employees will each contribute to the team? Of particular interest for a manager facing the Internet are two key points: the need to use information technology to better manage people and its limitations.

Employee Needs and S^3PE Fit

The Internet is about information and knowledge which means that the individuals who have this knowledge are extremely important. In designing organizational strategies, structures, and systems for a good S^3PE fit, a firm needs to know more about what makes each individual tick. Sure enough, on average, employees may want stock options in their firm. But there may be software engineers who would rather have their names in some part of the software so that their friends and relatives can access it and see that they actually played a major part in developing the software. Moreover, what happens when everyone offers stock options to their employees? The point is that managers need to know more about each employee in order to better decide to whom they should report, how their performance is measured, and how that performance is rewarded.

Physical Colocation

Many of the properties of the Internet indicate that distance is less of a constraint than it used to be for many activities. As general managers structure their organizations, however, it is important for them to remember that certain transactions may still require in-person physical interaction. Some kinds of tacit knowledge are difficult to unstick and encode in a form that can be transmitted and received over the Internet. In pharmaceuticals, for example, doctors can post data from the clinical testing of a new drug on a website for sharing with other doctors, thus increasing the efficiency and speed of testing. This can lead to faster approval of drugs for marketing by the Food and Drug Administration and an increase in a firm's profits over the life of the drug's patent. However, the Internet is no substitute for the informal exchange of ideas that takes place over the water cooler, in the parking lot, in the cafeteria, and in the hallways that is critical during pharmaceutical drug discovery. Physical colocation is still critical for such R&D activities.[21] To the extent that people have emotions, it may also be a good idea to visit customers even if there is a website that people use for transactions.[22]

PERSONAL ROLE OF THE GENERAL MANAGER

General managers have been described as thinkers, controllers, leaders, champions, sponsors, and doers.[23] While some of these characteristics are desirable in general managers, we will concentrate on two that would serve managers well in the face of the Internet: champion and sponsor. The importance of these characteristics rests in part on the tendency for leadership and power in firms whose products are knowledge-based to reside with those individuals who have the knowledge—and these individuals are not necessarily the managers. Thus, a manager is more a facilitator of knowledge exchange than the controller of resources. Facilitating means the ability to articulate a vision of what the firm and its business model are all about. Champions and sponsors do this best.

Champions

Champions are individuals—sometimes called advocates or evangelists or entrepreneurs—who take an idea (theirs or that of an idea generator) and do all they can within their power to ensure its success.[24] In the process, they risk their position, reputation, and prestige. They actively promote the idea or business model, inspiring others with their vision of its potential. Jeff Bezos, of Amazon.com, was a champion for his firm in the late 1990s and early 2000. Champions must be able to relate to the whole value configuration and therefore require T-skills.[25] (T-skills are deep expertise in one discipline combined with a sufficiently broad knowledge in others to see the linkages between them.) Despite frequent opposition, especially in the face of disruptive technologies like the Internet, champions persist in their articulation and promotion of their vision of the technology. They usually emerge from the ranks of the organization and cannot be hired and groomed for the purpose of being champions. By evangelically communicating the vision of the potential of an innovation, a champion can go a long way in helping an organization better understand the rationale behind the innovation and its potential. General managers could benefit from having this characteristic. The other characteristic is being a sponsor.

Sponsors

Also called a coach or mentor, a **sponsor** is a senior-level manager who provides behind-the-scenes support, access to resources, and protection from political foes. Such support and protection serve two purposes.[26] First, in the case of a bricks-and-mortar firm adopting the Internet, for example, a sponsor's support sends a signal to political foes of the Internet that they are messing with a senior manager and sponsor. Second, it reassures the champion and other key individuals that they have the support of a senior manager. Lee Iacocca, former CEO of Chrysler, was the sponsor of the company's minivan. Edward Hagenlocker, Ford's vice president for truck operations, backed and boosted funds for a radical new approach to designing new cars that was instrumental to the success of Ford's trucks such as the F-150.[27]

Summary

In the face of the Internet, the primary responsibility of general managers is to guide their firm to gain or reinforce a sustainable competitive advantage. The extent to which they can meet this challenge is a function of three factors: whether their firm is an incumbent or a pure-play Internet new entrant, how they can guide the firm through the formulation and execution of a good strategy, and the characteristics of the general manager. General managers should understand some important differences between incumbents—the bricks-and-mortar or legacy firms that were in their industries before the Internet was adopted by those industries—and new entrants, the pure-play firms that entered using the Internet. Incumbents have to deal with the legacy problems of dominant managerial logic, competency traps, channel conflicts, internal political power, co-opetitor power, and emotional attachment to older technologies and capabilities. On the other hand, they may have complementary assets that they can use. Moreover, portions or all of many Internet business models can be imitated, giving incumbents a chance to catch up. New entrants do not have the legacy handicaps of incumbents and attract more equity capital and knowledgeable employees. However, they do not have complementary assets and must build them from scratch.

Whether a firm is an incumbent or a new entrant, it must formulate and execute an Internet strategy if it is going to have a sustainable competitive advantage. This entails answering four important questions: (1) *Where is the firm now?*—that is, how well is it doing? What is the basis of its performance? What are its strengths and weaknesses? Are there any threats or opportunities that it faces? (2) *Where does the firm go next?* Given the firm's performance, its positioning relative to its rivals and competitive and macro environments, it may want to pursue different goals. (3) *How does the firm get there?* Pursuing new goals usually means finding different ways to achieve them. (4) *How does the firm implement the decisions to get there?* Deciding where to go to next and how to get there is one thing. Executing the strategy is another. Guiding a firm through this strategy requires a general manager to have certain characteristics, among them being a champion and sponsor.

Key Terms

cannibalization, *206*
capabilities gap, *216*
champions, *219*
channel conflict, *206*
competency trap, *206*
competitive advantage, *203*
complementary assets, *204*

co-opetitor power, *207*
dominant coalition, *207*
dominant managerial logic, *205*
educational acquisition, *217*
emotional attachments, *208*

equity capital, *209*
genetic mix, *208*
incumbents, *204*
joint ventures, *209*
legacy firms, *204*
managerial logic, *205*
new entrants, *209*
new game strategy, *214*
political power, *207*

Discussion Questions

1. Why do incumbents have such a difficult time adopting radical technological changes?

2. When is an incumbent more likely to win an Internet race against new entrants?

3. In the face of the Internet, what type of firm would you rather manage: an incumbent or an attacker? Provide detailed evidence backing your choice.

4. It has been said that the best way to beat change is to change first. Does this statement apply in the face of the Internet? Any industries in particular?

5. What areas of government regulation do you think would have the most influence on the Internet: taxation of e-commerce, intellectual property laws, or privacy laws?

6. In a firm's Internet strategic management process, which of the four major steps do you believe require the most attention from a general manager: Where is the firm now as far as the Internet is concerned? Where does the firm go next? How does it get there? How does it implement the decisions to get there? Explain.

7. Apart from being sponsor and champion, what type of person do you believe the general manager of a firm should be? Does the type of industry in which the person manages make a difference?

8. It has been said that with the Internet, geography no longer matters. Do you agree or not? Explain.

Notes

1. For the first three questions in a "bigger" picture, see C. A. de Kluyver, *Strategic Thinking: An Executive Perspective* (New York: Prentice Hall, 2000).

2. S. Oster, *Modern Competitive Analysis,* 3rd ed. (Oxford: Oxford University Press, 1999), pp. 128–140.

3. R. M. Grant, *Contemporary Strategy Analysis* (Malden, MA: Blackwell, 1995), p. 151.

4. This section draws on A. N. Afuah, *Innovation Management: Strategies, Implementation, and Profits* (New York: Oxford University Press, 1998), pp. 217–222.

5. G. M. Hamel and C. K. Prahalad, *Competing for the Future* (Boston: Harvard Business School Press, 1994), pp. 49–71; R. A. Bettis and C. K. Prahalad, "The Dominant Logic: Retrospective and Extension," *Strategic Management Journal* 16 (1995), pp. 5–14.

6. D. C. Hambrick, M. A. Geletkanycz, and J. W. Fredrickson, "Top Executive Commitment to the Status Quo: Some Tests of Its Determinants," *Strategic Management Journal* 14 (1993), pp. 401–18.

7. D. Leonard-Barton, *Wellsprings of Knowledge* (Boston: Harvard Business School Press, 1995).

8. Bettis and Prahalad, "The Dominant Logic," pp. 5–14.

9. J. Pfeffer, *Managing with Power: Politics and Influence in Organizations* (Boston: Harvard Business School Press, 1992).

10. ———, *Power in Organizations* (Mansfield, MA: Pitman, 1981).

11. C. H. Ferguson and C. R. Morris, *Computer Wars: How the West Can Win in the Post-IBM World* (New York: Time Books, 1993).

12. C. M. Christensen and J. L. Bower, "Customer Power, Strategic Investment and Failure of Leading Firms," *Strategic Management Journal* 17 (1996), pp. 197–218.

13. R. A. Burgelman, "Fading Memories: The Process Theory of Strategic Business Exit in Dynamic Environments," *Administrative Science Quarterly* 38 (1994), pp. 24–56.

14. Hamel and Prahalad, *Competing for the Future,* pp. 49–71.

15. The General Mills, Hewlett-Packard, and 3M examples are based on a homecoming speech given by General Mills's CEO Steve Sanger at the University of Michigan Business School on October 26, 1995; S. Hickman, "General Mills Delivers Success Story," *The Monroe Street Journal,* October 30, 1995; K. Labich, "The Innovators," *Fortune,* June 6, 1988, p. 49; R. Mitchell, "Masters of Innovation," *Business Week,* April 10, 1989, p. 58; K. Kelly, "3M Run Scared? Forget about It," *Business Week,* September 16, 1991, pp. 59–62; M. Loeb and T. J. Martin, "Ten Commandments for Managing Creative People," *Fortune,* January 16, 1995.

16. For a fascinating account of the dynamics of technological change in the automobile and other industries, see J. M. Utterback, *Mastering the Dynamics of Innovation* (Cambridge: Harvard Business School Press, 1994).

17. A. A. Thompson and A. J. Strickland, *Strategic Management: Concepts and Cases* (Homewood, IL: Richard D. Irwin, 1990).

18. Hamel and Prahalad, *Competing for the Future,* pp. 129–290.

19. S. C. Johnson and C. Jones, "How to Organize for New Products," *Harvard Business Review,* May–June 1957, pp. 49–62; E. B. Roberts and C. A. Berry, "Entering New Businesses: Selecting Strategies for Success," *Sloan Management Review* 26, no. 3 (1985), pp. 3–17.

20. Roberts and Berry, "Entering New Businesses," pp. 3–17; see also M. H. Meyer and E. B. Roberts, "New Product Strategy in Small Technology-Based Firms: A Pilot Study," *Management Science* 32, no. 7 (1986), pp. 806–21.

21. T. Allen, *Managing the Flow of Technology* (Cambridge: MIT Press, 1984).

22. T. Peters, *Liberation Management* (New York: Alfred A. Knopf, 1992).

23. H. Mintzberg and J. B. Quinn, *The Strategy Process: Concepts, Contexts and Cases* (New York: Prentice Hall, 1996).

24. The concept of champions was first developed by D. A. Schön in his seminal article, "Champions for Radical New Inventions," *Harvard Business Review* 41 (1963), pp. 77–86; see also J. M. Howell and C. A. Higgins, "Champions of Technological Innovation, *Administrative Sciences Quarterly* 35 (1990), pp. 317–41; E. B. Roberts and A. R. Fusfeld, "Staffing the Innovative Technology-Based Organization," *Sloan Management Review* (Spring 1981), pp. 19–34.

25. M. Iansiti, "Real-World R&D: Jumping the Product Generation Gap," *Harvard Business Review,* May–June 1993, pp. 138–47.

26. Roberts and Fusfeld, "Staffing the Innovative Technology-Based Organization," pp. 19–34; M. A. Maidique, "Entrepreneurs, Champions, and Technological Innovation," *Sloan Management Review* (Winter 1980), pp. 59–76.

27. K. Naughton, "How Ford's F-150 Lapped the Competition," *Business Week,* July 29, 1996, pp. 74–75.

Chapter **Twelve**

Sample Analysis of an Internet Business Model Case[1]

In this section we apply several of the theories and frameworks discussed in prior chapters to a classic question, Should a company diversify into a new business model? We use the case of Amazon.com's decision in 1999 to inaugurate the zShops as an example of analyzing and appraising a business model.[2]

AMAZON.COM: zSHOPS*

On May 15, 1997, Amazon.com completed one of the most successful initial public offerings (IPOs) in history. Its success ushered in a new era in the Internet, the era of e-commerce (electronic commerce). As the market price continued to rise, many at Amazon became overnight millionaires, and Jeff Bezos, its founder, a billionaire.

By October 1999, with Amazon's market capitalization at $28 billion—substantially more than Sears, Roebuck & Co. and Kmart Corp. combined—Bezos needed to look at new products to maintain Amazon's growth rate. The company had added no new product categories that year until July, when it opened toy and electronics shopping, and annual quarter-to-quarter growth had slowed, to 7 percent from 33 percent the previous year. That growth rate did not justify its market value (see Table 12.1).

*New York University Stern School of Business MBA Candidates Youngseok Kim, Myriam E. Lopez, Suzanne Schiavelli, Heshy Shayovitz, and Steve Yoon developed this case under the supervision of Professor Christopher L. Tucci for the purpose of class discussion rather than to illustrate either effective or ineffective handling of an administrative situation. Copyright © 2001 by McGraw-Hill/Irwin. All rights reserved.

TABLE 12.1

Amazon Timeline

Source: *Seattle Times;*
Amazon.com press releases.

July 1995	Amazon begins selling books online.
May 15, 1997	Amazon goes public.
March 1998	Amazon.com Kids books available on the Web.
June 11, 1998	Amazon diversifies to include CDs.
August 4, 1998	Amazon purchases Junglee Corp. and PlanetAll
November 16, 1998	Amazon introduces video and gift stores.
March 29, 1999	Amazon releases its auction site to counter eBay.
July 1999	Amazon opens toys and electronics stores.
September 29, 1999	Amazon announces zShops.

Seeking to generate more growth, Amazon introduced the *zShops*. The zShops were a bazaar of online stores that make up an online mall. The zShops concept allowed other companies to open online stores under the Amazon.com brand and customers to benefit from a larger selection of products. As Bezos sat in his office, he wondered whether he had made the right decision to move Amazon away from e-tailing history and refocus the company as an e-commerce mall.

Amazon.com

After graduating summa cum laude from Princeton in 1986, Jeff Bezos joined FITEL, a high-tech start-up company in New York. Two years later Bezos moved to the Bankers Trust Company, where he led the development of computer systems that helped manage more than $250 billion in assets. He became the bank's youngest vice president in February 1990. From 1990 to 1994, Bezos helped build one of the most technically sophisticated and successful quantitative hedge funds on Wall Street for D. E. Shaw & Co., becoming their youngest senior vice president in 1992. Bezos said that he had a quarter of the company reporting to him at the time he came up with the idea for Amazon. He considered the consequences of pursuing the idea:

> I projected out to being 80 years old and put myself in a regret-minimization framework. Would I ever ask myself, "Boy, what would my 1994 Wall Street bonus have been?" Not likely! But I could sincerely regret not doing this . . . [3]

With that, he quit his job and drove west with his wife. At the time, he didn't even know where to ship his furniture. As his wife drove, he tapped out Amazon.com's business plan on a laptop computer and lined up financing on his cell phone. Eventually, he settled on Seattle, mainly because of its proximity to the Roseburg, Oregon, warehouse of Ingram, the giant book distributor. Before the truckload of his belongings arrived, Bezos and four software designers had set up shop in his garage to create the foundations of their company's website. His team spent a year developing database programs and creating the website. Amazon.com opened its virtual doors for business in July 1995.[4]

Amazon.com's greatest strength may be that it was the first online bookseller armed with substantial capital from its IPO, impressive service (including innovations like "1-Click" shopping), and a gigantic selection of titles (the company claimed to have a virtual inventory of 3.5 million books by 1996). Its strategy marked a clear challenge to established book chains like Barnes & Noble, whose superstores generally stock only 175,000 titles (see Table 12.2). In 1996 Amazon earned revenues of $15.8 million (see Table 12.3 and Figure 12.1).

Amazon's Diversification Strategy

The company's success did not go unnoticed. Both Barnes & Noble and Borders bookstores entered the market. The former represented a particularly strong challenge. Amazon responded by securing a contract to sell books to America Online's 8 million subscribers.[5]

Amazon meanwhile extended its existing online stores to appeal to more customers. In March 1998, for example, it opened Amazon.com Kids, which it dubbed "the most comprehensive resource for children's and young adult books on the Web." With its success in the book market firmly established, Amazon was poised to proceed with the next phase of its plan. Its scalable architecture (the ability of its information infrastructure design to handle growth) allowed it to sell additional items other than books. "The real benefit is for our customers," said Amazon.com spokesman Bill Curry. "We want to be the leading destination for e-commerce"[6] (see Table 12.4).

On June 11, 1988, Amazon extended its product line by introducing compact disks (CDs), with the ability to select among more than 125,000 music CD titles—10 times the CD selection of the typical music store. At the time Roy Satterthwaite, Gartner Group's electronic commerce analyst, thought that Amazon.com might be making a mistake. Satterthwaite said that in most e-commerce markets, companies need to concentrate on their specific categories, for example, Amazon.com and books. Because those companies specialize, they can concentrate on consumers "who limit their choices to the top three in each category."[7]

It took just four months to roll over the leading online music retailer, CDnow, to post music sales of $33.1 million during the fourth quarter of 1998 compared to $20.9 million for CDnow. Seeing their formula was successful,

TABLE 12.2

Amazon versus Barnes & Noble: Some Statistics

Source: *Business Week,* December 14, 1998, www.businessweek.com/ 1998/50/b3608006.htm.

	Amazon	Barnes & Noble
Number of stores	1 website	1,011
Titles per superstore	3.1 million	175,000
Book returns	2%	30%
Sales growth*	306%	10%
Sales per employee (annual)	$375,000	$100,000
Inventory turnovers per year	24	3
Long-term capital requirements	Low	High
Cash flow	High	Low

*Third quarter, 1998.

TABLE 12.3   **Amazon Financials at the Time of the zShops Introduction**

Source: Zacks Investment Research.

AMAZON.COM INC
Annual Income Statement
(in millions except EPS data)

Fiscal Year End for AMAZON.COM INC (AMZN) falls in the month of December.

	12/31/98	12/31/97	12/31/96	12/31/95
Sales	609.99	147.76	15.75	0.51
Cost of goods	476.11	118.94	12.29	0.41
Gross profit	**133.88**	**28.81**	**3.46**	**0.10**
Selling and administrative, and depreciation and amortization expenses	195.62	58.02	9.44	0.41
Income after depreciation and amortization	**(61.74)**	**(29.21)**	**(5.98)**	**(0.30)**
Nonoperating income	(36.15)	1.90	0.20	0.00
Interest expense	26.63	0.28	0.00	0.00
Pretax income	**(124.54)**	**(27.59)**	**(5.78)**	**(0.30)**
Income taxes	0.00	0.00	0.00	0.00
Minority interest	0.00	0.00	0.00	0.00
Investment gains/losses	0.00	0.00	0.00	0.00
Other income/charges	0.00	0.00	0.00	0.00
Income from continuing operations	N/A	N/A	N/A	N/A
Extras and discontinued operations	0.00	0.00	0.00	0.00
Net income	**(124.54)**	**(27.59)**	**(5.78)**	**(0.30)**
Depreciation Footnote:				
Income before depreciation and amortization	(49.67)	(24.47)	(5.69)	(0.29)
Depreciation and amortization (cash flow)	12.07	4.74	0.29	0.02
Income after depreciation and amortization	**(61.74)**	**(29.21)**	**(5.98)**	**(0.30)**
Earnings Per Share Data (EPS):				
Average no. of shares	**296.34**	**260.68**	**271.86**	**227.20**
Diluted EPS before nonrecurring items	(0.25)	(0.10)	(0.02)	(0.00)
Diluted net EPS	**(0.42)**	**(0.10)**	**(0.02)**	**(0.00)**

Bezos and company leveraged the brand to expand into more markets. In November 1998, just before the start of the holiday shopping season, Amazon introduced a video and gift section on its website. The video part of Amazon.com opened with 60,000 video titles and 2,000 digital videodisk (DVD) offerings, providing direct competition for online stores like Reel.com. In addition, several hundred gift items were added, ranging from Barbie dolls to Nintendo video games. Most of the gift items were chosen because they related either to what Amazon.com offered in books, music, or videos or "because they would appeal to [their] regular customers."[8]

FIGURE 12.1

Amazon's Annual Sales

Source: Zacks Investment Research.

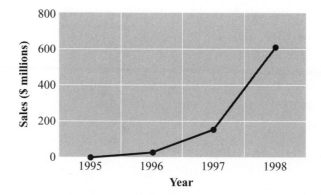

Hoping to counter eBay's success in the online auction market (see the eBay case in Part V of this book), Amazon introduced its own person-to-person auction site in March 1999. The auction included many trust-building features that made eBay such a success. In addition, the company reimbursed customers up to $250 if they could prove they were victims of fraud or did not receive paid-for auction items. In July Amazon introduced another store to sell electronics.

Adding another piece to the company's strategy, Amazon built a massive, $300 million, 5-million-square-foot warehouse in Fernley, Nevada, the first of seven it was to open by the end of 2000. It then hired Wal-Mart's logistics chief, Jimmy Wright, as vice president and chief logistics officer. This hire suggests that Bezos took seriously the challenges of establishing a powerful, rapid supply and distribution network.

Amazon's dream was to become a place where people can find not only books, but everything. Amazon has defined e-commerce as we know it: 1-Click shopping, customer reviews, online gift-wrapping—Amazon has invented them all. Amazon now offers 19 million items. Despite the huge number of items it sold, Amazon realized that it could not sell everything. Thus, the idea for the zShops emerged.

zShops

The zShops concept was a bazaar of online retailers who wanted to set up shop under the Amazon umbrella. Amazon opened its website to these merchants for a minimal fee. In return, the selling powerhouse gathered huge amounts of information on consumer buying habits. Amazon expected to help these companies and to expand well beyond its base of books, CDs, and so forth.

The biggest benefit for Amazon was a steady cash flow without the costs associated with a warehouse of products. Each online store paid a $9.99 monthly fee, which was less than the average for such a service, and commissions of 1 percent to 5 percent in return for access to Amazon's 12 million customers (see Table 12.5). If the zShop chose to have Amazon process its billing, the shop paid an additional 4.75 percent of the total sale. This arrangement also

TABLE 12.4   Amazon Properties

Source: www.companysleuth.com/askjeeves/index.cfm?INFO-AMZN.

Internet Domains	
amazon-electronics.com	zshop.com
amazon500.com	prizewinners.com
book-ology.com	amazontelevision.com
bookmatcher.com	amazon-electronic.com
amazontube.com	acimages.com
zpays.com	bookology.com
zdvds.com	zshoppe.org
amazonvideo.com	zsearchs.com
amazonelectronic.com	z-shoppe.net
friend-click.com	filmlovers.com

Listing of All New Trademarks Filed in Late 1999

Trademark No.	Description
75-775431	Book-ology
75-770523	zShops
75-765373	Quickclick
75-765372	Powerclick
75-765371	First Bidder Discount
75-765370	Crosslinks
75-765369	Charitylinks
75-765367	2-Click
75-765366	0-Click
75-760190	Crosslinks
75-755296	Selling circles
75-755295	Buying circles
75-755294	Bidding circles
75-755292	Auction circles
75-755291	Purchase circles
75-775431	Book-ology
75-770523	zShops
75-765373	Quickclick
75-765372	Powerclick
75-765371	First Bidder Discount

Patent No.	Description
5,963,949	Method for data gathering around forms and search barriers

TABLE 12.5
Price Range for Selected Companies

Source: Compiled from each company's website, www.msn.com, www.ebay.com, and www.amazon.com.

MSN:	1.5% and 5%, based on the purchase price.
eBay:	Sliding listings fee based on the opening bid; then received a final fee of between 1.25% and 5% of the selling price.
Amazon:	5% for $0–$25, 2.5% for $25–$999, and 1.25% for $1,000 and over.

gave Amazon valuable information for its database on consumer preferences and habits and provided target-marketing capabilities.

This new business model had two strategic implications. On the one hand, its move to become an unlimited shopping mall was an attempt to compete with Internet portals like America Online and Yahoo!, which offered links with millions of websites and had substantially more monthly traffic. On the other hand, it provided an opportunity to take away some of the small-business revenue flooding into auction sites like eBay, Microsoft, Excite@Home, and Lycos, which agreed to share their auction listings.

Amazon's zShops was organized essentially by product and product category, not by stores. After a customer picked an item from a list, he or she was sent to a merchant-controlled page that included a picture and description of the item. Amazon temporarily offered for free (until Christmas 1999) several of the marketing tools it had refined, and let any merchant offer 1-Click shopping in return for a percentage of the sale.

E-COMMERCE INDUSTRY

According to Forrester Research, consumer sales over the Internet would increase to $184.0 billion by 2004 from $3.9 billion in 1998,[9] and most major merchants are trying to develop a business strategy that will ensure a dominant position in this emerging marketplace. A few years ago Amazon had cyberspace largely to itself. Now the Internet was teeming with e-tailers. Buy.com, for example, was programmed to scan Amazon.com's prices and automatically undercut them.

Competitors

Online malls provided convenience, helping shoppers find an array of items in a single place. Portals, including Yahoo!, America Online, Excite@Home, MSN, and Lycos, were competing in this market with large customer bases and different services, such as online wallets and shopping carts that let buyers pick and choose from multiple stores with minimal hassle. The performance of online malls had been mixed. Big merchants, from Eddie Bauer to FAO Schwarz, continued to buy space, but Amazon was trying to put an end to marketing tie-ins with Internet portal sites. America Online was among the most successful online shopping destinations to that point, luring more than 1 million first-time shoppers in December 1998 alone and generating sales of

$1.2 billion over the holiday season. Yahoo's online mall rivaled Amazon's, with 7,000 stores and over 4 million items, including books, clothes, music, and toys. In July 1999, Excite@Home bought iMall, a Santa Monica, California, company that provided Web hosting and design services for the 2,000 small and midsize merchants listed in its online mall.

Smaller sites were consolidating their listings and their users, seeking "critical mass" to build competencies against much larger players. Where the small players would otherwise wither away in an unknown corner of cyberspace on the Web, alliances offered customers many points of entry to a central location and represented a threat to Amazon's zShops.

Threats

In reality, Amazon was having trouble with every one of its new categories. It was getting clobbered in auctions by competitors: eBay had 3 million listings; Yahoo!, nearly 4 million; Amazon, at last count, only 140,000. The electronics store launched in July 1999 was off to a bad start: Pioneer and Sony, two of the biggest manufacturers, said they would not allow Amazon to sell their products and they would take action against third-party dealers that tried to sell their products through Amazon's consumer electronics site. Amazon's toy shop had similar problems. Some manufacturers were either refusing to supply Amazon or were in a "test mode" with the company. The lack of confidence in Amazon's distribution capability seemed to be the issue. Thus, the biggest challenge for zShops was to attract top-tier, best-of-breed, name brands. Unless it could promise a full range of merchandise, the appeal of the zShops would be limited and could potentially hurt Amazon's credibility.

With zShops, Amazon risked losing control over its famed customer relationship management. Seventy percent of Amazon's revenues came from repeat business because the company was famous for its customer service. But now a retailer—known only by its online ID—was responsible for sending the product ordered from Amazon.com. If there were any problem with the delivery, Amazon's reputation would surely suffer. The company said it was trying to solve those problems, many of which were the growing pains of a new business. It offered customer reviews of each zShop merchant. Amazon said it would guarantee merchandise up to $1,000 if it handled the credit card payment and up to $250 if it did not. The risk to Amazon could be well worth it if the company became the preeminent vault of information for Internet shopping habits.

Proponents said that just because Amazon could sell books online, it did not mean it could sell everything else. Amazon had yet to turn a profit. However, at that time, Amazon could afford to make mistakes. In late 1999, it had $1 billion in cash from its bond offering. So, even if the stock market continued to head south, Amazon would still be able to carry out its plans.

The zShops Dilemma

Bezos insisted zShops were a winner. He figured customers of zShops would wind up buying more from Amazon, especially as it moved into new areas such as travel. "The number of items that Wal-Mart can offer online will certainly pale next to what Amazon with other merchants can sell," said Ken Cassar of Jupiter Communications.[10]

But the jury is still out on the e-mall concept. Yahoo! and Excite had been running online malls for some time, but the customers were not flocking in. Online specialty foods purveyor Greatfood.com was part of zShops, but CEO Ben Nourse conceded, "I wonder if the mall strategy is the right one."[11]

"Brand names are more important online than they are in the physical world," Bezos once said.[12] As Bezos sat looking at the plans for the warehouses being built, he wondered if Amazon was risking too much. Amazon's brand, positioning, and reputation could all be affected by how it implemented its diversification strategy. Should the company cut its losses and pursue other expansion ideas, stick to the zShops concept, or try to focus on the categories in which it was already established? A decision would need to be made soon if Amazon was to exit this latest market.

WHAT IS THE zSHOPS NEW PRODUCT CONCEPT AND HOW DOES IT ADD VALUE TO STAKEHOLDERS?

The first questions that we must ask with any new product are, What is the concept? How does this concept add value? These questions help us appraise the first component of the business model.

In 1995 Amazon established an unbeatable online bookseller brand name. Since then, Amazon has diversified its product offerings while remaining within the pure retailer model. Its new product line includes CDs, videotapes, gifts, toys, auctions, and electronics. Amazon's auction site is the only product that steps out of the boundaries of the pure retail model and extends the company into the world of the market-maker (intermediary).

In September 1999 Amazon added another new category, the zShops, which offered an unlimited number of independent shops and products. This action made it clear that Amazon had the intention not only of diversifying its retail business, but also of solidifying its position as a market-maker by diversifying into zShops and the e-mall concept.

Unlike retail, where Amazon sells and controls the service to the customer, Amazon acts as an intermediary in zShops, offering a cyber shop space where zShops can sell their products to customers. (Figure 12.2 shows zShops' purchasing procedure.) Amazon charges a monthly flat fee and a commission on the transaction. (See Table 12.6 for the revenue structure of zShops.)

zShops have a common attribute with Amazon's auction site because, at that site, Amazon also acts as an intermediary. However, these two models have different customer expectations and product availability. While auction customers expect sporadic product availability and do not have an identified performance level for the auctioneers, zShops' customers are likely to expect a higher product selection and high-quality service.

FIGURE 12.2
Purchasing Procedure

1. Customer places order in Amazon's zShops website.
2. Amazon processes order and notifies zShops stores.
3. zShops stores deliver the product directly to customer.

TABLE 12.6 **Revenue Structure of zShops in 1999**

Source: www.amazon.com/.

A. Hosting fee	$9.99 per month (for up to 3,000 products)
B. Transaction commission	
Order size:	Commission (%):
• Less than $25	5.0%
• $25 to $1,000	2.5
• Over $1,000	1.25
C. 1-Click service fee	4.75% of price and $0.60 per each transaction

Finally, zShops allow Amazon to offer a very large number of products and to become the premier shopping destination for online shoppers by exploiting Amazon's brand recognition and large and growing customer base.

How the zShops Add Value to Customers

- *Convenience of one-stop shopping.* With zShops, customers enjoy a dramatically increased product selection from one site, Amazon, instead of spending time "surfing" on the Web for every product they want to buy. In addition, customers avoid having to type their shipping address and credit card information every time they complete a transaction.

- *Reliability and credibility.* Customers are using a more reliable and credible service provider when they buy a product through Amazon than through an unknown individual online retailer. When customers order the product and give their credit card information, they feel comfortable because of Amazon's reliability and credibility.

- *Guarantee by Amazon.* Amazon's A-to-Z guarantee gives protection to its customers by providing a $250 guarantee for "regular" purchases and a $1,000 guarantee for purchases made through its 1-Click ordering capability.

How the zShops Add Value to Shop Merchants

- *Brand recognition.* By operating under Amazon's umbrella, zShops bene-fit from the brand recognition Amazon has been able to build, thus attract-ing customers who value Amazon's reliability and credibility. An individual store would be unable to build a strong brand name and customer recogni-tion level in such a short period of time.

- *Access to a large customer base.* By being affiliated with Amazon, zShops obtain a large distribution network that gives them access to the large num-ber of customers who visit Amazon. It would cost the individual zShops too much in advertising and marketing expenses to obtain even a fraction of Amazon's large customer base.

- *E-commerce package from Amazon.* It is too costly for a small retailer to open an independent online store that has the e-commerce capabilities Amazon currently has. By joining zShops, they can avoid this information technology expenditure and enjoy Amazon's information technology infra-structure.

- *Guarantee and credibility.* The individual stores in zShops obtain credibil-ity by being under Amazon's umbrella. In addition, Amazon's guarantee to customers of up to $1,000 for each purchase gives the zShops site an aura of quality.

- *Access to Amazon's client database.* zShops can potentially share the infor-mation on customers accumulated and analyzed by Amazon. Thus, they can have a better understanding of customers' needs and carry out a more focused business.

How the zShops Add Value to Amazon

- *Additional stable source of revenue to increase profitability by means of the subscription model.* In 1999 Amazon observed only a 4 percent sales growth in the U.S. market, compared to the 40 percent it experienced in 1998. (See Figure 12.3 for sales growth data.) zShops bring an additional and stable source of revenue to Amazon through the monthly fees paid by the stores. Since Amazon has a strong brand name and a growing customer base, it should be relatively easy for it to attract retailers and have them join the zShops network. Thus, we see a diversification from what we described in Chapter 4 as a merchant model to a merchant plus brokerage plus subscription model.

- *Customer information.* In the bookselling business, Amazon has been extremely successful in turning its first-time customers into repeat cus-tomers (see Figure 12.4). Amazon has been able to achieve this customer loyalty by offering not only competitive prices, but also community features such as book reviews from various sources and recommendations for other

FIGURE 12.3 **Amazon's U.S. Book Sales and Growth Rate pre-zShops**

Source: Mark J. Rowan, "Amazon.com Inc.," Prudential Securities Research Report, September 23, 1999, p.12.

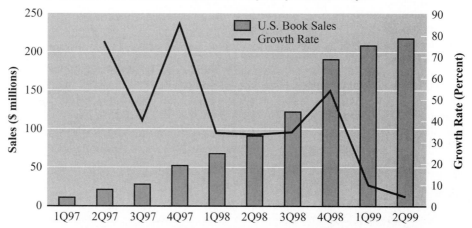

FIGURE 12.4 **Revenues from New and Repeat Customers pre-zShops**

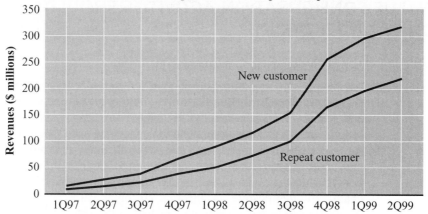

Source: Mark J. Rowan, "Amazon.com Inc.," Prudential Securities Research Report, September 23, 1999, p.11.

books. These community features have been made possible by processing and analyzing the data that have been obtained over a long period of time on the purchasing behavior of customers. As an intermediary of every single transaction in the zShops network, Amazon will be able to accumulate and analyze customer behavior data in the much broader product range offered by the zShops. The ability to provide better and more tailored information to the customer is likely to result in attracting and retaining an increased number of customers. For example, when a new PC camera is on sale in Amazon's zShops or in its proprietary electronics shop, Amazon could e-mail customers who they believe might be interested in buying this product based on the customer's purchasing history, thus fostering additional revenues for Amazon.

TABLE 12.7 Value Network Components for Amazon as an Intermediary

Network promotion and contract management
- Brand name and awareness
- Customer acquisition
- Merchant acquisition
- Merchant monitoring and evaluation

Service provisioning
- Providing recommendations based on interests or previous purchases
- Wide range of products
- Convenience
- Reliability
- Guarantee

Infrastructure operation
- Consumer interface
- Knowledge database
- Technological infrastructure
- Logistics expertise (although this would not be the primary source of value)

WHAT VALUE CONFIGURATION ACTIVITIES SHOULD AMAZON BE UNDERTAKING?

Value Network Components

Amazon has the capabilities to support the components of the value network. As we discussed in Chapter 7, firms should focus on one value configuration and pursue the connected activities that are most appropriate for that configuration, rather than simply pursuing the connected activities of the value chain. We also mentioned in Chapter 7 that Amazon.com is an example of a company that appears unfocused in its value configuration, simultaneously pursuing both a value chain and a value network approach, with the emphasis on value chain activities despite its apparent customer value as an intermediary. If Amazon were to pursue activities related to the value network rather than to the value chain, the components of the value network shown in Table 12.7 would be natural places to start.

DOES AMAZON HAVE CONTROL OVER KEY ASSETS?

Complementary Asset Framework

Please refer to the imitability and complementary asset framework (see Figure 12.5) that we developed in Chapter 5.

- *Imitability.* Amazon.com possesses tight control over the intellectual property associated with the most important aspects of its product development, implying that it is difficult for competitors to imitate or replicate. Amazon's brand awareness, customer interface, knowledge database, and technologi-

FIGURE 12.5
Viability of the zShops Strategy for Amazon

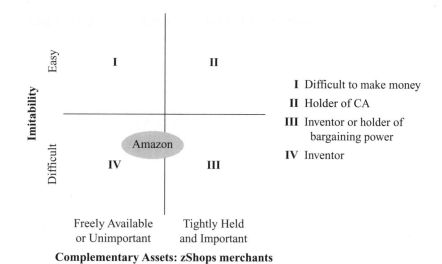

I Difficult to make money
II Holder of CA
III Inventor or holder of bargaining power
IV Inventor

Complementary Assets: zShops merchants

cal infrastructure are all necessary attributes that are difficult to replicate and provide Amazon with an advantage. Not all of these attributes are pure intellectual properties, but the company has protected those that are with trademarks, patents, or trade secrets.

- *Complementary assets.* The complementary assets necessary to create a viable online mall are freely available. Thousands of potential zShops participants would benefit from a relationship with Amazon. These participants are powerless to demand more from the relationship than Amazon is willing to provide because there are so many potential substitutes. It could be argued, however, that Amazon should selectively seek relationships with websites that already have some brand recognition, quality products, or other attributes, which would enhance the power of zShops participants.

- *Summary.* Low imitability combined with freely available complementary assets places Amazon's zShops model in quadrant IV bordering quadrant III in Figure 12.5. Existence in quadrant IV implies that the inventor will be the extractor of revenue from the invention. Therefore, Amazon is in a good position to make money from the zShops concept. If we consider Amazon's existence in quadrant III, the company is still in a good position to extract revenue from the zShops concept because it is both the inventor and the holder of superior bargaining power.

ARE THE zSHOPS A VIABLE GROWTH STRATEGY FOR AMAZON?

The zShops may be a viable growth strategy for Amazon.com. Amazon has been seeking to grow through diversification of its product lines within the boundaries of the retailer model. zShops provides an opportunity to diversify Amazon's product offerings at a much faster rate than would be possible as a stand-alone retailer. Amazon has the capabilities necessary to make zShops a successful online shopping destination. They include the following:

- *Large and growing customer base.* Among e-commerce companies, Amazon has the number one presence in terms of customer reach (percentage of a given population that is a customer). As of May 1999, it had a 17.5 percent customer reach, whereas barnesandnoble.com, which was in third place, had only 7 percent. This large number of customers, many of whom were repeat customers, demonstrates Amazon's strong presence in the e-commerce business.

- *Technological infrastructure.* Amazon has the technological infrastructure in place to offer customers superior service in their shopping experience. Product recommendation services and a secure transaction system are two of them. For zShops, this infrastructure can be easily adapted and utilized without significant cost.

Finally, the presence of other online market-makers implies that this business model can work. eBay, for example, has succeeded in bringing a large number of buyers and sellers to its unique community. Today it is regarded as a differentiated Internet-based company. From a financial point of view, eBay also has been successful, with revenues growing eightfold and net income growing by 275 percent between 1997 and 1998.[13] Projections show high growth rates for 1999 as well. As of late 1999 Amazon had not recorded positive earnings.

Analysis of Business Model Components

Amazon's move from a pure retailer to a retailer + market-maker is not an unequivocal win—although it may have some merit—according to our analysis of business model components (Table 12.8).

- *Customer value.* This was discussed above in the section on the zShops product concept. As a pure retailer, Amazon has knowledge of its customer preferences and uses that knowledge to recommend new products to the cus-

TABLE 12.8   **Appraising the Move to Retailer + Intermediary Models for Amazon**

Component	Pure Retailer	Retailer + Market-Maker
Customer value	High	High
Scope	High	Medium
Revenue source	Low	Medium
Pricing	Low	Medium
Connected activities	Low	Low, or worse
Capabilities	High	High
Sustainability	Low	Medium
Implementation	High	High

tomer. As a market-maker, it may not use this knowledge in such a proactive manner. Thus, customers may not consider Amazon to provide value at the same level as a pure retailer. On the other hand, customers may appreciate having a larger selection of items to choose from, much as they do in the bricks-and-mortar world. In addition, the avoidance of retyping (and redistributing) credit card information might be potentially valuable. It is difficult to reconcile these conflicting predictions, but it is most likely that customer value would remain at a high level.

- *Scope.* The primary identification of populations served is and remains B2C (business to consumer). As a pure retailer, Amazon had economies of scope in its prior diversification moves (e.g., from books to CDs). As a market-maker, it is only taking advantage of the economies of scope with its brand name, customer interface, and technological infrastructure, not of its knowledge database, warehouse infrastructure, or expertise in logistics. Therefore, Amazon's scope value would move from high to medium in its move to the zShops model.

- *Revenue sources.* As a pure retailer, Amazon's revenue was generated by end-user consumers. They were squarely in the "markup" (merchant) revenue model we discussed in Chapter 6.[14] As an intermediary, Amazon is also receiving revenues from the stores that form the network of zShops. The zShops merchants also pay a fixed fee to be affiliated with Amazon. Therefore, Amazon will expand into two new revenue models: *commission* (transaction fee from consummating each zShops purchase) and *subscription* (the flat fee paid monthly by each affiliated merchant). Thus, it is moving from a low to a medium outlook in terms of revenue sources.

- *Pricing.* As a pure retailer, Amazon's revenue stream was variable and dependent on the number of transactions. As a market-maker, Amazon has both a variable and fixed revenue stream, the latter due to the flat fee it charges retailers when they become affiliated with the zShops. From past behavior it seems that Amazon had little control over pricing in the retail market. The addition of the zShops may bring an improvement in its pricing power. Thus, it could be argued that Amazon is moving from low to medium control over pricing.

- *Connected activities.* As discussed above in the section on value configuration activities and in Chapter 7, Amazon has always pursued a somewhat schizophrenic approach to its connected activities. While its main value-added has been personalization, book reviews, and product suggestions—suggesting the value network approach—in practice its connected activities have been centered around the value chain. For example, it has focused on logistics, buying warehouses, shipping, and distribution. If Amazon continues in its current activities and simultaneously becomes more of an intermediary through the zShops, its connected activities will become even more of a mismatch, moving from an outlook of low value to something worse than low. However, if Amazon focuses more on the appropriate value configuration activities, as discussed above, it may be possible to move from an outlook of low value to something much better than that. Assuming that the company continues down its current path, we assign Amazon a low value for both the pure retailer and the retailer + market-maker models.

- *Capabilities.* As discussed in the section on the viability of zShops as part of Amazon's growth strategy, in both business models the company is providing a customer value that is higher than that of its competition. That is difficult to imitate because of several factors, including expertise in product development, customers and customer needs, interfacing with personalization software, data collection and mining, protection of intellectual property in terms of trademarks and patents (e.g., software and algorithms, including 1-Click), brand name, and logistics. Thus, we expect Amazon's capabilities to remain at a high level with or without the zShops.

- *Sustainability.* As a pure retailer, Amazon has been able to sustain its growth rate by "running": diversifying its product line, providing higher customer value by means of its knowledge database and investment in its brand equity. As a retailer, Amazon has sustained its leading position through several extensions, although it remains to be seen whether its current business model is truly sustainable in financial terms. Will Amazon become the next AOL (which lost money for years acquiring customers but eventually became profitable and dominated its market) or will it simply lose money until investors run for the exits? Comparing the sustainability of Amazon's retailer model with that of the retailer + market-maker, it seems as if this new business model is certainly no less sustainable than the old one. As discussed in the section on the viability of Amazon's growth strategy, it appears that relative to the zShop merchants, Amazon has reasonable control over the key assets. Further, it appears to have the upper hand with respect to other alliance partners. Therefore, we conclude that Amazon's sustainability could actually improve from low to perhaps medium or better.

- *Implementation.* As a pure retailer, Amazon has appeared to execute its chosen strategies well, regardless of whether one thinks those strategies are valid. The case does not give enough information to recognize whether Amazon's systems, structure, people, and environment fit well with that strategy. It seems plausible that Amazon's ability to execute and implement its strategies would be largely unaffected by the move to the market-maker model. Thus, we conclude that the outlook for Amazon's implementation is rather high in both the retailer and the retailer + market-maker model.

In summary, Amazon's move from a pure retailer to a retailer + market-maker results in a business model with some promise but not without pitfalls. Of the eight components listed in Table 12.8, three improve when moving to the intermediary model. On the other hand, two get worse. Therefore, this might be a reasonable move, especially if Amazon reconfigures its connected activities to reflect the increasing importance of the value network configuration in its new business model.

RECOMMENDATIONS: IS AMAZON RISKING TOO MUCH FROM THE STANDPOINT OF BRAND NAME AND REPUTATION?

One of Amazon's most important assets is its brand and reputation. Amazon has been able to build a strong brand name synonymous with quality products and reliable service. This success has come despite the hesitancy of a large proportion of shoppers to shop on the Internet because of their concern about reliability, privacy, and security. Amazon cannot afford to dilute its brand or harm its reputation. If it does, it risks losing its large installed customer base and growing percent of repeat users as well as the potential to attract new customers. The customers' experience with the various zShops will reflect directly on Amazon, even though the shops are independent entities. Amazon ties its own reputation to that of zShops participants by acting as an intermediary. If a customer has a bad experience utilizing the services of one of the zShops, it is likely to reflect badly on the other zShops and Amazon itself. Once customers become alienated, it is very difficult to convince them that the issues have been ironed out. It is often said that it is seven times more difficult to win back a lost customer than to gain a new customer.

Amazon also needs to be aware that externalities that were not part of the pure retailer model are important aspects of the market-maker model. In the market-maker model, both network size and quality as well as the size of the customer base matter. A small zShops network will not attract customers, which will lead to a small customer base, which in turn will influence potential zShops participants' decision to participate (see Figure 12.6).

Amazon has faced several situations where strong brands, such as Sony, have threatened to withhold products from distributors if they participate in Amazon's zShops. The negative press could affect consumers' perception of

FIGURE 12.6
Vicious Circle of Customer and zShops Participation

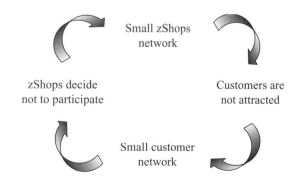

Small zShops network

Customers are not attracted

Small customer network

zShops decide not to participate

the quality of the zShops as a destination. Other brands state that their relationship with zShops is experimental, which lacks the permanency necessary to establish zShops as a viable alternative mall.

Amazon must try to mitigate these issues through some proactive steps.

1. Develop a large, high-quality zShops network.
   a. Obtain the best players in the categories.
   b. Establish relationships with branded product manufacturers.
2. Protect its brand name and reputation.
   a. Liberally live up to its guarantee.
   b. Exercise due diligence in the selection of participants.
   c. Remove negligent zShops merchants from the network.

Amazon needs to walk a fine line between building a large network and protecting the quality of the consumer experience. The large network is probably the most important factor at this stage of the game, although Amazon should not neglect protecting the consumer experience.

Notes

1. Case adapted from Youngseok Kim, Myriam E. Lopez, Suzanne Schiavelli, Heshy Shayovitz, and Steve Yoon, "Amazon.com: zShops," New York University Stern School of Business, Case #991-121, December 1999. © 1999 Christopher L. Tucci, reprinted with permission; sample analysis is adapted from Youngseok Kim, Myriam E. Lopez, Suzanne Schiavelli, Heshy Shayovitz, and Steve Yoon, "Amazon.com: zShops Analysis," New York University Stern School of Business, Note #991-125, December 1999.
2. We realize that Amazon.com is one of the most overstudied companies in the world. Still, this case illustrates many of the concepts from this book and provides a familiar backdrop for students.
3. www.edventure.com/pcforum/pc97/agenda/panel4.html#bezos
4. www.redherring.com/mag/issue44/bezos.html
5. www.redherring.com/mag/digital/amazon.html
6. www.cnnfn.com/digitaljam/newsbytes/113186.html
7. www.cnnfn.com/digitaljam/newsbytes/113186.html
8. www.sjmercury.com/business/center/amazon111798.htm
9. Seema Williams, David M. Cooperstein, David E. Weisman, and Thalika Oum, "Post-Web Retail," *The Forrester Report,* September 1999, p.1.
10. www.businessweek.com/1999/99_41/b3650116.htm
11. www.businessweek.com/1999/99_41/b3650116.htm
12. inc.com/articles/details/0,6378,ART1314_CNT53,00.html
13. eBay 10-K filed on March 29, 1999.
14. Do not confuse the "merchant" model (e-tailer) with the transition to an intermediary between Amazon and so-called zShop "merchants."

Appendix

Internet Protocols, More Details, and Further Reading

In this brief appendix, we provide a few more technical details as a reference for those interested in learning more about the technology of the Internet.[1] We describe the basic idea behind the main protocols and discuss domain names, the client-server model, and a few other technical details.

How Does the Internet Work?

Internet Protocol

The most important feature of the Internet is the Internet Protocol, which was developed years ago under the auspices of the Advanced Research Project Agency (ARPA), which was part of the United States Department of Defense. Indeed, the Internet was originally called the ARPAnet. The Internet Protocol (or IP for short) is a specification for how to share information across a network. It was called "Internet" in its inception because it was designed to connect disparate networks across the country and even the world.

IP was designed to break large amounts of information into small *packets* which were to be identified with a source and destination. The source was called the "sender's IP address" and the destination the "receiver's IP address." When a computer received a packet, it looked at the destination and decided where to send the packet next. It therefore routed the packet to the next stop-off point on the way from the source to the destination. The specialized computers that performed this task, for obvious reasons, became known as *packet switches* or *routers*.

Domains and the Domain Name System

Where do the addresses come from? Any organization or person can register for an IP address through a company (formerly, an agency) that administers the addresses. The organization can request any name that has not already been registered. Most companies would like to get a name that is identical to their actual name. For example, ABCD Corp. would most likely prefer abcd.com ("com" stands for "commercial," "edu" stands for "educational" institution, "gov" stands for "government," "mil" for "military," "net" for "network" (ISP), and "org" stands for nonprofit "organization," to name the most popular *domains*). If no one has reserved abcd.com, then ABCD Corp. will get the name and have a main IP address (and possibly a range of IP addresses) affiliated with that name.

Now, when a computer would like a document served up from across the network, there needs to be some way of mapping the Universal Resource Locators, or URLs, to numbers. In the early days, all computers stored all the IP addresses for all the other computers in a huge table. This, however, was not very efficient as the mapping of names to numbers occasionally changed, which meant the tables had to be reconstructed. The domain name system (DNS) was designed to manage this mapping of names to numbers. Assume you would like the document <http://www.abcd.com/corporate.html>. You need to know which IP address to put in the destination field of your packets. So your computer puts in a request at a local domain name server (also called a DNS) to see if it knows the IP address. If you are within the abcd.com intranet domain, the DNS will have this number available. However, if you are anywhere else, your request will be forwarded on to an appropriate DNS. It could go to a certain "master" name server called the InterNIC name server, which could give a primary and secondary DNS to contact. One of these servers should have the correct IP address for the host you are searching and will send that address back to you so you can make contact.

Client-Server Model

Many if not all of the interactions described here take advantage of an abstraction called a *client-server model*. The *client* runs on the end user's computer. It requests information or requests that a task be performed remotely by a *server.* For example, your electronic mail client executes on your computer. When you "check your e-mail," your client program will most likely send a message to a post office server where your e-mail is being held. It requests that all messages delivered since the last time you checked be delivered to your computer. The server sends the messages to the client and you can then read your e-mail on your own computer.[2]

Another example is a file server. On many systems that involve multiple users, such as those in an office, there are so-called *shared drives.* These shared drives are actually file servers, and a client program runs on the office computers that treats the shared drives as local drives in a manner transparent to the employee. An example is the Netware product by Novell. When you start your computer, the client program asks you to log in. If this were your own personal computer with its own hard drive, there would be no need to log in. However, the client program asks you to log in so it can "mount the shared drive." When you look in the shared drive, the client program on your computer sends a request to the file server for the directory information. When you open a file on the shared drive, the client requests the contents of the file from the server. The server complies with these requests as long as you are an authorized user. Thus, the log-in procedure.

The client-server model therefore decouples the *processing* of information from the *storage* of information and accomplishes both in the most efficient way. File servers are highly specialized computers that are optimized to hold and deliver large amounts of data, while your computer is a more general purpose tool that is, in general, useful but lacks both storage space and speed. The development of the client-server model thus led to a more distributed computing environment, making the rise of the Internet possible.

Other Major Protocols

IP is not the only protocol currently in use. The other main protocols are (in order of level of abstraction) TCP, FTP, and HTTP. TCP (transmission control protocol) keeps track of large amounts of information, breaking it into packets at the sender's computer and reassembling the packets into the original data stream at the recipient's computer. The reason you see IP/TCP written together is that they are almost always used in tandem. TCP breaks up the packets, numbers them, and sends them off with the correct IP headers so that the remote version of TCP can put them back together again. Since the information is broken up into packets and is not sent as a data "stream," it is highly likely that a later packet may arrive before an earlier one. Or a packet may get lost on the way and never arrive at all because of a failure in the computer hardware or a bug in the software. TCP keeps track of all of these things and makes various requests (by sending messages to the source's computer) to reassemble the original information stream in the correct and complete order. Most of the time, this happens so quickly that the average user does not notice it.

FTP is the file transfer protocol, which uses both IP and TCP to send a complete file across a network from an FTP server to an FTP client. HTTP is the hypertext transfer protocol, which is the specification for sending and receiving a World Wide Web page from a Web server to a Web client which is also called a *browser*.

Universal Resource Locator (URL)

After HTTP was developed, a general way of specifying a specific Internet address using *any* of the protocols came into use. This came to be known as the Universal Resource Locator (URL). The URL comprises three parts: the protocol, the separator (://), and the path to a specific file resident on a specific computer.[3] By 2000, URLs had become almost synonymous with HTTP, but theoretically, they can be used with other protocols, such as FTP or Telnet. For example, a typical URL is:

http://www.best.edu/students/list.html

which means, "connect to the host called www.best.edu using the hypertext transfer protocol, look in a subdirectory called 'students' and deliver the file in there called 'list.html' so I [the client/browser] can display it."[4] A non-HTTP example is:

ftp://ftp.mycompany.com/employees/list.doc

which instructs the computer to connect to the host ftp.mycompany.com using the file transfer protocol, look in a subdirectory called "employees," and deliver the file called "list.doc."[5]

Companies Supporting the Protocols

What sort of companies support these protocols? Internet service providers (ISPs) are basically in the business of renting IP addresses. Since the average consumer does not actually own a personal dedicated IP address, the ISP provides a telephone service (usually called PPP or SLIP) or other relatively low bandwidth network connection that lets the consumer borrow an IP address for the duration of the session. The user's own computer must support IP and TCP although the ISPs may sometimes provide the software that supports these protocols. The ISP also provides a connection to the Internet by connecting the user by means of the telephone network to its servers (such as e-mail servers or file servers) and packet switches. In addition, Last Mile providers (those companies providing the physical connection to the home as discussed in Chapter 2) introduced in 1999 a Digital Subscriber Line (DSL) service that involves a dedicated IP address and an "always on" connection over normal twisted-pair copper telephone wires. Large, industrial-grade ISPs do the same thing for companies except the service is often provided on high-capacity lines rather than individual telephone lines and may involve dedicated IP addresses for employees' computers.

Other software companies make applications that run on personal computers or workstations that support one or another of the Internet protocols. For example, some companies make electronic mail packages that support POP3 (one of the protocols for delivering e-mail to users) and SMTP (the protocol for sending e-mail from a user) clients and that organize e-mail into "inboxes" and allow the user to send replies to incoming messages. Other companies make Web browsers (supporting HTTP) that allow a user to view hypertext documents across the Internet. Still others provide packages that support FTP which allows the user to store documents on and retrieve documents from remote computers. Some software companies provide the server software to support these clients. For example, companies make software that stores e-mail until users request it, or software that organizes users' files so that e-mail is delivered to them on demand. Many companies provide both client and server software, although some companies specialize in one or the other. Electronic commerce is another example of an application that runs over the Internet, involving both client and server software. Examples might include payment processing systems that support customers typing in credit card numbers.

Some companies provide the content that resides on the servers, especially the Web (HTTP) servers. These companies could be "portals," sources of information that users turn to first when they get on the Internet. Most of the so-called content providers, content creators, or aggregators are pure providers of information compared to most other companies, which sell products or services using the Internet as one possible medium.

Further Reading

This appendix has attempted to give a brief glimpse into some of the details behind the technology of the Internet. We have not provided details on all the different formats or types of multimedia information available, nor have we given other details on related technologies. Examples of these missing topics include details on routers, ISDN, network computers, satellite protocols, Usenet newsgroups, Internet Relay Chat and Instant Messaging, World Wide Web form interfaces, Java, Javascript, CGI scripts, audio and video formats, encryption, firewalls, proxy servers—and the list goes on. On our website, we have collected more information on many of these topics. However, as mentioned earlier in this appendix, the basics of how the system works have remained relatively constant for over 20 years!

For more information, the reader should consult the many computer science, information technology, and electronic commerce texts. The best book at an intermediate level of technical detail is the sixth edition of Preston Gralla's *How the Internet Works,* published by QUE Press, 2001. Another good resource is Gail Honda and Kipp Martin, *The Essential Guide to Internet Business Technology,* Prentice Hall, 2002. The classic computer science books in this area are Paul E. Green, Jr. (ed.), *Computer Network Architectures and Protocols,* Plenum, 1982; and Andrew S. Tannenbaum, *Computer Networks,* 3rd Edition, Prentice Hall, 1996. For more information on the client-server model consult Robert Orfali, Dan Harkey, and Jeri Edwards, *Client/Server Survival Guide,* 3rd Edition, John Wiley & Sons, 1999. For a good overview of electronic commerce issues with an emphasis on Internet security, see Marilyn Greenstein and Todd Feinman, *Electronic Commerce: Security, Risk, Management, and Control,* McGraw-Hill, 2000. For a managerial perspective on electronic commerce, consult Ravi Kalakota and Andrew B. Whinston, *Electronic Commerce,* published by Addison Wesley, 1997. Finally, for a history of the Internet based on primary interviews with its architects, refer to Stephen Segaller's *Nerds[2.0.1],* published by TV Books, 1999.

Notes

1. The basics of this technology have not changed very much in the last 20 years, although some details do occasionally change: Technology advances every day and the physical infrastructure of the Internet along with it. Businesses merge, rename themselves, sell off business units, or go bankrupt. Companies launch new products and whole new segments are created seemingly overnight. While the basic ideas do not change very frequently, we have

prepared as a service to our readers an up-to-date synopsis of developments; feel free to point your browser to <http://www.internetbusinessmodelsand strategies.com> for some late-breaking news in both the technology and the business of the Internet.

2. Unfortunately, the word "server" refers to both the hardware (especially if dedicated) and the software that executes on that hardware to perform the server functions.

3. There are other usages of the URL. One is simply to connect using the Telnet protocol to a specific computer, thereby eliminating the need for a file name. Another use is to instruct the remote server to run a program, such as a CGI script, rather than serving a document (file) using http. This second usage is ideal for tailor-made situations where the served document must be created on the fly. For example, when you request a quote for a stock price, the price is constantly changing; therefore, the quote provider cannot leave a static file to serve. When you request the quote, the price is checked and a new document is created with the most recent price in it.

4. When no file name is given, the default file name is "index.html" or "home .html." Thus, when you see a URL such as "www.mycompany.com," this actually refers to the file "index.html" in the uppermost directory of the computer www.mycompany.com.

5. Astute readers may wonder whether there is unnecessary redundancy in this system as computers beginning with the name www always seem to be http servers, while computers beginning with the name ftp always seem to be ftp servers. While this naming convention usually holds, it is not necessarily the case, as the same computer can theoretically support multiple protocols. Thus, it is possible that you could ftp from a site whose name begins with www, or Telnet to a site whose name begins with ftp, and so on.

Part **Five**

Cases

Case One

Broadcast.com

Mark Cuban and Todd Wagner carefully contemplated their options. The past two days had been a whirlwind of activity as their Dallas-based firm, Broadcast.com, had been approached by Yahoo! During the Big Picture media conference, sponsored by *Variety* in New York City, Yahoo! CEO Tim Koogle made a tender offer to acquire Broadcast.com. Two days earlier, the news hit "the street" as a *Business Week* online story speculated about the potential merger. Shares of Broadcast.com surged 37 percent in one day of trading amid the rumors.[1] During the media conference, Tim Koogle declined comment on the rumor, but fueled the flames by announcing that Yahoo! was indeed seeking strategic acquisitions.

Broadcast.com was the current leader in audio and video broadcasting over the Internet. Since its inception, Cuban and Wagner had built superior Internet audio and video capabilities, and locked in predominantly exclusive contracts with over 300 radio stations, 40 television stations, 400 sports teams, and 600 business customers. However, its 4.6 million monthly viewers paled in comparison to the 30 million viewers of Yahoo![2] Additionally, Broadcast.com reported an operating loss of almost $15 million for the year ended 1998.

At the time, Yahoo! was the leading Internet portal with over 30 million visitors a month, but it was locked in a fierce battle with Microsoft and America Online (AOL) to retain its title. Despite its success, Yahoo! was mainly a text-based site that lacked "rich media" content. "Rich media" was the new phrase used to describe the mix of text, graphics, audio, video, animation, and interactivity. Koogle believed that users, advertisers, and online consumers all wanted TV-like content and services. A recent survey by Home Network found that users recalled seeing multimedia ads 34 percent more often than traditional banner ads.[3] The acquisition of Broadcast.com could place Yahoo! in position for a rapid shift to high-speed multimedia Internet services.

As the night fell on Gotham City, Cuban and Wagner mulled over the future of Broadcast.com.

New York University Stern School of Business MBA Candidates Sandy Chen, Arial Friedman, Darren Landy, Mark Stencik, and Joey Shammah prepared this case under the supervision of Professor Christopher L. Tucci for the purpose of class discussion rather than to illustrate either effective or ineffective handling of an administrative situation. Copyright © 2001 by McGraw-Hill/Irwin. All rights reserved.

THE HISTORY OF BROADCAST.COM

Mark Cuban and Todd Wagner were both Indiana University alumni living in Dallas, Texas. During the winter, they missed attending Hoosiers basketball games and wished that there was some way they could at least listen to the games. During the summer of 1995, Wagner wondered if the two would someday be able to listen to the games over the Internet.

With this idea and $5,000, Broadcast.com commenced in a spare bedroom in Cuban's house. Cuban bought a Packard Bell 486 PC for $2,995, $1,000 worth of network equipment, and spent $60 a month for a high-speed connection. The two then approached a local Dallas radio station, KLIF. They explained that in the near future, technology would lend itself to create a radio superstation on the Internet, and they wanted to work with KLIF to make this a reality now. Although KLIF agreed to give it a try, existing technology enabled Cuban and Wagner only to tape the broadcast, digitize the recordings, and post it on their website. However, in September 1995 the two aspiring media moguls figured out how to broadcast live radio over the Internet. Their idea was primitive, but it worked. They hooked up a $15 radio tuner to the sound card of Cuban's computer and began to broadcast live.

Their initial marketing strategy was not much more sophisticated than the $15 tuner. Cuban, over the Internet, began delivering his sales pitch to the local Dallas market. He invited anyone interested in Dallas area sports to come visit his website. The response was incredible and soon Cuban and Wagner had a feeling that they were on to something big. The e-mails continued pouring in from Dallas natives living elsewhere as well as from office workers in the Dallas area.

Backed by the confidence from the overwhelming response to their website, Cuban and Wagner decided to launch their own company, AudioNet.com. The name was later changed to Broadcast.com to reflect the diversity of their programming and services. They felt that the success of their company was tied to their ability to attract content providers, such as radio stations and sports teams, nationwide. Wagner knew that it would take a little more to assure long-term success. He recognized the need to block out potential competitors and control as much content as possible. Wagner set out to sign up as many content providers as possible, usually with multiyear, exclusive agreements. Wagner and Cuban got their big break by giving up 5 percent of the company's equity to Host Communication, which owned the radio broadcasting rights for 12 NCAA basketball teams and the NCAA tournament. Because they were the first movers in live "Internet" broadcasting, they were able to build a large portfolio of content providers.[4]

At the time, Internet broadcasting rights were simply unheard of. However, in November 1995 Congress enacted the Digital Performance Right in Sound Recordings Act, which gave owners of sound recordings certain exclusive rights to retain fees for broadcasting. The Act, however, had not been sufficiently interpreted, and Cuban and Wagner believed that Broadcast.com was exempt from inclusion under this law.[5]

THE BUSINESS MODEL

Broadcast.com was different from other Web-based companies in that Cuban and Wagner were quite focused on actually generating profits from the start. Their business model was based on the premise that all content providers would want to expand their listener base by using the Internet, thereby increasing their bargaining position with advertisers. Consequently, content providers would be willing to pay to "webcast" their programs.

Broadcast.com had three distinct sources of revenues: (1) Content providers paid to broadcast over the Internet, or bartered to provide free commercial airtime during programming. Broadcast.com used this airtime to promote its own site or resold the time to a third party. (2) The Business Service Group was established to provide cost-effective Internet and intranet broadcasting business services, such as earnings conference calls, investor conferences, press conferences, trade shows, stockholder meetings, training sessions, and even distant college courses. (3) Advertising space was sold on the site, including gateway ads that were broadcast prior to requested user programs with guaranteed click-thrus, channel and special event sponsorships, and multimedia and traditional banner ads.

Cuban and Wagner continued to build brand awareness through their exclusive agreements with most major colleges and universities and the NFL, including live coverage of the Super Bowl. However, by late 1995 they had spent close to $1 million, most of which was personally funded by Cuban. Feeling financial pressure and needing the infusion of a bit of cash, Cuban and Wagner turned to their friends who were eager to invest. Cuban and Wagner sold shares in $30,000 increments to their friends and local Dallas investors. However, since this new infusion of capital was only a short-term solution, Cuban and Wagner approached the services of investment bank Alex. Brown to handle their first private placement in 1996.

INTERNET BROADCASTING

The infusion of capital enabled Broadcast.com to expand its own private network. Broadcast.com received analog audio and video signals from its 22 satellites at its home office in Dallas. The company relied on streaming technology to convert the analog feeds into compressed digital information to feed directly through the Internet in real time. Its network consisted of over 550 multimedia-streaming servers that streamed the feeds and pumped them out to major net backbone providers through direct lines of 45 and 155 Mbps. Cuban and Wagner negotiated deals with the four largest backbone providers, GTEI, MCI, Sprint, and UUNET, which connected over 80 percent of the downstream Internet service providers (ISPs). The direct connections to the backbone providers allowed users to avoid congestion and delays normally caused by going through the downstream ISPs themselves.

Broadcast.com also relied on Unicasting technology, which sends a single stream of digital video, audio, or data to each requesting user over the Internet. However, end users needed to download free software from Microsoft or RealNetworks in order to hear or view the audio or video broadcast. In September 1997 Broadcast.com started using the latest technology, multicasting, whereby a single stream of content was sent to multiple destinations without flooding all network connections. Cuban and Wagner signed a deal with UUNET to develop the first multicasting network to allow over 500 simultaneous live events, and provide content to 100,000 simultaneous users over a single connection.

Broadcast.com also leveraged its reliance on third-party technology through strategic relationships with key Internet companies. Cuban signed an agreement with RealNetworks to allow users to download RealPlayer in exchange for a link on RealNetworks' home site. Then, early in 1998, Cuban signed a distribution deal with Yahoo!, allowing this leading portal site to take a minority stake in Broadcast.com.

Armed with the latest technology, Broadcast.com aired a live webcast of NBC's top-rated television show *ER*. Later, it broadcast live, on-demand coverage of ABC's 1998 Academy Awards. In February 1999 Broadcast.com set the record for simultaneous viewers, when more than 1.5 million people logged on to see the live broadcast of a Victoria's Secret fashion show, which was later dubbed "the quintessential net event."[6] However, the ISPs could not handle the enormous demand of viewers, and thousands of additional viewers could not log on to view the show.

COMPETITION

The rapid shift toward streaming technology and attention generated by live webcasts caught the eye of other firms. The increased competition began to mount on several fronts: streaming media sites, videoconferencing, and traditional media firms.

Streaming Media Websites

The emergence of similar websites that provided streaming media content increased rapidly. Most sites specialized in one medium such as Netradio, which allowed users to create their own radio stations over the Internet, or CBS Sportsline, which aired certain sporting events each week. In August 1997, however, RealNetworks and MCI formed a strategic alliance to create a service called Real Broadcast Network to provide a wide array of streaming media content. But, unlike Broadcast.com, RealNetworks only provided a link to news and entertainment content providers, such as ABCNews.com and CNN.com.

Videoconferencing

Broadcast.com also competed with videoconferencing and teleconferencing companies, as well as with other companies that provided Internet broadcasting services to businesses. By 1997 the Business Services Group accounted for 30 percent of the total revenues of Broadcast.com (see Exhibits 1.1 and 1.2). The competition in this arena also increased rapidly as new sites such as Vcall.com and BestCalls.com provided free audio versions of conference calls and other business meetings. Additionally, as the cost for this technology continued to decrease and the quality of transmission improved, industry experts expected more companies to perform these services in-house. This meant greater competition for fewer available revenues.

Traditional Media

Broadcast.com competed with traditional media including radio, television, and print for a slice of the advertiser's budget. Some traditional services, such as CNN and the *New York Times,* established a viable presence on the Internet and had the benefit of existing relationships with advertisers and advertising agencies. Additionally, Broadcast.com competed with traditional media companies to sell its inventory of radio and television ad spots, which it obtained from content providers in exchange for the content provider's Internet broadcasting rights.

EXHIBIT 1.1
Total Revenues for Year Ended December 31, 1997

Source: Broadcast.com
Prospectus, July 17, 1999.

	Year Ending December 31, 1997
Business services	$2,820,449
Web advertising	2,955,259
Traditional media advertising	942,090
Other	138,235
	$6,856,033

EXHIBIT 1.2
Revenues by Percent for Year Ended December 31, 1997

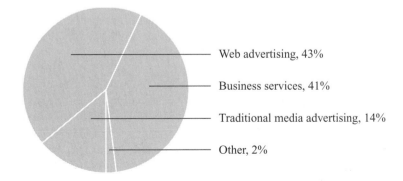

Web advertising, 43%

Business services, 41%

Traditional media advertising, 14%

Other, 2%

EXHIBIT 1.3 **Broadcast.com Balance Sheets**

Source: Broadcast.com Prospectus, July 17, 1998.

	Year Ending December 31,		Quarter Ending March 31,
	1996	**1997**	**1998**
Assets			
Current assets:			
Cash and cash equivalents	$ 4,580,286	$21,337,116	$22,400,176
Accounts receivable	406,802	1,976,765	2,448,561
Prepaid expenses	65,760	1,032,198	1,382,182
Other	17,912	11,311	52,986
Total current assets	5,070,760	24,357,390	26,283,905
Property and equipment	1,186,182	2,812,971	3,289,255
Prepaid expenses	1,715,000	935,720	369,834
Intangible assets	182,414	126,733	191,480
Total assets	8,154,356	28,232,814	30,134,474
Liabilities and Stockholders' Equity			
Current liabilities:			
Accounts payable	91,545	362,214	674,333
Accrued liabilities	454,926	677,662	1,154,149
Total current liabilities	546,471	1,039,876	1,828,482
Stockholders' Equity			
Common stock	57,341	85,763	89,835
Additional paid-in capital	10,807,309	36,838,152	40,669,584
Accumulated deficit	(3,256,765)	(9,730,977)	(12,453,427)
Total stockholders' equity	7,607,885	27,192,938	28,305,992
Total Liabilities and Stockholders' Equity	$ 8,154,356	$28,232,814	$30,134,474

GOING PUBLIC

On July 17, 1998, Broadcast.com went public with the stated goal of becoming the top broadcasting portal on the Internet. After one day of trading, Broadcast.com set another high-water mark as the stock appreciated over 249 percent.[7] Cuban and Wagner were now millionaires. However, unlike many Web-based entrepreneurs, they never viewed their IPO as an exit strategy. Instead, the IPO process enabled them to build the company's brand name, and the infusion of capital allowed them to continue to build upon its strategic position. (See Exhibits 1.3 and 1.4 for financial information.)

CURRENT SITUATION

Following the success of its IPO, Broadcast.com continued to expand the volume of its content agreements and business services. In December 1998 Cuban

EXHIBIT 1.4   **Broadcast.com Statement of Operations**

Source: Broadcast.com Prospectus, July 17, 1998.

	Year Ending December 31,		Quarter Ending March 31,
	1996	**1997**	**1998**
Revenues:			
Business services	$ 535,201	$ 2,820,449	$ 1,126,515
Web advertising	1,090,629	2,955,259	1,322,911
Traditional media advertising	0	942,090	516,707
Other	130,270	138,235	209,811
Total revenues	1,756,100	6,856,033	3,175,944
Operating Expenses:			
Production costs	1,301,253	2,949,641	1,224,957
Operating and development	1,506,449	4,659,249	2,247,141
Sales and marketing	717,547	3,389,069	1,670,727
General and administrative	751,785	1,416,276	588,179
Depreciation and amortization	544,003	1,129,120	442,456
Total operating expenses	4,821,037	13,543,355	6,173,460
Net operating loss	(3,064,937)	(6,687,322)	(2,997,516)
Interest and other income	76,090	213,110	275,066
Net Loss:	$(2,988,847)	$(6,474,212)	$(2,722,450)

and Wagner formed an alliance with NASDAQ for live streaming coverage of corporate quarterly earnings for the NASDAQ 100 Index companies. They then acquired Net Roadshow, which was the first company to receive permission from the Securities and Exchange Commission (SEC) to provide IPO Roadshows over the Internet. Net Roadshow was also the leading provider of Internet Roadshows and had contracts with nearly every major investment bank. Finally, Broadcast.com set its sights on the global market when it established a joint venture with Soft Bank to launch Broadcast.com Japan with audio and video content in Japanese.[8]

When the Media Metrix rankings came out in March 1999, Broadcast.com was ranked 6th in news/info/entertainment and was classified as the 14th largest website overall. The company had clearly established itself as the leading Web portal for Internet broadcasting. Cuban and Wagner had developed an impressive network of content providers. They secured contracts with 385 radio stations, 40 television stations, and 420 sports teams. Among its more than 600 business clients were leading U.S. blue-chips firms such as AT&T and General Motors.[9]

In 1999, Broadcast embarked on a new medium: film. It accomplished this by signing a deal with Trimark Holdings, Inc., to license the rights to broadcast Trimark's entire film library over the Internet. However, given the nature of the Internet, Broadcast.com still lost $14.1 million for the year ended 1998.[10] In addition, the company prospectus came with the conspicuous caveat to potential investors that "the Company expects to continue to incur significant losses on a quarterly and annual basis for the foreseeable future."

THE OFFER

In April, Yahoo! approached Wagner and Cuban with an offer to acquire Broadcast.com in a pooling of interest deal valued at $5.7 billion or $130 per share. At the end of March, shares in Broadcast.com traded in the $30 range. Yahoo! initially considered offering $110 to $120 per share, but feared a bidding war from rivals Microsoft and AOL.[11] As Wagner and Cuban considered the lucrative offer, they wondered about the benefits and risks of giving up their independence. Broadcast.com had built an impressive collection of licensing agreements and contracts with content providers and business clients, as well as a state-of-the-art network to "webcast" the content received. The $5.7 billion stock offer represented a hefty premium above the company's market value. However, the two moguls could not help but wonder if partnering with Yahoo! was the best strategic option for both parties to maximize synergies in the future.

Notes

1. Kara Swisher and Evan Ramstad, "Yahoo! Holds Talks on Acquiring Broadcast.com, Boosting Shares," *The Wall Street Journal,* March 23, 1999, p. A3.
2. Don Jeffrey, "Yahoo! Eyeing Broadcast.com?" *Billboard,* April 3, 1999.
3. Linda Himelstein and Andy Reinhardt, "Putting More TV on the PC," *Business Week,* April 5, 1999, at www.businessweek.com/1999/99_14/b3623079.htm.
4. Richard Murphy, "Making a Killing on the Internet," *Success,* May 1999, pp. 54–59.
5. Broadcast.com Prospectus, July 1998.
6. Bob Trott, "Victoria's Secret for Webcasts Is IP Multicasting," *InfoWorld,* August 16, 1999.
7. Richard Murphy, "Making a Killing on the Internet," *Success,* May 1999, pp. 54–59.
8. Morgan Stanley Dean Witter Investment Research, April 30, 1999.
9. Broadcast.com Prospectus, July 1998.
10. Morgan Stanley Dean Witter Investment Research, April 30, 1999.
11. "Yahoo! to Acquire Broadcast.com as the Internet Leans toward Audio and Video Streaming," *Weekly Corporate Growth Report,* April 12, 1999.

Case **Two**

Webvan: Reinventing the Milkman

Webvan will go down in history either as the next Federal Express or as one of the biggest failed infrastructure bets in history.[1]

On November 5, 1999, Webvan completed its much-anticipated initial public offering (IPO) and made headlines across the business world. Despite tiny sales and big losses to date, shares of the two-year-old company, which combines Internet grocery shopping with home delivery, shot to an 80 percent premium on its first day of trading. As the trading day ended, Webvan had a total market value of more than $8 billion, nearly half the capitalization of grocery industry leaders such as Safeway, Inc., and Kroger Co.[2]

Webvan Chairman Louis Borders, founder of Borders Books, felt at once exhilarated and terrified. Naturally he was extremely proud of the company's achievements. While Webvan had operated for a mere five months in the San Francisco area, more than 10,000 people had signed up for the service—not bad considering that it has taken rival Peapod, Inc., 10 years to amass a customer base of 100,000 households. Borders was confident that Webvan could prevail over its existing online competitors by expanding aggressively. In the Internet economy, Borders argued that first-to-scale, not first-to-market, counted.

On the other hand, the lofty valuation caused concern. For one, Webvan's 1999 sales were expected to amount to $11.9 million—less than large grocery chains make in one day—while losses would amount to $35 million (see Exhibit 2.1).[3] Borders found himself already thinking of how he could ensure the sustainability of his company. Could Webvan deliver on its huge promise and potential now that expectations had catapulted? Moreover, he suspected, Webvan's IPO had been a huge wake-up call for traditional grocers. How

This case was prepared by University of Michigan Business School MBA candidates Denise Banks, Otto Driessen, Thomas Oh, German Scipioni, and Rachel Zimmerman under the supervision of Professor Allan Afuah as a basis for class discussion. © Copyright 2001 by McGraw-Hill/Irwin. All rights reserved.

Webvan Group, Inc.
Consolidated Statement of Operations

	Year Ending December 31,	
	1997	**1998**
Net sales	0	0
Cost of goods sold	0	0
Gross profit	0	0
Operating expenses:		
Software development	$ 244	$ 3,010
General and administrative	2,612	8,825
Amortization of deferred stock	0	1,060
Total operating expenses	$ 2,856	$ 12,895
Interest income	85	923
Interest expense	69	32
Net interest income	16	891
Net loss	$(2,840)	$(12,004)
Basic and diluted net loss per share	$ (0.08)	$ (0.18)

would they—and perhaps other online competitors—react? Finally, Borders pondered possible new revenue streams. What additional, if any, delivery markets and products could Webvan pursue in the long term?

BORDERS BOOKS: REVOLUTIONIZING THE BOOK INDUSTRY

Back in 1971 Louis Borders and his brother Tom opened a "serious" bookshop in the heart of Ann Arbor, Michigan. Customers could expect friendly, well-informed store staff to help them locate their selections or let them browse solo for hours. With an unrivaled selection of topics, the first Borders store became known as one of the finest bookstores in the world.

Drawing upon Louis's study of mathematics, leading to a degree from the University of Michigan, and his graduate work at the Massachusetts Institute of Technology, Borders Books pioneered technologies and strategies that revolutionized the bookselling industry.

Inventory Management

Through its nationwide expansion, Borders Books devised and developed the most sophisticated computer inventory system in the book retailing business to date. As each store's purchases were recorded, the system used artificial intelligence technology to constantly adjust the store's inventory, thereby adding more books on topics that were selling and eliminating books on topics that were not. This technology allowed most Borders Books stores to stock over 200,000 book, music, and video titles, a selection unmatched by any other book or music store.

Customer Service

Not only did Borders Books cater to its customers through unparalleled selection, but it also offered exceptional service. From the day the first store opened, Borders focused on hiring well-educated book lovers. Special efforts were made to hire people who were passionate about books and music. In addition, all potential employees were required to pass a book or music quiz. This process ensured that well-informed and trained staff provided personal in-store attention and expertise to customers who requested it.

Borders Books selection and service competencies converged when attending to special customer orders. If a certain book or CD was not available in the store, the computer system searched for the item across all Borders stores in the country. If the item was not in inventory within the Borders Books chain, a salesperson would query publishers, wholesalers, suppliers, and smaller bookstores. Wherever it was available, the Borders Books staff would secure the item and ship it to the location that was most convenient to the customer.

Through their inventory management innovations and customer focus, Louis and Tom Borders were widely recognized as single-handedly revolutionizing and increasing sales in the over $10 billion bookselling industry. In 1999 the Borders Group, Inc., was the second largest book and music retailing chain in the United States and an independent, publicly owned corporation with its shares traded on the New York Stock Exchange.

A NEW CHALLENGE: THE GROCERY INDUSTRY

Energized by the staggering success of his initial venture, the 48-year-old Louis Borders sought a new challenge. He discovered it one day in 1997 as he opened a catalog order that had arrived at his Silicon Valley home by Federal Express. At that moment, Borders recognized that retailing through the Internet, a phenomenon that had exploded throughout the 1990s, would never become really big unless someone could discover a more efficient and cheaper way to deliver products to people's doorsteps. This untapped business proposition intrigued Borders. By transferring the inventory management and customer focus learning he established in the bookselling business, Borders was confident that he could reinvent the colossal $453 billion traditional off-line grocery market. With this goal in mind, Borders founded Webvan, an online grocer that was "arguably the most ambitious e-commerce initiative to date."[4]

HISTORY OF THE ONLINE GROCERY INDUSTRY

Although the traditional off-line grocery market was huge, the online grocery market emerged slowly. The online grocery industry originated in the late 1980s, when small local companies began taking orders by phone and fax and hired "professional shoppers" who would purchase the groceries from existing grocery stores. Orders were then delivered by the local companies or held in the store for pickup. In 1990 Peapod emerged as a front-runner in this industry, and many smaller players followed suit. However, since these smaller players relied on partnerships with traditional grocery stores, they were not able to sell goods cheaper than the actual store. The grocery delivery industry stayed afloat by charging delivery fees.

The rapid growth of Internet usage by consumers in the 1990s facilitated the transformation of the grocery delivery business into an online version. With more consumers using the Internet for informational and e-commerce purposes, online grocers tried to benefit from the efficiencies associated with Internet technology. New competitors, such as Webvan and eGrocer, sprang up in the marketplace, while more seasoned competitors, such as Peapod and Streamline.com, attempted to stay competitive. The original phone-and-fax players who were already in the marketplace were anxious to take advantage of the Internet channel and soon developed websites with product offerings that included not only groceries, but other items such as videos, flowers, music, and toys.

The latest trend in online grocery delivery was a distribution-centric prototype system. Its primary aim was to achieve a sizable customer base, respectable levels of customer service, satisfaction, and repeat usage. New entrants to the grocery delivery businesses planned aggressive national expansion programs by rapidly rolling out high-capacity customer distribution centers in most major metropolitan areas. Their goal was to steal market share from the enormous off-line grocery market and also to create new market opportunities by providing combinations of delivery services that did not yet exist in the bricks-and-mortar world.

MARKET POTENTIAL

Opportunities

The primary benefit the online grocery channel provided to consumers was convenience. The average "stock up" grocery store trip took 47 minutes[5] so online grocery shopping returned this valuable time to busy consumers. Moreover, after a 45-minute initial setup, subsequent orders could be processed extremely fast and efficiently. In addition, since many online grocers achieved less overhead by using centralized warehouses and employed fewer people than traditional stores, cost savings could potentially be transferred to the end consumer. Lastly, eliminating the costly real estate and other expenses related to bricks-and-mortar companies made for exciting business propositions and growth.

Research indicated that the online grocery channel was making inroads. The vast majority (89 percent) of people who tried purchasing groceries online visited the grocery store less often.[6] This indicated that online shopping could become habit-forming, potentially providing a constant stream of revenue for online grocers.

Challenges

Despite the hype of Internet companies and e-commerce as the "wave of the future," analysts and grocery industry experts were unsure about the actual growth potential of the online grocery market. Industry analysts estimated online grocery sales of $156 million in 1998, less than 1 percent of the entire grocery market. Market projections for the year 2003 ranged from $4.5 billion (Andersen Consulting) to $10.8 billion (Forrester Research). With such vastly different market projections, it appeared difficult to predict which online companies would do well, if any. Additionally, of the 53.5 million people who were online in the United States, only 435,000 ever purchased food online. This number represented less than 1 percent of the 14.5 million users who had made purchases online.[7]

The biggest challenge in the development of the online grocery industry was to attract and retain enough customers to use this alternative method of purchasing groceries. While online grocery shopping was deemed incapable of replacing the desire to "touch and feel" items such as fresh produce, the most common type of groceries purchased online were perishables.[8] Other common customer criticisms of online grocery shopping included lack of selection, the amount of time it took to set up an order, and the high cost of delivery relative to the service's perceived value. In addition, the demographic population that was most likely to use the online service was also the segment that was least willing to sit around and wait for deliveries.

Margin structures were razor thin in the highly competitive grocery industry, causing some competitors to diversify beyond mere grocery delivery. The savings associated with online ordering were partially offset by expensive home delivery and servicing requirements and, like all e-commerce ventures, could vanish when faced with the costs incurred by building brand recognition.

WEBVAN'S VISION

We are building the Last Mile to the consumer. It's a huge logistical problem.

—Louis Borders

Even in an industry rife with razor-thin margins, Louis Borders believed that by eliminating store costs, he could reap sizable profits. Instead of stock clerks and multiple warehouses, Borders envisioned giant distribution centers that would service major metropolitan warehouses around the globe.

Using Borders' analytical expertise, Webvan created a more efficient way to assemble customer orders, store them while in transit, and deliver them to homes within a 30-minute window. Borders estimated that Webvan could achieve 12 percent operating margins compared to the industry's traditionally low margins of 4 percent. To replicate this system nationwide, Webvan in

1999 signed a $1 billion agreement with Bechtel Group, an engineering and construction firm, to build distribution centers and delivery infrastructure in 26 new markets over the next two years. In addition, Borders foresaw a safe, secure online customer experience that offered nearly double the selection of products of a typical grocery store and at comparable prices.

With his compelling idea and vision in place, Borders set out to convince the business community that he had the retailing management expertise to crack the online grocery code. To build his business model, he duplicated the best operating practices from a myriad of cyber- and real-world businesses. Webvan looked to Federal Express as the blueprint for its hub-and-spoke delivery system, to traditional grocers as the model for maintaining food quality in transit, and to Wal-Mart as an example of breadth of product selection. Webvan's website emulated Yahoo! for speed and Amazon.com for the shopping experience. More than a few people were impressed as Webvan secured more than $120 million from hallmark investors such as CBS, Yahoo!, LVMH, Softbank, and respected venture capital firms Sequoia Capital and Benchmark Capital. In addition, Webvan was able to successfully recruit top, experienced management talent to join its mission. In a major coup, just prior to its IPO, Louis Borders convinced George Shaheen, CEO and 32-year veteran of Andersen Consulting, to forgo his imminent hefty retirement package and become Webvan's CEO.

THE WEBVAN MODEL

Building upon Borders' experience and expertise, Webvan differentiated itself within the online grocery market in two distinct areas: operations and customer service.

Operations

Webvan's 80 software programmers created proprietary systems that automated, linked, and tracked every part of the grocery ordering and delivery process. A new 330,000-square-foot distribution center in Oakland, California, utilized these proprietary systems to service customers within a 40-square-mile radius around the San Francisco Bay Area. The $25 million distribution center, a prototype for the 26 other centers Webvan intended to build, included 4.5 miles of conveyor belts, temperature-sensitive rooms for specialty items, and the ability to serve as many customers as 20 normal supermarkets.[9] The Webvan model could do all of this with half the labor and double the selection of products of regular supermarkets. Because of these innovative efficiencies, Borders believed that each of these facilities would make money within nine months of launch.

Once orders were placed on the Web, they were automatically routed to the warehouse. "Pickers" were stationed throughout the distribution center to assemble the orders in plastic boxes or totes, which were color-coded depending if the items were refrigerated, frozen, or dry. The pickers traveled no more than 19.5 feet in any direction to reach 8,000 bins of goods that were brought to the picker on rotating carousels.

A conveyor belt transported the totes throughout the facility until they were loaded onto refrigerated trucks. These trucks took the orders to one of 12 docking stations throughout the Bay Area where they were loaded onto one of more than 60 vans so that drivers could take the orders directly to people's homes. None of these vans traveled more than 10 miles in any direction and the route was mapped out by a system that optimized travel time. At peak performance, Webvan expected that each facility would handle more than 8,000 orders a day, totaling 225,000 items, and generate annual revenues of $300 million. In comparison, a conventional stand-alone supermarket brought in $12 million a year.

Customer Service

Webvan customers could order a shopping list of items and receive the groceries the next day within any specified 30-minute time period. Deliveries could be attended or unattended, meaning that the customer could either be home to receive the order, or the Webvan associate could drop off the order while the customer was away from home. Webvan couriers were not allowed to accept tips from customers, and were thoroughly screened and trained before starting their professional lives as Webvan "ambassadors." As of December 1999, delivery was free for orders over $50; delivery fees were $4.95 for orders under $50.

Additionally, Webvan aimed to provide its customers with 50,000 products from which to choose compared to a normal grocery store that carried 30,000 items.[10] Personalized shopping lists, which appeared after a customer's initial order, were also designed to provide faster and easier shopping services for the time-strapped customer. Webvan's market position as the quality-driven gourmet online grocer with everyday grocery prices was an attempt to differentiate itself from competitors. Webvan even employed its own culinary director, who was responsible for creating chef-prepared meals that catered to the lifestyle and tastes of Webvan customers. In addition, Webvan partnered with some highly regarded Bay Area suppliers to offer high-quality produce, meats, fish, and baked goods.

WEBVAN'S FINANCIAL PERFORMANCE

With high operational costs and low initial grocery sales, Webvan's 1999 losses were forecasted to be $35 million. Total sales for 1999 were expected to be only $11.9 million.[11] Forecasts called for Webvan to have sales of $518 million by 2001, with an overall loss of $302 million for the year. Sales of $518 million would be less than 1 percent of the entire grocery market (including bricks-and-mortar sales). Factors affecting these sales targets included on-time development of distribution centers and an increase in demand for online grocery services.

Gross sales were important to the company, but average order size and repeat customer business were also key drivers in overall profitability. Webvan's average grocery order, as of September 1999, was $71. This was significantly below the average order size of approximately $101 that was needed to generate annual targeted revenues per distribution center of $300 million.[12] However, Webvan's services had only been operational for a few months, so management believed that the average order size would increase over time.

Webvan received revenue solely from sales of grocery products and delivery fees. The company did not intend to sell its customer data to third-party database firms, nor did it receive online advertising fees, since it wanted to remain neutral among the different product brands that it sold online.

COMPETITION

Although the online grocery industry was relatively new, a number of companies competed with Webvan in trying to capitalize on its vast potential.

Peapod.com

Peapod was the oldest and largest online grocery player. Founded in 1989, its pioneering customers—400 households in the greater Chicago area—had to download proprietary software to use the service. "Personal shoppers" would then fill customer orders in local supermarkets. In 1998 Peapod claimed an estimated 44 percent of the Internet grocery market.[13] By 1999 Peapod had its software online and operations in Austin, Texas; Boston; Chicago; Columbus, Ohio; Dallas/Ft. Worth; Houston; Long Island, New York; and San Francisco/San Jose.

To keep up with demand—approximately 100,000 customers in 1999—Peapod switched from the personal shopper model to a warehouse model for filling orders, though its warehouses were significantly smaller than Webvan's. As of 1999, Peapod's personal shoppers picked their products inside Peapod warehouses and prepared them for delivery in temperature-controlled delivery bins. In November 1999 Peapod started shipping nonperishable packages across the country by UPS. Moreover, the company also established strategic membership alliances with Walgreen's for delivery of health and beauty aids, and was considering delivery of nongrocery items such as books, dry cleaning, and flowers.

Membership at Peapod actually decreased over 1999.[14] While analysts felt that Peapod's stock was underrated, it seemed that Peapod might have lost focus. In any case, it missed out on the investor mania that impacted so many Internet stocks. In November 1999 Peapod released disconcerting information, claiming that its funds would run out in the third quarter of 2000.[15]

Streamline.com; Shoplink.com

Originating in Boston, both of these companies positioned themselves as a "complete lifestyle solution, simplifying the lives of busy suburban families." For a monthly fee, Streamline and Shoplink delivered a wide variety of products and services at one's doorstep once a week. Unlike conventional home-delivery grocery services such as Peapod and HomeGrocer, Streamline and Shoplink delivered using either a portable cooling container or a leased, pre-installed refrigeration/shelving unit located in the customer's garage that was accessible only to authorized delivery workers. Products and services included groceries, prepared meals, pet food and supplies, postage stamps, dry cleaning, video and video game rentals, film processing, bottled water, as well as package pickup and delivery.[16]

While their delivery model allowed for more delivery flexibility, these companies also had to overcome additional customer reservations about privacy, theft, and safety. Furthermore, apartment dwellers were not eligible for these services. According to some, the high fixed and variable costs of this model appeared unattractive, yet deeper customer retention might prove a long-term advantage.

Netgrocer.com

Founded in 1997, Netgrocer was the first online grocer to employ the warehousing delivery strategy. From its northern New Jersey warehouse, Netgrocer shipped groceries anywhere in the 48 contiguous states, using Federal Express three-day delivery. Thus, Netgrocer was the only online delivery service that charged by weight rather than by order.

Netgrocer could be thought of as an "automatic pantry restocker." The company delivered only nonperishable goods, and its selection was far from comprehensive. As observed, "the best way you use it is to compile shopping lists of the things you know you buy every month and then just hit one button to have the same order delivered on a recurring basis. Paper towels, toothpaste, diapers, pasta, cat food, cans of soup, that sort of thing."[17] Thus, Netgrocer was betting on consumers' preferences to separate recurring nonperishables from more instinctive or short-term fresh produce purchases.

Hannaford Brothers; eGrocer.com

Hannaford and eGrocer employed a "collection center" strategy, whereby collection centers could be located in convenience stores, office buildings, drive-through facilities, gas stations, or in existing grocery stores, as in the case of eGrocer.

Hannaford, a Boston-area grocery store chain, began offering HomeRuns Online Worksite Delivery toward the end of 1999. This service utilized the corporate parking lot as its outlet, as grocery and prepared meal orders taken online were delivered there at the end of the working day.

At eGrocer, a Palo Alto, California, association of existing grocery stores, customers selected the products they wanted to buy online. These data were transmitted to a local, affiliated supermarket which fulfilled the order. The customers then picked up their groceries at their local supermarket in a designated area during a predetermined time window. This approach not only saved customers time in the store and at checkout lines, but also offered customers the opportunity to select certain items themselves. Thus, customers got convenience and the ability to "squeeze the tomatoes." While the online grocer avoided the cost of a distribution infrastructure, it had to share its margin with the supermarkets.

Niche Players

Niche players such as Pink Dot and EthnicGrocer.com competed on speed and tailored selection, respectively. Pink Dot created a "Domino's Pizza meets 7-Eleven Stores"[18] model for delivery of groceries, sandwiches, salads, and beverages. It sought to counterbalance higher prices by offering delivery in 30 minutes or less. However, this remained a strategy focused on the fulfillment of "emergency" or "last-minute" needs. Accordingly, order sizes were smaller, while the delivery time proved a sizable task in Pink Dot's city of origin, Los Angeles.

Players like EthnicGrocer focused on nonperishable and high-margin "hard-to-find" products. Similar to Pink Dot's "speed" strategy, the economics of this business model looked more dubious because it was likely to encounter difficulties in achieving economies of scale independently.

REACTION OF INCUMBENT SUPERMARKETS

The reaction of the bricks-and-mortar supermarket chains to the impending online grocery invasion would undoubtedly alter the online grocery landscape. Wall Street analysts had not encouraged bricks-and-mortar grocery chains to make big bets on the Internet. Bricks-and-mortar chains needed to determine if they should dismiss the online grocery phenomenon as a passing fad, or if—and when—they should invest heavily to remain competitive in a completely new marketplace. Many incumbents were looking for appropriate ways to acquire the competence necessary to compete online.

In a reaction to emerging online grocery stores, the biggest grocery chains such as Kroger and Safeway planned to launch experimental online delivery in selected areas. While these were only trials for companies that served much larger markets, incumbents were struggling to determine to what degree they should react to the new competition. Despite its growth, the online grocery delivery segment was forecasted to capture only an insignificant part of the total grocery market between 1999 and 2002. This was poised to change, however, with more ambitious projections calling for 20 percent of all grocery orders to be placed online five years later.[19]

Once incumbents did make the leap into the online segment, they would be formidable competitors. Incumbents already had an existing logistics and distribution model in place, which in most cases would require modest investments compared to the investments Webvan was taking on. Some grocery chains in the United Kingdom had begun to make the transition. For example, Safeway UK gave away free PalmPilots with a dedicated shopping application to its best customers. Tesco, the self-announced "biggest Internet grocer,"[20] with an estimated 240,000 customers, was selling a bar-code scanner that allowed customers to scan products while cruising the aisles. These data would then be downloaded directly to the store's back-end facilities so that the items selected were prepared for home delivery at a convenient time.[21]

LOOKING TO THE FUTURE

Now that Webvan had become a public company, the pressure of investor sentiment would be a major factor in Webvan's future strategic choices. Every decision made would directly affect the company's stock price and standing among Wall Street analysts and individual investors. To meet the high expectations and become the dominant player in the industry, Webvan faced some important strategic choices for the immediate future.

Should Webvan use its large market capitalization to buy regional grocery chains in markets it was interested in pursuing? These regional chains already possessed supplier networks as well as their own distribution centers. Webvan could possibly leverage some equipment from these distribution centers while attempting to replicate its existing distribution centers. This option would also eliminate a few competitors in these regions. On the other hand, should Webvan ever consider a takeover offer from a large grocery chain? Although Webvan's lofty valuation provided some protection against takeover, this certainly did not provide a permanent guarantee.

Furthermore, should Webvan continue to push forward with additional product lines? As of December 1999, sales demand was modest, and the Oakland, California, distribution center operated at only 20 percent of capacity. Would Webvan remain an online grocery company or would it become the "Last Mile" pioneer for all consumer products and services?

With all of this weighing on his mind, Borders decided to leave the office early in celebration of a successful IPO, but also to think about these strategic options for Webvan.

Notes

1. Mohanbir Sawhney, "The Longest Mile," *Business 2.0,* December 1999, p. 238.
2. George Anders, "Webvan's Splashy Stock Debut May Shake Up Staid Grocery Industry," *The Wall Street Journal,* November 8, 1999.
3. Ibid.

4. Linda Himelstein, "Can You Sell Groceries Like Books?" *Business Week,* July 26, 1999, pp. EB44–EB47.

5. "Market Spotlight: Grocery Shopping Online," *The Standard,* September 7, 1998.

6. Ibid.

7. Forrester Research, *Online Grocery Exposed,* December 3, 1998.

8. "Market Spotlight: Grocery Shopping Online," *The Standard,* September 7, 1998.

9. Linda Himelstein, "Innovators: Louis H. Borders," *Business Week,* September 27, 1999, p. 28.

10. Ibid.

11. Anders, "Webvan's Splashy Stock Debut . . . ," p. B1.

12. Webvan, SEC Prospectus Filing, Form 424B1, November 4, 1999.

13. Andrew Edgecliffe-Johnson, "Online Grocer's Funds Eaten Away," *Financial Times,* November 9, 1999.

14. Rick Aristotle Munarriz, "The Online Grocer Invasion," www.fool.com/specials/1999/sp991201groceries.htm, December 1, 1999.

15. Edgecliffe-Johnson, "Online Grocer's Funds Eaten Away."

16. Sawhney, "The Longest Mile," p. 238.

17. Don Wilmott, "So Long, Supermarket!" http://www.zdnet.com, December 5, 1997.

18. Sawhney, "The Longest Mile," p. 238.

19. Munarriz, "The Online Grocer Invasion."

20. Susanna Voyle, "Tesco Biggest Internet Grocer," *Financial Times,* December 1, 1999.

21. Penelope Ody, "Online Delights for the Adventurous," *Financial Times Information Technology Survey,* December 1, 1999.

Case **Three**

Reflect.com: Burn the Ships

At Reflect.com, your state-of-the-art skin care, hair care and cosmetic products don't exist until you create them. Simply create your beauty profile and our scientific process then blends your requests with the best technology to custom make your products. Delivered free. Unconditionally guaranteed.[1]

It was a warm October day in San Francisco as Ginger Kent, CEO of Reflect.com, sat at her desk and pondered whether the company would receive its recently requested second-round financing. Kent and her colleagues felt that the funds were desperately needed to redesign the website and improve the consumer purchase process. Reflect.com, an e-commerce site that allows women to customize beauty products, was about to celebrate its first anniversary. At this time, however, it needed a capital infusion from its original investors, which included the consumer packaged goods leader Procter & Gamble. While Reflect was hitting its monthly sales targets, it was difficult to ignore the turmoil that was ravaging the online beauty industry. Ingredients.com, Eve.com, Beautyscene.com, Beautyjungle.com, and countless others had closed down business, and it was rumored that others were not far behind. But Reflect.com's business model was unique, and Kent felt it was superior to other online third-party retailers. Still, the question loomed: Was it strong enough? Would women ever feel comfortable enough to buy their cosmetics and beauty needs online without a chance to touch, smell, or see them first?

NYU Stern School of Business MBA candidates Jean Pierre Divo, Margaret Higgins, Molly Milano, Juan Montoya, and M. Anne Wickland prepared this case under the supervision of Professor Christopher L. Tucci for the purpose of class discussion rather than to illustrate either effective or ineffective handling of an administrative situation. Copyright © 2002 by Christopher L. Tucci. All rights reserved.

COSMETIC INDUSTRY OVERVIEW

The health and beauty care industry, a $24 billion market, was one of the fastest growing and most profitable sectors in the United States over the past 50 years. It was expected to top $29 billion in 2003. According to Jupiter Communications, online beauty sales were projected to reach $100 million in 2001 and perhaps $360 million by 2003.[2]

The total cosmetics market (approximately $10 billion in sales) comprised two segments: the mass market and the prestige market. Mass products were sold through drug stores, grocery stores, health and beauty stores, and mass merchandisers. According to Information Resources Inc., mass cosmetic sales (excluding the nail segment) rose 10.5 percent to $2.8 billion for the 52-week period ending May 21, 2000. Including the nail segment, sales were $3.2 billion. Prestige products were sold through department stores and upscale retailers. In 1999, prestige beauty market sales were $6.5 billion in the U.S. Overall growth for the market was 3 percent.[3]

Online Consumer Trends

Both mass and prestige products were sold on the Web, either directly by manufacturers or through third-party vendors. By 1999 a Media Metrix/NPD E-Visory Report estimated that more than one-third of Internet users had ventured onto a beauty e-tail site, with women making up the majority of beauty buyers. The most popular purchases were in the bath and body category, while color cosmetics was the least-purchased category. Women's scents led sales dollar shares.[4] The study also found that buyers were not very experimental: only 6 percent said they bought things they had never tried before. The websites that had the highest recognition were pure-plays (i.e., websites without off-line operations) that focused on health and beauty.[5] Nevertheless, the outlook was promising. Women comprised nearly half of Internet users in 1999, representing 27 million women online in the U.S. In addition, approximately 58 percent of new Internet users were women, up from 44 percent in 1998.[6]

Competition: Chaos in Online Cosmetics

Reflect.com competed for the same wallet share as all of its competitors—mass, prestige, online, or offline. However, first and foremost, it competed against traditional manufacturers and marketers such as Procter & Gamble, L'Oreal, and the Estee Lauder Companies. (See Exhibits 3.1 and 3.2.)

Only one year prior, the beauty e-tail scene was thriving. Site after site opened, each better than the last. Then, however, the industry underwent a shakeout, with many of the sites that once seemed promising shutting their virtual doors.[7]

> **Beauty.com** was acquired by drugstore.com in February 2000; in late October 2000, the site terminated 10 percent of its workforce and announced that it would close its New York office.[8]

EXHIBIT 3.1   Top 20 Beauty Companies

Name	HQ	Sales ($ billions)	Subsidiaries/Main Brands
L'Oreal Group	Clichy, France	$11.20	L'Oreal Paris; Laboratoires Garnier; Gemey; Maybelline; Club des Createurs de Beaute; La Scad; Laboratoires Ylang; Soft Sheen; Lancome; Biotherm; Helena Rubinstein; Lanvin; Parfums Armani; Cacharel; Ralph Lauren; Paloma Picasso; Kiehl's; Guy LaRoche; Vichy; La Roche-Posay; L'Oreal Technique Professionelle; Kerastase; Redken; Inne; Matrix; Galderna; Sanofi-Synthelabo (20%); Carson Inc.
Procter & Gamble	Cincinnati, USA	7.50	Olay; SK-II; Cover Girl; Max Factor; Physique; Pantene; VS Vidal Sassoon; Head & Shoulders; Pert; Rejoice; Old Spice; "G" Giorgio; Hugo Boss; Red; BOSS; Reflect.com.
Unilever	Rotterdam & London	6.92	Elizabeth Arden; Calvin Klein Cosmetics; Parfums Karl Lagerfeld; Parfums Cerruti; Parfums Valentino; Scherrer; Helene Curtis; Cheeseborough Pond's; Elizabeth Taylor; Elida Gibbs; Faberge Brut; Atkinsons; Timotei; Clear; Sunsilk; Organics; Rexona; Sure; Axe; Lynx; Vaseline; Impulse.
Shiseido Co. Ltd.	Tokyo	4.90	Shiseido; Carita; Beaute Prestige International; Jean Paul Gaultier; Issey Miyake; Cle de Peau; Tony & Tony; Ayura Co Ltd.; D'ici la Co. Ltd.; Et Tu Sais Co. Ltd.; Zihr International; Nars; Za; 5S; Inoui; Auslese; Naturals; Qiora; Praudia; Pureness; Vital Perfection; Bio-performance Super Revitalizer; Basala; Femininite du Bois.
The Estee Lauder Companies, Inc.	New York, USA	4.20	Estee Lauder; Clinique; Aramis; Tommy Hilfiger; Prescriptives; Origins; MAC Cosmetics; Jane; La Mer; Donna Karan; Aveda; Stila; Jo Malone; Bumble & Bumble; Kate Spade.
Johnson & Johnson	New Brunswick, New Jersey, USA	3.40	Neutrogena; Clean & Clear; Purpose; pH5.5; RoC; Aveeno; Penaten; Johnson's; Renova; Retin-A.
Avon Products Inc.	New York, USA	3.20	Anew; Avon Techniques; Avon Beyond Color; ColorTrend; Perceive; Women of Earth; Far Away; Starring; Josie; Sweet Honesty.
KAO Corporation	Tokyo	2.60	The Andrew Jergens Co.; Goldwell; Guhl; Ikebana; Biore; Curel; Qualite; Jergens; Trendline; Merit; Blaune; Levenus; Sofina; Aube.
Biersdorf AG	Hamburg, Germany	2.53	Cosmed Division; NIVEA; 8x4; Atrix; Basis pH; Labello; Gammon; Juvena; La Prairie; Medical Division-Dermatology.
Wella Group	Darmstadt, Germany	2.43	Wella; Cosmopolitan Cosmetics; Sebastian International.

(continued)

EXHIBIT 3.1   *(continued)*

Name	HQ	Sales ($ billions)	Subsidiaries/Main Brands
Bristol-Myers Squibb	New York, USA	2.40	Clairol; Aussie/Redmond Products; Hydrience.
Kanebo Ltd.	Tokyo	2.28	Kanebo Cosmetics Europe; Kanebo Home Products, E'quipe Ltd./Kanebo Silk; Exclusive Bio; Sensai; Cosmetia; IB; Mild Coat; Medicated Shidenkai XD; Dada; Testimo; Kanebo Bio; Revue; RMK; Twany; Fila; Naïve.
Intimate Brands Inc.	Ohio, USA	2.05	Bath & Body Works; Victoria's Secret Beauty; White Barn Candle Co.
Alberto-Culver Co.	Melrose Park, USA	1.97	Alberto-Culver; Cederroth International; Alberto VO5; Tresemme; St. Ives Laboratoires; Sally Beauty Company; Molnlycke Toiletries; TCB; Pro-line; Motions.
Henkel KGAA	Dusseldorf, Germany	1.92	Schwarzkopf & Henkel; Poly Color; Fa; Schauma; Drei Wetter; Taft; Gliss Kur; Diadermine; Aok. Schwarzkopf Professional; Schwarzkopf & Dep Inc.; L.A. Looks; Morris.
Revlon Inc.	New York, USA	1.86	Revlon, Colorstay; Ultima II; Streetwear; Almay; Flex; Charlie.
LVMH Moet Hennessy Louis Vuitton	Paris, France	1.81	Christian Dior; Guerlain; Givenchy; Parfums Kenzo; Parfume Loewe; Hard Candy; Benefit Cosmetics; Make Up Forever; Urban Decay; Bliss
Coty, Inc.	New York, USA	1.80	Coty Beauty; Lancaster group/Vanilla Fields; The Healing Garden; Stetson; Adidas; Calgon; Davidoff Cool Water; Jil Sander; Exclamation; Vivienne Westwood; Isabella Rossellini; Rimmel; Yue-Sai.
The Boots Company PLC	Nottingham, England	1.60	Boots the Chemist; Boots Retail International; Boots Opticians; Halfords; Boots Properties; Boots Healthcare International; E45; Nobacter; Solubacter; Boots Contract Manufactoring; handbag.com.
Colgate-Palmolive Company	New York, USA	1.50	Colgate; Palmolive; Speed Stick; Lady Speed Stick; Skin Bracer; Afta; Protex; Caprice.

Beautyjungle.com laid off 60 percent of its staff and undertook a review of its strategic operations in late October 2000.[9] The site closed its doors for business by mid-November 2000.

Beautyscene.com went out of business in late November 2000.

Bliss/Blissworld.com, a growing spas and cosmetics company, developed successful lines of skin care and home spa products under the brands Remede and Bliss, which were distributed in selected locations. Bliss

EXHIBIT 3.2
Average Price Points for Reflect, Lancome, and Oil of Olay

Sources: www.reflect.com; www.lancome.com; local drugstore.

	Reflect.com	Lancome	Oil of Olay
Lipsticks, shampoos, conditioners	$12.00	$18.50	$8.29
Foundation makeup	16.50	32.50	10.99–12.99
Moisturizers	19.50	36–77	7.59
Facial mask	24.00	22.50–27.00	N/A
Eye gel	28.00	44.00	9.99
Night cream	29.50	59.00	9.99
Fragrance	40.00	32–80	N/A

also distributed a wide variety of its distinctive beauty products through its Blissworld.com website.

Eve.com shut down operations on October 20, 2000, less than 24 hours after its parent, Idealab, pulled financing from the site.[10] Eve.com's domain name and remnants have been acquired by competitor Sephora.com.

Gloss.com relaunched in March 2001. It featured all of the Estee Lauder Cos. brands as well as Clarins and Chanel. Industry sources believed Estee Lauder's presence may have a significant impact on the online industry by drawing more customers online.

Ibeauty.com, a certified AOL merchant, hired a new CEO, Gabriella Forte.

Lab21.com was an online laboratory that formulated skincare products to a customer's specific needs and requests. The site claimed it was capable of formulating 21 million unique skincare products. Customers answered an online questionnaire about their skin and its needs.

Sephora was an international beauty retailing venture owned by LVMH, which drew wide client and industry praise for its innovative store design and fresh approach to merchandising presentation. Sephora.com, launched in October 1999, extended the Sephora retail beauty concept to a worldwide audience.

PROCTER & GAMBLE

Started in 1837 as a soap manufacturer in Cincinnati, Procter & Gamble offered over 300 brands of consumer packaged goods in nearly 140 countries. P&G, a global leader in the industry with sales topping $38 billion annually, manufactured products in a wide range of categories, including fabric & home care, baby care, feminine care, tissues & towels, beauty care, health care, and food & beverages products.

With leading market shares, P&G's beauty care segment represented approximately 20 percent of P&G's total sales, or $7.5 billion annually. This category included three cosmetic labels, each targeted toward a different segment of the mass market:

- *Cover Girl:* P&G's Cover Girl line of cosmetics, launched in 1960, catered to girls and young women 14 to 24 years of age, who were concerned with clean skin, a natural look, and having fun.

- *Max Factor:* This line started as a line of theatrical makeup in 1909 created by Max Factor, Sr., who began as a make-up man for the Royal Ballet in Czarist Russia. In 2002, Max Factor was positioned as a cosmetics line used by makeup artists, but it was available to consumers through mass channels. Brand promotions centered around Hollywood themes such as blockbuster movie hits like *Titanic.*

- *Oil of Olay:* The Oil of Olay brand was the youngest of P&G's beauty lines. Launched as a full cosmetics line in 1999 as an extension of the popular moisturizer used by many women, this line was targeted to middle-aged women who wanted to look and feel younger. Benefit claims included reduced wrinkles and younger-looking skin.

The Beauty category also included noncosmetic brands, such as hair care, including VS Vidal Sassoon, Pantene, and Physique. Distribution for these products was almost exclusively in drug, grocery, or mass merchandisers such as Kmart and Wal-Mart.

Project Mirror

A corporate behemoth known for innovation and brand marketing prowess, P&G had long been a leader in new product development. However, in the early 90s, the consumer giant began to stumble.

The new product development process itself had become too bureaucratic and too slow to market. With so much time and money at stake, P&G could not afford another debacle like Olestra, the fat substitute that took 25 years and $250 million to develop. P&G began an initiative to foster more innovation and to shorten the new product development cycle. Major changes in its product development process included:

- Implementing new collaborative technologies that promote sharing ideas and information.

- Instituting global e-mail systems that linked 93,000 users.

- Creating virtual libraries and "collaboration [chat] rooms."

- Developing an internal innovation fund.

- Providing desktop video conferencing capabilities.

All of these corporate initiatives aided in reducing product development time and bureaucracy at P&G. As of late 2000, product development time was down 50 percent.[11]

In addition to revamping its product development process, P&G pursued another important initiative: embracing the Internet age. At a 1995 advertising industry meeting, P&G's CEO Ed Artzt warned, "Our most important ad medium, television, is about to change." Artzt believed that if marketers did not keep up with new digital media, years of brand building would be lost. Keeping up was vital for P&G. Artzt issued a mandate: "We have a lot of work to do. Let's get going."[12]

P&G reacted by building websites for virtually every brand they offered, even trying to sell products over the Web. However, much like the company brand structure, the attempt was uncoordinated and lacked a unified corporate vision. The company was simply "not uniquely prepared to capitalize" on Artzt's vision and had not harnessed the power of the Internet.[13] Additionally, P&G could not risk alienating its traditional distribution channels.

During this time, P&G's Interactive Marketing Team, a group of approximately 10 brand managers who received corporate funding to execute interactive projects with select brands, was quietly developing an idea in Cincinnati. Within a few months, the team came up with a plan, developed technology to customize products, and created a prototype website.[14] Thus, the idea of Project Mirror was born: a mass customization website that would allow women to make their own formulations of makeup, shampoo, and fragrance, complete with their own personalized label.

What began as a skunkworks project with $1 million from an internal innovation fund quickly ran into P&G's limited knowledge about the Internet.[15] P&G began to look outside its doors for help.

Armed with a list of venture capital firms from P&G's investment bankers, Denis Beausejour (P&G's worldwide VP of marketing for beauty care), Nathan Estruth, and other P&Gers flew to Silicon Valley to talk to the top venture capital firms. They grilled executives and venture capitalists about the secrets of Web success. The executives also learned the benefits of stripping out extra layers of management and increasing the pace of innovation and decision making.

REFLECT.COM

Reflect.com was financed with $35 million from Procter & Gamble and $15 million from Institutional Venture Partners (IVP), the investment firm famous for backing Excite Inc. (See Exhibits 3.3 and 3.4.) IVP's Geoff Yang summed up his enthusiasm for the deal saying, "What energized us was that this wasn't just another e-tailing deal. They were going to do something no one's done before."[16]

However, there were some sticking points in ironing out the details of the partnership. Where IVP was used to conducting informal negotiations with

EXHIBIT 3.3 **Institutional Venture Partners (IVP)**

Source: www.ivp.com.

> IVP has been venture investing since 1974 and has funded more than 200 companies. It now manages more than $1 billion. IVP has marshaled 60 IPOs and over 25 successful IPO-like acquisitions. The company has consistently funded companies that have become dominant players in new industries:
>
> •*Internet:* Excite, Mpath, Ask Jeeves, Concur.
> •*Communications Equipment:* Bay Networks, MMC Networks, Aspect Telecommunications.
> •*Enterprise Software:* Clarify, Concur.
> •*Semiconductors:* LSI Logic, Altera, Atmel, Cirrus Logic.
> •*Storage:* Seagate, Exabyte.
> •*Computing:* Stratus, Sequent.
> •*Life Sciences:* Aviron, Biopsys.
>
> IVP's investments have combined revenues of more than $20 billion and a combined market value of more than $30 billion. IVP employs more than 125,000 people.

EXHIBIT 3.4
Investors' Strengths

IVP	P&G
• $15 million invested	• $35 million invested
• Extensive Silicon Valley network	• Branding/marketing expertise
• Internet start-up experience	• Extensive R&D infrastructure
• High-tech recruiting muscle	• Launch team
• Speed	• Existing cosmetic business *with formulas*
• Credibility with Net establishment	• Credibility with media and Wall Street

young entrepreneurs that were finalized quickly with a handshake, the P&G lawyers went over every detail.[17] IVP's typical negotiations lasted just one day, whereas with Reflect.com, they took three weeks. Issues arose regarding equity, control of future financing events, and the new company's governance. "Yang wasn't interested in being a mere midwife for a P&G development project. He wanted to build a killer freestanding company that could pursue its own best interests. He put forward an argument he remembers this way: 'If you guys want control, it might as well be inside P&G. We can't allow you to call the shots. If we can't take this company public, then you're capping our upside.'"[18]

Despite the sticking points, P&G "threw caution to the wind on some key points." The investors agreed upon the 65/15/20 split (for P&G, IVP/Redpoint Ventures, and Reflect.com employees, respectively). IVP received the same number of board seats as P&G, as well as "an equal say over such pivotal issues as whether and when to take Reflect.com public." P&G, however, retained control over any reorganization or sale of the company.[19]

A. G. Lafley, then president of Procter & Gamble's global beauty care division and interim CEO of the new company (now P&G CEO), summed up

P&G's feelings about the site: "We very strongly believed we had to get out in the middle of the start-up environment and see if we could deliver innovation and speed at that rate."[20]

Independence Day—"Burn the Ships"

In order to make the Web venture more authentic, P&G forced employees to resign from the consumer goods giant, take pay cuts in exchange for stock options, and move to San Francisco. On October 1, 1999, a team of 15 people left P&G to join Reflect.com. The night before, Denis Beausejour hosted a sendoff party at his home, ceremoniously presenting each team member's spouse with one share of Reflect.com stock. "You don't have a lifeline back to P&G," Beausejour told the troops. "All you've got left now is your Reflect.com stock and your teammates. Now make it happen." The lifeline bit was no joke. A. G. Lafley decided that the 15 people sailing off on the Reflect.com lifeboat would not have the option of returning to P&G. "Burn the ships"—a reference to the conquistador Cortes's decision to stay in the New World—became a Reflect.com mantra.[21]

The Site

The Reflect.com site launched in December 1999 as a personalized line of beauty products (including skin and hair care and cosmetics) and services created for and available solely through the Internet, using a patent-pending system for a mass-customization model.

With access to P&G's global supply chain and R&D facilities, the site had the capability to create more than 300,000 different products and packages. By asking the consumer a series of questions and letting her control the experience, the site created customized products and packages. Additionally, Reflect.com owned its unique manufacturing process that resembled a virtual plug-and-play. The company was able to produce product in very small lots (25 vs. 10,000 for competitors), and reduced changeovers to 5 to 7 minutes. The industry average was 90 minutes. (See Exhibit 3.5.)

The site capitalized on P&G's beauty care expertise while leveraging the Internet's capabilities to create a consumer experience that could not be duplicated in a typical bricks-and-mortar environment. Using an interactive question-and-answer process to determine each woman's needs and P&G's research and development lab, Reflect.com created unique products for each customer.

The product creation process began on the site and ended with a fulfillment center in Cincinnati called Direct Site.[22] Sourcing from multiple suppliers along with technology as a delivery tool dictated order fulfillment. This process, from front to back end, was proprietary and was pending patent approval.[23] Reflect.com also enjoyed the benefits of lower inventories and reduced cost of sales.

The company allowed a customer to build her own brand of upscale beauty products that were created, manufactured, packaged, and distributed on an individual basis. "Reflect.com acts as a channel to serve the high-performance

EXHIBIT 3.5
Beauty Companies with Customized Offerings

Company	Products	Prices	Where	Waiting Time	Repeat Orders	Service
Three Custom Color	Concealer, blush, lipstick, lip gloss, eye shadow, and brow powder.	$33.50–$50.00	Henri Bendel, select Sephora stores, *three custom.com*	3 weeks, including shipping time; lipsticks and glosses about 45 minutes at Henri Bendel.	The shades used to create a color are logged, but the exact formulas are not. Matching depends on the skill of the blender, which we found to be consistently high.	Consultants explain how colors look on different complexions.
Prescriptives	Foundation, loose and pressed powder, and lipstick.	$30.00–$50.00	Major department stores; lipstick currently only at Bergdorf Goodman	Foundation or powder in about 10 minutes; lipstick fine-tuning can take 2 days.	Each store files a customer's formula, though duplication may vary slightly depending on who makes the batch.	Consultants lead you through the process, making it almost foolproof. If you don't like the finished product you can request changes on the spot.
By Terry	Anything and everything from liquid bronzer to false eyelashes, created by former Yves Saint Laurent cosmetics exec.	Beginning at $500 for a year's supply of lipstick, powder, cream or shadow packaged in a silver case.	011-33-1-44-76-00-76 or 21; Passage Vero-Dodat, Paris 75001	30 minutes to 1 hour	Absolutely precise, according to client's file.	De Gunzburg will go through as many "fittings" as the client needs— preferably in person or through product testing via mail.
Creed	Fragrances created by mixing existing Creed scents.	$350–$800 for the 2.5 ounce blend, which includes a bottle of each fragrance used in the mix.	Barneys in NY, Neiman Marcus, Bergdorf Goodman, Creed store in NY, 877–CREED-NY	30 minutes to 1 hour	The same scent can be recreated from ratios kept on file	A "blender" familiarizes customers with existing scents and mixes their favorites, typically going through 3–5 variations to reach the right proportions.

(continued)

EPILOGUE

Two days shy of its first birthday, Reflect.com received a $30 million round of financing, in which its original investors returned. (While the details of the second round were not made public, the terms were reported to be similar to the first-round financing.)[30] "Our investors are pleased with what we've achieved in the time we've been up and the response we've been getting in terms of orders and reorders," says Richard Gerstein, VP of design and marketing.[31]

Reflect.com officials claimed that they did not need the second-round financing because the site had burned through the first, but that it was necessary to invest in infrastructure and to further build the business. One of the first projects with the infusion was a relaunch of the site in response to customer feedback. As of November 2000, the site offered a more streamlined system and additional shopping benefits. For example, the site still profiled customers' needs, but the customer had the ability to start customizing her product as early as the first page. Previously, she had to navigate through several screens before reaching this step. Another new feature enabled shoppers to see aspects (e.g., package selection, choice of graphics) of their product as it was being created. Customers could also window-shop, viewing what types of products could be made, in what sizes, etc., before starting the creation process. In this browsing section, the shopper might click on the creation area anytime she wanted if she saw something she liked. The site incorporated a navigation bar across the top of each screen that provided visitors with more flexibility to move around the site.

Notes

1. http://www.reflect.com.
2. Kerry Diamond, "Taking Stock of Beauty's Net Worth," *Women's Wear Daily,* November 3, 2000, p. 6.
3. Laura Klepacki, "The Star Report," *Women's Wear Daily,* May 19, 2000, p. 2.
4. Janet Ozzard, "Understanding Beauty's Web Appeal," *Women's Wear Daily,* August 11, 2000, p. 10.
5. Ibid.
6. Alev Aktar, "Women on the Web," *Women's Wear Daily,* January 28, 2000, p. 9.
7. Diamond, "Taking Stock of Beauty's Net Worth."
8. Ibid.
9. Ibid.
10. Ibid.
11. Marianne Kolbasuk McGee, "Culture Change: Come Together: The Idea Behind Collaboration Rooms," *Information Week,* October 5, 1999, www.informationweek.com/758/prga3.htm.
12. Dale Buss, "Procter & Gamble Faces the Future," *The Industry Standard,* March 27, 2000, www.thestandard.com/article/display/0,1151,13264,000.htm.

13. Buss, "Procter & Gamble Faces the Future."
14. Linda Himelstein and Peter Galuszka, "P&G Gives Birth to a Web Baby," September 27, 1999, p. 87.
15. Jerry Useem, "Can These Marriages Be Saved?"*Fortune,* November 8, 2000, p. 102.
16. Ibid.
17. Linda Himelstein and Peter Galuszka, "P&G Gives Birth to a Web Baby."
18. Ibid.
19. Ibid.
20. Scott Herhold, "Web Site a Thing of Beauty for P&G," *San Jose Mercury News,* September 14, 1999, p. 1C.
21. Jerry Useem, "Can These Marriages Be Saved?"
22. Richard Karpinski, "Beauty Site Gets Personal—Reflect.com Delivers Fully Personalized Web Customer Service," *Internetweek,* November 29, 1999, p. 33.
23. Ramin P. Jaleshgari, "An Alternative Culture: Reflect.com's Unique Approach," *Information Week,* October 25, 1999.
24. David Ticoll, "The Beauty of the Internet—Letting Customers Create Their Own Brand Results in 'Ultimate Stickiness,'" *Teledotcom,* June 5, 2000, www.techweb.com/se/directlink.cgi?TLC20000605S0067.
25. Beth Cox, "Ah, the Sweet Smell of Eau de E-Commerce," *Ecommerce Guide,* September 6, 2000, http://ecommerce.internet.com/news/insights/trends/article/0,,10417_454021,00.html.
26. Jerry Useem, "Can These Marriages Be Saved?"
27. Betsy Spethmann, "Beauty Treatments," *Promo,* August 2000.
28. Ibid.
29. Lindsey Arent, "Procter Makes Up a Gamble," *Wired News,* September 17, 1999, www.wired.com/news/print/0,1294,21795,00.html.
30. O'Connor, Colleen, "Venture-Backed Beauty Site Reflects Potential," *IPO Reporter,* September 18, 2000. (No page number from Lexis/Nexis.)
31. Christopher Heun, "Per$onalizing Cosmetics," *Information Week,* September 18, 2000, *www.iweek.com.*

Case **Four**

VerticalNet: The New Face of B2B

After showing the last reporter to the door, Mark Walsh finally had a chance to return to his office and reflect on the incredible events of the prior 48 hours. Only the day before, on February 11, 1999, his company had staged a spectacular initial public offering (IPO). Shares of VerticalNet, Inc. (NASDAQ symbol VERT), had opened at $16 and skyrocketed 184 percent to $45 before the closing bell. This made Walsh the CEO of a company with a market capitalization of $738 million—and that company was less than four years old.[1]

Walsh was thrilled by the IPO results, but he also recognized that with the limelight came extensive public scrutiny and an intense pressure to perform. The business model he had developed for VerticalNet was solid enough not only to increase the growth of the company to its current IPO-ready size, but also to firmly establish VerticalNet as a leader in the business-to-business (B2B) electronic commerce arena. This market had evolved slowly over 15 years, but the pace of change had quickened considerably in the last 18 months. New players were rapidly entering the B2B marketplace and competition was increasing. With analysts' projections that B2B e-commerce would grow to a $1.3 trillion industry by the year 2002,[2] Walsh knew the stakes were extremely high: If he didn't continue to innovate and reinvent his firm, VerticalNet could be quickly overtaken by the competition.

University of Michigan Business School MBA Candidates Angie Bohr, Quitanne Delano, Paul Hofley, Paul Linton, and Brad Stewart prepared this case under the supervision of Professor Allan Afuah as the basis for class discussion rather than to illustrate either effective or ineffective handling of an administrative situation. © Copyright 2001 by McGraw-Hill/Irwin. All rights reserved.

EVOLUTION OF BUSINESS-TO-BUSINESS E-COMMERCE

Beginning in the early 1980s, businesses transferred information electronically using a system known as electronic data interchange (EDI). This system utilized a synchronous connection between two host computers to share various types of information, such as parts catalogs, delivery schedules, purchase orders, and payment verifications. EDI provided a more efficient way for businesses to transmit information compared with traditional mail or fax machines, but operated on a proprietary network, which limited its ability to support multiple users. In addition, the proprietary nature of EDI systems made enterprisewide expansion difficult.[3]

B2B e-commerce overcame some of the shortfalls of EDI through Web-based Internet applications. Businesses initially used the Internet to connect to and communicate with other businesses through the use of electronic mail (e-mail). Eventually, as Web browsers evolved and Internet access grew more commonplace, businesses developed a practical method for transferring business-related information through the Internet. The development of extensible markup language (XML) used in conjunction with hypertext markup language (HTML), among other languages, provided the backbone upon which B2B exchanges were built.

Businesses originally used the Internet much in the same way as EDI: The Internet acted as the conduit between businesses but offered greater flexibility among users. Unlike EDI, the Internet did not require a single, dedicated computer line but connected users instead through a system network which allowed multiple users to access information from individual workstations. Some of the first companies to embrace the Internet for business transactions were large technology companies, such as Cisco Systems, an Internet networking company, and computer companies such as IBM and Dell, which turned to the Internet as a means to complete supplier purchases and business sales. Other businesses quickly followed suit as companies recognized the Internet's ability to fundamentally change business communications and reduce transaction times and costs.

A few key traits distinguished a successful B2B exchange: high availability, transaction support, XML, security, and timeliness. High availability translated into anytime, anywhere access for both buyers and sellers using the exchange. Transaction support involved standardizing quantity and quality information so that a fair price could be agreed upon. XML tags provided a common set of data fields so that information transfer could be streamlined and formatted properly. Security remained a vital issue for all Internet transactions. Advanced B2B exchanges used "digital certificates" to confirm the identification of users. Finally, timeliness was representative of network capacity, with bandwidth and processing power needed to support the requests of the users.[4]

Digital marketplaces evolved into three different business models: e-Communities, e-Distributors, and e-Exchanges. These business models demonstrated the current trends in the business-to-business electronic commerce arena, and each model had a different approach to revenue generation. Accordingly, value recognized by the marketplace was hard to determine.

e-Communities

Composed of buyers and sellers exchanging information concerning a single vertical[5] market, e-Communities are digital publications that follow industry trends and news. Websites develop a user base through traditional advertising intended to draw traffic to the site. Revenue is generated primarily through advertising, sponsorships, and transaction fees. The viability of this revenue-generation model is unclear, which motivated companies to migrate to the distributor and exchange models.

e-Distributors

E-Distributors establish a single source for goods and services within a single vertical industry. Typically, goods and services from multiple vendors are aggregated to one comprehensive location, which helps to streamline the purchase process. In turn, the intermediary collects a transaction fee related to the services it provides. Traditional companies are adopting the e-Distributor model in addition to their existing bricks-and mortar operation to provide customers with an alternative channel for purchasing goods and services.

e-Exchanges

This model brings together buyers and sellers within the setting of a vertical industry marketplace. Exchanges use an auction-pricing model to provide buyers with a competitive environment and lower costs, which makes the intermediary attractive to large purchasing organizations. The marketplace offers both commodity and custom-made products. Custom-made products require more information about design, functionality, and quality in order to be considered by buyers. B2Bs that use this model typically collect a transaction fee as a means of generating revenue.

As each of the e-business models evolves, industry experts expect online marketplaces to incorporate elements of each model and envision successful digital marketplaces to include varying levels of community, content, and commerce.

HISTORY OF VERTICALNET

In 1995 Mike McNulty began selling advertising space for a wastewater industry trade publication. His clients often complained about their inability to track the number of leads generated by the ads they placed in the publication.[6] As a result, many customers were unsure whether they were getting a sufficient return on investment from their ads. McNulty was convinced that he could develop a more efficient and effective method that would not only bring buyers and suppliers together, but also provide businesses with lead tracking and qualification. The Internet, he thought, could be the answer.

From the beginning, McNulty envisioned a website that contained up-to-date industry news, trends, and information, as well as a list of suppliers that offered related products and services. His hope was that users would come to the site to locate current industry information and highlights while buyers would use the site as a convenient and reliable place to source goods and services.[7] McNulty first pitched his revolutionary idea to his boss, but got nowhere. Undeterred, he called Mike Hagan, a long-time friend and vice president at Merrill Lynch Asset Management. Upon hearing McNulty's idea, Hagan immediately saw the great potential for this venture.

Enthusiastic about the new business idea and cognizant of the importance of gaining "first mover" advantage on the Internet, the two quit their jobs and established VerticalNet in Horsham, Pennsylvania, in August 1995. VerticalNet's first "online vertical trade community,"[8] WaterOnline, was introduced shortly thereafter, and McNulty heavily leveraged his wide-ranging industry contacts to drum up business. Initial revenues were derived from selling online advertising spaces, dubbed "storefronts," to various wastewater industry suppliers. Buyers could browse the storefronts free of charge and, with the click of a button, send an e-mail request for product information or quotes. Search engine functionality was soon added to facilitate this process, followed quickly by a tool that let buyers post specific requests for proposals/quotes (RFPs and RFQs) that suppliers could then browse and respond to as appropriate. Additionally, McNulty and Hagan hired editors to develop and monitor news, job postings, and informational content posted on the site.[9]

Initially, McNulty and Hagan funded their young company through credit cards and personal savings, together contributing $75,000 to get through the first year. Hagan's contacts on Wall Street helped them to secure much-needed venture capital in 1996, which they received in the form of a $1 million equity investment from Internet Capital Group (ICG). The two founders knew, however, that the initial funding would not be enough to make the company a major player in the emerging B2B market. Both McNulty and Hagan recognized that to raise the necessary level of funding—potentially millions of dollars—VerticalNet would need an experienced and well-respected leader to bring credibility, confidence, and business knowledge to the company in order to attract investors.

In August 1997 the company found the leadership it was seeking when Mark L. Walsh signed on as CEO. Walsh's background included several years as a general manager at CUC International, an early pioneer in online interactive services, as well as extensive experience with other online ventures, including the management of General Electric's online services and a position as senior vice president for America Online's B2B division. When Walsh was first approached for the VerticalNet position, he was immediately smitten with the idea. "This is sweet," Walsh recalls saying at the time. "This is a total pure play for what I believe is the future of the Internet."[10]

By the time Walsh joined VerticalNet, it had expanded into five verticals with a staff of less than 50. With Walsh's help, in late 1997 and again in 1998 the company secured additional equity-based funding from ICG, ultimately giving the investment group a 49 percent stake in the company.[11] VerticalNet moved quickly to take advantage of the new funding by developing several new verticals (including PollutionOnline, SolidWasteOnline, ChemicalOnline, and SemiconductorOnline), and by nearly doubling the number of its employees. As a result, the company booked revenues of almost $800,000 during the 1997 calendar year and headed into 1998 with highly aggressive growth plans (see Exhibit 4.1).[12]

In May 1998, VerticalNet won the coveted Tenagra Award for "Successful Internet Business Model" in recognition of VerticalNet's profitability and success with online publishing and "community building" across multiple industries.[13] VerticalNet's oldest and most profitable site, WaterOnline, was receiving approximately 80,000 unique visitors per month and generating more than $500,000 in revenue annually. Walsh expected most of the other sites to follow suit. Throughout the year the company added 14 more verticals, bringing the total to 29. The rapid growth was essential to lock in first-mover advantages, but expansion came at a high price as expenses outpaced revenues. As the year drew to a close, VerticalNet had accumulated an operating deficit of over $14 million and would soon run out of venture capital.[14]

Rather than go back for another round of financing, Walsh decided it was time to capitalize on the recent positive press coverage and to take advantage of an IPO-hungry market by taking VerticalNet public. On February 11, 1999, the IPO date, VerticalNet offered 29 communities and employed 190 people. The 29 sites together drew more than 650,000 unique visitors a month, resulting in the generation of over 40,000 sales leads.[15] Despite the company's expectation that it would not be profitable until 2000 or 2001, the optimistic public markets traded over 4 million shares during the IPO and drove up the price some 184 percent. Clearly, investors believed that VerticalNet's business model positioned the company to capture a significant portion of the B2B e-commerce space.

BUSINESS MODEL

VerticalNet created a scalable platform that made it the industry leader in the development and launch of verticals. These industry-centric portals served the business-to-business sector of the Internet. As the number of verticals was projected to grow from 29 to 150 by 2005, VerticalNet expected to benefit from its ability to launch new sites efficiently, spreading costs across the sites. Each vertical was an independent profit center. Users accessed verticals to view content developed by VerticalNet's editorial staff, while advertisers paid for banner ads or sponsored newsletters that were e-mailed to registered users. Technical, sales and marketing, and administrative personnel worked across multiple verticals to achieve economies of scale.[16]

EXHIBIT 4.1   VerticalNet Selected Financial Data (in $000s, except share, per share data)

	July 28– December 31, 1995	Year Ending December 31,		
		1996	1997	1998
Statement of operations data:				
Revenues	$ 16	$ 285	$ 792	$3,135
Expenses, editorial and operational	24	214	1,056	3,238
Product development	22	214	711	1405
Sales and marketing	147	268	2,301	7,895
General and administrative	33	292	1,388	3,823
Amortization of goodwill	—	—	—	283
Operating loss	(210)	(703)	(4,664)	(13,509)
Interest, net	(1)	(6)	(115)	(85)
Net loss	$ (211)	$ (709)	$ (4,779)	$ (13,594)
Basic and diluted net loss per share	$ (0.19)	$ (0.27)	$ (1.89)	$ (5.29)
Shares outstanding used in basic and diluted net loss per share calculation[1]	1,096,679	2,583,648	2,526,865	2,570,550
Pro forma basic and diluted net loss per share	$ (0.19)	$ (0.21)	$ (0.77)	$ (1.28)
Shares outstanding used in pro forma basic and diluted net loss per common share calculation[1]	1,096,679	3,326,284	6,184,326	10,635,489

(1) As described in Note 1 of the consolidated financial statements. The unaudited pro forma balance sheet as of December 31, 1998, reflects (a) our capitalization subsequent to the initial public offering closing, including the sale of 4,025,000 shares of common stock on February 17, 1999, resulting in approximately $58,322,000 of net proceeds; (b) all of the then-outstanding shares of our convertible preferred stock automatically converted into 9,734,845 shares of common stock on the basis that the Series A preferred stock converted to shares of common stock on a ratio of 4.7619:1 and the Series B, C, and D preferred stock converted on a ratio of 1:1; (c) the $5.0 million of convertible notes from Internet Capital Group and certain holders of the Series D preferred stock converted at the $16 offering price into 312,500 shares of common stock; (d) the repayment of the $2.0 million bank note.

	Year Ending December 31,			
	1996	1997	1998	Pro forma
Balance sheet data:				
Cash and cash equivalents	$329	$ 755	$5,663	$61,985
Working capital (deficit)	150	(2,536)	938	59,260
Total assets	637	2,104	12,343	68,665
Short-term borrowings	—	2,651	2,288	288
Deferred revenues	216	710	2,177	2,177
Long-term debt, less current portion	167	400	5,352	352
Total shareholders' equity (deficit)	105	(2,424)	(276)	63,046

Why Visit a Vertical?

Content

Each vertical served as a comprehensive resource for new product information and had a dedicated editor who managed the mix of news and commentary and ensured that the content was current and relevant. While the editors added original content, such as objective analysis of new products, the sites also provided recent press releases and news stories pertinent to the industry. Additionally, industry professionals could access product case studies or industry "white papers" to stay informed of recent innovations and could utilize an archived information service for research. Finally, e-mail newsletters containing news updates, highlights, and special features were sent weekly to help generate repeat visits.[17]

Community

Verticals leveraged the power of the Internet to bring together industry professionals who could communicate efficiently and share information about upcoming trade shows and other industry events. VerticalNet planned eventually to offer its registered users free e-mail accounts as a way to both increase potential site usage and form a common community "identity." The proposed addresses would indicate the user's "community" by including the industry vertical name (e.g. "fredrickpoweronline.com"). Another community-building endeavor was the anticipated addition of a career center to provide employment services such as resume distribution and employment listings. Reports on companies would be available to assist the user in researching prospective employers and preparing for interviews.

Commerce

To ensure efficient and effective marketing, the sites provided products and services targeted at a narrow audience of users. The VerticalNet marketplace invited users to purchase a predetermined selection of books, videos, and software, and provided a library of demo-software and software sales service. Some verticals offered selections for continuing education and training services while third-party providers offered online courses with focused content and research to VerticalNet users. These services were of particular interest to those individuals looking either to acquire industry-specific licenses or to maintain specific industry certifications by regularly upgrading skills.[18]

Developing a Vertical

VerticalNet had a refined process for developing a new vertical through a series of steps. First, the company used various criteria to identify an industry sector that might benefit from a vertical portal (see Exhibit 4.2). Usually, industries with a substantial number of highly fragmented buyers and suppliers were prime targets. Next, VerticalNet recruited well-respected industry editorial talent who acted both as a content producer and a credibility builder

EXHIBIT 4.2
VerticalNet's
Vertical Trade
Communities

Source:
www.verticalnet.com/
communities.html.

Communities	Website Address
Environment and Utility	
Water Online	wateronline.com
Pollution Online	pollutiononline.com
Solid Waste Online	solidwaste.com
Pulp and Paper Online	pulpandpaperonline.com
Power Online	poweronline.com
Public Works Online	publicworks.com
Process Industries	
Chemical Online	chemicalonline.com
Pharmaceutical Online	pharmaceuticalonline.com
Semiconductor Online	semiconductoronline.com
Hydrocarbon Online	hydrocarbononline.com
Paint and Coatings Online	paintandcoatings.com
Food Online	foodonline.com
Adhesives and Sealants Online	adhesivesandsealants.com
Electronics	
Computer OEM Online	computeroem.com
Medical Design Online	medicaldesignonline.com
Test and Measurement Online	testandmeasurement.com
Life Sciences	
Bioresearch Online	bioresearchonline.com
Laboratory Network Online	laboratorynetwork.com
Services	
Property and Casualty Online	propertyandcasualty.com
Food and Packaging	
Food Ingredients Online	foodingredientsonline.com
Packaging Network	packagingnetwork.com
Beverage Online	beverageonline.com
Bakery Online	bakeryonline.com
Dairy Network	dairynetwork.com
Meat and Poultry Online	meatandpoultryonline.com
Telecommunications	
RF GlobalNet	rfglobalnet.com
Wireless Design Online	wirelessdesignonline.com
Photonics Online	photonicsonline.com
Fiber Optics Online	fiberopticsonline.com

for the site. A common site template provided the foundation for each new site, which would be formatted specifically to the site's industry. Finally, the company hired sales professionals to develop an industry buyer guide and a potential list of advertisers.

The resources required for each vertical included an editor, an industry manager, and a sales manager. The editor worked full-time to write original content and identify relevant news, and usually worked from home. The industry manager was responsible for establishing relationships with key industry players and trade association representatives and for attending trade shows. Trade shows provided a prime venue for the industry manager to make new contacts and sell advertising. The sales manager targeted organizations whose products and services were typically purchased by vertical visitors. The sales staff usually had a background in trade publication advertising and sales.

VerticalNet Revenue Sources

Advertising was expected to account for roughly 97 percent and limited e-commerce for the remaining 3 percent of revenues in the first quarter of 1999. The primary sources of advertising revenue were storefronts, banners, and sponsorships. Historically, the company renewed 90 percent of all advertising contracts and expected to maintain this rate going forward. VerticalNet hoped to grow its e-commerce revenues as a means of diversifying its revenue streams.

Storefronts

The storefront product provided a simple means for advertisers to display company information and product overviews. Users were directed to storefronts from banner ads on a vertical's front page or through links from a keyword search. Storefront visitors interested in a particular product could request additional information, which the vendor then delivered by e-mail. These inquiries often materialized into high-quality leads. As lead tracking was an important part of VerticalNet's value to its advertisers, the company installed a lead-generation system similar to lead "scorecards," which traditionally were used by trade magazines.[19] Instead of a paper postcard, VerticalNet offered a service, called VirtualOffice, to its advertisers whereby all user inquiries were tracked on the vertical but monitored by the advertiser itself. This allowed each advertiser to respond quickly to inquiries and to evaluate the effectiveness of individual banners.

Storefronts accounted for 85 percent of revenues in 1998, but were expected to fall to 50 percent of revenues as other products (e.g., banner sales and sponsorships) became more popular. The number of storefronts grew from 67 in 1996 to 1,300 in 1998 and nearly 1,600 by the time of the IPO. Meanwhile, the average number of storefronts per vertical had risen from 22 in 1996 to 48 in the last quarter of 1998. Typically, an advertiser paid $6,500 annually for a storefront. VerticalNet was exploring ways to generate additional storefront revenues, including options that would allow vendors to add e-commerce functionality to their storefronts.

Banners and Sponsorships

Banner and sponsorship-related revenue was expected to reach 47 percent of revenues in the first quarter of 1999, up from just 5 percent in the same period in 1998. Banner ads were available in two formats: large banner ads, which usually appeared near the top of a page, and smaller banners, similar to buttons, which appeared throughout the website. Advertisers purchased two types of banners: general and vertical-specific. They paid a monthly fee for banners as opposed to the more common "cost-per-million" (CPM) pricing used by many consumer portals. Advertisers chose from two types of sponsorships: (1) sponsorship of a specific area, or channel, of a vertical or (2) sponsorship of a vertical's newsletter. Sponsorship of a specific area gave the advertiser prominent placement of a banner ad within a vertical. If a vendor sponsored the newsletter, the vendor's name and a link to its storefront were included in the newsletter. Vendors were charged $0.10 if the user clicked on the storefront link and $0.20 if the user clicked through to the vendor's external, company-run homepage.

e-Commerce

E-Commerce revenue was generated from the sale of an industry vertical's products and services, such as books and software, and accounted for roughly 3 percent of total revenue at the time of the IPO. VerticalNet also received a commission from the sale of books, computers, software, gifts, apparel, accessories, and entertainment purchased from external websites that were accessed through a VerticalNet vertical.

VerticalNet Expenses

Personnel Expenses

The primary expenses related to operating a vertical were salaries and marketing costs. Editors, sales staff, and engineers received salaries while compensation for industry and sales managers was commission-based. Each vertical had one dedicated editor and shared a pool of nine technical writers who provided editorial support. A total of 44 direct sales and support personnel were employed at the end of 1998. The telesales group, made up of 15 individuals, performed customer prospecting, lead generation, and lead follow-up activities. A staff of 43 engineers supported the day-to-day operation of the websites. As of the IPO, the company expected to add approximately 10 engineers annually. In-house product development was carried out by a staff of programmers that was expected to grow at the rate of two per quarter. Approximately $1.2 million was spent to develop proprietary technology in 1998.

Advertising Expenses

Marketing expenses were divided into two major categories: off-line advertising and online advertising. Off-line advertising for the verticals was placed in trade magazines and exhibited at trade shows. Because some companies produced multiple magazines or shows, VerticalNet negotiated up-front, multiple ad placements for several verticals at a time. However, future advertising in trade magazines could be limited because of VerticalNet's position as a direct competitor of traditional industry publications.

For online advertising, VerticalNet negotiated agreements with two major Internet portals: Excite and AltaVista. A three-year sponsorship agreement with

Excite allowed VerticalNet to build and operate up to 30 industrial channels. The channels provided a preview of a vertical's front page, content, and features. Excite guaranteed minimum performance—exposures or impressions—in return for annual fees of $1.3 million in 1999, $2.3 million in 2000, and $2.0 million in 2001. VerticalNet also has a renewable one-year agreement with AltaVista. VerticalNet and AltaVista agreed to 31 "cobranded" or reciprocal-hyperlinked websites, while AltaVista guaranteed a negotiated number of site visits for an annual fee of $1 million. In addition, AltaVista and VerticalNet agreed to exchange $300,000 in advertising over the term of the agreement. Both the Excite and AltaVista agreements allowed VerticalNet to share advertising revenue generated from the cobranded websites.

COMPETITION IN THE ONLINE MARKETPLACE

Online B2B Intermediaries

FreeMarkets

FreeMarkets, Inc., manages and hosts business-to-business auctions for buyers of industrial parts, raw materials, and commodities. In 1998 online auctions covering approximately $1 billion worth of purchase orders were completed, with an estimated 30 buyers and 1,800 suppliers having participated in auctions through the end of 1998.[20] General Motors and United Technologies Corporation accounted for 77 percent of FreeMarkets' 1998 revenue of $7.7 million (see Exhibit 4.3). FreeMarkets' primary customers are large companies that purchase custom solutions. Buyers exchange confidential specifications with suppliers, and FreeMarkets designs an auction customized to the buyer's purchasing processes.

The custom market requires four to eight weeks of preliminary work. FreeMarkets helps potential clients identify products that would benefit from online auctions. These are usually products that are custom-made to buyer specification and that are available from many suppliers. The buyer prepares a request for quote (RFQ) that is sent to selected suppliers who in turn prepare bids. Suppliers are selected from both the FreeMarkets database and the company's vendor list and must be approved by the buyer. Once the vendors are trained to use FreeMarket's proprietary Internet-based BidWare software, the auction is held. The client can see the identity and current bid of each supplier, but the suppliers can see only competing bids. FreeMarkets staff monitor each auction and provide real-time assistance in over 20 languages.

Revenue is generated through service agreements with clients or may come in the form of fixed monthly fees or incentive payments based on volume or savings. Some supplier agreements allow FreeMarkets to earn a sales commission as well. Primary costs include staffing and general overhead. Sales and marketing expenses and general and administrative costs were 8.4 percent and 26 percent of sales in 1998, respectively.

EXHIBIT 4.3   **Selected Competitor Income Statements (in $000s, except per share amounts)**

Source: Respective Company SEC filings.

	FreeMarkets, Inc.		PurchasePro.com	
	1997	**1998**	**1997**	**1998**
Revenues	$ 1,783	$7,801	$ 675	$ 1,670
Cost of revenues	1,149	4,258	214	446
Gross (loss) profit	634	3,543	462	1,225
Operating costs:				
Research and development	292	842	802	971
Sales and marketing	586	656	1,179	3,841
General and administrative	837	2,026	1,345	2,896
Total operating expenses	1,715	3,542	3,326	7,708
Operating (loss) income	(1,081)	19	(2,865)	(6,483)
Other income	20	215	(120)	(117)
Net (loss) income	$(1,061)	$ 234	$(2,985)	$(6,600)
Earnings (loss) per share:				
Basic	$ (0.10)	$ 0.02	$ (0.39)	$ (0.83)
Diluted	$ (0.10)	$ 0.01	$ (0.36)	$ (0.78)

	Penton Media, Inc.	
	1997	**1998**
Revenues	$233,118	$204,931
Operating expenses:		
Editorial, production, and circulation	94,560	101,793
Selling, general and administrative	78,523	93,886
Depreciation and amortization	6,551	10,720
Total operating expenses	179,634	206,399
Operating income	25,297	26,719
Other income	209	(6,586)
Income before income taxes	25,506	20,133
Net income	$ 14,874	$ 10,890
Earnings per share:		
Basic and diluted	$ 0.70	$ 0.50

PurchasePro

PurchasePro.com, Inc. (NASDAQ: PPRO), is a leading provider of Internet B2B e-commerce services. The company offers proprietary software that enables businesses to buy and sell products over the Internet. The Las Vegas–based company got its start by signing up Mirage Resorts, Inc., which in turn recommended the software to its vendors. Originally designed as a bidding tool for large hospitality companies to communicate with suppliers, the company has since expanded into a range of other industries such as the food and beverage, furniture, fixtures, and equipment industries where productivity of purchasing departments is a constant challenge. In two years PurchasePro.com grew from about 20 employees in its Las Vegas office to more than 100 employees with new offices in Phoenix, Arizona, and Lexington, Kentucky.[21]

The PurchasePro.com e-commerce solution is composed of public and private communities called "e-marketplaces" where businesses can buy and sell a wide variety of products and services over the Internet in an efficient, competitive, and cost-effective manner. CEO and founder of PurchasePro.com, Charles "Junior" Johnson, commented, "The buzzword is vertical marketing. We wanted to be the first electronic procurement application to cross every vertical line. Every other e-commerce (system) has pieces of what we do, but nobody has an aggregate of what we do."[22] PurchasePro.com levels the playing field by providing each business, from "mom and-pop" shops to megastores, with the same software. PurchasePro.com makes its money by charging each of its businesses a nominal subscription fee of about $100 per month. Subscribers boast of making up the monthly fee with one purchasing order as lower prices are available in the e-marketplaces due to efficiency in purchasing and orders.

Industry-Specific Online Sites

Chemdex

Chemdex Corporation (NASDAQ: CMDX) is a provider of e-commerce solutions for the life sciences industry. Chemdex is part of a new breed of groundbreaking B2B e-commerce companies that leverage the Internet to unite buyers and sellers in a single, efficient virtual marketplace. Chemdex offers more than 240,000 products from some 100 suppliers—more than five times as many products as the industry's most comprehensive catalog.[23]

In December 1998 Genentech (NYSE: GNE), one of the world's leading biotechnology firms, fully implemented the Chemdex enterprise solution. With Chemdex, Genentech will be able to access hundreds of thousands of products from suppliers by means of the Genentech intranet, which links employees to a customized Chemdex site. The Chemdex system also allows suppliers to publish an unlimited amount of product and technical information, providing Genentech and other researchers with the resources they need to make purchasing decisions.[24]

E-Steel

In the past, manufacturing technology companies have focused on production in an attempt to squeeze time and cost out of the process and then rely on a network of distributors, brokers, and representatives to sell their goods, resulting in an inefficient imbalance between supply and demand. E-Steel, an ambitious online steel industry marketplace, was launched in March 1999 and plans to combat those inefficiencies by leveraging the Internet.[25]

E-Steel will use one-to-one profiling software to deliver customized content to registered steel buyers. This software will also put suppliers' fears to rest as strategic information will not be available to competitors, and no general price lists will be posted. It is e-Steel's goal to allow buyers and sellers to mirror their existing relationships on the Web, while enjoying increased efficiency over the Internet. The company also hopes its marketplace will offer not only convenience to its patrons, but also an opportunity to reach more people through the Internet than through conventional means. E-Steel will earn its keep primarily through charging its sellers a transaction fee of less than 1 percent on all purchases initiated on its site and, secondly, by selling advertising.[26]

Traditional Trade Magazines and Publications

Penton Media

Penton provides its customers with a portfolio of advertising options including trade magazines, trade shows, and websites. Penton's 50 trade magazines had a 1998 circulation of 3.2 million.[27] Two of its publications, *Electronic Design* and *Machine Design,* rank among the top 10 trade magazines by advertising revenue.[28] Advertising revenue for business magazines was an estimated $8.9 billion in 1998.[29] To justify higher advertising rates than consumer magazines, Penton uses annual questionnaires to verify the job responsibility and purchasing authority of its subscribers. Dedicated editorial and sales staffs ensure that the needs of readers and advertisers are met.

Penton is also one of the largest trade show managers in the United States and, along with other top operators, is expected to produce an estimated 16 percent of the 3,900 trade shows in the United States and Canada.[30] Penton has increased the number of worldwide trade shows it produces to 118 since it started in 1990 and has developed relationships with more than 7,000 exhibitors, many of which also advertise in their magazines. Internet World, one of Penton's fastest-growing trade shows, is currently produced in 23 countries.

Penton targets its websites to professionals in many of the industries it serves through magazines and trade shows. Its network of 42 online communities benefits from proprietary content created for its magazines; however, online content is updated in real time to maintain and increase a loyal reader base. Advertisers generate sales leads and track customer purchase behavior to aid in their marketing decisions. Penton generates revenue through banner advertising, sponsorship of sites, user fees, and transaction fees based on users who click through to e-commerce sites. In 1998 electronic media accounted for less than 1 percent of its $207 million in revenues.

Cahners

Cahners Business Information has a rich history of business-to business publishing dating back to 1855 when *Iron Age,* the company's first magazine, premiered. The magazine's essence is incorporated into Cahners' modern-day publication *New Steel.*[31] Through the years Cahners' portfolio of publications grew into a variety of markets including *Hotel & Travel Index,* a staple guide for travel agents worldwide, and *Modern Materials Handling,* an operations publication.

Cahners has emerged as a major B2B publishing and trade show management company. The company was particularly busy during the 1980s with an aggressive acquisition program. Cahners also boasts a well-respected research information service in Cahners Advertising Research Reports (CARR). The service is designed to help customers better understand B2B publications and advertising (print and online) by providing benchmark research and strategic advice to advertisers about the bottom-line effectiveness of communications programs.

Distributors

W. W. Grainger

E-Distributors that consolidate goods and services offered by multiple vendors stand as competition to the VerticalNet business model. These sites offer a simple search process for a buyer to select a specific product. In addition, traditional bricks-and-mortar distributors such as Grainger Industrial Supply have moved to the Internet as an alternative channel for its customers. Grainger built its business through catalog sales, but now offers the full range of its products through its website, www.grainger.com. Grainger expects that online sales will exceed $160 million, making it one of the largest-volume sites for Web sales.[32]

NEXT STEPS

Walsh thought about his options as he gathered his things and prepared to leave. Now that VerticalNet was public, where should he take the company from here? How could he capitalize on the tremendous opportunity that lay before him? For starters, he wondered whether the company should continue to add new industry segments as aggressively as it had in the past, or if VerticalNet should slow down and entrench more deeply into the 29 communities it had already entered?

Furthermore, Walsh wondered about the company's revenue model. Thanks to the successful IPO, VerticalNet now had almost $57 million in the bank, but Walsh knew that the company would burn through that in just a few years unless it could find ways to become more profitable. Should the company stick with its current storefront model and focus on signing up more vendors as well as perhaps raising the price? Or should it expand into new offerings and services? And if so, what should those be? Finally, was it time to start looking for new partnerships and/or acquisitions? What types of companies would make the most sense?

Walsh left for home far more wealthy than he was just two days before, very excited about the challenges ahead and yet cognizant that choosing the wrong strategy at this critical juncture could mean the end of VerticalNet.

Notes

1. Andrew Cassell, "VerticalNet Embraces Capitalism," *Philadelphia Inquirer,* February 15, 1999.
2. Andrew Marlatt, "Creating Vertical Marketplaces," *Internet World,* February 8, 1999.
3. Mary Addonizio, "Chrysler Corporation: JIT and EDI (A)," *Harvard Business School Case,* February 11, 1992.
4. Alan Zeichick, "B2B Exchanges Explained," *Red Herring,* November 1999, pp. 188–90.

5. A "vertical" is short for "vertical industry," "vertical market," or "vertical trade community" and refers to all buyers and suppliers (essentially the whole supply chain) within a given industry.

6. Martin Donsky, "VerticalNet Gets the Paper out of Publishing," *TECH Capital,* November 6, 1998.

7. Peter Kay, "VerticalNet Seeks to Raise $30M," *Philadelphia Business Journal,* December 14, 1998.

8. www.VerticalNet.com.

9. Bob Brooke, "Trade Pubs Moving Up and Online," *Philadelphia Business Journal,* January 19, 1998.

10. "Interview with Mark Walsh," *eMarketer,* August 17, 1998.

11. Kay, "VerticalNet Seeks to Raise $30M," p. 1.

12. Brooke, "Trade Pubs Moving Up and Online," p. 1.

13. "The 1998 Tenagra Awards," awards.tenagra.com/cat1vertical.html, May 1998.

14. "VerticalNet Shows Business Acumen," *Techweb,* December 23, 1998.

15. Darren Chervitz, "IPO First Words," *CBS Marketwatch,* March 18, 1999.

16. VerticalNet SEC filing, 1999.

17. Thomas Isakowitz, "VerticalNet Basic Report," *Janney Montgomery Scott,* June 22, 1999.

18. Ibid.

19. "Scorecards" are postcards that list vendor names and are placed in trade magazines. Interested subscribers check off a vendor of interest and send the card to the magazine, which in turn records the "lead" and then notifies the vendor.

20. Company information taken from FreeMarkets preliminary prospectus, September 8, 1999.

21. www.PurchasePro.com.

22. "Purchasing Pipeline," *Hoovers,* company press release, November 8, 1998.

23. Chemdex company press release, *Hoovers,* December 14, 1998.

24. Ibid.

25. C. Wilder, "E-commerce—Old Line Moves Online," *Information Week,* January 11, 1999.

26. Ibid.

27. Lauren Rich Fine, "Penton Media, Inc. In-depth Report," Merrill Lynch & Co., June 9, 1999.

28. *1999 Tradeshow Week Data Book,* Tradeshow Week, Inc.

29. *1998 Communications Industry Forecast,* Veronis, Suhler & Associates. The business magazine market is estimated at $10.8 billion and projected to grow at a compound rate of 8 percent through 2002.

30. *1999 Tradeshow Week Data Book,* Tradeshow Week, Inc., and Veronis, Suhler & Associates.

31. www.cahners.com.

32. Douglas Blackmon, "Selling Motors to Mops, Unglamorous Grainger Is a Web-Sales Star," *The Wall Street Journal,* December 13, 1999, p. B1.

Case **Five**

LiveREADS: Valuing an E-book Start-Up

READING AND A NEW FRONTIER

At 2:34 A.M. on Friday, November 17, 2000, Neal Bascomb finally turned off his computer. Five errors—he had found and corrected five errors in the final version of *Orpheus Emerged,* a newly discovered novella by Beat legend Jack Kerouac. Bascomb's new e-book publisher LiveREADS would introduce the novella in a revolutionary new e-format three days later on Monday, November 20. *Orpheus Emerged* would be the first e-book published to include an interactive, multimedia design. Too restless to let things go, CEO and cofounder Bascomb had insisted on reading both the Adobe GlassBooks and Microsoft Reader editions himself to be sure that there were no errors. Now, over 600 pages later, he was ready for bed. Later that day, he would deliver both versions to bn.com, the exclusive e-tailer for this inaugural LiveREAD.

As he attempted to fall asleep, Bascomb ticked through the implications of Monday's launch in his mind. After raising about $700,000 in a series of angel rounds, cash was starting to run low. He and cofounder Scott Waxman had used the bulk of the money to enter into contracts with 20 *New York Times* best-selling writers, paying them for options to original works the company had to exercise within four to six months (see Exhibit 5.1). They desperately needed to make the leap to the next level and raise $5 million to begin publishing the next series of LiveREADs before the options expired. Venture capitalists had been lukewarm on a content play but might be swayed if *Orpheus Emerged* made a big enough splash. And then there was the question of a strategic investor. The venture arm of a major media company had recently

NYU Stern School of Business MBA Candidates Diane Bartoli, Chris Lemmond, Ashok Sinha, Daniel Urbas, and Stephen Wells prepared this case under the supervision of Professor Christopher L. Tucci for the purpose of class discussion rather than to illustrate either effective or ineffective handling of an administrative situation. Copyright © 2002 by Christopher L. Tucci. All rights reserved.

EXHIBIT 5.1
Author
Qualifications

20 brand-name, best-selling authors
6 *New York Times* #1 bestsellers
The #1 travel writer in America
The #1 personal finance writer in America
The #1 adventure writer in America
The #1 popular science writer in America
The #1 sports writer in America
National Book Award winner
Over 75 million copies sold by authors

approached the founders to merge LiveREADS with an e-book publisher it had been incubating in an all-stock deal. Should the founders take the deal or hold out for a venture capitalist that would let them retain control and a larger piece of the pie? How would the founders even know what to accept from a VC or from this entertainment behemoth? How much was their company worth to these two different investors, and what other factors should they take into consideration?

ONCE UPON A TIME, THERE WAS LIVEREADS . . .

Nearly a year before, cofounder Neal Bascomb had been an agent at one of New York's more exclusive literary agencies, Carlisle & Co. He had helped Michael Carlisle, a respected veteran in publishing, break free from the giant William Morris Agency to go out on his own. Previously an editor at St. Martin's Press, Bascomb was one of the first employees at Carlisle in the summer of 1998 and quickly set to work building a long and profitable client list. Competitors joked that if he didn't pace himself he would be the Prefontaine of the agenting world, making reference to the champion runner who started with a flash and ended as fast. But pacing wasn't in Bascomb's vocabulary and by the end of year 1 he laid claim to nearly $1 million in book contract sales with major publishers, one of the most successful first years for an agent witnessed by the industry.

After that banner first year, Bascomb started to dream about running his own publishing house. First he went to his boss, Michael Carlisle, and talked about how the agency could be a bit more entrepreneurial in how it made money. Perhaps they should do more in exploiting the digital rights for their clients' works. But it seemed this was outside the scope of what Carlisle felt they were capable. Nearly a year and a half after starting at Carlisle, Bascomb decided to venture out on his own.

Bascomb began writing the business plan for what would eventually become LiveREADS. He called on every entrepreneur and visionary he knew in the business and interviewed them about future trends and the viability of an e-publishing model. Among the first of these interviewees was Scott Waxman, a young industry player who had started his own very successful agency a few years before. Although only 32, Waxman had a full head of salt-and-pepper hair and the self-assuredness of a veteran. In fact, when he learned that Bascomb left Carlisle & Co., he immediately attempted to convince him to join The Waxman Agency as a partner. But when Bascomb introduced the idea of an e-publisher, Waxman realized the true potential of a different kind of partnership. Shortly after reading Bascomb's business plan he called to say he wanted to help launch the business. Knowing that Waxman had a host of expertise as well as publishing and e-world contacts to bring to the table (Waxman's brother was a founder of Flooz.com), Bascomb was eager to accept the offer.

After officially incorporating in February 2000, the two founders immediately set about trying to find funding for their new venture. They talked to venture capitalists, angel investors, investment arms of media companies—anyone who would take a meeting with them. Rather than money, what they mostly got was advice. But they also found a lead angel investor in former Sony Corp. chairman Michael "Mickey" Schulhof, who helped finalize their e-publishing model as a business-to-consumer play that would build on the brands of established best-selling writers. In addition, LiveREADS would use the full extent of the digital medium by enhancing e-books with video, audio, animations, live links, and additional information all keyed to the text (see Exhibit 5.2 for information on characteristics of the LiveREAD product). Schulhof based his investment on a series of milestones the founders had to reach. These milestones were mostly in the form of author contracts, initially targeting a total of 15 contracts.

LET'S MAKE A DEAL

Since they had limited funds, Bascomb and Waxman constructed a contract similar to a movie option contract that would allow LiveREADS to gain access to some of the most successful writers in America for a relatively small cash outlay. In a traditional book contract, a publisher pays an author advance

EXHIBIT 5.2
Hoped-for
Characteristics of
LiveREADS
product

- Original—A new experience that surpasses other mediums.
- Size—Digestible size of 50–100 pages long.
- Compelling—It has to be worth the time it takes to read; holds reader's attention.
- Unique—No other comparable online options available.
- Frequently refreshed—Sense of urgency and timeliness.
- Topical—Meets the reader's expectations.
- Professional—Clean and easy to read and maneuver; accurate.
- Entertaining—Delivers written word in a fun, immersive way.
- Thorough—Leaves the reader satisfied.

against royalties in three stages: on signing, on delivery of the manuscript, and on publication. LiveREADS adapted that model by paying each author $10,000 in cash on execution of a contract that locked the writer into an option for four to six months. The remainder of the advance would then be made in the same stages as in a traditional contract, minus the option price of $10,000. All the works commissioned had never been published. In addition, LiveREADS specifically commissioned medium-length works to avoid the "book length" options most writers were bound to with their traditional publishers. Live-READS was not responsible for the remainder of the advance unless it chose to exercise the option. Payments for the remainder of the advance were tied to exercise of the option, delivery of the manuscript, and the publication of the work, thereby limiting LiveREADS's overall exposure. LiveREADS did not retain the print rights; however, it did retain rights for electronic text, multimedia, dramatization, worldwide translation, audio (which can be worth as much as half the value of the total advance), and perhaps most importantly, an option on the author's next midlength original work in the electronic medium, which held the author bound to LiveREADS for 18 months to two years.

With this blueprint in mind, Bascomb hired a publisher to help sign the authors. Paul Bresnick had most recently been an executive editor at William Morrow, a large traditional publisher. But his 30-year career spanned from *Spy* magazine to *Penthouse* to Doubleday Publishing. Over the course of his career, Bresnick had published renowned authors James Baldwin, T. C. Boyle, Betty Friedan, Joyce Carol Oates, Lawrence Block, and perhaps most notably, Bill Cosby. Cosby's *Fatherhood* was one of the biggest bestsellers of the eighties and one that announced the dawn of the celebrity book. Now Bresnick was onboard at LiveREADS to use his deep connections in the old world to see the dawn of yet another revolution in publishing—the emergence of the e-book. Bresnick's traditional experience was a neat counterbalance to the e-knowledge CTO Tim Cooper brought to the table. Cooper was the founder and president of a technology and programming consultancy that, among other things, developed digital products for the publishing industry.

By the beginning of September, the team at LiveREADS had met with virtually every major literary agency in the business and concluded deals with more than 20 major *New York Times* best-selling writers. Each deal required a long and complicated contract negotiation because LiveREADS was breaking new ground in the assignment of digital rights in respect to the combination of electronic text with multimedia (audio, video, animation) as well as e-commerce and advertising/sponsorship sales. This investment of time was vital to the success of the company—Bascomb and Waxman considered their contracts with these major agencies as valuable assets and key barriers to entry protecting LiveREADS from other fledgling e-publishers looking to compete in the space.

Having signed the targeted number of authors, and with the remainder of the angel financing in the bank, the company was ready for the next step in the business plan: raising the Series A round of financing. In preliminary meetings with venture capitalists, the founders soon learned that despite their impressive roster of writers, VC investment would not happen without more proof of concept. To prove themselves and their business model, and gain credibility with potential investors, they needed to publish their first LiveREAD.

MAKING THE LEAP

With time working against them, Bascomb and Waxman rallied the team. They had to publish their first LiveREAD within one month. Bresnick called literary agent Sterling Lord and told him the company would be exercising the option for a never-before-published novella by Jack Kerouac, *Orpheus Emerged*. Over the next month, LiveREADS would not only design and produce the interactive e-book, but also put together a series of marketing and distribution deals necessary to reach its target market. But before they could get started, they first needed to determine the price for their first LiveREAD.

There were a few factors to be considered in setting the price. There was a relatively short history of established e-book prices that ranged from $1 (Stephen King's *The Plant*) to as much as 10 percent below the traditional book price (about $18). In addition, mass-market paperback books (the most inexpensive books on the market) ranged from $5.50 to $9.00. Bascomb and Waxman wanted to price *Orpheus Emerged* inexpensively enough to encourage customer adoption. At $3.95 the founders felt it was cheap enough to encourage readers to take the leap. Plus, at $3.95 Bascomb estimated that they would need to sell only 20,000 copies to break even, a mere fraction of Kerouac's sales.

LiveREADS chose bn.com, the online arm of the Barnes & Noble superstore, as the exclusive distributor on the guarantee of a significant marketing campaign (including advertising and keyword searches on Yahoo!, AOL, MSN) and affiliate network push (over 400,000 sites would be offered the opportunity to carry the title). Furthermore, bn.com would build a boutique within its site that promoted LiveREADS and its first publication. With that distribution deal in place, LiveREADS began building its own marketing network based on revenue-sharing deals. Apple, Blah-blah Network, Flooz, Adobe, Salon.com, and tens of other sites would promote the lost Kerouac classic. On the day of the launch direct online marketers EMAIL SHOWS and Zooba would email over 300,000 people. Tens of thousands of flyers would be distributed on over 50 college campuses across the country. And a national publicity campaign, including stories in the *LA Times* and on National Public Radio's *Fresh Air*, would begin on November 20. As the head of bn.com's e-book division said: LiveREADS was the first company to actually be "publishing" an e-book instead of simply making a digital version of a pre-existing work available.

THE BURGEONING E-BOOK MARKET

The e-book market gained a legitimate toe-hold in 2000 by attracting the attention of the most powerful players in new media, including Rupert Murdoch's News Corporation, Microsoft, Adobe, Amazon, Barnes & Noble, and the world's largest publishers, including Bertelsmann and Time Warner.

Still in its infancy, the e-book and digital publishing industry was marked by a virtual cacophony of players staking claims and forming alliances, all with public pronouncements of tempered, cautious optimism about the future of the market. Lower forecasts of the market potential reflected sheer derision of the format, while higher estimates reflected the belief that e-books would inevitably dominate book publishing.

Some analysts estimated the market would grow to $218 million by 2002.[1] An industry-financed study performed by Andersen Consulting estimated that e-books would represent $2.3 billion, or 10 percent of the book market by 2005.[2] Forrester, on the other hand, forecast an e-book market share of only 2 percent by 2005.[3]

As of November 2000, bn.com carried 2,700 e-book titles in three competing formats,[4] and Amazon carried 1,000 e-book titles available in the Microsoft Reader format.[5] Tom Turvey, e-books manager at bn.com, remarked:

> Digital content is something that began slowly a few years ago and now is something that really has picked up steam. Even a year ago, this may have been a smaller part of our business, but with the strong partners, and now the strong original content from within the author community, it really has gained a lot of traction even in the last six to eight months.[6]

How fast the industry would grow would depend on the settlement of issues that had similarities to those facing the music industry. Importantly, authors and publishers wanted to ensure that published works were protected from piracy and that technologies and standards protected their intellectual property rights. Additionally, booksellers were cautious about the potential of cannibalization of their current bound-book business, and printers and distributors feared that they would be disintermediated out of the book publishing supply chain.

COMPETING AND DISTRIBUTOR FORMATS, PUBLISHERS

One of the most crucial issues for the growth of the e-book industry was the extent of consumer adoption of the digital format. Consumers had three ways to view digital content at the end of 2000. Consumers could download books directly to their personal computers to be read off the computer screen; they could download e-books to a specialized e-book reader; or, for a smaller portion of book titles, consumers could download to a personal digital assistant (PDA) using Microsoft's Reader or Reciprocal software.

Faced with these options, a number of manufacturers were striving to become the dominant standard. However, the existence of competing, incompatible formats exacerbated the problem for the industry. The main players included two of the largest software providers, Microsoft and Adobe, and Gemstar International's e-book reader format. Additionally, Reciprocal, a small software provider, was introducing a format to download e-books to personal computers as well as PDAs using the Palm operating system. Except for Adobe's Glassbook Reader, all competing formats adopted the 'Open E-Book' (OEB) standard, which used common HTML and XML Web programming. The first LiveREAD, *Orpheus Emerged,* was made available in both Adobe Glassbook and Microsoft Reader formats. It is important to note that only Glassbook allowed for the full effects of the connectivity and innovative design LiveREADS developed, despite the fact that it was impossible to print the novella from this edition. Although only plain text, the Microsoft Reader edition was printable. Exhibit 5.3 outlines the various attributes of the competing formats.

While concerned about cannibalization of their current bound books, the major publishers embarked on various initiatives that encompassed selling e-books on their own content websites, to distributing to traditional book e-tailers, to developing entirely new content. For current, fast-moving titles, the e-book model would be "time phased," where e-books would be released prior to print publication at print or print discount prices. Industry incumbents Random House and Warner Books had already announced new e-publishing divisions. In addition, new pure-play companies were coming on the scene. The most notable of these was Mighty Words (see Exhibit 5.4). Internet book retailers and other content sites had announced their own plans to distribute e-books (see Exhibit 5.5).

EXHIBIT 5.3   Competing Formats

Source: Company websites.

	Microsoft	Gemstar International	Adobe	Reciprocal
Products	Microsoft Reader	Rocketbook & Softbook	Glassbook	Reciprocal
Availability	MSN.com, online bookstores, Windows CE 3.	Retailers	bn.com	TBD
Price	Free	$299–$699	Free	TBD
Standard	Open	Open	Closed	Open
Additional Comments	Over 1 million downloads in 3 months after 8/2000 launch	Murdoch-backed company, encryption supported by publishers.	Preferred by LiveREADS.	New (launched in Nov. 2000), allows for download to Palm o/s.

EXHIBIT 5.4   **Publishers' e-Book Initiatives**

Random House (Bertelsmann)

Mary Bahr, editorial director of @Random, scheduled to launch in January 2001, said the new division would offer titles for consumers who "don't necessarily read book reviews or frequent bookstores."[a]

Warner Books (Time Warner)

Warner announced the March 2001 launch of iPublish.com, which would utilize digital content to test-market new talent and develop printed books. Greg Voynow, general manager, announced that iPublish might offer a subscription series of romantic short stories for "an insatiable fan to read at her desktop or print it out, on her lunch hour or at work, or before she puts her kids to bed."[a]

Mighty Words

A first mover in digital publishing, Mighty Words' parent, Fatbrain, received $35 million in funding from Microsoft cofounder Paul Allen. With an existing large-scale operation, the bulk of its operations related to vanity press–type publishing. Like LiveREADS, most of its works were short, original works. In November, bn.com agreed to carry Mighty Words content. According to Chris MacAskill, Mighty Words' CEO, "Business, technology and mind/body titles make up about 80 percent of our titles, with fiction and other nonfiction titles comprising only about 20 percent. Our bread is buttered by professional titles today, because at this stage it's still an early adopter market. On BN.com today, there are 120 titles, 85 percent original and exclusive."[b]

a. Paul D. Colford, "Hot Copy Publishers Ponder Paperless Books," *New York Daily News,* November 7, 2000.
b. Paul Hilts, "Mighty Words Titles to Be Offered at BN.com," *Publishers Weekly,* November 6, 2000.

EXHIBIT 5.5   **Retailers' e-Book Initiatives**

Amazon

Amazon created a special e-book section for its website and supported the Microsoft reader format only. Amazon would not push e-books for the holiday 2000 season, as it had not yet worked out secure encryption technologies to enable e-book gift-giving. Amazon typically retained 55 percent of revenues from its e-book offerings.

bn.com

The Barnes & Noble website, 40 percent owned by Bertelsmann, offered e-books available in the Microsoft Reader, Gemstar e-book, and Adobe Glassbook formats. Like Amazon, it retained 55 percent of e-book revenues.

Contentville

Contentville offered a limited range of titles that utilized the Microsoft, Gemstar, and Adobe Glassbook formats.

Lycos

In November, Lycos announced that it was entering into a five-year, nonexclusive commitment to carry Random House's "Modern Library" collection of downloadable new and old classics, available at Lycos Shops.

SELLING OUT?—ACQUISITION BECOMES AN OPTION

In early November, LiveREADS management was approached with an all-stock buyout offer. A newly formed investment and incubation group majority owned and backed by a global entertainment giant had spent the previous few months creating an e-book company and hoped to merge with LiveREADS to create a digital publishing and distribution company and website. Bascomb and his partners would receive shares in the resulting new company in exchange for their entire equity stake in LiveREADS.

The incubator had been formed as a subsidiary of the parent's music, motion picture, television, and related entertainment division. Its mandate was to create, incubate, operate, invest in, and acquire digital media companies. Given his business's dependence on consumer acceptance of new forms of entertainment technology, Bascomb saw this mission as a natural complement to LiveREADS.

The incubator focused on core digital media technology areas including broadband services, wireless, personal broadcasting, e-mail/direct marketing, digital asset management, e-commerce facilitation, and professional Internet services. In addition to equity financing, it provided portfolio companies with critical support in areas including: strategic planning; infrastructure needs ranging from office space, phones, administrative assistance, computers, network, and Internet connectivity to full human resources support, accounting, access to credit and financial administration; Web development and design; recruitment; product management; marketing; and a rich network of distribution partners in both online and off-line channels.

Bascomb was impressed with the company's portfolio and expected that if LiveREADS was acquired, many synergies could be realized for the new digital publishing company. These included a private, high-speed broadband network, a full-service digital rights management (DRM) solution, and a leading global infrastructure technology platform for the aggregation, distribution, and seamless integration of digital content to websites, portals, and wireless networks. The incubator had also helped manage well-known media and technology start-ups that had ultimately gone public or had been acquired by industry heavyweights.

The potential acquirer was focused almost exclusively on enabling technologies that would help consumers optimize their online entertainment experiences. The merger would provide LiveREADS with access to the parent's rich library of entertainment content, which could be integrated into future products. But Bascomb worried about the management and direction of the acquiring firm: it had received a substantial sum from its parent company, and although it had been operational for only a few months, there was little evidence that any real progress had been made.

Bascomb wondered how to value the new stock offer. His partners, investors, and he would receive stock in the merged publishing entity. But what would that be worth? How could he justify accepting an all-stock offer when he and his colleagues had worked for so long with little income and when his investors had already given him much cash? Should they accept stock in the new merged entity, and if so, how much?

GETTING MONEY "THE VC WAY"

Like every other start-up, LiveREADS embarked on the campaign of raising money. LiveREADS had started by raising $700,000 from angel investors. In the four angel rounds, equity was distributed to the investors in installments amounting to 10 percent each. This meant that the LiveREADS founders ended up keeping 60 percent of the company (see Exhibit 5.6 for details of previous financing rounds). Now LiveREADS was considering the first round of venture capital fund-raising, hoping to raise $5 million.

When asked about how the VCs place a money valuation on LiveREADS, Bascomb replied, "VCs look at your stage of business development, the type of company—in our case it is a content driven company, and the valuation from the last angel round."[7] VCs would then look at projected net income after a certain period (for instance, five years) to determine how much of the company they would need to own to realize an appropriate return on their initial investment. Exhibit 5.7 shows a typical calculation, with the appropriate P/E multiple crucial in determining the value of the company after an appropriate investment horizon and the amount of equity VCs will require.

In terms of the stage of development, LiveREADS had accomplished a few significant milestones, and the initial launch would also demonstrate a viable business model, if successful. Nevertheless, much needed to be done (see Exhibit 5.8 for future milestones).

The fact that LiveREADS was a content-driven company could also prove to be an issue. While plenty of funds were available for investment, and the VCs had substantial amounts of funds, there was a perception that funds were not being invested in companies. In particular, content companies appeared out of favor with the VC community.

However, translating these generalities into a specific valuation to take to the VCs would be difficult—Bascomb needed to know what specific factors the VCs would take into consideration when valuing the company in order to come up with a value. Bascomb knew that the core assets of the company, specifically the contracts with the authors, would play a large part. Achieving

EXHIBIT 5.6
Previous Financing Rounds

Date	Premoney Valuation	Amount Raised	Postmoney Valuation
15 May 2000	$900,000	$100,000	$1,000,000
1 July 2000	1,350,000	150,000	1,500,000
1 September 2000	1,800,000	200,000	2,000,000

EXHIBIT 5.7   VC Money Valuation for LiveREADS

Time to Exit	5 years	(Investment horizon, generally between 2 and 7 years.)
Year 5 Net Income	$1.7M	(LiveREADS projections.)
Year 5 Valuation	1.7 times X	(X is an appropriate P/E multiple.)
VC Investment	$5 M	
Est. VC Annual Return	40%	(Required return varies between 40% and 70%, depending on the risk of the company. LiveREADS was shipping product, so estimated return is lower.)
Cumulative 5-Year Return	5.4 times	(5 years of 40% growth per annum.)
Future Value of VC Investment	$26.9M	($5M investment multiplied by required 5-year return.)
VC Equity Share	26.9/year-5 valuation	(Amount of the company the VC would require to obtain the required return.)

EXHIBIT 5.8   Milestones

Based on the company's projections, the following milestones are instrumental to LiveREADS's plans:

2nd/3rd Quarter, 2000
- Develop online demo and begin site development.
- Hire a chief technology officer, vice president of content development.
- Sign 25 *NYT* best-selling writers.
- Begin investigating content delivery platforms.
- Secure $700,000 in angel financing and set Advisory Board.

4th Quarter, 2000
- Sign 10 *NYT* best-selling authors.
- Secure $5 million in financing.
- Coordinate content partnerships with portals and major media sites.
- Build out website and technology infrastructure.
- Hire chief operating officer, vice president of marketing, vice president of business development, and creative director.

1st Quarter, 2001
- Create 6 LiveREADS for launch.
- Develop strategic e-commerce partnerships for LiveREADS.
- Launch version 1.0 of website.
- Further integrate production/packaging abilities in-house.
- Obtain 50 content affiliates.

2nd Quarter, 2001
- Launch 8 LiveREADS.
- Develop key strategic partnerships.
- Sign 20 additional *NYT* best-selling writers.

their required return on investment, ownership and control issues, and other factors would also be under consideration in dealing with the VCs.

From a control perspective, Bascomb knew that if he went the VC route, the LiveREADS founders would end up giving away another 30 to 40 percent of the remaining equity. On the other hand, if he chose to accept the buyout offer, LiveREADS founders' equity would likely be diluted to 5 percent of the new company.

CONCLUSION

In deciding which avenue to pursue, Bascomb also had to take a number of other factors into consideration. LiveREADS was burning approximately $30,000 per month, which gave the company a fume date of mid-February 2001, although the company could theoretically proceed at a reduced pace without the additional capital. While cash outflows could be slowed, the company was anxious to exercise its author options before they expired and deliver the product to market. Aside from generating revenues, it would also provide credibility and assist in signing additional authors and raising capital.

Strategically, Bascomb had to determine how each financing route fit with potential exit strategies. The feeling of the founders and angel investors was that if all went according to plan, the best time to exit would be within two years, with a trade sale the most likely outcome. While recognizing that start-ups don't often proceed according to plan, Bascomb also felt the natural urge to ensure that any exit would allow them to reap some of the reward from the sweat equity invested in the company and would be liquid to a certain degree. Control issues were also important in the overall decision, as was the value that each of the different investors would bring to the company in addition to their capital contribution.

These and other issues were under consideration as CEO Neal tried to decide which route to pursue, and how he should value the company to present his "price" to each of the potential investors.

Notes

1. *The Sunday Patriot-News* (Harrisburg), November 5, 2000.
2. John Dorschner, "E-Books Still Long Way Off From Joining Best-Seller List," *Chicago Tribune,* October 16, 2000.
3. Mary Jo Foley, "New Flare-Up in Battle Over E-Books," *ZDNet News,* November 6, 2000.
4. Paul Kendall, "A New Chapter in the History of the Book," *Daily Mail,* November 7, 2000.
5. Paul D. Colford, "Hot Copy Publishers Ponder Paperless Books," *New York Daily News,* November 7, 2000.
6. Kevin Featherly, "Barnesandnoble.com Set to Sell Bevy of E-Books," *Newsbytes News Network,* October 30, 2000.
7. Team interview with Neal Bascomb, November 13, 2000.

Case Six

Beyond Interactive: Internet Advertising and Cash Crunch

So how do you start a successful Internet business? Any MBA student might state the following success factors: an experienced management team, well-funded investors, technical employees, stock ownership plans, and a Silicon Valley headquarters. Jonn Behrman, CEO and founder of Beyond Interactive (BI), would have to disagree. In just over three years, Jonn had built a $4.6 million online advertising services firm with a management team all under 25 years of age. He had no outside investors, mostly nontechnical employees, no employee equity program, and a headquarters in Ann Arbor, Michigan. Asked about the primary reason for BI's recent success, he would immediately answer "our people." Jonn boasted, "We haven't lost a single employee since I started this business." However, when asked about the challenges facing BI, the big grin quickly disappeared. . . . "Cash flow and competition are what keep me up at night."[1]

Behrman's strategy to combat the competition was simple. Grow—and do it fast! He realized the old method of slow growth through earnings was not enough to create a sustainable business model on the Internet. COO Nick Pahade agreed:

> We have more business than we can handle at the moment. We want to expand by hiring more people and opening more sales offices, but we just don't have

University of Michigan Business School MBA Candidates Charlie Choi, Patti Glaza, Ashesh Kamdar, Rich Lesperance, and Kevin White prepared this case under the direction of Professor Allan Afuah as the basis for class discussion rather than to illustrate either effective or ineffective handling of an administrative situation.

the capital. We have no tangible assets, so our bank line of credit is just $50,000. Additionally, more and more customers are paying us later. Jonn and I agree that we need more money, but we're not sure which option is best. We're exploring the vulture [venture] capital route, alliances with traditional advertising agencies, and angel [private] investors. We're not interested in being acquired at this point. Our biggest concern is giving up equity and losing control of our business. Also, I know we need to get our bookkeeping in order before we attract investors. We're looking for a CFO right now![2]

On December 11, 1998, Jonn had more than the BI holiday party on his mind. Strong competitors in Internet marketing were entering the company's market space every day. Traditional agencies or well-funded start-ups could catch up to BI in months. BI needed to stay one step ahead of the rapidly changing environment in Internet marketing. His young but relatively experienced staff was being courted by competitors offering higher salaries. The list of expansion projects seemed to be growing daily, while the cash flow situation wasn't improving. As Jonn looked out from his new office, he thought hard about the right financing and growth strategy. He had to make the right decisions not only for his company but also for his loyal and motivated "fraternity" at BI.

BACKGROUND

BI had its beginnings in the undergraduate business program at the University of Michigan. After a summer internship in real estate, Jonn became interested in the real estate industry's use of the Web. This interest led to an academic project during the fall semester of 1995. During the project, Jonn became extremely frustrated with the time it took to find relevant information on the Internet. He saw a business opportunity for website promotion and in October founded Wolverine Web Productions (WWP). For over a year, the business focus was website optimization and targeted e-mail services. The company website, Web Production Resource Center (WPRC), not only promoted WWP but also provided general resources for Internet marketing. During this early phase of WWP, Darian Heyman and Nick Pahade joined the company as partners (see Exhibit 6.1). Heyman's enthusiasm and knack for selling helped WWP land its first large account: Ameritech. WWP stayed financially afloat through its clients who paid for marketing services up front, while BI's vendors required payment within 30 days.

In 1997 WWP added Internet media planning and buying to its portfolio of services. This decision spurred significant growth for the company. By the end of 1997, the company added another partner (Matt Day), employed 16 people, and billed clients $1.4 million for marketing services. Additionally, the company created a new business website separate from its resource site WPRC. The goal was to provide unbiased information about Internet marketing to the Web community.

EXHIBIT 6.1
The Founders of
Beyond Interactive

Jonn Behrman, CEO

Jonn Behrman was born in Venezuela and moved to the United States in the mid-1980s. He graduated from the University of Michigan's School of Business with an undergraduate degree in Computer Information Systems (CIS) and marketing in 1996. BI (then called Wolverine Web Productions) opened in 1995, when the industry was still in its infancy. Started without any external financing, the company's original focus was search engine optimization. Working out of his apartment, Behrman and his small team set out to make it easier to find sites on the Web. Within a short period of time, Behrman refocused the company toward online media buying and campaign management. Jonn Behrman is 25 years old.

Nick Pahade, COO

Nick Pahade graduated from the University of Michigan in 1996 with an undergraduate degree in biopsychology and marketing. Originally pursuing a career in medicine, he had been published in three Web medical journals and was a featured speaker at numerous premed symposiums. Pahade became involved with BI to develop a student housing locator. The relationship continued to grow until Pahade decided to commit to the company full-time in 1996. Shortly thereafter he was made both partner and vice president. As COO, Pahade is ultimately responsible for the company's profit and loss as well as operating budgets. He manages the financial and administrative personnel, develops operational processes, and ensures that they are deployed companywide. He is also in charge of developing and managing relationships with outside vendors, suppliers, and clients. Nick Pahade is 25 years old.

Darian Heyman, VP Business Development

Darian Heyman has been vice president of business development at BI since he graduated from the University of Michigan in 1996 with a degree in international relations. He first turned down a business development opportunity with Procter & Gamble, as well as an opportunity to study in Mexico on a scholarship, to get involved with Internet advertising. Heyman has played a critical role in pushing the company's growth; in 1997 his efforts brought in $1.4 million worth of advertising sales. Darian Heyman is 25 years old.

In 1998 WWP changed its name to Beyond Interactive and continued its client-financed growth. By the end of November, billings reached $4.6 million with 42 full-time employees. The growth in revenue was the result of winning larger clients who could commit to larger Internet marketing budgets. Recently, BI instituted a policy of doing business only with clients that spent a minimum of $30,000 every three months. BI also opened a satellite sales office in San Francisco to build closer ties with potential West Coast clients. BI had learned that selling Internet marketing services actually required face-to-face selling. Finally, the company hired Kevin Hermida, a recent computer science graduate from the University of Michigan and Microsoft employee, as its chief technology officer (CTO).

THE BI "FRATERNITY"

"It's like my college fraternity around here," Jonn commented with a smile as he observed the activity around his office. Rows of cubicles littered with huge toys were a short distance from the Ping-Pong room, the site of numerous company tournaments. Above an oversized gum ball dispenser hung a sign announcing a contest for employees. Employees at BI were 22 to 25 years old, had no dress code, and passed around bottles of beer in the office on Friday afternoons. Jonn is genuinely excited when talking about the environment he has created: "People are the key to success in this business. I am better at motivating people than any head coach you will meet. It's my gift. My people love me, they adore me. They love their jobs."[3] In stark contrast to other firms in the advertising industry, BI has had zero turnover since its founding in 1995.

To stay competitive, BI planned to grow from 42 to 100 employees within the next year. Employees were generally undergraduates with liberal arts degrees looking for their first job. Their qualifications? Passion and energy: "We often win business based on our enthusiasm."[4] This fun atmosphere was a big benefit to employees, who were willing to work for less than half the typical wages in the industry in order to support the company's aggressive growth. However, top management worried that rivals with far more resources, such as Avenue A, would lure away BI employees by offering fatter salaries and incentives. Employees in turn were becoming more concerned with the possible impact of growth on BI's culture. One employee complained that the Ping-Pong table might be removed to make room for more cubicles.

THE ONLINE ADVERTISING INDUSTRY

In 1998 the opportunities for online advertising were staggering. E-commerce was expected to reach $425 billion by 2002. Ad spending was predicted to reach $2.3–3 billion by 1999 and as much as $25 billion by 2002. While online advertising in 1998 made up only 1.3 percent of all ad budgets, on average, this proportion was expected to increase rapidly as more users came online.[5]

Three forms of online advertising were dominant in 1998: banners, sponsorships, and interstitials. While these were the most popular, new forms were expected to emerge as a result of changing technologies.

Banners: Rectangular ads that allow users to "click through" to advertisers' websites.

Sponsorships: The advertiser is given a prominent position on a website, often on the top of the page, for its company name and logo, and usually given "sponsored by" credit. Content on the website is typically correlated with the advertiser's industry.[6]

Interstitials: Ads that interrupt users, regardless of the users' actions. Similar to television ads that interrupt programming, users have no control over interstitials, which could take up the entire viewable area in the users' browsers. Users have to click on interstitials to close them.

How effective were these ads? Opinions varied. A study conducted by WebCMO found that the three most effective methods to generating sales and site traffic were (1) search engine submission, (2) solicited e-mail, and (3) off-line promotion. While banners were being used more frequently than off-line promotion in 1998, their value had increasingly come under attack.[7] In 1997 only 9.1 percent of online users said they looked at banner ads "very often" or "often," and the number of users that said they "never" looked at banners jumped from 38.7 percent to 48 percent between 1997 and 1998.[8] Martha Deevy, a senior vice president at Charles Schwab & Co., made a good analogy: "A lot of Internet banner ads are like billboards on the side of the highway. People drive right past them and don't bother to look."[9] An additional challenge facing advertisers was that looking at ads did not necessarily mean the user "clicked through."

ONE-TO-ONE VERSUS MASS MARKETING

An important difference between traditional advertising media and the Internet was the capability for one-to-one targeting on the Web. Based on unlimited access to customer information, "the information superhighway is enabling direct marketing to fulfill its goal of nurturing that neighborhood-store feeling among customers."[10] No longer were companies forced to market general ads toward broad segments, they could specifically target *you* based on where you lived, how much income you made, and what types of products you bought.

The key element for taking advantage of these trends was a company's ability to analyze and act on the information it gathered. For most companies, this gap was filled by third-party advertising and data-mining agencies.

While being able to offer personalized service was a critical requirement for advertising, a company's brand name also continued to play a major role. A recent survey showed that 69 percent of Internet buyers considered brand familiarity as critical to their buying decision. Unfortunately, in the race to get online quickly, many retailers, catalogers, and direct marketers forgot to leverage the branding that they worked so hard to create.[11]

TECHNOLOGY TRENDS AFFECTING INTERNET MARKETING

Centralized Ad Serving

More and more Internet ads were being managed by third-party ad serving systems. These vendors managed customer ads from delivery to the destination website to reporting traffic statistics. The advantage of using a third-party ad server was consistent ad delivery and standard reporting for clients regardless of the chosen websites in the media plan. One company that provided this service was DART for Advertisers (DFA).

Internet Video Technology

Hardware limitations in processor speeds, monitor resolution, disk storage, and especially Internet connections led to software innovations in data compression and audio and video processing. For example, video "streaming" allowed users to download video clips in small data chunks in succession, so that the video could be viewed as it was being downloaded. In the past, the entire clip had to be downloaded (taking several minutes with a telephone modem) before it could be viewed. However, limited bandwidth (a measure of how much data could be sent simultaneously across a data line) on most Internet connections could still make online video slow, choppy, and grainy.

The typical modem used downloaded data at a speed of 56,000 (56K) bits per second (bps), but to get video approaching television quality required speeds of 1 million (1M) bps and higher. Two of the more promising technologies aimed at solving the bandwidth problem were cable modems and Digital Subscriber Line (DSL). Forward Concepts projected 9.6 million cable modems and 1.86 DSL modems in North America by 2003, less than 10 percent of U.S. households.[12] Given the rapid rate of innovation, it was almost impossible to predict with any accuracy where the next innovation would come from or what the online world would look like in the future. But as things stood now, due to the limited availability, high cost, and technological limitations, it did not seem likely that Internet connections of 1 Mbps and above would be commonplace for home users for at least another five years.

Boomerang Cookies

Many websites tagged visitors' computers with small files, known as "cookies," that helped identify users on return visits. With current technology, these data were useful only if the customer came back to that particular site. Starting in 1999 DoubleClick planned to introduce powerful software to let advertisers spot those visitors, even weeks later on other websites. Then those "visitors" could be greeted with more ads for the original merchant, and their surfing habits could be tracked for future targeting. DoubleClick called this boomerang technology.

Search Engine Submission Software

Most customers could not find a company's homepage/website if their address was not listed in the online "yellow pages"—the search engines. Posting addresses on these search engines could be extremely time intensive if undertaken manually. While most online advertising agencies assisted clients with this service, new software packages performed a similar function, all for under $100. CyberSleuth Internet Services' product offered fully automated submission to hundreds of search engines and directories, and also offered semiautomated support for hundreds of others.[13]

Media Convergence

In 1998 *The Wall Street Journal* reported: "Media companies are moving from the traditional analog to a digital environment."[14] Though high definition television (HDTV) was in its infancy, digital technology went far beyond simply better television pictures. Digital signals opened up the traditional world of "push" programming to "pull" scheduling. No longer would consumers be forced to watch specific programs or commercials at set times, but they would instead choose what and when they watched.

Digital cable broadcasting would allow two-way, interactive communication through a television set, similar to what the Internet currently provided. This had two major implications for the advertising industry: (1) one-to-one marketing would become the dominant form of advertising,[15] and (2) advertising agencies could use digital technology to increase economies of scale by integrating television, print, and online media campaigns.[16]

COMPETITION

There was no lack of available online agencies to take the growing ad dollars. Any search on the Web for "Internet advertising" brought back long lists of potential companies. These companies took all shapes and forms, but there were three typical models in 1998: traditional agencies, design shops, and specialty agencies.

Traditional Agencies (Integrating Print, Television, and Radio Campaigns)

While late to the game, traditional agencies moved quickly to develop expertise in online advertising. Either through hiring, buying small shops, or creating alliances, traditional agencies started to capture big accounts. Large portals that captured significant online viewership spurred the smaller upstart agencies to focus on developing integrated online and off-line campaigns. In mid-October, Excite hired Lowe & Partners/SMS, Geocities chose Young & Rubicam, and Snap released TV ads created by Saatchi & Saatchi. Though Snap had been open to nontraditional/specialty agencies, its final decision came down to "we needed an agency that could build a mass brand, and had experience with both television advertising and alternative media."[17]

Design Shops

Most of these companies were primarily focused on producing Web pages for clients. They assisted in the design and layout of the Internet site that the end customers visited. In order to offer a broader range of services to their clients, many of these design shops were "busy acquiring people, skills and companies with traditional media strengths such as brand strategy and media planning."[18]

Specialty Agencies

These companies focused on one or two types of advertising media exclusively. Instead of being a "one-stop shop," specialty agencies tried to maximize their value through dedicated resources. A large number of firms had entered Internet advertising to meet the growing needs of the marketplace for search-engine effectiveness, e-mail campaigns, and online ad creation. Specialty firms had survived intense competition in other media such as television, radio, and print.

With the rush to gain a piece of the online pie, companies spent a great deal of time trying to define themselves. "There is a pissing match going on over who offers the most services, not over who is creating the right model," stated the managing director of Grey Interactive. Mergers between technology and media companies, such as US Web/CKS Group and Sapient Corp./Studio Archetype blurred the lines between where technology ended and marketing services began.[19] How far clients would expect their ad agency to understand and handle the technology aspects of online services had not been established.

Not fitting into one of the standard company models, DoubleClick, Inc., offered standard creation and placement services, but also developed sophisticated tracking technologies. This allowed advertisers to target specific segments based on customers' country or metropolitan sign-in point. To expand its customer base, DoubleClick, Inc., sold its services and some of its technology to other ad agencies. For example, competitors could buy certain DoubleClick software tools to manage their own marketing campaigns.[20]

Back-end technologies also helped smaller specialty shops add value for their clients. Beyond standard offerings such as managing ad campaigns, conducting research on ad placement, negotiating prices, and delivering effectiveness reports, Avenue A Media used a proprietary planning system. This system contained performance and demographic information on tens of thousands of sites. Based on client objectives, budget, and product category, the system created a list of viable ad spaces that could be integrated into the media plan.

CUSTOMERS

BI's client list contained a variety of both famous and less well-known organizations. Some of the blue-chip companies include IBM, Ameritech, *The Economist,* and NextCard Visa. While these businesses are quite different, they all shared an interest in building their cyberspace brand. The following clients were recently added:

Fallon McElligott

Fallon McElligott (FM), a traditional advertising agency, needed an Internet marketing partner to assist with its client's cyberspace marketing needs. Its client, United Airlines, wanted to target business travelers on the Internet. BI won the contract on its ability to negotiate lower advertising rates on behalf of clients. BI also improved the media plan targeting. With BI's help, FM was able to concentrate on traditional media planning and still provide a complete marketing solution for United Airlines.

NextCard Visa

NextCard Visa (NV) wanted to attract prequalified traffic to its website. It hoped the Internet would enable the company to achieve aggressive customer sign-up goals. NV chose BI to assist with its Internet marketing plan. BI ran test campaigns on a variety of websites and established long-term relationships with the most effective sites. NV eventually reached its sign-up goals over the Internet and also locked up advertising on strategic websites.

SERVICE OFFERINGS AND OPERATING ROLES: VALUE DELIVERY AT BI

Although BI began by offering limited online advertising services, by 1998 its service portfolio had matured to include search engine optimization, targeted e-mail, press release distribution, and interactive banner advertising.

Service Offerings

Search engine optimization was initially provided to increase total traffic on client sites by using the many engines prevalent on the Internet. Not only did BI provide tips to optimize clients' pages for user searches, it also provided manual and automated URL submission services. Targeted e-mail and press release services were also used to promote client offerings. For e-mail advertising, BI aided clients in choosing the appropriate target audience and developing an advertising message that spurred consumer interest. Press release services were designed to communicate a client message through information releases in traditional media forms. Information had to be framed to interest not only the prospective end customer, but also the media channel used as the message conduit.

Although BI used these limited advertising solutions to expand the business, Jonn and his team knew that they had to provide greater value to customers to sustain growth. In early 1997 interactive banner advertising was identified as the engine that would power BI's growth. Partnerships were developed with vendors who could provide the services with less value added that had traditionally been the staple of BI's service offerings. The company began to optimize its systems and practices to efficiently provide services to its clients using this more sophisticated technique.

Interactive banner ads provided many advantages over their less sophisticated predecessors. Visual appeal, improved targeting, and customer-tracking options proved appealing to BI's growing customer base. Keys to banner advertising success were proper placement, design effectiveness, and cost, and BI's services addressed all three of these success factors. By using tools such as @plan media planning software, InterWatch AdSpend Report, and independent research, BI was able to identify advertising techniques and banner locations tailored for each customer. It also worked with clients to design the interactive banners and mediate appropriate vendor pricing options, including flat fee, CPM (cost per thousand impressions), and cost per click-through.

BI charged clients through a service-specific compensation structure, as follows:

- A standard 15 percent agency commission for media buys and targeted e-mails.

- An hourly charge for strategic linking and nonmedia programs.

- A flat fee for search engine optimization, press releases, and/or copywriting.

- Varied fees for creative services.

Key Operating Roles

There were three primary functional roles that supported business development activities at BI: business developers (BDs), account managers (AMs), and media planners (MPs).

- *Business developers.* Primarily responsible for follow-up on initial business leads, these individuals screened potential customers and spearheaded the development of the marketing strategy overview (MSO). During the early days of BI, Jonn and Nick performed this function. As the number of customers grew, the business developer position was created to shoulder the initial screening and burden of MSO preparation. However, Jonn and Nick continued their involvement with large, strategic clients.

- *Account managers.* There were seven to nine account managers (AMs) at BI in November 1998 who managed the ongoing relationship with each client. AMs acted as the focus between the client and the vendors outlined in the media plan, providing ongoing campaign support throughout the duration of the advertising initiative. AMs did not necessarily appear early in the history of BI; however, as BI's client list grew, it became increasingly important to have a single point of contact for the customer, and an internal expert who was familiar with that customer's expectations and idiosyncrasies. When describing the evolution of the position, senior AM Moses Robles commented:

  > Early in the process, everyone was doing business development. The method for allocating accounts to people in the company was based primarily on who took the initial phone call. Our AMs were chosen based upon natural talent, not necessarily specific experience. Later on, we began to specialize in industry and vendor areas, with many of us developing

strong working relationships with our vendors. In those cases, we were able to leverage such relationships to garner very competitive prices and offer them to multiple customers.[21]

AMs also acted as troubleshooters when things did not go as outlined in the media plan, managing vendor and customer expectations to arrive at reasonable conclusions. As client size increased, so too did the need to expand BI's services beyond an individual advertising campaign. It was the responsibility of the AM to set in motion repeat business from his or her clients and to cross-sell or expand services into other divisions or business units within that client. Robles reflected:

> We need to maintain a good repertoire with our vendors for the long term, and we try not to overwork them on prices. On the same token, we feel that repeat client business will guarantee future revenue. Our [AM] #1 goal is to grow our existing client accounts and cross-sell services to other groups at that client. To do that, we rely not only on our knowledge of the client's industry, but also on our people skills.[22]

- *Media planner.* The backbone of the business development process, media planners (MPs) were responsible for much of the creativity in BI's client offerings. Although they were largely responsible for developing media plans for prospective clients, MPs also conducted vendor and industry research to support new or ongoing client needs.

BUSINESS DEVELOPMENT PROCESS

The business development process at BI consisted of five steps: lead follow-up and needs assessment, developing and submitting a marketing strategy overview (MSO), developing and presenting a media plan, project kickoff and campaign management, and cultivating future business opportunities.

Lead Follow-up and Needs Assessment

By November 1998 the flow of incoming business leads had evolved into three main sources. The bulk (about 50 percent) came from the websites, both WPRC and BI, which offered potential clients a free consultation on how they could benefit from online advertising. Although the highest volume of leads came through this channel, most of these were for smaller clients.

Another 20 percent of business leads came from trade shows, where BI employees gave ad technology seminars and descriptive presentations of BI services. The other main source of leads (about 30 percent) was through word-of-mouth referrals, either from past clients or companies that provided complementary services. BI had developed working referral relationships with a number of these companies, including traditional advertising agencies, design shops, and online media consultants. Overall, approximately 80 percent of customers contracted BI directly to provide services, while 20 percent came as subcontracts from traditional agencies or design shops. In that 20 percent, it was not uncommon for the end customer to have no idea that BI provided the Internet portion of its campaign.

These informal partnerships were reciprocal in nature. BI often referred new clients to these partners when it could not provide appropriate services to meet a client's advertising needs. According to Nick Pahade:

> Many traditional ad agencies do not have interactive [online] media departments. When their clients need those types of services, we want to be considered for such services. Unfortunately, it is often a catch-22 with these agencies—we can get referrals for large clients this way, but we may not get to pitch the client directly. In those cases, the client may not know who we are. What we really want to foster is relationships with traditional agencies where we can pitch the client with them, so that we can build our equity in the marketplace. Ultimately, we would like to be included directly on the RFP [request for proposal] lists of big customers.[23]

Once a lead had been identified, Nick, Jonn, or one of the two business developers took it and performed a needs assessment for the potential client, using a standard form and telephone or e-mail conversations. If the client had a clearly identified need and scope in mind, the BDs and MPs immediately began a media plan. If the client was unsure of its needs and budget, or if it was new to online advertising, an MSO was developed as an interim step to highlight BI's service offerings in the context of that specific client.

Developing and Submitting an MSO

The BD worked with the media planning department to create the initial pitch to the client. This pitch, termed the marketing strategy overview (MSO), outlined the services BI would offer the client, general advertising channels that would be pursued, the types of interactive advertising recommended, and estimated prices. The MSO was mailed to the client free of charge, and the BD, sometimes with the assigned MP, held a teleconference with the client to review it. A description of typical MSO content is shown in Exhibit 6.2.

EXHIBIT 6.2
Media Strategy Overview (MSO) Contents

A typical MSO contains the following key elements:
- Overview of pricing models, including:
  - Cost per acquisition (CPA).
  - Cost per thousand impressions (CPM).
  - Cost per click-through.
  - Flat fee.
- Description of online advertising opportunities, including:
  - Content site advertising.
  - Inexpensive run of network.
  - Search engines.
- Overview of Beyond Interactive skills, creative services.
- Overview of campaign performance tracking and analysis.

Developing and Presenting a Media Plan

If a client was interested in employing BI, cash was requested to develop and implement a media plan. The commitment and payment typically covered the first three months of BI services. The MPs developed a detailed media plan which spelled out what types of ads would be designed for which websites, and how much they would cost.

The MPs used many complementary tools to develop this plan. AdPlan was an online service that reported (for a fee) which sites have worked best for different types of companies/industries advertising on the Internet. AdSpend was an online service that reported (for a fee) historical ad spending on the Internet by specific companies. Jupiter researched the effectiveness of different advertising techniques and shared the results of research for a fee. Various ad networks like doubleclick.net and 247media.com negotiated rights to vast networks of websites and could help prospective advertisers choose the sites frequented by customers in their respective target markets. In combination with these services, MPs used their personal experience and the group's collective experience to tailor a unique plan that best served a client's needs. Data acquired from the process were stored in a media plan database that housed valuable client, technology, and vendor information. This comprehensive database proved an invaluable resource to MPs and AMs as BI's client list grew, allowing new employees to leverage key lessons from previous campaigns. A description of typical media plan content is shown in Exhibit 6.3.

The finished media plan was then sent to the client for approval before ads were actually created and placed. A letter of engagement was also forwarded to the client. Upon receiving the signed letter, BI assigned an AM and proceeded with the campaign.

Project Kickoff and Campaign Management

Account managers (AMs) closely monitored campaign execution and tracked advertising performance using tools such as Doubleclick's DART for Advertisers. Through the use of such tools, BI could evaluate how well a campaign was reaching its target audience, and if that audience was following through

EXHIBIT 6.3
Media Plan Contents

A typical media plan contains the following key elements:
- Online vendor information for any/all sources for the campaign, including:
  - Vendor name.
  - Flight dates.
  - Cost per thousand impressions (CPM).
  - Monthly/total impressions.
  - Monthly/total cost.
  - Site descriptions, URL, and creative specifications for each vendor.
- Special vendor notes (as applicable).

to a purchasing decision. This information could be fed back to the client to modify or lengthen the ongoing campaign as necessary.

Cultivating Repeat Business Opportunities

During the client campaign, AMs attempted to make additional contacts at the client and leveraged those into new business opportunities. They also tried to develop a relationship with the client whereby they (AMs at BI) became the preferred online advertising provider for all future campaigns. Any new client work that entered the process through this channel usually skipped the MSO stage and went directly into media planning. AMs were informally evaluated on their ability to drive repeat business with existing client organizations.

LOOKING TO THE FUTURE

The management team at BI had a long list of growth projects for the company. Potential investments included new people, offices, and technology. Employees were needed in every area of the company. Additionally, BI was seeking an experienced chief financial officer (CFO) to improve its accounting and manage its financing. The management team was also committed to geographic expansion. Next year, Jonn planned to open offices in New York and London. Finally, BI would invest in the company's technological infrastructure in order to build their information-sharing capabilities, especially with other offices. Jonn summarized BI's strategy:

> We want to be the Rolls-Royce of the industry, both in the breadth of our online services and in their quality. We also want to grow the size of our accounts. To better serve our clients, we need to have offices in key areas around the U.S. and the world. We feel this expansion will help support, and actually drive, our revenue growth.[24]

These ambitious growth objectives required cash, which was in limited supply. (See Exhibit 6.4.) Larger clients were demanding "net 30" payment terms, which meant that for the first time in BI's short history, it would need to rely on outside funding. Nick explained the following financing options:

- *Venture capital (VC).* BI started approaching VC firms in the fall of 1998. The management team was not excited about this option because they were afraid of losing management control. The team also knew that VC firms would probably pressure them into taking the company public within a couple of years. However, BI recognized that VC funding might be necessary as a last resort.

- *Acquisition.* BI had received several unsolicited offers from other advertising agencies to sell its business. These offers were turned down by the management team, who believed that they had the ability to develop BI into a premier digital advertising agency with a global reach.

EXHIBIT 6.4
Income/Expense
Structure

	% of Total Income
Income	
Media planning/buying	96.5%
Other services	3.5
Total income	100.0%
Expenses	
Ad placement costs	76.7%
Other services costs	.4
Wages & benefits	11.2
Travel & entertainment	1.2
Office & supplies	5.5
Marketing	2.3
Other expenses	2.2
Total expenses	99.5%
Net income	.5%

- *Strategic partnerships.* A third option was to form an alliance with a traditional advertising agency. This option could increase the client list overnight, but the management team had some concerns. Would BI be able to pursue other clients or would the traditional agency demand exclusivity? Would the traditional agency eventually want management control?

- *Angel investors.* Another option would be to attract private investors into the business. This option sounded appealing to the management team. Angel investors might settle for a lower level of control in the business than professional VC firms, but they offered little or no management expertise.

Jonn was leaning back in his chair, thinking about these different financing alternatives. Even if BI was able to secure financing, how would BI best use the funds? He knew 1999 would be a very interesting year.

Notes

1. Casewriters' interview with CEO Jonn Behrman, November 1998.
2. Casewriters' interview with COO Nick Pahade, November 1998.
3. Casewriters' interview with CEO Jonn Behrman, November 1998.
4. Ibid.
5. Jesse Berst, "Don't Be an E-commerce Victim," *ZDNet,* November 12, 1998; "Ad & E-commerce Revenue Streams Swell . . . ," *Min's New Media Report,* October 26, 1998; Jeff Lehman, "Bring TV, Radio Commercials to the Net," *Advertising Age,* September 28, 1998, p. 50.
6. Kate Maddox, "Sponsored Content's Next Level . . . ," *Advertising Age,* August 31, 1998, p. 23.
7. Nancy Dietz, "Survey: Banners Losing Effectiveness," *Business Marketing* 83, no. 9 (September 1998), p. 40.

8. Kate Maddox, "Survey Shows Increase in Online Usage . . . ," *Advertising Age,* October 26, 1998, p. S6.

9. George Anders, "Internet Advertising . . . ," *The Wall Street Journal,* November 30, 1998.

10. Lois K. Geller, "The Internet: The Ultimate Relationship Marketing Tool," *Direct Marketing* 1, no. 5 (September 1998), p. 36.

11. Ibid.

12. *European Broadband Networking News,* August 6, 1998.

13. Melissa Campanelli, "Hit List," *Entrepreneur* 26, no. 10 (October 1998), p. 49.

14. Raju Narisetti, "New and Improved," *The Wall Street Journal,* November 16, 1998.

15. Ibid.

16. John Owen, "The Interactive Future," *Campaign,* September 18, 1998, p. 41.

17. Randal Rothenberg, "Web Portals Invite Mad Ave to Spin Point of Difference," *Advertising Age,* November 9, 1998, p. 46.

18. Kate Maddox, "Online Agencies Seek Identity as Borders Blur," *Advertising Age* website www.adage.com/news.

19. Ibid.

20. *Hoover's Online,* December 8, 1998.

21. Casewriters' interview with Moses Nobles, November 1998.

22. Ibid.

23. Casewriters' interview with COO Nick Pahade, November 1998.

24. Casewriters' interview with CEO Jonn Behrman, November 1998.

Hotmail: Free E-Mail for Sale

THE PROPOSAL

Sabeer Bhatia and Jack Smith, cofounders of Hotmail, looked across the table at the six Microsoft managers dressed in suits. The cofounders listened with excitement as the Microsoft managers went through the terms of the offer for their young Silicon Valley company. Hotmail was the fastest-growing free Web-based e-mail system in the world. It had more than 9.5 million subscribers and was the 12th most visited website as of December 1997.[1] Microsoft's first offer of $200 million served as an appetizer for the discussion. Bhatia countered the offer by commenting that Microsoft must be "very poor" to make such a small offer. The room was filled with tension as Microsoft began to "pile cash on the table."[2] It made it difficult to avoid facing the decision: trade in the future potential of the company for immediate gains. Tempting as the offer was, was it enough to compensate Bhatia and Smith for the loss of independence and future gains?

THE FOUNDERS

Sabeer Bhatia, the CEO of Hotmail, was originally from India. He came to the United States in 1988 to attend Caltech and went on to receive a master of science degree from Stanford University in 1993. While at Stanford, Bhatia met many entrepreneurs and decided then that he eventually wanted to start his own company. After Stanford, Bhatia worked as a systems integrator at an Apple Computer subsidiary, Firepower Systems, where he met Jack Smith, Hotmail's current CTO. Bhatia and Smith saw their peers making fortunes on

New York University Stern School of Business MBA Candidates Brian Faleiro, Dana Porter, Siddharth Rastogi, Vitaly Shub, Christine Stokes, and Lanchi Venator prepared this case under the supervision of Professor Christopher L. Tucci for the purpose of class discussion rather than to illustrate either effective or ineffective handling of an administrative situation.

Internet ideas and decided that they wanted to do the same. Bhatia said, "Here were all these young guys getting rich on Internet ideas and we started saying 'Hey, we could have thought of that.' "[3] With only their engineering backgrounds and no experience in management or starting companies, the two entrepreneurs set out to build the company that is now Hotmail.

THE CONCEPT

Bhatia and Smith originally thought their fortune was in writing a Web-based personal database tool called JavaSoft. Their concept was to build a relational database that was accessible through the Web. As they were both working full-time, they had to find time outside the workday to strategize, plan, and prepare for their database. This proved to be a challenge for both of them.

They were having difficulties effectively communicating and exchanging ideas with each other when they were in different locations. This problem led to an idea. One day while Jack Smith was driving to his home in a suburb of Silicon Valley, he came up with the idea to use the Web as a means for personal communication. At this point in its history, the Web was a directory of information more than a direct communication tool. He immediately called Bhatia, who exclaimed, "Eureka! We found it!"[4]

Bhatia and Smith began to focus their energy on this new concept of allowing everyone to access e-mail from any Web browser. They recognized the huge potential demand for this product. The work world was gravitating toward a more global and mobile workforce. For people on the move, it would mean gaining access to e-mail from any portal, desktop, laptop, or dial-up. By removing the physical constraint of having to subscribe to an Internet service provider (ISP) or an e-mail provider, Bhatia and Smith's idea was poised to make messaging communication faster and more convenient.

Instead of making money on the service, Bhatia and Smith decided to provide the service for free. This was the best way to ensure that the service would catch on. Their money-making concept was to charge advertisers for access to their subscriber base. Not only would they provide access to subscribers but their ability to track subscribers' surfing habits and demographic information would allow advertisers to customize advertising information as well.

As they developed their new business idea, Bhatia and Smith never gave up on the relational database concept. They continued their work in this arena. In the meantime, the Hotmail concept crystallized. Bhatia and Smith realized that their next step was to raise capital. Their combined personal investment of $4,000 was not going to be sufficient to make their dream come true.

ENTER THE VCS

In December 1995 Bhatia and Smith approached the venture capital firm of Draper Fisher Jurvetson (DFJ) to sell their idea of a Web-based database. They originally had no intention of mentioning the free Web-based e-mail;

they were afraid the venture capitalists would steal or exploit their idea. However, DFJ was unimpressed with the database idea. Recalls DFJ partner Tim Draper, "They were promoting a database product that other people already had. We were about to show them the door when they mentioned the free e-mail idea."[5] Forced to show their hand early in the game, Bhatia and Smith had to reveal their trump card. Once on board, DFJ granted Bhatia and Smith approximately $300,000 in funding in exchange for 15 percent of the company.[6]

Aside from monetary funding, DFJ gave Hotmail its start in what proved to be one of the most successful campaigns of "viral marketing." Viral marketing refers to product or service design that induces the users themselves to market the product (or service) simply by using it. The venture capitalists suggested that each Hotmail message should end with an "advertisement" directing recipients to the Hotmail site for their own free e-mail account. Recalls Draper, "When we first suggested it, they were taking the purist point of view, saying, 'We can't do that—it's spamming!'[delivering junk e-mail]. But by the end of the conversation, it dawned on them that it wasn't much different from running a banner ad."[7]

The result of this simple marketing device was an explosion of Hotmail's subscriber roster. Hotmail expanded its user base rapidly on very low advertising spending. Much later, *Red Herring* would write, "Draper Fisher Jurvetson came up with the concept of viral marketing, perhaps the most influential idea in the Internet Economy right now."[8]

IN THE BEGINNING

Success at gaining funding from DFJ allowed Bhatia and Smith to focus on their concept. They worked out of a two-room office all day and all night and took breaks only to go home and sleep. A lot of strategic decisions were made right there, in the initial stages of the business. Initially, they identified three marketplaces. One was the consumer market, which was huge. The second was the corporate market, which meant becoming an application service provider for e-mail over corporate intranets and extranets. And the third was to create a packaged Web e-mail product with Hotmail's software and actually sell it to corporations. Early on, however, Bhatia decided to stay away from the last two market areas because he did not feel they had the resources to build those, and decided instead to concentrate exclusively on the consumer market.

A month before the product launch, Hotmail's burn rate had eaten through all of its cash. But Bhatia persuaded the original 15 employees to stay with Hotmail for only stock options. At that time in Silicon Valley, jobs were instantly available and high salaries and stock options were used to attract employees from other companies. Bhatia commented later, "My greatest accomplishment was not to build the company, but to convince people that this is their company. I showed people how this would ultimately benefit them. . . . We initiated the avalanche."[9]

The product was launched on July 4, 1996, operating on two primitive computers. That day, the founders constantly received the number of new subscriptions to the site by beeper. After starting with 100 subscribers in the first hour, Hotmail grew to 100,000 subscribers in a month, and reached a million in less than six months. Hotmail was universally and easily accessible because, like other websites, it could be reached through any Internet service provider.

GROWING PAINS

This explosive growth did not go completely without problems. Early on, Hotmail experienced intermittent service outages because of very high consumer demand. But unlike Juno, an early competitor, Hotmail never restricted how many users could adopt the service. Instead, Bhatia was continuously beefing up the service's networks, firewalls, and security programs.

Bhatia understood that reliability and convenience of the service were the key ingredients of success and the creation of a powerful brand. In early 1997 Hotmail implemented a new, highly scalable and redundant architecture. This new architecture was capable of sustaining more than 50,000 new users a day, sending and receiving millions of e-mail messages daily, and achieving response time in less than a second regardless of system load. The system itself was outsourced to Exodus,[10] a leader in managing data centers for mission-critical Internet operations, to ensure constant uptime of all basic operations, including the Internet connection, server hardware, and power. Hotmail was trying hard to keep pace with the demands of its growth and to implement innovative technologies.

Hotmail's Web-based model and fault-tolerant system architecture were uniquely designed for high-volume traffic and reliability. Its system architecture featured dynamic load balancing and fully redundant storage, power, and processors that would allow the Hotmail system to scale well beyond the 10 million users it had in January 1997 and to provide a highly reliable and responsive service worldwide. "We're particularly excited about the load balancing design of this architecture," said Jack Smith. "When [users log] on to Hotmail, they get the least busy path to their e-mail, which dramatically enhances their online experience."[11] Hotmail's performance goals included providing millisecond system response time and delivery of Hotmail-to-Hotmail messages within five seconds. Every Hotmail Web server was backed up by hot standby and hot swappable servers that immediately would pick up the workload in case of a failure.

Indeed, Microsoft cited technology as the main reason for its interest in Hotmail. Hotmail had proven that its technology and systems could handle an enormous amount of e-mail, and could easily handle even more.

Another round of service slowdowns was caused by "vicious attacks from e-mail marketers using the service to deliver unsolicited electronic mail."[12] After numerous user complaints about junk e-mail, Hotmail developed several methods to help users deal with junk e-mail, or so-called spamming.[13] For example, users were provided with filters that redirected junk mail directly to the trash bin. Additionally, Hotmail installed automatic controls that observed the mailing behavior of individual customers.

GROWTH AND COMPETITION

Hotmail grew very quickly, attracting thousands of new users daily (see Exhibit 7.1).[14] By July 1997, Hotmail had over 5 million subscribers, making it the largest e-mail provider in the world after America Online (AOL). The site generated more than 8 million page impressions per day and had 30,000 new users sign up daily.[15] It was reported that 25 percent of free mail users logged on every day and 50 percent logged on every week, making the business even more attractive in terms of eyeballs for advertising dollars.[16]

While Hotmail was establishing its presence as a free Web-based e-mail provider, it had a number of competitors in the market that were segmented into Web-based e-mail providers and Internet service providers (see Exhibit 7.2).

Web-Based E-Mail Providers

Juno was a service launched in April 1996, just three months prior to Hotmail, and offered customers a free e-mail account.[17] This solution required users to install software and use a dial-in modem in order to access the e-mail account. Therefore, unlike Hotmail users who were required to have their own Internet access, Juno users received the access as part of the offering, but this access could be used for e-mail purposes only.[18] In terms of user characteristics, 40 percent of Hotmail's users were international compared to Juno's strictly domestic user population. Demand for free e-mail was so great that in early 1997 Juno had to limit the number of new subscribers.[19] By October 1997 Juno had about 3 million subscribers. In November 1997 Juno struck a marketing alliance with Market Facts. Market Facts was attracted to Juno for one major reason. Juno claimed that its own subscriber base visited its site with more frequency than competing subscriber bases.

EXHIBIT 7.1
Subscribers

	Total Number of Subscribers	New Subscribers per Day
July 1996	20,000	
August 1996	75,000	3,000
October 1996	250,000	8,000
November 1996	500,000	10,000
January 1997	1,200,000	12,000
March 1997	2,000,000	20,000
July 1997	5,000,000	30,000
September 1997	6,500,000	40,000
October 1997	8,500,000	60,000

EXHIBIT 7.2   **Competitors**

Company	Product	Description	Revenue Model	Date Launched	Number of Questions New Subscribers Must Answer to Get an Account
America Online	ISP	ISP	Subscriptions + Ad	1985	(a)
CompuServe	ISP	ISP	Subscriptions + Ad	1979 (b)	(a)
Juno	Juno	Free e-mail	Ad	April 1996	20
USA.Net	NetAddress	Web-based	Ad	April 1996	None
Hotmail	Hotmail	Web-based e-mail	Ad	July 1996	5
Four11	RocketMail	Web-based	Ad	March 1997	5
WhoWhere	WhoWhere	Web-based	Ad	March 1997	(a)

(a) Information not available.
(b) Date when it began offering e-mail to personal computers.

Four11, an Internet white pages directory of e-mail addresses, launched a free Web-based e-mail service in March 1997.[20] The service was named RocketMail and had a user base of 700,000 by September 1997 with 7,000 new users a day. DFJ, the same venture capital group that sponsored Hotmail, supported the company. The service was acquired by Yahoo! in October 1997 for almost $100 million.

Other Web-based e-mail providers included iName, which began offering free e-mail in mid-1996.[21] WhoWhere launched its Web-based free e-mail in March 1997 and reported more than 1 million users by December 1997. WhoWhere partners with other websites, one of which is Excite. The Excite Web engine launched its own version of free e-mail, MailExcite, in July 1997 and had established a user base of 100,000 in just two months. USA.Net launched NetAddress, a Web-based e-mail service, in April 1996 and had almost 2 million members by December 1997. The NetAddress service also would forward messages to any other e-mail account, a feature not available on Hotmail.[22]

ISPs/OSPs

As of late 1997 AOL, Microsoft Network, and CompuServe were the largest e-mail providers. These companies were ISPs that allocated an e-mail account to any customer that purchased Internet access. Their revenue model differed since their accounts were based primarily on subscriptions that cost between $10 and $20 a month.[23] The service is also limited since a user can access his or her account only from a specific machine.

HOTMAIL'S OPTIONS

With the free Web-based e-mail market heating up with an increasing number of competitors and consolidation in the industry, Hotmail had to figure out quickly how it should continue to grow and achieve profitability. One option was to merge with a large portal such as Microsoft's MSN. Microsoft had much to gain through a marriage with Hotmail. Up to this point, Microsoft had only 2.3 million subscribers and was one of the few portals without a free Web-based e-mail system. At the same time Microsoft offered services such as travel and car purchases for its customers. Hotmail's list of subscribers and market information would provide Microsoft with the ability to expand its market reach and tailor its services.

Hotmail's second option was to go public. Major e-mail competitors such as AOL and CompuServe were public and had deep pockets from the cash generated from the IPO and their own valuable stock currency to market their services and buy smaller companies. A third option was to remain private. Hotmail's competitors, Juno, USA.Net, and WhoWhere, each remained private and continued to thrive. The very independent Hotmail founders could continue to control and build their company.

Bhatia and Smith shifted in their seats. Should they consider Microsoft's offer of over $200 million and risk losing the company's independence? Or should they try to go public or remain private? For the company's very survival, they knew that they had to expand the firm quickly and either develop partnerships or risk giving away potential profits to the growing number of competitors.

Notes

1. Steve Young and John Defterros, "President of Hotmail Discusses Recent Investor Interest," *Digital Jam,* October 16, 1997.
2. Po Bronson, "What's the Big Idea?" *Stanford Magazine,* September–October 1999, www.stanfordalumni.org/news/magazine/1999/sepoct/articles/bhatia.html.
3. Janet Rae-Dupree, "Everlasting E-mail Will Help Pitch Products," *San Jose Mercury News,* August 26, 1996.
4. Ibid.
5. Luc Hatlestad, "Free Mail Explosion," *Red Herring,* no. 55 (June 1998), www.redherring.com/mag/issue55/explosion.html.
6. Pramit Mitra, "A Capital Idea," *Far Eastern Economic Review,* September 17, 1998.
7. Hatlestad, "Free Mail Explosion."
8. Ibid.
9. Ibid.
10. Gregory Dalton, "Custom Web Service-Business Moves Beyond ISP to Specialized Hosts," *Information Week,* August 4, 1997, p. 73; John T.

Mulqueen, "From Selling Web Access to Running Data Operations," *Communications Week,* April 21, 1997, p. 69.

11. Bronson, "What's the Big Idea?"
12. Lee Copeland, *Computer Reseller News,* January 12, 1998.
13. Sean Butterbaugh Wolfe, "Revamped Hotmail Hits 2 Million Users," *Media Daily,* February 28, 1997.
14. "E-mail Devotees," *Ad Week,* July 29, 1996, p. 94; "Hotmail Subscriber Base Doubles to 500,000 in One Month," *BusinessWire,* November 11, 1996; "Hotmail Corp," *InteractiveWeek,* July 14, 1997, p. 19; "Juno Survives Where Others Falter," *InteractiveWeek,* July 21, 1997, p. 28; "Hotmail Subscriber Base Tops One Million," *PR NewsWire,* January 21, 1997; "Hotmail Is Now the Cyber Home to More than 2 Million Users: Popular Service Has New Architecture, Interface and Features," *PR NewsWire,* February 27, 1997; Young and Defterros, "President of Hotmail Discusses Recent Investor Interest"; Paul M. Eng, "E-mail: Fast, Fun and Now It's Free," *Business Week,* September 15, 1997, p. 68; Dupree, "Everlasting E-mail Will Help Pitch Products."
15. "Hotmail Celebrates One Year Anniversary and Five Million Users: Second Largest E-mail Provider in the World," *PR Newswire,* July 7, 1997.
16. Leslie Miller, "Supported by Ads, Free E-mail Is a Booming Business," *USA Today,* December 10, 1996.
17. Ibid.
18. Julia Angwin, "Another Free E-Mail Service Launched—Net Address," *San Francisco Chronicle,* December 3, 1996, p. C4.
19. Joe Terranova, "Nielsen, Eat Your Heart Out," *Media Daily,* November 13, 1997; Wolfe, "Revamped Hotmail."
20. Eng, "E-mail: Fast, Fun and Now It's Free," p. 68.
21. Brian E. Taptich, "A Brief History of Web Mail," *Red Herring,* November 1998, www.redherring.com/mag/issue60/mail.html.
22. Jamie Murphy, "Free E-mail Finds a Place on the Internet," *New York Times,* December 26, 1997, at www.nytimes.com/library/cyber/week/122697email.html.
23. Ibid.

GMBuypower.com: Dealer Beware

On May 29, 1997, Ann Blakney hung up the phone in her office in Thousand Oaks, California, and took a deep breath. She had faced many challenges in her 25-year career at General Motors (GM), including the last four years in California rebuilding GM's West Coast share. This latest assignment, however, could be her most challenging and highest profile project to date. She had just received a call from Ron Zarella, the VP of GM's North American vehicle sales, service, and marketing group. He had asked her to devise a way for GM to sell a significant volume of cars over the Internet and had given her 90 days to have the service operational. Ann thought about the rapid growth of Internet-based automotive sales and information companies such as Auto-By-Tel and the threat they represented to the traditional way of doing business at the world's largest automaker. She also thought about the difficulties she would have convincing GM's dealers to support a sales tool that would effectively cut the average profit margin on each vehicle it sold.

GENERAL MOTORS AND THE AMERICAN AUTO INDUSTRY

The Origins of GM

The roots of General Motors can be traced back to 1886 and a ride hitched in a horse-drawn cart in a small Michigan lumber town. William Durant was so impressed with its innovative spring suspension that he bought the manufacturing rights and founded the Flint Road Cart Company. Thus were planted the seeds of what would eventually become the world's largest industrial corporation.

University of Michigan Business School MBA Candidates Mark Crisan, Chris Reid, Manuel Valencia, and Andrew Vickers prepared this case under the supervision of Professor Allan Afuah as the basis for class discussion rather than to illustrate either effective or ineffective handling of an administrative situation.

In 1903 troubled automobile manufacturer David Buick approached Durant for help. Always looking for new opportunities, Durant tested one of Buick's cars for three months and subsequently bought the ailing company. Within three years, Buick's sales had risen from 37 to more than 8,000 cars per year.[1] This success cemented Durant's future strategy of aggressive growth through acquisitions and mergers.

By 1908 automakers were going in and out of business at a frenetic pace as tastes and technologies changed and standards emerged. Durant approached the heads of the other two major automotive manufacturers, Henry Ford and Ransom Olds. He proposed that the companies join together in a consortium as a buffer against the whims of the market. Henry Ford rejected a stock offer, preferring cash, but Ransom Olds accepted. The General Motors Company was incorporated with Buick and Oldsmobile as its first two divisions. Expansion continued over the next 10 years as GM acquired the Oakland Motor Car Company, Cadillac, and Chevrolet. By 1918 all of the modern-day divisions were in place, with the exception of Saturn. By 1927 GM was outselling Ford.[2]

The market for automobiles grew steadily over the next 50 years, and so did GM. The company expanded overseas, diversified its portfolio of businesses into radio and aircraft, and was a major contributor to the Allies' victory in World War II. The Big Three automakers, GM, Ford, and Chrysler, both fueled and prospered from the growth of the United States through the 20th century. As of 1997 General Motors was the largest company in the world by revenue, reporting $166 billion in sales and generating net income of $6.7 billion. The corporation employs 608,000 worldwide.[3] Exhibit 8.1 contains recent financial data.

AUTOMOTIVE DISTRIBUTION

Automakers Develop the Franchise System, 1900–1950

The original automobile manufacturers were small companies that applied their scarce capital to the development and manufacture of new products. Lacking the resources necessary to establish fully owned nationwide distribution networks, auto manufacturers turned to entrepreneurs to be the retail dealers of their products. What emerged was a franchised distribution system created out of a highly fragmented network of independent businesses.

The franchise system was based on loose sales and service agreements that gave dealers flexibility in the day-to-day operations of their businesses in return for a steady supply of vehicles to sell. The agreements gave automakers power over the dealers through the control of product supply, as well as the right to grant and revoke franchises. The system satisfied both sides as demand for cars grew steadily through the 1920s and 1930s.

Demand for new automobiles surged after World War II and by 1950, U.S. vehicle demand was at full production capacity. The Big Three were able to

EXHIBIT 8.1   Selected Financials of General Motors (in $ millions)

Source: *Hoover's Online.*

	1997	1996	1995
Income			
Revenue.	$166,445	$158,015	$163,861
Cost of goods sold	146,644	158,015	163,861
Gross profit	19,801	22,253	138,557
Gross profit margin	11.9%	14.1%	15.4%
SG & A expense.	16,192	14,580	13,514
Operating income.	3,609	7,673	11,789
Operating margin	2.2%	4.9%	7.2%
Net income	6,698	4,963	6,880
Net profit margin	4.0%	3.1%	4.2%
Full diluted earnings per share	8.62	6.02	7.14
Balance Sheet			
Cash	$ 11,262	$ 14,063	$ 11,044
Net receivables	66,363	66,614	68,720
Inventories	12,102	11,898	11,529
Current assets.	101,449	100,774	96,892
Assets.	228,888	222,142	217,123
Short-term debt.	51,055	47,226	46,648
Current liabilities	66,837	61,447	58,547
Long-term debt	41,972	38,074	36,674
Liabilities	211,382	198,724	193,777
Common stock equity.	17,505	23,417	23,344

dictate terms to their dealers who complied to ensure a steady supply of new vehicles. Manufacturers used this power to force dealers to hold bloated inventories of cars and parts, purchase expensive repair tools, and contribute to national advertising funds that did little for local sales. Dealers that did not comply could be punished by having new competition licensed in their territories or their franchises canceled.

The Courts Shift Power to Dealers, 1950–1960

As the postwar boom subsided, it became increasingly difficult for dealers to pass on the financial burden of the automakers' demands to the consumer. The National Automobile Dealers Association (NADA), founded in 1917, intensified its government lobbying effort for a check on the power of the automakers. The Automobile Dealer's Day in Court Act of 1956 was passed after a U.S. Senate subcommittee investigation. This legislation outlawed many of the automakers' most aggressive tactics, such as withholding product supply and dumping car and spare parts inventory. Perhaps more importantly, individual states were emboldened to pass their own acts expanding and refining their dealer franchise laws. One result of these legislative initiatives was that automakers in the United States are not allowed to sell their vehicles directly to end users. Even large fleet sales had to be channeled through dealers.

Under this new regulatory environment, dealers and manufacturers were bound by state and federal franchise laws, which superseded historic sales and service agreements. Automakers lost the power to strip dealers of their franchises and could no longer seriously punish dealers for low sales volume, poor customer service ratings, or substandard facilities. Automakers also lost the right to veto the sale or transfer of a dealership except to known felons.

The Industry Matures, 1960–1990s

Throughout the 1960s and 1970s, growth in overall demand buoyed dealer profitability, but by the 1980s, annual sales growth had slowed to 1.1 percent. Demand in the United States was expected to follow population trends as the U.S. market was mature and most households requiring a car already had one. As overall growth slowed, dealers turned to other methods to boost revenues. Many dealers entered new franchise agreements to represent additional brands.

The 1990s brought increased pressure on dealer and manufacturer margins, as it became difficult to differentiate between automobiles on quality or style. Quality had been improving across the industry since the mid-1980s. Accelerated design and development processes had greatly reduced the time period in which a company could enjoy an advantage from innovative technology and styling. In 1991 the Big Three's average model was over five years old. In 2001 the average model was expected to be just over three years old.

The automotive distribution system did not change significantly from 1960 to 1990, though the number of dealers declined. The decline in dealerships can be largely attributed to the marginalization of dealers in response to changing American demographics. By 1990, 80 percent of the U.S. population lived in metropolitan areas, compared with 63 percent in 1960.[4]

The Purchase Experience

Traditionally, purchasing a new car from a dealer involves going to several dealerships to compare models, test-drive cars, and negotiate prices. Customers generally work with a single sales representative at each dealer while choosing a model and options based on personal taste, availability, and price. The sales representative negotiates not only the car price, but also the trade-in price, financing fees, extended warranty or service contract costs, and other licensing and processing fees. It is common for a customer to obtain a rock-bottom purchase price only to have the dealer increase the margin on one of these other products. Customers often visit multiple dealers representing the same automaker in an attempt to get the car they want at the best price.

Although product quality has increased over time, customer satisfaction with the sales and service processes has not kept pace. Average car quality has improved by over 40 percent since 1989, while customer satisfaction with the purchase process has improved by about 20 percent.[5] Conventional wisdom has most consumers ranking purchasing a car right up there with a trip to the dentist. The largest contributor to this dissatisfaction is the negotiating process. Currently, 85 percent of franchised dealers still practice negotiated selling. Most of these dealers compensate salespeople heavily on the profit they are able to extract from the customer.

NEW DISTRIBUTION MODELS

CarMax

In 1991 the management at Circuit City Stores, Inc., began to contemplate ways in which the company could sustain growth once its electronics superstores business matured. They decided to apply the retail skills learned in the electronics business to another fragmented consumer durable goods market, automobile sales. Circuit City quickly found that state franchise laws and manufacturer relationships would inhibit them from dealing in the new car market. Based on market research indicating widespread dissatisfaction with the vehicle purchase process and the dealership experience as a whole, Circuit City developed a new sales model for used vehicles. The first CarMax was opened in Richmond, Virginia, in 1993 and introduced the public to a new way of buying cars, the auto retailing superstore.

The CarMax model is different from the traditional dealership in several ways. CarMax stores are larger, offer a wider selection, and employ a no-haggle pricing strategy. Each car acquired by CarMax is reconditioned as necessary, is within a specified age and mileage range, and is guaranteed after purchase. CarMax sales representatives receive a salary and a bonus based on unit sales and customer satisfaction, not dealer margin.

CarMax planned to cover much larger territories with its superstores. For example, the entire Atlanta area supports 135 franchised dealerships and over 440 independent used car dealers, but was covered by only three CarMax superstores.

AutoNation

The most aggressive competitor to CarMax is AutoNation, a superstore chain started by Wayne Huizenga's Republic Industries. Huizenga is famous for his success in driving consolidation in the video rental idustry with Blockbuster Video. AutoNation's business model is to establish a single retailer that provides the complete range of automotive products and services, including new and used car sales, finance, insurance, rental services, parts and accessories, and maintainance. Unlike CarMax, AutoNation plans aggressive growth through acquisition, and has purchased numerous new and used car dealerships, several car rental companies, and has formed its own finance company. AutoNation plans to have 2 or 3 used car megastores and 9 to 10 new vehicle superstores in each major metropolitan market. Responding to AutoNation, CarMax has also purchased several new car dealerships.

ONLINE AUTO RETAILING

A Challenge to the Dealer Model

Another more radical model for the sale of automobiles, online auto retailing, is having a profound effect on the industry. The detailed dealer cost data provided by these sites removes the asymmetry of information between buyer and seller that has for so long allowed dealers to extract the maximum economic rent from each customer. In the traditional process, the customer started at the vehicle sticker price and negotiated downward to his or her best price, unsure of the true dealer margin. The average buyer left the lot wondering whether or not he or she had obtained a fair price for the new car from a crafty and experienced sales staff.

The initial impact of the Internet was to provide shoppers with immediate access to information about the actual price paid by the dealer to the auto manufacturer for the automobile. Included on the sites were not only vehicle invoice costs, but also the arcane credits and rebates typically offered by automakers that determine the dealer's true cost. The customer was now armed to negotiate a fair margin above true cost with the dealer.

Newer, more sophisticated online models have further reduced the necessity to negotiate the sales price. The customer now can use these sites to receive price quotes directly from dealers. These sites also typically sell complementary products such as automotive financing and insurance. A buyer specifies the type of vehicle and the options he or she desires online and receives a best-price quote from a participating dealer. The customer then makes the trip to the dealer to execute the transaction and take delivery of the vehicle. The leading sites contain a comprehensive selection of vehicles from multiple manufacturers' product lines, allowing buyers to compare features and receive quotes on several types of cars. This process allows customers to feel confident that they have negotiated a fair price for the vehicle and eliminates the stressful and unpleasant good cop/bad cop negotiations with the sales representative and his offstage and perpetually displeased Loch Ness Monster, the "sales manager."

Online referral services offer various pay structures and levels of training to participating dealers. Many of these services sign an exclusive agreement with dealers in a particular region and charge start-up fees of up to $6,500, and monthly fees of $300 to $9,000.[6] Many also provide training in computer literacy and sales (see Exhibit 8.2). The auto manufacturer's margin is unchanged by this new structure. The online companies in effect return a portion of the dealers' profit margin to the customer and charge dealers a fee into the bargain. The dealer would rather book the sale at a reduced margin than see it funneled to a competitor. Additionally, the dealer does recoup some of the lost margin by realizing savings on sales commissions for these transactions. Finally, if the dealer has an exclusive referral agreement for his or her brand in a territory, a portion of the online customers are incremental to the dealership because otherwise customers would have bought their vehicles from a competitor's lot.

EXHIBIT 8.2   **Online Referral Services Fees and Training, 1997**

Source: *Automotive News* survey, 1997.

	Auto-By-Tel	AutoWeb	CarPoint	AutoVantage	CarSmart	Stoneage Corp.
Start-up fee	$2,500–6,500	None	$2,500	None	$800–1,500	$495
Monthly fee	$500–2,500	$475–975	$600–1,600	$6,000–9,000	$300–750	$20/lead
Training	2-day on-site 3-day at headquarters	Regional seminars, manual	Training thru Reynolds & Reynolds	On-site training by request, manual	On-site as needed, manual	No formal training

Dealer Margins Are Squeezed

The Internet reduces dealer control over vehicle purchases. Because consumers can more easily research dealer cost, dealers wind up with lower profit margins. On average, the gross profit drops to $100 to $200 when a customer has shopped the Internet. Some dealers feel that they are deriving significant profit from the Web despite a lower margin per unit. Bruce Bendell, president of Major Automobile Group based in Long Island City, New York, says Internet shoppers represent 12 percent of the 400 new vehicles he sells each month.[7] He acknowledges that the Internet lowers gross profits, but these are offset by reductions in advertising costs. He pegs the cost of promoting cars online at $25 to $75 per unit, far less than the $300 to $500 it takes to market a car through conventional channels.[8]

For many dealers such as Pat Condrin, who owns a Cadillac-Oldsmobile-Subaru dealership in Altoona, Pennsylvania, new car sales were always close to a break-even proposition. He relies on his service department for the bulk of his profit. Pat feels that online auto sales have little value to his dealership: "You sell a car to a guy 200 miles away for invoice and then never see the guy again. You are not really getting a customer. A lot of our future is in fixed operations." Although dealers may disagree on the benefits of online auto sales, none will disagree that the Internet will change their business. The top four online auto sales sites, Auto-By-Tel, AutoVantage, Autoweb.com, and Carpoint, estimate that they generate about 702,000 new vehicle sales a year; this already represents 5 percent of annual new unit sales volume.[9]

Auto-By-Tel

Auto-By-Tel was started in 1995 by Peter Ellis, a former automobile dealer who owned 16 dealerships throughout California and Arizona. Forced into bankruptcy during the automotive sales recession of the early 1990s, Ellis had a vision for a new type of automotive showroom on the Internet without the expensive overhead of traditional bricks-and-mortar facilities. He enlisted a partner, OSP Prodigy Services, Inc., and together they rolled out a site that generated 1,300 auto sales by its fourth day.[10]

In 1996 the company received 345,000 purchase requests through its site and had 1,206 subscribed dealerships. In early 1997 Auto-By-Tel was receiving 55 million hits a month on its site and had over 1.2 million unique customers. Auto-By-Tel provides training and support, real-time sales reports to dealer management, and requires dealers to contact customers within 24 hours of a purchase request. In addition to car sales, Auto-By-Tel partners with American International Group (AIG) and Chase Manhattan Bank to sell vehicle insurance and auto financing online. Despite the convenience of one-stop shopping and additional value-added services, Auto-By-Tel still has not shown a profit due to high expenditures in marketing and technology development (see Exhibit 8.3).[11]

AutoWeb.Com

AutoWeb.com is an online broker founded in Santa Clara, California, in 1994. AutoWeb allows users to research new and used cars for purchase, as well as advertise vehicles for sale. The company's "AutoWeb Affiliate" program pays participating online partners a commission for each customer sent by hotlink who either completes a purchase request or advertises a vehicle for sale. AutoWeb provides a fee-based service to participating dealers, allowing them to access data on the site's customers and receive statistics on local demand for used vehicles. AutoWeb partners with State Farm Insurance and Nations-Bank to sell automotive insurance and financing. In 1997 AutoWeb had 750 participating dealerships and expected rapid dealer membership growth driven by a new "fee-per-lead" pricing structure.[12]

CarPoint

Microsoft Corporation founded CarPoint in 1995 as a feature site on its new Microsoft Network (MSN) portal. It was originally introduced as an

EXHIBIT 8.3   **Auto-By-Tel: Selected Financials**

Source: Company financial statements and case writer estimates.

| | | Three Months Ended | | | | Year Ended |
	December 31, 1995	March 31, 1996	June 30, 1996	September 30, 1996	December 31, 1996	December 31, 1996
Revenues	$ 274	$ 436	$ 952	$ 1,434	$ 2,203	$ 5,025
Operating expenses:						
Marketing and advertising	476	475	678	1,247	2,039	4,439
Selling, training, and support	454	362	563	851	1,417	3,197
Technology development	99	67	78	294	954	1,393
General administrative	275	134	258	740	1,027	2,159
Total operating expenses	1,304	1,038	1,577	3,132	5,437	11,184
Other income (expense) net:	—	—	(6)	22	108	124
Net loss:	$(1,030)	$(602)	$(631)	$(1,676)	$(3,126)	$(6,036)

informational website where prospective car buyers could see a 360-degree view of over 900 car models and check "spec sheets" provided by auto manufacturers.[13] Users could compare similarly priced cars, use the site's loan calculator to compute monthly payments, and locate dealers with a regional search feature. Customers were able to request detailed road test reports from partner IntelliChoice and were directed to partner Auto-By-Tel if they wished to purchase a vehicle. The disappointing initial operating results were attributable primarily to the low overall interest in MSN. In 1997 there were 560 new vehicle and 800 used vehicle dealerships participating in Microsoft's CarPoint service.[14] Subsequently, the site was redesigned in cooperation with Reynolds & Reynolds, a manufacturer of automotive dealer back-office software, into a stand-alone online buying service for vehicles, insurance, and financial services in the manner of Auto-By-Tel.

Kelley Blue Book

Kelley Blue Book (KBB), the long-time publisher of automotive pricing guides, introduced an Internet site in July 1996. KBB online provides users with information on new car manufacturers' suggested retail prices and used-car retail and trade-in values. Users have access to the values of more than 15,000 types of cars, trucks, and vans covering most popular models of the past 21 years.[15] In the first six weeks of operation, the site received requests for over 1 million used-car reports from its database. The site generates revenue from advertisers and a fee-based service that allows customers to trace the title history of a car based on the vehicle identification number. KBB online has successfully levered the ubiquitous Blue Book brand to generate impressive traffic to the site.[16]

AUTO MANUFACTURERS ON THE WEB

Ford and Chrysler

Currently, neither Ford nor Chrysler offers buying services on their websites, following instead a strictly informational model. Ford encourages its dealers to use the Web as a supplement to traditional marketing efforts and provides technical and creative assistance to dealers in establishing sites.[17] Chrysler runs banner ads to promote its new car models and has recognized the value of Web advertising and promotions. Chrysler rewards its 5-star customer satisfaction dealerships with three free home pages on the Chrysler.com website.[18] Customers visiting the corporate site are shown a list of the eight dealers closest to their location, highlighting the 5-star service award winners. Both Ford and Chrysler are experiencing heavy traffic volume on their corporate websites and are encouraging dealers to take advantage of marketing opportunities online.

Toyota

Foreign car manufacturers began to introduce multilingual online sites in late 1995. One of the pioneers was Toyota, the leading import brand in the United

States, which offers its Toyota Internet Drive site in Japanese- and English-language versions. The site offers over 2,600 pages of information on Toyota's new vehicle models and data on Japan's automobile industry. Based on research indicating that over 56 percent of Toyota car owners and over 80 percent of luxury-division Lexus owners had access to a PC, Toyota has invested heavily in feature-rich CD-ROMs and online marketing campaigns to assist its dealers. In late 1996 a national Web development and corporate guideline training program was started across Toyota's 12 U.S. regions. As an additional feature, Toyota has partnered with international marketing and advertising giant Saatchi & Saatchi to add content on gardening, travel, sports, and other special interests in an effort to develop affinity groups centered around the @Toyota site.

Volvo

Swedish automaker Volvo has made the most innovative use of the Web. When the company launched its website in October 1994, it incorporated links from the corporate site to the Web pages of 50 of its 385 North American dealers. Volvo is a small manufacturer with an affluent, highly educated customer base that often uses the Internet. The company was a pioneer in adopting online content to complement and possibly reduce its reliance on expensive advertising. Sweden's lax dealer franchise laws have allowed Volvo to explore ways to eliminate costs by restructuring its traditional value chain using the Web.[19]

GM'S RESPONSE—GMBUYPOWER.COM

The Team

Ann Blakney began working for GM as a summer intern in 1974 while completing her MBA at Stanford and has spent the bulk of her career at the automaker in sales and marketing positions. Ann also has a bachelor's and master's degree in psychology. Charged with turning around GM's performance in California, which had long been a stronghold for imported cars, Blakney changed a number of long-standing dealer practices to improve the consumer purchase experience. She created the "Value Pricing" program to eliminate the unpopular haggling between the dealer and customer. Under this program cars are offered at a set price incorporating a moderate dealer margin (11 percent instead of 17 percent).[20] She also broke an industry taboo by putting independently compiled competitor price information in the showroom. This was a break with the existing unspoken rule to never say too much about the competition. These moves to develop a less adversarial purchase experience for the consumer have contributed to a 20 percent increase in sales and a 22 percent increase in GM's market share in California over the past four years.[21]

In the first days after Zarella's call, Blakney put together a team to undertake her new Internet assignment. She brought together six people with a variety of backgrounds to handle operations and technical issues, finance, field marketing (working with dealers), advertising, and public relations. It was decided to test the concept in four western states—California, Washington, Oregon, and Idaho. Technology development and website hosting was outsourced to former GM subsidiary Electronic Data Systems while website design was performed by Catalyst Resources.

The Process

The challenge of initiating GM's Internet sales program within 90 days meshed with Blakney's conviction that speed to market is critical for success in online sales. Blakney says of the Internet, "It's different from the traditional business model in which you evaluate all of the eventualities. You don't have time. You have to make a commitment of first to market, first to learn. It's much more aggressive."[22]

Blakney and her team envision one of the key roles of the site as providing an in-depth source of information about GM and competitor vehicles, allowing customers to research their options before entering the showroom. This concept differs from the accepted industry marketing philosophy, which seeks to entice the customer onto a dealer's lot where the sales department can close a sale. Blakney's goal was to empower online consumers with information that would streamline the buying process. She sought to create a competitive advantage for GM in attracting consumers who were using the Internet to escape the misery of the traditional vehicle purchase process.

Ninety-eight days into the project Blakney's team began the crucial process of enlisting dealer participation in the experiment. Blakney's team began an exhaustive road-show pitching to dealers across the four test states. It was very difficult to convince the dealers that it was a good idea to give your "best price" to consumers on the Internet. Each dealer that signed up had to have a salesperson trained in effective e-mail communication to handle the correspondence with customers. The team would eventually enroll dealers supplying 70 percent of GM's volume in the four-state region.

GMBuyPower.com was launched on October 27, 1997, just 137 days after its inception. The site was hyped with a blitz of Internet, print, radio, and TV advertising. The press had been introduced to the concept two weeks earlier, and GM set up a studio in Hollywood with a bank of PCs for reporters to try identifying, configuring, and pricing vehicles on the site.

The Website

GMBuyPower.com is currently active in four states: California, Washington, Oregon, and Idaho. GM's initial plan was to roll out the site to the rest of the country in the first quarter of 1999.

The website provides consumers with:

- Extensive vehicle information.

- Third-party competitive comparison.

- Access to dealer inventory.

- A personal message center to communicate with dealers.

- A "no-haggle" online list price good for 24 hours.

- GMAC financing options.

Consumers who visit the GMBuyPower.com site can browse through descriptions and specifications covering over 200 car models. Detailed information allows users to develop the option packages that they want to include on their target vehicle. The consumer can also view third-party competitive comparisons provided by the Automotive Information Center of their chosen car with similarly equipped cars from other manufacturers. Real-time inventory tracking allows buyers to locate dealers that have their ideal GM car in stock and then communicate with the dealer staff using online message forms. Finally, the consumer and the dealer can negotiate the terms of the transaction by e-mail. GMAC financing options are available and the consumer can apply for credit online. The site even provides the buyer with directions to the dealer's showroom to pick up his or her new vehicle. "There's a very aggressive effort to give dealers the tools to meet the demands of customers in the Internet age," said Ann Blakney. "We offer dealers the ability to have a very sophisticated website and to be able to communicate in a way that customers have asked for."[23]

Results and Dealer Reaction

Many dealers and analysts have been disappointed with the performance of GMBuyPower.com. Only 60 percent of the total dealers in the four pilot states have signed on to the program and only 8,000 vehicle sales were attributed to the website as of September 1998.[24]

One of the disappointed GM dealers who signed up for GMBuyPower.com has received eight leads, which have generated only one sale in the 11 months the site has been active. This same dealer sells 15 cars a month through Auto-By-Tel. Jim Begier, general manager of Ben A. Begier Buick in San Leandro, California, believes that GM's long-term goal is to phase out privately owned dealerships in favor of company-owned facilities. However, Begier is convinced that car buyers prefer a more traditional approach. "BuyPower has been a failure. People still want to see, touch and feel a new car. GM is in denial on the whole thing."[25]

According to Boston Consulting Group consultant Oleg Khaykin, "GM is only recycling its existing customers on the Web. The only way that the website sells a car is if the consumer has already decided to buy a GM car."[26]

Whatever the reason, GM is underperforming its rivals online as evidenced by data provided by Auto-By-Tel (see Exhibit 8.4). Auto-By-Tel's founder, Peter Ellis, feels that GM needs the high-pressure sales techniques used by its traditional dealers to move GM products. A more charitable explanation may be that GM's traditional buyers are less likely to purchase cars over the Internet. Another faction of GM dealers believes that the company is not moving

EXHIBIT 8.4

Sales as a
Percentage of U.S.
Auto Market

Source: "Can General
Motors Learn to Love the
Net?" *Business 2.0,*
September 1998.

	Toyota	Honda	GM	Chrysler
U.S. market	8.0%	7.0%	31.0%	16.0%
Auto-By-Tel sales	12.0	12.0	19.0	18.5

fast enough to capitalize on e-commerce opportunities. These dealers would prefer that GM satisfy its online customers with a corporate site rather than have these consumers give a piece of the margin to a third-party broker. They feel that developing online auto retailing in cooperation with GMBuyPower offers the best means to preserve their profit margins.[27]

The Next Step

As Ann heads out of town for Memorial Day weekend, she is thinking about the whirlwind events of the past year. On balance she feels that the results to date have been inconclusive. Certainly the site has not been as effective as Auto-By-Tel, but the company has gained valuable online sales experience. Stuck in Los Angeles traffic, Ann has time to reflect on the big picture issues that surround her efforts. Should GM be developing its own site or working with existing brokers? What opportunities do online sales offer to restructure other areas of the business? Is an online auto store that offers only one automaker's products a compelling model for consumers? If online sales weaken GM's traditional dealer network, what will it mean for the company? Ann doesn't have all the answers, but she does know that the way the industry sells cars is being fundamentally transformed by this new technology. Unless changes are made to existing federal legislation, GM will continue to rely on dealers to retail its vehicles. However, the auto industry would dearly love to cut the estimated $100 billion tied up in new car inventory across the nation.

Notes

1. www.gmcanada.com, accessed 1998.
2. Ibid.
3. www.gm.com, accessed 1998.
4. U.S. Census Bureau.
5. J. D. Power Associates.
6. *Automotive News,* January 12, 1998.
7. Ibid.
8. *Automotive News,* February 2, 1998.
9. *Automotive News,* January 26, 1998.
10. "Auto-By-Tel Drives Car Shoppers through the Internet," *Bank Technology News,* October 1998.
11. Ibid.

12. "AutoWeb Doubles Dealer Count with per Lead Fees," *Automotive News,* August 17, 1998.
13. "Microsoft Pitches Auto Mall on the Web," *Automotive News,* July 21, 1997.
14. "CarPoint Revs Up to Overtake Rivals," *Automotive News,* October 12, 1998.
15. "Smart Sellers, Buyers Use Kelley Blue Book in Their Automotive Dealings," *Sacramento Bee,* September 19, 1996.
16. "Kelley Blue Book Sets Up on the Internet," *Ward's Auto World,* January 1997.
17. "Court: Ford Had Right to Veto Dealership Sale," *Automotive News,* March 25, 1996; "Surf's Up: Ford Dealers Hit the Web," *Automotive News,* June 10, 1996.
18. "Chrysler Web Touts Best–CSI Dealers," *Automotive News,* February 24, 1997.
19. "Volvo Starts Selling on the Net," *Automotive News Europe,* May 25, 1998.
20. "GM on the Web," *San Francisco Chronicle,* September 9, 1998.
21. "Can General Motors Learn to Love the Net?" *Business 2.0,* September 1998.
22. Ibid.
23. "GM Revs Up Web Sales," *San Francisco Chronicle,* September 9, 1998.
24. "Heard on the Beat; GM Expands Online," *Los Angeles Times,* September 28, 1998.
25. "GM Revs Up Web Sales."
26. "Can General Motors Learn to Love the Net?"
27. Ibid.

Case Nine

*i*Village: Innovation among Women's Websites

Candice Carpenter, cofounder and CEO of *i*Village, looked out the window of her New York City office and reflected on the stunning achievements of her company. The women's online network had experienced an extremely successful initial public offering (IPO), raising approximately $292 million in market value on its first day of trading in March 1999. *i*Village, having established a name for itself as the ultimate women's online resource, had reached a pivotal moment in its growth cycle. However, over the last four months, competition was heating up.

Three of the most powerful women in entertainment had teamed up to form Oxygen Media, a new company set up to offer integrated media and entertainment services by broadcasting over different channels. Launched in 1998 by Geraldine Laybourne, Oxygen, like *i*Village, recognized the value of this powerful and growing consumer audience. However, in addition to offering a stand-alone website, Oxygen planned to launch a cable station on January 1, 2000. Oxygen's long-term business model was highly innovative in that it revolved around convergence of the Web with television. The firm's website was slated to go online May 1, 1999.

Knowing that *i*Village's current business model would not create the sustainable revenues Carpenter needed, she speculated on what to say to the new stockholders at their first meeting the following morning. How should *i*Village

New York University Stern School of Business MBA Candidates Carol Foley, Falguni Pandya, Anne Shiva, Jonathan Singer, and H. Dassi Weinstein prepared this case under the supervision of Professor Christopher L. Tucci for the purpose of class discussion rather than to illustrate either effective or ineffective handling of an administrative situation. Copyright © 2001 by McGraw-Hill/Irwin. All rights reserved.

innovate its product offering in the face of new competitive threats, notably Oxygen's arrival, and not alienate its current customer base? Carpenter started outlining ideas for product development.

THE CHANGING FACE OF THE MEDIA INDUSTRY

Since the Internet has infiltrated the home and become increasingly popular, it has redefined the role of media on a massive scale. The number of Internet users was estimated to reach approximately 320 million by the end of 2002.[1] The widespread acceptance of the Internet, its low-cost infrastructure, and the nature of its interactivity raised an uproar of excitement throughout the world by allowing anyone who had access to a computer and modem to establish a presence on the Internet. Moreover, worldwide commerce revenue on the Internet was expected to increase to more than $425 billion in 2002.[2]

In the wake of the Internet phenomenon, traditional media were going through a shakedown. Since the Internet could serve purposes that other media have served in the past, as well as offer entirely new functions of e-commerce, distribution, and interactivity, traditional media had to refocus their approach in order to retain audiences. The Internet, however, has not managed to replace other media. Rather, it was blurring the lines between different forms of media, forcing traditional radio stations, magazines, newspapers, and broadcast TV stations to build a presence in other media channels. These traditional forms focus more heavily on the strength and "elasticity" (the suitability for different forms and end-user devices) of their content to retain their audiences.[3] In this respect, those who have a hold on a specific content niche are dominating the new paradigm. *i*Village created a dominant brand that had a strong hold on a specific niche market—women aged 25 to 49.

WOMEN AS A MARKET

According to the Women's Consumer Network, women control 85 percent of all personal and household goods spending. Women also consume more media than men per day (8.8 hours versus 8.2 hours), and they currently account for 43 percent of Internet and online service users. In addition, women comprise 57 percent of new Internet service provider subscribers.

Moreover, according to an *i*Village Women's Net Monitor poll taken in February 1998, the Internet was no longer a place to gather information passively; rather, women were using it to actively solve real problems. The poll was conducted with 700 online respondents, split between men and women. Once on the Web, more women than men met and kept new friends. In addition, more women rated the online community as an important part of their lives.

An *i*Village online survey conducted in 1999 revealed that 77 percent of women went online primarily to explore, but 86 percent stayed because they found information that helped them get through their daily lives. The survey results validated what *i*Village believed from the beginning.

Bearing in mind these statistics, we can understand why women's websites have grown and flourished. Prior to 2000, three dominant players had emerged: *i*Village, Women.com, and the latest, Oxygen Media, Inc. Each company in its own way attempted to capitalize on this powerful niche market.

THE COMPETITION

Carpenter was concerned about emerging threats from other online start-ups that were targeting women such as Oxygen Media, Inc., and Women.com. Allison Abraham, *i*Village's chief operating officer, commenting on the competition, said that "We must stay focused as opportunities are ours to keep."[4]

Women.com

Women.com, partly owned by Hearst New Media and Technology, a subsidiary of the publishing giant, was originally founded as a content site. During the creation of the Women.com site, the firm was able to exploit Hearst's rich database on women customers. Like other women's sites, Women.com evolved to have some community features, and most recently, has started a small commerce venture.

Oxygen Media, Inc.

Oxygen Media, Inc., backed by strong media personalities and heavy investors, generated a wave of interest partly because of its innovative approach to satisfying women's needs. It was a multimedia company, aimed primarily at women, and combined the entertainment power of television with the power of the Internet to create interactive television. The combination of Oxygen online and Oxygen cable was a futuristic, visionary approach that would shape the future of the new media industry. Its vision was to create a comprehensive "Home Base" for women online, which would go beyond the offerings of *i*Village. Oxygen's model was innovative, more comprehensive, and hard to imitate.

Oxygen Media was founded by Geraldine Laybourne, one of the most powerful women executives in the television industry. The formation of the Oxygen network for women represents a partnership between Laybourne, Oprah Winfrey, and the Carsey-Werner-Mandach production company. Oxygen Media also acquired investments from America Online (AOL) and ABC, a Disney company. Oxygen planned to raise revenue through charging operators license fees per subscriber and by attracting a broad range of advertisers and e-commerce partners.

WWW.*i*VILLAGE.COM

History

Cofounders CEO Candice Carpenter and editor-in-chief Nancy Evans established *i*Village in June 1995. Carpenter began thinking about the idea for *i*Village while working as a consultant to AOL. As a single mother of two children, Carpenter knew that "women today are so pragmatic and time-pressed that they use the Web to find out how to get things done."

The company, headquartered in New York City, humanized cyberspace by providing a relevant online experience for women. Carpenter and Evans originally created a one-stop destination for women looking for information on topics such as children, health, and family. They developed a site that was primarily a content site without any intercommunication. However, because of the way women use the Internet and the site's dynamic information, *i*Village then evolved into an online community where members exchanged advice and developed relationships. In this case, the consumers drove the site's innovation. The firm had to respond by further developing its offering to fit the needs and wants of its users.

Target Market

*i*Village was one of the most demographically targeted online communities on the Web. The network of sites was tailored to the interests and needs of women aged 25 through 49. The average household income of the *i*Village customer was $55,000; most were married, employed full-time, and had attended college—an attractive market segment for potential advertisers and sponsors (see Exhibit 9.1). As such, the site was recognized as a leader in developing innovative sponsorships and commerce relationships. This leadership position was vital to the company's revenue growth through the 1990s.

Product

*i*Village.com was the world's largest online destination for women. By actively participating in the network's communities, members learned from experts and from each other, gained empowerment to find solutions, and inspired fellow members to handle everyday challenges more effectively. Candice Carpenter summed up the goal of *i*Village's offerings: "We strive to help women navigate through increasingly busy lives and maximize their potential in their various roles as parents, friends, spouses, partners, career women, breadwinners, employees, and individuals."[5]

*i*Village was the first company to offer this type of online product to women. Moreover, the firm innovated its product offering into what could be called the "un-content" provider. The firm developed its site into a community-oriented site from its original content-only product. Offering support groups, bulletin boards, and buddies, *i*Village developed a community for every interest. *i*Village's channels and sites included: Better Health, Career, Relationships,

EXHIBIT 9.1
*i*Village
**Demographic
Profile**

Gender	Female/Male	80%/20%
Age	Average	33.7
Household Income	Average	$54,744
Marital Status	Married	59.6%
	Living w/ partner	7.6%
	Single	21.7%
	Separated/divorced/widowed	11.2%
Employment Status	Full-time	55.0%
	Part-time	9.7%
	Work from home	9.3%
	Unemployed	5.6%
	Full-time parent	8.7%
	Student	9.1%
	Retired	2.7%
Education	Attended/graduated college	61.2%
	Attended graduate school	6.4%
	Postgraduate degree	12.7%

Food, ParentsPlace, Shopping, Fitness & Beauty, Work From Home, Travel, Pets, Astrology.net, Book Club, and Money Life. Also, *i*Village and Intuit, the makers of Quicken, launched Armchair Millionaire in an online partnership.

Beyond Armchair Millionaire, *i*Village offered little information on finance or world news, although it did offer a group of experts available for consultation on many topics. At any one time, there were some 1,400 ongoing discussion boards which brought together groups of like-minded women who shared experiences or helped each other solve problems. For example, the Work from Home section offered a software library filled with bookkeeping, billing, legal, payroll, and sales-lead shareware. From the Health page, members could access the huge store of medical information in its database. In contrast, competing aggregate sites tended to resemble traditional women's magazines, carrying mostly articles and lacking any chat or message board functions.

Traffic

In terms of traffic, *i*Village was the most successful women's website. Traffic flow was vital because it was a concrete definition of success and future potential in Internet business models at the time. According to Relevant Knowledge, a Web measurement company, more than 2 million different visitors visited *i*Village sites during June 1998 alone. This was more than twice the traffic of its nearest competitor, Women.com. April 1998 statistics revealed that *i*Village had the largest reach (3.8 percent) of any women's site and it claimed 65 million page views a month. Traffic to the site continued to increase exponentially.

Financial Issues

A growing number of industry watchers and executives have begun to question how a volume-driven Internet can survive, let alone grow, when its native businesses can bring themselves to utter the "P" word only in the negative. "No profit for the foreseeable future" is now a boilerplate disclaimer in the prospectus of an Internet company preparing an initial stock offering.[6]

—Susan Karlin, Upside Magazine

Like many companies based on the World Wide Web, *i*Village had yet to turn a profit. Indeed, it had accumulated a substantial deficit; the company was still spending more money than it brought in. Analysts surmised that the company's profitability was not a near-term goal; losses grew in 1998 to $43.7 million from $21.3 million in 1997 (see Exhibit 9.2). Clearly, accumulating losses were a consideration when reviewing and restructuring *i*Village's business model.

*i*Village's Business Model

Like many new sites based on content and community, *i*Village generated most of its revenues by selling banners, text-links, and sponsorships from other business. As traffic, or volume, was the key to attracting advertising clients, this business model became known as the "volume-based" model. This model, however, may not be sustainable. According to Jupiter Communications, Internet advertising was expected to total only $1 to $2 billion, or roughly 1 percent of the total advertising spending in the United States. Combined with this fact, more and more websites were competing for the same revenue dollars from advertisers. Along these lines, advertisers had become less willing to post ads on pages that were increasingly congested with other sponsors' banners and links. As such, pages were limited in the number of ads they could post, which in turn capped their ability to generate revenues.

This trend forced most online companies to experiment with other revenue-generating models such as e-commerce. However, the e-commerce business model, too, had yet to be proven as a reliable means for generating profits. For instance, Amazon.com sold 2.5 million books over the Internet, yet it closed 1998 with $124.5 million in losses. However, in venturing into e-commerce, *i*Village maintained a distinct advantage. Whereas Amazon had to spend vast amounts of money marketing its product and service, *i*Village was able to launch *i*Baby with little or no promotion due to its existing customer base and online community. *i*Village should be able to capitalize on this advantage in future e-commerce ventures.

EXHIBIT 9.2   *i*Village Financials

Source: Company SEC filings.

	Income Statement		
	1998	**1997**	**1996**
Revenues:			
Sponsorship, advertising, and usage	$ 12,450,620	$ 6,018,696	$ 732,045
Commerce	2,561,203	—	—
Total revenues	15,011,823	6,018,696	732,045
Operating expenses:			
Production, product, and technology	14,521,015	7,606,355	4,521,410
Sales and marketing	28,522,874	8,770,581	2,708,779
General and administrative	10,612,434	7,840,588	3,103,864
Depreciation and amortization	5,683,006	2,886,256	108,956
Total operating expenses	59,339,329	27,103,780	10,443,009
Loss from operations	(44,327,506)	(21,085,084)	(9,710,964)
Interest income (expense), net	591,186	(215,876)	28,282
Loss on sale of website	(503,961)	—	—
Minority interest	586,599	—	—
Net loss	$(43,653,682)	$(21,300,960)	$(9,682,682)

	Balance Sheet	
	1998	**1997**
ASSETS		
Current assets:		
Cash and cash equivalents	$ 30,824,869	$ 4,334,721
Accounts receivable	3,147,561	2,199,520
Other current assets	715,161	153,985
Total current assets	34,687,591	6,688,226
Fixed assets, net	7,380,366	3,802,823
Goodwill and other intangible assets, net	4,535,148	5,598,233
Other assets	187,860	146,801
Total assets	$ 46,790,965	$ 16,236,083
LIABILITIES AND STOCKHOLDERS' EQUITY		
Current liabilities:		
Accounts payable and accrued expenses	$ 11,559,711	$ 3,989,945
Capital leases payable	136,573	247,943
Deferred revenue	2,909,740	1,004,199
Other current liabilities	162,859	332,531
Total current liabilities	14,768,883	5,574,618
Capital leases payable, net of current portion	—	139,346
Total liabilities	14,768,883	5,713,964
Stockholders' equity:		
Convertible series	21,851	9,486
Common stock	21,133	18,197
Additional paid-in capital	112,848,505	43,180,649
Accumulated deficit	(76,274,895)	(32,621,213)
Stockholders notes receivable	(565,000)	(65,000)
Unearned compensation and deferred advertising	(4,029,512)	—
Total stockholders' equity	32,022,082	10,522,119
Total liabilities and stockholders' equity	$ 46,790,965	$ 16,236,083

The Shift to E-Commerce

In March 1998, *i*Village ventured into electronic commerce with the acquisition of an online store, *i*Baby, a one-year-old online commerce success. This shift in revenue generation marked a milestone for *i*Village. The company began as a content site, evolved into a community site, and, with this latest move, further developed its product to include e-commerce. *i*Village's latest product development was a clear response to heightening competition for sustainability and revenue.

*i*Baby delivered the most extensive selection of baby products and gift services worldwide. *i*Village was striving for a quick and convenient shopping experience for its consumers, offering more than 14,000 baby-related products, access to over 800 vendors, and a baby gift registry. Already, *i*Baby had a unique position as a young venture touting $1 million in sales and a database filled with thousands of loyal customers.

In the agreement, *i*Village offered *i*Baby more than 65 million page views per month, the ability to strategically target segments of its online communities to market *i*Baby's products, and an expertise in building compelling and functional online environments. *i*Baby brought to the table complementary areas of expertise such as product sourcing, established vendor relations, warehousing, inventory control, and customer service.

As a stand-alone business, *i*Baby would retain control of the inventory management and shipping operations to guarantee a top-quality experience for customers. This gave *i*Baby the ability to track both inventory and shipping flow precisely, efficiently, and effectively. Considering that e-commerce was outside of its original model, *i*Village's venture with *i*Baby was a first step toward further product innovation.

Carpenter viewed *i*Baby to be a strong step toward innovation into e-commerce. But how far should her company venture? Was *i*Village ready to make such a sharp turn in product development into a new area of business? Would it affect the existing community experience? How would its business model have to change? Carpenter knew that all of these issues had to be viewed in light of the competition. Every day new players were encroaching on *i*Village's territory.

LOOKING TO THE FUTURE

As Carpenter outlined her thoughts for the stockholders the next morning, she considered the events over the last four months. She needed to consider how growing competitive threats and dynamic customer needs would reshape *i*Village's revenue stream. The decision regarding product development into electronic commerce needed to be made soon.

Notes

1. *i*Village website statistic: www.corporate-ir.net/ireye/ir_site.zhtml?ticker= IVIL&script=2100.
2. Ibid.
3. Lisa Allen, Bill Bass, Chris Charron, and Jill Aldort, "Old Media's New Role," *The Forrester Report,* no. 5 (January 1999), p. 6.
4. Allison Abraham, "Internet Communities," Presentation in Electronic Commerce class, New York University, Stern School of Business, April 12, 1999.
5. Heather Green, "For Women, *i*Village is a Site of Their Own," *Business Week,* businessweek.com/1998/29/b3587126.htm, July 20, 1998.
6. Susan Karlin, "It Takes an *i*Village," *Upside Magazine,* www.upside.com/ texis/mvm/story?id=3665bcf40, December 2, 1998.

Case **Ten**

eBay, Inc.: Diversification in the Internet Auction Market

eBay Agrees to Buy Butterfield & Butterfield

—eBay press releases, April 26, 1999

eBay Purchases Respected Automobile Auctioneer

—eBay press releases, May 18, 1999

eBay Halts Auction of Human Kidney; Bidding Had Reached $5.7 Million

—CBS MarketWatch, September 2, 1999

eBay Comes to Tampa-St. Petersburg with New Local Web Site

—PR Newswire, October 27, 1999

eBay Starts Business-to-Business Auctions

—Reuters, November 4, 1999

New York University Stern School of Business MBA Candidates Mark Abramowitz, Theresa Harpster, Justina Nixon-Saintil, Carol Szeto, and Josh Witz prepared this case under the supervision of Professor Christopher L. Tucci for the purpose of class discussion rather than to illustrate either effective or ineffective handling of an administrative situation. Copyright © 2001 by McGraw-Hill/Irwin. All rights reserved.

Nineteen ninety-nine was a tremendous year for eBay, the champion of the person-to-person online auction business. Gross merchandise sales rose 280 percent, to $741 million from $195 million the previous year, and registered users jumped 509 percent, to 7.7 million from 1.3 million.[1] eBay has emerged as one of the leading Internet companies among online giants such as Amazon and Yahoo! However, given the increasingly competitive online auction market, Margaret C. Whitman, the CEO of eBay, knew that the battle ahead would not be easy. As she retraced the events that happened in the last six months, she pondered eBay's strategy to manage both the external competitive situation and the internal hypergrowth of the company.

Several issues were troubling Whitman. eBay had always focused on the person-to-person auction market. But given the recent hype about the growth prospects in the business-to-consumer (B2C) and business-to-business (B2B) markets, was eBay missing out on these opportunities? Besides, this year the company started pursuing a regional and international expansion strategy as well as an off-line strategy by purchasing two auction houses. Even if eBay did enter the new markets, would it be spreading itself too thin? How could it integrate these different ideas without losing focus on the core business? eBay's revenue model was another concern. Some competitors were relying on their retail revenue and offering auction services for free. Was eBay's main revenue stream from placement fees and commissions on transactions sustainable?

THE HISTORY OF eBAY

We started with commerce, and what grew out of that was community.[2]

—*Meg Whitman, CEO of eBay*

eBay was conceived initially as a result of a conversation between Pierre Omidyar, an engineer at General Magic, and his fiancée. His fiancée was an avid Pez collector and trader. She commented to Omidyar how great it would be if she were able to trade dispensers with other collectors over the Internet. As an early Internet enthusiast, Omidyar knew that people needed a central location to buy and sell unique items and to meet other users with similar interests. He started the first online auction website to fulfill this need.

With a BS in computer science from Tufts University and years of experience running start-ups, Omidyar was not a newcomer to the Internet industry (see Exhibit 10.1 for company biographies). He brought in his friend Jeff Skoll, a Stanford MBA, as the company's first president. Together, they wrote the company's first business plan and launched the first online auction service, Auction Web, on Labor Day in September 1995. Within a few weeks, buyers and sellers began flocking to the service as news of it spread by word of mouth. A few months of heavy traffic later, Omidyar realized he had a company on his hands and quit his job.[3]

EXHIBIT 10.1 eBay Management Biography

Source: *Red Herring.*

	Pierre Omidyar	**Jeff Skoll**	**Margaret C. Whitman**
Title	Founder	First president	Current CEO
Education	BS, computer science, Tufts University	MBA, Stanford University	MBA, Harvard University; BA, economics, Princeton University
Experience	Engineer, General Magic; Cofounder, Ink Development (online shopping)	Founder, Skoll Engineering (computer consultancy); Founder, Micros on the Move, Ltd. (computer rentals)	General manager, Hasbro; CEO, Florists Transworld Delivery (FTD); President, Stride Rite; Senior VP, Disney's Consumer Products unit; VP, Bain Consulting; Brand manager, Procter & Gamble

Auction Web was incorporated in 1996 and changed its name to eBay in 1997 when it began promoting itself through banner ads and advertising. By the middle of that year, eBay was boasting nearly 800,000 auctions each day. eBay was profitable from the beginning and unsolicited offers from venture capitalists began to pour in. It secured a $3 million round of venture financing from Benchmark Capital that it put in the bank and never touched. "We wanted a good mentor, not money," explained Jeff Skoll.[4]

In early 1998 Omidyar turned over the CEO position to Margaret ("Meg") Whitman, formerly of Bain Consulting, Procter & Gamble, Disney, StrideRite, FTD, and Hasbro, so he could concentrate on strategy. eBay's highly successful IPO occurred in September of that year. With heavy marketing through national advertising campaigns and alliances with America Online and WebTV, eBay had become a household name identified with the largest online auction trading community. The number of registered users had grown to more than 6 million (see Exhibit 10.2) and eBay was deemed the "stickiest" site on the Internet, according to the Nielsen/NetRatings research in the first quarter of 1999 (see Exhibit 10.3). One year after its initial public offering (IPO), eBay now had a market capitalization of $19 billion. Unlike most of the Internet start-ups, eBay was actually making a profit—$2.4 million on sales of $47.3 million in fiscal 1998 (see Exhibit 10.4 for eBay's quarterly financial statements).

HOW DOES eBAY WORK?

Online Auction Mechanism

Functioning as an Internet-based garage sale, consumers participated in eBay's online trading community for four main reasons: It was fun, you met people with similar interests, you got a great deal (most of the time), and you found

EXHIBIT 10.2   **Number of eBay Registered Users**

Source: Deutsche Banc Alex. Brown estimates; company reports.

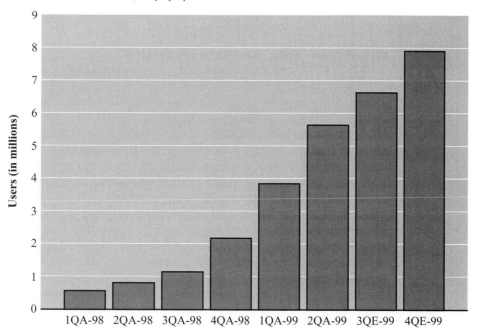

EXHIBIT 10.3   **"Stickiest" Online Activities**

Source: Nielsen/NetRatings, March 1999.

Property	Type	Monthly Rank Time Spent (hours:minutes:seconds)	By Unique Audience	Pages per Person
eBay	Auction	3:08:19	17	233
Yahoo!	Portal	1:02:34	2	75
MSN	Portal	1:00:03	3	48
Uproar	Gaming	0:44:21	65	33
The Excite Network	Portal	0:33:10	7	30
AOL sites	Portal	0:32:01	1	24
Prodigy	Portal	0:31:47	56	11
Knight Ridder Real Cities Network	Newspapers	0:29:18	59	22
GO Network	Portal Plus	0:27:46	5	27
CNN	News	0:26:43	20	25

EXHIBIT 10.4A   eBay, Inc., Annual Financials

Source: eBay 10-K filed on March 29, 1999.

eBAY INC.
CONSOLIDATED STATEMENT OF INCOME
(in thousands, except per share amounts)

	Year Ended December 31,		
	1996	**1997**	**1998**
Net revenues	$ 372	$ 5,744	$ 47,352
Cost of net revenues	14	746	6,859
Gross profit	358	4,998	40,493
Operating expenses:			
Sales and marketing	32	1,730	19,841
Product development	28	831	4,606
General and administrative	45	950	9,080
Amortization of acquired intangibles	—	—	805
Total operating expenses	105	3,511	34,332
Income from operations	253	1,487	6,161
Interest and other income, net	1	59	908
Interest expense	—	(3)	(39)
Income before income taxes	254	1,543	7,030
Provision for income taxes	(106)	(669)	(4,632)
Net income	$ 148	$ 874	$ 2,398
Net income per share:			
Basic	$ 0.02	$ 0.04	$ 0.05
Weighted average shares—basic	6,375	22,313	49,895
Diluted	$ 0.00	$ 0.01	$ 0.02
Weighted average shares—diluted	$42,945	$82,660	$114,590

valuable collectibles. Goods were sold through an auction that lasted several days. Many bids were usually garnered for each item. Each day, more than 2 million new auctions were conducted and over 200,000 new items were listed.

Conceptually, the online auction was similar to that of physical auctions. In a nutshell: Items were listed and viewed, bids were entered, and items were purchased and delivered (see Exhibit 10.5 for the eBay trading community). Since only very expensive rare items were typically sold at physical auctions, an online auction filled the void for all other goods.

Before bidders could bid and sellers could list items for sale, each had to register with eBay, indicating some personal contact and credit card information, and acknowledging acceptance of disclaimer and disclosure rules. Like the off-line world, a bid invoked a legally binding contract.

To list an item for sale, a seller had to choose which category to list it under. Categories included antiques, collectibles, sports memorabilia, dolls,

EXHIBIT 10.4B   eBay Quarterly Financials

Source: eBay 10Q filed on November 15, 1999.

eBAY INC.
CONDENSED CONSOLIDATED STATEMENT OF INCOME
(in thousands, except per share amounts; unaudited)

	Three Months Ended September 30,		Nine Months Ended September 30,	
	1998	**1999**	**1998**	**1999**
Net revenues:				
Fees and services	$ 20,816	$ 57,632	$ 52,143	$147,827
Real estate rentals	915	893	3,056	2,978
Total net revenues	21,731	58,525	55,199	150,805
Cost of net revenues:				
Fees and services	3,947	16,687	8,635	34,821
Real estate rentals	420	394	1,509	1,182
Total cost of net revenues	4,367	17,081	10,144	36,003
Gross profit	17,364	41,444	45,055	114,802
Operating expenses:				
Sales and marketing	9,414	27,230	21,317	67,104
Product development	1,514	6,851	3,062	14,490
General and administrative	4,249	11,779	11,049	29,481
Amortization of acquired intangibles	327	328	477	983
Merger related costs	—	—	—	4,359
Total operating expenses	15,504	46,188	35,905	116,417
Income (loss) from operations	1,860	(4,744)	9,150	(1,615)
Interest and other income, net	190	7,524	686	14,880
Interest expense	(351)	(449)	(1,279)	(1,491)
Income before income taxes	1,699	2,331	8,557	11,774
Provision for income taxes	(1,238)	(979)	(3,923)	(5,841)
Net income	$ 461	$ 1,352	$ 4,634	$ 5,933
Net income per share:				
Basic	$ 0.01	$ 0.01	$ 0.12	$ 0.06
Diluted	0.00	$ 0.01	$ 0.04	$ 0.04
Weighted average shares:				
Basic	48,385	115,980	39,002	105,864
Diluted	113,619	140,082	109,625	135,358
Supplemental pro forma information:				
Income before income taxes	$ 1,699	$ 2,331	$ 8,557	$ 11,774
Provision for income taxes as reported	(1,238)	(979)	(3,923)	(5,841)
Pro forma adjustment to provision for income taxes	274	—	(1,239)	(677)
Pro forma net income	$ 735	$ 1,352	$ 3,395	$ 5,256
Pro forma net income per share:				
Basic	$ 0.02	$ 0.01	$ 0.09	$ 0.05
Diluted	$ 0.01	$ 0.01	$ 0.03	$ 0.04

EXHIBIT 10.5 **eBay Trading Community**

Source: eBay and BT Alex. Brown Research Report, October 27, 1998.

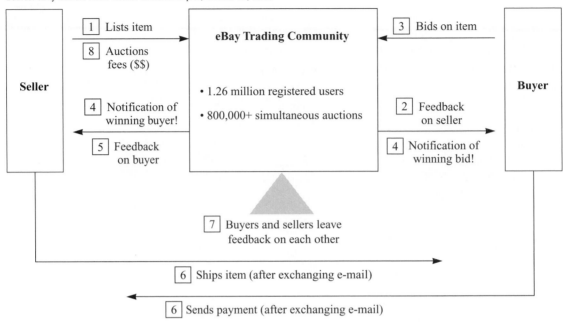

jewelry, pottery, toys, and so forth. Each category was divided into more specific subcategories. For example, the computer category was broken up into hardware and software; the hardware subcategory was divided into areas such as modems, printers, monitors, and so on. Once selected, the seller indicated the duration of the auction (three days minimum), lowest bid acceptable, purchase description and photo (if available), payment (currency specified), and delivery terms.

During the auction period, eBay updated bidders about the status of their bid—whether they were high or had been outbid. To avoid having to monitor an auction continuously, bidders could invoke the "bid proxy." Here, bidders specified up front the maximum they would pay for an item; eBay then monitored the auction and adjusted the bid as needed without exceeding the maximum level. Upon auction closing, eBay sent e-mail messages to seller and bidders notifying them of the results and reminding the high bidder of the need to contact the seller within three business days to claim the item.

Security and Technology Issues

Trust was an important element in the online auction environment. eBay addressed fraud and unscrupulous deals in two primary ways: a feedback system that encouraged users to rate each other and indicate comments regarding the reliability and credibility of the buyer or seller, and an optional escrow system (i-Escrow) through which payment would be released to the seller only when the buyer gave approval. With these additional value-added services, eBay was able to address consumer concerns about security and to attract more users to its site.

Another factor vital to eBay's existence was technology. In the second and third quarters of 1999, eBay experienced several outages that resulted in the company's loss of millions of dollars in revenue. While eBay traditionally relied chiefly on internal resources to maintain and service its technology infrastructure, it announced that it would outsource its back-end Internet technology to Abovenet Communications and Exodus Communications. Thus, the maintenance and performance responsibilities for Web servers, database servers, and Internet routers would switch to an external provider. As eBay continued to grow, it hoped these measures would help ensure success.

INDUSTRY OVERVIEW

The public has embraced online bidding ever since eBay pioneered person-to-person online auctions. The Internet has collapsed the distance between buyers and sellers, thereby creating a dynamic marketplace where prices were more fluid than ever. Now, the market had evolved to include not only personal collectibles, but also surplus inventory offered by retail merchants. The auction market had become increasingly crowded because barriers to entry were very low. Auction technologies such as LiveExchange and AuctionNow were readily available, essentially allowing any online merchant to offer these services. In the consumer auction space, eBay competed with many players, including Amazon, Yahoo!, and FairMarket.

Amazon.com

Amazon.com was the largest and broadest online consumer retailer, with close to 12 million registered customers as of the second quarter of 1998. The company's mission was to help people find almost anything they wanted to buy online, including books, toys, pets, and furniture. In March 1999 Amazon moved into the online auction space to compete head-to-head with eBay. Its online auction house was called "zShops" and it conducted both person-to-person and business-to-consumer auctions.

To distinguish its auction services, Amazon provided a $250 guarantee for consumers, and a $1,000 guarantee if the transaction was conducted through its 1-Click ordering capability. These guarantees addressed the fraud issue. The well-known brand name, an established customer base, and the ability to cross-market its retail and auction merchandise certainly helped Amazon build a strong presence in the online auction world.

Yahoo!

Yahoo!, founded in 1995, was at the time the most popular Internet portal site. It offered a branded network of comprehensive information, communication, and shopping services to millions of users daily, and it boasted more monthly usage hours than any other site on the Internet. To start its own auction service, Yahoo! first licensed Onsale's technology and then took over Exchange, Onsale's person-to-person auction service. The Yahoo! auction was free and supported only by advertising revenues.

FairMarket AuctionPlace

FairMarket, founded in 1997, represented the newest competitor in the online auction market that posed a significant threat to eBay. In September 1999 it announced a plan to aggregate the bidders and sellers across about 100 portal, retail, and community sites, including MSN, Excite, Lycos, Dell, and Ticketmaster Online, and allowed goods to be shared among these member sites. This meant that someone listing a used Palm Pilot for sale on Lycos, for instance, would automatically have the gadget posted on the auction sites of Microsoft and Excite as well.[5] Pulling together an instant critical mass of a combined 50 million users, FairMarket was helping companies to extend their reach to consumers and challenge the leading auctioneer eBay.

STRATEGY FOR GROWTH

As the pioneer of online person-to-person trading, eBay had been able to exploit its first-mover advantage into the creation of critical mass. With roughly 80 percent of the person-to-person auction space on the Internet and the largest offering of individual auctions (over 3 million items), eBay had created a solid brand name and a loyal customer base. Over the prior year, the company had employed an aggressive growth plan to solidify its leadership position in the auction market. This included a focus on product and service offerings, and regional and international expansion.

Product and Service Offerings

Since eBay was a virtual company—one that never actually physically handled merchandise—the company believed that it must offer better customer service and marketing than most. To foster a stronger community, eBay offered a number of venues such as News Features, Library, and Charity to help users meet and exchange information. Additionally, the company forged innovative partnerships with companies like Kodak (for digitizing customer photos), Mailboxes Etc. (for shipping), i-Escrow (for releasing funds after items are received), and Collectors Universe (for authenticating auction items) to improve its customer service. In 1999 the company acquired Billpoint to enable customers to pay with credit cards.

To expand its product portfolio, eBay took an unprecedented step in April 1999 to acquire Butterfield & Butterfield, the 134-year-old auction house, for approximately $260 million. A month later it bought Kruse International, the high-end automobile auction house.[6] Before these acquisitions, eBay had focused on collectibles that were worth less than $500. These new businesses signaled eBay's drive in hosting higher-value auctions. But more importantly, they also marked the beginning of the company's off-line strategy.

Regional Auction Strategy

In October 1999 eBay shocked the market again by creating yet another source of new revenue. It rolled out regional auctions in 10 new markets and the list continued to grow. For example, "the San Francisco site has a Grateful Dead section, bundled-up Minneapolis residents can buy ice-fishing equipment, and Atlantans might bid on Braves paraphernalia."[7] Through further segmentation of the auction market, eBay attempted to reach more customers and capture the share from smaller regional and niche market players.

International Expansion

As eBay continued to penetrate the auction market in the United States, it also planned to leverage its knowledge in this core market across international borders. In June 1999 eBay purchased alando.de, a German online trading community. In addition, the company developed separate Web pages for several communities abroad and mechanisms to allow cross-border trading. eBay had been building up its management team according to specific markets, including (1) Germany, Switzerland, and Austria, (2) the U.K., France, and Scandinavia, (3) Asia (Japan and Korea), (4) China, and (5) Australia and New Zealand.[8] It was expected that eBay would invest aggressively in these target markets to secure a leadership position in the online auction market.

THE FUTURE?

With the person-to-person auction market becoming increasingly competitive, Meg Whitman wondered what should be the next step for eBay. Although she repeatedly told the press that the strategy for eBay was to focus on the person-to-person (P2P) market, the opportunity to bring in name-brand partners to offer business-to-consumer (B2C) auctions certainly sounded attractive. Forrester Research predicted that while P2P auctions constituted 70 percent of 1998 online auction sales, B2C auctions would gain momentum and generate 66 percent of total online auction market revenues by 2003.[9] Competitors such as Amazon and FairMarket were already entering that market. Should eBay follow the lead?

Another opportunity for eBay was business-to-business (B2B) auctions. In fall 1999, eBay started offering a B2B sales category on its German auction site alando.de. In addition, eBay made a capital investment in a U.S. privately held company, Tradeout.com. Tradeout.com provided auctions for corporate surplus materials, a fast growing segment of the B2B auction revenues. These two investments provided eBay with a foothold into this new market, but the plan to aggressively pursue this business was still questionable.

Whitman also wondered about the sustainability of eBay's revenue model. With competitors like Yahoo! offering their auction service for free, could eBay justify its placement fees and commission on sales? How should eBay integrate its product and service offerings in the person-to-person market, and regional and international sites?

Notes

1. Carolyn Koo, "eBay Beats Estimates But Stock Takes a Bath," www.thestreet.com/_yahoo/brknews/internet/805387.html.
2. Linda Himelstein, "eBay vs. Amazon," *Business Week,* May 31, 1999, p. 128.
3. Cate T. Corcoran, "Does eBay Represent a New Way of Doing Business?" *Red Herring,* www.redherring.com/mag/issue69/news-auctions.html.
4. Ibid.
5. Jon G. Auerbach, "Internet Giants Pool Their Bids for Auction Site to Rival eBay," *The Wall Street Journal,* September 17, 1999, p. B1.
6. Christina Stubbs, "Internet Upstarts Are Acquiring Complementary Real-World Operations to Expand Their Markets," *Red Herring,* www.redherring.com/mag/issue70/news-physical.html.
7. Adam Lashinsky, "eBay's Not-So-Secret Strategy for World Domination," www.thestreet.com/comment/siliconstreet/805456.html.
8. Research on eBay Inc., Deutsche Banc Alex. Brown, August 11, 1999.
9. Evie Black Dykema, Kate Delhagen, and Carrie Ardito, "Consumers Catch Auction Fever," *The Forrester Report,* March 1999.

Microsoft: Xbox Online

Greg Canessa gazed at the Cascade Mountains as the evening sun settled in the west. Canessa, business development manager and lead planner for Microsoft's Online Games (and a lifelong gamer), was contemplating the outcome of the online strategy the team had selected for the console. The brief historical landscape of online video games was strewn with failed ventures, but Microsoft was counting on a new technology environment to create a golden era of global multiplayer interaction. For a company that could easily rest on its laurels, Microsoft was taking a huge and very public gamble that its new Xbox game console would become a centerpiece of delivering online gaming.

Microsoft was a behemoth in the software industry. The company frequently recorded more annual profits than the rest of the software industry combined and was sitting on a $36.2 billion war chest of cash.[1] By 2001, the ubiquitous Windows operating system ran nearly 95 percent of the personal computers in the world.[2] Since Bill Gates and Paul Allen founded Microsoft in 1975, the company had always been noted for being aggressive in defending its "home turf," and relentless in attacking new ones. However, this entry into the gaming business was Microsoft's biggest leap ever outside of its core software business, putting the company in an unfamiliar role as a consumer electronics and game maker.

Why was Microsoft betting so much on the home gaming console industry? The industry appeared to be attractive, but a respected competitor had recently exited the market. Was there enough market potential to justify Microsoft's hefty investment? Would online gaming provide a market opportunity for consoles? There were many PC gamers online, but fewer than 1 million were paying for access. Could the game console potentially reduce the importance of the PC? Sony was betting that the multimedia and online capabilities of the

This case was prepared by Ira Hall, David Ibrahim, Hemant Mandal, Clint Perez, Bryan Richards, and John Schumacher under the direction of Professor Allan Afuah at the University of Michigan Business School. Copyright © 2002 by McGraw-Hill/Irwin. All rights reserved.

PS2 would move the consumer away from the computer and in front of the television. Would the Xbox, with its advanced technology and online capabilities, trump the competition?

Greg leaned back and wondered whether the Internet-connected Xbox would preserve Microsoft's place at the top of the technology food chain for a third decade.

THE VIDEO GAME INDUSTRY

History

In 1975, an agreement between Sears Roebuck & Co. and Atari ignited the home video gaming industry. Sears gained exclusive rights to sell a console that played Pong to the home consumer, and, consequently, Atari reached overall sales close to $40 million.[3] This milestone marked the beginning of the highly profitable home computer and video game console industry. In the late 1970s, Atari launched the 2600, a gaming console that played games on cartridges. While not the first cartridge system, the 2600 was the first commercially successful console, with high sales and market penetration. Meanwhile, the precursor to modern online gaming emerged in the form of multiuser dungeons (MUDs), which offered users access to a shared adventure game over a computer network. Most MUD gamers were university students and research scientists from the 1970s through the 1990s.

In 1985, the introduction of the 8-bit Nintendo entertainment system propelled the mainstream consumer gaming industry to new heights. Soon thereafter, Sega launched its highly popular 16-bit* Genesis. In 1995 and 1996, game-hungry consumers rushed to purchase Sony's PlayStation1 console and Nintendo's N64, ushering in yet another generation of video game consoles. The industry reached loftier heights with the appearance of Sega's 128-bit Dreamcast console in 1999 and Sony's PlayStation2 (PS2) in fall 2000. The Dreamcast included a 56-kilobyte modem for online gaming and the PS2 allowed users not only to play games but also to watch DVDs and listen to audio CDs.[4]

Online Gaming

By the late 1990s, online gaming had begun to show potential for mass consumer appeal. According to the Interactive Digital Software Association (IDSA), approximately one-third of Internet users regularly played online games. Forty-three percent of those playing online games had been doing so for less than a year, a signal that this form of entertainment was in an early stage of growth. Seventy-nine percent of online gamers were between the ages of 25 and 55.

---

* The difference between 8-bit and 16-bit is a significant increase in processing power. Sixteen bit essentially doubles system power, allowing games to contain higher resolution graphics and better sound.

The IDSA study showed the potential of the online game market, but it also offered a cautionary note: 89 percent of those who played games online indicated that they were not willing to pay to do so, and only 1 in 10 online game players paid for a subscription to any of the online game services.[5] Leading technology analysts predicted that the American video game market would grow to $40 billion by 2003. They also forecasted that online gaming subscription revenues in the U.S. would grow from $270 million in 2001 to $4.6 billion in 2005.[6] Experts estimated 35.1 million people played online games in 2001.[7] By 2001, the two most comprehensive gaming websites were the Microsoft Game Zone ("the Zone") and EA.com, Electronic Arts' online and e-commerce business. The Zone and EA.com offered to connect PC gamers to other players who had the same game installed on their PCs. They also offered games directed toward families and casual players.

Industry Segments

While online gaming was beginning to attract attention, in 2000 the home video game industry consisted primarily of three main segments: hardware, software, and accessories. The hardware segment included game consoles (e.g., the Sony PlayStation), portable game players (e.g., the Nintendo GameBoy), and personal computers. The software segment featured the games that ran on the hardware. The accessory segment consisted of game controllers and other peripherals. Online communities had just entered the stage. These communities ran games through the Internet but did not sell hardware or software. In 2000, industry revenue breakdown was 70 percent software, 20 percent hardware, and 10 percent accessories.[8]

Business Models and Pricing

Software generated 70 percent of the total revenues for the home video game industry. Console manufacturers sold hardware for minimal to negative margins and then earned higher margins on sales of video games and accessories for the consoles.

Historically, console makers profited from this loss leader strategy in three ways:

1. Console manufacturers produced game software and earned revenues directly from the game sales.

2. Console manufacturers negotiated royalty agreements with third-party software publishers to publish games for their system. Console manufacturers received payments upon the sale of each game. Third-party software game sales accounted for 75 percent of all video game sales in 2000.[9]

3. Console manufacturers profited from selling accessories and peripherals for their systems. They also licensed rights to create accessories to third-party hardware manufacturers like MadCatz and Gameshark.

Industry observers monitored the success of the loss leader strategy through metrics such as the "attach rate." This rate measured the number of games sold for each individual console in a given year. The greater the attach rate, the greater the likelihood the console maker would achieve its profitability goals via the loss leader strategy. Exhibit 11.1 charts historical attach rates for three of the leading consoles from 1995 to 2000.

Online gaming communities were all PC-based to date and some charged subscription fees for the use of their services. For example, EA.com charged individuals a $10 monthly fee for each premium game title a user wanted to play online and allowed the user to play less popular games for free. In other cases, users had access to free online games, usually through an individual's private server. A gamer might host a game like Quake, with other users buying a CD version of the game and playing online through the host's server without additional fees. Under a third model, game publishers sold titles through retail stores and then matched gamers against one another at no additional charge. The gamers were responsible for finding servers and Internet connections through which they could play online. Games such as Blizzard Entertainment's Starcraft used this model, though the company's Battle.net website auto-assigned servers.[†]

Unique Online Gaming Challenges

As console makers, software developers, and online communities sought new online gaming opportunities, they grappled with two major points of uncertainty. These companies questioned how readily consumers would change their video game playing behavior. Gamers were accustomed to playing at

EXHIBIT 11.1
Historical Software Attach Rates
Retail Sales of Software Units Per Installed Hardware Base (units)

Source: NPD, Bank of America Securities LLC estimates.

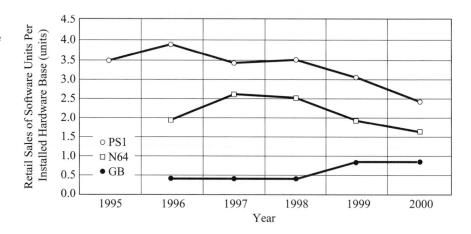

† Auto-assigning a server means the software picks the best server for the gamer. The choice of server is based on connection speed, server load, etc. Conversely, gamers may also pick the server they want to play on, perhaps because their friends are on it as well or for other reasons.

EXHIBIT 11.2
Narrowband versus
Broadband

Source: *McKinsey &*
Company, Narrowband
3/2000, Broadband 9/2000.

	Percent of Time Spent	
	Narrowband (15.9 hours/month)	Broadband (21.4 hours/month)
News	4%	4%
Consumer transaction	1	9
Community*	43	35
Entertainment**	14	32
Portals/ISPs	8	5
Other	19	15

*Includes e-mail, chat, personal Web hosting, and interest group.
**Composition of the time increase: gaming 75%; others (animation, multimedia, kids) 12%; sports 10%; adult sites 3%.

home by themselves or against visiting friends by simply inserting a disk or cartridge into the console and starting a game. They were used to using the Internet for Web browsing or electronic mail exchanges. Microsoft and its rivals were betting these individuals would comfortably move online to play against unseen competitors.[10] These companies were also uncertain about whether traditional off-line console gamers would pay to play for the extra features online gaming offered.

Online gaming also had to deal with varying qualities of connectivity to the Internet that dictated the type of online activity that could be reasonably expected. Low broadband‡ penetration restricted online gaming to parlor games that required little bandwidth over phone/modem lines (e.g., Solitaire). In 1997, two role-playing games achieved popularity online in the PC arena, primarily across narrowband modem lines. Electronic Arts' Ultima Online and Sony's EverQuest each attracted 200,000 to 250,000 subscribers at $9.95 per month. The combination of Ultima Online and EverQuest captured 55 percent of the $106 million online gaming market in 2000.[11] These online communities were counting on rising broadband usage to trigger heavy usage. By 2001, 21 million households had gained broadband Internet access.[12] See Exhibit 11.2 for differences in narrowband and broadband usage patterns.

COMPETITIVE LANDSCAPE

Microsoft's Xbox would face competition on various fronts. At the start of the 21st century, two players dominated the video game console market. Sony and Nintendo, both Japanese manufacturers, controlled roughly 70 percent of worldwide industry revenues in June 2001 through their PlayStation (1 and 2) and N64 lines.[13] The companies enjoyed extensive user bases, popular products, tremendous brand recognition, and widespread distribution.

‡ Broadband is considered any service that provides 128kbps bandwidth or higher.

EXHIBIT 11.3
Game Franchises

Source: NPD, Bank of
America Securities LLC
estimates.

Title	Publisher	Platform (1)
Crash Bandicoot	Sony	PS1
FIFA	Electronic Arts	PS1
Final Fantasy	Square EA	PS1
Gran Turismo	Sony	PS1
Madden NFL	Electronic Arts	PS1
Mario Brothers (2)	Nintendo of America	N64, GB
Tekken	Namco	PS1
Tetris	THQ (3)	GB
Zelda	Nintendo of America	N64

(1) Platforms listed represent those on which titles dominate; title may appear on other platforms as well.
(2) Includes all Mario games, including Donkey Kong.
(3) Formerly published by Nintendo of America.

Console manufacturers also faced competition from the video game software industry. Software accounted for 70 percent of the total industry's revenues in the U.S.[14] With the bulk of profits coming from royalties on video game sales, Sony and Nintendo published their own titles and relied upon third-party software developers to broaden the product line. While third-party support was vital for console survival, in-house and third-party games often competed with each other for sales. The third parties were responsible for 76 percent of all retail game sales with the remaining 24 percent coming from the manufacturers' in-house game development.[15] Competition in the software arena came from games developed by Sega, Electronic Arts, Activision, and Take-Two Interactive Software, among others.[16] Popular titles sometimes became "franchises" in their own right. Franchises commanded premiums for developers and even drove sales of consoles via increased user loyalty. See Exhibit 11.3 for a list of some popular game franchises.

Together the hardware and software companies competed for an $18.7 billion worldwide market in 2000.[17] With the 2000 release of Sony's PS2, the June 2001 release of Nintendo's GameBoy Advanced handheld system, and back-to-back launches of Microsoft Xbox and Nintendo GameCube in November 2001, the competition had reached an epic scale. "We are entering a golden age of video games!" exclaimed John Steinbrecher, CEO of Electronics Boutique Great Britain, a mall-based game retailer. "You get a big console release. You sell a lot of hardware that year. The following two years you sell a lot of software to support it. We have an 18-month period where there will be four console releases. That's unheard of in my 15 years in the industry."[18]

Online communities added a new twist to the video game industry. These communities frequently hosted video game competitions via the Internet that featured PC gamers from across the globe. MSN Gaming Zone, EA.com, and Gamespy emerged as early pioneers in this area. In addition, these sites offered free and subscription-based services that either complemented CD-based games or stood alone as entertainment products. EA's Majestic was one such product that combined a $9.95 per month subscription with CD-based content. Microsoft and Sony both saw potential for adding an Internet subscription model to their game consoles.

VIDEO GAME SYSTEMS

Sony

Sony towered over the video game system industry. Between 2000 and 2001, it had sold over 20 million PS2 consoles worldwide. Between PS1 and PS2, Sony had achieved 50 percent market share throughout the world, with its largest sales volume coming from the United States and Japan.[19]

Sony, a consumer electronics and entertainment colossus (with total dollar sales double those of Microsoft), distributed its products through national American consumer retailers (Wal-Mart, Best Buy, etc.), specialty gaming retailers (Electronics Boutique, Funco), online retailers (Amazon.com, etc.), and Sony's Playstation.com website.[20] Sony stimulated frenetic demand for PS2 by undersupplying its consoles during the October 2000 product launch, creating long lines and shortages to heighten consumer interest.

Sony began establishing an online gaming presence for its console in 2001. Sony partnered with Cisco Systems to offer high-speed Internet access and joined America Online in developing e-mail and instant messaging.[21] Sony aimed to get PS2 users online in 2002 through the sale of a broadband attachment for the console.[22]

Nintendo

Nintendo had successfully entrenched itself in the console market, displacing earlier manufacturers like Atari and Intellivision. Nintendo introduced the N64 in 1996, expecting this machine to be the market leader. To the industry's surprise, Sony's PlayStation1, introduced a year earlier, took the lead instead. Hobbled by reliance upon cartridges, the N64 endured higher production costs than Sony, which played games on cheaper, higher-memory CD-ROMs.[23]

Over the years, Nintendo's in-house development efforts spawned several popular franchises such as Super Mario Brothers, Zelda, and Pokemon.[24] Nintendo also expanded its scope with its wildly successful GameBoy handheld system. GameBoy sold 100 million units worldwide and controlled 95 percent of the handheld gaming market.[25]

By the fall of 2001, Nintendo was preparing to launch a new console, the GameCube. Applying lessons learned from the N64, Nintendo utilized proprietary DVDs instead of cartridges and planned to increase its portfolio through greater reliance upon third-party developers. In fact, only 2 of the 15 launch titles would be in-house games, the rest coming from external developers like Electronic Arts and LucasArts.[26] Additionally, Nintendo would leverage its installed base of GameBoy Advanced users by allowing the new GameBoy and Game-Cube to interact with each other.

Over 60 percent of Nintendo's consumers were under 18. The company intended to use that segment as a starting point for future growth. As one Nintendo executive explained, "Our goal is to keep the core demographic we're so strong in and build on it by having more games for older audiences. We'd like to keep them for a lifetime by getting them while they're young, but we want to compete in the entire market."[27]

GameCube also featured an expansion port for future modem/broadband adapter to permit play over the Internet.[28] Still, Nintendo showed little faith in this prospect. "The revenue model for online gaming is still uncertain," argued Atsushi Asada, executive vice president at Nintendo. "It may have some potential in the future, but it will take time. The infrastructure simply does not exist."[29] Nintendo was also concerned about its young core audience. These young consumers had little disposable income and no credit cards to buy online services.[30]

SOFTWARE

Through deals with companies such as Activision, Take Two Interactive, and LucasArts, the three console makers hoped to convince consumers they offered the greatest variety or quality of video games. Some deals were for exclusive rights to a game. Others were nonexclusive and allowed developers to create game versions for all three consoles. Each console manufacturer sought exclusive titles that could attract more consumers to its machines. Game margins for third-party developers are shown in Exhibit 11.4.

Sega

An international leader in the arcade and home video game industries throughout the 1980s and 1990s, Sega had recently fallen upon hard times. Sega was in the console business until its Dreamcast product, launched in late 1999, failed on the worldwide market. Although it sold 2.9 million units in the U.S., Dreamcast suffered from a lack of third-party developer support (EA did not develop games for Dreamcast). Additionally, its launch date was so close to PS2's that many consumers simply held out for Sony's product.

EXHIBIT 11.4
Game Gross Margins (Third-Party Titles) per Disk/Cartridge

Source: Company reports, Bank of America Securities LLC estimates.

	PS1	PS2	N64	PC	GameBoy
Retail price	$39.99	$49.99	$49.54	$54.00	$29.99
Wholesale price	32.00	40.00	42.00	40.00	22.00
Royalty and manufacturer costs	9.00	9.00	22.00	4.00	13.00
Gross income	23.00	31.00	20.00	36.00	9.00
Gross margin	70%	78%	47%	90%	41%

Dreamcast was the first product to offer Internet access through a built-in modem. Sega built SegaNet, an online network for Dreamcast players to play each other online, which cost $100 million to develop. While a first mover in online gaming for consoles, Sega ultimately suffered $420 million in losses in 2000 and terminated production of the console.[31]

In 2001, Sega decided to focus on developing games for Xbox, PlayStation2, and the GameCube.[32] Sega agreed to produce 13 games for the Xbox during 2001 and signed agreements to provide additional gaming software for both PS2 and GameCube. All three console makers sought Sega's software due to the company's groundbreaking success in building three-dimensional graphics and voice-recognition software into video games. According to an executive at Electronics Boutique: "There's good will toward Sega from consumers. The quality of their game play is top-notch, and they have great franchises."[33] With high quality games, Sega could draw many consumers toward the Xbox, or it could lure them toward PlayStation2 or GameCube.

Electronic Arts

With $1.3 billion in annual revenue, Electronic Arts (EA) was the top independent game publisher worldwide. EA was known for successful sports franchises such as FIFA Soccer, Madden NFL Football, and NHL Hockey, which had large followings in the console market. EA was also known for PC games, including Ultima Online and The Sims (developed through its Maxis subsidiary). EA had the resources to develop games for all three next-generation consoles at once. Microsoft, Nintendo, and Sony all expected to win console buyers and software royalties through the games, but it was not clear whether consumers would gravitate toward one console or another based on the fact that EA planned to produce for all three. All three manufacturers hoped to sign agreements for exclusive rights to certain EA games in the future.

Companies like EA emphasized both online and off-line gaming. Even though console games sold more, the game product life cycle was much shorter than that of online games. The typical life cycle of an off-line console game was six months as compared to several years for an online game. On average, a company such as EA would invest $10–20 million to develop a high-quality game. Developers could prolong life cycles by offering upgrades and updates. Even if companies initially sold fewer copies, they could expect residual revenues for several more years.

ONLINE COMMUNITIES

AOL Time Warner

Sony partnered with AOL Time Warner to create a broadband strategy that would bring AOL's electronics, media, and communications businesses to Sony devices via four gateways: TVs, PCs, PlayStations, and mobile phones. Under the agreement, Sony would incorporate AOL tools and features into the

PS2 platform, enabling consumers to use instant messaging, chat, and e-mail on their gaming systems. The alliance provided Sony with access to AOL's 32 million online subscribers and Time Warner's 12.7 million cable television subscribers.[34] AOL Time Warner also owned substantial content in the form of magazines, movies, music, television, and the Web. In addition to the Sony alliance, AOL had an existing online entertainment agreement with Electronic Arts, which ran the AOL games channel.

Yahoo!

Yahoo! created and maintained its own online gaming site for members of the Yahoo! community. With 2.8 million users per month, Yahoo! Games tended to offer low-tech parlor games like backgammon and hearts that could be played with other members of the community.[35] While Yahoo! had no plans to create a community for more sophisticated PC and console gaming, it did have an alliance to manage, maintain, and cobrand with many of Sony's websites.

Other Online Communities

Many smaller gaming communities existed on the Internet with varying degrees of success. Some communities like Gamespot (owned by Ziff-Davis Publishing) and Adrenaline Vault existed as game information services, posting game reviews, previews, and forums for players to communicate with each other. Other communities were more robust, offering software that allowed gamers to connect to and play each other online. Gamespy was one such community, offering Gamespy Arcade for Windows PC users.

XBOX CONSOLE

The future of gaming starts today, and it starts with Xbox. Xbox is a key part of our strategy to drive the digital entertainment revolution and deliver the future of interactive entertainment to the home. It's a great example of how Microsoft is innovating. But, most important, it's incredibly cool.[36]

—*William H. Gates III, CEO of Microsoft*

Xbox Launch

Against the backdrop of stiff competition, Microsoft muscled its way onto the scene with a $500 million marketing campaign and a rumored $2 billion in development costs. Microsoft entered with only a modest history in designing video games for PCs, with 4 percent market share for the PC game industry.[37] Microsoft had no experience in manufacturing game consoles. Even so, the company brought its Xbox to market in mid-November of 2001 and garnered high initial praise from the industry and gamers alike.

Sony watched Microsoft's entry with a combination of confidence and concern. The Japanese rival wondered whether its new competitor might fundamentally alter the industry. Sony CEO Kunitake Ando cautioned, "The biggest threat to PlayStation2 is that the Xbox changes the industry's life cycle. It is unclear how long we can keep [our] business model." Traditionally, consoles sold in five-year product life cycles, allowing manufacturers time to recover startup costs for hardware, but Xbox might reduce the life cycle to three years or even less. Similarly, if Sony were to respond by unveiling a PlayStation3 on a shortened production schedule, it could jeopardize Microsoft's ability to recover the Xbox's high entry costs.[38] In the meantime, Sony prepared to defend its flagship product with a $750 million worldwide marketing assault and an army of gaming software developers.[39]

Factors Fueling the Xbox Launch

Industry analysts pointed to three major factors driving the company's product launch decision:

- **Booming industry.** According to Bank of America, the industry would generate $18.7 billion in revenues during 2001—more money than the entire Hollywood movie industry would generate that year.[40] The revenues would derive from the sale of video game consoles, console games, personal computer games, and arcade games. The U.S. market alone was worth $8.1 billion in 2000.

- **Trojan horse strategy.** Video game consoles demonstrated a growing breadth of functionality. In the 1999 Comdex trade show, Sony CEO Nobuyuki Idei declared, "The PlayStation2 is more than a game machine. It can be more than a communications product . . . more than a personal computer!"[41] This statement concerned Microsoft executives. In 2001, Microsoft's Windows software loaded on consumer PCs was the company's fortress into the home market, with 95 percent market share in operating systems. Sony's statement signaled a new threat to this dominance. Perhaps Sony would soon offer a potent substitute to the home PC, directly challenging Microsoft's lock on the home market.

- **Supplement PC revenue stream.** The PC industry was in its fourth decade and as such was beginning to show signs of saturation and maturity, lowering growth rates and hurting profitability.

Building the Box

With design feedback from developers, the Xbox team set out to engineer the actual console. The company had to overcome two major hurdles. First, its competencies were firmly grounded in software development, not hardware. Second, PS2 had a one-year head start. The Xbox team had to create a quality product quickly before Sony's PS2 built an insurmountable lead in the market.

Microsoft first focused on deepening its team. The company scored a coup by hiring away two Sony veterans, Toshiyuki Miyata and Naoto Yoshioka, to work on designing and developing the Xbox. Both men had been instrumental in the launch of PlayStation1, and they would greatly shorten the development process.

Next, the Xbox team faced a critical design decision: Should the console's internal chips be created from scratch; use existing, off-the-shelf technology; or use some mixture of the two? The biggest concern was the console microprocessor. Sony had partnered with Toshiba to design and manufacture custom microprocessors for its consoles, while Nintendo had partnered with IBM. These companies engineered their microprocessors from the ground up to achieve high-quality CD sound and fast processing of complex graphics. Though creating a custom processor might seem ideal, development time and costs dictated otherwise. Microsoft settled on a processor already on the market, the Intel 733 MHz Pentium III, which was slightly modified for the Xbox. The Intel chip also guaranteed that the system would be able to run a stripped-down Windows operating system.

Using a Windows/Intel environment had three beneficial effects. First, Microsoft could shortcut a lengthy and expensive operating system development process by just adapting its established Windows 2000 software. Second, developer tools would be more "PC-like," giving some game programmers an instant familiarity with the design process. Third, Windows-based tools would draw in PC game developers who had never created or ported games to consoles before. "We can do our next Doom on the Xbox, but it won't run on the PlayStation2," explained John Carmack, cofounder and owner of id software, the company responsible for the wildly popular Doom and Quake series for PCs.[42]

Microsoft contracted NVIDIA Corp. to manufacture a derivative of its high-end GeForce3 chip for graphics processing. One of the most costly components to the system, the NVIDIA chip allowed the Xbox to render polygons[§] at twice the speed of PS2. Other off-the-shelf components would allow the Xbox to get to market quickly while trimming development costs.

Cracking the Consumer Electronics Business

Microsoft now sought to enter a market dominated by two highly respected companies, Nintendo and Sony. Over the past 20 years, the console gaming industry had existed as a duopoly, with two console makers dominating the market at any given time. Microsoft had some experience in the PC gaming and peripherals space, but home consoles would present a different set of challenges for the organization. On top of that, Microsoft sought to penetrate the online gaming sector, which had its own set of competitive dynamics.

---

§ Polygons are the most basic element in creating 3D video game graphics. Programmers can greatly increase a game's realism by "painting" more polygons per scene.

For Microsoft to build a sustainable and profitable Xbox customer base, it faced issues regarding:

- Target market
- Developer support
- Competitive pricing
- Product differentiation

Identifying a Target Market

Both Nintendo and Sony had been successful because they realized early on who their target consumers were. Nintendo attracted children and adolescents, typically aged 6 to 14. The Sony PlayStation1 and PS2 attracted older, more casual gamers aged 18 to 34. Both companies' consoles also sold well beyond their target markets. Significant crossover existed between age groups and levels of interest.

After lengthy discussions, Microsoft decided to position the Xbox to attract older gamers, aged 18 to 34. Market research indicated that these players were key influencers for younger players. By targeting this segment, Xbox would compete head to head with PS2.

Priming the Developer Pump

To concentrate on bringing Xbox successfully to market, Chief Xbox Officer Robbie Bach moved his handpicked team from the company's main headquarters to its own office a few miles down the road from the Microsoft campus headquarters. This move allowed Bach's team to focus solely on developing the Xbox apart from Microsoft's famously strong culture.

Traditionally, Microsoft was a tough negotiator with software developers, extracting very favorable terms. In the console market, the tables turned. Microsoft had little market power in video games, but desperately needed a network of third-party developers. Ed Fries, VP of games publishing, pushed the organization from dictating terms to listening to developers:

> We were the new guys, and everybody was really anxious to tell us what was frustrating and limiting about the development process with the existing consoles. Then we went out and built the system they said they needed to make great games.[43]

The Xbox team not only abandoned the company's usual hard-nosed tactics but also consulted with industry game developers for nearly a year before beginning design work. By fall 2001, Microsoft had signed agreements with over 200 companies to develop games for the Xbox. Sony had approximately 300 developers at that time. Microsoft's contractors ranged from small development firms to powerhouses like Activision and Electronic Arts.

While the Xbox team seemed to be attracting significant interest in the developer community, the question still remained about how to differentiate the console from the PS2 and GameCube. After all, major developers could easily place their bets on all three consoles to maximize their profits and hedge their bets against any one console failing. Without differentiating factors, there would be little reason for consumers to buy the Xbox, especially from an untested newcomer. Gamers would likely continue flocking to the PS2 with its huge installed base of titles and backward compatibility with PS1 games.

Pricing against Competition

The Xbox would enter the market at a price of $299, believed to be a $125 per unit loss for Microsoft.[44] The GameCube would enter the U.S. market at $199 during the same week as the Xbox, and Sony was already selling its PS2 for $299 in the U.S. To remain competitive, Microsoft would have to monitor how the market responded to the aggressive GameCube pricing, and how Microsoft priced online services and accessories for the Xbox.

Achieving Differentiation

To differentiate itself from the pack, Xbox's design team inserted an Ethernet port for broadband Internet access and an 8-gigabyte hard drive directly into the console. Broadband access would allow Xbox users to play games online, talk to other gamers over the Internet, surf the World Wide Web, and download game enhancements. The hard drive would allow users to store digitized music, create and save personalized game scenarios, load detailed graphics more quickly, and add other applications to Xbox in the future.

Not to be outdone, Sony announced the release of a broadband/hard-drive add-on module for the PS2 for early 2002. Users would have to purchase the module at an additional cost, estimated to be between $100 and $150. Nintendo also planned to release a broadband adapter for the GameCube at some point in the future but was intent on developing an online gaming strategy first. Clearly, the next battleground for console manufacturers would be fought online. However, add-ons traditionally sold poorly in the console market, never penetrating more than 20 percent of the installed user base. Exhibit 11.5 provides some of the differences between the Xbox, GameCube, and PlayStation 2.

MICROSOFT ONLINE GAMING

Getting into the Zone

Electric Gravity, Inc., created the Internet Gaming Zone in October 1995. With slow connection speeds, the website offered turn-based games such as bridge and chess to about 1,500 gamers. Microsoft purchased the Zone—as it

EXHIBIT 11.5   Product Spec Comparison

Source: *Deutsche Bank Alex Brown, "Microsoft: Innovating Beyond Windows," September 25, 2001.*

	Microsoft Xbox	Nintendo GameCube	Sony PlayStation2
Hardware cost	$299	$199	$299
Average game cost	$49.99	$49.99	$49.99
Games available (expected by Christmas 2001)	15	7	130
Central Processing Unit speed	733 MHz	405 MHz	295 MHz
Graphics processor	250 MHz	202.5 MHz	148 MHz
Polygon/second	116.5 million/second	6–12 million/second	66 million/second
Audio channels	256	64	48
Online gaming	Yes (broadband)	Optional	Expected (broadband)
DVD playback	Optional ($29 remote)	No	Yes
RAM	64 MB	43 MB	40 MB
Built-in hard disk	8GB	No	Expected (40GB)
U.S. release date	November 15, 2001	November 18, 2001	October 2000

was casually known—in June of 1996. AOL and CompuServe had also offered similar gaming options for several years. Meanwhile, *Doom* by id Software was taking the PC gaming world by storm. This program offered fast-paced, first-person, shoot'em-up style action, and, for the first time, a killer app for online gaming. The game allowed players to fight each other in real-time. (Exhibit 11.6 shows a software value chain while Exhibit 11.7 shows an online gaming value chain.)

In 2001, the Zone was the largest online gaming site on the Web. Choices for entertainment ran the full spectrum from puzzle and card games for beginners, to complex strategy and action games such as MechWarrior for hard-core players. The site counted more than 22 million gamers as members, with 800 weekly tournaments and 130 games.[45] Many of the major game titles even had annual online championships that crowned supreme gamers and awarded $50,000 prizes. For nine of the titles, Microsoft offered individual subscriptions ranging from $1.95 for 24-hour access to $99.95 for a year.

A game development and publishing unit, the Zone.com and the Xbox formed Microsoft's Games Division. This division was separate from the MSN division, though there were overlapping interests and technologies. The MSN website was the home page for Microsoft's Internet Service Provider (ISP) arm. From all outward appearances, the Zone.com fit smoothly into the MSN general site. Microsoft's aim was to offer exciting content and a compelling community, thereby driving Internet users to MSN.com.

EXHIBIT 11.6 **Software Value Chain**

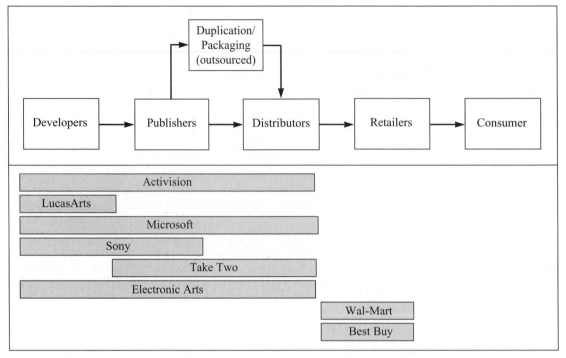

Developers: Game developers design and write the software code for video games.

Distributors: Game distributors warehouse and ship the game titles to small- and medium-sized retailers, and ship direct to consumers (i.e., fulfillment) for some websites.

Publishers: Publishers produce, market, and distribute the titles created by the developers. Most publishers are also developers and distributors. Some analysts also estimated that publishers themselves develop 50 percent of all game titles. This trend is due mainly to the fact that in-house development of software is more profitable than third-party software, and publishers desire a steadily growing inventory of titles.

Retailers: Retailers are the front-end to the consumers. The major retail distributors, like Wal-Mart, have a growing influence and are demanding greater discounts on game titles.

Widening the audience also required MSN to put a more beginner-friendly face on the site. According to Eddie Ranchigoda, a product manager for the Zone.com, "We've always had a strong hard-core following, but in the last year or so we've really seen a spike in casual gaming, mostly due to our puzzle games. . . . Casual gamers tend to "turn and run" when they see a registration process or a dark, gloomy hard-core gaming site."[46]

Microsoft Television Interests and Investments

Microsoft's other foray into consumer electronics was in the cable television and direct broadcast satellite market. Microsoft offered a digital video recorder/interactive television appliance known as Ultimate TV for sale to consumers.

EXHIBIT 11.7 **Online Gaming Value Chain**

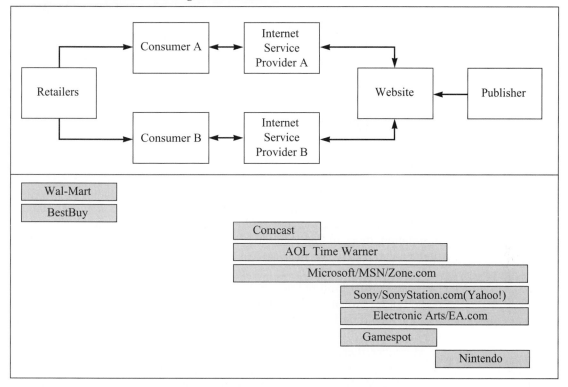

Retailers: Retailers are the front-end to the consumers. The major retail distributors, like Wal-Mart, have a growing influence and are demanding greater discounts on game titles.

Internet Service Provider (ISP): ISPs provide consumers the means to access the Internet. This is accomplished with dial-up or broadband modems on the consumer side and connection/hosting hardware on the ISP end (modems, servers, etc.). Comcast is an example of Broadband-only service provisioning through their cable network.

Website: These are Web-based communities that host games, usually charging a monthly fee for premium games. Gamers can meet and play interactively by using local PC game CDs or by using a browser online.

Publishers: Publishers produce, market, and distribute the titles created by the developers. Most currently available games have online gaming codes built in to allow interactivity. Publishers provide technical support and cobranding to online communities.

In 2001, the company offered the product to DirecTV satellite cable service subscribers only. For the television system operators (cable companies, satellite companies, terrestrial broadcasters), Microsoft offered the Microsoft TV platform. The platform allowed system operators to develop a variety of interactive TV services for consumers, including e-mail, Internet, interactive programming, electronic program guides, and digital video recording.

Additionally, Microsoft invested in various system operators. Microsoft made a $3 billion investment in Telewest, the number-two cable TV operator in the United Kingdom, a $1 billion investment in U.S. cable operator Comcast Corp, and a $5 billion investment in AT&T.[47] Microsoft also publicly announced its intention to support either Comcast or Cox Communications in the bid to buy the AT&T Broadband cable business, the largest cable operator in the United States.

WHERE TO GO FROM HERE?

Canessa noted that "the Zone is really the only successful example in the games business of a 'hybrid gaming site'—meshing a web-based card, board, and puzzle game experience for casual gamers with a premier PC gaming destination for hard-core gamers." It might be unwise to upset this successful formula. On the other hand, the Zone.com could return to its roots as a hard-core player destination, more in line with the Xbox demographic. Could Microsoft MSN find a balance between mass appeal and gamer cool?

With complete system control and significant influence over developers, Microsoft might limit online Xbox play to the Zone. Alternatively, Microsoft could opt for an "open" platform allowing players to choose any online community, including EA.com. Theoretically, this would allow Xbox consoles to play against PS2, GameCube, even PC gamers.

Moreover, there was a question of pricing. Only a handful of MSN's games had subscription pricing and those games generated little in the way of revenues. The MSN division compounded the challenge with expensive pricing schemes for broadband access, $39.95 per month for 10 hours, $1.50 each additional hour.[48]Although the Zone could generate more revenues through a subscription model, gamers might not be willing to pay additional fees. Conversely, offering free access would generate a huge community, but Microsoft's profits would hinge on volatile banner ad revenues. Could either model compensate for losses Microsoft incurred on console sales?

Now that the Xbox had launched, Greg knew there would be tough decisions ahead. As he turned back to his desk, he thought about how to capture his ideas in a memo to his boss.

Notes

1. Microsoft 10-K. September 30, 2001.
2. Deutsche Bank Alex. Brown Analyst Report, September 25, 2001, p. 19.
3. Donald A. Thomas, Jr., "I.C. 1977," www.icwhen.com; revised 1/12/01.
4. Stanley A. Miller, "Gaming Experience," *Milwaukee Journal,* November 20, 2001; "State of the Industry Report," *Interactive Digital Software Assoc.,* 2001.
5. "State of the Industry Report."
6. Rodney Chester, "X Marks the Spot," *Courier Mail,* November 17, 2001.

EXHIBIT 11.8   Xbox Financial Data[1]

Source: Composite of data from various media, broker, and market research sources including Bank of America, Deutsche Bank, Lehman Brothers, and case writer analysis.

	FY '02	FY '03	FY '04	FY '05	FY '06
Console Sales					
Unit sales (# of Xbox units sold in millions)	4	10	11	12	13
Console Prices and Costs					
Retail price per unit	299	249	249	249	199
Wholesale price per unit[2]	209.3	174.3	174.3	174.3	139.3
Production cost per unit	350	300	250	250	250
Operating Income					
Operating $ loss per unit	−140.7	−125.7	−75.7	−75.7	−110.7
Total operating $ loss on console sales	−562.8	−1257	−832.7	−908.4	−1439.1
Software Game Sales ("Attach Rates")					
Unit game sales per customer in first year of a customer's Xbox ownership	3	3	3	3	3
Unit game sales per customer per year after first year of Xbox ownership	1	1	1	1	1
Software Game Prices and Costs					
Retail $ price per unit	49.0	49.0	49.0	49.0	49.0
Production $ cost per unit[3]	36.3	36.3	36.3	36.3	36.3
Operating Income					
Operating $ margin per unit	12.8	12.8	12.8	12.8	12.8
Total operating $ profit on software game sales	153	578.5	1,106.75	1684	2,310.25
Total Operating Income					
Total operating profit or loss	−409.8	−678.5	274.05	775.6	871.15
Cumulative profit or loss	−409.8	−1,088.3	−814.25	−38.65	832.50

[1]Microsoft's fiscal year ends on June 30.
[2]Assume wholesale price is 70 percent of retail price.
[3]Assumes 75 percent third-party software sales with royalties of $7/game for Microsoft and 25 percent sales of in-house software with $30 gross margin for Microsoft.

7. Jupiter Media Metrix.
8. Bank of America Analyst Report; May 5, 2001, p. 30.
9. Bank of America Analyst Report; May 5, 2001, p. 35.
10. Ibid.
11. Bank of America Analyst Report, May 2001, p. 68.
12. Alorie Gilbert, "Report: Broadband Home Users Jump," *News.com,* December 11, 2001.
13. Deutsche Bank, September 25, 2001, p. 19.
14. Bank of America Analyst Report, May 5, 2001, p. 30.
15. Bank of America Analyst Report, p. 35.
16. Larry MacDonald, "Video Games Are Hot," *Montreal Gazette,* November 21, 2001.

17. Bank of America Analyst Report, May 5, 2001, p. 29.

18. Catherine Wheatley, "Good at Games," *The Independent* (London), June 13, 2001.

19. Jane Black, "This 3-Way Slugfest Is No Game," *Business Week Online,* December 13, 2001.

20. Lila LaHood, "Scoring the Game," *Fort Worth Star Telegram,* October 27, 2001.

21. Melanie Farmer, "PlayStation Wins More Net Support," *CNET News.com,* May 16, 2001, http://news.cnet.com/news/0-1006-200-5945953.html.

22. Alex Pham, "Where the Net's Your Playing Field," *Los Angeles Times,* November 8, 2001.

23. Sharon Pian Cain, "Let the Games Begin," *The Seattle Times,* October 25, 2001.

24. Ibid.

25. Ibid.

26. Tom Ham, "Have a Super Monkey Ball with the Cube," *Washington Post,* November 16, 2001.

27. Sharon Pian Cain, "Let the Games Begin."

28. Alex Lau, "GameCube Stripped for Action," *The San Francisco Chronicle,* November 14, 2001.

29. Paul Abrahams, "Gaming War Faces Fresh Battles," *The Irish Times,* May 25, 2001.

30. Alex Pham, "Where the Net's Your Playing Field."

31. Stanley A. Miller II, "Gaming Experience," *Milwaukee Journal Sentinel,* October 25, 2001; Alex Pham, "Sega to Charge for SegaNet Access," *Los Angeles Times,* October 25, 2001; and Kelly Zito, "Corporate Spotlight: New Path for Sega," *The San Francisco Chronicle,* August 12, 2001.

32. Tommy Cummings, "Sega Sports Titles Go Multiplatform," *The San Francisco Chronicle,* November 22, 2001.

33. Kelly Zito, "Corporate Spotlight: New Path for Sega."

34. Frank Robert, "Who Will Sign Up for AT&T Broadband?" *The Wall Street Journal,* December 13, 2001.

35. Nielsen/Netratings, June 2001.

36. Rodney Chester, "X Marks the Spot."

37. Prudential Financial Analyst Report, p. 7.

38. Paul Abrahams, "Gaming War Faces Fresh Battles."

39. Ibid.

40. Dean Takahashi, "The Game of War," *Red Herring,* November, 2001.

41. James Surowiecki, "The Paranoia Principle," *The New Yorker,* November 26, 2001.

42. Dean Takahashi, "The Game of War."

43. David Becker, "It's a New Playing Field for Microsoft," *Zdnet,* November 15, 2001.

44. "Can Xbox Save Xmas?" *Lehman Brothers,* November 12, 2001.

45. Bill Hutchens, "Microsoft's Zone.com Offers Easy Intro to Online Games," *The News Tribune,* November 2, 2001.

46. Ibid.

47. "Software Giant to Pay $3 Billion for British Concern," *Reuters,* October 23, 1999.

48. MSN website on 11/15/01.

Case **Twelve**

Sun Microsystems: Jumping for Java

In the past, power and success in the computer industry all boiled down to who controlled the key technological choke points. . . . Customers don't want that kind of industry domination anymore. . . . That's why Java is different. Sun is leading it, but by design nobody really owns it.

—Irving Wladawsky-Berger, IBM's Internet czar and chief Java strategist

Scott McNealy, CEO of Sun Microsystems, was thinking about the future as he walked back to his office. He had just met with Alan Baratz, president of Sun's JavaSoft subsidiary, to discuss Sun's next move regarding Java, the company's platform-independent programming language. Since its launch in May 1995, Java had been a rousing success. It was adopted more quickly across the software industry than any other new technology in computing history. Realizing its potential, many of Sun's competitors, including Microsoft, had rushed to license Java. Sun currently had over 200 licenses outstanding and 900,000 software developers working on new applications.

Java's proliferation had quickly convinced Microsoft that the "write once, run anywhere" software represented a real threat to its entrenched Windows monopoly. McNealy had boasted about the demise of Windows and how Java would be running on everything from cell phones to household appliances. Sun held to the belief that large networks of Java-enabled devices powered by massive servers would someday render the PC obsolete. Microsoft began to move aggressively to counter Sun's every move. They were able to persuade

New York University Stern School of Business MBA candidates Sarah Bennett, Eric Berman, Hally Burak, Jonathan London, and Sujatha Shan prepared this case under the supervision of Professor Christopher L. Tucci for the purpose of class discussion rather than to illustrate either effective or ineffective handling of an administrative situation. Copyright © 2001 by McGraw-Hill/Irwin. All rights reserved.

thousands of software developers to use Microsoft's version of Java. Sun continued to win the battles, but who would win the war?

As McNealy sat down in his office, he contemplated Sun's next move. Java represented a major part of Sun's future success. Its continuing development would spur sales growth for Sun's Internet servers, software tools, and microchips. In the past, Sun's tall promises, late releases, and tight grip on Java development had allowed Microsoft to counter Java. Now other partners were beginning to follow suit. What began as collaborative agreements with partners to make Sun's Java the standard programming language was quickly evolving into a struggle for control over development. McNealy considered the consequences of giving up some of this control.

SUN MICROSYSTEMS

Sun was regarded as "the last standing, fully integrated computing company, adding its own value at the chip, [operating system], and systems level."[1] The company first made a name for itself by making high-powered computer workstations, but was better known for building the servers and software that power the Internet. Sun's major products included the UltraWorkstation, Solaris Operating Environment, Sparc Microprocessor, and Java and Jini Connection Technologies (see Appendixes 12.1 and 12.2). In 1996 Sun was generating nearly $1.3 billion in revenues from server sales. Driven by the rapid growth of the Internet and increased demand for networked systems, the server market reached quarterly sales of over $16 billion in 1998 (see Exhibit 12.1). As Sun's server business flourished, intense competition and shrinking margins began to erode the company's core workstation business. Despite these pressures, the company

EXHIBIT 12.1   **Server Industry Market Share**

Source: IDC Research, 1999.

Vendor	4th Quarter 1997	Market Share (%)	4th Quarter 1998	Market Share (%)	Growth
IBM	$ 5,234	31%	$ 4,553	28%	−13%
Compaq	1,430	8	2,072	13	45
Hewlett-Packard	1,782	11	1,886	12	6
Sun Microsystems	**1,275**	**8**	**1,508**	**9**	**18**
Fujitsu	766	5	776	5	1
NEC	630	4	638	4	1
Dell	319	2	603	4	89
Siemens	381	2	599	4	57
Hitachi Ltd.	693	4	500	3	−28
SGI	392	2	271	2	−31
Others	4,038	24	2,796	17	−31
Total market	**$16,940**	**100%**	**$16,202**	**100%**	**−4%**

still managed to increase product revenues by $856 million or 11 percent in 1998, following a 21 percent growth year in 1997 (see Exhibits 12.2 and 12.3).

Sun was founded in 1982 by a group of four young pioneers brought together by a shared vision of decentralized, heterogeneous computing systems. In 1987 Sun adopted the slogan, "the Network is the Computer" to promote this open-systems philosophy. McNealy described Sun's vision as:

> a networked computing future driven by the needs and choices of the customer. It is a vision in which every man, woman, and child has access to the collective planetary wisdom that resides on the network. . . .[2]

McNealy's pugnacious attitude helped define Sun's culture in its early years. He promoted a coach/team-like atmosphere in which head-to-head competition was encouraged, and was quoted as saying, "If everyone believes in your strategy, you have zero chance of profit." Those who worked for him saw him as an inspirational corporate rebel who "made you want to win one for the gipper." Those who competed against him recognized his belligerent charm; one anonymous competitor told an industry publication, "Sun sells UNIX, a boring techie thing. You think if not for McNealy they'd be so successful and have so much name recognition?"[3]

THE BIRTH OF JAVA[4]

With the technology market booming in the early 1990s, a group of Sun's top computer programmers grew restless and thought about leaving the company. Included among them were programming gurus James Naughton and James Gosling. Keenly aware of their value to Sun, McNealy sat down with the two and made them an offer they couldn't refuse: The company would give them

EXHIBIT 12.2
Sun Microsystems Revenues

Source: *Business Week*, January 22, 1996.

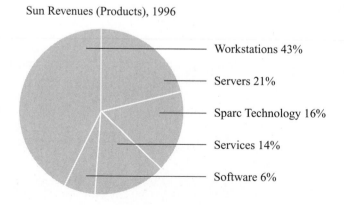

Sun Revenues (Products), 1996

Workstations 43%

Servers 21%

Sparc Technology 16%

Services 14%

Software 6%

EXHIBIT 12.3   **Abbreviated Financial Statement (in $000s)**

Source: Company SEC filings.

	Years Ended June 30,		
	1998	**1997**	**1996**
Net revenues:			
Products	$8,603,259	$7,747,115	$6,392,358
Services	1,187,581	851,231	702,393
Total net revenues	**9,790,840**	**8,598,346**	**7,094,751**
Growth	13.9%	21.2%	N/A
Cost of sales:			
Products	3,972,283	3,790,284	3,468,416
Services	721,053	530,176	452,812
Total cost of sales	4,693,336	4,320,460	3,921,228
Gross margin	52.1%	49.8%	44.7%
Research and development	1,013,782	825,968	653,044
Selling, general, and administrative	2,777,264	2,402,442	1,787,567
Purchased in-process R&D	176,384	22,958	57,900
Operating income	1,130,074	1,026,518	675,012
Margin	11.5%	11.9%	9.5%
Gain on sale of equity investment	—	62,245	—
Interest expense, net	(46,092)	(32,444)	(33,862)
Income before income taxes	1,176,166	1,121,207	708,874
Provision for income taxes	413,304	358,787	232,486
Net income	**$ 762,862**	**$ 762,420**	**$ 476,388**
Other data:			
Total assets	$5,711,062	$4,697,274	N/A
Total debt	$ 47,169	$ 100,930	N/A
Total stockholders' equity	$3,513,628	$2,741,937	N/A
Estimated number of stockholders	341,000	289,000	N/A
Total employees at year end	26,343	21,553	N/A

a team of top software developers with the freedom to pursue whatever they wanted. The only requirement was to make something "cool."

Rising to the challenge, Naughton and Gosling went into self-imposed exile with their new team, code-named Green, at a site miles from Sun's headquarters in Palo Alto, California. There they were no longer distracted by the everyday workings of Sun's office. The team was referred to as a modern-day version of the scientists on the Manhattan Project. They were intrigued with potential opportunities in the consumer electronics market that could make it possible for household consumer devices to communicate with each other. With this in mind, they set to work trying to create a language that would allow TV devices, such as a universal remote control and an interactive set-top box, to interact seamlessly. Meeting with little success, Gosling realized that the usual computer languages were too bulky and unreliable to program these types of devices. He began to develop a new, streamlined language called Oak, named for a tree outside his window. The Green project continued to evolve into a Sun-owned company called FirstPerson.

In 1993 the National Center for Supercomputing Applications introduced Mosaic, and the World Wide Web was born. FirstPerson recognized that the seamless programming language it had been unsuccessfully trying to apply to consumer electronics was well suited for online media. Sun began to market the product as a "language-based operating system," meaning the system itself became the product instead of part of a device. By March 1995 Oak had become known as Java.

WHAT IS JAVA?

Java is software for writing programs that can run on any device connected to a network. Unlike other programming languages such as C, C++, Pascal, or BASIC, which depend on an underlying operating system, Java can run on any operating system and on any computer. This unique versatility means that people working on completely different operating systems can work on the same document or play the same game as long as the program is written in Java. This is a fundamentally different vision of computing from the PC and fits perfectly with the World Wide Web's way of doing things. In essence, the Web is what Java was designed for—to be a network application—fitting into Sun's vision of the network as the computer (see Exhibit 12.4).

JAVA IN THE MARKETPLACE

Java was poised to affect the technology market in four important ways.

Versatility

Java's "write once, run anywhere" capability would enable programmers to create a single piece of software that could be understood by any major operating system. This would significantly cut development time for individual programs and expand the market potential of a program. From a programmer's perspective, this meant that all operating systems would be equal. Computers would interpret each line of Java code separately and translate it for the operating system. In turn, the operating system would translate the code for the microprocessor chip.

Savings

Java would not only cut development time, but also help users save money. Java would significantly reduce creative, distribution, and transfer costs because its applications run on any kind of computer.

EXHIBIT 12.4   **An Architectural View of Java and Jini Technology**

Source: www.sun.com.

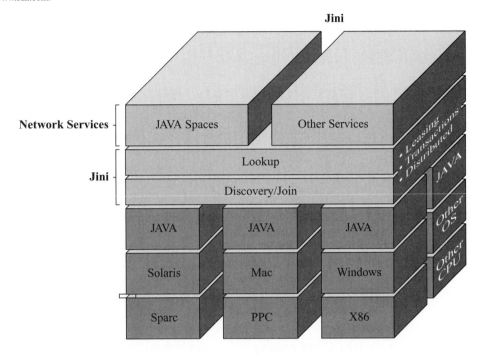

Competition

Java would make it possible for a new class of cheap network computers to compete with the elaborate Wintel operating system. According to McNealy, this was a pipe dream come true: "We always thought we were onto something with Java—that it was our one big chance to challenge Microsoft and change the economics of the business."[5]

Providing "the Dot in .Com"

With the dawning of the Internet age, perhaps the most important implication of Java is that it would adopt the role of the language best suited to the Internet. By nature, Java doesn't discriminate against specific machines and is inherently virus proof.

EXPLOITING JAVA

If the standard gets fragmented then Java fails.[6]

—*Ken Morse, chief technology officer of Power TV, Inc.*

Alliances and Partnerships

To exploit Java's full potential, Sun entered into a series of alliances and partnerships. In its quest for ubiquity and market acceptance, rather than profitability, Sun killed its own HotJava browser to enter a licensing agreement with Netscape. In September 1995 Netscape launched Navigator 2.0 with support for Java applets, giving Java unprecedented market penetration and a major presence on the Web. Several companies, including Oracle, Novell, and IBM, recognized Java's potential for network computing in the Internet age and embraced Java, hoping it would blunt Microsoft's hegemony. Appendix 12.3 lists the strategic alliances in which Sun was engaged.

Microsoft had initially dismissed Java's potential as overblown, but quickly reversed its position. In March 1996 Microsoft licensed Java for its Internet Explorer 3.0, which touted the best Java performance of any browser at the time. However, Sun's victory was limited. When Microsoft launched Internet Explorer 4.0 in 1997, it contained a Java source code optimized for Windows. This meant that certain Java applets would run smoothly only on Internet Explorer. Java as a standard universal language was under fire.

The Creation of JavaSoft

In January 1996 Sun announced the development of a new strategic business unit named JavaSoft. Its mission was "to develop, market, and support Java technology and products based on it." The overarching goal was to work toward building Java into an OS. This involved decreasing Java's association with UNIX and making it "cross-platform" as the architecture promised. JavaSoft was staffed by 100 people broken into developer services, products, and marketing. They received additional help from 200 volunteers working on developing the Java platform. By 1998, however, JavaSoft began to turn its sights away from platform development, moving to office application development, much to the chagrin of large and small third-party developers such as IBM and WebLogic.

RECOGNIZING JAVA'S WEAKNESSES

Sun's vision for the office application market was that all kinds of programs written in Java would reside on networks. Instead of a PC, offices would use bare-bones network computers. When employees needed to use an application, such as a word processor, they would download the application from the network, use it, and then the program would disappear. By centralizing software rather than duplicating it on individual terminals, businesses would reduce the costs of upgrading and fixing mismatched or corrupted systems.

Implementing this vision was not easy for Sun. Customers found that Java office applications had limited functionality and were unstable. The Java Virtual Machine, an "environment" that sat between the Java program and the machine it was running on, did not behave consistently across all computing platforms. This made it difficult for Java to live up to its versatility and speed claims. Java's "write once, run anywhere" technology meant that applications catered to the lowest common denominator. Thus, Java applications tended to run slower than programs honed for platforms like Macs or Windows. Additionally, many companies had already made a significant investment in the Windows platform and were not receptive to rewriting all of their software to be compatible with Java.

THE FUTURE OF JAVA

The WebTone

Sun continued to pursue its mission to make Java the platform for a "platform-less" technology. The company's future strategy was to supply all of the hardware and software necessary to build a 100 percent reliable Internet system—much like the dial tone offered by telecom companies. McNealy explained this concept of "WebTone":

> Information will become a utility, rather than people having a mainframe on their desk. . . . That's why so much of our effort this year has been directed toward what we call the WebTone—computing that's as powerful as a supercomputer, yet as reliable and as easy to use as a telephone.[7]

Open Licensing Agreements

Sun maintained its philosophy to offer open licensing for Java. This meant that other technology companies could develop their own versions of Java, provided that it passed the "100 percent Pure Java test." Open licensing agreements spawned more than 900,000 third-party software developers including IBM and Borland. These 100 percent Pure Java programs competed directly against Sun's package, the Java Development Kit. In 1998, Sun's revenue from licensing had reached $130 million.[8]

Internet Alliances

Sun continued to promote Java as the language of the Internet. In November 1998 the Internet community was rocked by news of a merger between AOL and Netscape. Behind the deal was a strategic alliance between Sun and AOL. Barry Schuler, president of America Online Interactive Services, explained:

> There are two big phenomena that make this strategic alliance a compelling opportunity. First, consumers are coming online in droves, accelerating e-commerce. Second, businesses are embracing network computing on top of Internet standards as the architecture for all of their back-end systems. That's what this strategic alliance will do: enhance the value chain all the way from silicon to eyeballs.[9]

Microsoft

In a world of manias and emotions, I have to make rational decisions. Someone who thinks that because a language is magic, these guys can overthrow the world—that person can't even think two chess moves ahead. You're not even in the game I'm playing.

—Bill Gates, on the possibility that Java
will make Windows obsolete, 1996.

Scott McNealy's continuous belittling of Windows NT has added fuel to the competitive fire between Sun and Microsoft. Microsoft had begun an all-out assault against Java, influencing thousands of software developers to use its Windows-optimal version. Moreover, Microsoft Research developed its own Windows-optimal virtual machine based upon technology acquired through its purchase of Colusa Software.

In 1997 Sun sued Microsoft, alleging that the company had violated Sun's license to use Java and was "polluting" the technology by distributing incompatible software tools and systems, including versions of Windows. In October 1998 Sun won the first round of the legal dispute when a federal judge issued a preliminary injunction ordering Microsoft to make its Java products compatible with Sun's Java. However, the victory was limited. The court ruled that Microsoft could still ship versions of its development tools to third-party developers and was still free to distribute Java versions developed independently from Sun's technology.[10]

SUN'S DILEMMA

While McNealy continued to pitch Sun's audacious "WebTone" vision to Wall Street analysts, the standard that Sun had worked so hard to develop themselves seemed to be slowly slipping away:

- In November, Sun archrival Hewlett-Packard (H-P) announced the creation of the Real-Time Java Working Group (RTJWG) consortium of Internet companies to develop real-time application program interfaces (APIs). RTJWG's claim was that Sun was tardy in developing Java's real-time capabilities and that Sun's licensing fees were excessive.[11]

- Longtime allies IBM and Novell began to complain that Sun's licensing restrictions were too tight. IBM specifically wanted more control over how Java interacts with its own legacy systems. Frustrated, Novell teamed up with Intel to develop an "optimized" version of Java.

- Microsoft enlisted the aid of Hewlett-Packard to codevelop its own version of Java. Shortly thereafter, Microsoft and H-P targeted Sun's Jini by developing a Java-based version of Microsoft's Universal Plug and Play (UPNP) software. Jini is a Java-derivative programming code that enables "dumb" devices like cell phones to communicate with a network.

With Microsoft building momentum and longtime Sun allies growing impatient, McNealy knew that Sun had to act decisively. He also knew that Sun could not win the Java war alone. There was no doubt that Java's future was uncertain and Sun was vulnerable. McNealy kept thinking of the popular film *The Godfather* and the infamous words of wisdom spoken by Don Corleone to his youngest son: "Keep your friends close, but your enemies even closer."

Notes

1. John Doerr of Kleiner Perkins, quoted in David Kirkpatrick, "Meanwhile, Back at Headquarters," *Fortune,* October 13, 1997, p. 82.
2. www.sun.co.uk/jobs/graduates/.
3. Darryl K. Taft, "Top 25 Executives: Scott McNealy," *Computer Reseller News,* November 17, 1997, no. 764, pp. 108–110.
4. The story of Java's birth taken from the following articles: Jason English, "The Story of the Java Platform," November 16, 1998, java.sun.com/java2/whatis/1996/storyofjava.html; Kevin Maney, "Sun Rises on Java's Promise," *USA Today,* February 28, 1999, www.usatoday.com/life/cyber/tech/cta838.htm; "Where Did Java Technology Come From?," www.sun.com/java/comefrom.jhtml.
5. Brent Schlender and Eryn Brown, "Sun's Java: The Threat to Microsoft Is Real," *Fortune,* November 11, 1996, p. 165.
6. Power TV, Inc., is a consumer software toolmaker.
7. Robert D. Hof, Steve Hamm, and Ira Sager, "Sun Power," *Business Week,* January 18, 1999, p. 64.
8. Sun Microsystems, Inc., 1998 *Annual Report.*
9. Sun press release, March 30, 1999, www.sun.com/smi/Press/sunflash/1999-03/sunflash.990330.1.html.
10. Steven Shankland, "HP Works to Reverse Sun Java Victory," *CNET News,* March 26, 1999, aolsvccomp.cnet.com/news/0-1003-200-340418.html.
11. Mary Jo Foley and Deborah Gage, "Vendors Wrestle to Control Java," *Sm@rt Reseller,* April 2, 1999.

APPENDIX 12.1   Terminology

Source: www.sun.com.

The "Virtual Machine"

The breakthrough application of Java was its capability of creating a "virtual machine" (VM). In essence, the VM is an abstract computer that sits between the Java program and the computer it operates on, executing Java code and guaranteeing certain behaviors regardless of the underlying hardware platform.

100% Pure Java

100% Pure Java is Sun's Java language without the embellishment of other companies' designs. The 100% Pure Java initiative was formed as a reaction to competitors like Microsoft who made versions of Java that ran better in certain environments and on certain platforms. 100% Pure Java stands for Sun's commitment to a platformless Java that treats all systems equally.

Jini

Jini is a Java-based language that allows computers and devices to quickly form impromptu systems unified by a network. The system is a federation of devices, including computers, which are simply connected. Within a federation, devices are instantly on—no one needs to install them. Similarly, you simply disconnect devices when you don't need them.

Solaris

Solaris is a 32-bit and 64-bit UNIX operating environment for enterprisewide computing. For users who value distributed network computing, Common Desktop Environment (CDE) for Solaris offers a high-performance, industry-standard desktop environment.

SPARC Technology/SPARC Families

SPARC is the flagship processor family for Sun. SPARC is characterized by design simplicity, allowing shorter development cycles, smaller die sizes, and ever-increasing performance. The SPARC architecture enables a unique combination of semiconductor and design scalability. With its multiprocessor capabilities, high bandwidth support, and register window design, the SPARC design allows implementations through a range of price/performance levels. SPARC processors achieve a higher number of instructions per second with fewer transistors.

APPENDIX 12.2   Sun Product Portfolio

Source: www.sun.com.

Management Solutions

- System Management
- Intranet Management

Support Solutions

- Educational Services
- Professional Services
- Online Support Tools

Development Solutions

Workshop Development Products
- Java WorkShop
- Sun Visual Workshop for C11
- Project Studio

Java Products
- Java Developer's Kit (JDK)

Deployment Solutions

Desktop Computers
- JavaStation Network Computer
- Ultra Family of Workstations
- Creator and Creator3D Graphics Stations
- Sun Elite3D High-end Graphics Station

Servers
- Sun Enterprise family of servers
- Sun Enterprise Starfire data center
- Netra family of dedicated file servers

Storage
- Sun StorEdge family of mainframe class and desktop storage products
- Components and Boards
- UltraSparc
- picoJava

APPENDIX 12.3   Strategic Alliances and Licensing Agreements

Source: www.sun.com.

Computers/Information Services

- IBM

Consumer Electronics

- Sony
- Samsung

Digital and Wireless Communications

- Alcatel
- Nortel
- Motorola
- Ericsson
- Siemens-Nixdorf

Electronic Commerce/Internet

- AOL/Netscape

Enterprise Resource Planning

- Baan
- Oracle
- PeopleSoft
- SAP

Interactive Television

- OpenTV
- Scientific Atlanta

Java Development Tools

- IBM
- Symantec/H-P
- Borland
- BEA Systems

Network Software

- Novell

Case **Thirteen**

OSCar—The Open Source Car Project

Markus Merz's head was aching. Maybe he'd had one beer too many. The first "OSCar Come Together" had ended in a long night out at the Wurstmarkt, an Octoberfest-style fair in the Southern German town of Bad Dürkheim. The meeting had been a great success. Car developers and designers who had formerly known each other only via e-mail met for the first time to exchange ideas in a direct and personal way.[1]

During the day's discussions, they had been able to agree on many important issues of OSCar, the Open Source Car project. The OSCar project was unique from the start. As a community of automobile developers, their primary goal was to design and develop a car over the Internet.[2] It seemed possible for the project to succeed. Still, after the meeting, the most important question remained unsolved: How could they turn this idea into a profitable business? Markus looked to the traditional automobile manufacturers for answers.

TRADITIONAL AUTOMOBILE DESIGN AND DEVELOPMENT: AN INDUSTRY IN FLUX

At its inception, the OSCar project was satisfying an important market need. Markus thought about the signals he was seeing in the marketplace with regard to the development of new cars. At the DaimlerChrysler Innovation Symposium in October 2000, Hans-Joachim Schopf, head of development for Mercedes-Benz reported that "in the past ten years, development productivity

NYU Stern School of Business MBA Candidates Elena Blankman, Suzanne Escousse, Achim Schillak, Lisa Schmidt, and Melissa Slotnick prepared this case under the supervision of Professor Christopher L. Tucci for the purpose of class discussion rather than to illustrate either effective or ineffective handling of an administrative situation. No part of this publication may be used or reproduced without written permission of the Berkley Center. Copyright © 2002 by Christopher L. Tucci. All rights reserved.

(of automobiles) doubled while the average development time for a new production series had been cut in half, despite the increasing complexity of the process."[3] When the industry's leading figures predicted that development time would be reduced by another 25 percent, Markus saw this as confirmation that the traditional methods of automobile manufacturing would need to be reevaluated.

To meet the ever-increasing needs for shorter development cycles, the automobile industry was in the midst of fundamental changes. Consumers wanted more features to choose from when they purchased new cars so auto companies worldwide continuously reinvented their designs. Thus, speed to market became the primary focus of many automobile manufacturers.

The traditional development of automobiles was not flexible enough to accommodate this rapid speed to market. Traditionally, manufacturing was dependent on a lengthy set of laborious processes and little or no input from anyone but the most senior executives. Recently, however, car companies recognized that they had to overhaul these processes to meet the needs of their target markets.[4]

The industry was focusing on three primary initiatives:

1. **Centralization of car development.** Many companies had begun to implement more integrative manufacturing processes like concurrent engineering. New product development practices relied on implementing cross-functional teamwork through every stage of the development process. Contrary to the traditional approach where engineers were not privy to the design concept until just prior to production, this new approach ensured that all team members would be involved in every step of the manufacturing process. These insights showed Markus that the market was ready for a design concept that would promote the sharing of information while both reducing costs and increasing speed to market.

2. **Increasing complexity and communication needed during development.** To make the process of new product development more flexible, it was essential to successfully manage coordination efforts between engineers, craftsmen, employees, and suppliers. To facilitate this goal, many manufacturers found that bringing these capabilities in-house reduced dissention and quickened development time. Yet, Markus knew firsthand that many companies still didn't implement most of the suggestions made by their employees. This was the impetus for the OSCar project. Markus was acutely aware of the fact that firms still felt that it was better to rely on a web of suppliers and experts rather than to bring all these functions in-house. But, regardless of whether automakers chose vertical integration and a firm-centric focus or chose to rely on a small web of preferred suppliers, designers, and engineers, the process of building cars was no longer a static operation. With the increasing number of moving parts involved, controlling the process was no easy feat. This, thought Markus, was just another reason for automotive giants to give serious consideration to the OSCar concept.

3. **Implementation of the computer aided design (CAD) methods.** Markus had personally experienced the limits to the traditional approach while working for BMW. There, the product development process consisted of three major prototyping cycles—with each cycle requiring thousands of design prototypes.[5] Often costly and time-consuming, the creation of these design prototypes required that suppliers and manufacturers all have the equipment necessary to press the sheet metal needed for the car's production. This highly specialized process made it impossible to speed up development without jeopardizing craftsmanship. BMW was forced to adapt its traditional approach by using CAD models.

When BMW first began to implement the CAD system, traditional design experts praised the benefits of CAD models. By utilizing computer simulation, every aspect of production could be tested for functionality and safety earlier in the development process. This resulted in significant cost savings to the manufacturer.[6] Markus continued to muse. If the experts had seen the merits of CAD, then surely they would relish the OSCar.

The traditional approach to car manufacturing was fast becoming a thing of the past—and Markus hoped to capitalize on this trend.

OSCar: THE IDEA

The idea for the OSCar project was born during an Internet seminar in the autumn of 1999. A local politician was praising the blessings of the Digital Economy. In the audience, Markus stopped paying attention. A former marketing manager at BMW and CEO of a small consulting firm that provided e-business strategies to the car industry, Markus was no "Internet newbie" at all. However, he wanted to go beyond the usual e-commerce concepts. Markus was wondering how to apply the Internet to the automobile industry in a really new and creative way. Sure, e-procurement, e-commerce, and virtual market places started to change the way car manufacturers conducted their business. But wasn't there a way to go a step further? How could one use the World Wide Web to redefine the way autos were built and developed?[7]

In the software business, open source and open system models had started to revolutionize the business fundamentally.[8] Netscape had just made the source code of its browser software accessible to the public. Linux, the open system operating system, was considered as a reasonable alternative to established products of Microsoft, IBM, and Sun. Millions of computer programmers worldwide spent their free time working on these software products. An idea materialized in Markus's imagination. Why not do the same in the automobile industry? Why not design an open source car? Thus, the idea for OSCar was born.[9]

Car designers are a very special breed. They love cars. They live cars. From nine to five, they work in the office towers of DaimlerChrysler, Toyota, VW, and Ford. After work, they continue to think about cars. They continuously produce new ideas, design new car bodies, and create new engines. However, being just tiny gearwheels in the moneymaking machines of international conglomerates, most of their ideas are continuously ignored and never put into action. Moreover, there are millions of car enthusiasts all over the world who would love to contribute their ideas to develop new cars. So, why not use the Internet to collect all this creative potential for one worldwide car design project—the OSCar!

Markus knew that in the automobile industry, the design process had become one of the most elaborate and expensive phases in a car's development process. The actual manufacturing process, on the other hand, had become a commodity that often was outsourced to other companies. If the OSCar project led to a complete and feasible design of a new automobile, it should be possible to sell it to one of the major car manufacturers. Connecting the creative input of millions of car enthusiasts to one global development web could lead to a superior product, the car for the new millennium, the vehicle the established car manufacturers had never managed to develop.[10]

THE INITIATOR: MARKUS MERZ

Markus's career in the automobile industry had been somewhat unusual. Having been fascinated by cars since his childhood, he found his way to BMW as a visitors' guide for sightseeing tours at the company's Munich factory. From there, he jumped to BMW's marketing department in its German headquarters as well as in the American branch. In the early 1990s, Markus was the first one at BMW to embrace the idea of using CD-ROMs for multimedia marketing of the company's products. In 1995–96, he was involved in the development and launch of www.bmw.com, the company's highly acclaimed Internet presence.

In 1998, Markus left BMW to start Monocom, a boutique-consulting firm that delivered e-strategies and other consulting services to automobile companies, in particular BMW and its German competitors. Monocom's operations would facilitate the launch of the OSCar idea and provide the infrastructure for the OSCar project (i.e., office space, computer facilities, administration, and maintenance).[11]

THE OSCar MANIFESTO

Markus launched the OSCar project by writing a manifesto that attempted to structure and define the basic goals and principles of the project. This vision described the OSCar project as a development process without boundaries or limitations (see Exhibit 13.1).[12]

The basic rule of OSCar followed the open source principle of the computer world: Just as source code has no owner but is in the public domain, all design results of the OSCar should be freely available to everybody, that is, every member of the OSCar community. The entire community should make all major design decisions in a democratic manner. Everybody—including private designers, companies, universities, and other organizations—should be able to join this design community.

Furthermore, the manifesto defined that the first OSCar prototype should be developed within 36 months (see Exhibit 13.2).

EXHIBIT 13.1 **Excerpts from the OSCar Manifesto**

Source: OSCar website: http://www.theOSCarproject.org.

> "To build a car without engineering center, without a boss, without money, and without borders . . . but with the creative help of the internet community—that is the meaning of empowerment, the meaning of challenge, and the initial reason for the internet."
>
> "In the next 36 months we will together develop a car on the internet—the OSCar. This vehicle is to be free from barriers and competition. It will redefine mobility. . . . That is how I want to blow past the hype of the 'New Economy'—with OSCar."
>
> "We have an expandable forum that allows us to think and discuss about what OSCar means . . . about what OSCar looks like . . . about what kind of car we would like OSCar to be. We will join without regard to our past, our location, or what car manufacturer we like best. We will join together with a focus on the future—individuals, schools, colleges, companies, and hackers will join in and help define how we continue."
>
> "Engineers who are used to developing against other engineers might just find themselves in that same forum—working together to solve the same problems."
>
> "We will build the car as a web-based community. Without a boss . . . without hierarchies."

EXHIBIT 13.2 **Tentative Schedule for the Execution of the OSCar Project**

Source: OSCar website: http://www.theOSCarproject.org.

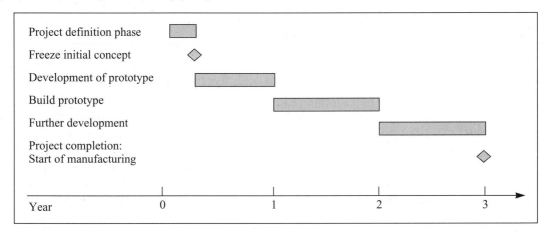

IMPLEMENTATION OF THE OSCar PROJECT

The heart of the OSCar project was its website, http://www.theOSCarproject .org. Markus and his team spent the first months thoughtfully designing and developing this site. Besides describing and advertising the OSCar project, the website was intended to be the communication medium for the developers. It offered various news groups, online chats, electronic whiteboards, forums, databases, and news servers that were designed to enable discussions and information exchange between auto experts. Having started entirely in German, the website soon was translated into the English language to allow car enthusiasts worldwide to participate in the undertaking.

The OSCar project was broken down into subprojects, following the typical structure from BMW. Every subproject—for example, engine, body (the "skin"), main frame, transmission, and electronics—had its own news group. The most important task for each discussion forum was to decide on a common platform.

To get a quick start, Markus found it necessary to strengthen the OSCar community by complementing the website with "real" meetings. Therefore, he initiated the "OSCar Come Together," a regular event where OSCar friends and developers from all over Germany met, socialized, and discussed their project. At this event, the first crucial decisions were made:

- The OSCar should be a modular concept—different design versions should be easily interchangeable.

- The OSCar should be a "world car"—simple, cheap, reliable, easy to maintain and repair.

- It should also be a high-tech tool—fun, innovative, full of features you would not find in a commercially available car.

- New, environmentally friendly engine types—for example, fuel cell, hydrogen, or electricity—should be taken into consideration.[13]

(Exhibit 13.3 shows several design outlines of the OSCar "skin," that is, the automobile's exterior design.)

DEFINING THE OSCar CAD PLATFORM

The OSCar team quickly discovered that a common CAD platform would be critical to the further progress of the project. In the international automobile industry, no software standard had yet emerged in regard to CAD programs. Almost every major car manufacturer used a different program. Because of this disparity, problems were apparent. While software tools were available to import/export data among different systems, this transfer always resulted in a loss of data. Furthermore, the professional autoCAD software ran exclusively on dedicated workstations. To allow car designers to work at home in their spare time, a CAD platform had to be agreed upon that would run on a personal computer.

EXHIBIT 13.3 **Early Concepts of OSCar's "Skin," That Is, Its Exterior Design—Artists' Views of the OSCar and Three-Dimensional Computer-Rendered Models.**

Source: OSCar website: http://www.theOSCarproject.org.

After many debates, the OSCar project team finally agreed to adopt CATIA, a CAD program that was also used by a large number of car manufacturers. The group even managed to identify a supplier of an open source clone of CATIA who would provide its program to the OSCar project. This choice was important in two ways. First, it allowed a large number of individuals to participate in the design process using tools they were acquainted with. Second, using CAD software that was industry standard enabled delivery of the final OSCar product to one of the major car manufacturers.

WHAT'S NEXT FOR OSCar?

Developing a Business Model

In the following months, the OSCar project continuously built momentum. The traffic on the OSCar website increased daily, as did the number of registered OSCar members. Car designers from all over Germany contributed concepts and discussed their ideas using the OSCar news groups and chat functions. These were mainly employees of the large Germany-based car manufacturers (e.g., Mercedes-Benz, BMW, Volkswagen, Ford, and Opel, a subsidiary of GM). Soon, an English website was launched to facilitate involvement from international developers. Companies sponsored and supported the project, and newspapers and radio stations ran stories about OSCar and its founder. Yet, Markus was facing the greatest challenge ever.

While OSCar had started as a personal vision as well as a public relations tool for his company Monocom, the project had now taken on a life of its own. It already occupied too much of Monocom's resources, including Markus's own time. To bring this idea to fruition, OSCar had to prove its viability as a profitable business for the long run.

The OSCar initiative surely created a lot of publicity for Monocom, but how could the company capitalize on this? Could there be money made by publishing and marketing the results of the OSCar project? Could Monocom achieve for the car industry what Red Hat had accomplished in the computer world when it started to publish Linux?

The OSCar organization knew it had its work cut out. It would be a formidable challenge to develop OSCar. But, even after it was developed, would anyone want the design? Everyone, and especially Markus, believed that the final design would have value. After all, it would be based on the best ideas in the industry and was clearly filling a market need. In addition, the design could be given to automobile manufacturers for free—why wouldn't they take it? There was one clear supposition that kept haunting Markus. The final OSCar design would be marketable only if it met the current needs of an automobile manufacturer. Markus had to make sure that OSCar attracted the attention of possible buyers. OSCar needed to be compelling enough with its modular design and fuel-efficiency to cause a major manufacturer to attempt to build it.

Markus knew he already had market momentum on his side. Several automobile manufacturers, including DaimlerChrysler/Mercedes-Benz, General Motors, and Ford had recently expressed difficulty in developing fuel-efficient cars with the capabilities of their current design teams.[14] An OSCar design should meet these needs. But fitting a specific design solution to a particular manufacturing facility would require moving away from the core OSCar ideals of open source and consensus design methods.

Markus and the rest of the management team began to mull over their options:

1. **An expanded OSCar line.** After the release of the first OSCar, the OSCar management team believed that the development concept could be used to accomplish many different goals. Utilizing open source development, OSCar could easily expand its online community to gain the expertise needed to develop the next generation of OSCars—whether a sport utility vehicle, a high-performance luxury car, or even an electric car. The fluidity of the OSCar developers would help change a company's capabilities to meet the market demand. Perhaps after OSCar gained credibility in the marketplace, future modular car designs could be *sold*.

2. **Partnerships and alliances.** In early 2000, Ford Motor Company had formed a joint venture with the women's community website *i*Village (www .ivillage.com), which allowed users to design "the car of their dreams" online. This way, Ford used the Internet as a channel to collect design suggestions from customers.[15] Obviously, the OSCar community of car enthusiasts and developers would be even more valuable. Therefore, another option for OSCar would be to pursue sponsorships and partnerships for the OSCar project. Notable sponsorship opportunities existed among the automobile manufacturers—just about any one of them could subsidize part of the OSCar project. In a way, each of the manufacturers is already sponsoring the project though indirectly, by having employees that contribute information and feedback while acting as OSCar developers in their spare time. The resultant community of developers may provide unexpected benefits to the automobile manufacturers since it serves as an idea exchange across firms.

   OSCar can also form business partnerships with consulting firms, marketing organizations, automobile suppliers, and component manufacturers. Since all of its current efforts are focused on design capabilities, OSCar must consider what other resources it needs in marketing and public relations services that it does not currently possess. Relationships with automobile suppliers and component manufacturers may be necessary if there are specific design features that are not adequately addressed during the open source design process.

3. **Consulting and value-added customization services.** Perhaps the largest potential revenue stream for the OSCar project will come from servicing and consulting revenues. Any automobile manufacturer that buys a design will not be as involved in the development process as they are in the typical development process. Therefore, the automobile manufacturers will need some advice on how to adapt the module to their specific needs and capabilities. But how exactly should the OSCar team construct the team to deliver these services? How should such services be priced?

There were other ideas that were being considered by the management team. One thought was to provide complementary services. For example, OSCar could offer its clients incremental additions to existing designs; they could develop research reports and recommend integration services and commercialization ideas.

As the day began to wane, Markus and his team wondered if they would ever be able to see OSCar available on the streets of Germany or anywhere else in the world. Further, they worried whether an automobile manufacturer that did adopt the modular design would agree to take on the risk of manufacturing. Markus couldn't help but ponder whether the OSCar project would ever become a profitable enterprise. Would automobile manufacturers be willing to give up control of their own product development processes? In today's competitive environment, the cars' unique design was seen as the secret that determined ultimate success in the market. Would a company be interested in building a car based on a generic design that was already known to the public? Would companies require exclusivity, or would they accept the fact that many manufacturers all over the world would be building "their" own OSCars?

On the other hand, having a functional, yet static, business model might jeopardize the success of the OSCar project. Auto enthusiasts were eager to participate in this project because they wanted to create a car that did ***not*** conform to established traditions. Would the creation of a formidable business discourage and damage the "Robin Hood" attitude of the OSCar community? Would Markus ever be able to transform www.theOSCarproject.org into www.theOSCarproject.com?

EPILOGUE

In a recent speech to shareholders, a high-level manager at DaimlerChrysler made a standing offer to support the OSCar project. Without mentioning OSCar or its founder directly, this DaimlerChrysler executive pointed out that his company would "support an open source car project in any way possible."[16] Would Markus become the Linus Torvalds of the automobile world?

Notes

1. Lukas Neckermann, *Interview,* New York University, Stern School of Business, October 27, 2000.
2. Radio broadcast, August 23, 2000: Antenne Bayern, Germany, *"OSCar— Das erste Internetauto"* (OSCar—the first Internet car), www.antennebayern .de/antenne/news/auto/rubrik/oscar/index.html.
3. Hans-Joachim Schopf, *DaimlerChrysler Innovation Symposium* (Sindelfingen, Germany), November 8, 2000.
4. Eric Taub, *Taurus: The Making of the Car that Saved Ford,* New York: E. P. Dutton, 1991.
5. Stefan Thomke, "BMW AG: The Digital Auto Project," Harvard Business School, January 14, 1999.
6. Ibid.
7. www.theoscarproject.org/english.html.
8. "Open-Source-Auto: Linux als Vorbild," *Linux-Magazin* (Germany), August 2000.
9. www.theoscarproject.org/english.html.
10. *"Das babylonische Automobile"* (the Babylonian automobile), www .heupferd.de/babylon.htm or www.stern.nyu.edu/~tucci/heupferd.html.
11. Lukas Neckermann, in an interview, New York University, Stern School of Business, October 27, 2000.
12. www.theoscarproject.org/english.html.
13. Michael Rieken, *OSCar Konzeptvorschlag,* (OSCar concept proposal), http://home.t-online.de/home/Michael.Rieken/oscar.html.

14. Larry Armstrong, "Honda's New Hybrid Laps the Field," *Business Week,* www.businessweek.com/bwdaily/dnflash/feb2002/nf2002027_2656.htm, February 7, 2002.

15. Debbie Reiching, Senior VP Marketing and Research, *i*Village, *Corporate Presentation at New York University, Stern School of Business,* November 29, 2000; "Women's Auto Center—Design your Dream Car" www.ivillage.com/auto/dreamcar/dreamcar.html.

16. Lukas Neckermann, interview.

Case **Fourteen**

E*Trade: "A Lust for Being Different"[1]

If your broker is so great, how come he still has to work?

—early E*Trade ad

In the winter of 2002, analysts who followed the brokerage industry wondered if E*Trade would make it in an industry that was still unraveling following the adoption of the Internet by industry incumbents. E*Trade, led by CEO Christos Cotsakos, a high-energy Vietnam vet known for his wild antics, now faced incumbents such as Merrill Lynch that had embraced the Internet. Cotsakos's goal was to take a group of highly creative, supercompetitive people and mold them into a family.[2] Many analysts wondered if E*Trade had the right business model to compete in the evolving brokerage industry.

BROKERAGE INDUSTRY OVERVIEW

Online brokerages have revolutionized the retail brokerage industry. The costs of trading to the individual trader have fallen to rates unthinkable just 10 years ago. Easy access to quality information, round-the-clock availability, and newly aggregated trading communities are creating new opportunities for individual investors and changing the way brokerages do business.

In the securities industry, brokerages are intermediaries between investors, who make trading decisions, and exchanges, which execute the transactions. Exchanges can be a single location, such as the New York Stock Exchange, a loose network such as the OTC market, or an established electronic network such as NASDAQ. Brokers can also "internalize" an investor's trade by processing the transaction through their own inventory—the securities they own in-house.

This case was prepared by Mathew Cobbett, Christine Miller, and Chieko Tsunoda under the supervision of Professor Allan Afuah for the purpose of class discussion rather than to illustrate either effective or ineffective handling of an administrative situation. Copyright © 2002 by McGraw-Hill/Irwin. All rights reserved.

Brokerages perform four primary functions within the securities value chain. They match buyers with sellers, determine prices through their intermediation, provide liquidity to buyers and sellers, and provide information about the market to investors based on their experience (see Exhibit 14.1).

Online retail brokerages represent the third major transformation in the securities business since its creation. The first was the creation of full-service brokerage houses. Originally, traders served as both financial advisors and transaction handlers. These two functions eventually split into groups of specialists, those who executed transactions and those who provided financial advice to investors. Full-service brokerage houses incorporated both of these groups of specialists under one roof. They sought to expand the market for stock trading by opening offices staffed with financial advisors. Traders in established trading centers would provide information to branch office advisors who would help individual investors on "Main Street" invest their savings in stocks and bonds.[3] This revolutionary approach meant that it was no longer necessary to be located near a major trading center to participate in the stock market. The development of full-service brokerages occurred in the immediate postwar period. Merrill Lynch represented the traditional full-service brokerage.[4]

Full-service brokerages provided a new value proposition to individual investors. They created new products, reduced costs of information and transactions, and provided customer service and support. Revenue opportunities for the brokerages were in commissions, account management fees, other services fees, and interest income. By tapping a new market in the investing public and providing a wide range of services to them, full-service brokerages

EXHIBIT 14.1 **Retail Securities Industry Value Chain (Simplified)**

Source: M. Chen, J. Huang, D. Wong, and K. Wong, "From Wall Street to Web Street: The Impacts of the Internet on Retail Brokerages," Haas School of Business, December 19, 2000.

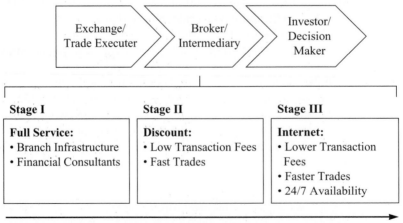

grew in size and power. They aggregated a huge amount of assets and controlled the flow of information to investors.[5]

The Securities and Exchange Commission's Act of 1975 permanently changed the securities industry by eliminating the fixed minimum commissions that brokerages were required to charge customers for the trade of listed stocks. Commissions could now be negotiated, resulting in lower prices for investors. Discount brokerage houses emerged, which charged lower prices for the execution of trades but also offered fewer services. The end result was the unbundling—again—of the financial services industry into transaction execution and financial advice. Trades could be executed for as much as 40 percent lower than at full-service houses.[6] Experienced investors, who did not need expensive advice, benefited from the lower prices. Novice investors could still obtain the advice from discount brokerages, but at a separate price. Charles Schwab represented the new breed of discount brokerage houses. Schwab aimed at "independent investors" who did their own research and did not want to pay for a staff of expensive financial consultants. Schwab's value proposition was reduced transaction costs, fast and efficient transaction execution, and a minimal amount of free consultation. Revenue opportunities for discount brokerages consisted of commission fees, interest income, and fees for other services. Discount brokerages tapped a new, more independent, type of individual investor and grew rapidly after 1975. Investors seeking faster transaction processing fled from full-service brokerages to the new discount houses.[7]

Each of these transformations was accompanied by the utilization of new technology. Schwab made a significant gamble in 1979; its technology investment at the time was worth $500,000, the value of its entire net worth.[8] The advent of computer telephony in the 1980s created new opportunities for the brokerage industry. The growth of the Internet in the 1990s provided new opportunities for E*Trade and other online brokerages, unleashing a third major transformation of the securities industry. By 2000, online transactions in the securities industry exceeded $1 trillion and represented over two-thirds of personal stock trades.[9] Online clients were expected to reach 14 million by 2003, with an estimated 35 million accounts. In 2000, the growth of online accounts exceeded that of off-line accounts. Online accounts now hold over half of the brokerage industry's assets.[10]

Many industries have approached the Internet with the intention of creating entirely new business models. For the securities industry, the Internet has meant another transformation similar to the two earlier transformations. The Internet further enhances geographic reach. Now, investors need not be near a brick-and-mortar branch office of an established broker. The Internet provides even faster execution of trades for online investors than a relationship with a financial consultant, and the lack of a branch office network lowers the barriers for online brokers, creating a highly competitive environment that pushes down costs to consumers. Low variable costs and unlimited geographic reach push online brokers to compete fiercely for a larger customer base over which to spread their high initial investment costs.

E*TRADE HISTORY

Trade Plus was founded in 1982 by entrepreneur Bill Porter, a physicist and inventor with over 12 patents to his credit.[11] Initially it was a service bureau on a private network providing online quotes and trading services to Fidelity, Charles Schwab, and Quick & Reilly. But Porter himself, an individual investor, wondered why he had to pay his broker hundreds of dollars for stock transactions. Combining this with his prediction that everyone would own a computer someday, he saw a need to allow individuals to make their own trades online.

On July 11, 1983, a doctor in Michigan placed the first online trade using technology developed by Porter's company. This led to the conception of E*Trade in 1992, the first Internet brokerage service. Initially E*Trade offered its online investing services through America Online and CompuServe. In 1996, the website www.etrade.com was launched and the demand for E*Trade's services exploded. The company now has over 3 million active accounts (twice as many as in 1999) and completes over 170,000 transactions daily.[12]

Christos Cotsakos, a decorated Vietnam War veteran and former Federal Express executive, was appointed CEO in 1996. Under his leadership the firm went public in August 1996 with a follow-on offering one year later. The company shifted into high gear, but there were hurdles for Christos. Computer failures resulted in E*Trade covering $1.7 million in customer losses when users were unable to gain access to their accounts. Computer backup systems were added. Technical glitches continued to hound E*Trade as the Internet volume grew and trading increased. In early 1999 "E*Trade stock prices were cut in half after its web site shut out traders and investors for hours."[13] The Securities and Exchange Commission reported a 330 percent increase in complaints concerning online investing in early 1999.

In 1997, E*Trade formed alliances with America Online and Bank One, ending the year with 225,000 accounts.[14] From there the firm took a global position. It expanded into Australia, Canada, Germany, Israel, and Japan. It now boasts four global divisions including North America; Latin America; Asia-Pacific; and Europe, Africa, and the Middle East. E*Trade is continuing to expand its global network with the inception of an exclusive agreement for staffed E*Trade zones and the world's third largest ATM network including installations at all traditional Target Stores and Target Greatland Stores across the United States. In April 2001, E*Trade opened a flagship bricks-and-mortar superstore in New York City. Acquisition of online brokerage firm Web Street was completed in August 2001. Web Street's corporate offices in Denver, Colorado, have been converted into another E*Trade financial superstore. Plans are in the works to create additional superstores in Beverly Hills, California; Boston; and San Francisco.

The E*Trade Group focused on entering the retail banking market in 2000. It bought Telebanc Financial and created E*Trade Financial. Telebanc Financial had a subsidiary online bank consisting of more than 100,000 depositors, which became E*Trade Bank. E*Trade Bank, the largest pure-play Internet bank, offers retail banking products on the E*Trade website. To further complement E*Trade Bank, the E*Trade Group acquired Card Capture Services (now E*Trade Access) by offering customers "real world" access to their money through a network of more than 10,000 ATMs across the United States. E*Trade Bank offers deposits, loans, credit cards, insurance, and other services. Most recently, E*Trade bought online mortgage originator LoansDirect and launched E*Trade Mortgage in June 2001.

VALUE PROPOSITION

"We're appealing to investors who do their own research and don't want to pay enormous brokerage fees," said Rebecca Patton, E*Trade's senior vice president of marketing.[15] Thus E*Trade's value proposition features cheap trades; no hassle, automated transaction execution; customized service and products; 24-hour account access; live telephone support; and easy access to research reports, resource links, tools and analysis, charts and news, customizable portfolio views, and checking and banking services. Their product offerings also include mutual funds, proprietary mutual funds, bond trading, automated teller machines, and the ability to access initial public offerings.[16]

E*Trade charges $14.95 a trade for listed market orders, such as those on the New York Stock Exchange, up to 5,000 shares. It charges $19.95 a trade for over-the-counter stocks, such as those listed on NASDAQ. Membership is free and includes free real-time quotes (up to 100 per day) and access to other tools and information. Opening an account with E*Trade gives customers the ability to place trades, get instant stock alerts, and apply for IPOs.

Customers open an account by filling out an application and making an initial investment of at least $1,000 for a cash account or $2,000 for a margin account. A welcome kit is mailed to the customer within 24 hours of receipt containing a user name and password along with an E*Trade quick investing guide. The account can then be accessed either online or by touchtone phone to begin investing.[17]

Customers place orders which are immediately transferred to the E*Trade computer system. The system verifies the account for adequate funds or the authority to trade on margin. Transactions are confirmed electronically and immediately posted on a Web page.[18]

MARKET SEGMENT

"E*Trade is truly separating from the other brokers," says analyst Gregory Smith of investment bank Chase H&Q. In just three years CEO Cotsakos has made E*Trade the number-two online stockbroker behind Charles Schwab. Cotsakos's drive has made E*Trade the fourth most recognizable brand name on the Web. It is ranked up there with Amazon.com according to Opinion Research Corp. International. Cotsakos is cutting deals so that E*Trade services can be zapped over cable TV, satellite TV, and wireless handheld gadgets. He wants E*Trade branded TV and radio programming.[19] E*Trade Group wants consumers to use its financial services for E*verything and marketing the E*Trade name has been a key component of its success. E*Trade is even developing a hip video game targeted at teenagers to help them learn about paying taxes, using credit cards, and managing their finances.[20] The E*Trade Bookstore through a link to Amazon.com offers CEO Christos Cotsakos's book titled *It's Your Money: The E*Trade Step-by-Step Guide to Investing.* These actions reflect E*Trade's awareness of a changing customer base.

When E*Trade began, the typical customer was an active, independent, empowered investor who was at ease with Internet technology. Low commission rates were attractive to these customers for two reasons, namely, they resented paying high brokerage fees and/or they traded frequently (five to six transactions per month), whereby savings in brokerage fees were significant.

To further grow, E*Trade has to continue to address new customer segments. E*Trade's next wave of customers will most likely be lower-volume traders, who are less price sensitive and are not as affected by the cost savings from trading electronically. They are less comfortable with Internet technologies and prefer the security of live telephone customer support. There is potential for these customers to be less profitable to E*Trade because they trade less frequently and the cost of attracting these customers and providing them with higher levels of service will be significant.

FINANCIAL OVERVIEW

In 2001, brand-name recognition and customer acquisition were the focal points of E*Trade's strategy to become a truly global, comprehensive online financial services company. Because customers still associate the Internet with some degree of uncertainty, customers look for brand names they know and trust. Over a two-year period, E*Trade spent $640 million on brand recognition and marketing; Schwab, which is 11 times the size of E*Trade, spent only $520 million in the same time frame.[21] High marketing and technology costs mean that economies of scale are a major factor for sustainability. E*Trade spent $50 million on marketing (down 50 percent from the same time the previous year), $20 million on technology development, and $55 million for general and administrative purposes during the third quarter of 2001.[22]

Competitors entering the deep-discount brokerage arena in the late 1990s forced E*Trade to renew its company strategy; E*Trade no longer offered the "cheapest" trades online. Board members needed to look beyond transaction fees for sources of revenue. Revenue from fees decreased in the second and third quarters of 2001 by two-digit numbers.[23] Therefore, the most important source of revenue became interest on customers' assets and investments. Interest contributes over half the revenues and is growing. Transaction fees contribute between 15 and 20 percent and are declining. Fees from other services such as banking, ATMs, and interest on mortgages and other assets represent other sources of revenue. (See Exhibits 14.2 and 14.3.)

EXHIBIT 14.2 **Balance Sheet for E*Trade: Fiscal Years 1994–2000 ($ thousands)**

Source: Disclosure, Inc., www.disclosure.com.

	9/2000	9/1999	9/1998	9/1997	9/1996	9/1995	9/1994
Assets							
Cash	175,443	157,705	52,776	38,235	50,141	9,624	692
Marketable securities	4,314,415	1,548,465	502,534	191,958	35,003	0	0
Receivables	10,715,262	5,136,585	1,365,247	724,365	193,228	1,936	535
Other current assets	0	0	24,287	6,970	2,203	470	623
Total Current Assets	15,205,120	6,842,755	1,944,844	961,528	280,575	12,030	1,850
Prop. plant & equip.	334,262	181,675	50,555	19,995	9,228	1,458	313
Net prop & equip.	334,262	181,675	50,555	19,995	9,228	1,458	313
Invest & adv to subs	985,218	828,829	59,276	5,519	2,860	676	0
Other non-cur assets	0	0	3,719	3,259	0	0	0
Intangibles	484,166	18,554	0	0	0	0	0
Deposits & oth assets	308,671	160,361	7,892	5,121	2,218	0	0
Total Assets	17,317,437	8,023,174	2,066,286	995,422	294,881	14,164	2,163
Liabilities and Equity							
Notes payable	3,531,000	1,267,474	0	9,400	0	0	0
Accounts payable	10,777,331	5,074,360	1,244,513	681,106	225,555	2,369	430
Cur long-term debt	0	0	0	0	0	0	1,314
Cur port cap leases	0	0	0	0	0	0	23
Accrued expenses	470,742	207,961	83,659	21,542	0	0	0
Income taxes	0	0	0	0	0	602	9
Other current liab	0	0	0	0	0	0	415
Total Current Liab	14,779,073	6,549,795	1,328,172	712,048	225,555	2,971	2,191
Mortgages	0	0	0	0	0	0	0
Deferred charges/Inc	0	0	704	0	0	0	0
Convertible debt	650,000	0	0	0	0	0	0
Long-term debt	0	0	0	0	0	45	64
Non-cur cap leases	0	0	0	0	22	0	0
Other long-term liab	0	0	0	0	0	0	0
Total Liabilities	15,429,073	6,549,795	1,328,876	712,048	225,577	3,016	2,255
Minority int (liab)	0	0	0	0	0	0	0
Preferred stock	31,531	30,584	3,000	0	0	1	0
Common stock net	3,101	2,838	2,313	399	295	149	150
Capital surplus	1,814,581	1,320,338	685,553	266,953	68,738	9,899	1,241
Retained earnings	−6,908	−26,060	33,786	16,022	271,	1,099	−1,482
Treasury stocks	0	0	0	0	0	0	0
Other equities	46,059	154,679	12,758	0	0	0	0
Shareholder Equity	1,888,364	1,482,379	737,410	283,374	69,304	11,148	−91
Total Liab & Net Worth	17,317,437	8,032,174	2,066,286	995,422	294,881	14,164	2,163

EXHIBIT 14.3 **Income Statement for E*Trade: Fiscal Years 1994–2000 ($ in thousands)**

Source: Disclosure, Inc., www.disclosure.com.

	9/2000	9/1999	9/1998	9/1997	9/1996	9/1995	9/1994
Net sales	2,157,958	955,470	335,756	234,128	48,991	23,340	10,905
	126%	185%	43%	378%	110%	114%	267%
Cost of goods	1,116,433	517,794	138,942	95,933	38,027	12,819	6,796
Gross profit	1,041,525	437,676	196,814	138,195	10,964	10,521	4,109
R&D expenditures	142,914	79,935	33,699	13,547	4,699	943	335
Selling, general, & administrative expenses	734,971	431,058	159,035	94,379	19,182	5,269	3,530
Income before depreciation & amortization	163,640	−73,317	4,080	30,269	−12,917	4,309	244
Depreciation & amortization	22,764	2,915	NA	NA	NA	NA	NA
Nonoperating income	−36,427	−7,174	−1,929	−946	13,529	NA	NA
Interest expense	NA	NA	NA	NA	NA	NA	NA
Income before tax	104,449	−83,406	2,151	29,323	612	4,309	244
Provision for income taxes	85,478	−31,288	224	10,130	−555	1,728	−541
Minority interests (Inc)	−181	2,197	NA	NA	NA	NA	NA
Extraordinary items & discontinued operations	NA	−2,454	NA	NA	NA	NA	NA
Net income	19,152	−56,769	1,927	19,193	1,167	2,581	785

ACQUISITIONS

E*Trade has acquired over 15 companies in the last three years. Early on, it acquired Clearstation.com, a community-based financial analysis site. They invested in E*Offering, a full-service online investment bank, and Archipelago, a leading electronic communication network (ECN).[24] E*Trade entered the stock market-making game with its acquisition of Chicago-based Dempsey & Company. eAdvisor is a venture with Ernst & Young to offer online financial advice. The company teamed up with State Street Global Advisors to offer college savings plans. E*Trade targets affluent customers with its premium trading and money management services offered through subsidiary PrivateAccounts.com. In addition, affluent clients have access to venture capital investments in young companies through E*Trade's alliance with Garage.com. E*Trade purchased Telebanc (now E*Trade Financial) with its more than 100,000 depositors and started E*Trade Bank, which offers retail banking services from the E*Trade website. Purchase of Card Capture Service (now E*Trade Access) gave E*Trade instant access to the third largest ATM network in the U.S. In May 2001, E*Trade purchased WebStreet.com, gaining physical locations in Boston, Beverly Hills, San Francisco, and Denver, and 34,000 active accounts. E*Trade entered the consumer lending market with its acquisition of LoansDirect.com (now E*Trade Mortgage).[25] In late October of 2001, E*Trade bank bought 33,000 customer accounts valued at more than $1.5 billion from Chase Manhattan Bank USA.

E*Trade has expanded its global presence through alliances and acquisitions. It purchased VERSUS Technologies, a Canadian-based firm providing electronic trading services. The company teamed up with UBS Warburg to allow non-U.S. investors to buy U.S. securities without needing to trade in dollars. E*Trade now has subsidiaries in Africa, South Africa, Asia, Germany, Japan, Sweden, United Kingdom, and other locations.

COMPETITORS

The securities industry is classified into three segments; full-service brokerages, discount brokerages, and pure-play online brokerages. The success of E*Trade in 1996 attracted the attention of the discount brokerage segment. Full-service brokerages showed no interest in online trading until later.

Charles Schwab

Charles Schwab established its online trading services in 1997 and is well known as the top online trading company (see Exhibit 14.4). In the first year, Schwab had the highest number of accounts and transactions. From the beginning, Charles Schwab had a long-running interest in trading with the use of communication tools. Schwab started both "Tele-broker" services using touch-tone telephones and online trading through personal computer connections in 1989. However, Tele-broker provided only basic, limited services, such as reference services and simple buy-and-sell orders. At that time, few people used personal computer communications, which impeded the reach and impact of its online trading services.

Although Charles Schwab provided online trading by private lines, it hesitated to provide services through the Internet because credibility and security were questionable. Schwab did not see the Internet as an appropriate marketing tool. However, after E*Trade's successful entry into the online trading market in 1996, Charles Schwab started to take Internet trading seriously.

Charles Schwab had already established a long list of loyal customers and tried to retain them by providing new services. It also wanted to gain a larger customer base by using brand-name recognition. At the outset, Schwab provided reasonable commissions as a discount brokerage firm. Schwab avoided price competition with E*Trade by setting a higher fee structure whose differentiating features included value-added additional services with the intention of unlocking blue-chip customers (see Exhibit 14.5). Taking advantage of its excellent reputation, strong customer relationships, and abundant research information, Schwab also established a firm position in the online trading market.

EXHIBIT 14.4
E*Trade Market Share by Total Assets*
*Data as of June 30, 2000. Source: Brokerages Need Banking to Keep Customers, *Web Finances,* 5 (7): April 5, 2001, Securities Data Publishing.

Charles Schwab	38%
Fidelity	30
TD Waterhouse	10
E*Trade	5
Ameritrade	4
CSFB Direct	2
Datek	1
NDB	1
Scottrade	1
Dreyfuss	1
Quick & Reilly	1
Other	6

EXHIBIT 14.5 Online Broker Comparison Table, 2000

Source: Investext ™ by The Investext Group: Putnam, Lovell, & Thornton, December 1, 2000.

Company	Number of Online Accounts	YOY Account Growth	Average Online Transactions per Day	Average Transactions per Account per Quarter
Fidelity	4,757,000	55%	100,771	1.4
Schwab	4,200,000	40	203,500	3.1
E*Trade	3,027,362	95	150,000	3.3
TD Waterhouse	2,272,000	96	151,900	2.7
Ameritrade	1,233,000	120	105,540	5.6
DLJ Direct	476,571	58	24,949	3.5
Datek	623,624	115	97,638	10.6
NDB	268,900	69	10,600	2.6

Targeted clients included those who use equity investment as a tool to reach their lifetime financial goal plans or those who prefer the convenience of an online trading company. These clients were not independently wealthy but had considerable amounts of money to invest in a long-term asset plan. In general, they do not trade frequently and are looking for a variety of services. The brand-name recognition of the brokerage is very important and they are willing to pay more for financial advice from these reputable firms. The characteristics of these customers are reflected in the volume per account. Schwab's average account balance is over $100,000, while E*Trade's is just $23,000 (see Exhibit 14.6).

Schwab has emphasized convenience in its online trading operations along with fast system response times. It provided exclusive Velocity software in 1999 to enhance the speed of operation for its heavy users. Power Broker was

EXHIBIT 14.6
Online Brokerage Trading Costs

Source: Piper Jaffrey, February 2, 2000.

Feb. 1996	E*Trade	$14.95/trade
May	Ebroker	$12
July	Datek	$9.99
Sep.	Scot deal	$9
Oct. 1997	Ameritrade	$8
Nov.	Suretrade	$7.95
March 1998	Brown and Company	$5

introduced in 2001 to provide mobile services. Schwab has utilized communication tools and new technology to develop new products and services. Schwab generated additional revenue by selling some of its technology to other traditional brokerage firms.

Merrill Lynch

Merrill Lynch (ML) announced its entry into the online trading market in June 1999, three years after E*Trade. ML had long been skeptical about online trading even after the success of E*Trade and the entry of many new brokerages into online trading. ML does not have interest in speculators, but instead in investors. The challenge and competition from online brokers, such as E*Trade, Charles Schwab, and Ameritrade, were considered a fad by ML's Trading Manager Steffans. Steffans further denied the possibility of ML's entrance into online trading in June 1998. Yet just one year after that, ML recognized that online trading was here to stay and decided to change its strategy and enter this promising market. Other large companies like Morgan Stanley Dean Witter and Salomon Smith Barney followed its lead.

Entry of a big, full-service brokerage firm created tough competition and a need for strategic reorganization by firms already in the online trading market. ML's minimum commission fee was set at $29.95, much higher than that of Ameritrade and E*Trade. Although online brokerages had a price advantage, it was uncertain how long they could sustain it given their rocketing advertising costs. Some of the recent entrants into the new discount online brokerage market had fallen into the red.[26]

ML took advantage of its strong advisory and information services supported by its over 15,000 financial consultants and gained customers at a steady pace. Against these kinds of powerful big securities companies, online brokers also have paid more attention to providing information services. E*Trade acquired Telebanc, a completely online Internet bank; meanwhile, Ameritrade and Charles Schwab established a joint online investment bank.

Merrill Lynch's target market is different from that of E*Trade. ML targets investors with a high net worth. These investors require a wide range of products and services, from access to IPOs, options, and bonds to account aggregators and sophisticated research tools. According to Credit Swiss First Boston, clients with net worth above $100,000 may want to consider the Unlimited

Advantage account. Unlimited Advantage provides investors with unlimited online trading and advisory services for a $1,500 annual fee.

Ameritrade

Ameritrade is a competing online discount broker similar to E*Trade. Ameritrade lets self-directed traders make stock, mutual fund, option, and bond trades, and also provides research and stock quotes. Ameritrade began in 1971 as investment bank TransTerra. TransTerra added deep-discount brokerage services and formed eBroker, a completely Internet-based brokerage service in 1996, which further evolved into Ameritrade. Ameritrade has followed in E*Trade's footsteps. However, due to the recent downturn in the economy, Ameritrade has struggled and plans to lay off 230 employees.

Datek

Datek puts a strong emphasis on response speeds and customer usability. Datek is especially conscious of heavy users like day-traders. Datek allows users free access to market news and information, and its primary focus and expertise are aimed at attracting active traders. The commission fee is $9.99 per trade for up to 5,000 shares, and Datek prides itself on providing lightning-fast trade executions, free streaming, and real-time quotes services.

In response to the special demands of its active trading customers, Datek has become one of the most technologically savvy online brokerages. Datek regularly upgrades and expands its state-of-the-art trading infrastructure. For active traders, Datek was recently regarded as the number-one brokerage according to Credit Swiss First Boston, and number three according to Gomez.

Following the dot.com crash, many analysts wondered if E*Trade had the right strategy to assure its survival. Had Cotsakos plotted a winning business model for E*Trade?

Notes

1. Quote by E*Trade CEO Christos Cotsakos from "Tricks of E*Trade," *Business Week,* February 7, 2000.
2. Ibid.
3. M. Chen, J. Huang, D. Wong, and K. Wong. "From Wall Street to Web Street: The Impacts of the Internet on Retail Brokerages," Haas School of Business, December 19, 2000.
4. www.merrilllynch.com.
5. M. Chen, J. Huang, D. Wong, and K. Wong. "From Wall Street to Web Street. . . ."
6. Ibid.
7. Ibid.
8. Ibid.
9. Nora Macalauso, "Online Trading Assets Roar Past $1 Trillion," *E-Commerce Times,* www.ecommercetimes.com, May 5, 2000.

10. M. Chen, J. Huang, D. Wong, and K. Wong. "From Wall Street to Web Street. . . ."
11. "About E*Trade," www.etrade.com.
12. Ibid.
13. "E-Brokers' Snafus Provide Lessons: Online Retailing Calls for Beefed-up IT, Strong Customer Service," *Computer World,* April 12, 1999, p. 24.
14. E*Trade Group, www.hoovers.com.
15. "E*Trade Grows a Brokerage Business on the Net," *Phillips Media Group's Interactive Marketing News,* Potomac, December 6, 1996.
16. M. Chen, J. Huang, D. Wong, and K. Wong, "From Wall Street to Web Street. . . ."
17. "Frequently Asked Questions," www.etrade.com.
18. "E*Trade Grows a Brokerage Business on the Net."
19. "Tricks of E*Trade."
20. "E*Trade Bank Teams with Laughlin/Constable to Help Underserved Teens," E*Trade Press Release, October 24, 2001.
21. M. Chen, J. Huang, D. Wong, and K. Wong, "From Wall Street to Web Street. . . ."
22. www.etrade.com.
23. Ibid.
24. "E*Trade: An E-Commerce Powerhouse," *GARP Investor,* August 22, 1999.
25. www.hoovers.com.
26. www.zdnet.co.jp, October 13, 1999.

Research In Motion Limited (RIM) and BlackBerry: Wireless E-Mail . . . The Killer App?

It was bound to happen, thought Mike Lazaridis, president and co-CEO of Research In Motion Limited (RIM), as he walked into Jim Basillie's office. Motorola, the undisputed heavyweight of the pager industry, had just announced a new wireless e-mail product that squarely attacked RIM's leadership position in the business market. The huge success of the wildly popular Black-Berry wireless e-mail solution had finally elicited a competitive response from Motorola. The chairman and co-CEO of RIM was already reading the press release when Mike entered his office. Mike glanced at the framed quote on Jim's wall from Michael Urlocker, a Credit Suisse First Boston Research Analyst:

> It's a very successful product that is technically superior. To best Motorola in the radio business is a significant accomplishment. It also sets up the brand-new product as front-runner in a market that could soon be worth hundreds of millions of dollars.[1]

NYU Stern School of Business MBA Candidates Oytun Altasi, Elizabeth Lim, James McNaughton, Rich Shirley, and Greg Wilmore prepared this case under the supervision of Professor Christopher L. Tucci for the purpose of class discussion rather than to illustrate either effective or ineffective handling of an administrative situation. Copyright © 2002 by Christopher L. Tucci. All rights reserved.

Mike sighed as he sat down and wondered how he and Jim would respond to the Motorola threat. Should RIM continue to improve its existing product with third-party applications or should the company redirect its sales efforts from the business market to the consumer market?

RESEARCH IN MOTION

Research In Motion Limited was founded in 1984 by Mike Lazaridis and Douglas Fresin in Waterloo, Ontario, and has grown to a $5.2 billion company. RIM's core technology centers around radio technology and mobile communications; the company's product line features items such as embedded radio modems, software development tools, wireless handheld devices, and the BlackBerry wireless e-mail solution. Research and development is a key to RIM's continued success, and strong manufacturing capabilities remove the company's dependence on others to produce its devices. Altogether, RIM's products yielded $85 million in revenues and $10.5 million in net income for fiscal year 2000 (see Exhibit 15.1).

EXHIBIT 15.1   Consolidated Statement of Operations and Retained Earnings

Source: RIM Annual Report, 2000.

	For the Year Ended		
	February 29, 2000	**February 29, 1999**	**February 29, 1998**
Revenue	$84,967	$47,342	$20,901
Cost of sales	48,574	28,767	14,404
Gross margin	36,393	18,575	6,497
Expenses			
Research and development	7,738	4,382	2,985
Selling, marketing, and adminstration	13,904	6,546	2,738
Amortization	4,683	2,783	1,472
	26,325	13,711	7,195
Income (loss) from operations	10,068	4,864	(698)
Investment income	5,968	3,790	1,319
Income before income taxes	16,036	8,654	621
Provision for income taxes	5,538	2,245	259
Net income	10,498	6,409	362
Retained earnings, beginning of year	7,632	1,223	1,123
Capital dividend paid	—	—	(262)
Retained earnings, end of year	$18,130	$ 7,632	$ 1,223
Earnings per share			
Basic	$ 0.16	$ 0.10	$ 0.01
Fully diluted	$ 0.15	$ 0.10	$ 0.01

ORIGINS OF BLACKBERRY

RIM's roots are in leading-edge radio technology, with some of the original products including radio communications hardware and modems. As early as 1997, RIM realized that traditional one-way paging was quickly becoming an outdated means of communication. Adding the ability to immediately respond to messages would increase the effectiveness and utility of a paging device, and thus two-way paging became a focus for RIM.

By 1998, RIM was ready to introduce the Inter@ctive Pager, which included not only two-way communications, but also Internet and Intranet connectivity, and the thumb-operated keyboard that characterizes the company's products today. Functions such as e-mail, faxing, and text-to-voice messages were included in this early product.

Over the next year, as the Inter@ctive Pager grew in popularity, RIM teamed with such providers as Bell South to access wireless data networks, as well as PageNet and SkyTel to distribute the actual devices. In addition, RIM called upon its software development team to build additional functionality for the wireless handhelds, coming up with a package for corporate customers that offered a "complete wireless e-mail solution." This overall product offering became known as BlackBerry.

BlackBerry combines the RIM wireless handheld devices (RIM 850, RIM 950, and RIM 957) with a software package that allows the user to access e-mail "anytime, anywhere." The handhelds also include peripherals such as docking stations to synch with personal computers, and other personal organizer functions such as calendars, address books, and task lists (see Exhibit 15.2).

The RIM 850 device is the original Inter@ctive Pager handheld and is still offered in conjunction with limited functionality two-way paging. The newer models, RIM 950 and RIM 957, have been tailored to fit well with BlackBerry,

EXHIBIT 15.2
**View of RIM 950
and RIM 957
Devices**

though they are still offered independently. The RIM 950 is pager-sized, and the RIM 957 is PDA-sized, with increased functionality and improved capability to view Web pages.

While BlackBerry is the most popular RIM package, accounting for 41 percent of RIM's revenues by the fourth quarter of the fiscal year 2000, RIM also sells just the handheld devices to providers such as Bell South. These relationships allow providers to include their own wireless solution for their customers, tailored to their specific needs. While these products may compete with BlackBerry, this has not been viewed as significant cannibalism of BlackBerry's current target market—corporate clients.

To date, RIM has focused on corporate clientele, striking deals with such financial service giants as Merrill Lynch, CSFB, and Salomon Smith Barney. The popularity of the BlackBerry product has become so widespread that advertising for the product is crossing over into the consumer arena, with a recent newspaper advertisement (free-standing insert) describing BlackBerry as the "Complete Wireless E-mail Solution for the Mobile Professional."

THE BLACKBERRY E-MAIL SOLUTION—HOW DOES IT WORK?

BlackBerry prides itself on being continuously online—the information is automatically available whenever the pager is on. The way this is possible is through continuous communication with a server that receives and sends e-mail.

Essentially, a server receives the user's e-mail and notifies the redirector (typically set up on the user's PC). The redirector then retrieves the e-mail, encodes it, and sends it over the Internet to a wireless network. The network contacts the user's handheld, where the message is decoded for the user to read. In sending e-mails from the handheld, the process is essentially reversed—the message is sent through the wireless network to the receiver's e-mail address via the Internet.

In the Enterprise platform edition, the redirector is eliminated (bundled with the server itself), and the server directly contacts the user with the encoded message. In this case, there is no need to move through the user's PC at any point in the communication.

While there is no need for the user to physically dial-in to the Internet to receive his/her e-mail, there is a need for continuous connection to the Internet. In the Enterprise solution, the server is continuously connected, but without the server, the individual's PC must maintain some type of connection with the Internet for continuous communication. This is typically easily achieved in a business setting, where the user has access to a company server that is connected to the Internet. (See Exhibit 15.3 for a graphic depiction of the set-up for both the Enterprise and Internet solutions.)

To address security concerns with e-mail transmission, BlackBerry uses a triple-DES encryption algorithm for encoding its messages. This coupled with randomly generated keys at the end-user's PC (based on random mouse movements) results in a highly secure system.

EXHIBIT 15.3 **Overview of BlackBerry System Setup (Internet Edition)**

Source: "Technical White Paper BlackBerry Exchange Edition version 2.0," Research In Motion Limited, 2000, p. 5.

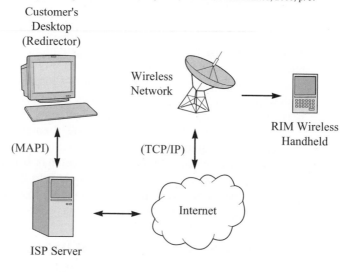

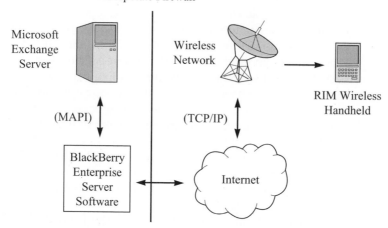

BlackBerry is run on an open source code operating system. Because RIM's core strengths are in the technology, and not in applications development, the company encourages third parties to develop applications for BlackBerry devices.

RIM also has a service called the BlackBerry Wireless Solution Provider Program, where it offers to help businesses provide a wireless solution to increase flexibility and availability of information access to the businesses' sales force and other employees.

TECHNOLOGY ALLIANCES

Throughout the BlackBerry new product development process, RIM entered into a number of technology alliances. RIM and Intel have a history of collaboration on wireless products and Intel has made an investment in the company. Intel in particular provided the company with the basic chip set for its BlackBerry pagers based on a standard Intel 386 architecture. Collaboration between the two firms has been well executed. In fact, in June 1999 the Canadian-American Business Council recognized RIM and Intel as having the "Most Successful Alliance in North America" by awarding them the 1999 Canadian-American Business Achievement Award.[2]

RIM's partnership with Sun Microsystems is extremely important for third-party application development. Announced in December 1999, the Sun/RIM partnership provided that Java 2 Micro Edition would be implemented on all RIM handhelds. This alliance expanded cross-platform software development opportunities because Java 2 Micro Edition was the "industry standard programming platform that significantly ease[d] the development and deployment of wireless technologies."[3]

DISTRIBUTION ALLIANCES

Telecommunications companies provide a major distribution outlet for Black-Berry services and are commonly cobranded with the partner's name, as mentioned above (see Exhibit 15.4). Commenting on RIM's distribution alliances, Jordan Worth, an analyst with IDC, stated:

> RIM really caught the attention of some huge U.S. players with BellSouth as their first major contract win for the two-way pager. Other phone companies that have the capacity to use their services would look at them because the more partners they have the more value they have to anyone who wants to partner with them.[4]

In addition to telecommunication providers, RIM has entered into significant distribution agreements with OEMs such as Compaq and Dell. In both cases, the company gains access to Fortune 500 businesses that are looking for an integrated server, PC, laptop, and/or handheld solution for their employees. The BlackBerry e-mail solution is particularly suited for these corporate accounts because it is optimized to work with Microsoft Exchange server, which is a predominant e-mail program for large businesses.

While ISPs are expected to play a major role in the distribution of Black-Berry Internet Edition to noncorporate users, penetration via this group of resellers is still somewhat limited. (See Exhibit 15.5 for a description of ISP partners.)

EXHIBIT 15.4   **Distribution Alliances—Network Providers**

Source: RIM press releases; http://www.rim.net/news/press/index.shtml.

Company	Description
Bell Mobility	Based in Canada, augments its line of cellular, paging data, and PCS services with both BlackBerry Exchange and Internet Edition.
Bell South	Longstanding strategic partner to RIM; its networks cover more than 93% of urban business population in the U.S. (Other networks include Ardis, Metricom, PageNet, PageMart.)
BT Cellnet	British Telecommunications provider; leverages its new GPRS (General Packet Radio Service) high-speed network to offer the Exchange service.
Group Telecom	Canadian CLEC that caters to small- and medium-sized businesses; offers the Internet Edition to those businesses.
Motient	Provides various communications services over a proprietary terrestrial/satellite network in the United States; offers BlackBerry Exchange to corporate customers.
Pagemart Canada	Provides paging services, voicemail messaging, and Web-based messaging to BlackBerry customers via 900 MHz FLEX network and two-way PCS paging network.
SkyTel	Subsidiary of WorldCom, offers BlackBerry services as a complement to a variety of paging, text, and messenger beeper products.

EXHIBIT 15.5   **Distribution Alliances—ISPs**

Source: RIM website.

Company	Description
EarthLink	Currently conducting market test of EarthLink Airmanager, a wireless service featuring BlackBerry Internet Edition.
OneMain	Regionally focused ISP that promotes the BlackBerry service on its website.
PageNet Canada	Canadian ISP partner.
RCN	Largest ISP partner, displaying BlackBerry offerings prominently on its website.
Rogers AT&T	Canadian ISP partner that distributes BlackBerry Internet Edition.

THIRD-PARTY SOFTWARE DEVELOPMENT

RIM's open platform for its wireless devices "enable[d] third party developers to create new applications and enable[d] manufacturers to enhance their products and services with wireless connectivity."[5] According to RIM's co-CEOs:

> We are encouraging the development of new third-party software development applications, such as mobile commerce, which are expected to drive demand for wireless technology beyond the pure e-mail market.[6]

Recognizing the third-party applications as a critical factor for its success both in consumer and business markets, RIM had many initiatives at the end of 2000. The company had relationships with the open source community providing software, technical support, and discussion forums with its "Developer Zone" website. By March 2000, over 8,000 free software development kits were distributed over the Internet.[7] In July, the company announced a joint Java Developers' Contest for RIM wireless handhelds with Handango, the world's largest Internet marketplace for handheld software applications. Laura Rippy, CEO of Hardango, explains:

> We want Java developers to focus on creating breakthrough mobile applications for RIM handhelds. . . . We will offer a full suite of services to the RIM developer community, including a featured area on Handango.com to promote and sell RIM handhelds and applications.[8]

Apart from its efforts to promote application development among the open source community, RIM assumed an active role in the development by working with third parties including network companies like Bell Mobility and professional service and hardware companies like Compaq (refer to Exhibit 15.6 for a list of alliances and applications). RIM's emphasis on the business segment underscored the importance of additional functionality expected from its devices. More and more companies relied on mobile devices for communication,

EXHIBIT 15.6 **Alliances and Third-Party Application Development**

Source: RIM Press Releases and Annual Report, 2000.

Alliance	Application
Bid.com	Wireless auction applications for B2B and B2C markets
OpenText	Integration of software with BlackBerry for dynamic supply chain collaboration
BellMobility/Neomar	Adaptation of Neomar's WAP microbrowser to BlackBerry Exchange
Compaq Professional Services	Customized solutions for corporate e-mail services and enterprise applications
Brience	Development of new services that will allow corporations to offer existing enterprise applications on BlackBerry
Handango	Jointly manage the development efforts of the open source community
Descartes	Dispatching services
Comtrack	Dispatching services
Millennium Softworks	Dispatching services
Aether	Stock trading and charting
w-Trade	Stock trading and charting
Outercurve Finance	Stock trading and charting
GoAmerica	Personalization and Web navigation
WolfeTech Corporation	Personalization and Web navigation
Sybase	Database access
Wynd Communications	Mobile communications to the deaf and others who can't use the phone

database access and updating, and customer relationship management. These functionalities typically demanded more development and customization effort together with higher reliability.

TURNING THE PAGE

Whether the BlackBerry is a two-way pager or something more, it is at the forefront of a shift in communications reminiscent of the introduction of the cellular phone in the 1980s.[9] An important aspect of this shift is that these devices are changing the nature of e-mail itself. Messages are shorter and jerkier than those issued from a desktop and are becoming more like phone calls. BlackBerry also gives the user the feeling of being many places at once. These facets together put BlackBerry in a position to eventually replace some phone calls.

Not surprisingly, many companies are working to redefine the competitive space and articulate their visions during this period of ferment. While all the players are willing to concede that the cell phone sales will explode in the years ahead, it is not clear that cell phones will crowd out other appliances. As one analyst observes, "about 33% of cellular telephone users have a pager . . . you see a division of labor—people use the phone for personal use or family contact and they use the pager for work contact."[10] A Motorola manager casts the issue of phone versus pager as "the ultimate Swiss Army knife question. The fact that you can collapse many functions into a single device doesn't mean that the specific functions that a given consumer wants to do are going to be met by that one device."[11]

THE COMPETITIVE LANDSCAPE

The wireless e-mail functionality is currently provided by three major categories of devices: e-mail capable mobile phones, PDAs (personal digital assistants), and two-way pagers. (See Exhibit 15.7 for major competitors in each of these categories.)

1. **E-mail–capable mobile phones.** Nokia, Ericsson, and Motorola are among the leaders in providing e-mail–capable mobile phones. The Wireless Application Protocol (WAP) has led to the emergence of WAP phones. WAP is a set of common rules that devices must use when adapting Web content for handheld devices, particularly mobile phones. However, there is still the question of whether these WAP phones can move beyond simply exchanging data to delivering the immediacy of BlackBerry e-mail exchange, as well as the power of enterprise applications.

2. **PDAs.** Like mobile phones, several PDAs have added e-mail functionality. While PDAs have larger screens and keyboards relative to phones, they require the user to log on to a server to collect his/her e-mail.

EXHIBIT 15.7   **Wireless Technology: Competitive Landscape**

Source: Corporate websites and adapted from: Carol S. Holzberg, "E-mail Unplugged: Explore Your Wireless Access Options," *E-Mail and More* 8, no. 7 (July 2000), pp. 22–25.

Category	Company	Product
PDA	Palm Inc.	Palm claims the only built-in wireless PDA, the Palm VII. Unlimited service plans are currently $44.95 per month, though OmniSky offers modems for the nonwireless Palm V at lower rates. Palm claims a 75% share of the PDA market, over 5,000 software programs, and an open source development community. The Palm Global Alliance Program includes companies like Computer Associates, Oracle, IBM, and Sun (also a RIM ally). Palm licensees include Sony, Nokia, Handspring, and Qualcomm.
	Handspring	The Handspring Visor has wireless messaging modules and uses the Palm OS. Handspring is planning a cell phone attachment that will transform palmtop into mobile phone. GSM compatibility will allow Handspring to go after the Europe market.
	HP	Wireless Pocket PCs have been slower to incorporate wireless connectivity. Nevertheless, Web access for laptop, handhelds, and other kinds of computers has improved as wireless modems have boosted downloads to nearly wired speeds. The HP Jornada uses the Sierra Wireless AirCard.
	Casio	Subscribers of AOL will be able to access e-mail through Casio and Compaq handheld computers.
Cellular Phone	Nokia	The largest cell phone provider. Like other smartphone providers, Nokia offers a range of wireless products and services including Mobile Chat.
	Motorola	The number-2 cell phone provider.
	Ericsson	Ericsson has partnered with Microsoft to offer cell phone access to Exchange-based e-mails.
	Samsung	Samsung has released numerous handsets designed for multiple wireless technologies, including Global System for Mobile Communications (GSM), second-generation Code-Division Multiple Access (cdmaOne), and Digital Enhanced Cordless Telecommunications (DECT).
	Mitsubishi	Provides cell phones to ATT Wireless among others.
	Sony	Sony is set to release its first personal digital assistant, based on the Palm operating system, this fall, and is expected to build wireless access into the device in the future.
	Qualcomm	Qualcomm is a broad technology company that provides a range of products and services based on its CDMA wireless data technology. It licenses technology to 75 communications manufacturers.

(continued)

EXHIBIT 15.7 (*continued*)

Category	Company	Product
Two-Way Pager	RIM	BlackBerry: wireless e-mail solution for mobile professionals.
	Motorola	Talkabout T900, Timeport P935; Motorola is also a major phone manufacturer and has agreed to cobrand a mobile phone with Palm.
	Glenayre Technologies	Glenayre Technologies, a once-promising competitor sued RIM in 1999 for an alleged patent violation, claiming damages from RIM's use of an "apparatus for generating power for use in a communications device." Glenayre offered to drop the suit for a one-time $4 million licensing fee.

3. **Two-way pager.** In reality, this is a poor name for this category, but it serves as a temporary placeholder for whatever type of wireless Internet device emerges from the ashes of the pager market. For fans of the Black-Berry, communicating by e-mail beats talking by phone. A typical user might cite a number of benefits: being able to do two things at once, communicating efficiently, not necessarily having to talk to all people by voice, worrying less about cancer, easier typing than phone keypads, not having to log on to get e-mail, broader network coverage than patched-together cell phone networks.

The lines dividing these categories have blurred as firms move toward all-in-one solutions. In spite of the intense competition and blurring of product concepts, strong consumer demand for wireless e-mail service is expected to drive growth of more than one firm and product solution. According to one estimate, wireless e-mail service may grow from the current base of 1 million Americans to 100 million over the next three years.[12] BlackBerry claimed 15,000 users in 1999. By contrast, Motorola sold 200,000 PageWriters in 1999.[13] Though Europe has higher penetration of cell phones (62 percent in Finland compared with less than half of that in the U.S.), RIM believes the European market is prime for the wireless Internet pager.[14]

Motorola

Motorola has certainly provided RIM with the most threatening competition in more realms than just two-way pagers. Its core capabilities parallel RIM's most closely and, in addition, Motorola has strong brand recognition with the consumer market. Motorola's renewed move into two-way paging has certainly given RIM pause.

Though Motorola's PageWriter series of pagers dominated the market, RIM caught the giant Gulliver snoozing on the wireless Internet device front. Motorola woke up angry and responded with two new products that created a buzz in the industry: the Talkabout (T900, targeted to the consumer market) and the Timeport (P935, targeted squarely at RIM's corporate segment). When considering whether Motorola should be taken seriously, one analyst offered, "When Motorola is bad, they're bad and when they're good, they're good—and right now they're good."[15]

Motorola is capable not only of inventing new products but also of bringing them to market. The company possesses strengths in key areas such as manufacturing, distribution, and marketing. The company has dominated the pager business, manufacturing 8 of 10 pagers sold in the United States and has the best-known pager on the market. Motorola's products operate over radio waves through a network built by Motorola. Motorola's consumer products are available through retail outlets such as OfficeMax and Best Buy.

In addition, Motorola plans to support the Talkabout and Timeport launches by spending millions of dollars on a national ad campaign. A cooperative advertisement with SkyTel features Motorola's Talkabout clamshells (in a variety of colors) facilitating a social chat about an upcoming party.[16] Motorola opted to extend the "Talkabout" brand from popular consumer two-way radios to its wireless e-mail solution. The company has strong preexisting marketing partnerships such as its relationship with the National Football League (NFL), whose coaches are seen pacing the sidelines with wireless Motorola headsets. Motorola's "Talkabout phone" is cobranded with a fan's favorite NFL team logo.[17]

Motorola's Talkabout T900

The Talkabout offers similar functionality to the BlackBerry (minus the more powerful enterprise solutions) and is targeted to the consumer market. At only $99.99 after a holiday season manufacturer's rebate of $80.00,[18] the price is significantly lower, and the service plans (as low as $19.95 a month) are also less than the $40.00 charge for BlackBerry. By making its product available in colors like "razberry ice," Motorola adds a "coolness factor" and sends a clear signal that it intends to preempt any attempt by RIM to market its brand to the masses.

Timeport P935

As if the Talkabout is not threatening enough, Motorola also weighs in with the Timeport. Unlike the Talkabout, the Timeport is aimed at the corporate user—RIM's core target market. The Timeport is positioned as an end-to-end solution for highly scheduled mobile business professionals, whose importance is somewhat measured by their accessibility. Appropriately, the Timeport offers round-the-clock connectivity, e-mail, Internet access, PC synchronization, PDA features, and third-party applications. These applications allow broader business functionality such as financial tracking, sales ordering, airline scheduling, and so on. Motorola's Wisdom Operating System 4.0 is billed as a "developer friendly" software platform for portable messaging products. The Timeport will be priced competitively with BlackBerry (at about $400), weighs 6.7 ounces, and has a Qwerty-style keyboard.[19]

HOW SHOULD RIM RESPOND?

As Jim finished reading the Motorola press release, Mike pondered RIM's options. Should RIM ignore the Motorola threat and continue to improve its existing product line? Could RIM fend off Motorola by simply decreasing prices? Should they attack Motorola in its own backyard, by aggressively entering the consumer market? Or should RIM focus on third-party application development to increase both the functionality of its handhelds and switching costs? Whichever option they chose, the co-CEOs would have their hands full protecting RIM's leadership position in the market.

Notes

1. Ian Austin, "Flavor of the Minute," *Canadian Business,* February 12, 1999, pp. 1–5.
2. RIM Press Release, "Intel/RIM Honoured As the Best Alliance in North America," June 17, 1999, www.rim.net/news/press/1999/pr-17_06_1999 .shtml.
3. RIM 2000 Annual Report.
4. Geoffrey Downey, "RIM's Dell Deal Rolled Out in U.S. While Canada Is Kept Waiting," *Computing Canada,* December 10, 1999, pp. 1–2.
5. RIM Prospectus October 1999.
6. RIM 2000 Annual Report.
7. Ibid.
8. RIM Press Release, "Handango and RIM Sponsor Java Developers' Contest for RIM Wireless Handhelds," June 6, 2000.
9. Amy Harmon, "BlackBerry Maker Thinks Wireless E-Mail Market Ripe for the Picking," *New York Times Wire Service,* September 25, 2000. (Accessed November 5, 2000, at http://chicagotribune.com.)
10. Patrick Cole, "Making a Run at the Next Wave in Wireless," *Chicago Tribune,* March 19, 2000, p. 1.
11. Ibid.
12. Amy Harmon, "BlackBerry Maker Thinks Wireless E-Mail Market Ripe for the Picking."
13. Patrick Cole, "Making a Run at the Next Wave in Wireless."
14. Brian D. Robinson, "When Will RIM's BlackBerry Win the Wireless War?" *Stockhouse,* April 3, 2000. (Accessed November 5, 2000, at http://www .stockhouse.ca/shfn/apr00/040300ca_rim.asp.)
15. Ibid.
16. Nokia takes a similar tack with a contemporaneous advertisement in which a young man uses his phone to type a message to a young woman sitting on the same couch (she would not have been able to hear him above the noise of the party music).

17. Motorola Consumer Catalog, http://commerce.motorola.com/consumer/ QWhtml/promo_nfl.html. (Not available with Baltimore Ravens or Carolina Panthers logos.)

18. *New York Times,* November 25, 2000, J&R Computer World, advertisement.

19. Motorola Press Release, "Motorola Introduces New Two-Way Wireless Handheld Device: Timeport P935 Personal Interactive Communicator," www.Motorola.com/MIMS/MSPG/Press/PR20000915_16957.html.

Case **Sixteen**

Sprint PCS: Winning the Wireless War?

In late 2001, Sprint PCS was poised to capitalize on the tremendous projected growth in wireless data services. With the only all-digital nationwide network in the United States, the company had a clear technology path to providing high-speed wireless data capabilities across the country. As the fastest-growing wireless carrier in the U.S., the company had announced third-quarter subscriber growth nearly double that of its closest competitor. Sprint PCS could attribute much of its success to the strength of its parent company, Sprint, with an impressive 95 percent brand awareness[1] and a vision of providing high-speed, always-on voice and data connectivity via wire-line or wireless, all from a single provider.

Still, the future was uncertain for Sprint PCS and as the company headed into 2002, management faced many strategic issues. The company was going against the grain, depending on a technology called code-division multiple access (CDMA) in lieu of other, more accepted global standards. They had just lost a major competitive advantage when the Federal Communications Commission (FCC) voted to remove limitations on the amount of radio spectrum each carrier could use. This gave competitors access to the bandwidth needed for their less efficient technologies. In addition, the market for wireless data was far from well defined. Despite massive industry growth projections, adoption rates were low with only 10 percent of Sprint PCS customers using its wireless Internet capabilities.[2] Analysts were uncertain of the real need for mobile users to access data and their willingness to pay for such services.

Sprint PCS's management faced some critical questions: What were the key success factors in the wireless industry? Would Sprint PCS be able to survive the threat of disruptive technologies? Were they being rational in betting on

This case was written by MBA candidates Mary Bruening, Jonathan Chizick, John Gearty, Ravi Gopal, and Srini Venkat under the supervision of Dr. Allan Afuah, Professor of Corporate Strategy at the University of Michigan Business School. This case is intended as a basis for class discussion rather than to illustrate either effective or ineffective handling of an administrative situation. Copyright © 2002 by McGraw-Hill/Irwin. All rights reserved.

CDMA technology and sacrificing worldwide compatibility? With mobile phone penetration at only 45 percent,[3] there was still substantial opportunity in the voice communications market, casting doubt on the company's data-focused strategy. Would customers pay more for data services? Would they pay enough to generate positive ROIs on massive 3G technology upgrades? Global standard technologies threatened Sprint PCS's position with lower supplier costs and global roaming capabilities. How could the company best capitalize on its massive investment in a nationwide network and its strong market position?

SPRINT PCS HISTORY

Sprint had been a major player in the U.S. telecommunications industry for over one hundred years. The firm began as Brown Telephone Company in 1899. Throughout the twentieth century, the company underwent tremendous growth and numerous name changes, emerging as one of the major U.S. telecom carriers. In 1994, Sprint announced a plan to partner with three major cable and television companies in a new venture to provide nationwide wireless personal communications service (PCS). In 1995, Sprint and its partners won the rights to wireless licenses in 29 major U.S. markets in an FCC auction. With these requisite assets in hand, the new venture was launched and named Sprint PCS. Under the agreement, Sprint held 40 percent of the venture. Its new partners held the rest, with Tele-Communications Inc. (TCI) owning 30 percent and Comcast Corp. and Cox Cable each owning 15 percent.[4]

After evaluating a number of analog and digital technologies, Sprint PCS decided on CDMA as the basis for its infrastructure. CDMA, developed and licensed by San Diego–based Qualcomm, was a digital protocol with voice and data transmission capabilities. CDMA had a number of advantages over other technologies. It was more "spectrally efficient," meaning it required less bandwidth, or wireless spectrum. It provided efficiency 10 to 12 times greater than analog technologies and at least twice that of other digital technologies.[5] Since the FCC capped spectrum usage at 45 MHz of bandwidth per carrier and since bandwidth licenses were expensive to purchase in government auctions, CDMA provided Sprint PCS a great competitive advantage. CDMA also offered inherent security, superior voice quality, and data transmission capabilities. Sprint PCS weighed these data capabilities heavily in its decision, as it expected business users to soon begin acknowledging a need for mobile e-mail and Internet access.

In just 18 months, the company built and launched a nationwide voice network serving 150 metropolitan markets. Revenues exploded, reaching $1.2 billion in only its second year of operation. Sprint PCS subsequently launched its Sprint PCS Wireless Web service in late September 1999,[6] allowing users to access e-mail and wireless-enabled Web pages from their phones. Later, the company introduced products that allowed its customers complete access to the Internet from their laptop PCs, either by connecting their mobile phones to their computers or by inserting a Sprint PCS wireless card.

In May of 1998, Sprint announced its intention to buy out its partners and acquire 100 percent ownership of Sprint PCS. In a series of steps, Sprint PCS became a unit of Sprint and an initial offering of Sprint PCS stock was issued, allowing Sprint and Sprint PCS to trade separately on the NYSE.

As of September 2001, the company's total customer base had reached 11.82 million subscribers, constituting over 10 percent of the total U.S. mobile telecom market. The Sprint PCS network covered 360 metropolitan areas and 85 percent of the U.S. population.[7] Subscriber growth for the previous quarter was 19 percent, while the industry as a whole grew at only 10 percent. Still, only 10 percent of its subscribers were using Wireless Web capabilities.[8]

INDUSTRY AND TECHNOLOGY

In 2001, the wireless market for voice services was maturing. Customer penetration stood at 45 percent with an estimated 121.3 million subscribers.[9] This represented growth of 27 percent from the previous year. The overall growth of the U.S. wireless market is shown in Exhibit 16.1. As wireless phone penetration approached saturation levels, which were estimated in the 60–70 percent range,[10] companies were left with tough decisions to make—continue to focus on voice or diversify into data services. The subscriber base for data services had reached 8.4 million by November 2001 and was expected to grow to 52 million subscribers in 2005.[11] The introduction of national flat-price plans by carriers was driving wireless voice into a commodity market.

Having access to a band of radio frequencies for transmission, referred to as spectrum, was a large barrier to entry in the wireless market. Spectrum available for wireless transmission extended from AM radio frequencies up to infrared frequencies. Improvements in wireless technologies allowed operators to move to higher frequency ranges in the wireless spectrum. Moving to higher frequencies allowed for more bandwidth and higher quality; however,

EXHIBIT 16.1
Growth of the U.S. Wireless Market

Source: Industry Surveys, "Telecommunications: Wireless," *Standard & Poors,* November 1, 2001, p. 1.

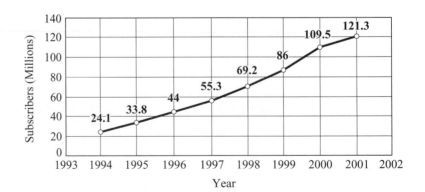

this also reduced the range of cellular transmitters and increased the cost of cellular deployment due to the need for additional transmission towers. In the U.S., the FCC regulated the spectrum and allocated narrow bands to wireless operators. Exhibit 16.2 shows the spectrum allocation in the U.S. at the end of November 2001.

By mid-2001, several wireless technologies were in existence. The most popular technologies fell broadly into three groups—cellular technology, satellite technology, and wireless local area networks.

Cellular Technology

First Generation (1G)

Bell Labs developed the first wire-free large area communication system in the 1960s. This was called a cellular telephone network because of the small geographic regions called "cells" into which a large contiguous land area was divided. The system used at the time was an analog system called advanced mobile phone service (AMPS). Introduced by AT&T in 1983, AMPS used the

EXHIBIT 16.2 **Wireless Spectrum Allocation in the United States**

Sources: eCompany.com, National Telecommunications and Information Administration.

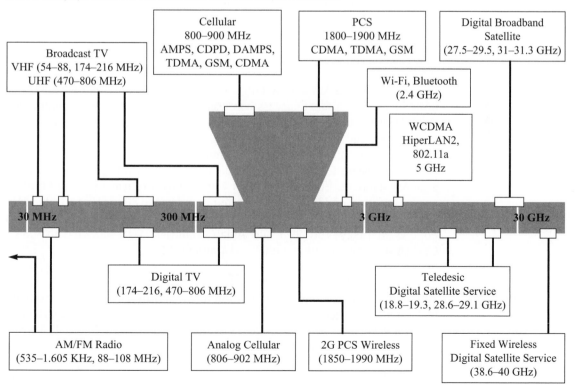

800–900 MHz frequency spectrum (known as the 800 MHz band) for cell phones. AMPS was referred to as a first-generation, or "1G" technology. This technology had some disadvantages: Links were poor and handoffs unreliable. The analog system caused excessive power consumption that resulted in heavy, bulky equipment that required frequent battery recharges.

Second Generation (2G)

Second-generation wireless used different technologies to divide the wireless spectrum and increase available capacity in limited bandwidth. Further subdivision of frequency spectrums using time-division multiple access (TDMA) resulted in digital AMPS (D-AMPS). D-AMPS provided a 3-to-1 capacity gain over analog technology. An alternative way to allocate spectrum was via code-division multiple access (CDMA). In CDMA, multiple digitized signals, each tagged with a unique code, are scattered across the frequency band. The receiving device can decipher only the data that are earmarked for it. The analogy from Qualcom below best illustrates the difference between TDMA and CDMA:

> Imagine a room full of people, all trying to carry on one-on-one conversations. In TDMA each couple takes turns talking. They keep their turns short by saying only one sentence at a time. As there is never more than one person speaking in the room at any given moment, no one has to worry about being heard over the background din. In CDMA, each couple talks at the same time, but they all use a different language. Because none of the listeners understand any language other than that of the individual to whom they are listening, the background din doesn't cause any real problems.[12]

Cellular digital packet data (CDPD) was a 2G technology that used TDMA protocol to allow users to access wireless data at 19.2 Kbps. It was optimized for TDMA networks and worked in the 800 MHz frequency band. CDPD had been in existence since the 1980s and had proven to be a reliable method of data transmission but had limited potential.

Global system for mobile communications (GSM) was gaining ground as a global standard. European carriers were almost exclusively using GSM. It used a variation of TDMA and operated in either the 800 MHz or 1800 MHz frequency band. Short message service (SMS), an instant-messaging service popular in many European and Asian countries, was started with GSM. CDMA was incompatible with TDMA and GSM.

Second-and-a-half Generation (2.5G)

Although there was no formal definition for what differentiated 2.5G from 3G technologies, General packet radio service (GPRS) was widely regarded as 2.5G. It was based on GSM technology and transmitted in the 56–114 Kbps range. More importantly, GPRS had always-on connectivity.

CDMA evolved into 2.5G with CDMA2000 1x, also developed by Qualcomm. This new version was already being deployed by Sprint PCS in late

2001 and demonstrated rates of 153–307 Kbps, the highest of the 2.5G technologies and arguably bordering on 3G capabilities. It was the first CDMA technology to allow always-on capability.

Faster technologies eliminated the need to use wireless middleware, increasing speeds at which users could access data on a mobile device. Other 2.5G protocols included high-speed circuit-switched data (HSCSD), which was a circuit-switched protocol with data rates up to 38.4 Kbps.

Third Generation (3G)

EDGE (enhanced data rate for global evolution), the next evolution of GSM, was essentially a faster version of GSM. Its top speed was 384 Kbps and it also used TDMA structure. It was regarded as an evolutionary step toward UMTS (universal mobile telecommunications service), which was a 3G, packet-based technology, capable of up to 2 Mbps (megabits per second) transmissions.

Qualcomm was busy developing its answer to the demand for 3G data services. Its response would come with the development of CDMA2000 1xEV, a direct descendant of CDMA2000 1x. This new protocol delivered data at speeds up to 2.3 Mbps, offered always-on connectivity, and was backward compatible with its predecessor. For carriers currently operating on CDMA, this would be the 3G technology of choice.

Another CDMA variant, called WCDMA, was a 3G technology supporting data rates up to 384 Kbps (for wide area access) or 2 Mbps (for local area access) and was optimized for multimedia applications. This technology was not backward compatible with other CDMA technologies but was arguably a slightly better technology for carriers building a 3G network from scratch or upgrading from GSM networks. It therefore became a more accepted standard for carriers not currently using CDMA.

Qualcomm's holding of many CDMA patents made it a giant in the market. Qualcomm had granted royalty-bearing licenses to more than 75 CDMA manufacturers, many of which covered 3G applications.

COMPETITION

Each U.S. wireless competitor faced a different migration path to 3G implementation (see Exhibit 16.3). For companies such as Sprint and Verizon, which used CDMA technology, the upgrade process to CDMA2000 1x was straightforward. This upgrade required only the installation of new "channel cards" at each of the transmitting base stations and three software upgrades at various points in the network. Such an upgrade was relatively inexpensive. However, for companies such as AT&T and Cingular, which used TDMA or GSM technology, the upgrade path to full-blown 3G was not as straightforward. These firms planned major network upgrades, from GSM to GPRS to EDGE and finally to WCDMA. The last step was more of a complete network rebuild than an upgrade. Since building a nationwide network costs in the

EXHIBIT 16.3 Major U.S. Wireless Telecommunications Firms

Source: Standard & Poor's, "Telecommunications: Wireless," November 1, 2001, p. 4.

	Sprint PCS	AT&T	Verizon	Cingular	Nextel
Technology	CDMA 1900	AMPS800, TDMA 1900	APMS 800, CDMA 800, CDMA 1900	AMPS 800, TDMA 800, TDMA 1900, GSM 1900	iDEN 800
Subscribers	11.8M	16.4M	27.9M	21.2M	7.7M
Market Share	11.2%	16.4%	27.9%	21.2%	7.7%
ARPU	$61.00	$63.80	$49.00	$52.38	$72.00
3Q01 Revenue	$2.3B	$3.4B	$4.4B	$3.6B	$2.0B

neighborhood of $10 billion, this cost was not negligible. In addition, customers needed new devices to receive service. Because of these costs and the spectrum demands, deployment of WCDMA was expected to be delayed until 2004 or later.

Verizon

On April 4, 2000, Verizon Wireless was created as a new coast-to-coast wireless network venture between Verizon Communications, with 55 percent ownership, and Vodafone Airtouch, with 45 percent ownership. As of November 2001, it was the market leader in the United States with 28.7 million customers and quarterly revenues of approximately $4.4 billion.[13] The company's network footprint covered nearly 90 percent of the U.S. market with 49 out of the top 50 and 96 out of the top 100 regional U.S. markets.[14] Part of Verizon's strategy was to expand its capacity in major markets such as New York, Boston, Los Angeles, Chicago, Philadelphia, Washington D.C., Seattle, and San Francisco. It was the winning bidder for 113 licenses in the FCC's January 2001 auction for 1.9 GHz of spectrum. This added capacity came with a high price tag of $8.8 billion but was seen as placing Verizon in a position to be prepared to launch 3G technology.[15]

Verizon used two types of technologies on its wireless networks: AMPS and CDMA. Verizon planned to upgrade its network to CDMA2000 1x, which would support data transmission speeds of 70–150 Kbps, and then to CDMA 2000 1xEV. The investment costs involved only software upgrades and the transition was a two-step process. However, there were two considerations that had the potential to slow this transition. Verizon and its partner Vodafone were contemplating how to effectively align Verizon's CDMA network and Vodafone's GSM system in the transition to 3G services. Secondly, with these multistandard networks, upgrades could be more costly.

Rough estimates indicated that in addition to the $8.8 billion recently spent to purchase licenses, Verizon would have to spend $1 billion to upgrade to CDMA2000 1x and an additional $7 billion to reach CDMA2000 1xEV.[16]

Cingular

Cingular Wireless was a joint venture of the wireless divisions of SBC and Bell South. SBC owned 60 percent of the company and Bell South 40 percent. Cingular was the second-largest player in the U.S. wireless industry, with 21.2 million customers as of the first half of 2001. Cingular posted second-quarter 2001 revenues of $3.6 billion and held a 21.2 percent U.S. market share.[17]

Cingular used three technologies in its network: AMPS, GSM, and TDMA. Future plans included evolving to EDGE later in 2001. Eventually, Cingular planned to upgrade to WCDMA technology.[18]

Cingular recently spent $2.3 billion in additional licenses, and rough estimates indicated that $1.4 billion would be required to upgrade to GPRS, $5.1 billion to upgrade to EDGE, and $9 billion to finally rollout WCDMA technology.[19]

AT&T Wireless

AT&T Wireless ranked third in mobile phone services provision in the U.S. It had 16.4 million subscribers with a 16.4 percent market share and $3.4 billion in second-quarter revenue.[20] AT&T Wireless was spun off in 2001 as part of its parent company's restructuring. NTT DoCoMo, which was partnering with AT&T Wireless to develop mobile multimedia services, owned a 16 percent stake, while the parent company AT&T retained 7 percent. AT&T Wireless offered service nationwide and had expanded its geographic footprint through a series of mergers.

As of November 2001, AT&T used AMPS and TDMA technology for its wireless network. AT&T's current CDPD network spanned across the U.S. but was likely to become obsolete in the short-term. Its future strategy included using a GSM-based approach to evolve its networks to 3G services. The first step in the migration involved the addition of GPRS channels. AT&T hoped to have this 2.5G solution in place by the end of 2002. The final step in their 3G migration plan would be to offer WCDMA technology in the 2004 time frame.[21]

AT&T Wireless spent $2.8 billion on additional license purchases and was expected to require $2.8 billion more to upgrade to GPRS, $5.1 billion to upgrade to EDGE, and $9.0 billion to upgrade to WCDMA.[22]

Nextel

Nextel was a smaller player, but was gaining market share. Primarily focused on business customers, in third-quarter 2001 it had 9.6 million subscribers, a 7.7 percent market share, and $2 billion in quarterly revenue.[23] Nextel used Motorola's integrated digital enhanced network (iDEN) technology for cellular phone service. Its features included paging, text messaging, and a two-way radio feature (Nextel Direct Connect) on a single handset. Announced on October 4, 2001, Nextel planned to upgrade its existing network with next-generation enhancements to double its voice capacity (via data compression) to enable the iDEN platform to remain competitive with other 3G technologies.[24]

As the only carrier using iDEN technology, Nextel alone carried the burden of supporting the Motorola standard in contrast to Qualcomm, whose many CDMA backers provided substantial revenue for technology development.

Mobile Virtual Network Operators (MVNO)

MVNOs were firms that contracted with major carriers to use their networks, while branding their own service. The MVNO phenomenon came to prominence in 1999, when Virgin Mobile (a subsidiary of Virgin) signed a deal with One 2 One to resell its wireless service in the United Kingdom. Virgin Mobile quickly became the UK's fastest growing wireless provider, signing up over 1 million subscribers in less than a year.[25] Other wireless carriers then began to consider similar deals to increase utilization of their networks. Sprint signed an MVNO deal with Virgin in October 2001, scheduled to rollout nationwide during the first half of 2002. Under the agreement, Virgin Mobile would initially focus marketing on the youth segment (15 to 30 year olds) where U.S. wireless penetration significantly lagged international markets. Other consumer marketing powerhouses such as MTV Networks and AOL Time Warner were rumored to be considering similar deals with other U.S. wireless carriers. Worldwide MVNO revenue was estimated to reach $1.1 billion in 2002 and grow to $13 billion by 2006.[26] However, some believed that by giving up some customer control to the MVNOs, network providers, such as Sprint PCS, may be relegated to providers of "dumb-pipes," similar to the fate of wire-line network providers.

SUBSTITUTE TECHNOLOGIES

In addition to direct cellular competitors, Sprint faced additional competition from substitute technologies. Two of the more prominent ones were wireless e-mail devices, such as the RIM BlackBerry, and wireless local area networks (WLANs). Both focused on data transmission, but with the advent of high-quality voice over IP (VoIP), a technology that allowed voice calls over pure data networks, they were poised to become serious competitors in the voice arena.

Research In Motion (RIM)

Research In Motion's (RIM) BlackBerry device was an always-on two-way pager that let users send and receive e-mail. By 2001 it had begun to reach large-scale adoption among enterprise users. Its subscriber base hit 164,000 in April 2001, compared with 120,000 during its previous quarter.[27] Between January 1999 and October 2001, RIM had shipped more than 1 million BlackBerry devices.[28] Its adoption was due in part to its ability to send and receive e-mail from corporate messaging systems, based on Microsoft Outlook. The Black-Berry utilized packet-switched networks, enabling an always-on connection using old two-way paging networks. Next-generation devices were planned to be voice-driven and based on the GPRS protocol. In a sign of its growing global acceptance, RIM had signed deals with a number of European telecommunications firms and had plans to run on GSM within the EU. In November 2001, RIM announced a deal with VoiceStream, allowing VoiceStream to resell BlackBerry devices that would run on VoiceStream's U.S. GSM/GPRS network.[29] On December 5, 2001, RIM announced a similar plan to launch GPRS-enabled BlackBerry devices in an alliance with Telecom Italia.[30] In addition, it was expected that RIM would introduce devices that could run on CDMA networks.[31] Analysts forecasted that these deals were precursors to RIM offering voice features on its devices.

Satellite-based Wireless Service

Satellites had been used for wireless communication over the past few years. Service was rendered by low-Earth orbit (LEO) satellites hundreds of miles above the Earth. A customer making a call using a satellite phone had the call routed through a gateway to the provider's satellites. Various satellites relayed the call among one another until a satellite with line-of-sight to the recipient's phone was located. The call was then conveyed to the recipient's phone. LEO satellites provided shorter connection times than higher, geosynchronous satellites (which hover thousands of miles above the Earth) and also required less power of the handset phone.

GlobalStar and Iridium were the two main players in satellite wireless services. This technology targeted underserved markets where the large telecommunication players had not installed enough cellular towers for users to receive a signal. Both firms targeted industrial users such as the military, emergency services, and heavy construction. GlobalStar had 48 satellites that routed calls using CDMA technology at data rates up to 9.6 Kbps. At the end of November 2001, the firm had roughly 60,000 customers, an increase of 14 percent over the prior quarter.[32] Iridium had 66 satellites in its network.[33] Calls were made in the 1.6 GHz frequency range. Iridium phones used TDMA technology to route calls and had transmission rates of approximately 2.4 Kbps. GlobalStar hoped to be cash-flow break-even in 2002.[34]

Iridium was founded on a $5 billion investment from Motorola but was considered a major business failure and filed for bankruptcy in late 1999. Iridium was subsequently purchased for only $22 million and shifted its focus from the consumer market to the niche government market. Iridium's troubled financial history led it not to publish sales figures, but it expected to be profitable by the end of 2002.[35]

A major factor holding back adoption of satellite wireless telephony is pricing to the end user. GlobalStar charged $119.95 for only 100 minutes of airtime, with each additional minute costing $1.39. Voicemail cost an extra $9.95/month.[36] Iridium charged upwards of $3/minute, on top of subscription and equipment charges.[37]

Wireless Local Area Networks (WLANs)

The dominant technology in the WLAN space was based on the IEEE (Institute of Electrical and Electronics Engineering) 802.11b standard, commonly referred to as "Wi-Fi." Wi-Fi provided short-distance wireless Internet access at a broadband speed of 11 Mbps. Wi-Fi was limited to a transmission distance of 100 meters, but the network could be easily extended with the addition of supplementary transmitters. Wi-Fi used the 2.4 GHz spectrum, which was unlicensed worldwide. This allowed anyone to set up a Wi-Fi network without having to obtain government approval. However, other wireless technologies such as Bluetooth, and consumer devices such as cordless phones, also utilized the 2.4 GHz spectrum, creating the possibility for interference. Wi-Fi equipment costs fell considerably in 2001, with some prices dropping up to 50 percent.

Two variations of Wi-Fi were in the process of being developed with the intent to increase transmission capacity. IEEE 802.11a equipment began shipping in fall 2001 and provided a data rate of 54 Mbps, although at a reduced range of 50 meters. Equipment costs for 802.11a were slightly higher than 802.11b but were expected to fall at a comparable rate. Additionally, because 802.11a operated in the 5 GHz spectrum, the possibility for interference with other wireless devices was minimized. However, there were concerns about interoperability in countries such as Japan, which did not make the 5 GHz spectrum available for unlicensed use. In addition, a European standard called HiperLAN2 (high performance radio local area network type 2) was being developed for the 5 GHz spectrum, causing further incompatibility possibilities.

Another variation, IEEE 802.11g, was being developed to extend the data transfer speed of 802.11b from 11 Mbps to 22 Mbps, while offering backward compatibility with 802.11b equipment. A draft IEEE standard for 802.11g was approved in December 2001, but 802.11g equipment was not expected to be available until at least fall 2002.

See Exhibit 16.4 for a summary of WLAN technology.

The biggest technological concern with WLANs was security. Although technologies such as wired equivalent privacy (WEP) and virtual private networking (VPN) were being developed, they were shown to be open to hacking and as such raised concerns with enterprise IT managers. WLAN networks based on Wi-Fi technology were growing significantly in popularity, particularly in corporate and education arenas. Hardware manufacturers such as Dell and Apple had begun to integrate WLAN capability into their laptop PCs, and Microsoft had built-in support in their latest operating system, Windows XP.

The main competitors in the 802.11 provider market were network operators such as Cisco, Wayport, and MobileStar. Wayport, MobileStar, WalkAbout Wireless, and other public wireless local-area solutions (PWLAS) began to implement WLANs in public places such as airports, hotels, and coffee shops. Wayport and MobileStar had received significant venture capital and boasted partnerships with companies such as Dell, Microsoft, Intel, and Starbucks. Initial adoption was slower than expected and MobileStar was forced to the brink of bankruptcy before being purchased by VoiceStream in November

EXHIBIT 16.4   **Overview of Wireless LAN Technologies**

Sources: Martin Johnsson, "HiperLAN/2—The Broadband Radio Transmission Technology Operating in the 5GHz Frequency Band,"
http://www.hiperlan2.com/presdocs/site/whitepaper.pdf, version 1.0, 1999; Brad Smith, "Another Standard in the Wind," *Wireless Week,* July 16, 2001.

	IEEE 802.11			ETSI HiperLAN2
Band	**2.4 GHz**		**5 GHz**	**5 GHz**
Standard	802.11b	802.11g	802.11a	HiperLAN2
Available spectrum	83.5 MHz	83.5 MHz	300 MHz	
Max data rate	11 Mbps	22 Mbps	54 Mbps	54 Mbps
Throughput	5-7 Mbps	10-11 Mbps	31 Mbps	20 Mbps
Range/corresponding data rate	100 m/11 Mbps	100 m/11 Mbps	50 m/9 Mbps	150 m/16 Mbps
Shipping	Now	fall 2002	winter 2001	winter 2001

2001. VoiceStream's purchase of MobileStar brought to light the possibility telecoms might consider WLANs as co-opetitors.

Cisco also recognized the potential of WLANs and during the COMDEX 2001 show announced a major initiative to implement Wi-Fi networks in public places and homes. This plan complemented its year-old mobile office initiative, which as of November 2001 had installed WLAN technology in 1,500 public spaces around the world. Cisco estimated the size of the market to be in the hundreds of thousands of locations and saw the market for WLAN gear (currently $1.5 billion) growing at about 50 percent annually.[38]

The increasing pervasiveness of WLANs provided both the potential for competition and the potential for cooperative synergies with telecom providers such as Sprint PCS. Estimates showed that by 2003, there would be over 10 million users and more than 15,000 WLAN hotspots in the U.S.[39] Another study forecasted growth of WLAN hotspots from 6,300 in 2001 to over 114,000 worldwide by 2006. The same study also forecasted 95 percent of all laptops and PDAs would be WLAN enabled by 2006.[40] Similar to the cellular industry, the goal of WLAN providers such as Wayport, MobileStar, and Cisco was to build out seamless coverage in urban areas across the world, enabling users to roam anywhere within the network without losing a connection. To facilitate this goal, companies such as Qualcomm, Ericsson, Nokia, and Mobilian were developing technologies to allow seamless connectivity between 802.11b, Bluetooth, and cellular networks.

WIRELESS APPLICATIONS

In late 2001, the wireless industry faced formidable challenges. In mature markets, competition was stiff and the transition to new technologies raised questions regarding feasibility and return on investment. Barriers to entry were rising as consolidation made size and scope critical at a time when capital was drying up. Most telecommunication operators' balance sheets looked weak and overleveraged. The amortization of capital expenditures just for wireless spectrum licenses was expected to severely impact net income for years. At the same time, competition was driving prices down, and the ARPU based on voice services was falling. Some analysts feared far more 3G licenses had been granted than some markets could support. Wireless operators were left with but one choice—find a "killer application" that would allow them to leverage their networks and drive ARPU up.

What did a busy professional expect from a wireless service? Mobility—anyone, anytime, anywhere—and reliability were the top two concerns of business users. The introduction of pagers revolutionized the way professionals went about their jobs. With one-way paging systems, people could send important messages to their counterparts irrespective of their location. With two-way messaging and mobile telephony, businesspeople could keep in touch continuously, unconstrained by wires. However, voice communications were fast becoming a commodity. Wireless service providers understood that growth in this area would be hard to come by. The key questions were then: Will businesses see value in data communications? If so, what are the key factors that would allow this value to be realized?

While the debate on wireless standards and technology continued, the focus turned to applications. The wireless value discovery process elicited mixed opinions among analysts and business executives. Speaking at the 2001 Cyberposium on the wireless landscape, David Berndt, director for wireless and mobile technologies at the high-tech market research firm Yankee Group, noted:

> The Killer App is voice. Ninety-eight percent of [wireless] traffic will be voice over the next five years.[41]

In return, NTT DoCoMo's executive director for gateway business, Takeshi Natsuno, asked rhetorically:

> Are 19 million people just buying this cell phone to download Mickey Mouse? I don't think so. . . . We don't need a killer app because we have a killer environment!

mCommerce Applications

mCommerce is broadly defined as providing mobile consumers and businesses with the ability to purchase and receive products and services via wireless channels. The vision for mobile commerce was to provide information and transaction processing tools that fully exploited the unique attributes of mobile technology—personal, anytime, anywhere, and location-aware. The first of the mCommerce applications originated in the 1996–1997 time frame, with the financial services industry leading the way. Mobile commerce applications were estimated to generate revenues in the range of $64.4 billion to $210.8 billion by 2005.[42] NTT DoCoMo's i-mode service was the largest mCommerce application success story.

In 2001, four types of mCommerce applications—payments, location-based marketing and directory services, comparative off-line shopping, and gaming and gambling—gained recognition. These applications were forecasted as possible means to drive mass consumer adoption. One initial application, downloadable ring-tones, generated US$300 million in Japan in year 2000 alone.[43]

Telematics Applications

One intriguing segment for cellular operators, infrastructure providers, content providers, and consumers was telematics—the convergence of telecommunications with the automobile. Telematics was broadly defined as mobile services delivered via wireless technology to in-vehicle devices. Telematics represented a niche application of wireless technology and was believed to be a killer app bringing together the automotive and telecommunication industries. The creation of Wingcast by Ford Motor Company and Qualcomm, and the aggressive rollout of OnStar by General Motors, refocused attention on vehicle telematics in the U.S. Telematics services fell into three main categories: safety & security, navigation & information, and entertainment. Safety & security services were expected to provide key buy-ins for telematics, and voice communications was expected to drive customer value. According to Forrester Research, telematics was expected to be a $20 billion market by 2006.[44]

The Opportunity for Wireless Data

By 2001, numerous applications for wireless data had been identified. The mobile workforce had a need to stay in touch while traveling. Many saw a need to provide navigation and data communication capabilities in the car. Marketers saw wireless as a new channel that would allow consumers to purchase airline tickets, news, and other information services while connected wirelessly. Wireless carriers had the unique opportunity to consolidate all billing services for mCommerce onto a single monthly bill. Location-sensitive applications could also provide value to customers by pinpointing one's location and providing information on the nearest hotels, restaurants, and retailers. SMS and e-mail were among the most popular immediately available applications for mobile phones.

In spite of all these applications, forecasts for the wireless data market remained questionable. Current data transmission rates were slow compared to high-speed home and office connections. Were businesses and consumers willing to pay to be connected all the time if they had convenient access at their desks? The number of U.S. wireless data subscribers was forecasted to increase to 52 million by 2005,[45] and mCommerce revenues were forecasted to grow from only $2 million in 2000 to over $2 billion in 2005.[46] But forecasts for wireless data services, once predicted to quickly reach tens of billions of dollars, had dropped. The most recent projections showed demand reaching less than $5 billion by 2004.[47]

SPRINT PCS APPROACH

Sprint PCS rested squarely in the CDMA2000 camp, along with Verizon. It had adhered to the CDMA standard and would therefore be able to leverage its existing network infrastructure in the years ahead. Backward compatibility was another advantage of Sprint PCS versus its TDMA-based competition (AT&T Wireless and Cingular, among others).

Sprint PCS had recently bid $280 million in an FCC auction, compared to Verizon's $4 billion, just for the rights to New York City. Its "spectral thriftiness" was a direct result of its dedication to CDMA. Sprint PCS claimed it would not require additional investments in spectrum in order to achieve 3G upgrades on its wireless data network. In late 2001, the company was upgrading its network to CDMA2000 1x at an expected cost of about $1 billion. This upgrade increased spectral efficiency by another 25 percent and provided average data rates of 40–60 Kbps. The upgrade was expected to be completed in late 2002. Another upgrade was likely to follow. The subsequent, more significant upgrade to CDMA2000 1xEV would cost in the neighborhood of $6 billion. This upgrade would provide maximum data rates of over 2 Mbps.

NEXT STEPS

As Ravi looked out his window, he pondered what this dynamic marketplace held in store for its numerous players. Which company would hold market power in the evolving wireless Internet landscape? What would be the impact of the FCC auctions? How would Sprint PCS respond to WLAN, satellite, not to mention other cellular competitors? What would be Sprint PCS's competitive advantage? How quickly would data services reach mainstream adoption? What did the cellular standards war foretell? Could Sprint PCS and its competitors generate positive ROIs on their planned 3G network upgrades? And what about the international impact of these answers? Ravi turned to his papers and began his research.

Notes

1. Sprint 2000 Summary Annual Report.
2. Sprint PCS, http://www.sprintpcs.com/aboutsprintpcs/mediacenter/2000/00_10_19A.html, accessed December 9, 2001.
3. UBS Warburg, Sprint PCS report, October 22, 2001.
4. http://company.monster.com/sprintpcs/, accessed December 12, 2001.
5. Silicon Insights: Spectral Efficiency, July 17, 2001.
6. Sprint PCS.
7. Sprint PCS Analyst Report, Lehman Brothers, October 25, 2001.
8. Sprint PCS.

9. Standard and Poors, "Industry Surveys, Telecommunications: Wireless," http://www.netadvantage.standardandpoors.com,accessed November 1, 2001.

10. Ibid.

11. Cahners In-Stat Group, *Wireless Week,* November 5, 2001, p. 24.

12. Archtronix, http://www.arcx.com/sites/CDMAvsTDMA.htm, accessed December 4, 2001.

13. Standard and Poors, Industry Surveys.

14. Verizon Annual Report, 2000.

15. Standard and Poors, Industry Surveys.

16. Sprint PCS, http://www.sprintpcs.com/aboutsprintpcs/Cdma_3g/, accessed December 4, 2001.

17. Standard and Poors, Industry Surveys.

18. "TDMA's Curious Road to 3G," *Wireless Week,* December 3, 2001.

19. Sprint PCS, http://www.sprintpcs.com/aboutsprintpcs/Cdma_3g/.

20. Standard and Poors, Industry Surveys.

21. "TDMA's Curious Road to 3G."

22. Sprint PCS, http://www.sprintpcs.com/aboutsprintpcs/Cdma_3g/.

23. http://www.wirelessnewsfactor.com/perl/story/14367.html, accessed December 4, 2001.

24. "Nextel and Motorola Announce iDEN Technology Upgrade," *Business Wire,* October 4, 2001.

25. Dan Briody, "Brand Power," *Red Herring,* November 2001, p. 54.

26. Ibid.

27. http://www.zdnet.com/zdnn/stories/news/0,4586,5081033,00.html.

28. Marcelo Prince, "The BlackBerry Quickly Became an Indispensable Tool for Many Professionals," *The Wall Street Journal,* October 15, 2001, p. R20.

29. "RIM Strikes Strategic Deal." *Wireless Week,* November 5, 2001, p. 26.

30. ZDNet, http://www.zdnet.com/zdnn/stories/news/0,4586,5081033,00 .html, accessed December 10, 2001.

31. Marcelo Prince, "The BlackBerry Quickly Became. . . ."

32. GlobalStar, http://www.globalstar.com/satellite_constellation.html, accessed December 10, 2001.

33. Iridium, http://www.iridium.com/corp/iri_corp-understand.asp, accessed December 10, 2001.

34. GlobalStar Corporate website, http://www.globalstar.com, accessed December 10, 2001.

35. TechTV News, http://www.techtv.com/news/culture/story/0,24195 ,3352821,00.html, accessed December 10, 2001.

36. GlobalStar Corporate website.

37. Network Computing, http://www.networkcomputing.com/905/905f2side 10.html, accessed December 10, 2001.

38. Ben Frankel and Stephen Wellman, "Cisco: Mobile Office Technology Will Grow Exponentially," The 802.11 Report, November 14, 2001, p. 8.

39. Arena Intelligence Group.

40. BWCS, "Wireless LANs and the Threat to Mobile Revenue," http://www
.wirelessdevnet.com/2001/207/news9.html, accessed November 2001.

41. George A. Chidi, "Wireless Killer App May Be Better Service," *Network World,* February 12, 2001.

42. *Reuter's Business Insight Report,* November 2000.

43. Dave Rothschild, "Guest Opinion," *Wireless Week,* November 5, 2001, p. 37.

44. "Voice Drives Telematics Boom," *Forrester,* June 2001.

45. "In-Stat Market Snapshot," *Wireless Week,* November 5, 2001, p. 24.

46. Chris Hayward, "Outlook for mCommerce: Technologies and Applications to 2005," *Reuters Business Insight Technology,* 2000.

47. InfoTech Trends, Gartner Group, December 11, 2000.

Case **Seventeen**

Napster: The Giant Online Pirate Bazaar

Napster: It's the future, in my opinion. That's the way music is going to be communicated around the world. The most important thing now is to embrace it. . . .[1]

—Dave Matthews (Dave Matthews Band)

[Napster] could end up being as powerful as the record companies are right now. And I would not predict that they would be any less greedy. They're [Napster] not doing it to benefit mankind. They're not doing it to help all the kids sitting around behind the computers in America who are musically starved. They're doing it because, sooner or later, here's my $50 million f—ing IPO, and I'm riding into the sunset.[2]

—Lars Ulrich (Metallica)

It was early December 2001. Konrad Hilbers, longtime media executive and current CEO at file-sharing pioneer Napster, had just watched the launch of MusicNet, the first subscription-based platform designed to download and play music online. Mr. Hilbers, a former executive vice president responsible for BMG Entertainment and CEO of Napster since July of 2001, watched the proceedings with some ambivalence. He was happy that BMG, Napster's corporate parent as well as major record label and partner in the MusicNet effort, would continue to be a trendsetter in the online entertainment industry. But he was also worried that this new subscription-based service, which included heavyweights such as Warner Music Group, EMI Recorded Music, and Real-Networks, would render futile his own efforts to transform Napster into a "legitimate" subscription-based business from its origins as a free file-sharing service.

"Stop the infringements, stop the delay tactics in court, and redouble your efforts to build a legitimate system"[3]—The comments issued by Hilary Rosen, president of the Recording Industry Association of America (RIAA), a trade group that headed the lawsuit against Napster on behalf of the five major record labels were still resonating in Mr. Hilbers's ears. In many ways his very appointment to the position of CEO had been among the first steps taken by Bertelsmann in that drive toward legitimacy after Napster had suffered a crippling legal blow in February 2001. That court-ordered injunction required Napster, the Internet's most popular file-sharing service, to disable transfers of any copyright protected material on its service. For a file-swapping service that at its zenith had boasted almost 60 million users and over 2 billion downloads a month, this ruling was tantamount to shutting down its operations. Napster was forced to install filters that prevented sharing of copyright protected material. When these filters failed to be fool proof in enforcing the court-issued mandate, Napster was forced to shut down its operations temporarily. Formerly loyal subscribers migrated in droves to competing services. In the meantime executives were left scrambling to chart a business future that was "legitimate."

It was just over two years ago that Shawn Fanning launched Napster, the "killer" application/service that enabled millions of users to quickly find the latest hot music and download it to their PCs. Napster became synonymous with the peer-to-peer (P2P) revolution, as the online community of music fans traded stories, swapped tunes, and built individual collections of music on their own storage devices—all for free.

Since its inception, Napster had been beset by unclear regulations regarding what constituted legal music sharing and downloading, and through what medium. Back in the mid-1980s, a similar theme ran through the courts when Sony was sued over its Beta recording system and whether copying television/video entertainment programming for personal use was legal. In 1984, the courts ruled that copying television shows or movies onto personal Beta tapes was legal, as long as the content was used solely for personal entertainment use and not broadcast or reproduced for profit. Similarly, cassette tapes could be used for copying music from other music tapes, CDs, and radio. Why was Napster so different? The answer: This was the Internet, and regulations surrounding online commerce were still in their infancy.

After fighting legal battle after legal battle since its official launch in June 1999, Napster had finally lost in the appeals court in February 2001. It had had to discontinue the free service and consider reopening under a subscription-based model that charged for the transfers of copyright protected material. But questions remained. Would the major record labels it had taken on in court consider licensing their content on Napster? How many of its 60+ million users, many of whom were already flocking to competing sites, would return if Napster began charging for its services? Could Napster continue to be a leading innovator in the face of a hostile music industry and unclear regulatory guidelines relating to music downloads and online file exchange?

COMPANY BACKGROUND

The coincidence of two major technological breakthroughs—ability to compress, store, and retrieve sound files from a computer with minimal loss of sound quality using MP3 technology and the explosion of the Internet and, in particular, the Internet Relay Chat (IRC)—led to the music file-swapping and downloading craze. Many companies and individual start-ups had developed software that allowed individual users to "rip" music from CD-ROM and store it on their PC hard drive or storage device in MP3 format. Critically, the MP3 format did not have a security layer that prevented indiscriminate sharing of files. Furthermore, you could trade these MP3 files without any loss in their quality. At the same time, on college campuses, IRCs were popular with many students. In the late 1990s, people were introduced to the IRC concept via instant messenger chats, such as ICQ, AOL Instant Messenger, and Yahoo! Messenger.[4] The concept of swapping music files arose because people were listening to MP3 files while chatting online and, as conversation turned to music, decided to trade files.

Napster was conceived in January 1999 by Shawn Fanning, a former Northeastern University undergraduate who left college on the belief that the Napster software he developed was a better way to find MP3 music files. (Exhibit 17.1 provides a chronology of events.) Fanning combined the practicality of sharing personal music and finding MP3s online with chat features. Unlike the concept of hosting music files on a central server, the Napster model involved having each user's hard drive act, in essence, as a server, with music files on each hard drive available to the worldwide community of fellow Napster users who were logged on to the service at that time. His uncle, John Fanning, believed that Shawn's venture had huge potential as a commercial success and backed his innovation. By May 1999, the company was incorporated. The success of Napster and its widespread popularity was foreshadowed when Shawn tested the beta version of the software by giving it to 30 friends in a chat room. In just three days, over 4,000 people had downloaded the software and proved Napster's potential industry power. Napster had launched the peer-to-peer (P2P) revolution.

Napster was an instant hit. Almost immediately, John Fanning contacted Andrew P. Bridges, a Silicon Valley lawyer involved in copyright laws applying to digital technologies (see the Appendix for details of copyright laws). Napster came into prominence at a time when MP3 players were becoming increasingly mobile and popular, while the price of CD burners was dropping.

EXHIBIT 17.1 Napster Timeline

Source: "Napster's Musical History," TheStandard.com.

January 1999	Shawn Fanning drops out of Boston's Northeastern University; asks his uncle to help commercialize the file-sharing software.
May 1999	Napster founded and incorporated.
June 1, 1999	Beta test, with friends; Napster begins operations.
October 1999	20–30 percent of Florida State University's pipes tied up with Napster traffic. Napster and major record companies begin talks, but Richardson's style sabotages cooperation.
December 1999	Recording Industry Association of America sues Napster for copyright infringement.
February 2000	Universities ban Napster. Students petition.
May 2000	San Francisco venture capital firm Hummer Winbald invests $15 million. Metallica asks Napster to bar access to the service for users downloading the group's music. Napster boots 300,000 members from its service for downloading Metallica songs.
June 2000	RIAA files for an injunction. Napster hires David Boies, the triumphant Microsoft attorney, to oversee legal matters during its antitrust case.
July 2000	Judge Marilyn Patel rules in favor of the recording industry and orders the company to shut down any trading of copyrighted files. Hours before the injunction is to go into effect, an appeals court issues a stay, keeping Napster alive.
October 2, 2000	A three-judge panel at the 9th U.S. Circuit Court of Appeals hears arguments from both sides on the validity of the earlier injunction.
October 31, 2000	Bertelsmann's e-commerce group strikes a deal with Napster, loaning it an estimated $50 million to develop a legal file-sharing system. The loan is redeemable for a minority equity stake in Napster. BMG, Bertelsmann's music arm and a member of the RIAA, agrees to drop out of the industry lawsuit if Napster is successful. BMG will make its catalog available to Napster only if it can figure out a way to distribute and charge for copyrighted files.
January 2001	Germany's Edel Music agrees to distribute its catalog over Napster. Napster cuts a deal with CDNow, an online Bertelsmann retailer, to include a link in Napster's interface that connects to CDNow's website. Simultaneously, the Dave Matthews Band, which records for BMG, issues a single on Napster. TVT Records, an independent label, drops its Napster lawsuit.
February 12, 2001	9th Circuit Court issues its opinion affirming that Napster violates copyright laws.
February 2001	Napster installs filters and blocks to prevent transfer of copyright protected material.
July 24, 2001	Bertelsmann appoints Konrad Hilbers as Napster's New CEO replacing Hank Barry.
September 24, 2001	Napster agrees to pay $26 million to settle its ongoing legal disputes with music publishers and songwriters.
December 4, 2001	MusicNet, the first subscription-based service owned by major record labels, is launched.

These technological advances made it possible not only to listen to music while on the computer but also to create one's own customized music on-the-go.

By fall of 1999, Napster was a major force for the universities to reckon with, as college students were tying up major amounts of bandwidth exchanging music files and chatting on Napster. Recognizing that they needed a CEO, the principals hired Eileen Richardson, a Boston venture capitalist. Richardson was inexperienced in this arena and confrontational as well, two qualities that some feel did not serve Napster well as it needed to simultaneously maneuver the legal battleground and raise venture capital. "This was the first time Richardson had run a company, let alone a Net startup that was challenging the giants of the music business."[5]

While the rest of the world was buzzing about Y2K doom, insiders at Napster spent a long, cold fall and winter, waiting for Richardson to help them land some financing. Napster had no need to initiate any of its own marketing, as the media, press, and word-of-mouth contributed to building the Napster user base. Despite the mushrooming popularity and membership of the site, Napster had difficulty articulating to VCs how it intended to make a profit.

On May 21, 2000, Napster finally raised $15 million from Hummer Winblad Venture Partners and acquired a new CEO: Hummer partner Hank Barry. John Hummer himself also joined the board. Eileen Richardson stepped down. The new regime began building a senior team capable of handling the challenge. Some key figures in the organization included Milton Olin, former senior vice president of A&M Records, who was named chief operating officer of Napster; and Claire Hough, VP of engineering who oversaw all technological aspects of Napster's operations and led the growth and implementation of its core technologies.

Brimming with Popularity, Boiling Over with Legal Troubles

With a steadily growing user base, fresh funding, and new leadership, Napster now had to address mounting legal turmoil. On April 13, 2000, Metallica sued Napster for copyright infringement, and Lars Ulrich of the band came forth to urge fans not to use Napster to download their songs. Ulrich claimed that fans would be hurting Metallica's creativity and future viability as a band. The lawsuit failed due to the continued uncertainty among the courts over the legality of Napster software. However, the Metallica affair reaffirmed for the industry that Napster was a strong force in the eyes of the consumers and a growing threat to the music labels and RIAA.

The first big victory for the music industry giants and the RIAA came on July 26, 2000, when the U.S. District Court slapped a preliminary injunction on Napster, ordering it to shut down services by July 29, pending the outcome of a civil trial over whether Napster violated copyright laws. But federal judges stayed the injunction, and Napster was allowed to stay open. The RIAA and major labels could have pursued more legal action to shut down Napster, but that would have alienated the millions of people who used the service. In fact, online message boards were filling up with pro-Napster rants. Moreover, with competitors popping up every day, it was felt that regardless of the industry or courts shutting down Napster, consumers would find ways to trade MP3s and songs on the Internet.

In response to the injunction, Napster officials issued a statement on July 29, 2000, declaring the upcoming weekend to be a "buycott" weekend. Napster wanted all of its users to go out and buy records by artists they had discovered on Napster, thereby proving to the RIAA and labels that Napster wasn't hurting them. The buycott was a bust. InSound and Soundscan reported no sale bumps or referrals that stirred album sales beyond averages, and the PR episode was embarrassing for Napster. Even though Napster stood behind Jupiter Research indicating that Napster users were 45 percent more likely to increase music spending, the failure to generate sales called into question the prevailing issue surrounding new business models for online music and whether the Napster argument regarding the legality of its business was weaker than it had originally appeared.

Then Napster attracted Bertelsmann, the world's third-largest media company and owner of the BMG record label, as an ally—and as a source of much-needed capital. Bertelsmann, a traditional media company that started off as a Bible publisher in 1835, was doing just fine without the Internet. The company's overall profit rose 45 percent in 2000, to $671 million on sales of $16.5 billion. Bertelsmann recorded music and magazine divisions were strong. But, Thomas Middelhoff, chairman and CEO of Bertelsmann, felt that in the future, media companies would be selling most of their wares over the Internet.

Bertelsmann's e-commerce group struck a deal with Napster on October 31, 2000, loaning it an estimated $50 million to develop a legal file-sharing service. The loan was redeemable for a minority equity stake in Napster. BMG, Bertelsmann's music arm and a member of the RIAA, agreed to drop out of the industry lawsuit if Napster was successful. BMG would make its music catalog, the fourth largest in the world, available to Napster only if Napster could figure out a way to distribute and charge for copyrighted files.

The deal alleviated financial pressures on Napster and put pressure on the other big labels like Sony, EMI, Warner Music, and Universal. BMG foresaw a tremendous financial future in Napster. Middelhoff proclaimed, "We have to develop business models that are legal, and somebody has to take the lead. . . . We have to find the second AOL." Middelhoff was eyeing the number-one spot in the global music business and in media e-commerce. *Business Week Online* called the move "recruiting the thief to protect the jewels."

On February 12, 2001, a court ruling declared Napster to cease and desist all exchange of copyrighted material on its website. The court order had many industry observers concerned that big label control would make Napster just another pawn in the music establishment. Users responded in many ways.

Some began flocking to competitors. Others began disguising the file names of songs they were sharing, using Pig Latin, for example, to avoid detection. Despite it all, Napster continued to pick up subscribers.

The lack of effectiveness of the filters intended to block trading of copyrighted material as well as the resourcefulness of Napster users continued to anger the RIAA which lobbied the courts that Napster was not following its mandate. Therefore, rather than risk further punishment, early in the summer of 2001, the management at Napster decided to shut down the service temporarily, its intention being to regroup and then launch a subscription-based model at a later time.

Given the projected importance of digital music in the future, Bertelsmann took a more active role in the reincarnation of Napster as a legitimate business. Hank Barry stepped down as CEO, and Konrad Hilbers, the head of BMG Entertainment, was appointed CEO on July 24, 2001, his task being to align all required resources and reopen Napster as a subscription-based digital downloading service. While the service had not been launched yet, he and Napster had made significant progress in signing up music publishers to license their content on Napster. But despite its close relationship with BMG, Hilbers's presence at Napster had not yielded any new alliances with major record labels.

NAPSTER'S STRATEGY

After 18 months, Napster had 50 million users. According to Media Metrix, from the period of January 1, 2001, through January 13, 2001, Napster was the 16th most visited web/application site, with 14.4 million unique visitors, being outranked mostly by media giants such as the likes of AOL, Disney, Time Warner, and Microsoft. (In February, Napster climbed to 13th place, with 16.9 million unique visitors.)

Despite its tremendous success Napster had never generated money from the daily operation of its service software/website. Indeed, Shawn Fanning's motivation was never to make money. "I didn't see us turning into a business," he claimed. "I just did it because I loved the technology." However, consumer interests showed that if Napster were to sell subscriptions to Napster users, 68 percent of the 40 million users in January 2001 would be willing to pay $15.00 per month for the Napster service, up from 59 percent in 2000 (Jupiter Reports). These numbers clearly showed the importance of Napster to users. If Napster lowered its monthly fee to $4.95, the anticipated percentage of customers with the intent to stay with Napster increased to a whopping 81 percent. Subscription/usage charges were estimated to eventually contribute 70 percent to Napster's operating bottom line in years 1–3 (Jupiter Reports).

Napster's prime real estate was its home page and download catalog pages. But the firm never opened its space to those interested in advertising on its prime, high-volume site. There were an estimated 35 different banner/text sponsorship spots available on the Napster website. In addition, these banner/ text spots could have been rotated as many times as once per user per page, thereby creating an exponential number of opportunities for sales to other advertisers. It is estimated that Napster missed out on potentially 15 percent of user revenues in 2000. Lastly, there was no marketing effort to e-mail the user base to provide value-added features to differentiate itself from the competition or to pave the way to a service that users might eventually agree to pay for.

In spite of its founder's beliefs and its lack of preparation for a transition to a revenue-generating business, people at Napster felt that they were well situated to make a success of the subscription-based model. Tentatively, it was suggested that they offer a tiered service to capture consumers with differing service-level expectations. Basic service with limited number of transfers would cost somewhere between $2.95 and $4.95 a month. Unlimited service would cost between $5.95 and $9.95.[6] But to operate a subscription-based model, its expenses would include rights to playlists from record companies, overhead for billing and customer service, technology development for a security standard to prevent songs from being passed around, record company fees per song, and songwriter fees per song.

NAPSTER AND ITS COMPETITORS

Napster was a peer-to-peer exchange system (P2P). In Napsterlike systems, every individual computer was both a receiver and a sender of information, whether MP3 files, dissertations, photos, or any other information. This was a large difference from traditional websites in which most users only received information from a central server—a method that made it feasible to keep tabs on content, usage, and payments. In peer-to-peer computing, once a user indexed each individual's files for upload, for viewing or for download, the user essentially created a landscape of information for other users to tap into. This chain effect made it very difficult for the system to track usage.

The difference between Napster and some other online file-sharing technologies was that Napster had a central index of users and their files. In many ways it had been easy for the court to classify Napster's as an illegal file-sharing system due to the perception that its central indexing system allowed Napster the ability to moderate and encourage copyright violations. However, other online offerings had no central indexes. Some could track users via IP addresses. Others encrypted all information and files, so a user or auditor could not tell who the sender or receiver was and, therefore, could not target a violator of copyright legislation—even if it was determined that the online sharing of music files did constitute such a violation.

New competitors were arriving on the Internet or disappearing with regular frequency. (Exhibit 17.2 provides a list of major competitors as of December 2001.) With so many file-sharing technologies emerging, record companies

EXHIBIT 17.2   **Napster and Its Competitors—At a Glance**

Name	Launched	Description	Features	Platform	Zeropaid Rating
Napster	June 1999	The king of the file-sharing networks with over 60 million downloads. The most reliable network for MP3 downloads, also works with Napigator.	Ease of use—Successful downloads—The largest user base—Quality content—Chat—Instant Messaging—Cool add-ons.	Windows, Mac, Linux, Unix	8.0633
Gnutella	March 2000	Released in early March 2000, Gnutella's decentralized network demonstrates the capability of peer-2-peer computing. Gnutella's user base has grown drastically due to the Napster case.	Decentralized unlike Napster and others—Connect and download directly from users—Share/Search/Download all media formats.	Windows, Linux, Unix, Macintosh, Java	4.7609
FreeNet		FreeNet is becoming something of a legend in the file-sharing community with its revolutionary technology. Recommended to advanced users.	Not centralized like some other clients—Users can remain anonymous—Information will increase in proportion to the demand for that information.	Windows, Unix/Linux	2.4000
iMesh	August 1999	iMesh is a file-sharing network that allows all media types to be downloaded or shared. iMesh is located in Israel, out of reach of the RIAA.	Simultaneous download—Share Wizard—Chat—Available Skins—Easy to use—Located outside the U.S.—Search on iMesh.com or via application.	Windows	5.9608
KaZaA		KaZaA is a file-sharing application based in the Netherlands that allows users to share all media types across the network.	No central server—Intelligent download capability—Automatic meta data assignment—Easy to use—Good download rate.	Windows	7.4872

(continued)

EXHIBIT 17.2 *(continued)*

Name	Launched	Description	Features	Platform	Zeropaid Rating
Morpheus		Morpheus is really a slightly altered version of KaZaA, modified to work with MusicCity's excellent array of servers.	No central server—Intelligent download capability—Automatic meta data assignment—Easy to use—Good download rate.	Windows	7.5500
LimeWire		LimeWire is a Java client that connects you to the Gnutella network. LimeWire is also a very stable client with few crashes and is a breeze to update.	Smart Downloading technology—Restrict uploads—Built-in client update—Web browser upload blocking.	Cross Platform, written in Java	7.2500

Note: Zeropaid.com is a peer-to-peer file-sharing portal that includes, among other things, a facility for visitors to rate various P2P sites. The rightmost column below, labeled "Zeropaid Rating," shows how users rated these sites.

were having a hard time tracking their growth. This was especially true as more servers were launched outside the copyright-friendly confines of the U.S. borders. Enforceability was going to be a problem against these foreign competitors.

Gnutella let people trade music files without revealing their locations on the Net. Gnutella was not a website but a "protocol," which is a set of rules that describe a way for computers to talk to one another. The Gnutella protocol outlined a method of sharing files among many computers. Its approach did not require a central database, as Napster's did. Because Gnutella allowed files to be swapped directly between individuals, the courts would have had to go after each user individually. Another anonymous trading service, Freenet, was especially designed to ignore copyright laws through its no sign-on/no registration, anonymous software technology, using encryption for both the sender and receiver of information. This created even more difficulty for record companies, as they tried to figure out who was sharing music over the Internet.

The creators of such services claimed to be more focused on the advantages of technology than on profits. There were key advantages to all distributed P2P systems—more efficient storage, with less dependence upon, and vulnerability to, a central storage site. As Ian Clarke, founder of Freenet, explained,

> The intention of the original Arpanet was . . . to create a decentralized system, the idea being that if there was a nuclear war, the only two things to survive would be cockroaches and the Internet. . . . I think that really Freenet in some ways is the realization of the original creators of the Internet. . . . On Freenet, popular information becomes more widely distributed, which means that you're not going to get what some people call "the slashdot effect," whereby

an extremely popular piece of information becomes unavailable. The availability of information on Freenet increases in proportion to its popularity. [Note: The more the file is requested, the more it is replicated on server sites.]

Despite the competition, Napster had been the clear leader in the category of free P2P music sites before the court-ordered filters rendered the service virtually useless. In addition to having an easy and efficient interface for trading music, Napster supported the "music community," hosting chat sessions, featuring new artists, including reviews of music, hosting message boards, and carrying the endorsements of many recording artists.

In the midst of litigation over free sharing of online music, legal business models for sharing files came into vogue. For example, Lightshare built a way to track files and asked users to pay a small fee for any that were downloaded. This P2P *sale* of anything digital made it the new, favored competitive model among labels and the RIAA. In addition, the music industry and its labels crafted their own competitive responses, which had the potential to significantly impact the road map for free technologies, copyright violations, and Napster's existence. Universal Music Group and Sony Entertainment had announced a joint venture to launch a paid music download service called pressPlay that included content from EMI as well. MusicNet was the digital distribution platform for the other major labels such as Warner Music Group, BMG Entertainment, EMI Recorded Music, and Zomba. Additionally, MusicNet had the backing of Real Networks, one of the pioneers and leaders in streaming entertainment.

TOWARD THE FUTURE

On December 4, 2001, as MusicNet became the first serious pay-for-download service supported by the major record labels, Napster's situation weighed heavily on Konrad Hilbers's mind. Thus far, Napster had not made any money. Moreover, there was a potential for even further monetary losses rising out of pending damage claims by the recording industry.

From a strategy execution standpoint, while they had developed a better rapport with major record labels, and even secured some licensing contracts from a number of music publishers, they were already several months behind the original plan of deploying a subscription-based model in late summer 2001. They did have a big advantage—a strong brand name. Moreover, services such as MusicNet and pressPlay were attracting antitrust attention due to the nature of the alliance between the partners, who were major record labels. In terms of their own services Napster had few options: create more transactional partnerships like the BMG deal; offer advertising, such as site banners, e-mails, content sponsorships, exclusive public relations; offer a free-to-paid migration strategy; offer some limited free service, such as chats or music previews, or noncopyrighted, new-artist previews; charge for copyrighted material, either on a subscription basis or pay-per-download basis. These options hinged on what the competition would do in response.

As Konrad Hilbers awaited the 2002 launch of Napster as a subscription-based service, he was left pondering several questions:

1. How could Napster become profitable? What subscription/pay-per-download model would work for sustaining Napster? Would banner/ad revenue offset losses on copyright fees and still help Napster turn a profit?

2. Would antitrust forces make life difficult for the label consortiums that were launching subscription-based online services? Moreover would the major record labels ever consent to licensing their music catalogs to Napster?

3. Should Napster remain sheltered as a subsidiary of Bertelsmann? In particular, would the subsidiary structure hinder technological innovation, the hallmark product of Napster?

4. What would happen to Napster's 60+ million users if Napster charged even a slight fee for music? Would they flee to other replacement services like Morpheus or iMesh?

5. Would copyright laws ever evolve in light of the widespread adoption of the Internet?

Notes

1. www.napster.com.
2. *Business Week Online* at www.businessweek.com, June 5, 2000.
3. Ibid.
4. In a chat session, members have e-mail conversations with each other, by having the words they type appear on everyone's chat window in real time. All members of a chat session are either logged in to an online service, such as AOL, or they know each other's Internet address and send messages back and forth.
5. S. Ante, "Inside Napster," cover story of *Business Week Online* at www .businessweek.com, August 14, 2000.
6. "Napster Keeps on Tryin'," *Geek News,* February 21, 2001, www.geek .com/news/geeknews/2001feb/gee20010221004438.htm.
7. Liam B. Lavery, "Rights and Wrongs: A Practical Guide to Rights in Internet Content," *WebBusiness,* December 1, 1999.

APPENDIX   Copyright Laws[7]

Audio recordings involve rights at multiple levels, much like photographs. A musical recording may involve not only a copyright of the person who made the recording but also the copyright of the composer and even the lyricist. Fortunately, various rights clearinghouses can help track down the relevant permissions.

For sound contained on a compact disc or other mass-published recording, the record company will typically hold the copyright in the sound recording itself, taking an assignment of the performer's rights in return for giving the performer a share of the royalty. A composers' group, such as the American Society of Composers, Authors, and Publishers (ASCAP) or Broadcast Music Inc. (BMI) in the United States, often has the authority to license a public performance in the underlying musical composition. The rights required depend on the type of Internet publication planned. A publisher providing a subscription-only music service will require different rights from someone who simply wants to use a single song whenever an end user accesses his or her home page. Organizations that grant permission are typically very sophisticated about distinguishing between various channels of distribution. Therefore, a publisher who has licensed a song for a radio commercial should not assume that the radio license will cover website use.

A publisher who commissions an audio recording may run into different rights issues. If the American Federation of Television and Radio Artists (AFTRA) or the Screen Actors Guild (SAG) union talent is used to perform the voice-over for an audio recording, the publisher will have to pay the talent at union rates for each distribution channel. Again, paying once for use on television or radio will generally not permit usage on a website. Frequently, publishers declare that the First Amendment permits them to use freely any content available for their websites. In fact, U.S. copyright law provides relief in the fair use doctrine. However, the fair use doctrine is subtle and frequently misapplied. If you want to rely on fair use when copying content from another source, you should talk to an attorney or an editor experienced in the exercise of fair use.

Section 107 of the Copyright Act lists four factors to be considered in determining whether a use made of a work in a particular case is fair:

- The purpose and character of the use, including whether such use is of a commercial nature or is for nonprofit educational purposes.
- The nature of the copyrighted work.
- The amount and substantiality of portion used in relation to the copyrighted work as a whole.
- The effect of the use upon the potential market for or value of the copyrighted work. How these factors apply varies from situation to situation. Generally, fair use protects noncommercial, educational, or journalistic use of content. The bottom line may be whether the claimed use takes away from the copyright holder's potential licensing market.

Index